FRANK LITTLE AND THE IWW

Frank Little and the IWW

THE BLOOD THAT STAINED
AN AMERICAN FAMILY

Jane Little Botkin

University of Oklahoma Press : Norman

Library of Congress Cataloging-in-Publication Data

Names: Botkin, Jane Little, 1952– author.
Title: Frank Little and the IWW : the blood that stained an American
    family / Jane Little Botkin.
Description: First Edition. | Norman, OK : University of Oklahoma Press,
    2017. | Includes bibliographical references and index.
Identifiers: LCCN 2016043996 | ISBN 978-0-8061-5500-5 (hardback)
Subjects: LCSH: Little, Franklin Henry, 1878–1917. | Industrial Workers of
    the World—Biography. | Industrial Workers of the World—History. |
    Western Federation of Miners—Biography. | Miners—Labor unions—West
    (U.S.) | BISAC: HISTORY / United States / State & Local / West (AK, CA,
    CO, HI, ID, MT, NV, UT, WY).
Classification: LCC HD6509.L58 B68 2017 | DDC 331.88/6092 [B] —dc23
LC record available at https://lccn.loc.gov/2016043996

The paper in this book meets the guidelines for permanence and durability of
the Committee on Production Guidelines for Book Longevity of the Council
on Library Resources, Inc. ∞

Copyright © 2017 by Jane Little Botkin. Published by the University of Oklahoma Press, Publishing Division of the University. Manufactured in the U.S.A.

1 2 3 4 5 6 7 8 9 10

To the Silent Generation—
Lee, Zora, Hazel, Tommie, Glen, and Thaylia

War will mean the end of free speech, free press, free assembly—everything we ever fought for. I'll take the firing squad first!

CONTENTS

Illustrations

COPPER TRUST TO THE PRESS: "IT'S ALL RIGHT, PAL; JUST TELL THEM HE WAS A TRAITOR."

From *Solidarity*, August 11, 1917. *Courtesy of the Industrial Workers of the World.*

PREFACE

Every family has secrets tucked away from prying eyes and curious hearts. In my family we have a ghost, hidden away for almost a century. My parents called this black sheep of the family, who was hanged ignominiously from a railroad trestle, "the socialist." I would pause to eavesdrop when the subject of my great-granduncle Frank H. Little arose, which it invariably did when we had relatives visiting. My parents would get out an ancient cardboard box of photos, and everyone would tell stories about the faces they saw. Although he was almost always mentioned, Frank's likeness was not included in the box.

Back in the 1960s, just a decade after the McCarthy era, I was a high school student developing an intense passion for gathering family genealogy and history overall. I pressed my parents to tell me more about Uncle Frank, but they volunteered little—only that he had died violently. Actually, they never knew him. Their parents' deliberate reticence had profoundly buried his story. Yet like a pebble dropped into water, my uncle's life had rippled through future Little generations, softly murmuring the tragedies of his life and death. I absorbed intermittent waves of family lore by quietly listening to rare stories that could not be found in any history book.

It was not until the 1990s, when they decided to discover more about Frank's murder, that my father and his sister took a trip to Butte, Montana. Once inside Silver Bow Library with their questions, they became instant curiosities, their presence prompting local reporting. As it turned out, my uncle was both notorious *and* famous. He outraged mine owners, governors, and perhaps even worried the president of the United States. Frank Little was an early organizer and agitator for the Industrial Workers of the World (IWW), a radical organization intent on inspiring economic revolution and improving quality of life for working men and women. Many in Butte revered him.

After that trip I became mildly interested in this famous relative, the "half-breed hobo-agitator" of whom no early history was published. I believed I had American Indian blood through Frank's mother, my great-great-grandmother, and early poetry and IWW stories about Frank seemed to confirm this. I was enveloped in the romantic notion of my ancestry with slight interest in who Frank Little really was and how his passion and actions influenced the American labor movement.

I also knew that my great-grandfather Alonzo Little had another brother, Fred, whose known family history yielded hints of a quixotic past. Family members told how Fred Little left home searching for riches in the Cripple Creek gold rush. Only Alonzo and their little sister Bessie remained in Oklahoma. Although I continued to interview my elders and ask for stories about my Little family heritage, years passed while I raised a family and taught school, with little thought to Frank or Fred Little.

One day, as I was helping my son prepare for an Advanced Placement U.S. History exam, we came across a cartoon of a lynched man whose body is labeled "Frank Little, IWW organizer." An armed, masked thug representing the Copper Trust is whispering into the ear of a character representing the American press, "It's all right, Pal, just tell them he was a traitor," as he hands over a stack of coins, perhaps symbolic of the thirty silver pieces paid for a more infamous betrayal. My son was asked to consider this cartoon as one of several primary sources for an essay on the early industrial labor movement. Not until I studied the cartoon did I realize how significantly my great-granduncle affected our country's history, and the uncertain circumstances of his death.

I began to explore why and how this young man left the family homestead in Oklahoma, radicalized, and participated in labor events prior to World War I. What occurred before Frank's murder in Butte that impacted my family so deeply afterward? Why had my family become silenced? Amid intense investigations over a seven-year period, I retraced Frank's journeys, trying to visualize his life, understand his decisions, and determine who he really was. What I discovered left me saddened, amazed, and proud. Not only had Frank Little been a radical, gutsy union organizer, passionately invested in the welfare of the dispossessed, but my great-grand-father Alonzo Little, my great-granduncle Fred Little, and Fred's wife, Emma Harper Little, also contributed to the turmoil of the period, all paying a price for their participation.

Almost all those family members who knew firsthand infor-mation about the Little family are gone. Fortunately, I was able to interview my grandaunts before their deaths, not knowing how precious their words would become later. Through years of previous investigation and ease of Internet connections, I also found cousins who, like me, were keepers of their family histories. Jack Little, grandson of Alonzo Little; Carolyn Leverich Atkinson, great-grand-daughter of Bessie Little Courtright; Wanda C. Kinsey, granddaugh-ter of Bessie Little Courtright; Susie Harper, grandniece of Emma Harper Little; and Barbara Clapper Lewis, great-grandniece of Almira Hays Little, shared sepia-colored memories, letters, photos, and the research they had compiled while unraveling their families' history. They, too, dedicated themselves to the minute details of our shared ancestors' lives. Our family keepsakes—letters, Bible pages, mysterious photos, puzzling notations written on scraps of paper, an IWW button, and most importantly, buried family stories—have enabled voices from the past to whisper the truth of our shared family. Together we were able to piece together our histories and understand the experiences that triggered secrets in our family closets. I am extremely grateful to them.

Frank Little is divided into three parts. The first, "The Forma-tive Years," presents historical influences and catalysts impacting

Little family members' life decisions. "One Big Union" begins the narrative of my family's involvement in the industrial labor union movement. Finally, "The Dissolution" not only climaxes with Frank Little's death, but highlights suspension of American common sense, the IWW as a victorious labor union, and Little family unity after the events in Butte. I have provided documentation and notations throughout the book so that other historians, journalists, and curious readers might review the evidence for themselves.

This book, woven with tattered stories, colored and textured with family perceptions, and shaped on a solid foundation of research, is not a family history; rather, it is a *revelation* of a family and the role it played in the United States' development as an industrial nation, and the punishments thereof. It is not an account of the IWW, but a chronicle of ordinary Americans who did extraordinary things during an extremely dark time in the American experience.

ACKNOWLEDGMENTS

When I first began this project eight years ago, I had no idea how many miles I would travel while tracing my family's journey from the late nineteenth into the early twentieth century, the era of American robber barons and adolescent labor unions. Nor did I realize how many individuals would assist me in unraveling the truth of my aunt's and uncles' radical participation in the time of the first Red Scare. The task was immense. Thankfully, my cousins Jack Little, Carolyn Atkinson, Susie Harper, Wanda Kinsey, and Barbara Lewis delved into their family history boxes for information, and their early investigations helped shape the manuscript's foundation. But there are many others who smoothed my path.

Foremost, I am deeply grateful to University of Oklahoma Press's editor-in-chief, Charles Rankin, for advocating the manuscript's publication and guiding its development. Chuck may believe I sought out OU Press because of his past directorship of publications at the Montana Historical Society. But he would be incorrect. In my naiveté, I approached OU Press because of the quality of its publications and the Little family's Oklahoma connection. What a blessing, indeed, to discover I had submitted the manuscript to an editor familiar with both Oklahoma history and Montana's Frank Little story! Chuck's able editorial assistant Bethany Mowry and freelance copy editor Kerin Tate guided the manuscript's final form, also earning my gratitude.

Three women initially moved the project forward. I am indebted to J. Marie Bassett for painstakingly reviewing my early work while providing wonderful insight involving historical perspectives; Debbie Font, who read as I wrote, encouraging me to write on and humoring me with conversations about labor movements and spies; and MaryJoy Martin, an immensely talented investigator and author of western labor history, who encouraged me whenever I needed a historical bridge to cross or just kind words when I became muddled in the baggage of my family's past. These people boosted me when I thought I would never finish this undertaking.

Various archives and libraries with their wonderful staffs deserve my thanks—William W. LeFevre of the Walter P. Reuther Library at Wayne State University; Elizabeth Catt, researcher in the Kheel Center at Cornell University; Julie Herrada, curator of the Joseph A. Labadie Collection in the Special Collections Library at the University of Michigan; Jacquie Zegan of the Alice Historical Society; Melissa Scroggins and staff at the Fresno County Library, Fresno, California; Colleen Holt of the Jerome Historical Society; Nancy Godoy and staff in Archives and Special Collections, Arizona State University; Verónica Reyes and staff in Special Collections, University of Arizona; and staff at the California State Library. I would like to thank Vernon Perry, president of the Gila Historical Society in Globe, Arizona; Tammy Posey, curator of the Drumright Historical Society Museum; Kay Little (no relation!) of the Bartlesville Area History Museum; Angela Haag of Central Nevada Museum, Goldfield, Nevada; Ellen Crain, Lee Whitney, and Nikole Evankovich of the Butte–Silver Bow Public Archives; and especially Richard I. Gibson, Butte historian and author. Butte was my favorite location to visit with its friendly people and beautiful atmosphere. Gone is the city of Poisonville.

I spent a delightful afternoon touring Miami, Arizona, streets with Delvan Burch Hayward of the Gila County Library and her wonderful friend John Michael Benson, both descendants of Arizona miners. Fred Barcón of Globe, Arizona, provided help with locations and understanding the racial atmosphere during Frank Little's stay in the Miami-Globe mining district. I am appreciative of Paul Espinosa, producer of the documentary *Los Mineros*, and his introduction of Dr. Christine Marin, retired archivist and historian of Mexican American studies from Arizona State University, whose recommendations introduced me to the minority perspective in Arizona labor conflicts.

I traveled in good company! Thanks to my dearest friends, Nancy Brunsteter Díaz and Ceci Brunner Pierce, who journeyed with me, following Frank's trail while skirting tornadoes in Oklahoma, border checkpoints in Arizona, and a new generation of bindle stiffs in California. I am grateful to my sons, Joshua, who guided me through Colorado ghost towns, and Chase, who helped map our Oklahoma family's travels. Finally, love and gratitude to my husband, Gary, who made the final journey with me to Butte, Montana, and shared in my excitement and wonder of this unusual family history.

I hope that my cousins are pleased. I never would have ventured into Frank, Fred, and Emma's world without their help and encouragement.

ABBREVIATIONS

ACC	Arizona Copper Company
AFL	American Federation of Labor
ASU	Arizona State Union (Western Federation of Miners)
AWO	Agricultural Workers Organization (Industrial Workers of the World)
BMMWU	Butte Metal Mine Workers' Union
BTW	Brotherhood of Timber Workers
GEB	General Executive Board of the Industrial Workers of the World
IUMMSW	International Union of Mine, Mill, and Smelter Workers
IWW	Industrial Workers of the World
M&M	Merchants and Manufacturers Association
MMWIU	Metal Mine Workers' Industrial Union (Industrial Workers of the World)
MOA	Mine Owners' Association
OBU	One Big Union (Industrial Workers of the World)

OWIU	Oil Workers Industrial Union (Industrial Workers of the World)
PLM	Partido Liberal Mexicano
SPA	Socialist Party of America
SLP	Socialist Labor Party
UMWA	United Mine Workers of America
WCU	Working Class Union
WFM	Western Federation of Miners
WULL	Women's Union Label League

FRANK LITTLE AND THE IWW

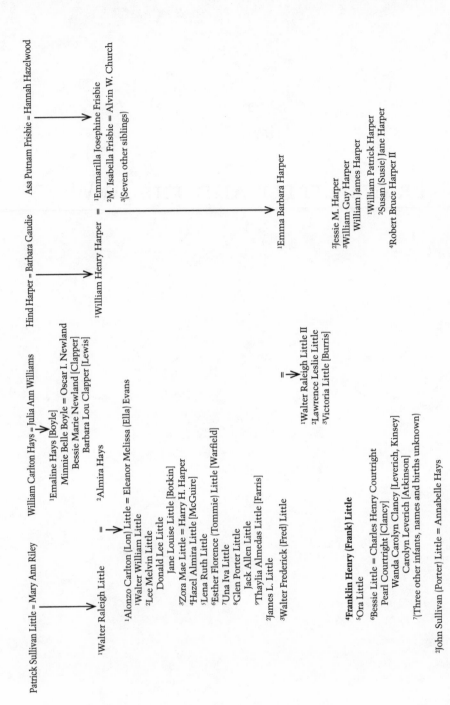

Patrick Sullivan Little = Mary Ann Riley   William Carlton Hays = Julia Ann Williams   Hind Harper = Barbara Gaudie   Asa Putnam Frisbie = Hannah Hazelwood

¹Emaline Hays [Boyle]
Minnie Belle Boyle = Oscar I. Newland
Bessie Marie Newland [Clapper]
Barbara Lou Clapper [Lewis]

²Almira Hays

¹Emmarilla Josephine Frisbie
²M. Isabella Frisbie = Alvin W. Church
³(Seven other siblings)

¹William Henry Harper =

¹Walter Raleigh Little =

¹Emma Barbara Harper

²Jessie M. Harper
³William Guy Harper
William James Harper
¹William Patrick Harper
²Susan (Susie) Jane Harper
⁴Robert Bruce Harper II

¹Alonzo Carlton (Lon) Little = Eleanor Melissa (Ella) Evans
¹Walter William Little
²Lee Melvin Little
Donald Lee Little
Jane Louise Little [Botkin]
³Zora Mae Little = Harry H. Harper
⁴Hazel Almira Little [McGuire]
⁵Lena Ruth Little
⁶Esther Florence (Tommie) Little [Warfield]
⁷Una Iva Little
⁸Glen Porter Little
Jack Allen Little
⁹Thaylia Almedas Little [Farris]
²James L. Little
³Walter Frederick (Fred) Little

=

¹Walter Raleigh Little II
²Lawrence Leslie Little
³Victoria Little [Burris]

⁴Franklin Henry (Frank) Little
⁵Ora Little
⁶Bessie Little = Charles Henry Courtright
Pearl Courtright [Clancy]
Wanda Carolyn Clancy [Leverich, Kinsey]
Carolyn Leverich [Atkinson]
⁷(Three other infants, names and births unknown)

²John Sullivan (Porter) Little = Annabelle Hays

The chart includes only persons named within *Frank Little and the IWW: The Blood That Stained an American Family*. Some parents, children, and spouses are omitted depending on relevancy.

PROLOGUE

In the early morning hours of August 1, 1917, a black Cadillac snaked slowly up North Wyoming Street from an old delivery barn below the hill in Butte, Montana. The weather had been arid and unusually warm, and tempers were heated as well. But in the serene coolness of night, there was an aural crispness—a heavy silence that descended on the city after days of strikers' demands for safer working conditions and fair employment, days after the great Speculator Mine had swallowed 168 miners in fire and toxic fumes. The Butte town was exhausted and anxious.

Six men quietly slid out of the idling car. One stood sentry while the other five entered a boardinghouse at 316 North Wyoming Street. Some said the men wore uniforms; others remembered indistinct attire. But all agreed that the six men, anonymous behind their masquerade masks and cloaked in darkness, were on a sinister assignment. Once inside, they crept to a downstairs room and violently kicked in the door, shattering the silence, only to find the room empty. Someone muttered, "A mistake somewhere." The men, apparently armed with misinformation from one of many paid informants, or "stoolies," hired by mine agents, moved to the next door in the hall.

While throwing on her robe, landlady Nora Byrne heard their frustrated, muffled voices just before her own door was opened several inches, a large pistol penetrating the darkness above her bed. A flashlight obscured the intruders momentarily from her sleepy eyes. A muted voice identified the speaker as a law officer, while the man with the menacing pistol demanded in loud whispers that Mrs. Byrne tell them which room Frank Little occupied. She murmured that Frank was renting room thirty-two, next to the room they had entered moments earlier.

Frank surely heard the locked door splintering at the same time Mrs. Byrne was awakened by the ruckus. He knew what was about to transpire, as he had received numerous threats and beatings in the past. As Frank reached for his pocket watch, he was yanked roughly out of bed, the watch rattling across the wood floor. Wearing only his underwear and a plaster cast protecting a broken ankle, Frank, oddly enough, reached next for his hat, but he was told he would not need it where he was going. By then he could make no response since his captors had gagged his mouth with a towel.

Only Mrs. Byrne and her two other boarders timidly peered through their doors to witness what was taking place: a struggling tenant dragged out of the boardinghouse to a waiting car. Typical of many bystanders, they provided Frank with no immediate assistance, waiting at least half an hour before calling local authorities. Frank twisted and thrashed, but with a broken ankle and six men restraining him, he was easily gathered and thrown into the backseat, where side curtains hid the crime. The beating had already begun, though the result would be different from the assaults he had received before.

The black sedan drove back south down Wyoming Street, stopping abruptly just before it turned west into Butte's business district. Wrenching Frank out of the Cadillac, his assailants tied him to the rear bumper and drove several more blocks, towing him in the car's wake over the granite-paved streets. Both of Frank's kneecaps were nearly ripped away, his toes and fingers reduced to bloody pulp. But he was still alive.

When the car was within sight of the Milwaukee Railroad trestle, about two miles south of town, it turned west onto a sandy road that led near the bridge. The car stopped directly underneath it, next to where a rope thrown over the ties above dangled in invitation. Someone quickly pinned a pasteboard placard on the right thigh of Frank's dirtied underwear. Scribbled in blood-red crayon, its message read, "Others take notice! First and last warning! 3-7-77," the numbers referring to an old Montana vigilante code. Added in lead pencil were the initials "L-D-C-S-S-W-T" with the L circled.

The men grasped Frank's body, pistol-whipped and now mangled from the dragging, and heaved him on top of the big black car. Between glimmers of awareness and flutters of dark unconsciousness, Frank must have felt the rough noose squeeze around his neck. Perhaps he could not command his body to struggle as a surreal heaviness hugged his brain while he slipped into nothingness. The assassin car suddenly moved forward, leaving Frank's slender frame to swing about five feet above the ground.

Then the mysterious hit men erased the evidence of their tracks and fled in their big black car, while Franklin Henry Little, youngest son of a quintessential American family, asphyxiated, alone, at the end of a hemp rope.

PART ONE

✧ ✧ ✧

THE FORMATIVE YEARS

1884–1899

1

✦ ✦ ✦ ✦

OKLAHOMA, LAND OF THE FAIR GOD

When Walter Raleigh Little drove his wagon southwest over the red prairie dirt in the summer of 1889, he was determined to establish a new home for his extended family. Now fifty years old, he had left behind at least three medical practices in Missouri, as wanderlust and the prospect of life in a new state beckoned him to the Unassigned Lands in what would eventually be Oklahoma.[1] On April 22, he had claimed 160 acres of land, free for the taking, in the first Oklahoma Land Run. After living in Indian Territory to the east for the past five years, he could now take legal residence in the newly formed Oklahoma Territory.

Walter was born March 20, 1839, near Vermont, Fulton County, Illinois. His father, Patrick Sullivan Little, was supposedly of Irish descent, but Walter's mother, Mary Ann Riley, was definitely Scots-Irish, her ancestors having immigrated to the United States in 1740 from Belfast, Ireland.[2] It is with her ancestry that the Little family most identified, originating ruminations of relationships with Sir Walter Raleigh and Mary, Queen of Scots.[3] One family member reminded her granddaughter that she was of Scottish ancestry and "to never be ashamed for they were from aristocracy."[4]

Riding along with Walter in the jangling wagon were Almira, his wife of thirty years, and their youngest child, Bessie, who was almost six years old. Bessie wore her dark-blonde hair parted in the middle, a widow's peak crowning her heart-shaped face. Only a dimple in her chin spoiled the perfect heart's symmetry. Just four of Walter and Almira's nine children had survived to make the trek into Indian Territory. Bessie's sister Ora died before she was ten. She had been extremely tiny—still able to walk under tables when she was nine.[5] Three-year-old James had also been left behind, buried in Fulton County.[6]

Now two of the Littles' three surviving sons, impressionable boys at the onset of their teenage years, helped drive the wagon with family belongings packed tightly in trunks, firmly strapped to the wagon bed and side boards. They were also responsible for the livestock, lumbering behind, and nervous chickens, caged in pens. Walter Frederick, called Fred by his family, was almost fourteen years old, and his little brother Franklin Henry, or Frank, was eleven. Both boys' honey-colored heads were turning coffee brown, much like their suntanned skin, and their blue eyes belied any evidence of Cherokee blood. Fred and Frank were likely eager to make the journey to a new, wild frontier. Bessie, who adored her older brothers, would have absorbed their excitement. Years later she still embraced her relationships with them—until fear of retaliation silenced her voice.

An autumn palette best describes Oklahoma during the summer. Bluestem and Indian grasses, green in springtime, transform to burnished gold, dusty orange, and sienna brown, with various hues of ochre melding into one endless prairie as dry spells set in. Travel along cool, green creeks with their thin river birches and lanky sycamores was not possible in a wagon, and shade was a fleeting mirage, transmuted only upon entering meadows shielded beneath canopies of black walnut and pecan trees. Perspiration drenched the family's clothing within minutes, with only a momentary coolness to chill moisture droplets on faces and arms, a passing reminder of drier climates left behind. The family wagons, having left Ski-a-took (present-day Skiatook in Osage County) sometime after June 1889, rumbled over summer grass mounds, straw-like undergrowth rolled into the rusty soil by other eighty-niners looking for the most direct route to their land claims. The animals were urged along as they yanked mouths of crisp grass along the way.

The Little family had scraped by for the past four and a half years, living illegally in Indian Territory in anticipation of momentous land openings for settlement and this final trip to their staked claims. Sometime after November 1884, the family had left Burdett, Bates County, Missouri, settling first in Vinita, Indian Territory (now Craig County, northeast Oklahoma), and then in Ski-a-took, Indian Territory, both locations in the Cooweescoowee district of the Cherokee Nation.[7] During these years, the children's unusual experiences enhanced their growth from early youth to adolescence. Most significant, their encounters shaped their values through identification with an ethnic mix of cultures. Years later Fred Little would describe his birth in Indian Territory, while Frank Little embellished even further—promoting his self-portrayal as a half-breed Indian, a deliberate stretch of the truth.

Twenty-five-year-old Oscar Ivanhoe Newland most likely accompanied the family on their trip from Missouri to Oklahoma since he had lived with them while employed as a farm laborer as early as 1880 in Grant, Cass County, Missouri.[8] An orphan, he had shown up on Walter's doorstep one day looking for work. The family adopted him as their own, and he and Walter's eldest son, Alonzo "Lon" Carlton Little, became best friends.[9] Oscar married Almira's niece Minnie Boyle in Indian Territory in 1886.

The newly incorporated Cherokee town of Vinita, a raucous shipping center for the thousands of brindle, black, and white longhorn cattle driven across Indian Territory's lush spring grasses, lay at the crossing of the first two railroads to enter what is now Oklahoma. A few miles east were major trails from the north and the east over which thousands of people traveled by horseback and wagons. The town was a logical destination for Walter and his family, who resided there about one year before moving to Ski-a-took and leaving Oscar Newland behind.

The trip to Ski-a-took was about fifty miles and took no more than three days. The family moved southwesterly by wagon, traveling among gentle, rolling hills. Osage Indians, living in colorful hide-and-canvas teepees dotting grassy valleys, welcomed the noncitizens, as they could collect rents from them to pay for better government-built houses.[10] Sitting under ancient walnuts, the old Ski-a-took trading post on Bird Creek was close to the line of the Cooweescoowee district and the Osage reservation.

Walter moved his family to Ski-a-took in part because of a Quaker mission school, which drew an influx of noncitizens whom the Cherokee Nation permitted to farm in the territory. Many of northeastern Oklahoma's most prominent men had been taught at the school. The decision would have a profound impact on Frank and Fred's moral compasses regarding fairness and relationships among diverse groups. Yet this was not their parents' sole reason for enrollment. After the 1884 death of Dr. George William Lloyd, who had negotiated with tribes to reserve a plot of land for Hillside Cemetery and Hillside Mission, a vacancy for a doctor opened.[11] Walter Little could fill that void.

In 1886, eight-year-old Frank and eleven-year-old Fred moved with other students to a newly constructed, larger mission-school building on a hillside two miles north of the original school. The enormous white clapboard building, incongruous among Ski-a-took's log cabins and wood pens, had three floors with two wings for dormitories, their windows projecting like giant bug eyes. At this time the school was renamed Hillside Quaker Mission School but was commonly called Friends' Mission School. Rich or poor, white or American Indian, everyone was treated alike.

Frank and Fred's first teacher taught only six months before being replaced by Quakers John and Lisa Watson. The teachers' curriculum was "rather elastic" as courses were added as the school grew.[12] Besides basic studies, including reading out of McGuffey Readers, the Watsons taught enrichment courses such as civil government, religion and dutiful responsibilities, general history, bookkeeping, and music.[13] The mission school even had a literary society, to which all students belonged, providing a valuable scholarly culture and drill in parliamentary usage. Frank utilized the latter afterward as a member of the IWW's General Executive Board (GEB).[14] The Watsons dedicated their lives to molding children into good neighbors and citizens while imbuing Quaker doctrine into students' young minds.

HILLSIDE MISSION SCHOOL

Frank and Fred attended the Quaker-run Hillside Mission School, first established for American Indian children. *Courtesy of the Bartlesville Area History Museum, Bartlesville, Oklahoma.*

After the Civil War, a strong sentiment against violence and brutality had driven the Friends' Society to criticize the conduct of the Bureau of Indian Affairs. As a result, President Grant allotted control of the Indians' general condition and their affairs to the Friends' Society. By doing so, the federal government hoped to instill a more peaceable attitude among the tribes toward white settlement. This history with the Friends gave Quakers prestige among American Indians. Students at Hillside, including the Little boys, deeply adhered to the Quakers' pacifist convictions. This early formative education would influence Frank's later behavior among his peers. His attitude toward conscription during World War I, in particular, was partially shaped by this early Quaker schooling in pacifism, despite the martial tone of his hard, inflammatory words denouncing the Great War and challenging the capitalists who supported it.

Frank and Fred studied and played among Indian children for two more years in an area with little racial division among whites,

Indians, and freedmen. Essentially all of them were settlers—many of Indian Territory's Native inhabitants were not even native to the area. The old mission school and its cemetery reflect a time during Oklahoma territorial days when prejudices were put aside for the purposes of education and evangelism.

The Little family, though, were likely considered *intruders*, individuals who illegally settled in Indian Territory and thus were subject to expulsion by federal troops unless they could produce a legal permit tied to economic development (such as ranching) or if they intermarried with a person of Indian blood. Tribal police regularly patrolled to see that these people had permits and to keep intruders from remaining within the Cherokee Nation.[15] However, it is doubtful that Walter depended on his wife's heritage for residency.

Almira Hays Little privately professed American Indian ancestry to the family, although she was most certainly not a full-blood Indian, or even a half-blood.[16] She was born in 1844 to shoemaker William "Billy" Carlton Hays and Julia Ann Williams in Fulton County, Illinois.[17] Julia, who is believed to have possessed Cherokee blood, was born in Indiana in 1820 and died during the cholera outbreak of 1851.[18] Little is known about Julia's background, but Almira acknowledged her noble Native ancestry, supposedly descending from a chief, when it bolstered her elevated position in the family and her condescension of her new daughter-in-law.[19] Almira's photographs reveal a prim, slightly framed woman, her mouth a slash across her face, her nose hawk-like between high cheekbones. Aside from these Indian characteristics, she was rather fair. In all of Almira's images, her dark, deep-set eyes peer into the camera, one eyebrow raised if as to express her impatience with the photographer.

The overland journey toward a permanent homestead continued after Ski-a-took, this time to the free land that Walter had claimed in April 1889. Traveling separately to their new land claims were Walter and Almira's eldest son, Lon, a stout young man of twenty-eight years, and his new wife, nineteen-year-old Ella Evans Little. Lon had his own trap, consisting of a wagon and team of

ALMIRA HAYS LITTLE
Frank Little's mother, ca. 1898.
Little Family Papers.

horses, a young colt, a cow, a pig, a plow, and the minimal household furnishings common to a newlywed couple.[20]

Eleanor (Ella) Melissa Evans, daughter of a Methodist missionary in Indian Territory, was one of nine children—seven daughters
and two sons. Her family had lived in a dugout near Ringo, Indian
Territory, after moving from Boone Township, Bates County, Missouri, to minister to Cherokees and Delawares in the area. Her
father, Rev. William Perry Evans, listed in 1883 as an intruder near
present-day Ochelata, Washington County, Oklahoma, was a busy
circuit rider.[21] His limited attention to his daughters, as well as
his wife Sarah's inadequate education, guaranteed Ella's shortcomings in both academics and genteel behavior. As family members report, Rev. Bill and Sarah Evans had their hands full trying
to keep their daughters from going "behind the bushes with the
Cherokee boys."[22]

At some point before 1889, while awaiting the opening of the Unassigned Lands, the Little family had hired Ella as a servant in their Ski-a-took household.[23] When Lon showed an interest in feisty, fair-haired Ella, Almira was not pleased, disdaining the girl's ignorance. She was not the only family member to scorn Ella. One family story tells how Fred and Frank were taught never to drink out of a glass someone else had used. To cause mischief, Ella, the "hired girl," would drink out of Fred's glass before serving him water. He would immediately throw a temper tantrum that she thought was funny.[24] Despite his mother's objections to Ella's commonness, Lon married Ella on June 22, 1889, in northeastern Oklahoma, with Ella's father possibly officiating, immediately before they began the trek southwest.[25] During the ensuing years, Ella proved to be an able bride for Lon with the requisite know-how and pioneering spirit, yet she and Almira continued to hate each other.[26]

Washington Irving may have been the first to describe the geographic beauty and wealth of Oklahoma's natural resources after he made a hunting trip in 1834 to the territory. He afterward described Oklahoma's beauty in his sketch "A Tour of the Prairies." Later, newspaperman Milton Reynolds, writing under the name Kicking Bird as special correspondent for the *Kansas City Times*, coined the phrase "Land of the Fair God" during his coverage of a campaign to open the land for settlement. He was not the only journalist to propagandize Oklahoma's attributes. In 1885 other headlines painted Indian Territory as "the land where milk and honey flows" and the "garden spot of the continent" with "cattle, cattle, everywhere."[27]

Although thousands of longhorn cattle roamed the territory, cattlemen who had leased lands there did not want settlers to encroach on their good arrangement, and they furiously lobbied against opening lands. On March 13, 1885, President Grover Cleveland issued a proclamation stating that anyone trespassing in Indian Territory would be arrested and that those who already lived illegally there needed to leave immediately or be evicted.[28] Yet public reaction pressured opening land for settlement. With the passage of the General Allotment Act, or Dawes Act, on February 8, 1887, and subsequent creation of Oklahoma Territory, Indian Territory shrank to its final form: the Five Civilized Tribes (Cherokee, Chickasaw, Choctaw, Creek, and Seminole) and the Quapaw Tract. These nations were assigned their own tribal areas, leaving a hole in the middle of Indian Territory. Known as the Unassigned Lands, this area further enticed white settlement since any land remaining after land allotments to individual Indians could become available for public sale.

Ignoring the presidential decree, people continued to flow to the border between Kansas and Indian Territory. They camped in tents and wagons while others, including the Little family, set up their camps within Indian Territory, evading patrolling federal troops. Many of these people were rootless settlers, folks who had failed at settlement elsewhere and were desperate for a second or third chance. Many were families that had never recovered their losses from the Civil War. Despite the government's attempts to restrict their settlement, contemporary newspapers prophesied that "Oklahoma will be wrested from barbarism and given to white settlement and civilization in the near future."[29]

After enormous public outcry and squatters' aggressive attempts to settle in the Unassigned Lands, Congress attached a last-minute amendment to an Indian appropriations bill providing release of lands for homestead settlement in March 1889. Finally, the Unassigned Lands would be opened for settlement, beginning with the land run in which Walter and his eldest son participated. Under the provisions of the 1862 Homestead Act, families could claim 160 acres of public land. Those who had leased acreage in the area prior to the land runs, including the cattlemen and those who already had 160-acre homesteads, were not eligible to participate.

The first land run of the future Oklahoma Territory included almost three million acres in what would become the territorial counties of Canadian, Cleveland, Kingfisher, Logan, Oklahoma, and Payne. Perhaps 100,000 people vied for fewer than 12,000 quarter sections, 160-acre tracts that had previously been surveyed and marked by stones at each corner.[30] Participants raced to drive a stake into a choice piece of land before a fellow "Boomer" could claim the property and then file claim in Guthrie, the new county seat.

Much has been written describing the excitement and motley participants in the 1889 land run. On a beautiful cloudless day, mounted blue-coated soldiers stood guard over scores of people— nervous riders on skittish horses, calmer drivers in sturdy wagons and all species of buggies angling for advantageous positions, and people on foot. The Santa Fe Railroad stood ready to carry carloads of future Oklahomans into the race. With instructions to the engineers to travel no faster than a horse or wagon, men and women could leap off the train to stake claims. While Almira, Fred, Frank, and Bessie waited safely to the northeast in Indian Territory, both Walter and Lon anticipated the race where they, too, would stake lands they had previously explored and selected for their homesteads.

At noon cavalry bugles trumpeted in cacophonous unison, and guns fired into a cerulean sky now tinged red from hooves churning prairie dirt in restless anticipation. The run had officially begun. Clouds of dust filled the air as people raced pell-mell for their choice claims. In the frantic melee, Walter successfully staked lots within what would be called Clayton Township in territorial Payne County.[31] The lots fringed the west and northwest side of the Cimarron River, adjacent to a crossing popular before bridges were built.[32] Evidently Walter claimed this land for investment and not for farming. Like Walter, Lon staked his own claim but not far from the starting line. Something happened to his horse, so Lon could not race to the property that he had scouted earlier. Instead, when shots were discharged for the run to begin, amid thundering hooves and excited shouts and frenzied screams, Lon simply walked a short distance west on foot and put his stake down.[33] This area was within the future Pawnee Township, also in Payne County.[34] Today the farm is located on Highway 51 east of Stillwater, about nine miles out of town.

Campfires dotted the prairies the night of April 22, 1889, and the tent city of Guthrie erupted by morning, blisters of white canvas tents spreading over russet-red dirt and trampled-grass town lots. Guthrie would serve as the unofficial capital of Oklahoma Territory:

1889 OKLAHOMA LAND RUN

Frank's father, Walter R. Little, and brother Alonzo C. Little both scrambled for land in the April 22, 1889, Oklahoma Land Run. *Courtesy of the Research Division of the Oklahoma Historical Society.*

a place for filing claims at a land office, a place to hang medical and legal shingles, a place to make money from selling the essential supplies that eighty-niners would need to establish their farms. Stores operated from the backs of wagons until prefabricated wooden structures could be quickly assembled to house their wares, and hotels opened in tents.

✦ ✦ ✦ ✦

Some distance from Guthrie, the wild prairie waited for Frank Little's family to arrive and break its red crust that summer of 1889. The trip from Indian Territory to their new homesteads took about four days, slow travel by wagon as there were no roads between Ski-a-took and their new claims—just grassy trails or tracks across the prairie and fords through streams and creeks.[35] The families

took a ferry southwest across the Red Fork of the Arkansas River
near a stage station of the same name on the old Chisholm Trail,
then turned due west through rugged hill country, following the
blood-red Cimarron River as it branched away from the Arkansas. They crossed the river north on another ferry about five miles
southwest of present-day Yale, Oklahoma, at the narrow, shallow stretch of water subsequently known as Clayton Ford, which
Walter's land abutted.

Ella Little later told her children that their journey was not
uneventful. Indians traveled the same path as the wagons, and the
land was untamed. Along the way wild animals tried to kill Lon's
colt and pig. At night the newlyweds put the smaller animals inside
their wagon to keep from losing them while the couple slept under
a wagon sheet outside.[36] Yet despite the dangers of the journey,
both families were excited to establish new homes on land that
the U.S. government had afforded them. Indeed, Oklahoma Territory
was a promising start for families that had gambled their futures
on uncertain weather, new territorial laws, and fickle politics.
When the future finally exposed her face, the means by which the
territory had met these conditions were blemished, fostering home-
grown radicals with progressive convictions.

2

HARDSCRABBLE, 1890–1894

Frank Little's family squeezed into a simple log cabin built on a red-clay bluff near the Clayton Ford of the Cimarron River. Locals subsequently called the bluff "Doc Little's Hill."[1] Running burgundy brown to crimson red, depending on the clay soils stirred by the rains, the wide Cimarron was a formidable barrier. Lined with rock outcroppings or with unstable sandy beaches formed from the red sediment, its sides made crossing difficult where there was no ferry. The saline, blood-hued water was also undrinkable, forcing settlers to dig wells or locate springs on their land. Below Walter and Almira's cabin, the river ran narrower and shallower, though it was rife with quicksand.

The meandering Cimarron River guided the formation of a zigzag string of communities near its banks. Ingalls, founded in 1889, was about four miles northeast of the Walter R. Little homestead, and "Old Clayton," which the family frequently cited as their residence, was about one mile west.[2] The family participated in social activities in both communities budding on the northern and western sides of the serpentine river. Founded where the line was drawn for the 1891 Land Run, Clayton overflowed with homesteaders. By February 1890, the little community would serve as the first post office address for the Little family.

The town of Ripley had sprouted by 1900—not on or near Walter R. Little's land, as he may have envisioned, but across the river. Ripley also served briefly as an address for the Littles after the Eastern Oklahoma Railroad bypassed Clayton for a new community named Mehan, two miles to the north. It was only after Walter's death and sale of his land that the railroad purchased right-of-way through the former Little homestead.

The Littles' land was rolling, with gentle hills sloping down to creeks, or "cricks," as Little family members called them. Today, hordes of red-berry juniper evergreen shrubs congregate atop hills, but land in the 1890s was mostly grassland with various hardwoods and grapevine lining the creeks. Enormous walnut trees along Stillwater Creek provided the lumber for Frank's family cabin.

The creek also afforded great adventure for Frank and Fred. Blackjacks produced heavy amber and red carpets of leaves during the fall, hiding the copperhead snakes that slithered beneath the boys' bare feet. After quickstepping to the creek bank, the boys fished for catfish hiding in cool, deep holes, or shot squirrels. It was a paradise away from home for the boys.

Bluestem and Indian grasses on the treeless hills provided forage for cattle and horses, but the land reluctantly yielded to early homesteaders hard-pressed to grow immediate sustenance. It was hardscrabble land that wrung sweat and fortitude out of the farmer for only marginal rewards. Oklahoma was no "land of milk and honey" unless one was fortunate enough to have an oil reservoir beneath one's parcel, but those discoveries were still ten years away.

In a 1937 interview, Walter's sister-in-law Annabelle Hays Little recalled life in newly opened Oklahoma Territory: "We all had a hard time but we had plenty to eat. There were plenty of deer and prairie chickens all over the country, so we always had plenty of meat. After the first year, everyone got along better as good crops were raised."[3] Other Little family members might have disagreed.

Both families had to "prove up" within five years after the run— that is, show improvements to the land in accordance with the Homestead Act's provisions. These first five years were enormously difficult ones. Arriving too late to plant a crop, most homesteaders began the 1889 summer by preparing ground for the next year's

planting season, building homes, and locating water. But 1890 was
a dry year, and once again, many farmers produced little. In September 1890, Congress provided $50,000 in relief funds to ease
homesteaders' hardships, fearing that some farmers would simply
abandon their claims rather than lose what little they had had
before the run. Nonetheless, many farmers were too proud to accept
government relief and suffered, while others picked up their com-
modities under cover of night.[4]

Essayist George Milburn described Oklahoma Territory as "a
place populated with failures," by a class of farmers experienced
in defeat after the Civil War.[5] Walter R. Little, a late bloomer,
may have shared some of their frustrations, as he, too, had been
swept along before finally settling on a fresh path at the war's conclusion. After selling his interest in his parents' family farm to his
brother James McElvain Little, Walter entered Abingdon College
in Abingdon, Illinois, graduating in 1869.[6] The small family then
moved to Schuyler County, Illinois, next door to well-known physician Hosea Davis, who mentored Walter in the field of medicine.[7]

Between 1874 and 1878, Walter R. Little formally attended
medical school in Keokuk, Lee County, Iowa. During the months
he was not in school, Walter farmed about twenty miles to the east
in Webster, Hancock County, Illinois. Fred was born during this
time, on August 28, 1875, and Frank was born between January
and mid-June 1878.[8] When Walter graduated on June 18, 1878, from
the College of Physicians and Surgeons in Keokuk, he was almost
forty years old.[9]

Some family members state that Walter went to Oklahoma
Territory because of a shortage of doctors there. Another theory is
that the federal government was paying gold to doctors who would
venture into Indian Territory to give smallpox vaccinations to Indians—and that Walter was one of these doctors. These beliefs are
not necessarily borne out by fact. Many doctors and dentists made
the 1889 Land Run, hanging their shingles on tents until their offices
were built. Like so many others, they were there because they were
interested in land.

A slight man, Walter now depended on his younger sons for
labor since Lon had his own farm to sustain. When not down at the
creek smoking grapevine or hunting, avocations in which many

Oklahoma boys partook, Frank and Fred did heavy work around the farm. It is possible that Walter might have been able to hire help, but most folks had little money.[10] As a horse-and-buggy physician who made home visits, with Bessie often acting as his assistant, he regularly accepted barter items in exchange for his medical services.[11] By farming and doctoring, Walter was able to make requisite improvements on his homestead, and he filed his patent for permanent ownership on October 31, 1896, in Guthrie.[12]

Life had also been demanding for newlyweds Lon and Ella Little. Several miles northwest of Walter and Almira's homestead, they dug out a winter home for themselves near a washed-out area on an oak-lined creek and another dugout for their livestock. In 1890 they built a one-room log cabin on a hill northwest of the dugout with shake shingles that Ella made by hand.[13] In August 1891 their first child, Walter William Little, was born, only to die one year later of "summer complaint."[14] Despite Ella's close relationship with her doctor father-in-law, who genuinely liked her, the baby could not be saved. Young Walter W. was the first Little to be buried in the new Ingalls Cemetery. After the summer of 1891, Lon and Ella built a new house on the hill, not far from the original log cabin and close to a spring where they dug down for a well. Yet Lon had to seek additional work in order to support his growing family, taking a job at Ingalls's general store by 1893.[15] With Ella's help and the extra income, Lon improved their homestead, and their patent record for land ownership was recorded on April 3, 1896.[16]

Other members of the Little and Hays families also moved to Oklahoma and Indian territories, meshing together a tightly woven extended family. Almira's sister and brother-in-law Emaline Hays and James H. Boyle and their daughter Minnie, who married Oscar Newland, had settled at West Cabin Creek, not far from Vinita. In 1891 Walter's younger brother Porter Sullivan Little moved to Oklahoma Territory on Walter's advice and later claimed land in the September 16, 1893 Land Run into the Cherokee Outlet. Unknown to the Littles, an enormous lake of oil lay underneath the claim.[17] No wonder Annabelle Little's recollection of the Little families' first years was cobwebbed with pleasant impressions.

Previously Walter and Almira had ensured that their children received as good an education as possible for the times in which they lived. Despite constant moves and uprooting from various schools, Lon was an avid reader who could have taught others.[18] Now his brothers and sister would have to get back to school. At sixteen, Fred was too old for the tent schools that sprang up shortly after the run. Besides, he had other plans. Avoiding the drudgery of farm work, Fred ran away to California with a friend during the summer of 1891, probably catching one of the trains rumbling west.[19] Bessie and Frank were still school age, though. In 1893, when Bessie was ten years old and Frank fifteen, Clayton Township built a one-room schoolhouse that taught seven grades. Many of the students were older farm boys who antagonized their teachers during the months they were able to attend school.[20] It is not known if Frank was one of these students.

At the time of the IWW's involvement in organizing western locals, Frank's critics painted him as an uneducated troublemaker. Radical William F. Dunn, editor of the *Butte Strike Bulletin*, wrote that Frank was "illiterate" and "embittered," while other governmental and corporate agents' depictions of Frank as an itinerant hobo also evoke this sense of ignorance.[21] Evidence to the contrary paints Frank as a humorously persuasive, albeit impulsive, writer and orator who spoke to native and immigrant laborers in a language that would endear him as one of their own. Where he learned his power of persuasion and confidence is a mystery, as neither of his parents is recorded as participating in local politics, though Walter did declare membership in the Republican Party while he lived in Missouri.[22]

In addition to a new school, citizens of the Clayton and Ingalls Townships built churches that different denominations used on alternating schedules. The Littles attended the First Christian Church in Ingalls. Despite what has been written regarding Frank Little's religious background, his family was not Quaker.[23] Perhaps the notion comes from Frank's ancestry one hundred years prior when his McIlvain family branch converted to the Society of Friends after intermarrying with Quakers in Pennsylvania. John McIlvain, Mary Ann Riley Little's great-grandfather, converted from Presbyterianism to Quakerism, the religion of his second wife.[24] Perhaps Frank's early education at Hillside Quaker Mission School in Ski-a-took played a role as well. However, both of Frank's parents were members of the Christian Church, as were his grandparents.[25] Thus, the Quaker story is just another of the replicated half-truths about Frank that add to his assorted romantic portraits.

The Little family's church did have an impact on family members' behaviors and belief systems. Strict in its doctrines, the Christian Church split into two separate organizations following philosophical differences about scripture, and the Church of Christ was formed in 1906. Almira and Bessie joined the new church. Its stringent doctrines possibly affected Fred's and Frank's actions in later life. Fred, who was raised in a temperate household, subsequently abused alcohol as an adult. Frank was an irreverent jokester who pulled pranks in the most inappropriate settings. Victoria Little Burris, Fred's daughter, recalled a story in which her grandparents were sitting in church when someone threw a dead cat inside the sanctuary, disrupting the service. Frank was blamed for engineering the prank, though he was sitting innocently beside them.[26]

Although the Five Civilized Tribes were exempted initially from the General Allotment Act of 1887, under the 1893 establishment of the Dawes Commission, the accompanying Dawes Roll would become a final database of census information on tribal members, used to dissolve Indian lands in exchange for land allotments. Individuals from the nations had to apply for roll numbers and were issued cards, known today as CDIB (Certificate of Degree of Indian Blood) cards. Almira claimed not to want public exposure as a mixed-blood Indian. As mentioned previously, whether she had enough Indian blood to qualify is subject to debate, though one Little granddaughter confided that Almira was "one-half Indian, a Cherokee" and ashamed of her Indian blood, and that she chose not to enroll despite her children's urging.[27]

Although everyday reminders that the land had formerly belonged to Indians surrounded its residents, Oklahoma Territory was now a totally different environment, with a new dawn of class, race, and politics defining a man's worth. To Frank Little these divisions were repugnant, and his witness to the territory's social changes would profoundly affect his disdain for robber-baron entities that treated laborers with the same measures.

3

OUTLAWS AND HEROES

The Little family had become accustomed to rebellion and rebellious ways—usually as accidental participants—long before they came to Oklahoma. Restlessness and hope for fresh opportunities, as well as disorderly social and political changes, influenced the family's history of moves. The circumstances and lessons of these life pursuits were not lost on Walter and Almira Little's children. In particular, Frank and Fred witnessed patterns of governmental intrusion that shaped their parents' most important life decisions, and stability always seemed to be out of reach. They began to associate rebels with heroic qualities, ultimately blending the personas of outlaw and hero into their favored archetype of an admirable nonconformist who bucked social and political traditions.

The first conflict in which the Little family took sides provided graphic examples of what happened to insurgents and their property, early cautionary lessons that would be passed down to subsequent generations. When President Lincoln called for a volunteer force to aid in the enforcement of laws and the suppression of insurrection on May 4, 1861, the Little men in Illinois, as Republicans, took the side of the Union. However, Walter and Almira were expecting their first child, who would be born one month before young men from Fulton and McDonough Counties registered. Walter declined to volunteer, while his youngest brother Porter lied about his name and age in order to enlist. In this context the family became well versed in civil disobedience and punishments thereof. Port, who later joined Walter in Oklahoma Territory, was captured early in his service in Memphis, Tennessee, spending seven months in the infamous Libby prison before he was released at the end of the war. Soon after the capture, General Sherman gave his well-known Special Field Order No. 120, his "scorched earth" directive in which his men were told to forage liberally in the country during the remaining campaign to the Atlantic Ocean, punishing any Southern sympathizers who stood in his way.

Still it was a prior federal response to militants' actions in Missouri that most impacted the Little family and its future. Militant abolitionist guerrilla fighters known as Jayhawkers had engaged in skirmishes with the Missouri militia as well as proslavery partisans on both sides of the border between Missouri and Kansas before the Civil War even began. In response to abolitionists' violent acts, outlaw Confederate guerrilla William Quantrill had led four hundred Missouri "bushwhackers" to Lawrence, Kansas, in August 1863, where his raiders pillaged, torched, and killed virtually all the male population, reportedly anywhere between 185 and 205 men.[1] This brutal massacre prompted Union Brigadier General Thomas E. Ewing Jr. to issue General Order No. 11. Residents of four western Missouri counties, including Cass and Bates Counties on the Kansas-Missouri border where the Little family would live, had just a couple of weeks to vacate their homes unless they lived within a mile of a military outpost and could prove loyalty to the Union.[2] The counties then were torched and their farms destroyed, leaving rock chimneys standing as solitary witnesses to the punishment for civil disobedience. Bates County was totally depopulated.[3]

The damage from General Order No. 11 was still evident when Frank Little moved with his family to Grant, Cass County, in 1879, with his father fresh out of medical college. Since many Missourians never returned to rebuild at the end of the Civil War, the emptiness of Cass and Bates Counties provided affordable real estate and opportunity for migrating families that wanted a new

beginning. Perhaps Walter R. Little wanted to fill a void within a
new town in need of physicians, or perhaps he merely saw the
scorched area as a place to create a new life for the family.

Not all Confederate Missourians fled from their home state.
Infamous outlaws Jesse and Frank James, hailing from Clay County
(north of Cass County), began their early education in guerrilla
warfare under Quantrill's bloody leadership. After the war they
reorganized as an outlaw gang along with their Younger cousins,
raiding primarily in Missouri and Kansas. Their escapades, both
invented and factual, were well known to the Little family while
they lived in Missouri. By the time Frank could read, newspapers
and cheap mass production of dime novels had firmly established
the outlaws' allure to Missourians in particular. Nationally, their
print characters were transformed into "social bandits," postwar
Robin Hoods who bucked elements of Reconstruction and capitalism. Reporters in western Missouri, where the Little family lived,
presented the James gang's operation as an extreme but "morally
justifiable form of resistance to the invasion of their region first by
Yankees and then by banks and railroads chartered by the Republican government of the state."[4] Editor John Newman Edwards of
the *Kansas City Times*, in particular, helped create Jesse James's
noble persona in life and death: "a noble lion" laid low by "Caesar's
servile minions."[5] Not surprisingly, despite its infamous deeds, the
gang and its acts of kindness permeated Little family lore.

In his study of the outlaw myth, historian Richard Slotkin
states that the countervailing ideology to progressivism was mythologized in a populist revision of the frontier hero in the "cheap
literature" of the dime novel. In the detective story, a "man who
knows Indians" is replaced by a "man who knows strikers"; in the
outlaw story, a social bandit uncovers and attacks the dark side
of modern capitalism. In different ways, both genres register the
discontent of lower-class readers with the division of wealth and
power in modern society.[6] A dime-novel outlaw such as Jesse James
was a "distinctly modern form of *social bandit* defending the
integrity of an old-style agrarian/artisanal community against the
aggressions of advanced capitalism represented by the corporation."[7]
Long after the James-Younger gang ended their lives of crime,

these dime novels continued to stuff young, impressionable boys, such as Frank and Fred Little, with romantic notions of outlaw careers comprised of robbing banks, stages, and trains—all vessels of big business. Dime novel production would continue into 1903, except for a six-year ban by the postmaster general between 1883 and 1889.[8] The "righteousness" of the post–Civil War outlaw would also inspire the next generation of outlaws, including the Dalton and Doolin gangs, who later became neighbors of the Little families in Oklahoma. Without a doubt, family tales of the James-Younger gang and subsequent relationships with the Doolin-Dalton gang planted incendiary seeds of rebellion against corporate monopolistic tendencies—specifically prominence of robber baron corporations that financed and profited from their lucrative operations of banks, railroads, oil drilling, and mining during the late nineteenth and early twentieth centuries.

Near the end of the James-Younger gang era of outlawry, Walter was practicing medicine but he also operated the farm on which Lon and Oscar Newland worked.[9] Like others who made the trip to Missouri, Walter and his family had to build their new farm and medical practice from the ground up. Their residency did not last long. When the Kansas City–Clinton–Springfield railway finally was constructed south near Creighton, it missed Grant, and the town simply died.

Just a year later, the Little family made their seventh move since Walter and Almira married. Again the family located within a county destroyed by General Order No. 11, Bates County. Walter began practicing medicine in another new community named Adrian, southeast of the Cass County line. By 1882 they had moved once again to the little community of Burdette, not far from Adrian, also in Bates County, where Walter finally had a "highly satisfactory" medical practice, and Bessie was born.[10]

The social and economic wounds on Missouri soil would take generations to heal. Many Missourians, who had returned to their state after the Civil War in poorer condition than before they fled, slowly began migrating south.[11] Walter too became restless for better opportunities and joined those from Bates County, Missouri, eager for a series of moves to southern Indian Territory.

All told, Walter and Almira moved at least twelve times before settling in Payne County, Oklahoma, with the younger Little children accompanying them on the last seven relocations. Clearly Walter was either an opportunist with itchy feet, or his failure at establishing any type of permanent, sustaining home compelled him to move on to greener grasses. Without a stable home environment, the children would become either restless nomads or anchors permanently entrenched in their home places. Both Frank and Fred were wanderers, risk-takers—apparently much like their father. Conversely, Lon and Bessie raised large families in relative stability, albeit with limited resources.

The family's travels shaped the two boys' senses of justice in other ways as well. While living in Ski-a-took, the Littles found that the laws of the Cherokee Nation were few but sufficient, and generally well enforced. All men were treated as equals under the law, one eighty-niner explaining that "family standing didn't cut any figure in dealing out justice, as all were treated according to the merits of the case which was being tried."[12] However, this simple governing changed rapidly with settlement in neighboring Oklahoma Territory. Frank and Fred, who thrived under the Cherokee Nation's simple, just laws, naturally would buck the ambiguous nature and complexities of territorial and later state and federal laws.

The federal legislation that opened the land for settlement initially provided no form of government. For a brief time, the people of Oklahoma Territory governed themselves by common consent. Surprisingly, good order prevailed while a majority of Oklahomans struggled to build their homesteads and businesses. Rigorous living conditions and lack of money did not attract crime. However, families that had made land runs with little money in their pockets and only their backbones for support found themselves unable to hold on to the land they had pursued so recklessly. Many mortgaged their properties, becoming indebted to lien holders. Oklahoma Territory began to acquire a reputation for lawlessness as farmers lost their independence. Amid the organization of a political landscape, outlaws began to rampage within Oklahoma and Indian territories and into other states, undertaking perceived heroic exploits against effects of capitalism. Eastern Oklahoma, then Indian Territory, became so conducive to banditry that it developed a reputation for being the most lawless part of the United States.[13]

In the absence of law enforcement, the Dalton brothers, who, like the Littles, had traveled to Indian Territory from Cass and Bates Counties, turned to illegal activities after finding it was easier to make a living on the wrong side of the law.[14] Between 1891 and October 5, 1892, when most of the Dalton gang members were finally killed in Coffeyville, Kansas, the Dalton brothers earned both notoriety and empathy as they robbed banks and trains as far west as California, stealing big corporation money.[15] Coincidentally in 1891, Bill and Grat Dalton spent jail time in Tulare County, California, where much later Fred Little claimed to have been jailed for five months for reasons unknown.[16]

Many folks knew the Daltons from their previous lives as neighbors and protectors in Indian Territory. Little family members were no different. Ella Evans Little told her children and grandchildren how she held horses for the Dalton gang when they arrived at a barn dance.[17] Lon's daughter, Esther "Tommie" Little Warfield, related to family members how sometime before 1892 Emmett Dalton stole a pony from a neighbor and ran the horse to death trying to escape from lawmen. After he was released from prison fourteen years later, he gave the family a pair of white mules in gratitude.[18]

Such stories of fairness and humility are ingrained in eighty-niners' family lore. Another old-timer from early Indian Territory told an interviewer in 1937 that "my sympathies were with them [Daltons] for they were not bad people. It was hard for anyone to get by without breaking the law in those days."[19] He added that "the outlaws were usually kindhearted persons who made a mistake and couldn't right it by making more."[20] Another Oklahoma resident wrote, "The nice thing about it [outlawry] in the early days[,] one knew who the outlaw was. . . . Many people in the early days would have gone hungry had it not have been for the train and bank robbers."[21] This view was not uncommon. This idea of resisting big business was rooted deeply inside the Little family

DALTON GANG IN CAVE, CA. 1891–1892

Gang members pose at their cave hideout near the Cimarron River, north of
present-day Oilton, Oklahoma. Dr. Walter Little made "house calls" to the
Doolin-Dalton gang in their hideouts. *Little Family Papers.*

and other struggling Oklahoma families that empathized with the
Daltons. Outlaws were neighbors and familiar sights in communities, such as Guthrie and Ingalls.

Living in Payne County, not far from Ingalls and the Little
families' homesteads, were the Doolins, who were part of what
became called "The Wild Bunch." The Wild Bunch was also known
as the Doolin-Dalton gang, since Bill Dalton rode with the Doolins
before 1893, as well as the "Oklahoma Long Riders," due to their
long dusters. The gang terrorized businesses, robbing banks and
railroads in Kansas, Arkansas, Missouri, and Oklahoma Territory.
Clayton was a favorite rest stop for the Doolin-Dalton gang in the
early 1890s, but Ingalls was where they socialized, shopped, had
shaves and haircuts, shod their horses, and even attended church.[22]

Everyone in the Little family knew Bill Doolin and his family. He was purported to be "a hard, but, they thought, fair man,"

according to Little family members.[23] The gang had a hideout at the Dunn Ranch on Council Creek, not far from the Cimarron River where rock outcroppings hid caves along the river and, with limited access, made perfect hideouts for outlaws.[24] It was not uncommon for Bill Doolin to cross paths with the Littles and their neighbors daily. Doolin's wife Edith, daughter of a Methodist minister who was also Ingalls's postmaster, actually lived in Ingalls where she worked as a nurse. In fact, Ingalls's citizens and their descendants emphasized for years that church activities, not illegal activities, took up most of their time.[25] One old Ingalls resident recalled a revival in a nearby brush arbor at which Bill Doolin, Arkansas Tom, and Bitter Creek Newcomb were present. All three were wearing their guns. Younger cowboys interrupted the meeting, at which point Bill Doolin arose and said, "Go ahead, preacher, and preach. I'll keep order."[26]

By the time Frank was fifteen years old, Dr. Walter R. Little had professionally encountered Bill Doolin at least two times, according to family records. Between 1890 and 1893, Walter was kidnapped for three days to set a gang member's broken leg, possibly at a cave hideout nearby.[27] Also, while hiding out on a nearby ranch, presumably the Dunn Ranch, Bill Doolin called for Walter to remove a bullet from his arm.[28] Walter diligently recorded the treatment in his medical journal and charged Doolin $1.50 for his services.[29]

The Doolin-Dalton gang, having been active for nearly five years, became a prime target of U.S. Marshal Evett Dumas Nix. On September 1, 1893, word reached the outlaws, who were visiting friends in Ingalls, that a Boomer wagon camped on the edge of town appeared to be hiding lawmen. Both townspeople and outlaws waited nervously throughout the morning, taking care of normal business but unsure of the wagon and armed men. By noon, Nix's assault on the town commenced, disrupting the clear, peaceful day.

The story of the gunfight has been exaggerated and mythologized with help from a 1914 Hollywood movie and the press. While versions vary as to the names of the saloon and hotel, how many bullets were actually fired, the time length of the fiery melee, the number of lawmen involved, and what the members of the gang were doing at the time of the attack, all stories agree that two bystanders, including a visiting teenager shot in the back by one of the deputies, and three U.S. lawmen lost their lives.[30] All but one of the outlaws escaped, only to be hunted down and killed violently.

During the shooting frenzy, Lon Little, who was working at the general store, hid behind a cracker barrel.[31] His account of the shootout passed down to Little family members, who continued to do business with the Doolin family and its enterprises for years afterward.[32] As for Ingalls, the bloodshed and ensuing publicity gave the town a perhaps unfair reputation for harboring outlaws, and the community died out. Today, Council Creek runs silently by the ghost town of Ingalls; a few weathered-gray wooden hulks are all that remains of its 1890s heyday. Only Ingalls Cemetery appears to be maintained, out of respect for the dead that inhabit its ordered rows. Walter and Almira Little and three of their grandchildren are residents of this serene hill.

The importance of the Little boys' social contact, if not intimate interaction, with individuals who were outlaws, socialized with outlaws, or did business with outlaws cannot be overstated. In a time period when the eastern United States was fascinated with outlaw stories and dime novels that presented heroic and daring feats as part of the outlaw's exploits, growing up within an area rich with the settings and characters of these semifictional novellas had an enormous impact on these young men's psyches. For Frank and Fred, the line between right and wrong became smeared with empathy. Gray areas consisting of justifiable challenges to authority and righteousness of civil disobedience began to blur expected and accepted social behaviors.

At nineteen, Fred was destined to be the family rebel. After his western tour, he returned home to face work on the family farm. His future options were limited. Probably under pressure from Walter, Fred enrolled as a freshman at Oklahoma Agricultural and Mechanical College, now Oklahoma State University, in the fall of 1894.[33] However, the young college could not hold Fred, who did not want to become a farmer. What discord was happening in the family is unknown, but Fred left Oklahoma with a more exciting plan for his future. His single-minded decision to change his destiny would leave sixteen-year-old Frank with all the farm work on his shoulders, while leading Fred to gold camps in Colorado.

4

✦ ✦ ✦ ✦

EMMA AND THE
TRAMP MINER

After Fred Little rode the rails to California, he set in motion a pattern of brief stays dictated by what he perceived as opportune moments in exciting places. This wanderlust lasted for the rest of his life as he chased pipe dreams from California to Colorado and back. He never returned to Oklahoma for any length of time, instead following miners, itinerant farm laborers, and his brother Frank during some of the more unsettling times in U.S. history. Like wind-driven tumbleweed, Fred bounced along paths of golden promises, collecting a detritus of thorny effects. Broken hearts and alcohol would plague his relationships with family and friends while gold prospecting tugged at his heart.

At some point after the first Cripple Creek strike of 1893–94, Fred left Oklahoma for the high mountains that surrounded gold mining districts nicknamed "World's Greatest Gold Camp" (the Cripple Creek mining district) and "Richest Square Mile on Earth" (the Central City–Black Hawk mining district).[1] He joined generations of other miners who had little in their pockets and were desperate to improve their circumstances. Like the thousands of men who sought instant wealth but ended up working in corporate-owned mines for three dollars a day, Fred had caught gold fever.

"Pikes Peak or Bust" was the slogan of the first prospectors, who crudely painted this early bumper sticker on their wagon canvasses and carts between 1858 and 1861, as they prepared to ascend the Rocky Mountains from Colorado's Front Range. Pikes Peak, with snowy stripes running down its grayish-rose shoulders, was the first prominent mountain top they espied upon reaching pink granite mountains, a major landmark guiding their trek.

At 14,115 feet, the peak reigned over smaller mountains and hills laced with gold. About seventy-five miles northeast, a struggling prospector named John H. Gregory had discovered a tremendous gold vein in a gulch that was to bear his name in 1859, establishing the rich Central City–Black Hawk mining district in Gilpin County, Colorado. In 1891, a carpenter named Winfield Scott Stratton located gold ten miles to the southwest of Pikes Peak, making him the first millionaire from the new Cripple Creek mining district. Once the ore was discovered, tens of thousands of gold seekers converged onto Colorado mountain hillsides prospecting for their own El Dorado. This second Colorado gold rush and ensuing labor war ultimately put Cripple Creek on the map.

The 1890 Sherman Silver Purchase Act, passed in response to a large silver overproduction in Colorado, required the U.S. Treasury to purchase silver using notes backed by either gold or silver. But mining districts required access, and an ensuing overbuilding of railroads into western states and declining gold reserves resulted in the Panic of 1893 and a general economic depression. Repeal of the act placed favor once again upon gold, as silver prices collapsed. Older gold mining districts were resuscitated with demand for more gold, including the old Central City–Black Hawk mining district in Gilpin County.

Newspapers across the country, including papers in Oklahoma, encouraged men to come to Colorado to discover and mine gold for the U.S. Treasury reserves. In 1894 the *Guthrie Daily* published a lengthy article on the resurgence of gold mining as a result of the fate of free silver coinage, advertising for men to come to Colorado, particularly back to "The Kingdom of Gilpin," to mine or to make new gold discoveries.[2] The author claimed there were "thousands of prospects located of which the surface has hardly been scratched."[3] No doubt Fred and other opportunistic Oklahomans read this article or others like it, and a flood of men from Oklahoma Territory moved into gold camps. Mining gold became a patriotic duty.

In a 1982 study, Dr. Jim Foster collected information pertaining to a group of young miners he dubbed "the ten-day tramps."[4] These men were strong and daring enough to endure rigors of life associated with working in various mines for short periods of time, often in dangerous conditions. They were ephemeral workers with blackened, youthful faces in dark cavities of the western Rocky Mountains; freeloaders who jumped freight trains to different camps. They acquired proficiencies along the way, becoming skilled laborers who easily could leave one job only to find another as quickly as they packed their traps and left.

Many of these miners were just teenagers, just as Fred had been when he first began his nomadic quest for gold in the Rockies. All of Dr. Foster's interviewees agreed that "it was a young man's game."[5] In one interview, an old miner reported:

> We were young, footloose, and fancy free. We could get work in any camp and the pay was pretty good. Besides there was always a camp just over the hill which we had never seen and a boarding house which was rumored to have the prettiest waitresses in the West. We'd usually work one job for no more than a month or two, long enough to sample the cooking, wink at the waitresses, and make enough to carry us to the next camp.[6]

Many early migrant miners initially did not look to union organizations for security as they generally had no families to support, were disinterested in planning too far ahead, or had yet to establish roots in any mining culture. They may not have been interested in the solidarity that union membership could provide or even the Western Federation of Miners' (WFM's) preexisting activities before the time that Fred first began working as a miner in Colorado. The second labor conflict at Cripple Creek had yet to occur, although in retrospect, tensions were rising in Colorado mining camps. Fred was no different from these tramp miners. His gold fever eventually led him above the Central City–Black Hawk mining district where the Big Alice Mine, the most extensive placer mine in Clear Creek County, drew his attention. Sitting below the crest of Saint Mary's Glacier at 10,083 feet in a small, piney valley, the Alice mining camp could be reached by a series of treacherous switchbacks following the Fall River near the town of Idaho Springs, twelve miles below, or from a rough road winding down Yankee Hill, one mile above. Yankee Hill sat on a saddle between Saint Mary's, Ninety-Four, and Alice mining camps in Clear Creek County and Nevadaville, Central City, and Black Hawk mining communities in Gilpin County, about ten miles away. With such a prime mining location before him, Fred just needed to find a job and a place to board so that in rare moments he could pursue the ore with which he was so enamored.

Colorado soon gave Fred more than a love for gold. Although exactly where Fred met Emma Barbara Harper is undocumented, it is probable that Fred was one of many transient guests in the Harper home in Alice. In 1886 the Harper family had built a well-known cabin that still stands today, its rustic image used as a key illustration for a Rand-McNally advertisement in 1972.[7] Emma's mother, Emmarilla, began to run a boarding house in the cabin after Emma's father William died at home of pneumonia in January 1897, leaving Emmarilla with two young sons and two teenage daughters.[8]

Emmarilla Josephine Frisbie epitomized the singular frontier woman who took certain risk in venturing west, away from safety of hearth and home. Since her father believed all women should be educated, have the right to vote, and voice their opinions, it is no surprise that Emmarilla struck out on her own after receiving enough education to qualify for teaching, graduating from Missouri's Stewartsville College.[9] Any adventures Emmarilla encountered between her graduation in 1870, when she is recorded as living in Clinton County, Missouri, and 1877, when she is known to be living in Colorado, are unrecorded. Her descendants tell stories of how she was a close friend of Buffalo Bill's, danced with him, and

HARPER BOARDING HOUSE

Fred Little likely met Emma Barbara Harper at the Harper Boarding House in Alice, Colorado. *Harper Family Papers.*

would have married him had he not "smelled like a buffalo!"[10] What is known is that in 1876 Emmarilla's sister Mary Isabella (Bella) married Alvin Church, and the couple moved to Gilpin County to try their luck in gold mining. Most likely Emmarilla joined them on the journey.

In the 1870s, Black Hawk, a stone's throw from the eastern side of Central City, had an abundant supply of water, necessary for milling precious rock, and the community became known as a center for most of the ore mined out of the area. Muddy streets were full of miners and millworkers, primarily from the British Isles: English and Irish, and eventually Cornish. The gulch where Gregory discovered his gold in 1859 already had become polluted with human and animal wastes, and dirty waters plagued the town. Yet the City of Mills had grown and attracted all sorts of people who yearned for riches and adventure. Though why Emmarilla proceeded to Black Hawk is uncertain, she was an eligible, single

EMMARILLA HARPER
Emmarilla Frisbie Harper,
Emma Harper Little's
mother, was a progressive
American woman who
claimed she would have
married Buffalo Bill Cody
had he not "smelled
like a buffalo!" *Harper
Family Papers.*

young woman who would add some degree of culture to the wild,
frontier mining community where she taught school. By the end
of 1877, when Black Hawk's smelters were processing half of
all ore mined in Gilpin County, twenty-five-year-old Emmarilla
married William Harper, who was hoping to stake his fortune in
Russell Gulch.[11]

Born in New York in 1843, the son of Scottish immigrants,
William Harper also respected education, and his love of reading
passed down to his daughter—passions that could be unsustain-
able in an isolated mining camp in the frigid Rocky Mountains.[12]
William also had proven that he could survive adverse conditions
and rebound with spirit, imbuing his daughter with the same character. While serving in Wisconsin's Company E, Twenty-Second

Infantry Regiment during the Civil War, William was captured and survived two months in Libby Prison in wretched conditions.[13] After prisoners were exchanged, William returned to fighting, taking part in Sherman's fabled march to the southeastern seaboard. Years afterward in a letter to President Woodrow Wilson, Emma would call her father "an old soldier" who "fought through three long bitter years of war to help preserve this Union" and "who marched with Sherman to the sea" as proof of her inherited loyalty to the United States during a time when Americans could not trust their next-door neighbors.[14]

Emma Barbara Harper was born to Emmarilla and William on October 12, 1879, on Bald Mountain, Gilpin County, Colorado. By 1880 Emmarilla had taken her one-year-old daughter home to her parents in Missouri, possibly to avoid extreme winter conditions that could easily take the life of an infant.[15] William remained in Black Hawk, living with mostly single immigrants in a boarding house on Main Street and working as a laborer.[16] During the next decade William's family and wealth grew as he and Emmarilla moved back and forth between Gilpin and Clear Creek Counties. Three more children were born: daughter Jessie in 1881, son William Guy in 1887, and son Robert Bruce in 1894.

In 1946 when Emmarilla J. Harper died, her obituary, presumably submitted by Emma Harper Little, stated that Emmarilla was "the widow of William Harper, mining capitalist."[17] The moniker "mining capitalist" may have a negative connotation when used in the language of a union organizer, but the characterization also suggests that William Harper accomplished much more after working as a mere laborer in Gilpin County, Colorado, in 1880.

While Emmarilla raised their children, William oversaw his mining acquisitions southeast of Saint Mary's Glacier, often riding for miles on steep, rocky terrain in deep snow. He acquired and patented the Little Lalla Lode on July 25, 1887, which was near Yankee Hill. He also acquired the Gold Anchor Mine in the Alice-Yankee Placer district and by April 22, 1891, acquired and patented the Little Mary Mine, all in the same general area. The pinnacle of his success was the acquisition and patent of the Little Lalla Mill on July 18, 1891, which enabled him to mine and process his own ore. William became president of Colorado Consolidated Mining and Development Company and Golconda Mining and Milling Company, thus crowning his achievements.[18]

In 1897 Emma finished her first teaching job in the new log school house in Alice, following her mother's footsteps as a frontier teacher.[19] She had grown into a confident, independent eighteen-year-old woman. Alice School was held in a two-room log cabin to the left of Fall River Road as it passed Alice on its way up to Yankee Hill. Quite conveniently Emma boarded in her own home, the rooming house for miners, and walked a short distance to the log cabin that had become the schoolhouse.

Teaching and all its accoutrements provided a rich medium for Emma's continued intellectual development in an environment generally bereft of scholarly notions and progressive ideas. Many early teachers such as Emma had only a high school education, and it was only after the turn of the century before an occasional applicant was found with a college degree.[20] But Emma was also well-read, having access to an extraordinary library supplied by both her parents. These books, which Emmarilla later donated to Idaho Springs Library, contained works that addressed nearly every subject that Emma would teach. Nonetheless, Clear Creek County made certain that its teachers were provided the most up-to-date educational methodology by sending them to Colorado State Normal Institute annually. During August 1897 the county sent Emma to the teaching institute in Golden, Colorado.[21] In a series of lectures, Emma listened to a variety of experienced educators describe practices in teaching discipline, reading, and science.

One lecturer planted a seed in her mind that may have helped her adapt to her future social status as well as challenge her political views. While speaking on civil government, a Professor Miller advised that one must become broader in political opinions and be willing to concede that each and every party has its merits.[22] Many mine-owning families, including Emma's Frisbie grandparents, tended to support Republican candidates.[23] The Harper family would not have supported Democrat William Jennings Bryan in his 1896 presidential campaign against Republican William McKinley Jr., since Bryan advocated against gold, banks, and railroads, all entities necessary for a successful gold mining business. McKinley won, yet progressivism and its social activist tenets were taking hold in both political parties, even as they developed in different directions. As a mine owner's daughter, Emma held an elevated class status when compared to mining laborers, both native and immigrant. As such, her choice in politics would be attributed to the social class with which she best identified at this time in her life. Dr. Miller's comments on political diversity may have been the first unbiased political exposition that Emma's ears ever heard.

Like the Harper Cabin, the first Alice School still stands, also a survivor of pioneer spirit and repurposing. A newer A-framed roof and barn-red second story today overwhelm the old chinked logs that formed the school's original structure. In the fall of 1897, after Emma's return from teacher training, the log walls embraced children's laughter and Emma's scolding.[24] Besides teaching diverse subjects, Emma had to model proper behavior. She was to be dressed properly, hair pinned up and shoes laced.[25] Since most children came from families that knew Emma, taking charge of the classroom was challenging as she was just a few years older than many of her pupils. Her teacher training instructed her to follow the biblical scripture in Luke: Do unto others as you would have them do unto you.[26] Still, living within the narrow realm of the Harper log cabin and Alice School, Emma was acutely receptive toward any escape off Bald Mountain.

By 1898 Fred had grown into a robust, attractive young man with thick, wavy russet hair and a strong cleft chin, a dominant characteristic inherited from the Little side of the family. A risk taker, Fred exuded exciting possibilities, including a dramatic flight from Colorado's frigid mountain heights. Subsequent events would reveal him as boisterous, impulsive, and self-destructive—attributes that would not help Frank's IWW mission. At this moment, he could honestly boast one accomplishment to Emma: he had been to California and would return to the Golden State one day.[27] Now that the 1897–98 school year was over, the handsome young miner with a dimpled chin talked his way into Emma's heart, whether during consumption of hot, filling meals or at some social activity held in or around Alice.

WALTER FREDERICK LITTLE
Walter Frederick Little, a
WFM miner (photographed
here ca. 1900), drew Frank
to California. *Courtright
Family Papers.*

Emmarilla was known to place a fine meal on her table, and
boarding houses were scarce in and around Alice. Just as Foster's
miner described looking forward to fancy food on a table and pretty
young ladies to serve it, Fred surely would have appreciated Emmarilla's cooking and Emma's self-assured presence nearby. Emma
was pleasing to the eye. Like her mother, she was petite and fine
boned, not much over five feet tall. Her dark tresses, pinned high
on her head, crowned arched brows framing large brown eyes. Her
nose turned upward slightly above full Harper lips that were not
femininely silent during conversations at the table during evening
meals. Emma had opinions, likely inherited from her mother. Inevi-
tably Fred became smitten with Emma Barbara Harper, probably
in lively supper conversations.

During the 1898 summer, Emma and Fred became involved in
a relationship that no doubt resulted in consequences for which
neither was prepared and that the school district would disapprove

soundly. By the end of August 1898, Emma found herself pregnant, and the nomadic father of her baby had gone prospecting somewhere along grassy slopes near Cripple Creek. Emma certainly could not return to the Alice school. Teachers were expected to be single, and assuredly not pregnant. She could not confide in Emmarilla since her embarrassing situation would cause scandal for the Harper family. Not surprisingly, an urgent letter reached Fred probably by late September 1898. He chivalrously agreed to meet Emma in Denver. In the largest city in Colorado, they could conceal the purchase of their marriage application; as a rural county, Clear Creek would have published their intentions to the Alice community. On October 6, 1898, Miss Emma B. Harper of Yankee, Clear Creek County, Colorado, married Mr. Walter F. Little (Fred) of Cripple Creek, El Paso County.[28] No one would have to know the actual date she and Fred married or that she was pregnant before marriage, and Emmarilla would be none the wiser.

No doubt uneasy about his new responsibilities, Fred began the journey back to Cripple Creek with his new wife. The newlywed couple would have taken the Colorado and Southern Railway (C&S), heading for Colorado Springs, where they could switch to the Midland Terminal Railroad for a fifty-five-mile ride into mountains, traveling through Ute Pass into Divide, Gillette, Victor, and finally, Cripple Creek. Like other prospective Cripple Creek residents who traveled trails and rails into the mountains, Fred and Emma passed red petrified giants, unusual sandstone formations along the lower elevations of their journey. Solid scrub oak and limber pine vied with taller blue spruce, their sad drooping arms giving the trees a wilted appearance on warm, red sandstone hills. Sitting next to a man she hardly knew, Emma naturally would have been anxious about the circumstances in which she had left her family and the context of her marriage.

The sandy route turned to red granite chat, and white-stemmed gooseberry bushes, well past flowering season, populated cracks and crevices in the pinkish elephant skin of granite embankments. Ponderosa pines, with silvery and cinnamon barks, and Engelmann spruce covered the hills until the train reached closer to the tree line. When the train looped through Victor and back north, Emma could see the scattered, vast mining camps that would soon be her new home. Here she found barren, windswept grassy hills, some quaking aspen colonies amid fewer pines—and the Cripple Creek town with its wide wintry-water-colored skies.

What Emma must have thought as she viewed the expansive skyline of head frames and hoists is unknown, but Cripple Creek was absolutely different from Alice in its constricted, green-alpine valley, and much unlike the gulch-squeezed streets of Nevada-ville, Central City, and Black Hawk. Emma certainly had no idea that within a few years, her charming new miner husband and his little brother would prove to be a wobbly springboard, launching her into a world of social reform.

5

CRIPPLE CREEK, 1898–1899

As idyllic as a fall journey may seem, winter and spring can be deadly in the high mountains of Colorado. Much like early miners in Clear Creek and Gilpin Counties, those at Cripple Creek braved cold, crude conditions in drafty tents and hastily constructed shacks at the base of Mount Pisgah, aptly named for the mountain from which Moses viewed the Promised Land. The similarity ended there. Many tents would evolve into wooden-framed buildings along busy Bennett Avenue where enterprising entrepreneurs conducted thriving businesses. Religion and the red-light district certainly did not converge; more like the disobedient worshippers of the Golden Calf, frequenters of nearby Myers Street were drawn by its brothels and saloons. It was said that the town never shut down as revelers sought "the hot time" they would have each night.[1] Life was bawdy and stimulating for miners who poured into the mining camp daily, flocking to boarding houses and hotels in order to refresh and warm themselves before looking for work in this supposed land of milk and honey.

Nearby, other camps and towns arose around head frames and hoists above mines with names such as Gassy (later Cameron), Goldfield, Altman, Independence, Anaconda, Lawrence, and Gillett, all encompassed within Cripple Creek mining district. The town of Victor, with its abundance of head frames and mounds of tailings, emerged in 1893 at the base of Battle Mountain, joining the "World's Greatest Gold Camp." By 1900 the Cripple Creek mining district had a population of about thirty-two thousand and by some reports was the fourth largest city in Colorado.[2]

Of the various mining camps in the district, only the towns of Cripple Creek and Victor have survived until present, although not to the same degree. Cripple Creek has flourished, while Victor appears to still struggle from the past. Other camps, towns, and gutted gulches have been absorbed by the vortex of an open ground mining operation, the Cripple Creek and Victor Gold Mining Company. A whirlpool in an ocean of aspen and grassy hills, spinning and swallowing old mining camps into some hell below, the company is the largest gold mining operation in the United States. Looking northward out of Victor today beyond Battle Mountain, the scenery has been reduced to this barren hole. Yet aspen, pine, and some spruce still decorate the remaining ancient timber head frames at mines that once had promising names—America Eagle, Vindicator, Ajax, Independence—all from a more propitious time. As a testament to the less technical past, burros amble freely along the Golden Loop Parkway that enters Cripple Creek.

Old photographs document lively streets in Cripple Creek between 1898 and 1900, providing clues as to what Emma and Fred espied when they arrived in October 1898.[3] Bennett Avenue was lined with its new brick-red facades, the street transporting bustling crowds of men, many new to mining and who were looking for work in one of the area's five hundred mines. New buildings on gray stone foundations lined Cripple Creek's other streets, some paved with bricks and tiny sparkles of turquoise residue, traces of earlier mining excavations of the beautiful sky-blue stone. Buggies and wagons crowded the streets, and women dressed in somber colors or sunlit calicos chatted on low boardwalks near business entrances. On surrounding hillsides above the buildings, various mine stacks smoked. Just two years earlier, a newspaper boasted that "[mining] camps build towns, mining camps build cities, mining camps build states, even empires, and Cripple Creek is the greatest mining camp on earth."[4]

As Fred and Emma walked down Bennett, Emma surveyed her
new surroundings that were, in some ways, similar to Nevadaville,
Blackhawk, and Central City. Yet Cripple Creek was much larger
and grander at first glance. Many boarding houses, hotels, and
chinked log and small frame houses offered residences for successful miners and their families. Delivery wagons dodged children
and dogs playing in dirt streets. Disparities in living conditions
were also evident. Many bachelor miners rented rooms, crude lean-
tos attached to larger buildings—some no larger than outhouses.
"Rented Rooms" signs were tacked onto many of these inferior
boarding houses, some only having black tar paper to insulate
their walls.

No record exists of Fred and Emma's residence; however, it
is doubtful that Fred would have been able to acquire substantial
quarters for his new wife immediately, let alone housing similar
to her previous environment. Fred probably first brought Emma to
a rented room, hardly comparable to the abode of a mine owner's
daughter. Surely Emma would begin to discern that her life would
be changed forever. Fred was only a miner, a laborer of the working
class, who would never own his own home despite the employment
opportunities available within Cripple Creek. The days of individual prospecting were gone, and industrial mining had replaced
dreamers with hard rock miners. As much as Fred wanted to continue prospecting, the reality was that he would work as a miner
in an absentee-corporate-owned mine in Cripple Creek.

The WFM had won a three-dollar, eight-hour workday in the
first Cripple Creek strike almost five years earlier, and with new
mines being worked, Fred probably had no problem finding work
at good union wages. Underground gold mining was so labor inten-
sive that it generated thousands of jobs with more than eight
thousand miners employed at the height of the Cripple Creek
mining district.[5] No record exists as to which mine employed
Fred, nor does any record of his WFM membership exist since the
1903–1904 labor war destroyed precious union records. However,
the Independence, owned by gold king Winfield S. Stratton, employed
many Cripple Creek miners, and it is likely that Fred Little was
one of them.

"Labor produces all wealth. Wealth belongs to the producer thereof," state WFM union cards issued in Cripple Creek mining district. This would have been an enormously attractive proposal for the struggling men who came from all walks of life to the mountains of Colorado to strike it rich independently, but who found themselves in the employ of huge mining corporations. Originating in Butte, Montana, during 1893, the WFM organized hard rock miners and smelter workers in the Rocky Mountain states of Montana, Idaho, Colorado, Utah, Nevada, and Arizona into an aggressive federation of labor unions. Not surprisingly, most mine owners and investors deemed the organization radical because of its violent strikes, militant action, and socialist leanings. In return, mine owners organized the Mine Owners' Association (MOA), employing armed guards and Pinkerton detectives to root out WFM agitators and undermine union activities, repeatedly using violent action themselves. Aggression was evident on both sides.

The 1893–94 Cripple Creek labor dispute created a foundation for successful labor agitation, thus attracting hard rock miners into the protective arms of the WFM. Hard rock miners in Cripple Creek mining district struck over long workdays and low pay—issues always at the forefront of early labor disputes. At the strike's conclusion, mine owners agreed to an eight-hour day, a three-dollar minimum wage, and the right to belong to a union.[6] Three hundred miners agreed to stand trial for their various crimes, but most were acquitted.[7] Beyond the concessions that the miners won, the most important victory was Cripple Creek's freedom to transform into a union town. For almost the next decade, Cripple Creek citizens would essentially govern their own, and the camp became a WFM utopia that other mining camps, including those within Arizona Territory where Frank Little would eventually live, sought to model. Certainly Fred joined WFM Local No. 40 in Cripple Creek, but the WFM itself would fundamentally transform Frank and Fred into future labor agitators.

While Fred worked daily at the mines, Emma became immersed in her life as a miner's wife. As a pregnant American woman who lived during the end of the nineteenth century, she would have begun a traditional period of confinement as soon as her pregnancy was evident. Most women disappeared socially during pregnancy unless economic circumstances demanded otherwise. Emma more than likely would have been confined to their rented room by early 1899. Even if Emma had not been pregnant, she could not secure work as a school teacher. As in Alice, Cripple Creek teachers were expected to be single. Interviewed by historian Elizabeth Jameson, longtime Cripple Creek resident Clara Stiverson stressed, "Women just didn't get jobs; women belonged in the home."[8] Emma could have taken in laundry, cooked, cleaned, or managed a boarding house, but she would not be able to stretch her intellect in a public business or union pursuit.[9] As the wife of a WFM member, Emma was expected to be a "good wife" who worked in the home, using Fred's union wage to buy union products while keeping a virtuous deportment. Thus, the WFM idealized women's domestic respon-sibilities, keeping them dependent on their husbands economically. This reality contrasted sharply with Emma's increasingly progres-sive attitude. Although she did not know Fred well when she married him, Emma embraced Fred's occupation, perhaps since her own father had risen from a laborer to mine owner. In doing so, she also pondered the discriminations that corporations placed upon a mining community. As part of a working class of immi-grants and uprooted Americans who found work in Cripple Creek, Emma found herself leaning left politically toward the Populist Party and later, Socialism.

While Emma was expected to preserve a moral center at home, Fred had more liberties and unique experiences due to his employ-ment in Cripple Creek. The WFM expected him to be inquisitive, aggressive, and competitive.[10] His success was measured by his production and work associations; Emma's, by her virtue and domesticity. As long as he provided the means to house, feed, and clothe Emma in a reputable fashion, he could visit the union lodge, taverns, and dance halls, where he could fraternize with other men and even loose women. This pattern of socializing sub-sequently impacted the marriage as Fred was not married to a tra-ditional woman.

As her pregnancy advanced, Emma spent short winter days reading about an intense political struggle that was simmering, a geyser ready to spew new indictments against mine and mill owners. She also became acutely aware of class struggles and pride of accomplishment from the first strike in Cripple Creek. Most families had been affected in some way by the first labor conflict. Between the first strike and Fred's arrival in Cripple Creek, fifty-four occupations unionized in the city, and the WFM was at the peak of its power.[11] Almost everyone who worked was in a union. This balance of power would exist until the second Cripple Creek strike in 1903, when miners used their strength to support other unions, including mill workers in Colorado City.

By 1900 Colorado Springs and Denver capitalists and foreign corporations owned 90 percent of the mines in Cripple Creek mining district.[12] Only 1 percent of the mine owners lived in the district; therefore, a strong sense of a working class community existed within.[13] Unlike William Harper or Winfield S. Stratton, most of these mine owners were a new generation of men who did not have a background in mining or in the working class.

Cripple Creek was also predominantly white. The WFM made certain that Italians, Greeks, Mexicans, and Slavs did not work in the district. Chinese workers were even more excluded. African Americans were not viewed as a threat because they typically did not seek the "traditional" work of white men. Even so, the WFM did not allow them to join, and most miners would not work with a black miner.[14] The various ethnicities that did live in Cripple Creek were mainly highly skilled Western Europeans. No matter their ethnicities or mining specializations, the district's miners were united in their resentment toward capitalist mine owners' management practices. Indignation for social injustice and readiness to fight ran in the Cripple Creek miners' blood.

Like Emma, many women in Cripple Creek were miners' daughters married to miners.[15] While there seems to have been no outward prejudice against Western Europeans among the working class, Emma expressed her disdain for the treatment various immigrant groups gave their own women. The Cornish miners, in particular, were noted for their skill after working centuries in tin and copper mines in Cornwall. Yet their Catholic Irish neighbors habitually spurned their "Cousin Jacks" and "Cousin Jennies," judging them to be uppity Protestants. While Cornish immigrant men were expert at extracting rich veins of ore that lay deep down inside the earth, their women were largely ignorant, tied to their homes raising children. Emma was irked that Cornish girls were kept home until their youngest brothers were old enough to go to school.[16] Her gut reaction to the Cornish treatment of women would complement the IWW's later support of female wage earners and education.

During their brief residency in Cripple Creek, Emma continued to study class struggles within the nascent microcosm of labor division in the camp. She and Fred became well aware of the strength found in a strong union setting. The couple's early chapter in Cripple Creek provided a foundation from which both Fred and Emma would evolve into IWW labor organizers with broader goals. More significantly, their experiences undoubtedly guided Frank Little's first foray into mining and union associations.

During the months that followed Fred's arrival in Cripple Creek, he sporadically mailed letters or wired messages to his family in Oklahoma. Through Fred's missives, Frank could envision new dramas. New heroes now replaced the social bandits of his youth—hard rock miners and their champions within labor unions now juxtaposed against mining corporations and their hired thugs. Payne County had not afforded the amusement that sporting with Indian children had provided both boys growing up back in Ski-a-took, and by 1894 most Oklahoma outlaws had been caught. Life on the homestead had become monotonous and lean for Frank.

In early December 1898, a gravely ill Walter R. Little drew his will. A little more than a month later, he passed away on January 13, 1899, at the relatively advanced age of fifty-nine. His obituary in the *Stillwater Gazette* modestly read, "Dr. W. R. Little, one of the oldest and most respected citizens of the vicinity of Clayton died at his home just east of Clayton last Friday after a short illness."[17] The heirs were listed as Alonzo, age thirty-seven, and residing in Ingalls; Frank H., age twenty, Clayton, OT; Bessie, age fifteen, Clayton, OT, and Fred W., age twenty-three, last known address, Cripple Creek, Colorado.[18]

With his father's passing, it was time for Fred to return to Oklahoma.

6

✦ ✦ ✦ ✦

BROKEN DREAMS

Like a child with growing pains, Oklahoma Territory stretched, flexing her legs and arms that were throbbing with clashing political views and economic hardships. The aches from these sudden growth spurts brought disappointments and misfortune for many Oklahomans with ebullience and successes for few. Perseverance and opportunity, sprinkled with a little luck, proved the most effective poultice for adversity.

According to Oklahoma historian Nigel Sellars, farmers believed that their land was their "last best hope, a refuge from the horrors of corporate capitalism and 'wage slavery,' a place where republican ideals of equal opportunity, the work ethic, and individual economic success still could be realized."[1] The year 1891 had been a productive one indeed. But two years later, the economic convulsions from the Panic of 1893 made many farm owners prisoners of their own land. Drought again plagued Payne County during 1895, and prairie fires popped up sporadically until the end of the year. Water became so scarce that livestock died outright or had to be shot.

In order to produce a crop, many farmers took out loans to purchase necessary supplies. Merchants held liens on purchase of the farms' yields—in essence, crops became collateral. In this way, the farmer became a tenant of the merchant. This agrarian business arrangement created a cycle of perpetual indebtedness for farmers. In an economic market where there were more sellers than buyers, farms were mortgaged routinely or lost.[2] Thus, private land ownership had not enhanced farmers' prosperity, as predicted by U.S. Senator Henry Dawes. Instead, economic self-sufficiency proved to be out of reach for many Oklahomans. By spring of 1899, economic mobility existed only by moving from land ownership to tenancy.

And so, the new territory was not immune to political change. The Populist movement in the 1890s was more of a farmers' revolt. Known as the People's Party, it pushed for government ownership of railroads, free coinage of silver, a graduated income tax, an eight-hour day (a long-standing point of contention), popular election of senators, prohibition of alien ownership, secret ballots, government ownership of telegraphs and telephones, and government-owned warehouses.

In 1896, three years before Walter Little's death, Populists supported the Democratic presidential candidate, William Jennings Bryan, who seemed sympathetic to some of their beliefs. In Oklahoma Territory, at least, both the People's Party and the Farmers' Alliance did not recover from the political loss. As a result, the Farmers' Union arose along with stirrings of popular socialist sentiments. At the same time, Oklahomans began to experience a transforming American economy where the growth of industrialization, with its accompanying mechanization and the rise of national corporations, redefined the meaning of opportunity. Such corporations came to dominate and sculpt Oklahoma statehood and government. The Democratic Party specifically controlled economic machineries of the territory, and it demanded statehood. The Populists—both radical and conservative—unsuccessfully opposed the change. In 1907 Oklahoma Territory became the state of Oklahoma. Humorist Will Rogers is rumored to have joked, "We spoiled the best territory in the world to make a state."

Not surprisingly, the Socialist Party attracted those excluded from the business progressive wing of the Democratic Party, and it successfully dominated politics in the years before World War I. Oklahoma became home to more radical forces of resistance to the emerging corporate order and was a perfect breeding ground for unionizing, all because of dissident tenant farmers and laborers whose needs had been largely ignored. In a letter addressed to *Solidarity* in late 1911, Frank Little wrote that Socialists had gained a stronghold of small farmers who were slaves to their farms.[3] Oklahoma farm owners and tenant farmers alike, under deep financial duress, met Frank secretly in moon-blanched woods to plead for membership in the IWW, an organization united solely for wage earners. Living in Oklahoma, "land of the fair God," had become a land of hell for the farmer.

Lon Little, who was almost a generation older than his siblings, was influenced greatly by the new politics of Oklahoma Territory. Lon had struggled since the first day he set foot on his homestead. He must have dreaded asking for a loan in order to make improvements and grow crops, mortgaging the homestead that he had acquired so freely.[4] Despair over forfeiting title of his farm to an outsider would have diminished any sense of relief. Debt would follow this Little family for generations as it suffered through drought and afterward, the Great Depression. Shrugging off the mantle of his father's Republican politics, Lon likely embraced the Populist Party and its tenets.

Walter R. Little's household fared even worse. Walter was simply too old to start anew. Frank, who had observed his parents' struggle to maintain the farm firsthand, may have sought work elsewhere, but one teenager helping support a family homestead was hardly sufficient.

In late October 1898, two months before his death, an already ailing Walter approached his neighbor William E. Berry for a fifteen-dollar loan. Berry, one of the cattle barons who had previously leased Indian lands in the area, was now a successful businessman, owning banks in Agra, Ripley, Pawnee, Norman, and eventually Stillwater. Instead of a formal bank loan, Berry personally loaned the money to Walter at 12 percent interest.[5] Berry, an opportunistic businessman who had been denied both of his staked claims after the 1889 and 1893 Land Runs because of his prior cattle leases, was waiting patiently for frustrated farmers to surrender their failed homesteads north and west of the Cimarron River. Berry's original stock-operation headquarters were located at the mouth of Stillwater Creek and the river, the same land that Walter R. Little owned. With his knowledge of many eighty-niners' financial crises, Berry and son Thomas slowly began to acquire relinquishments to claims. Their goal was to replace over a thousand-plus acres of leased grassland that the family had lost to settlement.[6] At the time of William's loan to Walter, the Berrys also purchased a relinquishment for a claim that abutted Walter Little's homestead, paying less than $500 to a man who had held the property just two years.[7]

Like many of the eighty-niners, Walter had not acquired much during the ten years since the land run. Upon his death, Walter left Almira a modest estate amounting to $1,400. The homestead was worth $1,200, and the remaining amount comprised a couple of horses and a wagon, cow, calf, and pig. He had no cash and, like many others, held outstanding debts, including the loan from Berry and a merchandise debt from Layton and Sain, a general store.[8] This was the Oklahoma to which Fred and Emma returned in early spring of 1899. Fred must have been disappointed to find neither financial gain nor home hearth to lay his hat on.

Almira Little's immediate situation was clearly dismal. She was fifty-five years old, in debt, and had no means of making a living and no hard cash to hire labor. She surely understood that her youngest son Frank could not be expected to remain home any longer. Fred was clearly a wanderer, and Almira could not move in with Lon, her most stable son, since she had created a barrier of hostility with Ella that would never be forgiven.

Amid Almira's quandary, Fred brought Emma home to the Littles' simple log cabin near Clayton. The train travel had been tedious for Emma as she was just weeks away from delivering their first child. Now travel worn and heavy with pregnancy, she probably blushed during her introduction to the family. Perhaps she did not take notice of Frank's own awkwardness during their first meeting.

A slender young man of twenty years, Frank's face was faintly disfigured. Slightly pinched at the outside corner, his left eye pulled his brow downward, the result of an accident when he was sixteen years old. Lon had been splitting logs when an errant piece of metal hit Frank in the face.[9] Walter Little had been unable to save the eye or prevent the minor facial disfigurement that followed the injury. Frank's mouth naturally curled upward, toward the corner of his bad eye, giving him a crooked smile. His famous lopsided grin subsequently would provoke anger from his enemies and amusement from his friends. From the moment of their introduction, Frank and Emma were close allies, both loving Fred for his high adventure and handsome charm.

Just about a month later, exactly ten years after the 1889 run, Emma gave birth to a son. Fred and Emma honored his late father by naming the baby Walter Raleigh Little II. The baby's birth surely supplanted ripples of grief with radiant joy, and the family momentarily paused their mourning to celebrate.

But there were still more changes to come. On May 29, 1899, Almira bought her children's interest in the family home for just one dollar each and then immediately sold the homestead to Harriet Berry, William E. Berry's daughter-in-law through his son Thomas, for $1,350. Harriet and her husband would live in the cabin briefly while constructing a larger home nearby on the homestead.[10] With cash in hand, Almira was able to pay off her debts and purchase a lesser farm in Mound Township, Payne County. She also gave permission for her underage daughter, Bessie, to marry Charles Henry Courtright, a cowboy who was one of the original Sooners. Soon after the couple married, Charlie began to farm Almira's new purchase.[11]

Fair-haired as a child, Bessie had grown into a brunette, blue-eyed beauty—and soon-to-be young mother. Unlike Emma, she happily assumed the traditional role of mother and wife. She was not interested in the progressive politics that would engage Emma within the next twenty years. But between 1899 and 1901, Bessie and Emma would share family and discussion on child rearing, not dangers of hard rock mining or mistreatment of immigrant

Bᴇssɪᴇ Lɪᴛᴛʟᴇ Cᴏᴜʀᴛʀɪɢʜᴛ

Bessie Courtright Little, shown here with daughter Pearl, ca. 1914, kept the Little family connected. *Little Family Papers.*

farm workers. Much like a flesh-and-blood switchboard, Bessie kept the family joined, even throughout the turbulent years to come, smoothing connections and amplifying needs.

While the Little families evidently embraced Emma as their new daughter and sister, Oklahoma itself held no attraction for Fred and his capricious plans. By May 1899, he set off once again to search for gold in California, leaving his bride and newborn son.[12] In her dismay at Fred's sudden departure, Emma still did not solicit help from her mother, instead moving to her Frisbie grandparents' family dairy in Guthrie.[13] It is probable that Emmarilla knew her daughter's situation by this point and chose to keep the embarrassing truth out of gossips' mouths. Like her mother, Emma would continue to be concerned with appearances, misrepresenting the date of her marriage in a court case almost twenty-two years later.

The widowed Almira wasted no time in finding a husband. After likely meeting her in church, Elihu Harlan Cox, an Indiana Civil War veteran and lonely widower, proposed marriage. Almira grabbed the opportunity for stability, marrying Cox in the Mulhall Church of Christ, just north of Guthrie, on June 19, 1900.[14] After their marriage, she moved with Elihu to Guthrie, not far from Emma's grandparents and her new grandson, leaving Bessie and Charlie to lease a farm of their own and join thousands of other Oklahoman tenant farmers. Sadly, Elihu and Almira's marriage would be a loveless, turbulent union.

Walter's death and Almira's real estate decisions provided Frank with the excuse needed to escape from the stifling atmosphere of Payne County. His earliest memories were of a hardscrabble childhood, his father dragging the Illinois family across seven communities in two states and two territories in his pursuit of fresh opportunities. Frank had witnessed a promising progression followed by a disappointing collapse of his family's economic condition in just ten years. Not much had been gained once government and large corporations seeded new rural communities with greedy entrepreneurs and self-serving laws, taking advantage of eighty-niners' shaky holds on their farms. James P. Cannon, a contemporary of Frank's, would later describe Frank's "hatred of exploitation and oppression, and of all those who profited by it" as "irreconcilable."[15] Frank most likely accompanied Fred to seek his fortune, the naive twenty-year-old following the trail of big brother, an absentee father with responsibilities. But while Fred merely served as an erratic catalyst, drawing Frank and then Emma to the mines and fields of California, it was the families' struggles to and within Oklahoma that augmented a foundation for their labor agitation.

By June 1, 1900, with Emma and little Walter still safely ensconced with her Frisbie grandparents, Fred already was settled in San Jose, California, working as a miner.[16] But Frank was not with him. Instead, Frank had embarked on a fiery seventeen-year-long odyssey, kindled by his Oklahoma experiences.

PART TWO

✧ ✧ ✧ ✧

ONE BIG UNION

1900–1916

7

BISBEE, 1903

After arriving in Bisbee, Arizona Territory, on an early Saturday afternoon, October 10, 1903, Frank Little stepped onto a wooden deck from a train loaded with passengers for the border town's business interests, mostly the Phelps, Dodge & Co. mining corporation (Phelps Dodge).[1] A miasma of decay and industrial fumes would stay in his nose until he left the mining town.[2] He came from San Francisco to find work, leaving his brother Fred and California's mining camps. Bisbee's Queen Mine beckoned.

En route, Frank had found a traveling partner in wealthy, French expatriate George Delaporte, a wholesale liquor salesman from San Francisco who planned to visit representatives of the numerous saloons in Brewery Gulch and on Main Street. Delaporte knew his way around the western states. He had been traveling them since the late 1890s and had a popular following as he pushed Yellowstone Whiskey in Bisbee and saloons in other Arizona camps as well.[3] Ignoring the stench as they began their trek up the hill, Frank joined the outgoing salesman, who had knowledge of the best accommodations plus a set of hospitable friends waiting at each of his stops.

As the two men crossed Main Street, Frank glanced upward at the blood-red brick offices of the Phelps Dodge General Office

Building before climbing steep steps to a new, grand hotel, strikingly inharmonious to Bisbee's streets. Stairs were everywhere, leading to private residences, churches, stores, saloons, and cribs as Bisbee planted into Mule Gulch, Tombstone Gulch, and Brewery Gulch. Bisbee was becoming a company town, Professor Douglas's copper town, set deep into rusty-soiled chasms of the Mule Mountains.

George Warren, for whom an upscale community nearby would be named, established the mining district after discovery of a silver-ore prospect in an outcropping thirty years earlier. Ironically, George Warren died in poverty and pity. According to legend, Warren drunkenly bet his claim in the Warren mining district that he could race one hundred yards, turn a stake driven into the ground, and run back—against a man on horseback. He lost, was relieved of his property, and subsequently was found insane for daring to make such a claim.[4]

The Queen Mine developed from Warren's lost claim when a California law firm bought the properties for $20,000, expecting to find a silver mine.[5] Instead, the Queen produced copper in great quantities, becoming the famous Copper Queen Mine. The surrounding camp was named Bisbee for one of the lawyers in the California firm, although Dewitt Bisbee never stepped foot in the town.[6]

Producing 23 percent copper ore, the mine attracted a new entrepreneur—Dr. James Douglas Sr., a Canadian metallurgist who was educated as a Presbyterian minister.[7] Customarily called Professor Douglas, he became an influential individual in the development of Bisbee and the Clifton-Morenci and Miami-Globe mining districts. His son Walter, who managed the Queen, became a nemesis to the IWW. Renaming the company Copper Queen Consolidated Mining Company after further exploration and drilling, Douglas invited miners, especially the Irish and Cornish, to come work there.

Bisbee, once in the heart of outlaw and Apache country, became a hot piece of real estate that Douglas sought to develop into a cultivated community. The town grew so suddenly and real estate became so costly that wooden frame buildings housing the town's businesses were built tightly together, often sharing common walls, a perfect recipe for spreading fire. Scrub oak, juniper, and Apache pine trees, growing on the steep hills surrounding Bisbee, provided wood for hasty construction. Their harvest denuded Bisbee's rocky slopes, creating a flood hazard.

When Frank arrived in 1903, however, Bisbee was between floods and fires. Booming, raucous sounds invited the curious to visit legendary Brewery Avenue, which wound uphill in a gulch to the north of the Phelps Dodge General Office Building. The large office building did not eclipse a beautiful forest-green-and-white, Italianate-styled building directly behind it, the Copper Queen Hotel.

The Copper Queen Hotel was not in Frank's budget, however, when he registered next to George Delaporte's name in a guest ledger resting on a heavy, tiger oak front desk. Frank could have shared a room with Delaporte for seventy-five cents a night or less, if invited, or he would have to pay at least $1.50 per night on a European plan.[8] His funds were limited, and since the hotel dining room posted dinner menu items that cost as much or more than a night's stay, Frank quickly moved to find cheaper boarding.

Frank may have tarried long enough to accompany Delaporte to the Copper Queen Hotel saloon. If he did, he strolled on Italian mosaic tiles through the Palm Room with its Tiffany-glassed cathedral ceiling, to a side room with a large oak bar where Delaporte was expected and welcomed. Frank may have gazed at Lillie Langtry's nude form above the bar, listened to a player piano, and planned what to do next, but he had to spend his money carefully until he found a job.

Bisbee was presently the largest city between San Francisco and St. Louis, and anyone who could read knew about the Copper Queen Consolidated Mining Company. Papers across the nation reported everything about capitalization, copper strikes, and mining accidents relating to Bisbee and the Queen Mine. Not surprisingly, a flood of miners had begun migrating into Arizona Territory's high desert, leaving Colorado gold and silver mining camps where Colorado governor James Peabody and mine owners appeared to be getting an upper hand over the WFM. The second Cripple Creek strike had begun, and this time the WFM would lose. Seasoned miners could find work effortlessly if they met certain Bisbee qualifications.

Copper Queen Consolidated Mining Company hired "big-hearted, rough-spoken, horny-handed sons of toil"—mainly white miners who worked three eight-hour shifts, sleeping or spending money when not working.[9] Although they might be skilled, Mexicans could work a few surface jobs but not inside the Queen or any other mine in Bisbee. As at Cripple Creek, Chinese were kept out of the mining industry completely while in Mexico they were shipped in to replace Mexican labor. Blacks were not tolerated. A daily lexicon that included such epithets as "Micks," "Niggers," "Dagoes," "Bohunks," "Mexes," "Injuns," and "Chinks" defined men in Bisbee as well as those in Arizona's other "white" mining camps. If not an American or Western European miner, a proprietor of a business establishment, or other gainfully employed immigrant, respectable residents were either wealthy, international stockholders or Princeton and Harvard graduates with connections to New York.[10]

A downtown Bisbee street scene might be painted with sombreroed Mexican vendors selling tamales, donkeys weighed down with bags of water from uphill in Brewery Gulch, miners standing around in their grimy overalls holding empty lunch pails, and well-groomed, mustached men in groups smoking aromatic cigars, discussing news of the day. Prostitutes in the red-light district were not permitted to enter downtown, but other women would clutch their plaid skirts to avoid the mud in making their way to a store or home. Frank would have heard myriad languages, but he would have listened only for his own tongue, otherwise dismissing the babble around him. Bisbee's culture made an exciting but awkward setting for twenty-five-year-old Frank Little of Oklahoma Territory.

After sampling indulgences that successful businessmen and investors customarily enjoyed at the Copper Queen Hotel, Frank found work in either the Phelps Dodge–owned Copper Queen Mine or mines owned by Calumet and Arizona Mining Company. As George Delaporte left Bisbee to continue his seasonal route through western states, buying drinks for other potential clients, Frank settled into an accustomed routine.

There were benefits to working in the Copper Queen Mine. It was a dry, horizontal mine, forty-seven degrees in its depths. Most other Arizona mines were vertical, hot, oppressive, and sometimes wet.[11] Frank worked an eight-hour—not a twelve-hour—shift, although Professor Douglas wrote in opposition to the eight-hour law.[12]

Without knowing the specific task assigned to Frank, his workday was nonetheless predictable. Frank "brassed in" or "tagged in," taking a numbered brass tag with him, indicating he was in the mine. He checked out a number of candles, carrying a candle holder that could be stuck in timber or a wall to provide light. He entered a cage with a complex bell system used to hoist miners between levels. Once deep in the mine, he probably worked several jobs depending on his skill. In a "stope," typically a forty-five-square-foot open area that had been blasted out, he may have drilled or packed dynamite to fracture ore-laden "ribs" (faces) of walls. He became expert in recognizing copper ore in the "head" (ceiling) or ribs of a stope. Whitish limestone rock had ruby hematite veins shot with gold, bright viridian malachite with copper ore, and some dark gray streaks of silver. He knew the "levida," or just "leave it alone" ore—it was merely rock.[13] Perhaps he worked as a crosscut miner, working to timber up heads of drifts, stopes, and new tunnels with pine. He might have goaded a mule to "tram" its four cars of ore, each car weighing three-quarters of a ton. Possibly he cared for the mule, which never saw daylight the remainder of its life, by mucking a stable area and feeding it. He even might have been a "mucker," removing debris after dynamiting, or just a "gofer" running back and forth delivering tools, materials, and messages. As he became skilled, he would progress through a hierarchy of mining duties, working with different men who came from all walks of life. He did pair with another miner working the same task, even when he needed to go to a "shit car," a two-seater—one car in each level.

Like other miners, Frank took a break midshift to eat his meal—whether breakfast, lunch, or dinner. His hands were dirty, covered in dangerous particles that he ingested with each bite. Only Cornish miners, who had generations of mining experience, typically avoided ingesting arsenic by packing "pasties" in their lunches, folded pie-like pastries stuffed with meat, cabbage, turnips, and other vegetables. A miner could hold onto a pastie's crimped, crusty edge while he ate, tossing crusts to the mine floor when finished.[14]

Frank faced hazards while working in the depths of the Queen. His knees and back hurt from climbing wooden ladders between levels, and his lungs were congested from dry silica dust, stirred in the air from drilling and blasting.[15] In 1903 he would have worn a soft canvas miner's cap. He had to listen for shouts warning of falling ore or cave-ins, but he plugged his ears when using noisy, steam-powered "widow-maker" drills or "buzzies" that shot out rocks and dust, causing blindness and even death. Miners were not allowed commercial cigarettes but hand-rolled their own, which extinguished themselves when dropped on the mine floor.[16] Smoking caused fires, the number one hazard, especially in areas where there was pyrite, a flammable mineral. So Frank chewed tobacco.

At the end of the day, Frank "brassed out" or "tagged out," indicating he had returned back to the top of the mine. He trudged home in filthy, sometimes wet work clothes in all kinds of weather because the company had not added a clean room for miners to shower and change clothing. He walked to his boarding room in a building on a hill accessed by countless stair steps. Staying at the Copper Queen Hotel was now a memorable respite when he closed his eyes to sleep between shifts.

Like other Bisbee mines, the Copper Queen Mine paid its white miners well when compared to what miners received in other western mining districts. Underground labor earned the union scale of three dollars per eight-hour day in 1903, in accord with an Arizona Territory law passed the previous June.[17] Employees were paid in cash so that on every Saturday payday, hard-earned

BISBEE UNDERGROUND MINERS

Soft-hatted miners, using only candles for illumination, had to listen for shouts warning of falling ore or cave-ins. *Courtesy of Bisbee Mining and Historical Museum.*

dollars would return swiftly to mining companies typically through a grocery or general store. Usually a miner could not pack quickly and leave for another mine if he still owed a "company" store, no matter how small the debt.[18] All debts had to be worked off first, an event that rarely happened because supplies had to be purchased each week.[19] When miners had "fun" money, they often spent it on Brewery Avenue, its red-light district beginning across from the store.

Brewery Avenue, coursing in the bottom of a gulch, was named for a brewery at its entrance, which paralleled O.K. Street. The gulch was lined with a mélange of saloons, gambling houses and opium dens. Higher up, houses of ill repute with steep wooden stairs led to various cribs whose tenants offered carnal delights. Overlooking the ravine of Brewery Avenue, wooden Mexican shanties lined on top of one another on Chihuahua Hill (today called "B" Hill). Their sewage flushed down into the gulch, making travel a nasty business if one wanted to play faro or walk home from mines to frame boarding houses above the red-light district. A Tucson newspaper, labeling Bisbee "the city of foul odors" and "sickening smells," reported the narrow street in Brewery Gulch "covered with slime several inches deep and four feet wide.[20] Frank may have walked through the constricted, smelly street on his way home each day, passing the Copper Queen Hotel to his left. He had no idea that one day he would stay in the hotel again under vastly different circumstances and a cloud of suspicion.

Bisbee was an "open camp," meaning no labor unions dictated working conditions. Professor Douglas theorized that he could keep labor unions out if *he* provided for his workers, whether goods and services, medical attention, or entertainment. His money eventually built and staffed the first hospital to counter the annual epidemic of typhoid, diphtheria, and smallpox. It also funded a church, a public library, a public water system to replace burro water trains, a YWCA (for women who had leisure time), and, through Bisbee Improvement Company, telephone service and electricity. The company produced a newspaper, the *Bisbee Review*, which promoted all things company-owned or company-managed. As long as he paid union wages for eight hours' work, Douglas

COPPER QUEEN HOTEL

Frank stayed in Bisbee's beautiful Copper Queen Hotel at least twice, the latter time under a false identity. *Author's postcard photo.*

reasoned miners had no reason to organize. His strategy worked. Despite many attempts by union organizers, Bisbee would be the last holdout to WFM organization in Arizona Territory.

Frank had become a member of the WFM sometime after following Fred to California, but no local union hall existed for him in Bisbee. There were subsequent attempts to organize a Bisbee WFM local in 1906 and 1907, but no benefits existed in late 1903, no place to fraternize with WFM boys after work, no place for union socials where he could meet girls, no union library, no brotherhood, no common purpose. Besides, few miners had time and energy to play basketball at the YMCA, built by Calumet and Arizona Mining Company for the leisure of Bisbee's employed.[21]

While Professor Douglas found ways to block WFM organization in Bisbee, he could not control political and social beliefs. In December 1903, Frank very likely went to hear attorney Harry A. McKee, a National Socialist, speak before a large Bisbee audience.

McKee had organized a Socialist Party of America (SPA) local that played an active role in Bisbee's economic and political community.[22] Much later McKee's life would intersect with those of Frank, Fred, and Emma Little in California.

At some point, Frank became a Socialist, hardly surprising because the WFM was composed of socialists predominantly, and the socialist structure in his home territory, Oklahoma, was evolving into the fastest growing SPA organization in the nation.[23] *Miner's Magazine*, the official WFM publication, extolled the virtues of socialism through such poets as Carl Sandberg, such authors as Jack London, and editorials from prominent union members. Joseph D. Cannon, a restaurant owner in Bisbee, became the leader of the SPA local.[24] Cannon influenced Frank's youthful belief system, and Frank would work with Cannon when Cannon became a WFM organizer.

His Bisbee sojourn was not wasted as Frank developed his social posture. The irony of an "open camp" closed to certain degrees of skin color and class was not lost as he calculated his next move.

After about one year in Bisbee, Frank returned to Oklahoma to visit the Little family. Almira had been married five years to Elihu Cox and, more than likely, did not tell Frank about trouble with her husband during Frank's visit to Guthrie during October 1904. She was embarrassed. Elihu had been teaching the Bible to a younger widow who lived nearby, prompting gossip and speculation in their neighborhood.[25] Almira was further humiliated that her husband provided only a meager allowance for her clothing and personal articles.[26] At sixty years old, she was running a household and farm with help of one farmhand, while Elihu spent his time politicking and speculating in land deals, routinely using Almira's name on transactions. He currently owned a feed barn in Guthrie and had been occupied as Logan County commissioner, leaving Almira to the drudgery.[27]

In a conversation with Elihu Cox, Frank mentioned a twenty-five-dollar loan that his mother had given him previously. It was hard-earned money from her butter making. After Frank left to return to Arizona, Cox was so enraged that Almira had not collected the debt from Frank while he was home that she feared for her safety.[28] In a nasty public trial, Almira sued Elihu Cox for temporary alimony. Some Oklahoma Territory newspapers covered the trial, reporting that the courtroom drama played to a good-sized crowd. One paper humorously said the dispute, which had begun over a son's debt, escalated to a scorching squabble. Something was said about a warmer climate, and Cox informed his wife that he "would furnish the fuel and she could raise the hell."[29]

Divorce was not compatible with her religious beliefs, but Almira remained separated from her husband. Elihu continued to purchase properties in her name but did not help with her support.[30] And so it was that Frank began sending Almira precious money that he earned from copper mining in Arizona Territory and afterward as an organizer for the WFM and IWW.

Bisbee would leave an impression on Frank. His encounters with the town's prejudiced racial, social, and economic hierarchy would inflame his resentment when he returned.

8

THE VISIONARIES, 1906

A perfect spring day greeted the 1906 May Day festivities in Globe, Arizona. Dignitaries on a wooden speakers' platform watched as a parade made a wide turn from Oak Street onto North Broad Street. Spectators had crowded the intersection, some shaded by broad-striped awnings of the handsome new Amster Building, when 1,100 miners suddenly appeared behind a procession of bartenders.[1] Although nearly all people in town observed the parade, practically suspending business, city officials glumly noted that socialists now controlled the occasion.[2] Apparently emboldened, miners and mill workers had walked off their jobs to participate without employer consent.[3] This May Day parade carried no American flag, played no patriotic tunes, and the American Federation of Labor (AFL) and WFM, usually adversarial unions, marched together exhibiting their solidarity in honor of the American worker.[4]

By the time the parade reached the platform supporting a covey of Socialist speakers just before noon, newspaper reporters and conservative businessmen took note of the altered celebration. May Day general committee chairman Fred C. White rose to announce the speakers. Instead of a prescheduled solo of "The Star Spangled Banner," White first introduced an address from former Bisbee restaurateur Joseph D. Cannon, who had come to Globe upon invitation of the Miners' Union. Tall and blonde, Cannon made a striking figure on the platform where, according to local newspapers, the theme of his and others' speeches was industrial unionism, and there was no mincing of words.[5]

The WFM often employed SPA speakers to travel among various mining camps, encouraging miners to join the federation. A decade later, the IWW would utilize the same model of traveling speakers to keep rank and file focused on a general strike. But this day, Cannon had another reason for speaking: he was running for U.S. Congress on the Arizona SPA ticket.[6]

Frank Little was now a close associate of Joe Cannon after Cannon helped Harry A. McKee successfully organize the Bisbee SPA local. Once Arizona State Union (ASU-WFM) No. 3 formed, after some mining corporations ignored the new eight-hour law, Cannon went to work as an ASU-WFM executive committee member helping organize Arizona's locals. Yet Cannon had failed to launch a Bisbee local, a necessary organization crucial to WFM success in Arizona.[7] Perhaps it was Joe Cannon's work with Globe socialists and the WFM local that induced Frank to leave Bisbee and join ASU-WFM's organizers, or perhaps it was Globe's reputation as one of the federation's "best and most aggressive camps in the jurisdiction."[8] One thing is certain—Frank Little was scheduled to be on the same Socialist speakers' platform for the evening's May Day festivities.

Much like the barnyard socialism of the Little Red Hen parable, ignoring the assumption that the tiny grain of wheat a capitalist farmer provides the Little Red Hen should be adequate, socialists believed that all workers should reap and communally share profits, or a loaf of bread in this case. While others have parodied the parable to fit various political and economic extremes of socialist economics versus capitalism, the SPA believed in reforming the nation's free-enterprise system and private ownership into cooperative and social ownership. Perhaps more confusing, complexities of socialist economic, social, and political viewpoints varied among different socialist groups, with many ideas over-lapping or at odds.

More simply explained within the context of the time period, WFM secretary-treasurer William "Big Bill" Haywood stated that he took the side of workers against mine owners who "did not find the gold, they did not mine the gold, they did not mill the gold, but by some weird alchemy all the gold belonged to them!"[9] In a time when owners of gigantic corporations were labeled "barons," the notion was not extraordinary, and it was alluring.

On the evening of May 1, 1906, Frank Little stood at a speakers' podium doing what he dreaded most—reciting poetry. His task was to deliver "Good Old Summer Time" before the main speaking event.[10] Ralph Chaplin, a poet, artist, and close friend of Frank's in later years, wrote in his memoirs that Frank did not like poetry particularly, preferring Chaplin's sketches.[11] However, in 1906 poetry was a fashionable way to both entertain and educate audiences, and this would not be the last time Frank employed verse to support a cause. Frank was not running for office like Cannon, but he would become recognized as the Clifton organizer from Globe.

In Frank, the spectators saw a young speaker with a crooked smile who was, perhaps, uncomfortable in his new role. At about twenty-eight years old, Frank was not particularly handsome like his brother Fred. But to those who actually met him after reading descriptions of his menacing expression, his face was surprisingly pleasant. Of all Almira's children, Frank looked most like his mother, and some noted a trace of American Indian ancestry when describing his features. Yet fair, brown-haired, and blue-eyed, Frank was not the dark persona that labor-activist Elizabeth Gurley Flynn characterized when stating that Frank was "tall and dark, with black hair and black eyes," his one damaged eye giving him a "misleadingly sinister appearance."[12] While Ralph Chaplin also described Frank's "deadly untamed look in that lone eye when his will was crossed," fellow IWWs described Frank as "gentle as a lamb" and a "slender, gentle, and soft-spoken man."[13]

The only surviving family photograph of Frank, taken several years later in Spokane, presents his countenance as one of a mustached young man, wide-eyed and possibly unsure of his path in

FRANK LITTLE, 1909
Frank Little mailed this photo postcard to his mother from Washington State, possibly Spokane, in late 1909. The rare photo is the only family photo to have survived Bureau of Investigation raids. *Courtright Family Papers.*

life—until one examines the photo closer. He is wearing a union pin, his hands are crossed, and he leans on a log-fence prop with a wide-sky background, an obviously contrived outdoor setting within a photographer's studio. He is looking directly into the lens, his lips pursed as if about to say something, a broad Stetson hat silhouetting his head. His square chin, dimpled yet strong, juts toward the camera, belying any doubts as to what he is about. Frank had matured from the farm boy who left Oklahoma's red dirt for shifting, sunburnt sands under Arizona's WFM foundation.

Much like the complexions of other mining districts in the American West, the character and style of Globe, Arizona, developed from the influx of opportunists who flooded the territorial town. One easterner wrote to a friend back home in 1906 that the town "is fine for health, a top-notcher for 'heat' and rocks and cactus, and a hell buster for 'copper,'" adding, "The way they hold you up for real estate would grow hair on John D. Rockefeller's bald spot!"[14] The letter writer further lamented, "I think all the human freaks we saw in the circuses must have gotten their start in the Arizona mining camp, eating their meals at a hash house."[15]

Infamous gamblers and criminals who called Globe home included some famous misfits, such as Big Nose Kate, Doc Holliday's lover, and the Apache Kid. The single main street called Broad Street ran north and south along the banks of an oft-flooding Pinal Creek. It boasted a hanging tree—a tall sycamore, directly in its center of wide dirt lanes—to handle the town's more notorious guests.

A few blocks south, the multibalconied Dominion Hotel attracted wheelers and dealers in grand style, its restaurant fit for Arizona Territory's colorful governor, George W. P. Hunt. Hunt, who also called Globe home, had walked into the town in 1881, his sole possessions on his back and the burro he drove. Annoying to mining corporations, Hunt became a proponent of organized labor. A political opponent later characterizing the successful, three-hundred-pound governor purportedly remarked, "Two circuses are in town today, Ringling Brothers and G. W. P. Hunt. Both are complete with side shows."[16]

All sorts of men traveled to Globe, but not for its seedy businesses or for the weather. They tolerated eating "with Chinamen" at chop houses "with the dirtiest cooks you ever saw" and paid high prices for mundane things such as a haircut and a shave when it would be cheaper to use a crock bowl and let their whiskers grow.[17] They endured expensive boarding houses sometimes sleeping three to a room and bought fifteen-cent drinks—all for a chance to work in the Old Dominion Copper Mine and smelter.

With the miners came the WFM, Globe Local No. 60, a solid union base for miners and mill workers that spread its organization into other mining camps of Arizona Territory. As such, Globe, with its influx of flourishing new businesses alongside the Old Dominion Mine, became an attractive work location for union members. By the end of 1905, when he moved to Globe, Frank Little would have agreed with the letter writer that Globe "will be the great copper country and [it] is only in its infancy."[18]

Globe also would become a center of labor agitation amid Phelps Dodge spies, loyalty leagues, and insidious ethnic bigotries, which, like Bisbee, would play a major role in Frank's evolution as a fiery labor agitator. In fact, early labor unrest in Arizona mining districts, including Globe, Bisbee, Jerome, and Clifton-Morenci, was merely a warm-up act to the main event about ten years later when Frank, threatening a general strike during wartime, would lead the IWW against copper mining companies and old WFM acquaintances.

Eighty miles east of Phoenix along today's U.S. Highway 60, Globe, Arizona, straddles Pinal Creek in the heart of Arizona's picturesque Tonto National Forest between spectacular vistas of the Apache Mountains on the east and the Pinal Mountains to the west. Western Apaches called it "Bésh Baa Gowąh" or "place of metal," but it became Globe in 1878 when a large spherical silver nugget was found.[19] The old Globe mining district was located between the Gila River on the south and the Salt River on the north, its back roads and subsequent train tracks serving as major arteries for transporting ore and miners between mining camps.

Just four miles to the west of Globe was Miami, an emergent mining camp in 1907 largely dependent on Miami Copper Company. Miami (pronounced "My-am-uh" by locals) also would provide an important setting for Frank Little's future agitation, but in this earlier time the close communities of Globe and Miami were isolated from the rest of Arizona except for the Gila Valley, Globe, and Northern Railway linking them to the outside world to the east. Like misshapen beads on a crooked wire, major mines strung the communities together through the valley with Old Dominion to the east, Miami Copper in the middle, and by 1909, the Inspiration to the northwest.

After he returned from visiting Almira in Guthrie, Oklahoma, in late 1904, Frank found no easy highway for traveling back to

Arizona and Globe. He took a train west through El Paso, Texas, and then on to Bowie, Arizona, (known as Teviston until 1908). From there a rough trail followed the Gila River valley west toward Globe, today U.S. Highway 70, which was used for freighting between mining camps, rail, and stage stops. Today, U.S. Highway 70 intersects U.S. Highway 60 in Globe.

Apache attacks had ended at least twenty-five years earlier, so a caravan might enjoy a scenic route traversing the upper Sonoran Desert along the river, the sun dancing pinks, golds, and yellows across the southern faces of the mountains to the north. Yet Frank probably chose to take the Globe and Northern Railway northwest to Safford, across the San Carlos Apache Reservation. No public stops were permitted on the lonely fifty-mile stretch across the reservation's bottomland where prized pima cotton is raised today. And no one wanted to be caught in extreme cold, heat, or violent monsoon rains that could transform the high desert quickly. When Frank finally could travel by automobile, he chanced misfortunes on the same Bowie-to-Globe trail that had evolved only to a narrow road, with perilous, rough inclines draining into sandy, cacti-covered arroyos. Such an accident actually may have saved him from being deported along with other Arizona copper miners in 1917.

Just before World War I, Frank listed his mailing address in Miami, but in early 1906 he maintained Globe as his residence. This was not uncommon, as miners living in both Globe and Miami mining camps sometimes worked at mines some distance away, walking or hitching rides back and forth.

The isolation allowed the WFM to dominate mining camps until 1904 when, amid financial duress, Professor Douglas and Phelps Dodge took over the Old Dominion Copper Mining and Smelting Company, renaming it Old Dominion Company.[20] Douglas was resistant to union organizing in Globe just as he had been in Bisbee, and, much like Douglas's management in Bisbee, Phelps Dodge began asserting itself against labor just before Frank arrived in Globe. Governor Hunt subsequently referred to Phelps Dodge as "the Beast of Arizona" because of its ruthlessness and "autocracy of wealth," a sobriquet that became commonly used for Phelps Dodge.[21]

The WFM, as a predominantly white organization, was able to hold on in Globe with tacit consent of mining companies, including Old Dominion Company. Local No. 60 initially had a membership of about three hundred, with Old Dominion Company being the primary employer.[22] By the time Frank arrived in Globe, the WFM had a national membership of twenty-four thousand, down from twenty-eight thousand in 1903, likely the result of the last Cripple Creek strike in Colorado. Cripple Creek, the utopian union mining camp, had ended in despair for many deported miners and their families, sending them in exodus across the desert to Arizona mining camps.[23]

As in Bisbee, Douglas again preferred to hire Irish and Cornish men. Cornish miners dominated as skilled miners and often held supervisory positions. As a consequence, when labor struck, the Cornish typically held with management, increasing divisiveness among other workers. This leaning would be borne out in Globe in 1917 strikes when the Cornish stayed true to the company. Happy with their jobs, they arrived each morning and sang while going down the shaft.[24]

Prejudice among ethnicities did not stop with the Cornish. Other ethnic groups that worked the Old Dominion Mine included Welsh and Eastern Europeans, primarily Bulgarians, Croats, Serbs, and Romanians, who had been excluded from Colorado mining camps, and a few American Indians.[25] Like Cripple Creek and Bisbee, Globe and Miami were white mining camps that supported the segregation of swarthy-skinned southern Europeans and other people of color. In particular, the Globe Miners' Union detested Mexican and Mexican American workers.

A tactic that Old Dominion Copper Mining and Smelting Company employed helped launch long-lived antagonism for Mexican usurpers among white miners. In 1896 a labor strike called for a reinstatement of wages after miners took a cut from $3.00 to $2.50 and then to $2.25 over a two-year period.[26] Company management was confident that it could hire Mexican miners at a much lower wage and starve out the new union.[27] In response, the WFM sent its president, Edward Boyce, to encourage the Globe Miners' Union to join the WFM, organizing Local No. 60 the same year.

Eventually, miners won back their original wage, and the WFM local became solidified although the company refused to recognize it.

Nevertheless, to white miners, Mexican labor became synonymous with scab labor, augmenting existing bigotry with resentment and limiting WFM membership.[28] For the next twenty years, as radical labor agitation in Arizona centered on the Miami-Globe district, often using Mexican labor as pawns, the white Local No. 60 earned a reputation as the most militant union in the territory.[29]

The killer sycamore tree and the elegant Dominion Hotel are long gone today but in 1905 were representative of the wide social divide in Globe. Also gone are racial animosities that made Globe a "white man's camp," although mining remains important to the city's economy. Mostly ruins are all that remain today of a mine that once produced millions of dollars in copper ore amid intense labor standoffs, soldiers and Arizona Rangers, and recalcitrant mine owners and miners.

At the time of the 1906 May Day Parade in Globe, WFM president Charles Moyer, WFM secretary Bill Haywood, and Colorado WFM leader George Pettibone were sitting in an Idaho jail awaiting trials for murder. They were accused of killing former Idaho governor Frank Steunenberg. Accusations against WFM leaders, who had butted heads with Steunenberg in the past, tarnished the union. Many called the WFM the "Western Federation of Murderers," blaming them for crimes that hired spies or gunmen initiated.[30] After George McPharland, a Pinkerton operative, convinced stoolie Harry Orchard to testify that the WFM had ordered him to plant a bomb at Steunenberg's front gate, Pinkerton agents kidnapped the WFM leaders in Colorado and illegally transported them across state lines to Boise, Idaho, for trial. President Theodore Roosevelt, who despised socialists, concluded with other government officials that WFM leaders were guilty, calling the men "undesirable citizens" in 1907.[31]

Money poured in from pockets of wealthy Colorado and Idaho Mine Owners' Associations and other state mining interests to prosecute the men and permanently break the WFM. The defense hired renowned Chicago lawyer Clarence Darrow, who was able to prove in two sensational trials that Orchard actually committed the murder independently. Darrow's bill between May 1906 and March 1907 alone was $14,803.75, an enormous sum for the organization to fund.[32] Still, Darrow was well worth the money as Orchard was finally convicted and sentenced to death.[33] Despite the blemish on the WFM, a timely merging with another organization—the IWW—had given new blood to the WFM, helping pour money into defense funds.

In June 1905, attending a founding convention in Chicago were prominent labor leaders, radicals, and socialists, including Bill Haywood, Vincent St. John, Ralph Chaplin, James P. Cannon, and William Trautmann. While the WFM had been the most militant labor organization in the country, those attending the convention united to create a more extreme union, one that demanded workplace solidarity in a battle against capitalist enterprises currently dominating America's industrial revolution. WFM leaders became convinced that one big union of all working-class people needed to be formed—one that attracted and included all crafts, ethnicities, and genders, a tenet that the WFM certainly had not embraced before. Its goal? To abolish the wage system and unite all workers as a single class.

In September 1905, the WFM became recognized nationally as the Mining Department of the Industrial Workers of the World. The IWW, whose members later became known as Wobblies, pushed the WFM further to the left. Although he did not attend the 1905 WFM Annual Convention in Denver, as a relatively new socialist, disenchanted laborer, and self-perceived victim of economic oppression, Frank was drawn naturally to the new radical union, adopting its vision for "One Big Union" (OBU).

If the IWW included all working men and women, then it would attract immigrants who had journeyed to the United States for better opportunities and increase WFM membership. While President Roosevelt decried immigrants as un-American "undesirables" unless they shed all their homeland vestiges, the IWW welcomed them with open arms of empathy, understanding, and equality.[34]

Frank promptly immersed himself in union activities along
with work, most likely in the Old Dominion Mine. His Scots-Irish
heritage was an early plus, and his WFM membership gave him
an open path for work. Frank had yet to use his Native ancestry
as an organizational tool, and neither company management nor
company-owned newspapers had yet made him notorious.

In February 1906, Frank mailed an editorial to the "Correspondence" section of *Miner's Magazine* from Globe:

Socialists and the IWW

Recognizing the fact that the working class and the
employing class have nothing in common. There can be
no peace so long as hunger and want are found among millions of working people, and the few who make up the
employing class have all the good things in life.

The working class must come together on the political
as well as on the industrial field, and take and hold that
which they produce (From Preamble of the I.W.W.).

And as the Socialist party is a working class organization on the political field.

And as the Industrial Workers of the World is a working
class organization on the industrial field. Both organized
to the same end; that of emancipating the working class
from wage slavery and abolishing the capitalist system, and
establish in its stead the Co-operative Commonwealth.

And as the two organizations are necessary one to the
other to more quickly bring about the social revolution.

And as there are speakers and organizers in the Socialist party who are aiding and supporting the American Federation of Labor, a capitalist-dominated labor union, and
as such organization is detrimental to the working class
on the Industrial as well as on the political field, therefore
in the opinion of the writer, all class-conscious Socialists
should refuse to aid, financially or otherwise, speakers and
organizers of the Socialist party who do not indorse the
Industrial Workers of the World.

Comrades, line up to the real revolution and aid us to educate the workers of the world to strike for their class interests, to vote for their class interests, and if necessary, fight for their class interests.

Globe, Arizona   F. H. Little[35]

Since his arrival in Bisbee three years earlier, Frank had risen quickly as a recognized proponent of industrial unionism and socialism. In Globe, Arizona, Frank Little found his voice.

9

THE ORGANIZER, 1906–1908

Saturday evening, October 1, 1904, an orphan train, sponsored by the Sisters of Charity Foundling Hospital in New York City, shuddered to a stop beside the old Coronado trail in Clifton, Arizona. Forty bewildered children, exhausted by their six-day journey, woke with a start. The littlest lay in the comforting arms of nuns and nurses who had accompanied them, while others peered uncertainly out the boxcar windows. Clifton would be a terminus for sixteen of forty children who had journeyed from Grand Central Station for placement in devout Catholic homes. The others would meet their new families next morning in Morenci, a tortuous corkscrew climb about one thousand feet above Clifton.

At the stop awaited a cluster of Clifton's Anglo women, curious about the orphan trains that had been delivering waifs all over the West. What they saw encouraged them to adopt. The nuns had dressed the little girls in starched white frocks, their hair curled and beribboned. The little boys made their Clifton debut in stylish sailor suits, incongruous with the dry rusty-red mountains looming above. The women pressed forward, eager to pick out children, unaware new foster families already had been assigned.

That evening at the wooden-framed Sacred Heart Catholic Church on Copper Street (today's Chase Street), darkly shawled foster mothers obediently formed a queue to collect children matched to their Catholic Clifton homes. Observers noted that all sixteen children were fair skinned with Irish surnames, and all new mothers were brown skinned. In fact, the new parents mostly came from mining families who earned a Mexican wage of $1.50 to $2.50 a day.[1]

Next day in Morenci, after the last child was placed into the arms of a Mexican family, a tempest erupted, as wicked as a thunderstorm wrecking a Morenci miners' strike the year before. And just like a flood of racism that had led to the 1903 miners' strike, this new conflict was built on a foundation of extreme prejudice.

During another downpour on the following evening, Morenci and Clifton Anglo women orchestrated a kidnapping from the Mexican mothers, generating mob rule that lasted several days. The *Arizona Bulletin* condemned Catholics for selling "sweet, innocent, white American babies" to "squalid, half-civilized Mexicans of the lowest class."[2] The priest was run out of town for having the stupidity to select parents from an obviously inferior race. Armed vigilantes "rescued" nineteen children while twenty-one children barely escaped with the nuns onto a train bound back east. After a failed, brief legal battle to return the children to their foster families, the orphans were gathered into the arms of white mothers while a patriotic band struck up "America" at their homecoming, and crowds celebrated, yelling until they could yell no more.[3]

Such was the racial atmosphere Frank Little entered nine months later. His job was to organize Mexican workers who surely had little reason to trust him.

Less than a hundred miles southeast of Globe, Arizona, veering northeast off U.S. Highway 70, is U.S. Highway 191, the old Coronado Trail. After leaving the flattened, lush landscape of the Gila River valley, U.S. Highway 191 branches the Black Hills Byway, a twenty-one-mile loop that traces the old Safford-Clifton trail. Years earlier, when Frank was called to Clifton from Globe, the old trail was just a rutted trace worn by a steady procession of men and mules through volcano-like mountains.

Not much has changed the landscape. Amid gray-green, lava-strewn hillsides, furry-coated cholla, midnight-green creosote, thorny mesquite, and some greasewood line the old trail that once carried men and freight to mines. Gradually the hills' faces, with pockmarked *malpaís* outcroppings, change from black to reddish castle-like projections, indicative of the state's geographic propensity to transform its colors abruptly, and in this case, hinting at great mineral wealth in the Clifton-Morenci mining district.

Emerging from the mountains, the byway rejoins U.S. Highway 191, usually presenting a panorama of blue sky, with Clifton, Arizona, stretched below along the green banks of the serpentine San Francisco River. To the northwest, a huge open-pit mining operation, its strata of ochre and turquoise hues, adds color to the crumbling, brown community that is Clifton today. When Frank arrived in 1906, the rough mining community sprawled along Chase Creek, more a dry wash that monsoon rains might transform into a raging river.

Chase Street, once the narrow main street running parallel to the creek, still offers remnants of the "tougher than Tombstone" town, which bustled with mining offices, boarding houses, general stores, theaters, saloons, and rough enterprises characteristic of mining camps.[4] Mostly vacant, two-story brick buildings have changed little since Frank's first arrival. Sacred Heart Catholic Church, scene of the orphan outrage, remains prominent on its raised foundation with a newer stone facade.

Just like Bisbee and Globe, mining rubble is strewn among dead buildings. On lower slopes of the desert mountains, shot with green-and-purple-shadowed canyons surrounding Clifton, are black maws of ancient tunnels, which formerly disgorged ore cars full of copper ore. The mountains hide scars of other mining wounds—the racism that dominated this mining district and contributed to Frank's failure in his first venture as a labor organizer.

Three mining camps formed the Clifton-Morenci mining district: Clifton, Morenci, and Metcalf, all interdependent communities contained in deep canyons within the White Mountain range.

Old Morenci, tied by the corkscrew railway to Clifton in 1901, was about six miles up in Morenci Canyon. It was mostly a Mexican and Italian camp with some of the most deplorable living conditions in Arizona. Most Mexicans lived on steep hills surrounding the isolated camp near smoky copper works, paying ten dollars in monthly rent to build on company-owned land.[5] The community had no streets, merely trails leading upward to flimsy Mexican shanties, many made of scrap lumber found on company grounds. No electricity or public facilities were provided, so company-owned mules hauled water in from the San Francisco River, almost five miles away. Businesses and the company store, built in "the hole" as the canyon was called, sold miners supplies, paid with *boletas*, or company scrip, and not with actual American dollars.[6]

The 1908 *Engineering and Mining Journal* is full of advice for supervising Mexican mine labor, including an explanation as to why Mexicans had no capacity for managing their wages. "The sooner you get his money away from the peon," one writer declared, "the better for him and the more work he will do . . . [he can't buy liquor]."[7] True to this writer's advice, Morenci's mining company controlled its camp, dictating how people lived, where they could shop, and what they could buy. It is no wonder that white women of Clifton and Morenci arrogantly believed that placing orphans into Mexican women's hands was akin to a Greek tragedy.

William Church purchased the Morenci Mine for Detroit Copper Company, later selling it to Phelps Dodge. As a result, Professor Douglas inserted himself into this mining camp just as he had in Bisbee and Globe.

Metcalf, another Mexican camp, was located in Metcalf Canyon, above Morenci. While chasing Chiricahua Apaches, the Metcalf brothers originally located and named Longfellow Mine (discovered on the poet's birthday), and then sold the mine to New York businessmen, the Lesinsky brothers, who later sold to a group of Scottish investors, the formidable Arizona Copper Company (ACC). James Colquhoun is best known for his Clifton management and innovation in this company.[8]

When current owner Freeport-McMoRan expanded its open-pit mining operation in 1983, the small communities of Metcalf and

Morenci were razed, the original ethnic neighborhoods having been built on company-owned property. A new Morenci exists today, and the town boasts that Freeport-McMoRan is the largest copper mining operation in North America, and Morenci Mine, one of the largest mines in the world.[9]

Clifton, below Morenci and Metcalf, housed mining companies' business operations and their concentrators and smelter. Unlike her sister camps, Clifton became the hub of all mining companies' activities and a natural place for Frank Little to begin labor organization.

Along Chase Creek were poor Mexicans and Chinese, victimized regularly by flooding. One witness, testifying to the 1917 President's Mediation Commission on Clifton-Morenci mining district's living conditions, said that before 1915, about 40 percent of Clifton's houses had no floors and about 60 percent had no furniture other than a candle, powder boxes for tables and storage, and other crude homemade articles.[10] Like Morenci and Metcalf, lack of services, including waste disposal and clean water, caused disease that struck the camp periodically like waves. Another witness testified that the only time the camp was cleaned was when Phelps Dodge officials were scheduled to visit.[11]

Generally, company management assumed that Mexicans were hardy, accustomed to living in squalor. Because of their simple lifestyles, efforts to provide cleanliness and improved hygiene were therefore thought wasted. As an example, no company dry rooms existed for miners to change clothes after their shifts. The men had to walk to their homes in wet working clothes even during cold weather.[12] Besides, improving workers' living conditions cost money. In fact, the prospect of additional capital outlay is what caused the 1903 Morenci wildcat strike.

Arizona legislators passed the eight-hour-day law for underground miners, effective June 1, 1903. The bill was supported by unions that wanted a closed shop and punishment for mining companies that contracted cheap, alien labor. Professor Douglas begrudgingly paid his white underground miners a standard wage of three dollars at Bisbee's Copper Queen, where Frank most likely had worked, but managing a Mexican camp, where a dual-wage system was in force, was different. Mexicans worked ten to twelve hours a day with a daily rate averaging $2.00 to $2.50. Their white counterparts worked only seven-and-a-half to eight hours, earning sometimes double what Mexicans were compensated.[13] If the Mexicans' workday was reduced by two hours and they were paid the same daily wages, it would amount to a 25 percent pay increase for them.[14]

In advance of the new territorial law taking effect, Professor Douglas and James Colquhoun announced that they would offer nine hours' "Mexican" pay for eight hours' work, about a 10 percent wage decrease for the Mexican worker, knowing full well that the Arizona WFM would not organize Mexicans.[15] Colquhoun cited exceptional conditions in Clifton-Morenci mining district, claiming additional labor costs would leave no profit for owners.[16]

The Mexican miners struck on Monday, June 3, after their demands for $2.50 a day and specified improved working conditions were denied. About three thousand men from ACC and Detroit Copper companies, in Metcalf and Morenci respectively, walked off their jobs.[17] Only after what was to be called "The Mexican Affair" was over, did WFM president Charles H. Moyer delegate a mild statement of verbal encouragement to the strikers.[18]

The *Bisbee Daily Review*, a Phelps Dodge Mining Company newspaper, supported mine operators and their contention that the companies should not pay more to Mexicans, especially because little skilled labor was required in operation of Morenci and Metcalf mines. The paper further noted that with no real labor organization guiding them, the Mexicans would stand loosely together and families would "become destitute before long and the strike won't last."[19] An editorial in the *Arizona Silver Belt*, which often supported WFM Local No. 60, blamed mining companies for hiring too many foreigners in the district in the first place, thus causing the problem.[20] In general, mine managers, believing Mexican workers docile, thought they would not fight back. The mine managers miscalculated.

Mexicans *had* united, taking initiative toward wage parity and improved working conditions, in part led by anarchists, predecessors to the Partido Liberal Mexicano (PLM), who later led a revolt against Mexican president Porfirio Díaz's regime and its pimping of Mexican labor. *Regeneración*, a radical periodical, surely was read in the Clifton-Morenci mining district. It urged political dissent and socialism as an attractive alternative for workers. Mexicans also had formed *mutualistas*, organizations that provided burial insurance, labor solidarity, political connections, and social events unifying a sense of community. In Clifton-Morenci, one mutualista called the Mexican Society, or Alianza Hispano Americana, helped organize the strike.[21]

Graham County Sheriff James V. Parks and thirty-two deputies arrived in Clifton in early June 1903, finding that mine owners were unwilling to negotiate despite Parks's conclusion that many of the workers' demands were reasonable: they *were* underpaid and working conditions *were* appalling.[22] Ignoring the sheriff's observations, mine management speedily implemented two commonly used methods to break the strike and avert bloodshed. Both tactics brought life to the dime novels of Frank's youth.

First, mining companies hired Thiel detective agents to infiltrate strikers, fearing Mexican political agitation would infect other mine operations in their Arizonan and Mexican mines. Because of high demand for information regarding labor activists, corporations routinely employed domestic spies to infiltrate company personnel and union inner circles. During his life, Frank would elude Pinkerton, Burns, and Thiel agents, many of whom were indistinguishable from general gunmen. By 1917 there would be nearly three hundred detective agencies across the country investigating labor activities.[23]

Mine officials also pushed for state militia support—in this case, the Arizona Rangers, an elite secret organization originally formed to catch cattle rustlers—who proceeded by special train to Clifton and Morenci on June 8.[24] The Arizona Rangers were not necessarily stellar representatives of the law, and this was their first assignment as strikebreakers. Frank afterward publicly criticized mining company misuse of state militia and federal troops for strikebreaking, intimidation, and inhumane punishment across western states.

The leader of the rangers, Captain Thomas H. Rynning, who had ridden with Teddy Roosevelt and his Rough Riders and who would become notorious in other strikebreaking activities, was "full of himself."[25] Under his leadership, rangers immediately identified troublemakers as "mostly Mexicans, but a lot of Dagoes, Bohunks, and foreigners of different kinds" that exacerbated the racially tense atmosphere.[26] Parks and his men worked to control Rynning and deflate the strike simultaneously.

James Colquhoun of ACC and Superintendent Charles Mills further pressured Fort Apache to send federal troops, inflating the strike into an incident that some feared could turn deadly.[27] Before the National Guard could arrive, on Tuesday, June 9, 1903, Morenci miners assembled by the hundreds, cheering speaker after speaker mounted atop boulders to address the strike in defiance of "gringo" rangers. Hundreds more of Metcalf's Mexican miners joined men gathered at a lime quarry before climbing upward to a rocky mountain overlooking Morenci Canyon and the lawmen. Then an unseasonable rain began to fall, suddenly becoming torrential, and a ten-foot wall of water swept down Morenci Canyon and into Chase Creek Canyon.

Chase Creek arroyo's water roared, overflowing into Clifton streets, snatching miners' modest homes, and destroying all in its wake.[28] The floods disorganized the strike, and miners returned to work for $2.25 a day within a few days, their demands unresolved. Six companies of the National Guard were needed to restore order.[29]

Unsuccessful in their action against American mining companies, Mexican labor now was ripe for some sort of organization, although perhaps not by an Anglo-American.

General organizer Marion W. Moor found conditions of Clifton workers "deplorable," so he met with the ASU executive board to discuss unorganized mining camps in October 1906.[30] Since the futile 1903 Clifton strike, no organization of laborers had taken place, in large part because of WFM locals' anti-Mexican policy. Now Moor and the ASU executive board, pushing bigotry into the shadows, strongly advocated including those previously shunned in an attempt to dominate the AFL. Moor took the initiative to hire two WFM organizers who directly began work in Clifton-Morenci mining district under the ASU—Frank Little and Fernando Velarde, a Mexican American blacksmith.[31] Velarde, an American-born citizen, had been enormously successful organizing an IWW mixed local (for mixed trades) in Phoenix, Arizona.

The Clifton-Morenci assignment was Frank's debut as a labor organizer. After Frank's death, the *Daily Missoulian* reported that his first IWW fight occurred in Goldfield, Nevada, a labor conflict that began in December 1906 and ended about two years later.[32] Wobblies claiming Goldfield in their labor pedigrees was not unusual—it was considered the first major IWW battle—but Frank was not there. He was busy in Arizona.

Eighty percent of workers in the Clifton-Morenci mining district were Mexican, and not one in five hundred spoke English, according to the WFM, so why would Frank, who did not speak Spanish, be assigned there?[33] It may be that Frank was perceived racially unbiased.

Racial bias greatly affected local organizational activities in Arizona, although ASU leadership voiced the benefits of including Hispanics, but Frank had no lengthy history in Arizona, no petri dish in which to culture racial prejudices. Instead, he had been raised in Indian Territory among American Indians, and although Frank had no opportunity to become fluent in secondary languages, he was willing to organize where other WFM locals resisted. Later history also illustrates his ability to empathize and align with immigrants, especially Eastern Europeans and Finns.

Clifton-Morenci mining conditions aside, perhaps Frank also saw the job as an opportunity to rise in the ranks. His relationship with Joe Cannon already had helped him climb a ladder of union organizing, and he had distinguished himself from other union members, using his quick tongue to compensate for his newborn knowledge of union organization. Perhaps most noticeable was his passion, although the bitterness ascribed to him in later years had yet to fester.

Moreover, organizing was a young man's game because organizers were always on the move, living in boarding houses and hotels and moving from mining camp to mining camp, and even from state to state. Typically, only WFM executive board members were paid field organizers; others organized on the job with no compensation.[34] For his first job as a professional organizer, Frank would receive a per diem rate comparable to what local underground miners received, plus expenses for mileage.[35] Frank's pay was based on a wage scale in one of the poorest-paid mining districts in the territory, but organizers typically did not take their jobs for the pay; in fact, many lost money. The other recompense was satisfaction from effectively organizing, often uninvited, in hostile locales. History shows that Frank thrived on the competitive edge of his work, and it beat working underground.

Frank Little and Fernando Velarde arrived in Clifton, Arizona, sometime in November 1906. Racial tension was palpable in the mining camp, and they immediately encountered a strong representation of AFL craft union members, who opposed organizing Mexicans.[36] Men holding AFL membership cards were horrified, especially at the idea of associating with the new WFM-IWW, which included people of color, immigrants, and unskilled workers.

Mexicans worked alongside Anglos in Clifton's mills and smelter, but they received lower wages. Despite the 1903 eight-hour law and subsequent strike, they were paid an average wage of $2.25 per ten-hour day.[37] These Mexican smelter and mill workers comprised the first group that Frank and Fernando Velarde approached for organizing a WFM local, and on November 30, 1906, they organized Clifton Mining and Smelting Local No. 158 with about two hundred new members, mostly Mexicans.[38] Either because of Frank's ignorance or inexperience or because no Mexican was nominated for candidacy, Local No. 158's officers were Anglos and not Mexicans. Along with Frank, Harry F. Kane and W. D. Stewart were named to head the new local.[39] Kane was not even a smelter or mill worker—he was a newspaper man who had just terminated his affiliation with the *Clifton Herald* and then edited the *Christian Advocate*.[40] The third officer, W. D. Stewart, was a machinist. Just as in the smelter in which they worked, Spanish-surnamed men held subordinate positions in the new union local, making it fragile at best.[41]

In an early article describing Frank's success in founding new locals in the Clifton-Morenci mining district, Kane reported organizational work was beset by difficulties "peculiar to the section of country and which are delaying the work of organization."[42] Language and skin color were obvious impediments that Frank would have to conquer singlehandedly in Metcalf and Morenci after Velarde was called to Phoenix unexpectedly for a family medical emergency.[43] Frank had no translator or Mexican counterpart to represent racial equality to men he hoped to win, Metcalf miners only earned an average wage of $1.80 for a ten-hour day, and the area was flooded with laborers from Mexico.[44] Frank had difficulties from the outset, including finding a central location to hold meetings.

The ACC owned all the ground for residence and business buildings. After observing Frank's activities in Clifton, the ACC made certain he was denied use of a public hall, and even if he could have used a public location, "well-paid white employees" could "be relied upon to throw every obstacle in the way of an organizer."[45] But by contacting groups such as mutualistas and circulating handbills, Frank successfully attracted disadvantaged miners and mill workers to assemble at private sites, likely open-air meetings. There Frank and new recruits dispensed more English, Italian, and Spanish-print WFM pamphlets and convincingly delivered tangible reasons for joining the WFM. More successful Mexican workers tended to be moderate and uninterested in unionization.[46] But when Frank's words hit their target, he was able to collect men's signatures or marks in order to obtain executive recognition for a new WFM charter. Frank prevailed almost three months later, on March 14, 1907, when Metcalf Miners' Local No. 159 was formed with a large membership.[47] He registered each worker on paper, collected dues, and issued a membership card with a dues-payment stamp. This time, besides Frank, a Mexican leader named Carmen Acosta was elected officer.[48]

At the same time Frank was organizing Metcalf, miners and smeltermen throughout Clifton-Morenci mining district began petitioning copper companies for a fifty-cent wage increase on a sliding scale, relative to the wholesale price of copper.[49] Morenci miners still had not acquiesced to union membership, but they supported the petition.

Morenci, worst of the mining camps in its stark, smoky setting, seemed an impenetrable wall. The 1903 failed strike and disgraceful treatment of Mexicans in the 1904 orphan abduction were fresh wounds. Like Metcalf, laborers received an average wage of $1.80 per day for ten hours' work, but unlike Metcalf, Mexican and Italian miners were driven independently and needed no Anglo to lead them.[50] After all, the previous miners' strike had begun in Morenci.

Frank was under pressure to bring the Morenci mining camp into the WFM fold. The WFM had finally established Local 106 in Bisbee on February 9, 1907. Bisbee was the toughest camp to organize thus far, and its tentative success highlighted other Arizona organizational activities. Morenci's organizational problems were quite different from Bisbee's, however. Frank not only had to oppose mining managers but also recalcitrant laborers, and his whiteness was a handicap.

While white mining officials entertained themselves at the Morenci Club, its lavish verandas hiding a bowling alley, theater, and library within, laboring families paid markups of almost 200 percent for goods in the Morenci store. Eggs and a pound of coffee took a day's salary, and many of the miners' children could not attend school because they lacked appropriate clothing. So many Mexicans died that Morenci Cemetery was renamed Catholic Cemetery.[51] While sentiment among Morenci workers was strong for an organization built on democracy and disregard for race or creed, distrust of an Anglo-led organization permeated the camp.

On May 9, 1907, a large number of Mexican and Italian laborers attended a meeting in a Morenci opera house. As each person entered, he was offered a red badge inscribed with "undesirable citizen."[52] Whether Mexicans generally understood that President Theodore Roosevelt publicly had labeled WFM labor leaders as such is doubtful, but they certainly knew local sentiment.[53] Headliner Joseph Cannon, now an ASU executive board member, spoke about the Moyer-Haywood trials, urging support for the indicted men and Bisbee miners who were contemplating a strike against copper companies' discharging and blacklisting union men.[54] Cannon also urged forming local unions in the Clifton-Morenci mining district, but few likely understood a word Cannon spoke. Frank was almost certainly present, but he did not speak. Instead Carmen Acosta, officer in the new Metcalf local, delivered words in rapid Spanish, carrying import to workers, many of whom were indecisive about forming a Morenci local, although the local newspaper perceived that his words were making their mark.[55]

Leaving Carmen Acosta at Metcalf and Harry Kane to deal with organizational issues and strike talk, Frank caught a train to Denver in early June 1907 to attend the WFM's Fifteenth Annual Convention held in Odd Fellows Hall from June 10 through July 3. This would be Frank's first participation in a convention as a delegate with two votes representing Clifton Local No. 158 and Metcalf Local No. 159. He was no doubt excited to make the journey, although the trip could not have occurred at a worse time.

After just two years, an ugly tempest brewed concerning the relationship of the WFM to its creation, the IWW, the result of a nasty internecine dispute. At question in the WFM convention was whether the WFM, a federation of miners' locals, would continue as the mining department under the IWW umbrella, an industrial union, or return to its prior independence. Frank unabashedly chose sides, despite being his first appearance at a union convention.[56]

Two factions within the IWW, supporters of president C. O. Sherman and supporters of secretary-treasurer W. E. Trautmann, had battled over the IWW Constitution, shady financial accounting, and seating of delegates at the second IWW convention about seven months earlier.[57] Frank likely read biased accounts of the convention in *Miner's Magazine* and heard alternate versions of graft and corruption from Joe Cannon and other Arizona organizers in a meeting held shortly before the WFM convention.[58] It is no surprise that after the seating of over 130 delegates, committee reports, and various housekeeping tasks, voting patterns began to manifest divisions among delegates.

Aside from recognition of his tepid success in organizing Clifton and Metcalf (no one realized how brief the life spans of the new locals would be), Frank voiced support for open meetings (it would keep the spies honest), guaranteed stenographic reporting, and abolition of contracts in opposition to the WFM's old guard, mostly Butte miners and engineers.[59] Antagonizing Butte No. 1 more, Frank spoke against their recent five-year contract with Anaconda Copper Mining Company, pronouncing that no union had a right to bind the membership to a time agreement that would set conditions for future workers.[60] Several of these Butte delegates would become Frank's enemies ten years later, shortly before his death in Montana.

By day fifteen of the convention, delegates had resorted to name-calling, from "aggregation of liars, crooks, scab herders" (Trautmann faction) to "miserable grafting sluggers" (Sherman faction) to "well fed, over paid mercenary parasite[s]" (*Miner's Magazine* editor John M. O'Neill).[61] The Butte, Montana, delegation was particularly critical of Sherman's opponents, including IWW organizer and Goldfield WFM delegate Vincent St. John, WFM-ASU executive board member Marion Moor, and Jerome delegate Alfred Ryan. As a tenderfoot at the convention, Frank was silent during most of this particular discussion, but his voting record favored St. John's, Ryan's, and Moor's votes, members of the so-called Trautmann faction.

Backbiting over socialist views and who was politically motivated infused all discussions, especially when amending the WFM preamble. Frank, along with St. John, Ryan, and Moor, lost a vote against amending the preamble to connect unionists to political action. Although a socialist, Frank openly criticized a "simple political ballot party," since in his view corporations owned political parties.[62] An open discussion of the WFM's responsibility to not endorse any political party, including the SPA, wove itself in and out of secondary issues as well. For WFM members to derisively bait other members for their socialist bents was a distinct change in attitude. After a brief union with the IWW, the WFM landscape was reverting to its original tenets. Soon the WFM would no longer affiliate with the IWW, reaffiliating with the AFL in 1911.

The tumultuous 1907 WFM Fifteenth Annual Convention defined Frank Little as a straight industrial unionist and propelled him forward toward IWW leadership. His participation thrust him outside the traditional WFM enclave as he fervently spoke his beliefs in opposition to the moderate leadership. During the convention Frank promised, "I will stay in the Western Federation of Miners and I will fight for it," but the WFM soon ejected him from membership for his stance on industrial unionism.[63] Frank was about to be labeled a "radical," and the verbal wounds he and others inflicted on Butte No. 1's dogmas and political contracts would barely scab over before splitting open in 1917.

Before leaving Clifton-Morenci for the Denver convention, Frank had tried to calm union membership in both the Clifton and Metcalf camps, urging men to refrain from the direct action spreading across Arizona until the locals had become stronger. But in his absence, talk intensified for striking in the Clifton-Morenci mining district. Even worse, Morenci miners rejected WFM representation completely. After ACC's management denied a miners' and smeltermen's petition for higher wages on July 21, 1907, stating it could not meet the Mexicans' demands, non-WFM Hispanic men immediately led a new Clifton-Morenci walkout, similar to the 1903 wildcat strike.[64] WFM men now had no choice but to support their coworkers. They did so reluctantly.

On Tuesday, July 23, 1907, Mexican miners called a meeting in the district and invited Frank, recently returned from Denver, to attend as an observer and not as an officer of No. 158 and No. 159. According to the *Morenci Leader*, "It was first surmised that Little . . . had something to do with the strike . . . but an incident took place . . . that does not make it appear that way."[65] Apparently Frank believed he should address the men, giving them some "fatherly advice," which played to the Anglo notion of knowing what was best for Mexicans and which most Morenci miners resented and rejected.[66] When Frank attempted to take the floor and speak, the chairman demanded he withdraw.[67] When Frank refused, he was escorted out physically. The *Morenci Leader* reported that Mexicans then "announced that they knew what they were doing and considered themselves capable of conducting their own business," despite an outsider's presence.[68]

The Clifton-Morenci strike, which Joseph Cannon called "hopeless," was lost in August and after the Panic of 1907, no miner was in a position to ask for higher wages. Cannon stated that the loss was due to the "inevitable result of any unorganized attempt on the part of workers to better or maintain conditions."[69] His moral was to organize.

Frank learned a different lesson. The experience at Morenci was an effective teacher of human nature. He later used his American Indian ancestry to cross ethnic lines. What better way to oppose large elitist corporations that typically viewed minorities as second-class residents than to represent oneself as a *true* American from the nation's first people? And, while the U.S. president simultaneously labeled many immigrants as "undesirable citizens," what better way to appeal to immigrant laborers than proclaim ancestry from what generally was considered an inferior race like theirs? Becoming a "half-breed hobo agitator" would work well for Frank.

Frank pulled out of Clifton-Morenci but not before reporting on conditions in the district to delegates attending the 1907 ASU Convention in Globe. In the report Frank admitted that mining officials had instigated the Clifton smeltermen's strike, sensing weakness within the new local.[70] Although Metcalf Local No. 159 was sustained under Carmen Acosta's leadership until the next year, the Clifton local soon disintegrated.

Not until 1946 would Clifton-Morenci Mexican Americans, as members of the International Union of Mine, Mill, and Smelter Workers (formerly WFM) strike successfully, winning equal pay, benefits, and job opportunities. Today, on Clifton's historic Chase Street, Morenci Miners' Union Local 616 of the United Steelworkers of America (AFL-CIO) occupies an old brick building, the labor union and building both survivors of manmade and natural misfortunes.

Despite his losses in the Clifton-Morenci mining district, Frank's decision to support the IWW and industrial unionism determined his future as a labor organizer and agitator for all classes of workers. But he could hardly foresee where and to what end it would take him.

10

✢ ✢ ✢

THE FOUR-WORD SPEECH

Downtown Missoula, Montana, buzzed with merchants, patrons, and itinerant workingmen crowding the intersection of Front and Higgins Streets on a typically busy September evening. Horse-drawn streetcars, stirring dust whirls with plodding hooves, traveled the middle of Higgins Avenue, deftly parting wayward pedestrians. The street's northward terminus melded into the Northern Pacific Railroad Depot and soft golden-green hills beyond. Other pass-ersby traveled southward one short block to where bridge recon-struction across the Clark Fork River, ongoing almost twelve months now and financed by copper baron William A. Clark, afforded "amateur-bridge inspectors" endless amusement in what a local newspaper called an "open-air vaudeville."[1]

The intersection was the heart of Missoula's business district. On the southeast corner of Front Street and Higgins Avenue, the Queen Anne–style First National Bank was closing its business for the day. Catercorner stood the grand Missoula Mercantile Store, its customers picking up last-minute purchases before night fell. Some glanced across the street at the Florence Hotel's canopied, corner entrance where four men and a girl were positioning boxes and barrels beneath a light pole. Already a circle of curious onlookers was forming in anticipation of repeat performances after five orators were arrested for disturbing the peace the night before.[2]

Upon further scrutiny, it appeared that the petite, auburn-haired girl was in charge. With one hand, she directed placement of boxes and barrels while her other arm cradled pamphlets, flyers, and newspapers. As she dispensed scripts to the men involved in the evening's soapboxing, police pressed toward the little group and the interested bystanders.

Nineteen-year-old Elizabeth Gurley Flynn handed Frank Little his oratorical topic for the evening, "On Temperance." Not a surprising treatise since the IWW had been crusading against alcohol recently. Too many workingmen were lured into saloons and prostitution houses where they were "rolled" of their hard-earned dollars before they could purchase much-needed shoes or clothing.[3]

The night before, September 28, 1909, Frank had prepared a speech on the Colorado labor wars to share with onlookers, but local police, announcing that the mayor had deemed such speeches too radical for the ears of Missoula citizenry, warned the soapboxers not to speak.[4] The city had just reinstated ordinances against public speaking and street assembly. This changed things.

At first the goal had been to educate masses of workers about "capitalist crimes" against workingmen through a series of prepared speeches. Since soapboxers were hauled down from their oratorical perches as soon as they opened their mouths, organizers had adjusted their protest goals. It was now their intention to fill jails to capacity and overwhelm the local court system. The fact that Missoula police were currently in the middle of a campaign to arrest prostitutes and their johns only aided IWW attempts to "pack the jails." Although not a conventional manner in which to grow membership, organizers hoped to increase awareness of industrial unionism as well as highlight the city's abuse of workingmen's constitutional rights. The right to speak went hand in hand with the right to organize.[5]

One at a time IWW members took a stand at the conspicuous street corner and began a speech with a customary greeting. No sooner was one arrested than another took his place. Soapbox tag-teaming had become an IWW pastime guaranteed to entertain hundreds of people who hoped to hear fiery speeches and watch city services at work.

Frank climbed atop a crate and began what the IWW would call the "four-word speech."

"Fellow workers and friends," he began.

Abruptly, before Frank could elucidate the evils of drink to a growing audience, police yanked him down and arrested him. Flynn's husband, Jack Jones, immediately took Frank's position, and he was arrested. But as George Applebee, a young logger, stepped up and was handcuffed, something curious happened. Herman Tucker, a U.S. Forest Service civil engineer, after watching the ruckus from his office window, rushed downstairs and tried to continue Applebee's attempt at the Declaration of Independence.[6] Then Tucker, too, was arrested.

In court the next day, Herman Tucker, Jack Jones, George Applebee, and Frank Little faced Justice of the Peace Harry Small. Small sentenced the men to fifteen days in the county jail after pronouncing them guilty of disturbing the peace despite their protests that they had a constitutional right to make speeches.[7] This was Frank's first experience with the American justice system and first of what would become many protest arrests. When Small offered immediate freedom if the men suspended their public speaking, the men chose to remain in jail and serve out their sentences.[8]

This was exactly what Elizabeth Gurley Flynn had planned. She sent out a call through the *Industrial Worker* for "all footloose rebels to come at once—to defend the Bill of Rights." Straightaway IWW members began streaming into Missoula, flocking in "by freight cars—on top, inside, and below."[9] The IWW had just given birth to the technique of free speech fighting in Missoula.[10]

Appalling conditions and low wages in logging camps are what prompted IWW secretary-treasurer Vincent St. John to send organizers to Missoula in fall 1909. The IWW had begun organizing in these camps as early as 1907, yet degrading conditions continued, and as one logger put it, men were paid "bum wages" for "bum work."[11]

Testimony from loggers in the 1918 Chicago trial against Bill Haywood and other IWWs revealed shocking living conditions that Elizabeth Gurley Flynn had briefly described in her speeches. Most men lived in bunkhouses that rarely had beds. Normally sleeping on hay (which they had to provide) on the floor, invariably there was not enough floor space for all the men. Those lucky enough to acquire a bed could expect to share one wooden bunk with no mattress or springs with a fellow worker.[12]

As many as fifty men typically shared a 28-by-40-foot room in an unventilated bunkhouse. They were rank with wet clothes, sweat, and unwashed bodies. Clothes were boiled in any available receptacle nightly, and then began the almost impossible feat of drying them before morning's first light called them to work again. For men who returned in the evening in wet clothes, steam rolling off them, there were no bathing facilities.[13]

At work, men were paid three dollars for a ten-hour day. They faced dangerous conditions on rivers where they drove logs and dynamited log jams, and on land where they broke apart rollways, piles of logs that could be compared to nails when dumped from kegs, strewn higgledy-piggledy.[14] Speedup prevailed with men already tired from working long hours, which increased accidents.[15]

The IWW chose Missoula because migratory workers, normally dispersed among mining and logging camps over hundreds of miles in remote areas, congregated in cities during off-season or between jobs. Employment agencies, in collusion with companies, scammed the vulnerable out-of-town workers by locating jobs for a fee. When a worker traveled to a job site at his own expense, he found no position awaiting him or was fired after brief employment. That meant starting over to find work and paying fees again. Meanwhile, the employment agency and the company foreman split the money. This practice guaranteed a large pool of unemployed laborers from which the mining and logging camps did their actual seasonal hiring.

Vincent St. John had directed Jack Jones to organize first in Missoula, Montana, and then in cities in other western states.[16] Elizabeth Gurley Flynn, now a seasoned agitator and fiery orator, was an added bonus to Jones's assignment. They had married the year before, and she intended to help him organize. Together they intended to expose the "sharks," or bogus employment agencies, using the jurisdiction of local lumber unions.[17] Flynn believed that the employment agencies, in league with mining and logging interests with whom they shared fees, had pressured the Missoula City Council to enforce the ordinance prohibiting street-speaking.[18]

The Jones couple opened an IWW hall in the basement of the Harnois, a leading theater located at 211 East Main Street, about September 22, 1909.[19] St. John had also called for Frank to meet them in Missoula, and Frank arrived about the same time after a year of agitating in California and Nevada. His travels had schooled him to the hardships that workingmen and their families experienced in fruit harvesting and in mountain mining and logging camps. Elizabeth Gurley Flynn had no need to tell him of logging-camp injustices, but he would soon learn from her how to soapbox.

Frank's eye-opening education had begun after the fractious 1907 WFM Convention in Denver and his dismissal from the WFM for his industrial unionist beliefs.[20] After Frank left Clifton-Morenci mining district in early fall 1907, he found work in Jerome, Arizona, "up the hill" in the United Verde Copper Mine where Yavapai County tax collector Thomas Campbell was manager until 1909.[21] Campbell later was elected governor of Arizona under dubious circumstances.[22]

Frank's fall 1907 activities are supported by a conversation he had with Governor Campbell in 1917. During a meeting, Frank told the governor that he had seen him a number of times, years past when Campbell was manager of the Haynes Copper Company and the Jerome Verde. "At that time I was a member of the Western Federation of Miners and worked a few shifts in the 'Big Hole,'" Frank said.[23] The "Big Hole" was the name miners gave to the hot

ELIZABETH GURLEY FLYNN

Frank learned to soapbox from the best, Elizabeth Gurley Flynn, shown
speaking at the Paterson silk strike in 1913. *Courtesy of the Joseph A.
Labadie Collection, University of Michigan.*

United Verde mine, with its many shafts, raises, large stopes, and
miles of drifts and tunnels, before there ever was an open pit.[24]
Frank had not remained long, later telling Governor Campbell that
"she was too hot for me, and I could not put up with 'the chow' at
the Old Mulligan (the company boarding house)."[25]

Frank's next stop was Prescott, Arizona, fifty-three miles southwest of Jerome. Prior union organization there had been tentative,
at best, with ASU general organizer Moor blaming the failure of
ASU's efforts on men's ignorance of industrial unionism and AFL
opposition.[26] By November 1907, Frank had organized a Prescott
IWW local successfully with thirty members.[27]

A miner named Chris Hansen, who had been working in Prescott, joined Frank on the trek to find work after the local organized.
Driving a wagon drawn by "four desert burros" and joking that they

had nothing to eat but "sage bush, cacti, and Gila monsters," the
men observed that special police patrolled the rails, preventing
men who were "thrown out of work" from hopping boxcars.[28] Frank,
a self-styled "Hobo Miner," described their adventures in the *Industrial Union Bulletin* on December 12, 1908.[29] He described his
experience as that "of a wage slave, seeking a master during the
panic of 1907–08."[30]

The word "hobo," originally referring to a migratory worker,
now also meant a homeless, penniless bum. With so many men
thrown out of work, railroad hubs and downtown areas became
anchors for this homeless proletariat looking for work, or as Frank
stated, a "master." The average IWW member, often a hobo, was
under twenty-five years old (Frank was twenty-nine), wifeless,
homeless, semiskilled, or unskilled. He harvested wheat, logged,
or worked on railroad or road construction, or he mined silver, lead,
copper, and tin in the western states.[31] Also called a "bindle stiff"
because of the blanket roll slung by a cord upon his shoulders,
the hobo jumped empty boxcars and worked job to job, taking
freight cars to other promising work sites.

Many of these men had left homes in the East or were recent
immigrants who found the American dream out of reach. If one
were to ask for an inventory of skills in a hobo camp, a diversity of
trades would be found. Yet American economic conditions between
1907 and 1914 had compelled even skilled men to search for sea-
sonable jobs, their homes and families often lost. Some preferred drifting with no responsibilities and required little to satisfy
their needs.

Freeloading train travel had inherent dangers. Because railroad
workers were unionized, a paid-up union membership card usually protected men and provided them with a free passage. Brakemen otherwise booted off freeloaders without union affiliations.[32]
But trains also carried bootleggers and hijackers who stole hoboes'
small valuables at gunpoint.[33] More recently, railroad detectives
patrolled to make sure "stiffs" could not board idle trains. Jumping
on and off slow-moving trains was dangerous in itself. Some men
died or lost limbs. As an example, in 1913 Frank miscalculated a
jump onto a Western Pacific train and badly sprained his ankle.[34]

Like Frank, hoboes were typically apolitical and rarely stayed in one place long enough to vote. While AFL's Samuel Gompers asserted that the lot of the migratory worker was worse than slavery, the AFL actually did little to help migrants who did not vote.

On December 5, 1907, Hansen and Frank left Prescott, driving the wagon a short distance over the desert to Octave, a nearby mining camp. One "overdressed, well-fed" Octave manager was a former Clifton Mine supervisor, and Frank knew he would not be welcome.[35] They continued on to Congress, "the worst scab hole in Arizona," and then south to Wickenburg, also crowded with "jobless slaves," during January 1908.[36] Realizing that no Arizona mining camp was hiring, Hansen and Frank continued west, crossing the Colorado River into California just a few miles north of Blythe in February 1908.

In his wake, Frank left a legacy of agitation and organization as well as a reputation that would follow him when he returned to Arizona. Now, however, he let the rails transport him into the immediate future. Without looking back, the men traveled northward, striking the main line of the Atchison, Topeka, and Santa Fe Railroad where they finally boarded.[37]

At Mohave, California, Frank found WFM membership in decline. On February 29, 1908, union members successfully passed a motion that Frank, a "Socialist," be barred from speaking in a meeting. Frank held his tongue until afterward when he spoke on industrial unionism despite the "good company tools," the miners influenced by their mining-company employer.[38]

Frank continued on, riding the train to a series of stops while they looked for work, joining masses of other itinerant workers. There the men found scores of lean, congenial faces, unemployed men who made camps, or "jungles," along the tracks, men whose lingo included other words that have become part of the modern American vocabulary: "chow" (food), "bull" (police), "can" (police station), "flop" (place to sleep), "crummy" (lousy), "fink" (strike breaker), "dump" (hangout), "ditch" (dispose), "haywire" (below standard), "hijack" (hold up), "idiot stick" (shovel), "mule" (corn alcohol), "rustle" (get busy), "wob" or "wobbly" (IWW member), and "stiff" (hobo worker or corpse).[39] Frank now spoke the language,

and the "stiffs" became his universal family. In March 1908, the
two men traveled "over the hills" to fruit country, after which
the train turned northward, stopping at Tulare, Visalia, Fresno,
Merced, and a myriad of other small towns along the way in the
San Joaquin Valley.[40]

Travel in California's fruit belt expanded Frank's empathies
for struggling Americans. A camera famously captured images of
wretched California workers during the Great Depression about
twenty-five years later, but no portraits of misery resonated with
Americans in 1908. "Conditions were in a horrible state," Frank
noted, because fruit workers had many mouths to feed on meager
earnings.[41] Many of these men and women could have been poster
subjects for want and suffering.

In describing migratory farm workers, Frank once wrote in
Solidarity, "When you see one tramping along the road, he generally has a load on his back that the average prospector would be
ashamed to put on a jackass. In fact, most of the jackasses would
have enough sense to kick it off."[42] During harvest season, he
added, a steady line of these bindle stiffs "tramping down the highway" begged for the "right to work to earn enough to buy a little
grub, take it down to the jungles by a river or beside an irrigation
ditch, and then cook it up in old tin cans which their masters had
thrown away."[43]

In Fresno Frank stayed longer than just a quick railroad stop.
His brother and sister-in-law were about to join his journey into
economic and social revolution.

Leaving her Frisbie grandparents in Oklahoma, Emma Little had
joined Fred in San Jose Township (renamed Pozo in 1902), San Luis
Obispo County, California, about 1901. Though the county's La
Panza gold district initially lured Fred west, the Pacific Ocean
offered significant benefits for the small family. The weather was
mild and healthy, and residents could camp in semipermanent
tent houses at Pismo Beach. Almost immediately, Emma became
pregnant and, when her son Walter R. Little was two years old, she

gave birth to another son. Lawrence Leslie Little was born in Pismo, California, on February 22, 1902.[44]

As in Colorado, Fred did not find his gold placer, just paltry wages in a local mining company. Eventually he left the dark tunnels although he remained a prospector at heart. Now Emma's aunt Bella and uncle Alvin William Church offered economic stability to the young family. Church, the Nevadaville mining engineer, and Bella, Emma's mother's sister, also had moved to Tulare Township, California, where they purchased a rancho.[45] Fred and Emma joined them there, moving into a rent house at 638 South D Street in Tulare by 1904. Fred found work as a laborer, possibly on Alvin Church's fruit farm, while Emma cared for the babies.[46] Frank, who had followed his brother into California mining camps, left the small family behind at some point before turning up in Bisbee in late 1903.

Perhaps it was Emma's progressive nature that goaded Fred to run for political office in 1906. Frank, who shared socialist philosophies with his brother, would have warned Fred not to trust the ballot box, especially in a Republican district, but on November 6, in a race for Tulare County Assemblyman in the 27th District on the Socialist ticket, Fred was whipped soundly.[47] Politics would not be this Little family's vehicle for carrying forward social reforms.

Alvin Church was presently in company with staunch Democrats who served with him on the Farmers' Irrigation Ditch Company in the Visalia-Tulare area, and he soon became director, a powerful position for landowners.[48] As the social gap widened between them and the Church family, Fred and Emma determined to move again. By 1907 Fred was working as a plumber at the Mariposa Hotel in Fresno, California.[49]

An early studio portrait of Emma shows a composed young woman dressed in an aproned, white linen dress, unadorned except for a lace collar around her throat. She sits casually, holding a magazine, titled *Make Your Own Movie*, a glint of humor perhaps just slightly peeking through unsmiling eyes, as she stares into the camera. She is thin, obviously having no need for a corset. Although she finally has escaped to California, the simple fabric of her dress and the texture of her hands betray the couple's lack of success.

For Emma now worked at the Mariposa Hotel as a chambermaid. Located on the northeast corner of Mariposa and M Streets, the hotel was across the street from the jail and courthouse.[50] The 1910 federal census lists her as a boarding employee (sans family).[51] Both Fred and Emma are listed as residing at the hotel during their separate times of service, indicating that boarding was a prerequisite for their employment.

Racial tensions were mounting in the San Joaquin Valley when Frank Little and Chris Hansen arrived in Fresno during the 1908 spring. Japanese were demanding higher wages, so fruit growers wanted cheap, Mexican labor. With no Cesar Chavez to organize them, migrant families found themselves adrift, much like Fred and Emma had been since they married. The two brothers and Emma discussed IWW organization, and shortly after the Missoula Free Speech Fight, Fred took early steps to becoming an organizer, joining the IWW and renting a union hall in fall 1909.[52]

Resuming their journey, Frank and Chris Hansen reached Graniteville by April 1908, a mining camp in northeastern California's Sierra Mountains. There, they finally found work. Frank's work résumé was shortened after only ten days when he was fired for agitating, forced to walk out of the camp, and blacklisted from other camps in the area.[53] Within a month, Frank had hitched a ride to Reno, Nevada, where he ended his tour looking for work, his head full of condemnation against capitalist corporations. With the exception of the oil boom (not yet born), Frank had surveyed a full spectrum of the western work force in its worst form.

Seven months later, Frank was still in Reno, working to organize an IWW local. He reported to *Solidarity* that like elsewhere, many men were out of work and "full of political dope."[54] Organizing would be difficult at best, but Frank remained optimistic. He stayed in Reno until early 1909 before rejoining Fred and Emma in Fresno. Not long afterward, Frank received marching orders from St. John. A fight was on in Missoula, Montana.

Missoula city fathers had a problem: the annual Apple Show was to be held October 18 through 22, 1909. Wobblies were literally

EMMA HARPER LITTLE
Emma Barbara Harper
Little, ca. 1904, holding a
California prop, *Make Your
Own Movie* magazine.
Harper Family Papers.

arriving each day by the trainload, camping out at railroad stations
and occupying downtown streets. They were an embarrassment
and a nuisance. The streets were now uniquely the IWWs' hall
for targeting audiences each evening, and their efforts were rewarded.
Despite the *Daily Missoulian*'s negative press, street speaking
began winning over a part of the public, which empathized with
the speakers.

Vaudeville acts regaled Missoula audiences in the opera house
above the IWW basement headquarters while below Elizabeth
Gurley Flynn taught newly arrived volunteers how to navigate the
Higgins Avenue and Front Street corner, climb a soapbox, and begin
speaking. If all went as planned, each IWW would be arrested after
the four-word greeting. If a speaker was able to continue speaking
before arrest, he could improvise a statement or read from a book.

Some nervous newcomers suffered stage fright. Flynn gave them literature they knew—the Bill of Rights and the Declaration of Independence—so that they could read slowly "with one eye hopefully on the cop, fearful that they would finish before he would arrest them."[55]

Meanwhile, Frank Little continued his sojourn in the old Missoula County Jail. Confinement was probably not the best use of his talents, but it taught patience. He was, however, able to report to *Industrial Worker's* readers the description of his first day in the jail.

The morning after his arrest, the men gathered in the southwest corner of the jail yard where they moved a table for Jack Jones to mount for speechmaking. Sheriff Davis Graham, presuming Jones to be inciting other prisoners to riot, ordered him to cease his speech and the men's singing. When Jones challenged Graham's edict, the sheriff grabbed him by the throat and threw him back on the table, slapping his face. Graham warned the men who crowded closer not to interfere, telling Frank, "You are a gentleman, but this fellow [pointing to Jones] is a damned _____."[56] Graham then shoved Jones into a cage, entered himself, and viciously beat Jones in the face with a big brass key. When Jones could or would not answer Graham's question as to whether he would be "good," the sheriff "grabbed Jones by the hair and seat of his pants, knocking him up and down on the steel floor."[57] One newspaper editor confirmed that Graham indeed had assaulted an "absolutely helpless" victim, who was a much smaller man than his two-hundred-pound assailant.[58] When the prisoners were finally able to reach Jones, he was unconscious, his eyes blackened and swollen. A doctor's services were refused after Frank asked for medical attention.[59]

Jack Jones was transferred to the city jail. Other prisoners in the city jail were transferred back to the county jail because they were deemed too noisy.[60] As both the county and city jails filled with speakers and protesters, city authorities began searching for alternative locations to billet prisoners.

The city finally recognized that the Flynn woman was the source of agitation as each new orator was arrested under the ordinance and sentenced to fifteen days. Missoula's Mayor Logan was "on" to the IWW scheme and claimed to have a "new salutary" tack for Wobbly (IWW) soapboxers.[61] So it was that on the evening of October 1, 1909, the Missoula Fire Department's horse-drawn hose wagon drove a quick three blocks down Higgins Avenue from the fire station located on Pine and Higgins, ready to put out fiery speeches and dampen morale. A mob of spectators, unaware of an impending drenching, had jammed each side of the intersection, making it difficult for police to clear a passageway to the soapbox speakers. Upon orders of the police chief, pressurized water shot out indiscriminately from a hose coupled to a hydrant, hitting all four corners of the intersection of Higgins Avenue and Front Street, soaking soapboxers and bystanders alike. Although the *Daily Missoulian* claimed that no one's clothing was spoiled and that the crowd was dispersed quickly, some townspeople protested that some individuals were hurt.[62]

Still, on Higgins Avenue and Front Street each evening, Elizabeth Gurley Flynn continued mingling among the workingmen, her arms full of industrial papers for sale. Other small squads, led by hand-picked men, dispersed throughout Missoula's business section. The plan was to give each speaker a chance to gather a crowd before police could stop the various street assemblies. Flynn predicted that the IWW message could not be suppressed if at least ten men were jailed every day, each demanding jury trials.[63]

Flynn herself was the last protester to be arrested—on Sunday, October 3, 1909—for speaking at an advertised open-air meeting. The local paper reported "that a crowd of nearly a thousand people followed the officer with the woman to the bastille," where her arrival was cheered by other inmates.[64] Flynn was relegated to the witness room overnight because the police department had no place to jail her. She most likely assessed her situation as positive, although the men jailed under the fire department might have disagreed.[65] With county and city jails full, the city had begun housing prisoners in a makeshift cell under the Missoula fire house. It, too, became full, and when watery excrement from horses stabled above leaked through cracks in the ceiling, the room became unbearable. The IWWs began playing "battleship," that is, making a ruckus through songs and chants so loud that it was unbearable to their

guards and general citizenry.[66] Guests at a fine hotel across the
street complained so much about the noise from the fire station
that the prisoners were moved back to county jail where they
could disrupt courthouse proceedings instead.

City officials soon faced a new burden. Speakers deliberately
had themselves arrested before supper so that the city would bear
the additional expense of feeding them. To make dinnertime in
jail, open-air meetings were held early. Soon police began turning
prisoners out before breakfast.

A worse problem for the city was that public opinion appeared
to be shifting. On October 7, 1909, *Industrial Worker* reported
that working people of Missoula were with the IWW in the matter
of free speech, and even the "scab sheet," the *Daily Missoulian*,
was withholding criticism after learning that some local police
were connected with prostitution.[67] Even the Butte Miners' Union
passed a resolution denouncing Missoula police.[68] Calls went out
for yet more men to descend on Missoula in the next two days, and
as fresh speakers were arrested, local citizenry jostled the police,
some throwing rocks.[69]

Flynn, released on bond after just two nights in custody, suspected that the Chamber of Commerce, in anticipation of the
upcoming Apple Show, wanted no more adverse press. In addition,
the city coffers were emptying as fast as a Wobbly could jump onto
a soapbox. Taxpayers complained, and when Robert "Fighting Bob"
La Follette Sr., a Wisconsin senator, arrived in Missoula to deliver
an address condemning the city's actions, acting mayor Herbert
Wilkinson knew he was whipped.[70] Despite calls from merchants
and hotels that street meetings obstructed streets and interfered
with business, city hall dropped all cases against the protestors on
October 8, 1909, declaring that IWWs could speak wherever and
whenever they pleased.[71]

Jail yards suddenly became silent. Without anticipation of future
agitation, the Missoula Free Speech Fight ended without a whimper.

Clearly Missoula was Elizabeth Gurley Flynn's victory, although
that victory went unrecognized for one hundred years. On October 3, 2009, the Missoula City Council resolved to have a historical marker placed near the site of the first American free speech

fight. After pronouncing that the Missoula Free Speech Fight was a watershed event in American history, bringing America's attention to the exercise of free speech, the City of Missoula proudly renamed the corner of Higgins Avenue and Front Street "Free Speech Corner."

For Frank Little in 1909, however, a new free speech fight loomed, and for his disobedience this time, his jailers would extract a pound of flesh.

11

✦ ✦ ✦

AN INJURY TO ONE, 1909–1910

It was eight in the morning Friday, September 2, 1910. Fresno's Courthouse Park streamed with people on their way to work. Atop the courthouse's main vestibule with its extended wings, the marble goddesses of justice and liberty gazed downward upon the visitors, their snowy stone faces impenetrable to a small drama playing out below them. More lively witnesses, passersby navigating the intersection at M and Mariposa Streets directly to the east of the park, surely noticed an officer with a gang of trustees, one clearly a reluctant prisoner, leaving the red-brick jail just north of the stately building. Park Officer Woods escorted his prisoners to the thickly treed grounds skirting the Fresno County Courthouse, assigned them various duties, and then shoved a rake into the unwilling prisoner's hands. Frank Little, in defiance of his machinated arrest, angrily tossed the rake to the ground in front of the other trustees, exclaiming, "The leaves can rot before I'll rake them up!"[1]

Originally charged with "creating a disturbance" in front of Fresno Beer Hall at 1827 Mariposa Street at nine in the evening on August 24, 1910, Frank was serving a twenty-five-day sentence for vagrancy after refusing to pay a twenty-five-dollar fine. His crime? He had argued "a trifle too loud" with two friends about rooms in a boarding house on H Street. When a patrolman named Pickens conveniently approached the men and told them not to talk so robustly, they ignored him. Officer Pickens promptly arrested the trio. When Pickens and his prisoners arrived at Courthouse Park moments later, Fred Little, now secretary of Fresno's Local 66, was arrested for "disturbing the peace and interfering with an officer" when he "impertinently" asked why his brother had been apprehended.[2]

While the men were being processed, Fred, who claimed to be a professional agitator by trade, boasted to a night jailer that he could bring two thousand men to Fresno to protest the arrests.[3] Having Frank in town had boosted Fred's self-image in IWW circles. Indeed, the next morning Vincent St. John wired Fred that not only did the IWW organization endorse a fight for free speech and the right of assemblage, but that reinforcements were on the way.[4] The telegram was leaked to the press, and the police had a quick response for the general public: they would be prepared for the IWWs' publicity stunts, "hurling themselves in the path of the police in order to be placed under arrest."[5] If the police were correct, then Fred would not mind spending his thirty-fifth birthday in jail three days later.

All afternoon on Wednesday, August 31, a crowd of mostly workingmen filled police court to watch testimonies during a jury trial where Frank and Fred represented themselves and the two other arrested men. Without censure from the judge, the prosecution's witnesses gave conflicting accounts concerning the subject of the Wobblies' conversation in front of the beer hall, ranging from a particular boarding house to "socialism and the present government."[6] The common theme was that the men talked too loudly. Afterward Fred filed perjury charges against Ira Hapgood, a forty-five-year-old teamster and one of the prosecution's witnesses, for swearing that Fred was actually inside the beer hall and thus causing confusion among jurors about the initial incident.[7] Drinking and the IWW were not compatible, and Emma Little would also have questioned her husband.

The Wobbly whom Police Chief William Shaw really wanted off Fresno's streets was Frank Little, who had led local IWW

organization since his arrival in March 1910. All the defendants
were charged equally, yet Frank would be the only man declared
guilty in the clearly contrived arrest and judgment.[8] After the verdict, he bravely stood and claimed, "Your jails and dungeons have
no terrors for me."[9] Local newspapers contemptuously mocked him
as an IWW martyr. His message was not intended exclusively for
the court but also for the IWWs in the audience, who would be
asked to put themselves under arrest in the months ahead.

The next day in court, September 1, 1910, at precisely 10:00
A.M., Frank rose to accept his sentencing in a courtroom packed "to
the walls" with Wobbly spectators and other interested onlookers.
As a bailiff led Frank off to jail, Frank smiled crookedly at the
audience and waved goodbye.[10] The next morning, he belligerently
faced a park guard whose sole job was to see that trustees carried
out their sentences by raking the courthouse grounds.

Frank clearly understood the consequences he would receive
for refusing to work. His early Arizona experiences had taught him
that the man who would work as a prisoner was no better than
one who would scab during a strike—and that park work should
be done by paid workingmen.[11] Packing his principles with him,
Frank was thrown into the "dungeon" where he "lustily" began to
sing IWW anthems.[12] A ten-day diet of bread and water in the warm
dark hole was nothing to what he had experienced in the arctic
freezer of Spokane, Washington.

After the victory in Missoula, calls had gone out for Wobblies to
storm back to Spokane where at least thirty-one employment
"sharks" were monopolizing employment agencies.[13] Since the
1908 winter, IWWs continued to be at war with these agencies
over their complicity with company managers. Purportedly three
thousand men were hired through employment sharks for one camp
during the 1909 winter, to maintain a force of just fifty men.[14] As
soon as a man had worked long enough to pay the shark's fee,
hospital dollar, and poll tax, he was discharged. Riots broke out on
Spokane's streets and, pressured by the employment agencies, the

city passed an ordinance prohibiting the holding of public meetings on streets, sidewalks, or alleys within the fire limits (or city limits). The IWW would have to use public parks and vacant lots away from populated stem streets, where they could make little impact.[15] The Salvation Army had been exempted.

Generally, IWWs detested organized religion and organizations such as the Salvation Army, and some members were atheists. Many simply objected to evangelists who competed in soapbox alleys, promising "pie in the sky" rewards to hungry, homeless hoboes. Both Frank and Fred more than likely fell into this group—men who had been fed strict religious beliefs, men who had thrown the ancient saddle of an organized church from their scripture-sore backs although their faith lay deeply embedded beneath their calloused skins. Frank and Fred Little had a fundamentalist religious background, and Emma Little was an Episcopalian from childhood throughout adulthood.[16]

The Salvation Army and preachers such as Billy Sunday incurred the wrath of all IWWs who wanted to improve living conditions in *this* life, instead of waiting for the rapture in poverty. Carl Sandburg encapsulated their collective belief:

You come along—tearing your shirt—yelling about Jesus.
    I want to know what the hell you know about Jesus?
Jesus had a way of talking soft, and everybody except a few
    bankers
        and higher-ups among the con men of Jerusalem liked to
        have this Jesus
    around because he never made any fake passes, and
        everything he said
    went and he helped the sick and gave the people hope.
You come along squirting words at us, shaking your fist and
    calling us all
        damn fools—so fierce the froth of your spit slobbers
        over your lips—
    always blabbering we're all going to hell straight off and
        you know all
    about it.

I've read Jesus' words. I know what he said. You don't throw
   any scare into
      me. I've got your number. I know how much you know
         about Jesus.[17]
                              Excerpted from "Billy Sunday"

Using hymns that most men and women knew, the IWW replaced
religious lyrics with IWW verses. Now when the Salvation Army
began singing a hymn on Spokane street corners, the IWW joined
in the melody and used their own words, exacerbating chaos amid
grinning bystanders. Originating with the Spokane local, much of
this music became the union's songbook, resulting in *The Little
Red Songbook*, first published in 1909. Frank loved to sing IWW
songs, although his refrains generally echoed off solid concrete and
brick walls in the gut of a jail house.

   Frank made his way from Kalispell, Montana, in early November 1909, after receiving a telegram from Spokane's local IWW
secretary, C. L. (Charley) Filigno, advising, "Fight on; send men!"
The success of the Spokane Free Speech Fight, already in progress,
depended on "an injury to one" becoming "an injury to all."[18] Just
three days after the first soapboxers were arrested on Tuesday,
November 2, 1909, Frank found himself handcuffed by Police
Chief John T. Sullivan, along with twelve other Wobblies. He had
been soapboxing on a crate earlier that morning, most likely on the
corner of Howard and First Streets. As he and others were arrested,
the crowd jeered the police before a fire hose was brought out to
disperse spectators.[19]

   Sporting a big black mustache under his large hawkish nose
and clad in a black Stetson and suit, Sullivan exuded malevolence.
By the end of the Spokane Free Speech Fight, he would be accused
in $120,000 of $150,000 wrongful-injury-and-death law suits brought
by IWWs and other innocent victims and forced to resign his position.[20] Because of Sullivan's distinctly notorious character, Wobblies
quietly celebrated his death when a bullet hit its mark as Sullivan
sat in his living room reading his newspaper two years later.[21]
After his Spokane initiation, Frank would encounter Sullivan's

breed, now endemic across police departments in western cities and villages, amid other labor conflicts.

The next morning, Frank refused to eat the hot steaming breakfast delivered to cells reserved for men who awaited hearings. A solidarity strike for the convicted who were on a starvation diet was presently in progress. The *Spokane Daily Chronicle* now derisively labeled the Wobblies the "Starvation Army." Reflecting a division in public opinion, the *Spokane Press* urged fair play and voiced concern for the IWWs' welfare.[22]

That evening in court, Frank, wearing a red ribbon, was asked what he was doing when he was arrested. He replied bluntly, "Reading the Declaration of Independence," and pled not guilty to disorderly conduct. When Frank refused to pay a $30 fine and court costs, Judge S. A. Mann declared, "Thirty days!" and set Frank's bond at $200.[23] Immediately Frank joined other unfortunates who would be introduced to a torture chamber deep in the Spokane city jail.

The sweat box was a dark, airtight room of about eight by ten feet. As many as thirty-six men were squeezed inside, packed so tightly that the strength of several policemen was required to force the room's steel door shut.[24] A four-inch hole transported a pipe that blasted hot steam on the men. If they could move, the men removed their clothing. When a man collapsed, he did not hit the human-waste-covered floor since the men were squashed together.[25]

After fifteen hours of being sweated, the prisoners were removed to vermin-infested, cold cells with open windows and no bedding. The men had no shoes, as these had been taken away when the men dared to stamp their feet to warm them.[26] When Frank arrived, one cell was already slippery with vomit. Jailers turned a fire hose on inmates when they sang or played "Battleship" on the prison bars, leaving them to stand in inches of frigid water all night. Then the prisoners were returned to the fetid sweat box to begin the torment all over again. Other newcomers were dumped into the chilly cells day and night, blood pouring down their faces after police beatings. By the time Frank was arrested, there were over 140 men in jail suffering this treatment.[27]

Some men agreed to work on the county rock pile and were soon chained to a fellow Wobbly with fifteen-pound balls attached to their ankles. As frigid rain pelted their heads, they marched to the rock pile on Broadway and Monroe Streets to pick at small boulders.[28] These men soon mastered the art of passive resistance, working at a snail's pace. One Wobbly reported that two men chained together tapped upon one rock the size of a wash bucket for four days until it was broken accidentally.[29] Still, the outside weather was arctic: they pounded rocks to keep warm or they froze to death.[30]

Frank Little refused to chip away at rocks.

Fred Little received a letter on November 15, 1909, from an IWW who began by saying, "I understand you are the brother of F. H. Little, the hobo agitator, in jail with two hundred more." The writer's descriptions matched later testimonies from men who survived the torturous treatments, detailing "3rd degree methods" that jailers and police applied to IWWs in order to dissuade them from intentional incarceration.[31] But as Fred collected monies for the jailed men's aid, Frank was suffering in worse conditions than the letter revealed, this time in a heavily guarded jail annex.

Spokane authorities had moved the increasing overflow of men who refused to work to an immense, empty, unheated school house at the corner of Front Avenue (today's Trent Street) and Grant Street. Philip S. Foner, noted for his analysis and collection of voices describing the early free speech fights, compares the appalling conditions in Franklin School to those in the Confederate Libby Prison.[32] These IWWs still were participating in the hunger strike when Frank arrived. Some prisoner-artists had drawn satirical pictures of Spokane officials on the blackboards. Weaker prisoners sat listlessly at tall windows in the northwest room on the second floor, looking down over lower, vacant, arched windows, while listening to whistles from locomotives approaching the Northern Pacific Roundhouse directly across from the school.

By November 11, their hunger strike was over, and a diet of bread and water resumed. Fed just one-fifth to one-third of a loaf of bread twice daily in these conditions, men became ill.[33] After they tore wooden molding from the walls to burn for warmth, the prisoners were beaten—noses and teeth broken, eyes blackened, and sides kicked. Nonetheless, the men would sing "The Red Flag" and other IWW songs as early as six in the morning, creating bed-lam in the building. Twelve special officers, armed with shotguns, guarded the school's high-stepped entrance in case a weakened man, who deliberately had endeavored to get into jail in the first place, miraculously decided to break and run.[34]

Once a week Frank and seven other men were shuttled from the school back to the city jail, to be hosed with scalding water, given an icy rinse, and then marched back on wintry streets to the unheated school building.[35] Sympathetic onlookers threw the prisoners all sorts of food that police guards kicked away. Other men were hit with clubs as they tried to grasp the proffered tobacco, sandwiches, and fruit. One unfortunate fellow had his nose broken when he desperately took a bite out of an apple.

On a rainy Friday, November 19, 1909, Frank returned to Judge Mann's warm courtroom to appeal his conviction. This time he had a young attorney, Fred H. Moore, represent him, although unsuccessfully.[36] The forms within Case No. 3943, the City of Spokane vs. F. H. Little, are filled with empty blanks—an incomplete historical record—suggesting that Mann's court was overwhelmed with appeals and that Moore's attention to individual cases was spread thin. In fact, criminal appeals had first begun on the previous Monday, when Mann judged sixty men individually, followed the next day with another fifty separate appeals that he completed in only forty minutes.[37] Although each Wobbly demanded a separate fair trial, Mann ran the cases in assembly-line fashion, directing the failure of most appeals.

Frank thus returned to the abandoned Franklin School where nighttime prison guards had begun to terrorize the emaciated men, chasing them from room to room.[38] At 4:00 A.M., the guards brutally roused men from the cold, hard floors, making inmates wait until 8:30 A.M. for a breakfast of bread and water.[39] Conditions were getting so bad that the starving were too weak to rise.[40] Some men's teeth began loosening, a symptom of scurvy. When one onion found its way into the Franklin School, it was divided carefully into sixty-five pieces so that all could share it.[41]

The cold rains that had caused heavy flooding finally left Spokane on Wednesday, November 24, leaving clear blue skies and a cheerful festivity across the city. The hopeful prisoners looked forward to a meal change for the next day, Thanksgiving. When lunch was brought to their jail dining hall, instead of a turkey and cranberry dinner, pails of water and plates of unbuttered bread decorated their holiday tables.[42] Police Chief Sullivan reportedly told them that they would find the water faucet in good order when the Wobblies pointed out that common criminals were receiving turkey dinners.[43] With empty stomachs, the IWWs proclaimed their thanks for having "men with moral courage to go to prison and fast and suffer hunger for the principle of free speech, on the day when American people are feasting and offering thanks for the blessings they enjoy."[44]

National criticism began trickling into the city now pinched with budget worries, after police resorted to arresting newsboys selling IWW papers on street corners. The tousled-haired children, wearing toeless shoes, were also sweated to secure information against IWW leaders.[45] Taxpayers were determined to change the ordinance, while national and local unions and civic organizations demanded that the prisoners be released. By February 1910, the city of Spokane was spending $1,000 a week solely on the Wobbly prisoners with 1,200 arrests on the books and half as many in jail.[46] Contributing to the enormous expenses were the prisoners' medical bills. In one month, 334 prisoners were hospitalized, and another month, 681.[47] Three men eventually died in the Franklin School, adding to the damage suits for police brutality. Famed lawyer Clarence Darrow was rumored to be coming to Spokane in order to take over the lingering defense of IWW leaders yet to be tried in conspiracy trials, a future expense for Spokane courts. Even more troublesome, a national call had gone out to all IWWs to converge on Spokane on March 1, 1910. Emulating the Parisian *sans-culottes* of 1789, they marched through the streets triumphantly singing "La Marseillaise."[48] On March 4, 1910, the city finally capitulated.[49]

And so, after surviving Spokane's Franklin School, Frank Little knew he could endure the "dungeon" of the Fresno City Jail.

12

REDS

Fresno, California, sits in the palm of an ancient lake bed in the San Joaquin Valley between the violet-shadowed Sierra Madre to the east and the southern Coastal Mountains to the west. Irrigated sandy-mush soils define the great produce-growing land where fruits, nuts, and vegetables suck the water to parch their thirsts. On ranchos' uncultivated fields, sand dunes are lapped by waves of golden-green grasses. Inside the heart of the Raisin City, red-tile-roofed suburbs surround a downtown area where, between 1910 and 1917, Wobblies made jungles near the train tracks. Still a mecca for the homeless, a tent-and-cardboard colony houses modern-day bindle stiffs, its blue-and-tan tarps fluttering in soft warm breezes. Fred and Emma Little's home in 1917 at 742 California Street once stood nearby, in what is today a light industrial district with packing houses and warehouses.

With a great palette of civic resources, Fresno has reinvented itself, painting over the ugly 1910–11 Free Speech Fight that occurred in its historic district. Sterile, modern city, county, and federal buildings frame the heart of Free Speech Plaza on Fulton Mall, a block southwest of Courthouse Park. On the corner of what were Mariposa and I Streets, a scarred historical plaque designates the general location of California's first fight for free speech. A venue for tourists and businesspeople during the day, the mall empties before dark, and the homeless begin milling aimlessly while others pack away their "Occupy Fresno" placards for the night after protesting on the identical location where Frank and Fred Little led an army of Wobbly rebels against the city fathers. A major difference, however, is that the bindle stiffs of 1910 had a single purpose—they desperately wanted to work at a fair wage.

Jobs should have been plentiful in fall 1909: heavy rains broke an uncommonly long, dry season, and the Fresno fruit crop was expected to break records. Fruit workers were needed immediately for harvesting and fruit packing. The migrant work force was illiterate, "common labor," and a cheap bargain—so long as IWW organizers stayed away.

When Fresno police chief William Shaw first noticed Wobblies distributing literature on Fresno's "soapbox row" near Mariposa and I, showing migrants how to agitate for a higher wage, he warned IWW leaders that he would run them out of town, since the large fruit crop had to be "cheaply handled."[1] Besides, President William Taft was set to deliver a speech at a Union religious service in nearby Courthouse Park on Sunday, October 10, and Shaw wanted no distractions near or along the parade route. He need not have worried, since Fred Little had already determined that the union was too weak to push aggressive organization until the new year. Ironically, during Taft's speech, the president reminded an estimated sixty thousand Fresno citizens and visitors that

> [popular government] rests in the common sense, and the self-restraint of the American people. It rests in the knowledge of the majority that it must keep within the checks of the law and the Constitution if the Government is to be preserved. . . . It rests in the knowledge of the majority that the rights of the minority and in the individuals of that minority are exactly as sacred as the rights in the individuals of the majority.[2]

On this point, it would seem that Fresno mayor Dr. Chester Rowell, who also owned the partisan *Fresno Morning Republican*, and his chief of police had deaf ears.

While Frank was surviving on bread and water in Spokane, Fred and Emma Little had quietly begun to organize the valley's unskilled migrant workers. With Frank's advice, Fred organized Local 66, its charter dated October 27, 1909, and rented Chance Hall at 1129 I Street to begin weekly Thursday evening meetings.[3] Fred received his own IWW membership card dated November 1, 1909.[4]

Then both Fred and Emma began a brief letter-to-the-editor writing campaign, hoping to soapbox from their kitchen table. *Morning Republican* readers perused pithy letters that pointed out social injustices in Fresno and the country at large. Emma, in particular, began a lifelong habit of espousing her political and social beliefs, bluntly questioning and criticizing government and business leaders by writing to this audience. (*Sacramento Bee* readers would become her target audience years later.) Hiding in the anonymity of her initials and maiden name in the November 23, 1909, issue, Emma compared the United States to Mexico, a country about to become besieged with revolution because of capitalism's "wage slavery." She advised socialism as a cure—not the political party but the economic organization of the working class.[5] In fact, the IWW now advertised boldly on the masthead of its new newspaper, *Industrial Worker*, that it was controlled by no political party, including the SLP and SPA. On December 12, 1909, with her brother-in-law in mind, Emma wrote, "The Constitution of the United States guarantees free speech. Can the laboring man or the laboring woman speak on the streets of Spokane?"[6] One week later, Fred and Emma had back-to-back letters—Fred's asserting that socialism is the only true form of democracy, and Emma's arguing that for human civilization to progress toward democracy, it must be through education and organization of the working people.[7] Of course, the Mexican migrants, who had fled Mexican president Porfirio Díaz's regime and whom Fred and Emma were trying to organize, could not read their black-and-white speeches. But the English-speaking general public, which surely did read their radical arguments with bored expressions, were about to become blindsided by IWW "hobo-agitators."

As soon as Frank's thirty-day sentence in Spokane's Franklin School was fulfilled in early December 1909, he, too, wrote an

article describing the barbarism occurring there, closing tongue-
in-cheek with "By a Graduate."[8] Frank underscored the continued
importance of fighting for the rights guaranteed by the Constitution—free press, free speech, and freedom to assemble—even when
the "Master Class" conveniently disregarded them.

An IWW agitator from Los Angeles, stopping in Fresno in
February 1910, noted that Local 66 had "a tough row to hoe" since
Police Chief Shaw had threatened to drive Fred Little out of town
if he attempted to organize the agricultural workers.[9] Fresno organization had been sluggish although Fred had rented a reading
room and new headquarters location for Local 66. On a limited
budget, he was able to locate the room in an alley between J and
K Streets, just forty feet off Mariposa Street, advertising the address
as 1114 Federal Alley.[10] Local 66's reading room attempted to
keep Fresno Wobblies, including women, connected to purpose
and direct action.

Fred was also actively involved in the SPA, having formed
the Fresno local. Yet the landscape had changed regarding which
Socialist avenue would best suit labor. By the Fourth Annual IWW
Convention in 1908, the Wobblies had split into two factions. The
more moderate SPA, headed by Eugene V. Debs, advocated political action. Daniel De Leon led a more radical faction within the
SLP that advocated both political and direct action, including general strikes, boycotts, and even sabotage. Although the SLP supported
the class-conscious unionism prized by IWW members, De Leon
was expelled from the IWW, which wanted no political party associated with the industrial union. However, Fred continued to support the Fresno SPA, even connecting with WFM members by
contributing Fresno SPA local monies for mutual causes.[11]

Frank, on the other hand, sided with IWW leaders Vincent
St. John and Bill Haywood, who promoted direct action to achieve
IWW objectives, including untraditional support of immigrants.
To the IWW, any Socialist party believing in arbitration and the
ballot box was espousing "yellow socialism," or "revolutionary
socialism," while the IWWs boldly adopted red, the Marxist color
of "revolutionary industrial unionism," as symbolic of their cause
and which subsequently accented the first Red Scare in the United

States. Frank agreed with the western Wobblies' mantra, "It's better to be called Red than be called Yellow."[12]

The relationship between the two Little brothers had also diverged, mainly due to the mishmash of Frank's experiences since moving to Arizona. While Fred had tentatively stuck his toe into the political pool to test his potential for success, Frank had leapt into a sea of union organization, agitation, and discipline. In truth, Fred was simply a dreamer; Frank, a doer. Frank loved the competition, the contest of beating city halls and unethical employers. But as more horrific events unfolded impacting workingmen and their families, his competitiveness curdled into a deep visceral response to injustices suffered by the vulnerable. Spokane had set in motion his increasing empathy for the downtrodden and passionate abhorrence of discrimination against immigrants and the homeless. His future would fuel hatred for the John D. Rockefellers and William Clarks of the world, as well as the private militias and gunmen their companies employed.

Although Frank had been a rank-and-file Wobbly in Spokane, he took the lead in Fresno. Terribly weakened from his incarceration in Franklin School, Frank jumped a Southern Pacific train for Fresno, likely moving in with Fred and Emma as soon as he arrived. Emma still worked as a chambermaid at the Mariposa Hotel and, as was customary, boarded there while Fred worked as a carpet cleaner. They had a home base for the family, a frame shotgun house at 394 Poplar Avenue.[13]

Frank and Fred began touring nearby work sites to assess labor conditions firsthand. By April 1910, they were ready to mount their soapboxes. Surprisingly, Chief Shaw had granted them a permit to speak, perhaps believing their efforts futile. Harvesting season had not yet begun, and Shaw felt little pressure to stop IWWs from organizing.[14] But the little group of Wobblies was growing, beginning with fifteen members and growing to over a hundred in a couple of weeks.[15]

Among Fresno's construction laborers were migrant Mexicans. At the Santa Fe Railroad, Fresno's migrant workers earned one dollar a day to be used for provisions purchased at a company store. Wobblies began encouraging them to join the IWW movement and walk away from store debt and pitiful wages.[16] Other Wobblies went to work at the Southern Pacific Railroad, beginning a "silent strike" by malingering, "poor work for poor pay."[17] The effects of the movement were soon felt. A contractor, building a dam outside the city, complained to Fresno city hall that he could not find cheap Mexican labor and blamed his troubles on the IWW.

After a Mexican socialist was stopped from speaking to his countrymen (whom the *Morning Republican* called "peons") by police near Fresno's Chinatown at the corner of F and Tulare Streets in mid-April 1910, Fred produced his permit to speak, taking over the soapboxing demonstration. The irritated officers told him he was not to disparage the police in his speaking, but they otherwise had no recourse.[18] Chief Shaw, however, wasted no time in revoking IWW speaking permits, telling Local 66 that to talk against business interests was treason. Writing to *Industrial Worker* in late May, Frank reported that Shaw warned that he would "vag" (arrest for vagrancy) any man turning down work, regardless of wages or conditions. Frank urged Wobblies to come to Fresno to be "vagged."[19]

On Sunday, May 29, 1910, an assembly of IWWs met on the courthouse square at the end of Mariposa Street to test Shaw's warning. Groups had been allowed to congregate and speak, but the Wobblies anticipated police interference. They brought along copies of the Declaration of Independence and the U.S. and California Constitutions, modeling Elizabeth Gurley Flynn's technique of soapboxing while propagandizing their constitutional rights. Instantly police, some in plain clothes, converged on the men, shredding the papers and clubbing Wobblies. Witnesses saw Chief Shaw angrily rip a California State Constitution into pieces.[20] Later that evening at an IWW meeting in Chinatown, police made no arrests, although Chief Shaw was offended by his description as a "petty official" for his declaration to arrest any man not gainfully employed.[21]

The next day, Local 66 presented a written statement before the Fresno City Council's regular meeting to consider their case for free speech. After giving a brief history of police interference in their organization, Frank boldly asked if the city council could afford a free speech campaign like Spokane's. His answer came when council members tabled Local 66's demands indefinitely.[22]

For the IWW, regular civil process had not worked—direct action was inevitable.

Late summer was looking hot as all parties began preparation for battle. The Fresno Employers' Association pressured Chief Shaw to squash the IWW by arresting any men who congregated on Fresno streets and charging them with vagrancy.[23] *Morning Republican* editor Chester H. Rowell (nephew of Mayor Rowell) stirred fear by expressing concern about militantly organized ethnic workers in his editorials. His paper went on to describe the IWWs as an anarchist mob that was unpatriotic for opposing local government.[24] Similar to Spokane, city fathers gave the Salvation Army permits to speak on soapbox row while denying the IWW, creating further consternation among the Wobblies.[25] In response, Frank reported that he expected a summer influx of Russians, Japanese, Germans, and Chinese to join the IWW.[26] Laborers across the country read Frank Little's calls to come to Fresno in *Solidarity* on May 10 and August 27, 1910, and *Industrial Worker* on June 4, 1910.

Frank and Fred Little decided to wait until the harvest was over to take the fight to the streets. Meanwhile they would organize quietly and grow their membership. Again Local 66 moved its headquarters to accommodate growth, this time to 1408 Tulare, a respectable street-front office.[27] Still more indicative of Frank and Fred's success, Fred requested a subscription for twenty-five copies per week of *Industrial Worker* for Local 66's growing readership.[28] IWW locals were indeed growing, primarily because of the press coverage of free speech fights. Between the 1909 and 1910 conventions, sixty-six new IWW locals had formed.[29]

Emma Little continued working through the summer at the Mariposa Hotel. But her life had just turned upside down. Whether Emma used Margaret Sanger's progressive advice for birth control and deliberately avoided pregnancy in the preceding years is unknown, but in late 1908, she had become pregnant for the third time. The unnamed baby boy was born dead on July 19, 1909.[30] Now less than a year later, Emma found herself expectant again. She would be inconveniently pregnant in the middle of an IWW fight, one in which she desperately wanted to participate. As a bystander, Emma surely bore dual emotions: exhilaration mixed with fear

for her unborn child and the impending free speech fight. Emma
could at least fight with pen and paper from her kitchen table as
soon as her pregnancy required her to quit her job.

Just prior to his Fresno arrest on August 24, 1910, Frank, too,
had used the papers to press a free speech fight. In a correspondence to *Solidarity* on August 17, Frank wryly noted that the Mexican jackass, which lived on cactus and sage brush, fared better than
the workers in the San Joaquin Valley. He reported to Wobbly readers
that he had successfully organized "the slaves of this country"
during street meetings, including in Selma, a small agricultural
community near Fresno.[31] His successes in the San Joaquin Valley
promptly triggered Fresno authorities to contrive arrests of key
IWW organizers before the harvest season concluded. Days afterward, Frank began serving twenty-five days on bread and water
in the bottom of the Fresno dungeon for refusing to rake leaves on
the courthouse lawn.

As Labor Day approached, Fresno newspapers publicized a
glorious parade honoring laborers, touting Fresno's legitimate labor
unions as the best organized in the country. In a blatant belittling
of the IWW's collective intellect and its war to raise wages among
immigrant workers, the *Fresno Herald* further claimed that Fresno's
labor organizations were composed "of a class of men far above
the average intelligence" and that "local working classes in general
are in thorough accord with their employers, and are thoroughly
cognizant of the fact that what is of benefit to those who pay wages
is also of benefit to them."[32] Meanwhile, the railroads brought an
endless stream of Wobbly soldiers who camped, waiting, in jungles
near the railroad tracks. Frank promised that at least five hundred
men were ready to go to jail.[33] A fight was imminent.

On Monday, September 5, 1910, Chief Shaw and two other
officers led the largest Fresno Labor Day Parade thus far on their
prancing steeds, just ahead of Mayor Rowell in his automobile.
Behind the group marched divisions of Fresno's trade unions, all
part of the AFL, which the city openly supported.[34] Frank surely
heard the cheers from the dank jailhouse dungeon as the lengthy
parade marched past the grand marshal's parade stand near Courthouse Park. Afterward, no IWW member attended celebratory events

REDS   139

for trade union members and their supporters, which included the basket dinner, dances, and other family activities at Zapp's Park.

Chief Shaw told newspaper reporters that the IWW had been restricted from participating since they had wanted to carry a large red flag.[35] Fred Little debunked Shaw's statements in a letter to the editor, decrying Shaw's words as yet another police story meant to prejudice citizens against the IWW. Against Shaw's allegation that a disgruntled IWW tore down the American flag in front of Union Hall, Fred claimed the IWW would never tear down an American flag or any other flag for that matter.[36] Yet Mayor Rowell, newspaper editor Chester H. Rowell (the mayor's nephew), and Shaw continued their campaign to discredit the IWW.

Two days later, Frank was offered a second opportunity to work on the courthouse grounds, but he again refused to lift a rake. He had been given a "square meal" just once during the previous six days and was beginning a new five-day cycle of bread and water.[37] Fred and Emma became increasingly alarmed about Frank's health, already weakened from the scurvy-besieged school in Spokane. In Chicago, IWW General Headquarters shared their concerns and sent a telegram ordering Frank to do park work. The condition of his health jeopardized his future ability to help the Wobbly cause. Local 66 discussed the telegram, admiring Frank's spirit, but immediately voted to send Frank the message to get out of the tank and rake leaves with other trustees. Fortunately, Frank had more common sense than Little hardheadedness, and he acquiesced to Local 66's instructions. After ten days on the bread-and-water diet, Frank obediently returned to daylight, park work, and regular jail rations.[38]

On September 25, 1910, Frank walked out of the old red-brick jail onto the courthouse grounds he had helped manicure. The historic Fresno Free Speech Fight could officially begin now that harvest season was winding down, and he was free. Wobblies, who had traveled to Fresno anticipating the fight, were jubilant with the release. They anxiously waited for Fred and Frank Little's plans to agitate.

Their celebration would abruptly morph to shock when, just three weeks later, Fred made a reckless decision that sucker punched IWW momentum and fractured his marriage.

13

FRESNO FREE SPEECH FIGHT

Frank had enjoyed just twenty-one days of liberty after his release
from the Fresno County Jail on September 25, 1910. He had
lots of time to scheme while imprisoned, so his new interlude of
independence was packed with deliberation and action. Frank had
boldly announced to the *Fresno Herald* that the anticipated free
speech fight would begin shortly before the November elections,
pending the outcome of another appeal for a speaking permit. Frank
had stated candidly to the press that he knew Chief Shaw detested
the IWW and that permission would surely be denied. At this point
the Wobblies would proceed to act on his war plan:

> We will place our speakers on the street with instructions
> to address those who gather about them. When an officer
> puts in an appearance and makes demands to see our permit
> for making a public address on the street, we will inform
> him that our permit consists of the Constitution of the
> United States, which gives any citizen the privilege of free
> speech. The officer then, should the speaker refuse to stop,
> and probably in accordance to instructions previously given
> him, will march our man off to jail. If he does this, the

speaker's place will be promptly taken by another man, and when he is arrested, another will take his place, and so on until the jail is full.[1]

Frank had promised that the IWW would not start any hostility—if violence began, it would start with city authorities. He had given the Wobblies instructions to go along peacefully with any officer who placed them under arrest.[2] The object was to pack the jail, bring attention to Fresno hiring policies and restricted constitutional rights, and effect change in those practices—in other words, passive civil disobedience.

A new competition of words—this time between the IWW's *Industrial Worker* and Local 66, and the mayor's *Fresno Morning Republican* and a new sheriff—heightened the battle to influence Fresno newcomers expecting a constitutional rights fight. Forty-year-old Fresno County sheriff Robert Dean Chittenden joined the walrus-mustached, silver-headed Chief William Shaw in protecting the public.[3] Both men hailed from Switzerland County, Indiana, and both resented the Wobbly invasion to their adopted home. But Chittenden had also recently suffered the loss of his first wife. Paired with his bitterness toward the growing IWW menace, his judgment proved imperfect and cruel.[4] Still, the *Fresno Morning Republican* loyally reported Chittenden's every move with assurance to its readers.

Fresno citizens already doubted Wobbly integrity, since the newspaper reported various small crimes by men who wore IWW buttons and carried IWW membership cards. Deliberately misreading their empty pockets for lazy "I Won't Work" or "I Want Whiskey" bindle stiffs, Chittenden and Shaw described arrested men as aimless vagrants who could not afford blankets to keep them warm.[5] In actuality, the IWWs knew better than to have valuables on their persons, as unscrupulous policemen had stolen their personal effects in Spokane. They were tradesmen for the most part—sailors, dockworkers, boilermakers, smelter workers, line workers, potter men, tool dressers, loggers, and miners. Some were common laborers who migrated up and down the San Joaquin Valley gathering the fruit in season.

In a perverse contagion across the city, housewives spread frightening gossip about IWW beggars offending them and stealing eggs and chickens. The *Morning Republican* reported that residents in the Belmont neighborhood, near where Fred and Emma presently lived, claimed a rash of petty thefts by IWW hands.[6] The newspaper bolstered housewives' illustrations of filthy, threadbare hoboes with a former Spokane reporter's warning: "What the city authorities want to do is to put a damper on the IWWs just as soon as they begin their appearance in the city." He disdainfully added that the average IWW was "unable to make a speech" anyway.[7]

An undercurrent of deep racial animus ran in some policemen's veins. One officer described a Wobbly agitator, whose name was spelled phonetically in the jail register, as "waving his arms like a windmill and chattering like a monkey."[8] The *Morning Republican* confirmed that the man was unable to spell or write his name and did not know his nativity, proving his ignorance. More likely the agitator simply could not understand English.

Morning Republican editor Rowell also drew negative attention to IWW activities in area towns. In one article that described various people and trivial happenings in Coalinga, California, Rowell deliberately headlined the article with "IWW Agitator in Wrong at Coalinga." The piece contained only a few sentences briefly mentioning Frank's trip to Coalinga to organize oil field workers. He had given two speeches upon his release from jail over the weekend of September 30—one from a soapbox on Front Street, and the other to a Socialist meeting in city hall.[9] A more serious story on October 25, 1910, claimed that an August explosion was in fact a bombing, undertaken by an IWW member who was found unconscious in the general vicinity after falling off a train. The *Morning Republican* reported that Sheriff Chittenden had "severely interrogated" Frank Little, a known IWW leader, about his knowledge of the man's activities, neglecting to mention that Frank had been in jail at the time of the explosion.[10]

Not to be outdone by the *Morning Republican*, the *Herald* editor chastised citizens to aid the police in their suppression of a growing IWW menace. Hamilton Gilmour editorialized that "a whipping post and cat o'nine tails, well-seasoned by being soaked in salt water, is none too harsh a treatment for the peace breakers."[11] Subsequent events supported Gilmour's mindset. The *Herald* also reported an influx of Wobblies arriving singly and in pairs for the past weeks. By September's end, more than three hundred IWWs were scattered throughout the surrounding vineyards and wineries.[12] With another army of experienced freedom fighters on their way from Washington State, the stage was soon set for Frank's war plan.[13]

On Sunday evening, October 16, 1910, Frank stood on a wooden crate at the corner of Kern and H Streets, exhorting a small cheering crowd to support industrial unionism. The location was not far from the train tracks where men congregated. Immediately Chief Shaw and a squad of officers arrested Frank, manhandling him. Twelve other Wobblies who took his place received the same treatment, one at a time.[14] According to one witness, the war plan went like "clockwork," producing the desired effect on the supportive crowd.[15] The brief incident officially began the Fresno Free Speech Fight, a struggle that has been described as three waves of passive resistance, punctuated with violent consequences.

The next morning all thirteen men, clothed similarly in overalls and black working shirts, stood together before Judge Herbert F. Briggs in police court, pleading not guilty. Frank smiled widely as each man delivered the same prepared speech, demanding a separate jury trial. But Briggs shrewdly set a single trial date for mid-November and bail at $250 each.[16] Individual jury trials cost money, so Frank would be the sole IWW tried. Depending on this test case, the other Wobblies would be released or tried.

That same evening at 7:00 P.M., a crowd gathered at the corners of Mariposa and I Streets to await an anticipated clash of IWWs and local police. They were not disappointed. Like an immense, choreographed foxtrot, soapboxers timed a twinkle of speeches on all four corners with the sympathetic crowd jostling lawmen who clumsily rushed out of step from corner to corner to make arrests.[17] Several other IWWs tried to distribute newspapers, leaflets, and pamphlets that carried the message of industrial unionism, also illegal according to Chief Shaw's rules. Officers, many in plain clothes supported by a large force of deputy sheriffs, circulated among the crowd, threatening charges of vagrancy to the men who

FRESNO SOAPBOX CORNER

Frank Little soapboxed at the corner of Mariposa and I Streets, Fresno, California
(left street corner). Once known as Soapbox Corner, today the location is
known as Free Speech Plaza. A scarred plaque marks the site of the first
California Free Speech Fight. *Author's photo postcard.*

dispensed literature. This time, seven more Wobbly speakers from
among a reported hundred IWWs and Fresno-citizen spectators
marched off to jail.[18]

Meanwhile, rail authorities reported to the *Morning Republican* that more men were expected to arrive in the next days to
replenish the rank-and-file Wobblies who had been arrested. The
police department received word that 176 men were on their way
to Fresno from the northwest as they had been seen camping along
the tracks below Sacramento.[19] Another 50 had arrived from southern California.[20] Most of those arrested, including E. F. (Red) Doree,
a close friend of Frank's who had arrived from Spokane to aid the
fight, demanded a separate jury trial.[21] Songwriter Joe Hill also

purportedly joined the mass of men who entered the Fresno fray and became arrested.[22] Many had just arrived on the "brake beams of the southbound trains" the day before.[23]

Sheriff Chittenden bragged to the *Morning Republican* that after arresting five more IWWs among a crowd of about five hundred on Thursday evening, October 20, 1910, he could make accommodations for three hundred more if necessary, stating, "I can, on a moment's notice, take all of the vags [vagrants] out of the bull-pen and turn it over to the 'workers.'"[24] But the cold, cement-floored bull pen, part of which sat underground in the northwest wing of the dilapidated jail, would belie Chittenden's claim. It was not nearly adequate, measuring only 20 1/2 by 40 feet and 8 feet in height. Eight small windows, nineteen beds, one bath tub, a toilet, and a water sink served the forty-seven prisoners within the pen's walls. Because of the crowded conditions, the starving, unwashed Wobblies slept in shifts. Despite their long-standing opposition, the IWWs also engaged in amicable conversations with Salvation Army soldiers to break the boredom.[25]

Matters were troubling outside of the jail as well. Chittenden had to post two police guards with sawed-off shotguns in plain view outside the jail walls, in case a Wobbly decided to chip through the fourteen-inch brick walls.[26] At night, three outside lamps were added to illuminate the perimeter.[27] These measures only increased concern for apprehensive business owners who walked past Fresno's Courthouse Park daily. Some began to meet en masse, their vigilante plans foreboding a wicked future.

Night after night a swelling crowd continued to gather at the Mariposa and I intersection to await Wobbly speakers and their arrests. Some gawkers held grudges against the police while others were delighted with the apprehensions. Chittenden's and Shaw's men were stretched across the four street corners, ready to seize any Wobbly speakers who mounted platforms to soapbox. Chief Shaw was not worried—Chittenden promised him a bull pen capable of holding several hundred men, and Fresno citizens were not affected by IWW propaganda. The two men soon received another wholly unexpected gift: the defection of Fred Little from the IWW cause.

On Friday, October 28, 1910, Fred reluctantly rose to his feet in Police Judge Briggs's courtroom. When Judge Briggs asked him if he still pled innocent, Fred unexpectedly changed his plea, begging mercy from the court. He explained to the honorable gentleman that he had a wife and family to support and could not sacrifice his workdays to reside in jail. In fact, to the absolute horror of the Wobbly audience in attendance, Fred stated he could not afford to waste any more time supporting the IWW cause. With such optimistic news, Briggs advised Fred that if he promised good behavior, his ninety-day sentence would be suspended. Now there would be no need for the jury trial that Fred had staunchly demanded almost one week earlier.[28]

The thorny hitch was that Fred had just admitted to public drunkenness when arrested for intoxication the past Saturday night.[29] Now the Fresno Beer Hall accusation in August did not seem so sinister, and former prosecution witness Ira Hapgood could be vindicated—if there still had been a case against him. Much pricklier were more intimate injuries from Fred's foolhardy actions.

Worse than facing Judge Briggs in police court was confronting six-months-pregnant Emma Little. Between his arrest on October 22, 1910, and his court date one week later, the Little household had been in turmoil with Fred caught between the proverbial "rock and a hard place." On one side was his marriage, in which an icy fissure was slowly widening the connubial chasm between Fred and Emma. Conversely, Fred was secretary of Local 66, an important position for the couple. If he were to claim innocence, Fred would continue to hold esteem among Fresno IWWs even if he went to jail, but Emma would not be able to support the family alone. To admit drunkenness in order to get a suspended sentence meant his continuance as the family breadwinner but the end of his IWW role.

Not until 1919 did the IWW Constitution explicitly state that any officer found publicly drunk would be removed from his position.[30] However in 1910, the constitution clearly gave instructions for members to be removed, based on personal conduct. Fred knew he would have to step down, demoralizing the men he had just organized. And to make matters worse, his infamous little brother was still sitting in an isolated jail cell, unable to influence the events that immediately followed Fred's pronouncements. While Fred was negotiating his fall from grace with Emma, and Frank sat alone in his jail cell, the momentum of the Wobbly train to Fresno's soapbox corners screeched to a halt. Hopes that the Fresno Free Speech Fight would suffer "a natural death" would soon be realized.[31]

On October 29, 1910, the *Morning Republican* reported that the prisoners took Fred's defection with much grumbling, and several of them suddenly changed their pleas to guilty to get a "floater" (parole) so that they could leave town.[32] Fresno Wobblies condemned Fred for his desertion of the cause, while the IWWs who had just arrived simply backtracked. Selective, disconsolate excerpts from a Wobbly prisoner's confiscated diary, printed in the newspaper for all to see, added another reason to abandon the fight.[33] With the diary in hand, Sheriff Chittenden confidently pronounced that a break in spirit was inevitable.

Some of the remaining prisoners had been sleeping four to a cell on bare concrete floors and eating just two meals a day. They had been allowed one cup of water daily and absolutely no tobacco. Bathing was not an option. But if they wanted a shower, all they had to do was sing, and they would get the "water cure."[34] Confined in a separate cell for fear of agitation, Frank continued their ballad and was also threatened with a garden hose.[35] Confronted with Fred's desertion, the men in the bull pen debated the merits of fighting for the cause. After discussing a hunger strike versus jail release, Red Doree began organizing men to plead guilty and get out of jail.[36]

The *Industrial Worker* carried news from the Fresno front. U. L. Leister of the "Jungles Press Committee" grabbed the red standard from Local 66, hyperbolizing that the fight was for their "very breath."[37] No stories of Fred Little's transgression filled the newspaper's pages. Instead a more urgent call went out to Wobblies to march to Fresno. But Leister's appeal was too late. By November 2, 1910, following Fred's model of courtroom decorum, fifty-three of the fifty-eight men who had been arrested pled guilty and received ninety-day suspended sentences as long as they left Fresno County within three hours. Frank had been bailed out.[38] The next day, the

**E. F. (Red) Doree and
Frank Little, 1913**

E. F. (Red) Doree (left) and
Frank Little (right) were
both imprisoned in
Fresno's famous bull pen
in 1910. *E. F. Doree
Papers, courtesy of the
Joseph A. Labadie
Collection, University
of Michigan.*

Morning Republican trumpeted "Industrial Workers Are Beaten
in Fight for Streets."[39] On Saturday, November 5, the jail closed its
register on IWW prisoners. An estimated sixty-five men had been
jailed and released in two and a half weeks.[40] The Fresno Free Speech
Fight was flatlining.

At home, Emma Little diligently clipped all newspaper articles
concerning the free speech fight. She intended to put together a

scrapbook—perhaps giving her a sense of active participation as she awaited the birth of her baby. More likely she wanted to openly protest the *Morning Republican*'s depiction of IWWs as illiterate, homeless pests. A November 9, 1910, *Industrial Worker* article looks suspiciously like Emma's work. The anonymous author eloquently shames the workers whose defections led to the halt of the free speech fight while heartening humble Wobblies who were the core of the movement. The article sharply contrasts the true "Industrial Unionist," modest and keenly conscious of his shortcomings but fair at figures and at taking stock of materials with which to fight, with the man who walks "around with a chip on his shoulder, telling the timid and modest members what he knows and what he would do in each and every case and what a splendid fighter he is."[41] Could the latter be an oblique description of Fred Little? The author points out that somehow this individual can never spare time for the IWW. He or she describes the faithful IWW as one who acts quietly, stays clean, and is a good listener, an industrial unionist who is "patient as the stars and constant."[42] If the dedicated IWWs all prepared together in Fresno, the author argued, then they "could storm hell" itself.[43] The article was simply signed "The Jungles Press Committee."[44]

Whether Emma penned the article alone, with the help of others, or not at all is of less consequence than its effect on readers. This article, and others like it, helped turn the tide. Swells of unionist workers slowly rose upward and washed toward Fresno, as a sea of workingmen revived themselves and moved to rinse off the shame from their fellow Wobblies' desertions. Along with Wobbly Fred Hickok, Frank hit the road for Visalia and Porterville to turn back defeated IWWs. Local 66 claimed that if they could recall at least fifteen men, the free speech fight could resume. The men began returning cautiously, avoiding railroad bulls.

IWW Local 66 had moved its headquarters once again in early anticipation of vast Wobbly numbers, this time to the floor above the Cosmopolitan Restaurant on Mariposa Street. This location, too, proved to be unacceptable, primarily because the local police could closely monitor who came and went. The growing population of visiting Wobblies also needed a place to "flop," but no other landlord was permitted to rent to Local 66 per orders of Chief Shaw.[45]

Sometime before their October arrests, the two Little brothers had found a five-acre former vineyard on Palm Avenue just north of Belmont, outside the city limits and Chief Shaw's jurisdiction.[46] Fred and Emma Little's (and probably Frank's) current residence at 555 Echo was conveniently nearby.[47] The owner of the lot, William Storey, was sympathetic to the Wobbly cause and leased the grounds to Local 66.[48] Storey was also the source of Frank's unexpected bond in early November when Frank realized that with Fred resigning leadership, he would need to take the helm of Local 66 quickly.[49]

The Wobblies erected a large tent they purchased from a local hardware store, using it to hold meetings, process IWW members, provide financial assistance, and board men arriving on freight trains for the second wave of protests. Incoming bindle stiffs jumped off trains at an area north of town called the "ditch" where a Local 66 representative directed them to the tent with a red flag. Along an avenue extending from the railroad yards to the tent, signs also efficiently guided men to their destination.[50] Upon arriving at headquarters, they were given a hot meal and a day's rest before they began agitating.[51]

To further obfuscate the authorities, other IWWs were told to go to the Fresno Coffee Store at 1128 I Street upon their arrival. They were to hand the clerk their questions, masked as written orders for goods, whereupon the freedom fighters would be given instructions surreptitiously.[52] All the men had to do now was melt away into Fresno streets and wait—other reinforcements were on the way.

On Monday, November 21, 1910, representatives from twenty-four IWW locals met at the "Jungles," as Wobblies now called their tent headquarters, agreeing to make one more attempt to get a legal permit to speak.[53] Surprisingly, Chief Shaw acquiesced, a decision he later regretted. Believing speakers' promises to broadcast "safe, sane, and conservative" remarks, Shaw had awarded speaking permits in good faith to four leaders of the IWW group—Frank Little, Charley Filigno, James Murdock, and J. S. Merrill.[54] The tenor of the soapboxers' remarks on K and Mariposa Streets changed, however, when men who previously had been awarded suspended sentences and told to leave town reappeared. Soon a freight conductor aboard a train from the north warned Chief Shaw that a large band of Wobblies, wearing red sweaters with "IWW" on their backs, was about one hundred miles north of Fresno.[55]

On Sunday, November 26, Frank stood in front of a life-size pewter boy holding a leaky boot, which drained water into the center of an ornate fountain at the intersection of Mariposa and K.[56] The sound of the tinkling water was muted by Frank's vigorous speech. Reminding them of what had occurred in Goldfield and Cripple Creek in the fight for the eight-hour day, Frank told the crowd how California law presently guaranteed the eight-hour day for wage earners. He pointed out that Fresno police worked ten-hour days, uncontested out of fear. He introduced the possibility of their organizing.[57] Policemen stood by nervously, unsure of whether to make arrests.

The Fresno Free Speech Fight was reborn when Chief Shaw decided enough was enough two days later.[58] His thin skin betrayed his primary motives: Shaw publicly expressed distaste for being called a "bean-shooter" and other "pet names." All soapboxers and IWWs who sold papers on street corners were immediately arrested for vagrancy, with bonds set at $500.[59]

Frank's test trial, which had been set tentatively for November 25, had been postponed while Judge Briggs sought a change of venue. Since other IWWs had been denied legal services while searching for help, Briggs agreed with Frank that he could not find a fair jury in Fresno.[60] After being rearrested on Tuesday, November 29, Frank notified the court that he had retained Los Angeles attorney Fred H. Moore to defend him in court. He further announced that he would not need a jury trial after all, mystifying Police Judge Briggs.[61] The blow to law enforcement came just ten days later. On December 7, Frank conducted his own defense without Fred Moore in a one-hour hearing in front of a courtroom in Selma, California, packed to the doors with curious onlookers. There was no jury at Frank's request. Just three witnesses were called to the stand.

Chief Shaw, the first witness, stated that he had issued a speaking permit to Frank just days earlier, claiming that Frank abused

Boy with the Leaky Boot

Frank Little soapboxed in front of the *Boy with the Leaky Boot* fountain in Fresno's Courthouse Square. Behind the fountain are the grounds where Frank finally agreed to rake leaves. *Author's photo postcard.*

it by "roasting" police and city officials.[62] In rebuttal, Frank declared that no law on the books prohibited street speaking. Like a gasping fish, William Shaw could only mouth that he had *believed* such a law existed after the judge's failed attempt to locate the ordinance. Briggs ruled Shaw's testimony as having no bearing on the case. Then the second witness, patrolman Jack Broad, testified that he had taken Frank into custody and charged him with disturbing the peace upon orders of Chief Shaw. Upon cross-examination, Frank asked Officer Broad if Frank had disturbed the peace. The patrolman answered he had not, but that Frank had no permit to speak either, this fact now moot. The third witness, P. [William] Brutsch, owner of a saloon and rooming house on the corner of H and Kern Streets where the soapboxing took place, likewise confirmed that Frank had not disturbed his peace.

Briggs acquitted Frank at once. Frank thanked the court and then turned around to shake hands with his raucous supporters.[63] Chief Shaw surely sat in shock. Fifty-five incarcerated Wobblies soon stood to be released.[64]

The next evening, soapboxers entertained a small crowd at Mariposa and I Streets, unmolested, to Chief Shaw's and Sheriff Chittenden's chagrin. While Fresno city trustees scrambled to call a special meeting to discuss passing a speech ordinance, law enforcement and the fire department turned deaf ears to vigilantes' growing whispers.[65] On Friday evening, December 9, Wobbly inmates, languishing in Courthouse Park's bull pen, peered out the small windows to see about six hundred men and boys, momentarily well-lit by the new outside lighting, melding into the darkness toward Mariposa and I Streets.[66]

When IWW soapbox speakers arrived at the illuminated intersection to address Fresno citizens, the crowd had grown. With no idea of the incoming storm, the Wobblies positioned a soapbox for the first speaker.[67] Then Onig "Nig" Normart and his cohort "Professor" Jimmy Quinn, both former prize fighters, edged close to a Wobbly who was about to mount the crate. A handsome Armenian immigrant, Normart had illustrated great athletic abilities as a boy although he was not overly large. When local firemen recognized his determination and speed with a punching bag, they invited him to the gym where they worked out.[68] From this point on, Normart enjoyed dual passions—boxing and firefighting. Fresno citizens knew the twenty-six-year-old firefighter as a scrappy pugilist who drank hard and had a history of bullying.[69]

As soon as the soapboxer opened his mouth with the words, "Fellow Workers," Normart and Quinn reportedly flew at him, pulled him to the ground, and pounded him severely, setting off mob madness.[70] Plainclothes police standing nearby made no effort to interfere in the brawl that ensued.[71] After Normart and Quinn rushed the first assault, the stunned IWWs in the congested audience made a panic-stricken dash for North Belmont and Palm Avenues, believing that the tent headquarters could provide some sort of safety. The mob followed them, thrashing any and all recognized Wobblies in the crowd.

Frank M. Shuck, another friend of Normart's and owner of the Acme Restaurant at 1057 I Street, positioned his car so he could collect rioters and drop them off at the IWW tent. Along with several other automobile owners, he allegedly made several trips back and forth, carrying the rabid crowd to its destination.[72] Other rioters jumped a streetcar to make the one-and-a-half-mile trip while scores chased IWWs on foot.

Emma could dimly see the large red banner flying atop the tent from her back door—the Little home was less than a quarter mile away. Her gut must have drawn into a queasy ball behind the baby she was carrying when she first witnessed smoke. The crawling, silvery swirl swiftly thickened to a spiraling black billow, with orange flames illuminating the dark clouds now fused into the night sky. The light rain was not enough to douse the inferno that burned all supplies, bedding, food, and personal belongings of the visiting Wobblies. Hanging damply above the tent, the crimson flag incited its own destruction, the red bunting torn into souvenirs of man's inner savageness triumphing over civilized dissent.[73] Police stood idly nearby, stating that the field on Palmer and North Belmont was out of their jurisdiction.[74] Wobblies, many of them in their underwear and carrying all their earthly belongings, scrambled out of the camp with rioters in hot pursuit.

Then the mob turned its attention toward the Fresno County Jail, where the captive group of IWWs made easier prey for tarring and feathering, lynching, or whatever else the rabble's frenzied brains believed was fitting. Chief Shaw and his deputies stood at the entrance of the red-brick jail in Fresno Courthouse Park. Another lawman posed on top of the steps directly in front of the door. Terrified men peeked out of the bull pen windows at the crowd that clearly demanded their blood. When Shaw's bulldog stance held firm, the mob finally dispersed to the relief of all inside.

Normart, Quinn, and Shuck, described as plotters and leaders of the mob, later vehemently denied their roles in the shameful attack on Fresno streets. *Morning Republican* editor Chester H. Rowell (Mayor Rowell's nephew) mourned that their actions would simultaneously draw national attention and more Wobblies to the city.[75] It was a valid prediction. Recent events of the free speech fight demonstrated that Fresno business interests had relied on undemocratic ordinances, violated constitutional liberties, and resorted to force and violence to keep workers from organizing. IWWs claimed that the "broadcloth" mob was bred not only of Fresno capitalists, but "Pinkerton agents, firemen, and pimps," organized by men who took the law into their own hands.[76] One Wobbly declared that two policemen and six firemen participated in the rioting. Quickly Fresno city authorities clarified that the policemen were on day detail and not in uniform or on duty when the rioting started. The firemen, too, were in civilian clothes. As such, they were not expected to act in any official capacity.

Wobblies sought redress at local and state levels of government. IWW general secretary-treasurer Vincent St. John telegraphed Sacramento for the governor's assistance. In response, the California governor's office wired back that it had no authority and to "appeal to Fresno local authorities"—that is, Chief Shaw, Sheriff Chittenden, and Judge Briggs—for help.[77] Frank Little also appeared in the Fresno district attorney's office the morning after the violence. A local attorney had advised him that Local 66 had a case against the mob's ringleaders. While waiting to speak to District Attorney Denver S. Church, Frank told Detective Tom Walton that Local 66 might bring criminal suits against Normart, Quinn, and Shuck.[78] Then Frank waited and waited. The district attorney never opened his door for a consultation, so Frank left. All legal avenues had now failed Local 66.

City officials remained less than helpful. Mayor Rowell insisted that not only had authorities possessed no knowledge of vigilante plans but also that "the industrialists received only what they preach."[79] Others claimed that he and Chief Shaw had incited the mob. Rowell promised that a street ordinance would be passed, giving police the authority to make legal arrests. Sheriff Chittenden, who was out of town at the time of the riot, stated that he deplored the citizens' actions, yet he regarded the mob violence as an effective tool. He believed it would occur again if the IWW rebuilt its headquarters. Likewise, Chief Shaw threatened landlord William Storey with nuisance charges if Storey permitted the IWW to rebuild on his lot.[80] The officers visited the scene of the devastation and described all that remained of the camp as "a heap of ashes and charred boxes," adding that "every bit of cloth, partly burned or otherwise, was carried off by members of the mob as souvenirs of the occasion."[81]

The scattered Wobblies regrouped again over the next few days while vitriolic speech on both sides increased. Fifty-seven men still remained in jail.[82] Another "test" case had just produced more effective results for Fresno law enforcement, and Shaw and Chittenden were once again positive that the Wobblies were whipped.

14

TRIALS AND TRUCES

Historian Melvin Dubofsky notes that IWW free speech fights were more about organizing tactics designed to illustrate that America's dispossessed could challenge established authority, and not so much about protecting civil liberties.[1] While this notion is strongly evident, Frank Little repeatedly and often earnestly engaged the justice system using his rights as guaranteed by the Constitution of the United States. He understood the nuances of Fresno's court system when acting as a legal representative and used the courtroom as both a platform for espousing IWW principles and protection of workingmen's civil liberties, especially when he knew the result would be a conviction. Yet Frank also denounced the Constitution as just a piece of paper when the document was blatantly ignored by those who should have upheld the law.

In some cases, Frank's defense strategies were so compelling that multiple ballots had to be cast before a jury presented a verdict acceptable to the court. Shortly before the mob incident, cartoonist James (Jack) Murdock, one of the four leaders in the free speech fight, was tried for vagrancy. Yet Chief Shaw accused Murdock of radical street speeches, including criticism of the local government and police department, in his trial. Shaw claimed to the *Fresno Morning Republican* that Murdock was receiving thirty dollars a

week from national IWW headquarters in a devious effort to turn
workingmen against their leaders.[2] Upon cross-examination, Murdock submitted receipts and checks proving that he was actually
receiving just two dollars per day for Fresno agitation.[3] After Frank
and three other men testified on behalf of Murdock, indecisive jurymen took eight ballots to achieve the verdict the city required, and
the charge finally stuck.[4]

Several days after Murdock's trial, Charley Filigno, another identified leader of the Fresno Wobblies, was found guilty of vagrancy
on the first ballot. Filigno, the Italian IWW organizer from Spokane
to whom Frank had responded from Kalispell in 1909, had been
dividing his stay in an Italian boarding house and the tent on Palm
Avenue. The evidence against him, provided by J. S. Merrill, Fred
Little, and Chief Shaw, resulted in an expedited, unanimous decision
and another six-month jail sentence.[5] According to the *Morning
Republican*, Filigno took his sentence calmly and did not file notice
of appeal. As he walked from the courtroom, he remarked that
he "asked no favors of any one."[6] Both Murdock and Filigno had
shown purposeful composure in receiving their sentences.

While Frank likewise had shown himself to be a patient man
with the courts, his temper lay shallow. Historians have generally
agreed that Frank Little was boldly confrontational in his passion
for industrial unionism. One measured Frank as "the toughest,
most courageous and impulsive leader the IWW ever had."[7] After
Frank's death, IWW songwriter and cartoonist Ralph Chaplin added,
"I liked Frank Little. I liked him because of his candor, courage,
and unfailing good humor."[8] Early evidence of these testimoni-
als is illustrated by what occurred on Sunday afternoon, December 11, 1910.

Despite the success of the vagrancy test case against Jack Murdock, Shaw's and Chittenden's threats, and the subsequent failure
of a judicial process regarding the mob, Frank still taunted civil
authorities. Six or seven Wobblies seated in a spring wagon paraded
up and down the streets of Fresno's business section for half an hour
or more.[9] Flowing crimson streamers, characterized by the *Morning
Republican* as "torrid," decorated the wagon. Its occupants also wore
red bands around their hats and red ribbons on their coats. The

understated reply to Sheriff Chittenden and Chief Shaw's threats was impulsive, bold, and quick-witted. The IWW needed no other proclamation. The final wave of the Fresno Free Speech Fight was about to commence.

Attorney Fred H. Moore arrived in Fresno to assist the incarcerated Wobblies at IWW national headquarters' request. Moore advised making a new agreement with the city to have all prisoners liberated, the sentenced men paroled, and then fighting out the city ordinance in court. The drawback was that the Wobblies would have to leave town at once, notify IWW headquarters that the Fresno Free Speech Fight was over, and to not send more men. The prisoners voted unanimously to reject the city's proposal. Shocked, District Attorney Church blamed the Wobblies' foolish vote on the basis that a "majority of them ran away from home when they were boys, refused to go to school and now they are a worthless outfit who are endeavoring to place the blame on the shoulders of deserving citizens."[10] Moore, who had underestimated the heart of the fight, returned to Los Angeles.[11]

One day later on December 20, the Fresno City Council finally passed an ordinance making street-speaking illegal except in outlying districts (similar to what Spokane authorities had proposed).[12] Seventy-four men stood in Sheriff Chittenden's bull pen and jail cells, men who had been arrested for vagrancy at Mariposa and I street corners.[13] A full press to implement the new ordinance began. However, this time the opposition had widened against Fresno city officials and the weighted court system. A *blitzkrieg* of propaganda bombarded Fresno city officials' heads. Circulars were scattered across neighborhoods and business districts, educating local citizens on how to request copies of the U.S. Constitution. Anonymous letters arrived in officials' mailboxes, warning that the city's illegal activities would be discovered. Across the state, newspapers carried stories of groups protesting the city's actions.

A more personal attack came from the pen of IWW poet Joe Hill in a poem that circulated among Wobblies.[14]

Who recommended the cat-o'-nine,
And wished to have it soaked in brine,

To make the workers fall in line?
> Der Chief.

Who said the working men were scum?
That we were tramps and on the bum?
And that he had us on the run?
> Der Chief.

Who was the despot who used his might?
Who broke the backbone of our fight?
Vagged all our leaders in one night?
> Der Chief.

Excerpt from "Der Chief, of Fresno," first
published in Solidarity, February 2, 1911, p. 3

And IWWs *were* coming to Fresno.

Fred Little had reinserted himself into the free speech fight after almost two months of humiliation. With Wobblies getting arrested on a daily basis, he again submitted communications to *Solidarity*, requesting money orders from the readership (made out to him) to be mailed to Fresno to assist the "boys in jail" and the Wobblies who needed to rebuild headquarters. Fred joined Frank as Fresno's new defense committee. This was Fred's first but not last role in creating such a committee for jailed IWWs.

Frank had still been the only IWW to be tried and acquitted. After Wobbly locals sent him telegrams updating their plans, he warned Chief Shaw that five hundred freedom fighters would invade Fresno.[15] In response, police looked for a new opportunity to rearrest Frank. On Wednesday, December 21, one day after the street ordinance passed, Frank served as defense advocate for William J. Andreas, who was charged with vagrancy. Andreas fully admitted that he had come to Fresno with the express purpose of agitating for free speech to get into jail. Frank asked Andreas about his occupation and length of residence in Fresno. When Andreas answered that he had no money or job, Frank humorously asked if he was an IWW because of the fact that he did not work. Judge Briggs had to use his gavel to restore order when the large crowd broke out in laughter. Knowing full well that Andreas would be found guilty,

Frank made final arguments to the jury, "confining his remarks to a review of the fight for free speech and matters pertaining to the I.W.W.'s."[16] More important than freeing Andreas was getting out the industrial union's message.

A day later Frank was arrested just as he emerged from the private chambers of Judge Briggs, with whom he had been conferring about trial dates for his fellow workers. He was escorted to jail where he too was charged with vagrancy, just in time for a new jail outrage. The riot that followed was blamed partially on Frank, supposedly one of the leaders of "the demonstration."[17]

At 7 P.M., animated Wobblies cursed the brutal beating of a handcuffed "drunk Mexican" (or Frenchman according to some witnesses) at the hands of four policemen while Sheriff Chittenden calmly stood by. The man allegedly became insane after his treatment.[18] As punishment, Chittenden ordered bread and water for the demonstrators. When breakfast was served the next day, Wobblies hurled bread loaves back at their jailer and sang on empty stomachs, pledging they would starve to death before taking a bite. Their impassioned speeches to the public prompted a white curtain to be drawn over the bull pen's closed windows.[19] When jailer Ed Jones threatened them with drenching, a prisoner pitched a bucket of cold water in his face. To the glee of the prisoners, Jones sprayed a garden hose into the bull pen, an ineffective remedy to their protest.[20]

Fred Little later described the newest "water cure" that the eighty prisoners, including Frank, next received in jail.[21] Chittenden had called for the fire department after the jail's water hose was found to be inadequate.[22] For two hours at a stretch, via a two-inch fire engine hose with 150 to 200 pounds pressure, the men received a forceful torrent of water that slammed their bodies "up in the air like toothpicks" and into jail walls and cement floors.[23] While windows were torn from their hinges, men tried to grab straw mattresses to protect themselves from the watery cannon. Two men had their ear drums perforated, and others earned blackened eyes.[24] Eighty beds floated when the sewer holes clogged in the tub-like bull pen. Water rose to the men's knees and remained at least nine inches deep late into the night on December 23. When the first light of Christmas Eve shone into the bull pen's small, opaque windows, the men were soaked and shivering.[25]

Christmas Day was more cheerful. The Wobblies received new mattresses and dry blankets. After eating regular jail fare, they spent the day singing in harmony. The night jailer, who was leaving his post a week afterward, came in after Christmas to wish the men good luck in their quest.[26] But one week later, pneumonia, severe colds, and tonsillitis had invaded the jail.

Jack Whyte, who was arrested the day after the inmate's beating, subsequently joined Fred as official spokesman for the Fresno IWWs.[27] Whyte had been convicted on a charge of vagrancy for allegedly reporting the news to *Industrial Worker* and *Solidarity*.[28] Both men wasted no time in propagandizing the cruel treatment delivered to the eighty IWWs in jail at the time of the riot, calling for more Wobblies to come to Fresno. Jack Whyte reported that the men had been starved; Fred, that the men were beaten with billy clubs. Six men had been sent to the hospital.[29] The bull pen was overfilling rapidly, incapable of holding its current occupants, let alone the three hundred men Chittenden had promised.

But Sheriff Chittenden retired at the end of 1910, the final months of his law career filled with conflict and frustration. New county sheriff William S. McSwain, who appeared more sympathetic to his prisoners and staff, soon found himself at odds with Chief Shaw when he called in the health department to inspect his jail at the beginning of the New Year.[30] On January 11, 1911, a health inspector, who told Frank he was on their side of the fight, listened to Frank's description of conditions in the crowded bull pen.[31] After further scrutiny, inspectors declared that the bull pen's air quality was unhealthy, the space barely adequate for fifteen to thirty men.[32] Doctors inspected prisoners for illness, and those found ailing were included in a written report for authorities.[33] The health department soon warned the public of an impending epidemic. Not letting a crisis go to waste, on the same day of the inspection, the new sheriff used jail conditions to propagandize taxpayers' support for financing and construction of a new jail addition. Sheriff McSwain also began releasing some of the prisoners who had been held almost forty-five days without a trial, perhaps because of their physical conditions.[34] Other men received brief time in the jail yard. A week later, the released men were rearrested for soapboxing without permits and once again demanded individual jury trials.

Fresno news had escaped to national presses that were sympathetic to the IWW cause. Emma Little appealed for help in a national, left-leaning magazine. Her plea was eventually read by members of the extended Little family, Boyle cousins who lived far away in Missouri and began a letter-writing campaign to Chief Shaw and Judge Briggs.[35] Their missives were added to the pile of other protests arriving from across the nation while American workingmen made plans to invade Fresno and send money for the men's defense funds and needs.

In a strange twist of events, the past December, United Presbyterian minister J. M. Gillespie had suggested using a chain gang that would move the prisoners outside in fresh air in full view of the public, instead of "catcalling" back and forth from the bull pen's windows in Courthouse Park.[36] A rock pile would surely deter workingmen from endeavoring to get arrested and impeding the police court with demands for jury trials. Almost a hundred Wobblies, gazing out their small windows, observed with interest the growing pile of granite blocks that had been dumped in the prison yard from a quarry north of town.[37] The county jail was just waiting on the sledgehammers to arrive.

For less than $150, Sheriff McSwain creatively added a jail extension to house the new rock crushing exercise—a wooden stockade built by inmates at the back of the county jail on courthouse grounds. The 127-by-75-foot structure was surrounded by a 10-foot "tight board fence" with barbed wire strung along the top, to shut out prisoners from public view. Yet the fence was still within 10 feet of the M Street sidewalk, close enough for citizens to hear sounds from within. The prisoners would access the new stockade by way of a delivery entrance, a small sheet-iron door in the rear wall of the jail. Trees provided shade for prisoners as they pounded granite blocks into gravel with 12-pound and 16-pound sledges.[38] Frank wryly commented that a "rock pile doesn't scare IWWs because in Spokane the city treasury suffered the most from the cost of replacing hundreds of broken hammer handles."[39]

Again Frank requested a change of venue for his second trial, this time for vagrancy. And again, he was acquitted—this time by a jury in less than four minutes on February 1, 1911. In an effort to turn the jailed Wobblies against Frank, the *Morning Republican* wrote that Frank and other IWW organizers earned three dollars a day, even on Sundays, whether in jail or not, the exact evidence that Frank had used to prove he was gainfully employed.[40] The paper propagandized that Wobblies, who were jealous of Frank's freedom and income, had pled guilty in order to get "floaters" and leave town. Wobbly inmate H. Minderman's diary records a different story. No mention is made of animosity toward Frank, and more men entered jail than were released.[41] Nevertheless, the newspaper forecast that there would be no industrialists in the bull pen by week's end. Frank endeavored to return to jail himself, pending business that he first needed to conduct.

Just like Spokane, the cost of boarding Wobblies was making a dent in the city's budget since Sheriff McSwain made sure that the city received the bill and not the county. And Frank, still soapboxing outside the district proscribed in the city ordinance, urged released IWWs to provoke arrests and grow McSwain's claims.[42] A new headquarters had been designated on Olive Avenue in a house that William Storey found. Frank prepared a set speech, copies of which were given to newly arriving IWWs. Besides a message of industrial unionism, he included an appeal to spectators "to refrain from blockading the sidewalks," a major complaint of local businesses.[43] Visiting IWWs, many of whom spoke English as a second language, tried to memorize the speech and deliver it proficiently. While the men practiced greeting their audience with "Fellow Worker," Frank worked on a general defense for the imprisoned Wobblies finally scheduled for trial.

The defense strategy was simple: each case would rest on the First Amendment. In the next weeks, jury after jury listened to Frank's impassioned summation exhorting them to rule on the basis of federal laws. He argued that the IWWs had a constitutional right to assemble and speak on public streets. If the Constitution could not be upheld, then the American flag was no more than a "piece of bunting."[44] Fresno newspapers roared their fury at his words. Nevertheless, a few of the Fresno citizens called to jury duty admitted that they were in sympathy with the IWW. They were rejected immediately.[45]

Frank was learning the art of law, if not by osmosis then by experimenting in a hostile court with Wobblies as his test subjects. He insisted that a test case should be made to decide the constitutionality of the new street-speaking ordinance. When he filed a demurrer to one defendant's claim questioning the ordinance, the court promptly overruled him.[46] Judge Briggs informed Frank that he considered the law constitutional and that the sole recourse the IWWs had was to appeal the decision to the Superior Court. After court adjourned for the day, Frank warned that over two hundred Wobblies were in route to Fresno. Exploiting McSwain's frustration from inheriting the free speech fight with limited resources, Frank added, "We will force the authorities to build an addition to the jail before we get through with this fight for free speech."[47]

Sheriff McSwain was not the only individual concerned about the growing number of IWWs. On Wednesday, February 15, a day when there were about one hundred Wobblies waiting in the bull pen and most of them were yet untried, a *Morning Republican* editorial supported the Ministerial Union's claim that not only had the new street ordinance and court system proved ineffective, but that religious speakers had become unfairly entangled in the new law's web. Local ministers demanded an exemption or modification to the law and a fast judicial process for the incarcerated Wobblies. Until convicted, men could not be punished on the rock pile. The editor mourned the blunders that Fresno police and mob members committed in growing "the IWW problem."[48]

That evening Frank deliberately achieved his fifth Fresno arrest. He was in the midst of a speech among a crowd of workingmen at the corner of H and Kern Streets when officers approached the group. Four more speakers attempted to take the soapbox in succession when they also were arrested. When the soapboxers joined other inmates who were laughing, Frank was uncharacteristically quiet.[49] Just the day before in court, while referring to a diatribe that he should be "strung up" for his activities, Frank had stated gravely to a Fresno jury his fatalist view: "If a noose were dangling in front of my face, I would laugh at it. I am willing to die for the cause, if necessary, as I have committed no crime, unless you call it a crime to help uplift the workingman."[50] His prescient reaction revealed the level to which Frank's devotion had risen.

Meanwhile, conditions in Fresno County Jail worsened. Three days later Dr. Burks, a county health inspector, informed the *Morning Republican* that besides backed-up leaking pipes, dilapidated floors, and unsanitary conditions, there was no more room in the bull pen for arrested or convicted prisoners.[51] But it was another news story, and not the health inspector's report, that ultimately led Fresno city officials to surrender. The *Morning Republican* began carrying stories about thousands of bindle stiffs on their way to Fresno from distant states. The first news on February 18, the same day that Dr. Burks's report went public, reported that ten thousand men were on their way to Fresno.[52]

The most interesting group was a band of Wobblies leaving Portland, Oregon, who were dedicated to reaching Fresno, no matter the snowy conditions or cruelties they endured along the way. A few optimistic officials believed the men to be traveling to Mexico to aid revolutionaries, and not to Fresno. Daily piecemeal reports of the group's progress made their way into the *Morning Republican*. And day by day, the group began arousing empathy in the small communities that met them. It soon became crystal clear that these Wobblies were dead set on joining the Fresno Free Speech Fight. The half-starved men, who had been booted off a Southern Pacific freight train in Ashland, Oregon, began trudging through the Siskiyou Pass amid a snow storm with six feet of snow on the ground. They made twelve miles a day, camping around fires in bitter cold weather at night. By the time Fresno citizens read of their trek, the 170-member group had walked into California.[53]

By February 20, the group had arrived 375 miles north of Sacramento. Hopeful officials reported that the men were dissatisfied; some had quit, and in general, the group was disorganized.[54] One man's feet were so frostbitten, he feared losing them. By now, Wobblies had perfected the act of organization and could police

themselves while aiding their members. Their crusade would continue—and they even paid train fare for the man with frozen feet
to go ahead. Compounding their perseverance were new reports
of five thousand Wobblies planning to make a spring invasion from
Denver, and another army of hoboes was set to leave straightaway
from St. Louis.[55] Both groups criticized Southern Pacific Railroad's
treatment of the Portland Wobblies.

Alarmed Fresno officials fought Chief Shaw for some sort of
compromise with the Fresno IWWs. Just two days earlier Mayor
Rowell and Sheriff McSwain had proposed offering to set aside a
strip of pavement, thirty-five feet wide, on K Street between Fresno
and Mariposa Streets, to be used for street-speaking for IWWs and
religious groups. But at the Chamber of Commerce meeting two
days later, on February 21, after McSwain informed the city that
he refused to accept any more prisoners, the majority of those in
attendance wanted to surrender all Fresno streets to the IWWs.[56]
By meeting's end, citizens reversed surrendering, instead offering
censorship of newspaper reporting and a local militia of "special
police" to fight Wobblies.[57] They voted not to surrender any street
to the free speech fighters, electing a five-man committee to work
on the problem. That same evening the Portland Wobblies stum-
bled into Weed, California, a mountain logging camp, foot-sore and
frozen. Railroad police made certain they could not climb into empty
boxcars for warmth during the night.[58] The next day, Wednesday,
February 22, the incarcerated Fresno Wobblies elected their own
committee of five to draft a set of resolutions to present to the newly
elected city committee. Frank naturally was selected to serve. A
democratic body, the Wobblies voted to accept their committee's
brief but purposeful resolutions.[59]

That evening an advanced guard of the Portland Wobblies
reached Sacramento while the main body was struggling along the
Siskiyou Trail to reach Dunsmuir. Concerned individuals began
aiding them. *Morning Republican* editor Rowell (Mayor Rowell's
nephew) had no idea that the IWWs had breached the Siskiyou's
snow-covered summit. In a February 23 editorial, he shamed Fresno
citizens for even contemplating lawlessness and censorship: "This
mob talk must cease! It is more dangerous and more wicked than

the talk for which the I.W.W.'s are being jailed. If Fresno is not able to deal with this problem by methods of law and order, it is not fit to deal with it at all and should surrender at once."[60] Since Sheriff McSwain was clearly not bowing down to city police, Rowell suggested building a temporary jail facility. Rowell believed that the city had time and that the Portland Wobblies would have to wait for spring's snowmelt to burst through the mountain pass.

While the Fresno Citizens' Committee met with Senator George W. Cartwright, recently arrived from Sacramento, to discuss a potential bill that would deny the right of trial by jury to parties accused of city ordinance violations, Sheriff McSwain made plans to move his overcrowded prisoners into the stockade. The granite pile would have to be moved to the railroad yard. To alleviate crowding during the day, prisoners would begin work on public projects, keeping streets, alleys, and draining ditches clean. Not surprisingly, on February 28, the IWWs refused to employ a shovel or broom on Fresno streets. They claimed that by working on the streets, an established precedent would be set wherein other convicted IWWs would be put to work beside them, and in the end many laborers would be forced out of employment. They did, however, agree to work the rock pile as it was "non-competitive."[61] The stockade was soon crowded with men chipping happily away at rocks. But the jail and its stockade would not be able to handle the hundreds of men about to invade Fresno.

An expedited meeting that evening between the special Citizens' Committee and Frank's IWW committee brokered an agreement that finally achieved what the IWWs wanted—free speech on Fresno streets. In return, nonresident Wobblies would leave Fresno, and the IWWs would curb new arrivals.[62] The great Fresno Free Speech Fight, which residents would call merely a "skirmish," was finally about to end. The same day, February 28, 1911, Emma Little gave birth to a baby girl. She named her Victoria—victory was theirs, after all.[63]

Sheriff McSwain began to liberate all 174 prisoners, releasing them in small groups so that they could find a willing boxcar to transport them out of Fresno once and for all. Many took pieces of the rock pile with them as souvenirs for friends and family.[64]

Frank was sitting in jail four days later on Sunday morning, March 5, along with the last four men waiting to be released.[65] He would be the last man to walk out. On March 6, about 261 miles to the north, Portland's "Fresno Brigade" trudged into Chico, California, where they finally disbanded after receiving a "royal welcome." Since conceiving the idea of the journey a month earlier, the majority of 113 men had walked almost 670 miles.[66]

The same day a cleaning crew assigned to erase all vestiges of the Fresno Free Speech Fight entered the infamous bull pen. While they expected to find human debris that typically accompanies crowded conditions, what they espied was quite extraordinary, a reminder of what the conflict had been fought over. Jack Murdock had drawn artful caricatures of city and national officials, using every bit of available space with the exception of the west wall. Chiseled into the brick-and-mortar west wall was the "Preamble to the Industrial Workers of the World Constitution."[67]

A local Fresno minister explained to his captive congregation what IWWs had tried to express to employers:

> We have not made an unwarranted distinction between labor with hands and labor with brains, that somehow it is more respectable, more high-toned, to work with one's brain than with one's hands. Manual labor is under a ban. I think we need to be reminded that our Christ was a carpenter. My contention is that these people, in view of all these things—and others which might be mentioned—have a cause.[68]

The Fresno Free Speech Fight is clearly Frank Little's defining chapter; his murder, the denouement of a remarkable life. He had proven his leadership to the IWW body, although this was certainly not his goal. His contribution? He had inspired a nonviolent approach to protest, encouraging hardy, weather-beaten faces to hold fast, despite receiving cruel treatment, inadequate food, and an absence of basic needs in an ancient jail. To many, the IWW had found recognition as an organization dedicated to preserving a basic principle of American democracy—the freedom to speak one's beliefs without fear of reprisal.

To others, it was a dangerous body bent on destroying the American way.

15

Hallelujah! I'm a Bum!

Trying to keep a straight face as he addressed the workingmen below the dais, IWW general secretary-treasurer Vincent St. John delivered a fine eulogy to a song about to be removed from the newest edition of *The Little Red Song Book*. But his rowdy audience, doubled over in laughter, were not about to bury the song they had sung at the top of their lungs. Sung to the tune of the popular hymn "Revive Us Again," the song "Hallelujah! I'm A Bum!" was more than a marching refrain—it was a proud acceptance of America's most recent identification of the Wobblies.

> Why don't you work like other folks do?
> How the hell can I work when there's no work to do?
> *Refrain*
> Hallelujah, I'm a bum,
> Hallelujah, bum again,
> Hallelujah, give us a handout
> To revive us again.

The twenty-four delegates in attendance at the ten-day Sixth Annual IWW Convention, beginning September 18, 1911, promptly amended the motion. "Hallelujah! I'm A Bum!" would remain in the songbook.[1]

The convention had commenced in the Schweitzer-Turner Hall, formerly Uhlich Hall, in Chicago. The hall had been the birthplace of the American Labor Union, and Chicago, an aged, industrial city of skyscrapers, made an appropriate setting for the industrial union's annual meeting. The conference was Frank Little's first as an IWW delegate, like many other attending "live wires," mostly young men unfazed by the typewriters, adding machines, and mimeograph machines required during committee work after hours.[2]

The city must have been eye-opening for the Oklahoma country boy. Aside from San Francisco, Chicago was the largest city Frank had ever visited, with its marriage of time-worn and contemporary architecture, cutting-edge transit systems, and progressive industries. Immediately south of the hall was the Chicago River, congested with all species of water crafts and traversed by the Clark Street Bridge. The old steel swing bridge transported green-and-yellow streetcars, horse-drawn wagons, and newfangled automobiles to "the Loop," the city's commercial core. West of Clark Street, bridge after bridge stacked like crooked ladder rungs across the fouled waters, while to the east more bridges obscured the murky river as it poured into Lake Michigan.

American poet Carl Sandburg, himself a bum years earlier, would describe Clark Street Bridge and its evening cessation of busy street rhythms, "dust of the feet and dust of the wheels" resulting from "voices of dollars and drops of blood."[3] His verses lamented Chicago's industrialist practices that spawned violent strikes, partisan press, and corrupt city officials. In this great industrial city, not all labor organizations were appreciated, although the Chamber of Commerce had wished the IWW convention "success in every respect."[4] The message brought roars of laughter from those who knew the Windy City's blustering politicians and blood-spattered episodes. To honor that history, they recessed Wednesday, September 26, to respect an event hallowed in all American labor unions: the upcoming anniversary of the 1887 Haymarket executions.

The delegates loaded into two "L" cars to make the long journey to Waldheim Cemetery. There they quietly paid tribute to the Haymarket martyrs, men who had been attacked at the end of a peaceful rally for an eight-hour day, indicted for murder when a bomb exploded amid the mob, and unjustly convicted by a meticulously constructed jury. They considered August Spies's "prophetic utterance" before he was hanged, the words inscribed on a grand monument commemorating the lost labor leaders: "The day will come when our silence will be more powerful than the voices you strangle today."[5] Frank had joined the others as they sang revolutionary songs during the outbound trip, but silence reigned on the return.[6] The reminder of the inherent danger in fighting for workingmen's rights could not have been more profound.

Yet Frank's star had just risen. The next day, September 27, 1911, he was elected to the General Executive Board (GEB) of the IWW. Frank had shown himself to be a staunch supporter of centralized leadership, a cool head among young men who had come "with war in their eyes."[7] Most importantly, he had proven himself to be a strong representative for the western states, and he was absolutely fearless.

With the Fresno Free Speech Fight, the first quarter of 1911 had begun an eventful year in American labor history. It ended when a sobering industrial accident elevated American ire. On March 25, 1911, fire broke out in the Triangle Shirtwaist Factory in Manhattan, New York. Panicked garment workers, many of them young girls, found all the stairwell doorways on upper floors locked on orders of the owners, who did not want workers to take unauthorized breaks. One hundred forty-six workers died from burns, smoke inhalation, and jumps from the towering Asch Building.[8] Labor unrest swiftly followed.

While the public digested the Triangle catastrophe, Frank remained in Fresno to direct Local 66. Local street-speaking presently offered no challenges, so he could spend time with his family, mending his thirty-three-year-old body while participating in inoffensive activities. Frank first embarked on a mild crusade, challenging the SPA in an effort to propagandize the differences between the political party and the industrial union. To celebrate the April opening of a new IWW hall, this time at 917 L Street, Local 66 invited SPA ex-organizer Wood Hubbard to debate Frank Little. The topic was "Resolved, that political and industrial action are efficient in the emancipation of the working class."[9] Frank took the negative, arguing that political action was a detriment to the working class. Hubbard offered a strong argument for the use of both approaches, despite the fact that the Fresno SPA had dismissed IWW members, including Fred Little, for using direct action.[10] In the crowded hall, audience members applauded loudly whenever one of the speakers scored a point. Jack Whyte reported to *Solidarity* that the debate "was of great educational value"—exactly what Frank had wanted to accomplish.[11] Now well-attended street meetings were held twice a week, and the IWW reading room was open twenty-four hours a day.[12] Yet the chasm continued to widen nationally between the two groups as more prominent IWW leaders left SPA membership.[13] The central issue was that, with more labor leaders getting thrown into jail without due process, the SPA still refused to endorse a general strike for their release.

Then two AFL steelworkers were arrested in April 1911, accused of what the *Los Angeles Times* called the greatest "crime of the century."[14] Brothers John J. and James B. McNamara had entangled themselves in the October 1, 1910 bombing of the Los Angeles Times building. Prior to the sensational crime, newspaper owner-mogul Harrison Gray Otis had antagonized organized labor in southern California for weeks, using his newspaper to whip up hysteria against immigrant labor and AFL unionization. When Socialists and unionists began to soapbox together on Los Angeles's streets, Otis helped form the Merchants and Manufacturers Association (M&M) to support his anti-union campaign. The M&M conspired with city officials to ban free speech on Los Angeles streets, antagonizing the AFL. Now Otis's building had been destroyed and an after-hours staff trying to meet a late deadline had been killed. All fingers pointed to the local structural ironworkers' union.

Despite their differences, the SPA and IWW joined the AFL's Samuel Gompers in supporting the McNamaras' innocence, rallying for the workers and due process.[15] The McNamara trial consumed almost the entire year of 1911 until the brothers unexpectedly admitted guilt in December. As a result, the *Times* convincingly presented the McNamaras as anarchists rather than the trade unionists they were, casting negative aspersions over all radical movements. Clarence Darrow, who had defended the McNamaras, was nearly ruined. Many IWWs, who still believed the McNamaras were innocent, claimed betrayal.[16]

After the Times Building bombing and Triangle Shirtwaist Factory fire, public outcry forced Congress to create a new federal commission on industrial relations that would investigate labor conditions in America's principal industries, especially those in corporate forms. During the three-year investigation, the commission investigated the Illinois Central and Harriman Railroad Lines conflict of 1911–13, where armed guards and strike-breakers clashed with shop men (machinists) striking for higher wages and improved working conditions; a 1913 IWW-led strike in a silk mill in Paterson, New Jersey, where workers were fined fifty cents if they laughed or talked during a workday; Colorado's 1914 Ludlow Massacre, where innocents died amid Gatling gunfire during a Rockefeller-owned Colorado Fuel and Iron Company strike; and of course, the western free speech fights, where the commission discovered that Californian migrant laborers worked in temperatures upward of 105 degrees as growers refused to supply water, and that Pacific Northwest lumber workers labored ten hours a day for twenty cents an hour.[17] Now the Justice Department, which had generally ignored state and local complaints about free speech fighters crossing state lines to arrive at new protest sites, had also started to take notice.

Recent IWW activities in Fresno and soon-to-be-deadly San Diego alarmed *Times* owner Harrison Gray Otis, who had connections in the Taft administration.[18] Amid rumors that Wobblies were crossing international boundaries to assist Mexican and Canadian workingmen who labored under American interests, Otis promptly combatted unionists and socialists, this time with federal support. With his son-in-law Harry Chandler, Otis owned thousands of ranchland acres in Baja California under the California-Mexico Land and Cattle Company. Many American capitalist giants, including Guggenheim, Rockefeller, Morgan, and Hearst, had joined Otis in unfettered control of Mexican acres, railroads, factories, and mines,

operating their interests with Mexican labor. If industrial unionists and Socialists interrupted the supply of cheap labor, both the
capitalists and beleaguered Mexican president Porfirio Díaz would
lose profits.

When questioned as to their intentions after the Fresno Free
Speech Fight, Frank and other IWWs denied they would join the
trek to Mexico to aid followers of Ricardo Flores Magón and the
PLM in what would become an absurd attempt at carving out a piece
of Mexico for a socialist utopia. Yet the liberation of Tijuana from
Díaz's control on May 9, 1911, resulted in heightened federal awareness of IWW anarchism. Among the Tijuana victors were IWW
rebels and other filibusterers, mainly soldiers of fortune, former
military veterans, con men, and common adventurers.[19] As IWW
Joe Hill said, "As long as the red flag flew in Baja California, as much
as I tried, I could not find a single 'important person' in the revolutionary ranks. I only found, in great numbers, ordinary everyday
workers."[20] Unfortunately for the Magonistas, three other revolutionary leaders with stronger native support also promoted their
own version of Tierra y Libertad! Emilio Zapata, Pancho Villa, and
their campesino liberation army rose in revolt, initially aiding presidential challenger Francisco Madero.[21] The Maderistas would ultimately win after La Vieja Bestia, the old beast Porfirio Díaz, resigned
in ignominy May 25, 1911. On June 22, the Liberales lost the second
battle of Tijuana against newly organized Mexican federal forces
under Madero. The ragtag Magonistas broke and ran for the border
where U.S. soldiers waited to arrest the anarchists. After raising
social consciousness of the plight of the Mexican peon under Porfirio Díaz, Magón and his brother Enrique were tried, found guilty,
and jailed for breaking neutrality laws.[22]

Some historians have suggested that both Frank and Fred Little
actively assisted the Magonistas in their crusade against Díaz.
However, their names do not appear in any eyewitness accounts or
reports. With his strained marriage and new baby, Fred would not
have left Fresno for any lengthy campaign.[23] As for Frank, he likely
ventured south to evaluate an emerging free speech fight amid
the McNamara fiasco in Los Angeles and also may have joined

spectators and tourists in the first Tijuana battle's circus-like aftermath.[24] He certainly could have assisted PLM organization in San Diego. However, by June 1, 1911, Frank was definitely not in Mexico, as proven by a 1955 interview with Wobbly Sam Murray, who had participated in the second Tijuana battle. While Murray definitively placed himself and his close friend Joe Hill in Tijuana in early June, both lugging ancient 30.30 rifles and wearing bandoliers slung across their shoulders, he never made mention of Frank participating in the battle or even arriving in Tijuana. Murray was one of the men arrested at the border, while Hill slipped back into the United States unscathed after the final battle on June 22.[25] The *Industrial Worker* also continuously ran eyewitness accounts from its members in Tijuana, including one letter that described Tijuana as a utopia where no one was arrested for vagrancy for not working; a direct reference, perhaps, to Fresno police chief Shaw.[26] Although the Magóns, along with Los Angeles and San Diego IWW leaders, appear to have strategized PLM operations from across their chess board on American soil, Frank's name was never mentioned in connection with the Mexican Revolution among the many reports to the *Worker*. He appears to have been an interested bystander amid the simultaneous conflicts in Tijuana, San Diego, and Los Angeles. One must also consider Frank's propensity for the courtroom rather than the battlefield. Collectively the McNamaras' trial, Harrison Gray Otis's *Times* editorial hysteria, the aborted Baja social revolution, and the arrests and trial of the Magón brothers ominously contributed to heightened tension in southern California.

The year had other injustices to address and, just after the IWW convention ended in Chicago on September 28, Frank found himself facilitating the next fighting match for workingmen. The free speech movement bled eastward to Kansas City, Missouri, when a workingman was arrested for blocking a sidewalk during a curbside speech. Leaving Fred again as Fresno's Local 66 secretary, Frank and fellow GEB member Thomas Halcro left Chicago, dodging railroad detectives to hop on boxcars for Kansas City. Rivaling Chicago in commercial and progressive enterprises, Kansas City was about

one-sixth Chicago's size in 1911. Built on a great bluff overlooking
the confluence of the Kansas and Missouri Rivers, the city served as
a busy railway center and river port where stockyards, meatpack-
ing centers, and grain markets supplied American pantries. It, too,
was ripe for industrial unionization with about 20 percent of the
population composed of African Americans and immigrants who
were typically barred from traditional union membership.[27] Now
Kansas City authorities met any civil disobedience with suspicion
and punishment. Echoing Chicago's police and business leaders' fears
of labor leaders, the city's police had begun to harass industrial-
union-organizing IWWs the previous March.[28]

On the afternoon of Saturday, October 14, Kansas City's Main
Street was a mass of buggies and automobiles, with street cars in
the center of its stretched brick-paved face. An aerial mesh of wires
crisscrossed above harassed pedestrians darting beneath a laundry
line of awnings linking store fronts. Blue-jacketed mounted officers
and Bobby-helmeted traffic police attempted to control the melee
of man, beast, and machine. The setting was too choked to tolerate
any provocative interruption, and any unusual commotion would
clog traffic flow and block sidewalks, aggravating police and business owners. Frank Little had been in midsentence at an open-air
street meeting on the corner of Sixth and Main Streets when police
officers arrested him, along with six other men, on charges of
obstructing sidewalks.[29] Afterward a barber named Miller was
named as the single complainant.[30] When bystanders crowded the
speakers and police, officers asked for IWW leaders to identify themselves. They retorted that there were no leaders, as being an IWW
was leader enough.[31] At this point the police began to arrest anyone
who identified himself as an IWW while they wove among the
entertained audience in the street.

Two days later, in the Honorable Clarence A. Burney's court,
a businessman waved a copy of "Appeal to Wage Workers" in front
of court watchers, convinced that the pamphlet was ample proof
of disturbing the peace on city streets. Frank asked to be recognized by the court, and despite the judge's warning that he did not
want to hear any "stump speeches," Frank expounded the purpose
for IWW organization and his desire to be tried in a jury trial in a

"real" and not a "kangaroo" court. Ignoring the reference, Judge
Burney suddenly stopped Frank midsentence and read a section of
the pamphlet: "If demands are not granted, turn out poor work, or
slow work so as to decrease profits until the employer will be made
to understand that he will gain most by granting the demands."[32]
Frank continued his oration at which point Burney censored him,
stating, "You are fined $25 and the rest $10 each!"[33] After the men
were led off to jail, a delegation from Local 61 met with the court,
warning of a free speech fight. Reconsidering the recent arrests,
Judge Burning released everyone but Frank, who was given twenty-
five days.[34]

With Frank's arrest, the Kansas City Free Speech Fight officially
began, and city officials responded much like their Fresno counterparts. Police Chief Wentworth E. Griffin presented a history
of the IWW to city commissioners on October 18, declaring that
the organization opposed "capital, labor, law, order, the church, the
Bible, and the dove of peace."[35] He forecast terrible consequences
of Biblical proportion if the IWW continued to speak, blocking
sidewalks and streets. But local authorities also recognized that
they had a prominent union leader in their custody. Local newspapers reported detailed narratives of the Fresno Free Speech Fight,
and Missoula and Spokane authorities had wired dire warnings to
city officials. Frank spent the entire free speech fight isolated in
Leeds Farm, a workhouse ten miles east of town, which housed
common criminals, dope fiends, and alcoholics. Authorities believed
that if Frank were sequestered, they could curb the fight more easily.
But Frank's arrest ignited IWWs across the country, sending in a
steady supply of Wobbly agitators straight to Kansas City.[36] While
Frank languished at Leeds, the free speech fight prospered as fellow
Wobblies endeavored to join him.

Leeds Farm would place a heavy toll on Frank in the brief time
he was incarcerated. Originally built in 1911 to relieve overcrowding
in the city's aged, castle-like workhouse, Leeds Municipal Farm was
soon redesigned to be a reformatory, where prisoners would learn
skills to use upon their release. Yet its early history reads more
like a movie-thriller plot. Dr. E. W. Cavaness, the prison superintendent, commonly administered belladonna, a highly poisonous

plant derivative, as a purgative cure. Patients frequently died. Others
reported that Cavaness was a sadist "who seemed to enjoy inflict-
ing pain" and whose care was "absolutely brutal."[37] But Cavaness
was influential and active in civic organizations, contributing to
his tenure at Leeds Farm. Eventually the good doctor would resign
his position after an extensive record of deaths, high recidivism,
and general mistreatment of prisoners. Despite new minister-
superintendent Jesse O. Stutsman's progressive administration
in late 1913 and early 1914, any earnest attempts at rehabilita-
tion utterly failed.

Frank was escorted from Jackson County Courthouse to Leeds
Municipal Farm in the early morning Tuesday, October 17, 1911.[38]
The institution's 125 acres of hills, bluffs, and heavily wooded
ravines contained barely 12 acres of tillable land, but the bluffs
provided plenty of rock for prisoners to hammer.[39] Built by prisoners,
the main building was 50 by 150 feet with a wing measuring 45
by 100 feet. About a mile west, a recently established potter's field
doubled as the cemetery for Leeds Farm, including those who died
from Dr. Cavaness's experimental "cures."[40] Upon his arrival, Frank
was stripped, weighed and measured, and medically evaluated. As
subsequent events would reveal, Frank was not healthy upon his
arrival to Kansas City. Although his incarceration at Leeds Farm was
brief when compared to his Spokane and Fresno confinements, his
condition deteriorated quickly.

Frank's clothes were sent out for fumigation and laundering
while he dressed in prison garb and prepared for his placement. Yet
he did not join the other inmates, who were convicted mostly of
misdemeanors and were there to work off their sentences. After
evaluation, a new inmate was typically assigned to a work area,
such as building roads, crushing stone, mowing weeds, planting
vegetables, or working on new construction projects within the
prison. Yet Frank and the Wobblies who later joined him were
singled out for harsh, solitary work assignments. No plans to reform
Wobblies existed, nor were they slated to learn new job skills.
Mayor Darius A. Brown's goals were to get Wobblies off Kansas City
streets and for word to get out describing how punitive Leeds Municipal Farm could be. A separate rock pile was established for IWWs

away from the general population. That way, they could "agitate among themselves" since there was "altogether too fertile a field to work" if turned loose on the farm.[41] Following the Spokane model, anyone who refused to work was punished with a diet of bread and water in "the hole," a basement consisting of three dark cells.[42] Frank's friend and fellow Wobbly Grover Perry claimed that no man was ever put on bread and water during the first Kansas City Free Speech Fight.[43] No one refused the rock pile but many, if not all, worked, at a snail's pace. One week after Frank's arrival, twenty-three other Wobblies filled the segregated section, working for fifty cents a day toward their fines.[44]

Escapes were common with an average of four men walking out of the facility daily. With just 15 to 20 guards for 240 prisoners, guards were neither able nor especially willing to be diligent in their duties.[45] But none of the IWWs attempted escape. Instead, the *Industrial Worker* proclaimed an IWW banner shouting "The Free Speech Fight Is On in Kansas City. On to Kansas City!"[46] To further exacerbate Police Chief Griffin's worries, the IWW promised that one thousand Wobblies would arrive in time for Thanksgiving dinner at Leeds Farm.[47] Meanwhile, Kansas City's Board of Public Welfare began to walk back its strategy of incarcerating Wobblies at Leeds. In a *Kansas City Star* report just days before, on October 24, a journalist noted the IWW "peculiarity" of using passive resistance in order to obtain their rights as well as their denunciation of violence.[48] These hoboes were not violent criminals, drug addicts, or alcoholics—and their numbers were growing.

By October 26, police began taking pamphlets thrust into their hands at street meetings, instead of manhandling street orators to jail. When the police actually read "Bulletin No. 1," they found it to be a "disappointing document" that set forth the rights of workingmen to free speech and cited the struggles of the IWW in other cities. Nothing anarchistic or inflammatory filled its paragraphs.[49] Two days later the Board of Public Welfare officially pressed Police Chief Griffin to stop all IWW arrests. While IWW civil disobedience galled Griffin and Judge Burney, who fundamentally disagreed with the board, future IWW participation promised to become too overwhelming.[50] On Sunday, October 29, IWW leaders, attempting to

gain permission to visit the Wobblies at Leeds, held an impromptu
meeting with the public welfare board and police. The three-hour
conference resulted in a deal struck that let everyone save face.[51]
As the *Star* reported, it had begun "to look as if there wouldn't
be hammers enough in Kansas City to equip all the IWW members
for stone breaking and the prospect of finding a building big enough
to hold them appeared hopeless. And, anyhow, maybe the speeches
weren't so bad."[52] That same afternoon, IWW GEB member Tom
Halcro carried parole applications to the municipal farm. Everyone, including Frank, agreed to the terms within. Every resident
IWW could speak on any street corner in Kansas City without secur-
ing a permit of any kind as long as the meeting did not "endanger
the life and limb of passersby" and nearby property owners raised
no valid objections. Out-of-town Wobblies agreed to leave Kansas
City immediately.[53]

On a mild Halloween day, the Board of Public Welfare examined Frank, questioning his consent to being paroled. Would he
leave Kansas City? Satisfied with his assurances, a board representative released Frank to the city where Police Chief Griffin formally
approved Frank's parole on Wednesday, November 1, 1911.[54] Early
the next morning Frank received his washed clothes. Had he been
a typical prisoner, he would have also received a small cash stipend,
but IWWs were not normal prisoners. Instead, twenty scruffy prisoners were escorted to Kansas City where a celebratory feast at IWW
headquarters awaited them.[55] The 1911 Kansas City Free Speech
Fight, the first easterly free speech fight of any importance, was
officially won.[56] The peace would not last, and Frank would return
to Kansas City two years later.

About November 3, 1911, Frank left town, but he did not return
to Fresno or Chicago. While some Wobblies likely returned to the
peripatetic nature of hobo-hood, Frank went home to Oklahoma's
familiar red dirt and his mother, Almira. Frank was sick.

16

SAN DIEGO, 1912

Sometime after 1908, Almira Little Cox returned home to care
for her semi-invalid husband. Since 1885, Elihu had collected a
fourteen-dollar-a-month disability pension from injuries sustained
in the Civil War.[1] Despite his disability, local newspapers reveal
that he participated in civic organizations, preached at camp meetings, and even planned an upcoming reunion for his fellow Indiana
veterans.[2] Elihu certainly had been sound in mind and body when
he participated in the 1889 Land Run, staking a homestead in Logan
County where he would run hundreds of horses, and when he purchased a house and multiple lots in Guthrie and Caddo County.[3]
The day after Frank Little left Kansas City for Oklahoma, Elihu
had speculated in an Old Soldiers' Colony near present-day Panama
Beach, Florida, where he purchased three lots from St. Andrews
Bay Development Company, and had hocked the original home-
stead to make these investments.[4] A year later, though, he and
Almira would lose everything to foreclosure except the Guthrie
house and the Florida lots.[5] But apparently Elihu H. Cox had no
plans to squeeze money from his stepson, as he had in 1904, when
Frank finally arrived at his mother's small Guthrie bungalow early
November 1911.[6]

No exact diagnosis has been given for Frank's illness in late 1911 and early 1912, although his contemporaries speculated that he suffered from rheumatism. Most likely Frank was feeling the effects of his life's work, its adrenaline rush no longer sustaining the demanding work schedule. By the time he looked to his mother for care, he likely had a chronic bronchial infection or perhaps pneumonia, writing that he had "been sick for some time."[7] Whatever his exact affliction, Almira had her youngest son home for over two months as Frank recuperated in a soft bed and ate home-cooked meals. Whether Elihu took issue with the living situation is unknown but interfering between a mother and her son clearly was not in his best interest. The two men surely had economic and political differences that may have caused heated discussions—especially when Frank began planning IWW organization from his sick room.[8]

As his health improved, Frank began to tour other farming communities and industrial areas, including Oklahoma City, where he attempted to build a new local.[9] The Mid-Continent oil field was expanding, and recently oil had been discovered in an enormous pool extending beneath Porter Little's homestead, about seventy miles northeast of the Cox home. Frank, however, focused on the Oklahoma farming conditions that affected his immediate family members. The Littles toiled on their farms like other original eighty-niners who had struggled since the Panic of 1907, with the exception of Uncle Port, who now reaped oil-lease dollars directly from the Lauderdale oil field discovery. Though open to ideas of cooperative farming, most of these small farmers had no desire to establish an agricultural commonwealth, despite a strong local Socialist presence. Like Frank, many of them no longer trusted politicians.

Frank had wasted no time in surveying Logan County farmers, including his brother-in-law Charles Courtright and brother Lon Little in Payne County, about drought conditions and their paltry cotton crops. Just before Thanksgiving 1911, Frank also met with other "small fry" farmers who wanted to join the IWW.[10] This was dangerous since politics and oil were dramatically transforming Oklahoma's ruddy face. Wobbly and *Voice of the People* editor Covington Hall recalled that many of these meetings occurred in the moonlight with armed "worker guards" watching over Frank as he questioned members of various SPA locals.[11] With wintry breaths, disgruntled farmers reported their current frustrations to the newly elected IWW executive, and Frank grasped that Oklahoma was now a prime example of corporate-created misery. Bankers, credit-store merchants, loan sharks, and lawyers controlled state economics and the political machinery, and the exploitation of eighty-niners had created a serfdom of tenant farmers. In 1900, tenants operated 47,250 of 108,000 farms.[12] By 1910, 125,308 of 190,192 farm operators rented their farms, including Charles and Bessie Little Courtright in Elm Grove Township.[13] Of the remaining 64,884 farms, 36,036 were mortgaged, including Lon and Ella Evans Little's farm.[14] By 1915, when the IWW finally organized and implemented an agricultural branch, 80 percent of the land owners were heavily mortgaged, and twenty-three years after thousands of claims were given away, 68 percent of the farm population in 47 counties were still tenant farmers.[15]

In a 1917 *International Socialist Review* article, W. E. Reynolds described general conditions of Oklahoma tenant farmers' homes:

These tenants are not only poor but destitute, their "homes" in the great majority of instances being without the simplest and generally considered, necessary conveniences. They have no cooking ranges, no sinks, no kitchen appliances (often no kitchen to put them in), no linoleum, no carpets, not enough dishes to set the table for the family. Their furniture is of the most rudimentary kind, boxes and benches doing duty in the absence of chairs. A bathtub is a luxury which not one in a thousand may enjoy. Houses without plaster, cracks you can kick one of the dogs through, floors uneven or missing, cardboard or rags doing duty for missing window panes, outbuildings dilapidated or absent;— this is not a description of an exceptional case, but of the average tenant's home in Oklahoma.[16]

When Frank explained to the farmers that only wage workers were eligible to join the IWW, they were profoundly disappointed.[17] Yet they promised to help him organize small meetings with others in the future.[18] He promptly reported the meetings to *Solidarity*.

While Frank assessed Oklahoma farm workers, Fred and Emma Little received reports of skirmishes between Wobblies pushing for free speech within a newly restricted forty-nine-block district in San Diego and an army of law enforcement and rabid vigilantes. IWWs had flooded into the city to help organize mill, lumber, and laundry workers, streetcar conductors, and motormen, many of whom were unskilled immigrants and women excluded from the AFL. Following his friend Harrison Gray Otis's model, John D. Spreckels, a sugar baron who owned a streetcar monopoly and various public utilities, had pressured the city council to pass the ordinance against the Wobblies and other anarchists, socialists, and religious sects. Spreckels still was incensed over the Baha California conflict where he, too, had had plans to expand his business ventures. Other businessmen, particularly realtors who wanted an IWW-free zone, worked with a Spreckels-owned press, to fuel negative public opinion with outlandish stories of anarchism, a bomb-making factory, weapons, and murder plots.[19] All of San Diego's city agencies and the general public were whipped into hysteria, mutually supporting extreme actions against the Wobblies who had journeyed to the city in early 1912. San Diego's citizens were particularly incensed, as their city was competing for federal dollars to host a 1915 international exposition heralding the opening of the Panama Canal. Some feared the radicals would influence the "moral character" of the city, if not cause the exposition to be moved completely.[20] In this tense atmosphere, even a planned, peaceful protest was a risky endeavor.

On January 9, 1912, the California Free Speech League formed, with Socialist attorneys E. E. Kirk and Frank's old Bisbee acquaintance Harry McKee as its leaders. The League organized orderly protests, most notably a February 26 parade that was planned to be two miles long with at least two thousand marching suffragettes and single-taxers, socialists and anarchists, religious groups and atheists, and AFL and IWW members.[21] One day later the Spreckels-owned *San Diego Evening Tribune* gleefully reported that the parade proved disappointing for labor activists as it was scarcely more than three blocks in length.[22] Simultaneously, in Lawrence, Massachusetts, the IWW made national news by organizing a textile factory strike to protest a pay cut, the result of reduced work hours to a fifty-four-hour work week. Between the distorted characterizations of the IWW in San Diego on the West Coast and the larger, successful Lawrence strike, the nation became further acquainted with the IWW, and fair and unfair accusations flew across news wires.

Early spring 1912 also brought familiar stories of overcrowded jails and deportations spreading northward, but when an elderly Wobbly named Michael Hoey died from injuries sustained in the San Diego jail, the IWW railed.[23] Calls went out for aid in San Diego, where Fresno free speech veteran H. Minderman was Local 13 secretary-treasurer. The protests instantaneously turned violent and deadly, prodded by the press and largely ignored by California's governor, Hiram Johnson. The *San Diego Evening Tribune* exemplified this antagonism in its March 4, 1912 editorial: "Hanging is none too good for them [hoboes], and they would be much better dead; for they are absolutely useless in the human economy; they are the waste material of creation and should be drained off into the sewer of oblivion there to rot in cold obstruction like any other excrement."[24] Citizens, wearing small American flags on their breasts, took the words to heart, and bolstered by the press, police, and court system, supported actions that would define the San Diego Free Speech Fight by its brutality.[25]

The most extreme occurrences involved drunken vigilantes, calling themselves "regulators," who beat men off trains and forced them face down in a manure-strewn cattle pen. The vigilantes then clubbed the men's heads and appendages, compelling their victims to run a medieval gauntlet in groups of five. The fifty-foot-long gauntlet was comprised of about one hundred armed regulators who used wagon spokes, axe handles, guns, and whips to cudgel their victims mercilessly after making them kneel and kiss the American flag. The most notorious gauntlet occurred around April 5, 1912, when drunken men wearing constable badges and white handkerchiefs around their left arms beat or broke the bones of approximately

ninety-three men on their way to San Diego. Before dumping the
maimed Wobblies at the county line, the thugs stole their valuables
and money. This group of unfortunates likely included Frank's former traveling pal Chris Hansen and fifty Fresno men. Hansen would
spend months in a hospital recuperating from his injuries.[26]

One week later, a mighty, unsinkable ship named the *RMS
Titanic* overshadowed all news when it slipped beneath the icy
Atlantic waters along with 1,503 souls, the majority of whom were
the poorest passengers trapped in steerage. The resulting debate
concerning consequences of class division had no effect on the
extraordinary abuse meted out to the working-class men and women
in San Diego.

It was the Littles' close friend Jack Whyte who caught Frank's
attention. Whyte had been jailed and bailed out in San Diego by
the time Frank read of his first appeal to aid Local 13 in *Solidarity*
on February 24, 1912, amid the overshadowing stories of the Lawrence textile strike.[27] A month later, Whyte pled again for IWWs
to come to San Diego, where two hundred men and women were
in jail. On March 30, after sixteen IWW men were taken from jail,
beaten, and dumped forty miles away, *Solidarity* reported that men
were now dying and missing.[28] Again Frank returned to California, and moved to a small house on Fairview Avenue near Sutter
Street in Fresno.

Fred and Emma had relocated, this time near Fred's place of
employment on K Street where he now worked as a plumber's assistant.[29] Frank was still in no condition to soapbox himself into jail
or worse, considering the extraordinary punishments of which he
had been hearing. The treachery and abhorrent details of a subsequent attack on anarchist Emma Goldman and her lover confirmed
that his life would have been be in imminent danger if he had participated openly in San Diego. Goldman had arrived at San Diego's
U. S. Grant Hotel in mid-May. She planned to lecture on Henry
Ibsen's play "An Enemy of the People," which describes a town's
corrupt base led by a tyranny of a majority, much like San Diego and
its businessmen-endorsed police who had murdered IWW watchman Joseph Mikolasek one week earlier.[30] Under a ruse, her manager
and partner Dr. Ben Reitman was separated from her, kidnapped,

transported out of town under police escort, and turned over to radical vigilantes. There he was urinated on, violated with a cane, tarred, and covered with sage brush. As if this were not enough, he was forced to run the infamous gauntlet. When he was returned to Goldman, she found "IWW" burned on his buttocks. Neither Reitman nor Goldman was ever a member of the IWW.[31]

After April's vigilante actions but before the Reitman kidnapping, Governor Johnson had finally called for an investigation. Colonel Harris Weinstock, appointed by the governor, began collecting testimony regarding civil rights violations and brutality from all parties.[32] San Diego waited for the investigation to officially approve of its violence.

During this time, Frank shifted from soapboxing to legal counsel. He acted as a perfect courtroom observer for 38 conspiracy cases, including Whyte's, all indictments that even the judge admitted were made by a prejudiced grand jury.[33] Another 141 men confined in jails in the San Diego area also awaited their futures.[34] When one man's trial dragged on for ten days before he was acquitted, Frank and other GEB members ordered Local 13 to put together a special publicity bureau to help raise additional legal funds for those traveling to San Diego to protest.[35]

During the pretrial hearings, no one was off limits from vigilante punishment. *San Diego Herald* editor Abraham R. Sauer, who had reported police atrocities, was kidnapped, mock hanged, censored, and forced to leave San Diego after his printing office was destroyed.[36] Attorney Fred H. Moore, again defending arrested IWW leaders and rank-and-file members, also received death threats.[37] When Moore asked for additional security for those attending court, the judge reportedly "sneered" at him, denying anyone protection.[38] Vigilantes openly approached jurors, warning that if any verdict of "not guilty" was found, all jurymen would be hanged.[39] Wearing an American flag on one's lapel safely identified where a person stood on the issues of restricting anarchists' speech and handling soapbox demagoguery.

When the governor's special commission report was released in mid-May 1912, the city erupted in a fury, denouncing it as a "rump inquiry."[40] Within the report, Investigator Weinstock flatly stated

he had been to Russia once, and "while taking testimony he won-
dered whether he were not now in Russia instead of the alleged land
of the free and home of the brave."[41] He summarized that the vigilantes had indeed "trampled" on the rights of other men and proven
to be "the bitterest enemies of law and order."[42] Weinstock further
affirmed that not one man among the two hundred arrested was
guilty of anything more than a misdemeanor for speaking on the
streets. Not one weapon had been found. Instead, Weinstock noted
that there was a stronger case against the vigilantes than the protesters. San Diego citizens retorted that no outsiders should judge
how they handle the "riffraff and tripe-visaged rascalry of the Industrial Anarchists."[43] The city's district attorney further cried slander
for being accused of ignoring citizens' and law officials' acts of violence against the Wobblies.[44] Under pressure, Governor Johnson
appointed another investigation in order to appease disgruntled
San Diegans.

The conspiracy trials began the first week of July 1912 with
Frank in attendance. He reported that just fourteen men remained
indicted and the rest had been released for lack of evidence, medical conditions, or because they had become weary of their two-
to-three-month jail stay. They had finally entered guilty pleas in
exchange for probation and a fine. Frank wrote:

> What was their crime? The city council passed an obnox-
> ious ordinance prohibiting free speech and assemblage in
> a district that for 30 years or longer had been known as the
> People's Forum. The common people protested in no uncer-
> tain terms, believing as they did that the best method of
> repealing a bad law is to make the officials enforce it. These
> men violated a law that carried as a punishment 30 days in
> the city jail. But instead of being charged with violating
> that ordinance, they were charged with 'conspiracy to vio-
> late such ordinance,' an offense that carried a penalty of one
> year in jail and $4,000 fine. Thus the law was stretched to
> silence the voice of our fellow workers.[45]

The jurors made short work of the defendants and before Frank's
first story could be published in *Solidarity* on August 10, he had

to augment the report. Six men had been found guilty of "conspiring to violate the traffic ordinance," including Jack Whyte and
Harry M. McKee.[46] Frank observed that all the men looked ill,
"without exception."[47] He went on to berate the IWW in general
for not calling attention to the remaining rank and file: nineteen
men charged with attempted murder stemming from the police
raid on the house where night watchman Joseph Mikolasek was
killed. According to Frank, unlike the Lawrence strikers, the San
Diego Wobblies' fame had not "spread across the nation"; hence,
"no special writers" told of "their bravery or their struggles."[48] By
most accounts the police had successfully sold their story of cached
weapons and attempted murder.

One week later, when he was sentenced for conspiracy, Jack
Whyte arose in defiance, declaring:

"To hell with your courts, I know what justice is," for I
have sat in your court room day after day and have seen
members of my class pass before this, the so-called bar of
justice. I have seen you, Judge Sloane, and others of your
kind, send them to prison because they dared to infringe
upon the sacred rights of property. You have become blind
and deaf to the rights of man to pursue life and happiness,
and you have crushed those rights so that the sacred rights
of property should be preserved. Then you tell me to respect
the law. I don't. . . . The prosecutor lied, but I will accept it
as a truth and say again so that you, Judge Sloane, may not
be mistaken as to my attitude: "To hell with your courts;
I know what justice is."[49]

With that, Jack Whyte sat down. Sloane drily remarked, "It is very
certain that free speech is not forbidden in this court, at least."
The judge saw the free speech fight differently, stating, "In this day
and land of initiative, referendum and recall, there is no excuse for
organized disobedience and defiance of the enforcement of law."[50]

On August 12, 1912, for lack of evidence, all prisoners were
released.[51] Attorney Fred H. Moore pronounced the real reason why
the charges were dropped. He declared he had evidence that the
San Diego police perjured themselves to the grand jury, and if the

policemen repeated their stories in court, he promised to expose them. Some of the liberated prisoners would yet encounter harsh acts of retribution. Jack Whyte was shot in the back while he was sitting down to dinner in a boarding house a little over two years later, after continuing his crusade to help labor in Tonopah, Nevada. Emma Goldman later called Jack Whyte "one of the most intelligent IWW boys in California."[52]

What Jack Whyte and other IWWs such as Frank Little had tried to do in San Diego was upset a labor hierarchy, a division that had been crafted and preserved so carefully, by calling attention to simple human rights. In response, the city showed that even the best citizens, unchecked, could retaliate with savagery and rationalize those actions as justice within a country of bystanders. Hysteria and violence, as evidenced in the San Diego free speech fight, could sweep like wildfire across the United States with the right fuel.

17

MIDWEST FOLLY

Bundled in their summer coats against a cool damp breeze, two men walked along a dock while ignoring railroad detectives' stares. The distant bellows of "Lakers," Lake Superior freighters, mingled with workingmen's shouts and hollow metallic and wooden clanging—early-morning sounds of Duluth's industrial center, the Mesabi ore docks. Across Superior Bay the mammoth railway system spread like fingers on a robotic hand, their jointed, rusty-colored bones crisscrossing underneath Duluth, Missabe and Northern Railroad's (DM&N's) platforms. Ore jennies, vat-shaped cars full of iron ore, queued for discharge and obscured the tracks beneath them. On the sides of the docks, mouths of giant chutes fed cargo into the enormous red-white-and-black freighters floating below. Just a few miles to the southeast, at the entrance to the bay, a similar scene repeated at the Allouez docks in Duluth's sister city, Superior, where Great Northern's day shift was beginning with few men on the job.[1]

Walking with one hand in his coat pocket, Frank Little was in deep discussion with James P. Cannon. Keeping a wary eye, the men walked directly past the gunmen employed by the railroad and mining companies whose ore was being loaded into the ships' holds. Day workers stood atop ore-laden cars while a few picketing strikers occasionally yelled out to the two men from a safe distance. It was a dangerous undertaking, crossing and recrossing company property. Yet Frank had insisted that Cannon accompany him on the walk to show that they were not afraid of these "special police." Besides, Frank had insurance—concealed within his coat pocket, a pistol rested in his hand. Recent setbacks had dictated protection.[2]

Duluth was not a typical setting for a western Wobbly who packed a pistol. The city sits on the lower base of an arrowhead-shaped region known as the Iron Range, which once included the vastly rich Mesabi, Cuyuna, and Vermillion iron-ore ranges. At first glance in 1913, the region appeared predominantly Scandinavian, dotted with Finnish halls, opera houses, and other buildings that housed federations, societies, athletic clubs, and schools. Yet employers had successively introduced other immigrant groups into the Iron Range's labor force, bringing strong Eastern European customs and beliefs. By 1912 over thirty different tongues could be heard in the range's villages and cities, and the diverse ethnic groups had fallen into distinct sociopolitical camps, contributing to prickly labor positions.[3]

First arriving with the Scandinavians were the Irish and Cornish. But after open-pit mining expanded in 1905, other unskilled Finns and eastern and southern European immigrants entered the labor force. The latecomers did the "dirty work" and were often exploited by earlier immigrant mine captains and shift bosses. Subsequently, Catholic Italians, Croatians, Bulgarians, Montenegrins, and Slovenians were brought in as strikebreakers after a contentious 1907 labor dispute.[4] Still the Finns dominated Duluth's and Superior's docks, staking their families permanently to cities and villages, many with mortgaged homes supported by their industrial jobs. Within this setting, Frank began forging a close relationship with immigrant labor, especially the Finns.

This blend of immigration and industry, where U.S. Steel dominated the iron-ore industry, controlling mines, railroads, and barges, created the conditions for labor conflict, including a wide range of sectors.[5] Iron Range miners extracted raw mineral aggregate from mines fortified with timber cut by lumbermen in Minnesota forests. Railway men pulled cars along docks where dock workers unloaded the iron ore. Longshoremen guided tankers alongside these docks to collect cargo for steel mills where factory workers processed the metal. With the stitching up of Great Lakes industries and employees, discontent saturated the narrow strip of land containing the richest iron ore in the Iron Range, running east and west on a high tree-covered Minnesota plateau down to the docks of Lake Superior.[6] Even so, the Great Northern Railway boasted that no strike could occur since men were plentiful and easily replaced.[7]

Agitating for industrial union membership in the Midwest was not as easy as in western states. While the West had been isolated and somewhat unsettled, its labor practices were in flux. This differed from the Midwest, where its labor maladies circulated in a static, hardened system clotted with well-established industrial plants, low pay, long hours, and unsafe conditions. The Mississippi River, its major artery, had guided industrial organization, and its major factories developed on its tributaries to transport products to river barges via rail. These industries typically controlled heartbeats of established communities, where workers were tethered to family homes, community centers, and fraternal organizations. Ralph Chaplin remarked that Frank especially disdained these "mighty" factories, "walking past them with the free-swinging stride of the logger or hard rock miner."[8]

Despite deep-rooted problems in some Midwest industrial centers, Frank Little and other IWWs viewed the region as a fertile ground to grow membership. The calculation was a mistake, and *Solidarity* was first to describe a "Taylorized" Peoria factory's free speech fight as folly.[9] But the lesson was not learned before agitating began in Duluth and Superior during the late summer of 1913. This time, organization would be fraught with ethnic division, kidnapping, and gunplay.

The Minnesota free speech fight had begun during the Peoria strike, just before a GEB special session in late June 1913 in Chicago.[10] Peoria's *Herald-Transcript* had posted a warning to other midwestern cities that their newspapers should be "minutemen

to warn the public of the insidious campaigns of the lawless disturbers."[11] Just days later, both Duluth and Superior's city authorities notified IWWs that they would not tolerate street meetings.
Vincent St. John warned Wobblies they would be met with night-
sticks and arrests for disorderly conduct and conspiracy.[12] The AFL,
which recently had terminated a three-year strike in Duluth, mocked
IWW foolishness for picking up the baton for Great Lakes workers
while the WFM focused on Michigan's copper mines. Still, the GEB
dispatched Frank from Chicago to assist IWW organizers James P.
Cannon and Red Doree, as well as Leo Laukki, a Finnish professor
of languages and former cavalry officer, on Lake Superior's ore docks.[13]

Recognizing the dangers of agitating near the ore docks, most
IWWs traveled in pairs. Yet on the evening of Tuesday, July 14,
1913, Frank was walking alone when he was knocked down from
behind, kicked viciously in the face, and left senseless in a Duluth
street gutter. Frank had been billed to speak to Local 68 at 907 West
Michigan Street later that evening. Strategically located amid bars
and employment agencies, the union hall stood near the railroad
tracks, not far from the docks where the local hoped to capture
migratory workers. Whether special police, railroad detectives,
or neighborhood thugs assaulted Frank is unclear, but the familiar pattern of abuse appeared to be calculated. When he failed to
appear at the event, uneasy committee members began a search
with little success.

The next morning Frank was finally located in a courtroom,
"still in a dazed condition," his face and head "fearfully beaten."[14]
During the late evening or early morning hours, police had discovered him, withheld medical attention, and placed Frank in a
holdover cell typically reserved for drunks. He was considered still
in "serious condition" at the time of the press committee's reporting on July 16.[15]

Meanwhile, IWW organizers continued to push for higher wages
and shorter hours. Dock workers, who earned two dollars daily,
were told they would receive a twenty-five-cent raise in months
to come. The night shift would increase to $2.40.[16] When disgrun-
tled Finnish workers on the Allouez docks demanded that raises

go into effect immediately, they were turned down, and rumblings of a strike filtered among the 1,200 men working on Duluth's Mesabi and Superior's Allouez docks. In response, Duluth newspapers published plans to blacklist Finns, and Great Northern Railway officials in Superior began hiring more Belgians, who "as a rule" were "more tractable."[17] The workers' strike talk stalled.

On July 29, Frank wired *Solidarity* from Duluth asking for men to help organize, this time for a new steel plant hiring both marine workers and miners. Despite his beating, Frank wrote that Duluth was "as good as any place as you can find" for organizing.[18] Police had recently stopped arresting street speakers, according to Frank. While the more moderate "right-wing" SPA clearly stated that it would not back IWW free speech fights, radical "left-wing" Finns, who were also socialists, enthusiastically supported IWW methods.[19]

What had begun as a free speech fight for workers' rights changed quickly on July 31. Workers struck after two ore punchers were crushed to death on the Allouez ore docks in Superior. After opening pockets (doors) under ore jennies' bellies, punchers helped push ore down chutes to freighters waiting below. The men typically stood on the sides of cars or upon piles of ore in the waiting hopper cars, breaking up frozen ore with poles. In this case, the two dead ore punchers and other injured men were thrown down open chutes and covered with ore when a string of rail cars collided with the cars being unloaded.[20] Many considered the Great Northern Railway's carelessness the root cause. Just a month earlier in Two Harbors, Minnesota, three similar accidents had occurred, also raising awareness of corporate negligence.[21]

The morning after the punchers' deaths, Frank spoke to dock workers at the West Superior ball park. He advised striking immediately and submitting their demands to the Great Northern Railway. Following his advice, the workers assembled as the Union of Ore-Dock Workers and decided on three safety demands: that one man from each shift be selected to supervise the switching of the railroad cars on the ore docks; that ore pockets be closed when not in use; and that workers should have the right to enforce the discharge of foremen whom they believed objectionable.[22] No request for higher wages was made at this point. Frank would be in charge of conducting the strike in Superior while James P. Cannon would organize Duluth's ore handlers, who had not struck yet.

Strike committee members and Great Northern's Lake District superintendent C. O. Jenks held a conference on August 6. The meeting did not go well. Previously, the committee had refused to accept the railroad's overtures of a fifteen-cent raise and some safety measures.[23] Now the DM&N dock workers demanded more pay, permission to place a man at each end of the docks to give proper signals for the transmission of trains, and the placement of blue lights on the ends of trains to protect workers. Jenks refused and withdrew the offer completely, announcing that he would import strikebreakers to operate his docks.[24]

Emboldened by the coroner's jury verdict finding Great Northern Railway indirectly responsible for the Allouez dock accident, a solid body of six hundred men struck, including Duluth's dock workers, who walked out in sympathy.[25] Immediately special police, most of them Oliver Mining Company guards imported from the Mesabi Iron Range, deputized by Sheriff John R. Meining, and "paid by the Steel Trust," began arresting and manhandling organizers and strikers.[26]

The afternoon of the mass walkout, Frank concluded a "rousing" speech to striking Allouez dock workers in Superior that the "bosses" did not appreciate.[27] The *Duluth News-Tribune* now reported that company officials blamed a particular IWW agitator for the present situation.[28] Unbeknownst to Frank, two carloads of special police and gunmen shadowed him after he left the strike meeting. About ten o'clock at night, after Frank stepped from the Allouez trolley at the intersection of Belknap Street and Tower Avenue, gunmen accosted him, forced him into an automobile, and covered his mouth. With the muzzle of one gun pressed into his temple and another into his side, he was told he was wanted at the police station.

Moments later at Great Northern Railway's crossing between Superior and Central avenues, the car paused while the other car's gunmen flagged down a passenger train. The train came to a stop as if prearranged. Frank was ordered out of the vehicle and lifted into an extra coach. Three men accompanied him, ignoring his questions about their destination. Instead, they told him that they intended to keep him until the strike was over, even if they had to bury him. No conductor came to collect their fares.[29]

After arriving in Holyoke, Minnesota, about thirty-five miles southwest of Duluth, Frank was taken to a hotel managed by a Swede, Andrew E. Erickson, and locked in a room. The next morning after breakfast, when Frank started to "raise hell on the street," the gunmen told a group of onlookers that they were deputy sheriffs and were holding the prisoner for extradition to Oregon.[30] Then Frank was ordered to get into another automobile, where he was taken to a deserted farmhouse about four miles west of town. The farmhouse was actually no more than an empty, tar-papered shack on the Joseph William Getty farm. Getty, a bricklayer by trade, lived in Duluth. It is no coincidence that Frank was taken to the Getty farmhouse. Among Frank's captors was a leader who stood "about six feet tall in his stockings," no doubt Matt R. Mannheim, a stout Great Northern Railway detective who boarded in the Getty city home.[31]

During the earliest hours of his abduction, Frank apparently had won over his captors in some measure, and they permitted him small freedoms. That Frank's character actually could diminish a hostile environment may be surprising. Yet James P. Cannon recalled Frank Little's time in Peoria's jail, just two months earlier. A seasoned free speech fighter with a wad of tobacco bulging one cheek, Frank's quiet dignity had brought a calming effect on both jail mates and jailers, men who likely viewed Frank with dual suspicion and downright awe.[32] Frank's demeanor contradicts the myths that Cannon also circulated about his Peoria jailing. He hyperbolized Frank's jail time as "double hell," his "wild Indian strain" chafing in jail "like a tiger in a trap."[33] Events at the Getty farmhouse illustrate otherwise. The Wobblies, who were frantic to find Frank, would have been surprised to know that, at the same time they were organizing a search committee, Frank was calmly reading newspaper accounts describing his kidnapping and the strike.[34]

On August 9, too late for newspaper reporting to reach Frank and his kidnappers, a meeting of sympathetic strikers near the

Duluth docks was broken up by fifty Steel Trust police. With the help of city police and deputy sheriffs, they "slugged" Leo Laukki and James P. Cannon when the two attempted to speak.[35] Duluth's mayor and chief of police broadcasted that no more IWW meetings would be permitted and that agitators would be jailed or run out of town.[36]

The news of Frank's kidnapping and the organizers' assault angered but also perplexed many strikers. Simultaneously the DM&N commenced a public relations campaign to win back workers. DM&N president W. A. McGonagle confidently announced that the strike "was at end."[37] Late that evening IWWs were tipped off as to where Frank might have been taken. With only twenty minutes to spare, three members of Local 68 and seven strikers, including Ero Sihto, caught the 11:10 P.M. train to Holyoke. Sihto, a Finnish painter, recalled years later seeing Frank on a picket line in Superior when company guards told Frank he did not belong there and "to get the hell away." In response Frank had responded, "I belong in this world, Mister."[38] The Finnish striker, fascinated with these words, jumped at the opportunity to aid in Frank's liberation. As the rescue unfolded, two newspapermen documented the details. Upon arrival at 12:37 A.M. on August 10, Erick (Gus) Ericson, a Finnish socialist from Portland, Oregon, was selected to lead the ten rescuers to the locale. The men had no time to gather weapons. Instead, they procured a lantern from the station agent and set out to find the deserted farmhouse. After locating Frank, Ericson's strategy was to return to Holyoke and recruit a posse that would surround the Getty farmhouse, arrest the kidnappers peacefully, and gain Frank's freedom.[39] Their plan proved to be both simplistic and flawed.

The morning air was brisk when the men arrived about a mile from the purported location of Frank's prison. The farmhouse sat on eighty acres in a level clearing bordered with Jack pines, scrub cedar, and other lowland brush, providing a blind for the rescuers.[40] After a brief discussion, Ericson and a man named Julius Weller returned to Holyoke to retrieve warrants and a posse while Wobbly W. I. Fisher took charge. Fisher and a scouting party wormed their way through tall grass and brush until they were one hundred yards from the shack. Despite the uncertain light, filtered through the fringe of trees in front of the gray house, they could see the dark huddle of a sleeping guard outside the front door. The men rejoined their group to wait for Ericson and the hoped-for reinforcements.[41] A staff reporter managed to wire the *News-Tribune* that at 2:30 A.M. the men were waiting patiently in front of the farmhouse believed to hold Frank.[42] Meanwhile, the other two rescuers arrived in Holyoke much too early to stir community assistance, and according to the *News-Tribune,* no one even listened to IWW leader Ericson. After waking Judge H. E. McCuskey to request warrants for the offenders, his constable William Sweitzer feigned illness, declaring he was too sick to get out of bed to carry out the warrants.[43]

Only Ericson and Weller returned by 7:15 A.M., Weller having been deputized to replace the ailing constable. Besides search and arrest warrants, Weller also had been provided a .22-caliber pistol.[44] As daylight illuminated the farm, the men quietly advanced three abreast toward the shanty's front door without being detected. Then newly appointed Special Deputy Constable Weller boldly demanded entrance, displaying his search warrant.

The door was opened by a "pale-faced and trembling" gunman, according to one reporter. The rescuers could clearly see Frank, haggard and unshaven, calmly chewing tobacco as he lay on a bed near his scantily clad captors.[45] Armed with Weller's arrest warrant for the gunmen, Gus Fischer declared their intention to place all detectives under arrest. He leveled the .22 on the largest of the group, probably Mannheim, who declared, "You can have Little, but you won't arrest me!"[46] At that moment Frank warily swung his legs over the side of the bed, quietly saying, "Boys, no gun play. Let them go."[47] Fisher covered another detective with a pistol he took from one of the three gunmen inside, just as the leader leveled his own gun back at Gus Ericson and the other rescuers and demanded that the intruders leave immediately. Determining that the detective leader meant business, the men beat a hasty retreat with bullets whistling at their backs. Reporters watched from a safe distance as the detective chased them for nearly one hundred yards, emptying his gun. Just after the pistol's last crack, Frank flew out of the shack for the trees.[48] Miraculously, no one was injured. The victors returned to Holyoke and headed back to Duluth. Fisher kept the pistol he confiscated as a souvenir.[49]

When Frank arrived in Duluth with his rescuers, a "monster" protest meeting at the old armory was already in progress, with three thousand people in attendance.[50] The crowd went wild as Frank made a dramatic appearance on the speaker's platform. Despite his obvious fatigue, Frank recounted his adventure, insisting that he had not been ill-used and had plenty to eat.[51] He said that after learning that agitators were using his kidnapping for propaganda, he did not worry and had settled down to enjoy a much needed vacation at the expense of the Great Northern Railway. Now Frank boldly claimed he intended to increase his strike activity despite the rail company's attempts to remove him.[52] The crowd threw their hats and cheered.

Unfortunately, strikers were not as enthused two days later, when James P. Cannon and Frank crisscrossed Duluth's ore docks to demonstrate that they were not intimidated. IWW bravado was not enough to instill courage into men who feared losing their homes, just as the AFL predicted. McGonagle's claim that the strike was over in Duluth appeared accurate. Picketers reportedly began "laying down on the job," their eagerness waning, perhaps because McGonagle had offered workers who had struck in sympathy their former jobs with no penalty.[53] Great Northern Railway's superintendent Jenks was not so generous after strikers refused to come back to work. The Allouez docks in Superior, where the strike had originally begun, had more men working than before the strike even began.[54] Jenks had awarded permanent jobs to the scabs.

Frank stood in front of a small meeting of Duluth strikers, along with Red Doree and James P. Cannon. Sorely frustrated at the outcome from recent events, Frank tempered his speech when he told Duluth's Mesabi ore-dock strikers, "Stick as long as you can. If you can not win this time, you will win the next strike. If you can not win the next strike, you can win five years later. Stick as long as you can, then go back."[55] One week later Frank stubbornly pushed for ore workers' assistance, though the strike officially had been called off and pickets withdrawn on August 15, "to enable old men who have families here and who own homes to obtain their jobs."[56] He wired *Solidarity*, asking for financial help to carry the strikers who had lost their jobs, writing "A little money spent here will bring great returns in a short time."[57] But men did not "stick," and Frank would be called to another strike three years later in the middle of the Iron Range.

In general, the SPA and AFL rejected Frank's contribution to the strike, dismissing his kidnapping as a public relations stunt and blaming IWW "bummery" for encouraging ore workers to begin a strike they could never win. AFL's *Labor World* reported, "IWW Leader Little claimed to have been kidnaped by special agents of the Great Northern last week. His explanation of the affair sounded so fishy that his henchmen dropped it like a hot potato."[58] The paper condemned the practices of the Steel Trust and Duluth and Superior city governments, as well as the *News-Tribune*'s biased reporting, but also called the IWW "labor pirates."[59] John McNeil, editor of the WFM's *Miner's Magazine*, added his analysis: "Little is well known throughout the West and his story about being kidnaped [*sic*] is merely another fabrication of a brain that has been seriously affected by chronic lying."[60]

Yet demand for safety equipment *was* won when the strike was called off, and IWW historian Fred Thompson later stated that additional concessions obtained in the settlement were spread by Finns to other docks. Despite the folly of challenging the Steel Trust, Thompson reported that as late as 1976, the same safety devices were used on ore docks—surely a contribution to generations of ore workers.[61] As to the veracity of the kidnapping episode, in hindsight no one can doubt that the crime was only the beginning. It was the first of three abductions, each one escalating in violence and brutality, as Frank Little's voice became more strident.

Three weeks later on September 9, 1913, Frank was back in Chicago for the Eighth Annual Convention of the Industrial Workers of the World. Unlike the previous year's large and animated attendance, a contentious debate loomed for the GEB among young, rebellious delegates and the IWW's old guard. A decentralization movement had rapidly spread among young western Wobblies who liked the autonomy of their isolated locals and felt no need for a GEB. To many, the conflict stemmed from the creation of mixed locals where membership of several trades had led to diverse self-serving philosophies and self-governance, and not to the One Big Union's idea of universal organization. To others, the conflict was between western Wobblies, who wanted to break "the discipline that comes from organization," and eastern Wobblies, who valued centralization from having worked in older industrial centers.[62]

To increase delegate participation from every local, the Chicago office issued voluntary mileage stamps to help pay for delegates' trips to the convention. Despite the availability of the stamps, no delegate represented Fresno's Local 66, citing lack of funds and distance.[63] Yet Local 66 notified the convention's delegates that it firmly supported centralization and the GEB. When a resolution for abolishing the GEB finally came to the floor for a vote, it failed with a vote of seventy-six to forty-four with some delegates abstaining.[64] Obviously, Frank had stood with centralization, and his "sound organizational instincts, fortified by wide experience, enabled him to recognize quickly the disintegrating tendencies of the 'decentralization' movement," a factor that James P. Cannon believed was most decisive in defeating the faction.[65] Once again Frank was elected to serve on the GEB, which he had fought to preserve.

While the decentralization-versus-centralization issue characterized the 1913 IWW gathering, a curious photo taken of mostly unidentified people in front of the meeting hall, many with smiles on their faces, captures the conclusion of the convention for two Little family members. Posing in the front row are activists Mary E. Gallagher and Thomas Flynn, Elizabeth Gurley Flynn's father. To Flynn's left is a diminutive young woman, warmly dressed in a homemade overcoat, its velvet lapels partially obscuring a familiar lace collar. On the woman's head, a stylishly feathered satin hat shades her eyes from the afternoon's sunlight. Her left arm cradles a scrunched-up brown paper bag, while her hand clutches a purse and possibly IWW materials. Like the others, she stands frozen, staring into the camera. But Frank, whose profile is featured in

1913 IWW CONVENTION WITH FRANK AND EMMA LITTLE

At the 1913 IWW Convention in Chicago, Frank Little, in profile at left edge of photo, looks toward Emma B. Little, posing second from right in the front row. *Courtesy of the Joseph A. Labadie Collection, University of Michigan.*

the far left of the photo, is leveling his gaze toward the woman: Emma Little.[66]

With Local 66's inability to send a delegate to the convention, Frank had evidently invited Emma to accompany him during the convention. Although she did not serve in any official capacity, Frank must have paid her way, and her relationship as the wife of his brother seems to have allayed any appearances of impropriety.[67]

18

✦ ✦ ✦

DRUMRIGHT, 1914

According to family consensus, Lee Little was a mean man. Perhaps "ornery" is a better descriptor of the brawny young roughneck. In 1914, the eldest son of Lon and Ella Little absconded from Drumright, Oklahoma, leaving his job at the Drumright-Cushing oil and gas field because of a foolish prank. The law, actually a loosely organized group of Drumright citizens, was looking to arrest Lee for damages. But Lee was headed for the state line. Kansas had oil fields too.

Lee's brother Glen occupied his empty hours riding a small white mule, simply called "the jack-ass," close to his parents' boarding house in Drumright. One day, Lee and another fellow caught the normally placid mule and squirted "High Life," a flammable liquid used for fumigation and insect control, under its tail. Even adolescent boys knew that when the turpentine compound was poured on an unfortunate victim, the animal would come to life, illustrating the product's name in a way manufacturers never planned. The mule charged through the mostly tent town of Drumright, barging through a newlywed couple's white tent, and was eventually found twenty miles away in Stroud. By then Lee had made it safely to Kansas. Meanwhile the authorities, such as they were, waited for his return.[1] But Lee was not the only Little in Drumright with a reputation for making trouble. By mid-March 1914, his Uncle Frank had arrived to help unionize the town's oil workers.

Like Colorado and Arizona, Oklahoma had a new boom: oil, the black gold. And like the thousands of miners who created camps in the Colorado gold rush, a new influx of unskilled laborers erected tent cities next to oil fields in the Mid-Continent region of the United States. Their ranks included roustabouts, men with absolutely no skill in the oil drilling business; roughnecks, who worked on drilling crews; pumpers; haulers; pipe layers; and drillers. Wildcatters, speculating on uncertain locations, drilled for their dreams.

Representatives from eastern oil field companies competed for lucrative leases on farms, most of which were owned by original eighty-niners now desperate for cash. In March 1912, wildcatter Tom Slick discovered oil on a 160-acre lease belonging to farmer Frank Wheeler in western Creek County. Without delay other investors competed to seize leases on neighboring farms, resulting in the Drumright-Cushing oil field, the largest oil field in the world at that time. Farmers gained even more wealth when Standard Oil Company began to acquire the oil companies and their leases.

A rush of humanity—single, rowdy, itinerant men—settled close to the field in which they worked. By 1913, the first gushers had blown in and the Drumright-Cushing field was "clotted with shack towns interspersed with clusters of derricks as far as the eye could see," including Drumright.[2] Other small camps honored town planner Aaron Drumright by naming their tent communities after him: Gasright, Dropright, Alright, Justright, and down by the dam on Tiger Creek, Damright.[3] Estimates put the total number of oil derricks surrounding Drumright at the 1915 peak somewhere between 2,500 and 3,000.[4] Lon and Ella Little decided that they, too, would move to Drumright after living the past two years in Yale, a small oil-fed community near their Payne County farm. Drumright offered possibilities of earning much more money than Yale, and their homestead had a mortgage.[5] In the household were Lee and Zora, 21 and 19 respectively, who both worked; 12-year-old Tommie

(Esther) and 6-year-old Glen, who were in school; and 3-year-old Thaylia, the baby.

At fifty-two years old, Lon Little was not a healthy man.[6] An old photograph shows that he was well-built but not tall, with graying light brown hair parted straight on the left, a drooping mustache, pale eyes, and the prominent Little chin. Standing above him is Ella, a stout woman who had purpose. She was determined to support her husband, and her entrepreneurial spirit helped the family survive until Frank's appearance almost thwarted the success of their venture.

The family packed Ella's stove, cookware, and other necessities to make a home and a business after deciding that her talent as an excellent cook might pay off. A family story boasts that American Indian Olympian Jim Thorpe loved Ella's fried chicken so much that he would help himself to more than his share when he visited Zora in Yale.[7] In Drumright, Ella's fried chicken could bring as much as thirty-five cents a plate if she wanted to compete with other cafés.[8] The elder children could work in Drumright: Lee in the oil fields, and Tommie and Zora in Ella's planned boarding house.[9]

The family might have rented one of the shotgun or boxcar houses in which many Drumright citizens lived, but most likely, they moved into a fourteen-by-sixteen-foot tent while Ella opened her boarding house in a shack. The boarding house likely had little more than a roof, walls, and floor. Tables, benches, and chairs were assembled to feed oil field workers with Ella's stove vented out the roof to the rear of the building. Between 1914 and 1917, January and February were so bitterly cold that one citizen described Drumright housing as "colder in the winter and hotter in the summer" than being outside.[10] Yet clients welcomed a warm boarding house, even if it was a shack, since many oil field hovels had cracks almost an inch wide that let in the frigid air.[11]

Glen Little suffered from the move since his opportunities for an education diminished quickly. Traveling to and from school each day was not a safe proposition for a young boy in Drumright, which now housed a strong criminal element. Routinely left to his own means of entertainment, Glen wandered around tents and shacks atop his mule.[12] Family photographs show Glen straddling his white

LON AND ELLA LITTLE
IN DRUMRIGHT, CA. 1914

Lon and Ella Little in
Drumright, Oklahoma,
where Ella's fried chicken
could bring as much as
thirty-five cents a plate.
Little Family Papers.

jackass, a serious look on his face as he posed for a camera behind
a white clapboard house in Drumright. Rarely does he smile in
these early photos.

Despite its primitive conditions, Drumright was conducive to
progressive ideas. The Socialist Party ticket, which currently distanced itself from the IWW, dominated in Drumright elections.
During the first half of 1914, the *Drumright Derrick* had a regular
one-page ad discussing the merits of cooperative farming as seen
in Western Europe. *Derrick* editor H. S. Blair, a Democrat who
extolled the virtues of progressivism, stated that Drumright was
"the greatest city of the Age."[13] Just three years prior, Blair noted,
there had been nothing except farm and ranch grazing land.[14] The
Derrick's glowing report of Drumright aside, the environment was

GLEN LITTLE ON HIS JACKASS
IN DRUMRIGHT

Frank's nephew Glen
Porter Little, shown here ca.
1914 on his white jackass,
witnessed a teamster's
death on Drumright's
muddy main street.
Little Family Papers.

not especially conducive to raising a family. Following a few
respectable families, like the Littles, came fraudulent stock pro-
moters, gamblers, hijackers, and prostitutes.[15] The law arrived
only after saloons, prostitution houses, and gambling halls were
already rooted and thriving. A. W. Rockwell, Drumright's IWW
586 secretary-treasurer, wrote a description of its disorder and
need for union organization:

> Where everybody is money-mad and where life is sacri-
> ficed on the altar of greed, where law, order, and decency is

set at naught, everything that goes to make a hellhole and to deprive a slave of reason, is here. Surface toilets, poor water, alleys one mass of decaying garbage and filth from the overcrowded restaurants, no sanitary arrangements whatever, fully one-third of the people sick with intestinal troubles, fourteen little babies died in one week, bootleggers plying their trade openly, cocaine peddlers, and fiends on every corner, the town full of human vultures known as pimps, lewd women by the hundreds, drunken men by the score, wages low, work the hardest, each slave or crew thriving on their reputation of being able to lay more pipe or drive more rivets than any man or crew in the field. . . . Men, calling themselves human, working hard under almost unbearable conditions, becoming completely covered with oil and forced off the job in a few days through physical exhaustion and without even buying themselves a clean shirt, hunting up a bootlegger or going to the drug store after "Mule," then to the jungles where they sleep off a beastly drunk. In all my travels I have never found a place that needs awakening like this place.[16]

But Drumright *was* booming and the smell of money was in the air, a rotten-egg smell of gas and crude oil. No one minded the oil, mud, and odors. One old-timer is quoted as describing oil fever as something "that gets into a man's nostrils and causes a delightful inebriation, the symptoms tending toward a magnification of wealth lying around loose in the country."[17] By November 27, 1914, the *Derrick* claimed Drumright was a town of ten thousand people, 95 percent of them men trying to get rich.[18] Tent photographers, ready to record the men who came with hopes for prosperity, captured their young, clean-cut faces on staged backdrops. Lee Little and a fellow roustabout appear in a cardboard hot-air balloon flying above an aerial view of Drumright, the card proudly proclaiming "Flying High in Drumright!" Lee was one of many grimy oil field workers in surface-pipe boots, overalls, and swedge-nipple pants, many from out of state, who typically gathered along muddy-plank sidewalks lining Broadway Street, Drumright's main avenue.

FRANK'S NEPHEW LEE LITTLE
AND PAL IN STAGED
DRUMRIGHT BALLOON
Frank's nephew Lee Little,
left, and a fellow roustabout
appear in a cardboard
hot-air balloon flying
above an aerial view of
Drumright, ca. 1914.
Little Family Papers.

Driving a wagon west on Broadway Street in 1914, one's eyes were drawn to black pillars of smoke rising from burning slush pits. Derricks were silhouetted against the sky, steely gray in morning, later emerging from midday's colorless haze to a bright copper, burnished by sooty smoke against a southwestern sunset. However, remarkable skies are not what most folks remember about Drumright. Instead, they remember the dramatic nature of Drumright at ground level. Broadway is the longest uphill-downhill main street in Oklahoma, and the drive east to west across the middle of the community is a roller coaster of hills of varying elevations. Locals call these hills "humps." To make matters worse, Broadway was rife with muddy clays, which churned into deep ruts after summer rains and winter snows. Despite the fifty-foot width of the avenue, navigation was difficult at best. Red mud stuck to a man's boots and pulled at wagon wheels. At least eight hundred horse- or mule-drawn wagons laden with steam boilers, lumber, barrels of oil, and store merchandise pulled through the muck in 1914.[19]

After Tiger Hill, the most famous and last hump on Broadway, a congested single-lane bridge over Tiger Creek transported the visitor near the new Tiger subdivision, a more upscale neighborhood west of town, or southwest toward the oil fields. Bartlesville Street had a famous gambling and prostitution business named after the challenging last hill on Broadway, likewise called The Hump. Further on was an aggregation of tents belonging to oil field workers. For them, "going over the hump" back to their tents was a double entendre. A confluence of growing illegal activities, which some local law enforcement ignored, was a reason for concern.

Oil changed labor in Oklahoma as it outpaced agriculture. However, just as within mining camps, both large and small drilling companies exploited labor. Crews worked seven days a week in shifts, often in hazardous situations, and accidents were common. One could identify a member of a cable crew just by his missing fingers. Lee Little lost his right index finger using a cable tool drill.[20]

Standard Oil Company now owned Prairie Oil Company, which oversaw much of the Drumright-Cushing oil field. To weary workers, Covington Hall's *Voice of the People* reported John D. Rockefeller's belief that "the freedom of the individual to work for whom he pleases and for what he pleases without being hampered by tyrannical labor unions" actually penalized the laborer.[21] In rebuttal, the periodical reported that Drumright teamsters were working from ten to twenty hours a day for $2.25. Roads were so bad that a typical eight-hour trip could take as many as twenty hours. A teamster and the team's owner received a day's pay for each trip regardless of how long the trip actually took. The paper suggested that Standard Oil representatives were not interested in repairing the roads, nor did management seem to appreciate how many horses were killed while hauling unreasonably heavy loads. The cost was all the same to Standard Oil Company: $2.00 for a single teamster,

DRUMRIGHT'S MUDDY MAIN STREET, BROADWAY

At least eight hundred heavily laden wagons pulled through the muck of Drumright's main street, Broadway, in 1914. *Courtesy of the Research Division of the Oklahoma Historical Society.*

and $5.00 for a man and a team each trip.[22] Other exhausted oil
field workers who worked from fourteen to eighteen hours a day
earned small wages, from $2.50 to $3.00 a day, and paid a high cost
of living. Board was reported to be $5.25 a week at oil camps, some
men paying an additional $1.25 a week to stay in Ragtown's room-
ing house, which consisted of two rows of bunks in a tent.[23] In
town, room and board was reported to be $1.00 a day. Teamsters in
grading camps paid a board of $5 to $7 per week.[24] And so, Drumright's new industry was ripe for unionization.

In early 1914, Frank Little had once again been arrested, fined,
and placed in Leeds Municipal Workhouse.[25] After his arrest, and
as part of a press committee release on January 8, Frank wrote an
appeal in *Voice of the People* urging fellow workers to converge
on Kansas City for another free speech fight. He related the poor
conditions in the newly "reformed" workhouse: broken or missing
windows in extreme winter cold, single-blanket beds on concrete
floors, and lack of medical attention. He reiterated that while arrests
of men had been peaceful in general, some men had been beaten
and others were living on bread and water.[26] After burdening the
city's coffers with arrests again, Kansas City authorities agreed to
IWW demands by March 8.

Just before the second free speech fight in Kansas City, the
IWW GEB had ordered organizers to Tulsa and Drumright to mus-
ter the growing labor force. Jack Law was sent to Tulsa, and A. W.
Rockwell and Frank to Drumright.[27] Law helped organize Oil
Workers Industrial Union (OWIU) Local 586 and within a month
had signed one hundred members, mainly pipe liners.[28] Simultaneously, *Voice of the People* urged out-of-work members of the
Louisiana Brotherhood of Timber Workers (BTW), an IWW affiliate,
to enter oil fields, especially Drumright's, to fight for economic
parity. Frank arrived in Oklahoma mid-March to help expand this
membership, a new nuisance to oil companies.

Frank Little was well known in the world of labor by 1914.
Young men who labored in mining, logging, harvesting, and other

industrial occupations knew of him, and a few even tried to emulate him by claiming to be part American Indian.[29] Ordinary Americans reading front-page news stories about the emerging war in
Europe had probably heard of Frank. The Fresno Free Speech Fight
made him well known on the West Coast, and his name had been
splashed across newspaper pages in Duluth and Kansas City. If
others did not consider him newsworthy, Oklahoma newspapers
surely did. Cries that Wobblies were unpatriotic and their efforts
to include "undesirables" in their membership fueled the state's
newspaper editors to call for action. Tulsa papers became especially critical of IWW and immigrant laborers. Oklahoma was turning ugly toward IWW members, and hostile businessmen and city
officials began forming vigilante groups.

In April 1914, national newspapers carried the gruesome story
of the Ludlow massacre, where a tent colony of 1,200 evicted,
striking coal miners and their mostly Greek and Italian families
were fired upon by armed thugs of the Rockefellers' Colorado
Fuel and Iron Company as well as the Colorado National Guard.
Amid Gatling gunfire, some women and children hid in a dirt cellar
beneath their fired tent, and most asphyxiated or burned to death.
Elizabeth Gurley Flynn reported that many Americans lost respect
for Standard Oil Company as a result.[30]

Within this explosive atmosphere, Frank returned to organize
the same men whom Ella Little fed every day, despite the possibility of his family becoming targets of retribution. Frank helped
organize the OWIU Local 586 in Drumright just six weeks later,
amid growing tensions among the crime element, oil-company-
hired thugs, and zealous civic leaders. Now additional calls went
out for more Wobblies to come to Drumright to help construct the
growing community. The new local would push immediately for
an eight-hour day, a $3.50 daily wage, a set price for meals in camps,
sanitary bedding, and tents set aside for reading, writing, and bathing, the latter derisively mocked by local papers.[31]

Every Wednesday, Saturday, and Sunday night from March
onward, soapbox orators appeared on Drumright street corners
to proclaim the benefits of joining an industrial organization. On

Saturday evening, May 23, A. W. Rockwell, new Local 586 secretary-treasurer of Drumright, began speaking on a street corner. A crowd had already gathered when a lawman asked Rockwell to stop and give way to an Oklahoma gubernatorial candidate who was about to speak just down the street on the next corner. Rockwell politely acquiesced but told the crowd, "You have just seen the Bull stopping me; well, he says, that there is a guy who is looking for a job as Governor of this state, so go and hear him, and tomorrow night F. H. Little will answer him."[32] The next night Frank spoke to a large crowd, though his speech is unrecorded.

In early July, Rockwell resigned as secretary-treasurer, and Forrest Edwards of Seattle took his position. Edwards announced grand plans to organize a national OWIU.[33] Perhaps by design, the timing of his pronouncement collided with developing American business interests abroad. Opportunities for enormous capital gains lay just across the Atlantic Ocean. Austria had just declared war on Serbia; followed by Germany on Russia and France; and then Great Britain on Germany. With the European War commencing and the prospect of oil profits rising, Standard Oil Company declared its own war on the OWIU-IWW. Oil-trust gunmen and thugs began to intimidate and interrupt IWW speakers. Organizers A. A. Rice and Charles Clinton were pelted with rotten eggs on Sunday, August 16, while speaking to Drumright residents.[34] The next day the men tried again. When eggs flew again, this time hitting residents, a small riot followed. The police told the agitators not to speak in town again.[35]

The small police force did not uphold the law or individual rights for many Drumright residents. On August 23, forty to fifty company thugs interrupted a soapbox oration and badly beat Clinton as he addressed a crowd of men. Drumright had four deputy sheriffs and a force of policemen, but all had business elsewhere when the assault occurred.[36] The *Derrick* reported in 1916 that the police department was probably the worst in the United States and just short of being "a little reign of terror."[37] From the time that the IWW first entered Drumright, the police department, although outnumbered by citizens three hundred to one, brazenly searched and ransacked citizens' homes without arrest warrants, using unnecessary force and intimidation.[38] The same paper reported that "they [police] have searched places where there was practically no evidence to warrant them in getting a warrant and searching the place."[39] Many good, law-abiding citizens of Drumright were threatened and ordered to leave the city. Yet, Rice encouraged IWW speakers to find a way to cooperate with antagonists while steering clear of politics and religion as they spoke about the merits of unionization.[40]

Alongside their refusal to protect street corner assemblies, policemen took bribes from bootleggers and turned a blind eye to "liquor dens" and brothels, permitting many illegal activities to continue. City officials determined that cutting off the men's entertainment would encourage workers to let off steam by committing more serious crimes.[41] So another side of Drumright was permitted to show its ugly face in the evening "when the saloons along Tiger Creek Avenue lit their kerosene lanterns, and fancy-dressed gamblers with diamond rings and thin cigars in their mouths, sat down at gaming tables with their marked cards" and prepared to strip wages from "grease-caked roustabouts who had come to town to 'tear loose.'"[42] Many oil field workers simply drank themselves into a stupor each night. Alcohol now became a problem for Drumright's residents, not only because drunken workers caused fights and even murders but also because oil company owners lost money to drunkenness and crime. Once again, Frank and other IWW organizers tried to dissuade men from alcohol abuse. IWW organizers encouraged roustabouts to join the OWIU and then work on labor issues instead of giving in to drunkenness. Still, talk began to circulate of bringing in U.S. marshals to clean up the town.

Sometime in 1914, Drumright's Knights of Liberty and the Ku Klux Klan (KKK), comprised of conservative businessmen, churchgoers, and law officers, silently began organizing to remove the town's radical element in the name of patriotism. The IWW, which welcomed men and women of all ethnicities, especially became a new target for KKK hostilities.[43] As future mayor W. E. Nicodemus's family reported, joining the Klan was the "peer group thing to do" although they claimed that Nicodemus himself never joined.[44] In short, oil company thugs, corrupt law officers, and vigilante justice

now made Drumright a dangerous place for a man who had enemies with deep-rooted biases.

On Sunday, August 24, the Standard Oil Company's thugs
halted their intimidation. A fire had begun when lightning struck
a 55,000-barrel oil tank. It burned for several days and spread to
other gas wells. One well producing more than twenty-five million
cubic feet of gas burned so fiercely that it created a blackened sky
to the southwest for days.[45] Residents mailed a variety of postcards,
picturing Drumright with great plumes of black smoke in the background, to their friends and relatives while Prairie Oil and Gas
Company dealt with the devastation. The respite allowed OWIU
Drumright Local 586 to organize without interference.

Frank and Glen Little were riding in Ella's buggy on Broadway,
their errand unrecorded. Glen was excited to ride with his Uncle
Frank in town. Frank was always fun, even bringing small gifts to
the younger children on the rare occasions he visited the family.
Recent rains had made the roller-coaster main street a wide trail
of red mud and ruts. The town was full of oil field workers, including teamsters in wagons moving equipment and oil barrels up and
down the hills in thick, sticky clay. As they approached the last hill,
Frank urged the horses for the climb.

Every teamster dreaded Tiger Hill. Repeatedly wagons became
stuck, and animals collapsed while straining under their heavy loads.
Sometimes a horse would fall on another horse and not be able to
rise, becoming bogged in three to four feet of mud.[46] When this happened, the animal was shot and dragged by chains to a ditch near
Tiger Creek and covered with dirt.[47] Tempers often flared, generally
as a release of human emotions caught in maddening circumstances.

The Littles passed a man who was mercilessly beating his team
of horses on the hump of the hill. His barrel wagon was loaded with
oil, and the straining animals could pull the onerous wagon no further. Frank yelled at the driver to stop whipping the horses, whereupon he was told to mind his own business. Frank pulled his horses

to a stop and jumped out of the buggy on the incline while Glen sat frozen in the seat. When the teamster raised the whip again, Frank grabbed it out of the man's hands. The driver leapt out of his wagon, and the two men began shoving and punching, punctuated by the curse words Frank was known to use.

Broadway's constant flow of traffic guaranteed recognition of Frank Little, a scrappy one-eyed Wobbly fighter, matched against an awfully angry and possibly hungover teamster, frustrated at losing time over his exhausted animals and an interfering "son of a bitch." Witnesses must have seen the two men wrestling in the muck, trying to stay afoot on the slant of Tiger Hill. But fights were common, and weariness can discourage intervention at terrible moments. Such men become silent spectators, only vaguely curious about the outcome. The teamster pulled out a knife, and a fight for life ensued.

When Frank finally stood, a man lay dying by his own blade. Frank left the driver in the mud and, collecting his Stetson, turned to a wide-eyed Glen and ordered him to take the buggy back to the boarding house. Glen was instructed to tell his father exactly what had occurred, and that Lon would know what to do. Muddied and bloodied from the fight, Frank gazed at Glen for the last time in his life, turned his back, and trudged away. He would never return to Drumright. Seven-year-old Glen bravely took the reins in his hands and navigated the buggy back toward home. Afterward, Lon told his family to never again discuss Frank with anyone, under any circumstance. The protective ring of survivor silence had begun.[48]

The savage side of Drumright's history leaves few official records. Too many men died in drunken fist-and-knife fights.[49] Only a handful of records are held at the Muskogee County Courthouse, and none in Drumright or in Sapulpa, the Creek County seat. Yet this culture of lawlessness benefited Frank, who eluded arrest.

Growing into statehood adolescence, Oklahoma's complexion had changed, shallow layers of civility peeling off her face, revealing nasty eruptions of extremism. Like a child sent to a chicken pox party, Oklahoma had caught the infectious disease of patriotic vigilantism spreading across the country. In 1916, Mayor Nicodemus bragged that he "wanted the people of Oklahoma to know that a damn Easterner could come and straighten out a wild oil boom town and make it a decent little city in which to live."[50] He had closed down The Hump, fought the IWW, and rid Drumright of "the worst element of people who would not fit into the environment as first class citizens."[51] Despite these progressive changes, no arrest warrant would be issued for Frank, and he would never see his brother's Oklahoma family again.

19

✧ ✧ ✧

WILHELM'S WARRIORS

A knock on the door in the late afternoon of Monday, July 3, 1916, brought Militza Masonovich to her feet. Her husband, Philip, a Montenegrin iron-ore miner and strike leader, was taking a nap. As Mrs. Masonovich opened the door of their Biwabik, Minnesota, house, Special Deputy Nick Dillon and three others burst past her. To her polite invitation to take a seat, Dillon responded they were not there to visit but to arrest her husband and John (Jovo) Orlandich for operating a "blind pig," a still.[1]

Just three days earlier, Minnesota governor J. A. Burnquist had wired St. Louis County sheriff John R. Meining to "arrest forthwith and take before magistrate, preferably in Duluth, all persons who are participating in riots (strikes) in your county. Use all your powers, including the summoning of a posse, for the preservation of life and property."[2] In response Meining promptly deputized over a thousand of the county's residents—never checking the character of the private gunmen he steeped with public authority.[3] Nick Dillon, a Pickands-Mather mine guard who had honed his aggression working as a whorehouse bouncer, perfectly exemplified the type of gunman Meining employed.[4] Any excuse for an arrest warrant could serve to remove strike leaders to jail.

Philip Masonovich came out of his bedroom, calling his wife to collect his shoes, while she argued that her husband should go only with "Old Man O'Hara," the Biwabik village marshal.[5] They knew of Dillon's antagonistic temperament and so had cause to fear his fellow special deputies, James C. Myron, Ed Hoffman, and Deputy Sheriff Edward Schubisky (the only "regular" deputy).[6] When Mrs. Masonovich moved to retrieve the shoes, Dillon blocked her way with a verbal warning. Having limited English, she did not understand, asking Dillon, "What 'ope' means? I am going to get shoes for my husband."[7] Dillon then threw the small woman into the bedroom containing her nine-month-old baby. Her eleven-year-old son Nick buffered her, protecting the infant.[8] The enraged mother then turned on her attacker and charged full force at Dillon. The deputies scurried for the front door while Nick Masonovich bolted with his brothers and sisters to the safety of the barn.

As Mrs. Masonovich rushed out on her porch, she was clubbed over the head, and Dillon punched her in the mouth.[9] The four men then turned their billy clubs on her husband Philip and their boarders, John Orlandich, Joe Nickich and Joe Cernogortovich, who had rushed to aid the screaming woman. Hoffman scrambled back to the mine to get help while Dillon and Schubisky shot their pistols wildly toward the house. As Nick Masonovich later testified, the barn door was ajar. The scared boy watched as Dillon shot toward "pop man" Thomas Ladvalla five times, striking him once in the neck. Ladvalla was selling sodas at the Masonovich boarding house when the four deputized gunmen arrived, and his unfortunate timing cost him his life.[10] Myron, who was standing near the doorway as he beat Orlandich, took bullets in his back from Schubisky's gun and died instantly. It was then that the diminutive Militza Masonovich walloped Schubisky over the head with a pole, sending the deputy sheriff to the ground where he feigned unconsciousness.[11]

The four Montenegrin boarders, all striking miners, had no guns and fired no shots according to most accounts (although the *Duluth News Tribune* quickly reported the men had armed themselves).[12] But what was actually resistance and self-defense became charged as "rioting" to fit Governor Burnquist's orders, and so the

News Tribune reported the incident as a "riot-murder."[13] For the deaths of a deputy and innocent bystander, the four miners and Militza Masonovich were arrested. She took her baby with her to jail.

Even though he had been organizing miles away from Biwabik at the time of the shootings, Frank Little was also arrested for the murders of Myron and Ladvalla early the next morning, July 4, 1916. Describing the ill-fated turn of events in a letter he wrote to *Solidarity* on July 9, Frank reported that he had been sleeping soundly in his hotel twelve miles away in Virginia, Minnesota, when at three in the morning someone rapped on his door. Various organizers, including Frank, had been stationed at distant points just before the Masonovich shootings occurred. Thinking it was "some of the boys," Frank opened the door to find "five big burly bulls" who took him to Virginia's city jail without a warrant.[14] When he awoke hours afterward, he found two of his fellow IWW agitators—Carlo Tresca, a well-known Italian anarchist and socialist, and organizer Joseph Gilday—in jail with him. Tresca had actually roused Frank at 11:00 the night before to warn him that IWW leaders would be arrested for the Masonovich shootings, asking him to stay at an Italian miner's safe house. Exhausted from his trip, Frank had refused, rolling over to go back to sleep. In the end both Tresca and Gilday had dismissed their Italian bodyguards and rented rooms in the same hotel.[15]

After hearing that Frank, Tresca, and Gilday had been jailed, almost three thousand iron-ore miners in the Hibbing and Buhl mining range towns (called "locations") began a twenty-five-mile march to Virginia.[16] They had no idea that by six o'clock in the morning, the three IWW organizers would join the five Montenegrins, all manacled in accordance with the governor's order, on a heavily guarded special train to Duluth's St. Louis County Jail and the Duluth magistrate without being informed of their charges.[17] Duluth was seventy miles from most range locations, all of which housed magistrates of their own. It was clear that the Oliver Iron Mining Company had exerted its hold on Governor Burnquist and moved to control subsequent events. After investigating the Mesabi Range strike for a report to the U.S. Committee on Industrial

Relations the following November, George P. West wrote that if Burnquist had "even halfway investigated" the alleged criminal actions of the strikers, he would have learned that "nearly all of the law violation(s) . . . was that of the armed thugs employed by the mining companies or inspired by them."[18] With the backing of the state of Minnesota, company gunmen had been given full authority to use deadly force against miners and organizers.

Oliver Iron Mining Company was notorious for breaking laws without fear of retribution, all to keep its miners oppressed and on the job. Bribery was regularly used, and often expected, in order to acquire a position. Anywhere from $5 to $130 in beer, cigars, and cash was the going rate for a living wage.[19] One miner testified that when and if a mining captain *liked* a miner's woman, the miner had to shut his eyes in order to keep his job.[20] Adding insult to injury, the company's contract system set arbitrary rates relative to each mining area. A contract miner's weekly supplies, including dynamite, blasting caps, tools, and wire, were automatically docked from his pay. The amounts could be severe; one worker stated "[if] we eat, we don't dress, and if we dress, we don't eat."[21] When an Italian contract miner named Greeni received his meager paycheck minus deductions for supplies, he walked off the job in disgust.[22] An entire shift of miners followed him, and so the great Mesabi strike began.[23] While the IWW was not involved in the strike's inception, IWW secretary-treasurer Bill Haywood published a declaration of war against the Steel Trust and other independent mining companies in Minnesota, reiterating the call for increased wages, an eight-hour workday, and abolition of contract labor.[24] He also sent Frank, among other organizers familiar with the area, to the Iron Range to direct the loosely organized immigrant miners.

The IWW's involvement in the Iron Range's labor unrest led mine company owners to take extreme actions and, just as in other conflict locations, they mobilized the businesses and municipal offices under their ownership. All mail and telegrams to and from Virginia were halted and reviewed.[25] In other locations, including Biwabik, Aurora, and Eveleth, general stores turned away miners and their families. When the strikers formed their own cooperative for supplies and groceries, Oliver Iron Mining Company pressured

wholesalers to serve notice that all credit would be curtailed pending the strike, and that payments for supplies must be made weekly.[26]
Meanwhile Sheriff Meining publicly announced new jail sentences
for other agitators and miners for simply saying, "Hello Fellow
Worker," carrying a red IWW membership card, or discussing
industrial unionism on public streets.[27] There was no room for nego-
tiation. When the mayors of Hibbing, Virginia, and Chisholm stood
for the rights of the miners and asked for mediation between the
U.S. Department of Labor and U.S. Steel Trust representatives, they
were flatly turned down by the mining companies. The Steel Trust
intended to crush its enemy, and Duluth was its central command.

Frank now awaited his preliminary hearing in the old Victo-
rian county jail on Duluth's East Third Street, wisecracking that
the accused "all had nothing to do but sleep and read. But we haven't
anything to read!"[28] Some of the defendants would spend over five
months in the jail building, whose red-brick facade with carved
brownstone trim, arched windows, gabled Palladian windows, and
iron-crested roof resembled a palatial home. Inside was a different
story. Hallmarks of an obsolete holding facility—poor ventilation,
insufficient exercise facilities, unsanitary conditions, and crowded
cells—led to a grand jury's recommendation, just two months after
Frank's arrest, to demolish the building. Strikers, women, and their
children were housed together with hardened criminals. Near
Frank's cell, one alcoholic inmate, dropped off to jail by his wife,
howled hourly from "the snakes [sic]" until he finally died.[29] In
retrospect the next weeks in the old jail were a respite compared
to Frank's hectic schedule since walking away from Tiger Hill
in Drumright.

In the late summer of 1914, Frank Little and IWW national organizer Jack Law had toured the harvest fields of Oklahoma, Kansas,
and Missouri, while they awaited the Ninth Annual IWW Convention and its accompanying GEB meeting to be held in September
in Chicago.[30] Based in part on their observations and conversations
with migratory grain harvesters and cotton pickers, convention

FRANK LITTLE,
IWW GEB CHAIRMAN

In 1914 Frank Little was
elected chairman of the
IWW General Executive
Board. *Courtesy of the
Joseph A. Labadie
Collection, University
of Michigan.*

delegates would renew discussion of a new branch, the future Agricultural Workers Organization (AWO).[31] Frank would push to organize itinerant men who followed harvests.

Upon his return to Chicago, Frank likely stayed with Vincent
St. John and his wife Clara at their Franklin Street apartment.[32]
Frank had known St. John since their early days in the WFM and
was welcomed to stay whenever he was in Chicago. Vincent St.
John would resign his position at the September meeting, with Bill
Haywood elected in his place. Frank himself would nominate five

other men to compose the new GEB, but his peers overwhelmingly reelected him to the executive board and elected him GEB chairman, in recognition of his leadership and fearless character.[33]

Now Frank had to work in tandem with Haywood, an extrovert whose love of the limelight made him a far different leader from St. John. Generally, Frank told others that they had to do what Haywood wanted, stating, "When Bill makes up his mind about a thing, we are all supposed to toe the line, and we do, or try to—even to not drinking whiskey. Bill calls that 'teamwork.'"[34] Although newspapers now derisively referred to Frank as "Haywood's lieutenant," Frank did dissent with some of Haywood's opinions. At the end of the 1914 convention, Haywood would put forth a resolution denouncing the European War with which Frank agreed.[35] This early resolution dogged Haywood three years later, when the United States entered the Great War and many American Wobblies became conflicted concerning their patriotism and military nonparticipation. Under a cloud of sedition, Haywood and Frank disagreed on the handling of a formal public IWW resolution on war. Haywood waffled, stating that enlistment decisions should be left "to the conscience of the individual."[36] Frank would die for his firm antiwar position.

After the IWW GEB met, just twenty-five delegates joined for the IWW convention on September 21.[37] Among various discussions, Frank spoke about the need to return to California that winter to support itinerant fruit workers, whom he saw as future AWO members.[38] He left Chicago as soon as the convention closed and headed where Emma Little was busy agitating.[39] Emma had not accompanied her brother-in-law to the convention, as she had been elected president of the Fresno Women's Union Label League (WULL).[40] Now she worked furiously for a California state proposition that would cement women's and children's minimum wage, eight-hour day, and safe working conditions in the state's constitution.[41] Her work went beyond the original scope of the WULL's goal of wives, mothers, and daughters helping union workers via their purchasing power. Under Emma's leadership, the Fresno WULL also joined other California feminists who pushed for labor legislation. Her busy October schedule was full of speeches supporting the local chapter's goals as outlined in a revision of its preamble and the proposed legislation.[42]

While Fred plodded daily to his colorless job doing rug cleaning, Emma began a project that validated her IWW role. IWW General Headquarters was collecting information regarding past free speech fights in response to a request from the U.S. Committee on Industrial Relations. Believing the "publicity to be worth the work it will entail," Vincent St. John made an appeal in *Solidarity* one week before the September convention.[43] Anyone who had first-hand experience was asked to submit personal narratives, pamphlets, bulletins, reports, and detailed histories regarding the various free speech fights. Emma was proud of her manuscript "Fresno Free Speech Fight," which she believed would be helpful in enlightening labor and governmental viewpoints. She even created a scrapbook of various newspaper clippings from San Diego and Fresno with photos of IWWs who took part in the historic labor fights. She also possessed Minderman's diary, providing a rich account of the Fresno free speech fight.[44] Her contributions were added to a mass of documents and sent to Washington, D.C. The committee later found that the United States' immigration policy had created industrial unrest because an enormous immigration influx had "undermined the American standard of living for all workmen except those in skilled trades."[45] Furthermore, the committee determined that non-English-speaking workers had prevented development of better employer-employee relationships, especially with the "unreasonable prejudice of almost every class of Americans toward immigrants."[46] With rumblings of a European war, the committee recommended immediate legislation for restricting immigration except for those who were "likely to make the most desirable citizens."[47]

Approaching American participation in World War I, suspicion arose regarding the primary loyalty of ethnic groups, disdainfully called "hyphenated Americans." A new spirit of nativism compelled people to prove their loyalty to the United States by packing away once-popular progressivism like last year's fashions, claiming "America first!" In 1915, Theodore Roosevelt stated that many immigrant Americans were only loyal to their mother countries and therefore untrustworthy, especially in a time of war.[48] In a barnstorming speech across western states, President Woodrow Wilson emphasized, "I cannot say too often—any man who carries a hyphen about with him carries a dagger that he is ready to plunge into the vitals of this Republic whenever he gets ready."[49] Wilson's attitude encouraged carte blanche for discrimination and violence against minorities, and xenophobia began to permeate the American atmosphere. One immigrant stated, "It is true that there are many foreign-born among us, but—strangely enough—we are entirely welcome when we are willing to submit to industrial serfdom. Only when we demand our 'rights to life, liberty, and happiness' so gloriously pictured as American, do we become undesirable foreigners."[50] The IWW stated in *Solidarity* that although "hyphenated Americans" were "causing the U.S. Government much worry nowadays. . . . With us there are no hyphenates—they're all one tribe . . . the world over."[51] The OBU continued to open its halls to men and women of all classes, colors, and ethnicities.

In April 1915, Frank returned to Chicago to meet with the IWW GEB and discuss various assignments and implementation for an AWO organizational convention. With Russian blockades contributing to a growing European economic depression, America's wheat production in Oklahoma, Kansas, Missouri, Nebraska, and the Dakotas was booming in response to worldwide demand, and harvesters were desperately needed. Following the meeting, the AWO formally organized in Kansas. Its purpose was to implement a plan of action to protect bindle stiffs and tenant farmers in the grain belt, the Tom Joads whose lives ebbed with growing seasons as they moved from farm to farm, often with their entire families. Frank was surely aware of his sister Bessie's family situation. A surviving Little family photograph shows Bessie Little Courtright, her sunburnt face sullen, standing in tall cotton along with two of her sons, canvas cotton sacks slung over their shoulders. Charles and Bessie Courtright rented their farm until 1919, raising seven children despite harsh economic conditions. One winter all they had to eat was canned peaches.[52] The AWO offered no solution for tenant families like them.

The Department of Labor announced that eighteen thousand men were needed in the grain belt during the 1915 summer. The

Bessie Little
Courtright and
sons picking cotton

The AWO offered no
solutions for tenant
farmers whose families
became slaves to rented
farms. Shown picking
cotton ca. 1920 are
Bessie Little Courtright
and sons Roy and Bill.
*Courtright Family
Papers.*

department added that wages would range from two dollars to three
dollars a day, and workers were expected to pay their own expenses.[53]
Advertisements deliberately called for vast numbers of workers to
come to specific harvest areas. When many men arrived in a single
location, a system of sorting applicants to remove vagrants pur-
posefully ensued, much like winnowing chaff from grain. Anglo
men were hired first, preferably English speakers who were not
floaters or bindle stiffs.[54] Then the undesirables were whisked out
of town by marshals and railroad police after this "flooding" of men,
a practice that farming communities used to lower wages and raise
working hours.[55]

With supply and demand favoring the wheat producer, the
laborer had little power in his employment negotiations. The AWO
immediately went into action. By fall 1916, the AWO had become

one of the most successful IWW unions, with a membership of eighteen thousand and an eight-hundred-mile picket line from Kansas
to South Dakota.[56] New beneficiaries included about 50 percent
of the Iron Range's embattled strikers, possibly the poorest paid
workers in the United States, who left the mines for short-lived
harvesting jobs. They could earn almost $4 a day in wheat fields
compared to the prevailing $2.80 a day underground in 1916, the
same wage Frank and his associates now hoped to change.[57]

Frank would be jailed three times in 1916, with Duluth as his second
arrest. His first had occurred near Webb City, Missouri, in June
1916, a year after the sinking of the *Lusitania*. Frank and other
organizers had been organizing a strike involving Local No. 603's
metal miners and hoisting engineers whose wages had just
been reduced.[58] They had been mining zinc and lead, necessary
for increased production of bullet casings. Each of Frank's incarcerations would be more tedious than its predecessor, as his participation in labor battles was more than a nuisance amid a changing
political landscape. The press had successfully redefined the acronym
"IWW" as "I Won't Workers" and "I Want Whiskey," influencing
public opinion with tales of IWW-induced "death and woe, widowed
wives, and orphaned children."[59] Corporations hoping to furnish
supplies for the European War and a willing media soon convinced
the American public that the IWW was a German army of saboteurs. Two years later, in front of the U.S. Congress, Arizona senator
Henry F. Ashurst would add "Imperial Wilhelm's Warriors" to the
list of epithets, further defining the IWW as a treasonous body.[60]
The tide was turning against organized industrial labor as American
corporations had their fill with labor unions and their agitators—
foreboding a wicked future.

20

THE CANARY

IWW songwriter Joe Hill's arrest, trial, and execution suggested
that no Wobbly should expect a fair judgment in the U.S. judicial
system. Hill's treatment also signaled shifting public opinion relating to IWW activities. While Hill's fate was not directly linked
to Frank's, like a canary in a coal mine, it ominously foretold the
destructive strength of the press's venomous pen and irrational
judicial policies against Wobblies and their cause.

Immensely liked by fellow workers, Joe Hill (Hillström) was the
infinitely talented Swedish immigrant musician-turned–dock worker
whom Frank likely first encountered in Fresno during the free speech
fight. The IWW's *Little Red Song Book*, which was revised yearly,
carried Hill's songs to the American West, helping unify the working class into a solo voice and contributing to a new genre of American folk protest music. Decades later American songwriter Woody
Guthrie, inspired by Hill's songs, wrote lyrics that described the
murder, trial, and execution of Hill.

In January 1914, Salt Lake City grocer John Morrison and his
son were murdered by two masked men just before their store's
closing. Nothing was stolen. The teenager got off one shot before
dying and allegedly hit one of the men, based on a few bloody stains
found in snow a block away and a missing bullet in a .38 caliber

revolver.[1] Later that same evening, Joe Hill appeared at Dr. Frank McHugh's house for treatment of a gunshot wound in his chest. Hill confided to the doctor that he had been shot by a friend over a woman.

When a couple claimed they saw a sandy-haired man matching Joe Hill's description near the store, Utah governor William Spry announced a $500 reward for information or his capture. Within days, McHugh stepped forward to report Hill's injury and claim the money. Authorities arrested Hill on McHugh's word alone, dragging him from bed after shooting him in the hand as he reached for his pants.[2] They ignored information that a felon of the same description, Magnus Olson (alias Frank Z. Wilson), had been in the area at the time of the murder.[3]

Woody Guthrie lamented in his song "Ballad of Joe Hill" that

> I was courting a woman and had a fight with a man
> He fired a pistol that lodged in me
> Old Prosecutor Leatherwood can beat out his brains
> But I'm not going to tell you this lady's name.[4]

If Guthrie's lyrics were correct, Hill indeed quarreled with a friend over a woman, resulting in a broken engagement and his gunshot wound. Yet he loyally refused to drag his friend Otto Applequist or Hilda Erickson, Applequist's former fiancée, into the criminal investigation, stoically accepting charges against him.[5] In 1949 Erickson corroborated Hill's story, describing the fight and gunshot.[6] Unfortunately, her account would be thirty-three years too late. Despite lack of concrete evidence, Hill was found guilty. *Solidarity* reported that the jury, assisted by "patriotic guff," based their condemnation solely on the coincidence of the gunshot wound.[7] It claimed that Hill's crime was that he was a homeless Wobbly, an immigrant worker who was arrested during a time of mounting IWW enmity. Under Utah law Hill was given the option of being shot to death or hanged at the gallows. Hill quipped, "I'll take the shooting. I've been shot a couple times before, and I think I can take it."[8]

The IWW did not sit idly by and wait for Hill's execution. Wobblies made impassioned pleas to Utah's Governor Spry and President Woodrow Wilson, and lodged a formal appeal to the Utah State Supreme Court. Even Emma Little wrote an emotional public appeal for Hill's release in September 1915, pleading, "Another crime is about to be perpetrated by the capitalist class against the workers. Our song bird is about to be executed—before he ever has a chance to sing for us the glorious songs of freedom—the freedom of the white slaves from wage slavery."[9] She admonished Wobblies to "get busy boys, boys get busy."[10] Ultimately Governor Spry did not help Hill's cause, and Judge Orrin N. Hilton, made famous for his successful defense of George Pettibone in the Governor Steunenberg murder trial, was ineffective in Hill's appeal.[11] Hill remained on death row.

Frank had been in Bill Haywood's Chicago office when the GEB received word of Joe Hill's impending execution during fall 1915. Ralph Chaplin later wrote that Haywood received Hill's farewell note in silence, made no comment, and then stared out a window. Haywood then shoved the letter across his desk to Frank, who haltingly read it aloud to the other men in the room. With his characteristic tongue-in-cheek humor, Hill wrote

> Goodbye, Bill:
> I die like a true rebel. Don't waste any time mourning—organize! It is a hundred miles from here to Wyoming. Could you arrange to have my body hauled to the state line to be buried? I don't want to be found dead in Utah.
> —Joe Hill[12]

Joe Hill was executed on November 19, 1915. After being strapped in a chair and pinned with a three-quarter-inch black bullseye on his breast, Hill shouted the orders himself to the firing squad.[13] His last will, written in verse, included a final request for his remains:

> My body? Of, if I could choose,
> I would to ashes it reduce,

And let the merry breezes blow
My dust to where some flowers grow.
***Perhaps some fading flowers then
Would come to life and bloom again.[14]

And so it was that, after attending Joe Hill's funeral in Chicago on Thanksgiving Day, 1915, Frank Little began carrying a small envelope of Hill's ashes.[15]

After Hill's funeral, Frank returned to California where a Western AWO conference was to be held, and Sacramento and Roseville AWO locals were organizing.[16] In February 1916, Frank reported to *Solidarity* that at a Fresno Labor Council meeting, the *Fresno Republican* representative conducting the gathering endorsed the AFL's role in building industry and called for IWW organizers to be arrested as criminals. Disgusted, Frank declared the *Republican* to be "one of the dirtiest, slimiest papers in the west." So frustrated was he with the disregard for California agricultural workers, that he signed off the article with a simple "Oh, Hell!"[17] Living with Fred and Emma, Frank continued to organize farm workers and miners, focusing next in Porterville, about seventy miles southeast of Fresno. He wrote to *Solidarity* in March that the European War had caused a boom in magnesite, a crystal-like mineral used to process steel, and Porterville Magnesite Company was screening potential employees for IWW membership before they hired them at $3.00 a day—except for Mexican laborers, who received just $1.25 daily.[18]

Out of respect for his sister-in-law's progressiveness and fighting spirit, Frank also called on the IWW to recruit more women and develop agitators. Emma, who had been shut out of WFM organization and who had worked as a domestic herself years ago, no doubt had Frank's ear as she pushed for more feminist inclusion. Although Elizabeth Gurley Flynn had helped organize women on the East Coast, no real organization had occurred in western states. When a feisty young woman, Jane Street, decided to organize house maids in Denver, Frank assisted Street in officially establishing the Domestic Workers' Industrial Union, IWW Local No. 113, at the end of March.[19] At the 1916 Tenth Annual IWW Convention,

Frank supported a motion to create special literature for women workers and feature it on one page in each *Solidarity* issue, and to form a women's league.[20] Afterward Frank joined Flynn on the speakers' podium in Chicago's West Side Auditorium in front of the Labor Defense League on April 2, with Hill's conviction fresh in their minds. They both spoke about a corrupt legal system that sent numerous IWW organizers to jail for "being rebels against the Industrial hell of American wage-earners."[21] The next day, Frank again met with the IWW GEB. They discussed increasing awareness that the federal government had begun reading their mail and instructed that all locals be notified to not send union materials, especially those with the IWW seal.[22] With mail being intercepted illegally, a new chapter had begun for the IWW, and the mechanics of cat and mouse oiled its rusty gears for a deadly contest.

Aside from the lengthy April GEB meeting and Chicago speeches, Frank spent the first five months of 1916 in Fresno. He planned a twofold attack that would begin in the spring with demands for increased pay in both mines and fruit orchards. Frank promised his fellow Wobblies plenty of work in the Golden West for the 1916 summer.[23] However, he would not be in California to see successful completion. Haywood had ordered Frank to the Iron Range to help some loosely organized immigrant strikers.

Across the nation, newspapers announced that the same Denver judge who had failed to help Joe Hill in his appeal was preparing to defend the Iron Range Wobbly organizers and strike leaders, who had been charged with the first-degree murder of James C. Myron and Thomas Ladvalla, pending results of their initial municipal court appearance.[24] Judge Hilton would then serve as chief counsel for cases sent to a grand jury. On July 21, the St. Louis County Municipal Courtroom and its halls overflowed with IWW sympathizers and curious court observers before the scheduled preliminary hearing. Already waiting within the courtroom were Philip and Militza Masonovich, John Orlandich, Joe Nickich, and Joe Cernogortovich. When Frank Little and "hyphenated Americans"

Sam Scarlett, Carlo Tresca, Joseph Gilday, Joseph Ahlgren, Joseph Schmidt, Veno Wesaman, and Leo Stark joined them, loud and enthusiastic applause erupted. An "army of bailiffs" had to clear the courtroom while Judge Smallwood repeatedly rapped his gavel to restore order.[25]

St. Louis County attorney Warren E. Greene set an ambitious goal of proving that the murders of Myron and Ladvalla were a result of "constructive presence," a commission of crimes in which the charged were not actually present.[26] Greene asserted that the IWW agitators' inflammatory addresses led to the murders. The State hoped to incriminate the defendants on this legal statute and, by extension, the IWW membership cards found in their coat pockets. The defendants were represented by attorney John A. Keyes, who immediately made a motion that all defendants be dismissed because the complaint contained no definite charge. Smallwood denied the motion.[27] Once everyone was removed to the crowded halls except testifying witnesses, Smallwood then allowed the witnesses to be called. Deputy Edward Schubisky's testimony had changed, and now he claimed that he had been overpowered by Joe Nickich and not the small woman Masonovich.[28] Young Nick Masonovich prepared to testify that he saw Special Deputy Nick Dillon fire the shots that killed Thomas Ladvalla.[29]

Prosecutor Greene then charged that Frank Little had been on the Iron Range between June 14 and June 26, 1916, where he made inflammatory speeches. He claimed his witness, Ansel Smith, could testify to this claim.[30] However, Keyes and the local IWW secretary both refuted Greene's claim, testifying that they had seen Frank at various places away from strike zones where the State had accused him of delivering incendiary addresses.[31] Indeed, Frank had arrived on the Iron Range on June 28, when he began organizing many miles distant of Biwabik. After agitating near Duluth, he had arrived back in Virginia strike headquarters at the Socialist Opera House on July 3, the day of the shootings.[32]

The State also presented testimonies that Schmidt, Tresca, and Scarlett had called for a retaliatory murder after striking-miner John Aller's death. Aller (Alar), a Croatian miner and family man, had been shot several times in the back and neck by an Oliver Mining

Company gunman on the morning of June 22 while standing in a picket line just outside his own home.[33] Seven thousand miners had marched in Aller's funeral procession.[34] Carlo Tresca and other strike leaders attending the funeral were arrested for criminal libel although they were jailed briefly.[35] Since Tresca had called for "an eye for an eye" in his eulogy, all Sheriff Meining needed was a murder—anywhere—to connect Tresca as an incendiary.[36] Philip and Militza Masonovich, Joe Nickich, and others, who attended the strike-organization meetings and marched in striking miners' parades, had been charged with following the agitator's instructions after Myron's and Ladvalla's deaths.[37] Still, witnesses for the defense claimed that in response to the "constructive presence" statute, the organizers had specifically advised strikers to refrain from violence, keep their hands in their pockets, and retaliate only if the life of one of the strikers was taken by a guard. Aside from the alleged incendiary remarks, the men's union cards were the principal evidence against them.[38]

On July 27, 1916, the State rested its case, and the Masonovich shooting participants were indicted for first-degree murder. Of the arrested organizers, Frank Little, Joseph Gilday, Leo Stark, and Frank Russell were released when Judge Smallwood dropped charges against them at 6:30 P.M. Frank immediately telegraphed *Solidarity* stating that they would win the strike.[39] Meanwhile, orders to arrest all organizers continued on the Iron Range.

Bill Haywood had supplied more forces to assist. Haywood wired Elizabeth Gurley Flynn and IWW general organizer Joseph Ettor to go to the Iron Range on July 7, 1916.[40] Along with Frank and others, they planned a speaking tour in various locations in order to grow strike funds and highlight the unreasonable charges. Flynn, now separated from her husband Jack Jones, was especially distressed as Carlo Tresca and she were known to be in an intimate relationship at the time.[41]

On the evening of July 30, Elizabeth Gurley Flynn and Frank addressed the Duluth Finnish Socialist Hall, speaking for the working class and the IWW.[42] As a fluent American woman, Flynn did not fit the portrait that the Steel Trust and press had painted of radicals. In some ways she was an anomaly to the Iron Range press.

The press varied their descriptions of her, anywhere from "the hope of the IWW" to "a virtual goddess among the devils."[43] At one speaking engagement, Flynn humorously retorted to her lawyers that she would talk to a certain *News Tribune* newspaperman only if "he does not call me 'The Flynn Woman,' 'Agitator,' 'Fire Eater,' or 'Anarchist,' and above all 'Fat.'"[44]

Now that Tresca would be held over for the grand jury, Flynn began to work furiously for his release and to call for contributions to strike funds. She visited location after location to assess the needs of striking miners' families that were living in shameful penury. She estimated that of eight hundred families dependent on others for support, four hundred depended on the IWW to help feed them.[45] Their need was urgent: striking husbands and fathers who had left their families to work as migrant farm laborers were about to find themselves unemployed again. The harvest was ending shortly, and Minnesota winters could be devastating.

While Flynn empathetically spoke about the inhuman conditions resulting from Oliver Iron Mining Company's labor practices, Frank's address was more bellicose. At the climax of the strike meeting, Frank called out to an audience interwoven with mining-company spies and special deputies, "I say the St. Louis county jail doors can be and shall be opened to release innocent men in connection with the range strike, and allow them to walk out as free men!"[46] Although the *Duluth News Tribune* reported next day that "county jail authorities took Little's boast of a jail delivery as idle talk," mining-company gunmen and special deputies took notice.[47]

By early August 1916, IWW organizers reported that Oliver Iron Mining Company gunmen "were giving strikers the choice of scabbing on themselves or being evicted, in some cases, out of their own homes built on company property held for a lease of one year."[48] Women and children were reportedly thrown out of company-owned houses on a county road, and one woman was beaten and dragged in a street by gunmen, losing both her life and unborn baby.[49] Inexperienced men and boys, who were scabbing in vacant mining positions, had begun to die in pointless accidents.

Kidnappings and "wholesale intimidation" also were reported in attempts to crush the growing strike. In Iron Range locations, Steel Trust gunmen constructed "forts" with cannons and shone searchlights over nighttime streets. The *Kansas City Star* stated that the "cannon" in the forts—actually old stove pipes—terrorized families.[50] In other villages, gunmen commandeered all roads approaching the mines. Their acts of sabotage were blamed on strikers in an effort to rouse public opinion and justify retaliation. In one case, gunmen planted dynamite under a bridge and then acted as if they had discovered a heinous plot by the IWW.[51]

Despite Oliver Mining Company's tactics, Frank, Flynn, and Ettor continued their tour of the Iron Range. On Wednesday, August 2, they spoke in the eight-hundred-seat Socialist Opera House in Virginia, their strike headquarters.[52] The three-story white building, built by Finnish miners with their own money, served as a symbol for the working class. Its ornately gilded spectator balcony witnessed fiery speeches and rallies supplied by the Wobblies and then translated into various languages, unifying the various ethnic groups. The next day Frank separately addressed a small Chisholm audience, advising strikers, "If a gunman abuses you, laugh at him, if he tries to make you commit violence and grabs you, go with him peaceably. If you are sent to jail, stay there quietly, do not seek bail or lawyers, but be glad you are in jail because you are then helping your fellow workers to win the strike."[53] Frank also suggested packing the jails, since the expense was already exceeding $2,000 daily.[54] That evening Frank brought greetings from "the boys in jail" in Duluth to about fifty strikers in the Buhl Finnish Opera House, adding that Tresca, Schmidt, and Scarlett were "in fine shape, and urged their fellow workers to stick together and not lose heart."[55] In response, calls went out for more deputies to guard Buhl mines.

On Friday, August 4, a parade carrying a red flag and the U.S. flag marched to the Duluth auditorium from the courthouse square where oratorical speeches appealed for funds and condemnations flowed. Elizabeth Gurley Flynn pointed out that the contract system led to the strike, and that babies on the range needed milk; strikers, bread; and women, clothes.[56] Joseph Ettor decried the loss of free speech and the right to picket and distribute handbills. After he threatened to close every U.S. industry unless the IWWs in the St. Louis County Jail were released and gunmen removed from the range strike zone, John A. Keyes confirmed that the IWW could indeed carry out its threats through efforts of laboring men.[57]

Frank was not in Duluth that day but in Virginia, where he had returned for a meeting at the Socialist Opera House. "To hell with the governor! To hell with the sheriff! The 'I-don't-give-a-damn' policy is the only method by which to win this strike," Frank unabashedly declared.[58] Even his expletives were translated in various foreign languages for the strikers. Frank again reminded his audience that there was no law against free assembly. "I once served six months for delivering an address of this nature," Frank told the audience, ending his speech with IWW verse and a call for release of the agitators.[59] After his speech, Frank and the other organizers began planning a public meeting in Hibbing for Sunday, August 6, that would be open to all "with mining company officials especially invited."[60] The IWW now claimed that at least seven thousand men had joined the organization, and thousands more were out on strike on the Iron Range.[61]

Oliver Iron Mining Company gunmen determined that if legal maneuvering and intimidation could not halt IWW agitation, then wholesale kidnapping and deportation of IWW and strike leaders might succeed. On August 12, a Duluth special report to *Solidarity* stated that organizers who had been arrested by deputies five days prior had been placed on a Rockefeller-owned train and driven out of town.[62] At the same time, Frank reported that AFL members had disrupted a dock workers' meeting in Superior's Finnish hall, supported by Mayor Conklin. Conklin told the men that if they joined the AFL, then he would help them win their strike, but if they joined the IWW, he would suppress them.[63]

On the same day that Frank's story was reported in *Solidarity*, he too disappeared. Frank had traveled to Michigan iron-ore mining country to raise money for Mesabi and Cuyuna strikers.[64] Upon his arrival in Iron River, he achieved his third arrest for 1916 when deputies promptly threw him in jail and beat him. He did not have time to ponder how he would spend his incarceration as he had in Duluth, and he had no means to wire for help. By August 16, gunmen—possibly from Pickands-Mather Mining Company, the same company that had employed Nick Dillon—fetched Frank from jail and escorted him on a joyride out of town.

Thugs began the first assault by viciously beating Frank. At some point the gunmen placed a hemp rope around Frank's neck, pulling tightly while they quizzed him about local Iron River labor leaders. After Frank could not or would not give names, he was beaten senseless, and his body was tossed from the car into roadside bushes with the rope still looped about his neck.[65] His unconscious body was later discovered in a ditch near Watersmeet, Michigan, thirty miles northwest of Iron River, an area today in part of Ottawa National Forest.[66]

A December 1916 settlement between prosecutors and IWW attorneys promised that Tresca, Schmidt, and Scarlett would be released, in exchange for the Montenegrins' agreement to manslaughter charges with a reduced sentence of one year. Instead, the duped miners were handed terms upward of twenty years for crimes they did not commit. Philip Masonovich, Joe Nickich, and Joe Cernogortovich served time in Minnesota State Prison as late as 1920, almost four years later.[67] Militza Masonovich, who was released with her baby, vanished into historical obscurity.

PART THREE

✧ ✧ ✧

THE DISSOLUTION

1917–1920

21

THE SON-OF-A-BITCH WAR

Rolling over Arizona mining camps like a great desert haboob, a dark disquiet crescendoed toward Montana. A subliminal drumroll heightened the Great War's advance, marking a soft staccato beat for union leaders and rank and file, as American patriots, capitalist giants, and the Bureau of Investigation consolidated a stand against organized labor. Frank, ignoring storm warnings, quickened his march into enclaves of exasperated miners, encouraging them to a different war front for economic revolution. Had he known the endgame, Frank Little's pace likely would not have slowed.

Every movement caused Frank pain. Wounded by injuries received in Michigan in 1916, some scars were so severe that they would be almost indistinguishable from those of another murderous attack nearly one year later.[1] Sometime between November 1916 and March 1917 in El Paso, Texas, gunmen jumped Frank, violently kicking him in the abdomen, the likely cause of a hernia he also suffered.[2] Whether Frank just happened to take the El Paso route after visiting his mother or planned to agitate the Guggenheim family's American Smelting and Refining Company (ASARCO) plant and meet with Mexican agitators there is unknown. Similar to the 1907 Clifton-Morenci atmosphere, the IWW had struggled with union organization after a failed strike in 1913, and ASARCO held control over El Paso's Smeltertown and its primarily Mexican residents.

If the assault on Frank was not in retaliation from ASARCO, other paid detectives could have had information regarding Frank's itinerary and sought him out for their own reasons. A network of spies operated throughout the mining districts. To facilitate encrypted messages, mining companies had implemented code books that spies and operators used when wiring advance warning of radical activities among camps and the locations of radical organizers.[3] No matter the particulars, two gunmen knew exactly where Frank would be.

Earlier, at the November 1916 IWW Convention, delegates had determined to infiltrate western copper districts, selecting those camps most disgusted with WFM leadership. Now, the WFM identified itself as the International Union of Mine, Mill, and Smelter Workers (IUMMSW).[4] With a recent fracture in union leadership, Arizona's WFM-IUMMSW was foundering. Taking advantage of this weakness, Frank zigzagged across Arizona, dipping into Cananea, Mexico, to bring IWW tenets to mine workers, particularly within the four main Arizona mining districts: Bisbee, Jerome, Miami-Globe, and Clifton-Morenci.

Boring into union locals was not a novel idea, and federal agents and copper company operatives countered IWW success by planting their own spies within both the IWW and IUMMSW, some of them in leadership positions. In Globe's Old Dominion Mine, an ex-Pinkerton operative working for the Thiel Detective Agency reportedly was paid a "fancy salary" while working underground as an ordinary miner.[5] This detective, unknown by sight to mine management, rose to head the Globe local even as he reported on radical workers and union activities.[6] Roger Culver, leader and organizer of Miami-Globe district, was arrested in the 1917 IWW roundup and about to be tried in Chicago when Judge Kenesaw Mountain Landis discovered that Culver had been planted by the federal Secret Service.[7] Culver, who maintained an intimate association with IWW leadership, was likely the Old Dominion spy.

Even Frank's friend from Clifton-Morenci days, H. F. Kane, was suspected a turncoat. Kane stridently demonstrated in Globe, perhaps too boldly, demanding that the federal government take control of the mines. Embedded spies often argued enthusiastically for local direct action instead of waiting for a general walkout, in order to disrupt union organization. Kane's protests, however, did support an early belief that a government takeover would give miners a fairer shake than the mine owners.[8]

Bisbee had spies, too. Outspoken IWW organizer James Chapman was probably a company-hired detective, a provocateur used to damage labor credibility.[9] Agents provocateurs such as Chapman, many of them Pinkerton detectives, typically and "coldly engineered a single provocative act designed to 'set up' leaders for roundup and arrest."[10] Frank warned that the Arizona area also "had been planted full of Burns men [detectives.]"[11]

Using company infiltrators such as these to create confusion, suspicion, and incrimination among the different unions, mining management successfully blanketed all Arizona unions with IWW-isms: radicalism, anarchism, and even Bolshevism.[12] Such tactics enabled Arizona's governor and mine operators to justify calling for state and federal military assistance to protect private interests in the name of national security. In response, the IUMMSW cried conspiracy, blaming mine operators for hiring IWWs to discredit their legitimate union goals.[13]

Joining Frank in attempting to outwit mine management's array of cloak-and-dagger methods was Grover Hazzard Perry, newly appointed secretary-treasurer of the IWW western copper and lead mining branch. Hailing from New Jersey, Perry seemed more comfortable writing than organizing. Yet in January 1917, the former *Solidarity* business manager and *Industrial Worker* editor/essayist was in Phoenix, Arizona, leading the new Arizona chapter of IWW's Metal Mine Workers' Industrial Union (MMWIU), No. 800.[14] Both veteran free speech fighters, Perry and Frank had been associates as early as 1911 when they were thrown into the Kansas City Jail.[15] Although they worked closely together, their goals diverged in Arizona. Perry was concerned with pragmatic issues, including higher wages and shorter workdays in safe mines, whereas Frank campaigned passionately for loftier causes such as IWW principles of education, organization, and emancipation.[16] Perry had received at least one letter warning him to be on his guard against double agents, "anti-conscriptionists or anti-war F. W.'s. [Fellow Workers] . . . masquerading in the guise of a rebel . . . in order to bring about certain results not to the welfare of the movement."[17] Despite these warnings, the shorthanded Perry continued to welcome assistance, even if unvetted.[18]

Assisting Arizona mining managers and their spies amid back-biting unionists were national and local newspapers that labeled IWWs as pro-German agitators. Editors leaped at any opportunity to create hysteria by manufacturing reports of German agents sending airships across the western states, IWW bombers, and IWW sabotage. In the rural West, the heart of radicalism, the enemy could surely conceal itself, plotting attacks on Americans with German money while infiltrating American labor forces. As nativism exploded, local justice reached a new level, with superpatriots taking the law into their own hands.

By April 6, 1917, when the United States finally entered into what Frank termed the "son-of-a-bitch war" amid dramatically rising copper prices, mining corporations no longer did the "dirty work"— they had their own local, inspired vigilantes.[19] As an example, in Globe a city ordinance passed requiring every household or renter to display the American flag.[20] Many workers railed at the requirement. Globe's Loyalty League, whose mantra was to "eliminate the IWW," circulated loyalty applications for all Miami and Globe citizens to sign. Those who refused were branded traitors, and their businesses were boycotted.[21]

With Registration Day set for June 5, 1917, amid vociferous objections countered by patriotic hallelujahs, men argued the merits and injustices of being forced to fight in the European War. Contrary to the public perception of an internal immigrant threat, most rural white Americans viewed the war as a "rich man's war; poor man's fight" waged for industrial barons.[22] Later, Grover Perry underscored that "when the stars and stripes are being used for a just cause, I think you will find every member of the IWW will be there to back it up just as quick as any dollar patriots."[23] The problem was that the IWW had no reason to trust the standard bearers.

According to *Solidarity* editor Ralph Chaplin, wartime hysteria was so great that thousands wrote asking about the IWW's official stand on war.[24] A frustrated Frank wired a mouthful to Bill Haywood on April 10: "Suggest that a conference of all radical organizations be called to prepare to fight compulsory enlistment[,] to prepare for and advocate the general strike of all industries[,] to strike for industrial freedom of the working class[,] must act at once."[25] Frank demanded a statement. Haywood did not respond—either frozen with indecision or simply and uncharacteristically closed-mouthed with caution.

Haywood had also not been sympathetic to Frank's deteriorating condition. Desperately needing a $150 hernia operation, Frank had turned to Haywood for financial assistance, at the same time asking for a replacement. Frank then wrote to Grover Perry from Jerome, Arizona, on April 11, voicing his frustrations that his health was "completely gone," although he did not want the WFM to know of his injury and thereby have "something to make noise about."[26]

Perry wrote to Frank the same day. Referring to Frank's request to organize the Kingman and Oatman mining camps, Perry advised him not to get too far away from Phoenix. Because of his customary enthusiasm, Frank had not let on how serious his injury was in earlier communications, so Perry even asked Frank to come to Phoenix before traveling to Bisbee again on June 1.[27] Perry also admonished Frank to use a typewriter whenever possible, as Frank's tightly scrawled handwriting apparently was difficult to read.[28] Frank wrote to Perry several days later, this time in a typed letter, to urge that they "must fight with all our power the efforts of the Capitalist Class to force [us] in to the Army. Even to the limit that some of us is lined against the Dead Wall and shot. The Fight is on. On with the fight to the end."[29] Frank made no mention of his medical condition.

Impatient, Frank wrote to Haywood on April 16: "It is the duty of the IWW to oppose war at any and all costs. . . . What in Hell are we going to do? Lay down like a bunch of curs and let them force us to war? I, for one, say no. By GD, I will not keep still and I want to see our papers express themselves. If we fight, let us fight for freedom, and now is the time to take a stand."[30] Frank also claimed to *Solidarity* readers that the IWW was looking out for Arizona's workers and workers alone. He promised more pay for less work hours and time for rest and study. The IWW would not support contractual agreements with "the boss" and demanded two men on a machine, something the WFM had never put into effect. Expressing his own opinion, Frank added, "All class-conscious workingmen are determined to stay at home and fight their own battles with their own enemy—the boss. . . . Don't fight the bosses' battles; join the IWW and fight your own."[31]

Bill Haywood finally responded to Frank on April 21, saying, "My advice in this hour of crisis is a calm head and cool judgment. Talk is not the thing needed now."[32] Haywood refused to address Wobblies' conscription questions definitively or publicly, and he did not address Frank's medical procedure. Dismayed, Frank confided to Grover Perry that he feared a "jolt behind bars would finish me."[33] He needed a man to take his duties so he could have surgery, fast. And so, the stage was set for a bitter summer.

After winning the first strike of the season at the Humboldt smelter near Prescott, Arizona, a groundswell of strikes involving both IWW and IUMMSW workers arose.[34] As a result, Frank had been extraordinarily busy. From Prescott, he traveled to Bisbee where he spoke at the city park in mid-May, making a good impression on the "mud-diggers," despite his worsening condition.[35] His pain was so severe during travel that he said he would "faint dead away" while on the road.[36] After his Bisbee speech, Frank wrote to Perry again to say he could only work "an hour or two at a time" before he needed to rest. Headquarters, he admonished, could "not afford to pay wages to a sick man."[37]

To compound his misery, Bessie Little Courtright wrote to Frank that their mother was seriously ill.[38] The letter, dated May 24, 1917, and addressed to Frank's Miami address, had been routed to Phoenix where Frank was meeting with Grover Perry.[39] Frank tucked the letter into his suitcase. The news could not have come at a worse time.

At the end of May, Grover Perry finally convinced Haywood that their best organizer could not maintain his demanding schedule. Frank wired James P. Thompson in Seattle to come immediately to help Perry with Arizona organization at the end of the month. On June 4, 1917, Haywood told Thompson that Frank was "in terribly bad shape physically, and has got to go to the hospital for an operation."[40] The GEB had approved funding for the procedure, but finding time was difficult, and Frank would put it off.[41] Besides, Frank was having second thoughts about his life's work. He grumbled to Perry that perhaps he should just get out and prospect if he could "get someone to grub stake me."[42] For the first time, Frank did not sound like Frank, but more like his brother Fred.

Nevertheless, Frank and Grover Perry were back to work in Jerome on May 25, 1917, when the IWW tentatively joined the IUMMSW in calling the next strike of about two thousand workers against United Verde Copper Company.[43] Frank had worked the mining camp since early spring, the locals nicknaming him "Wobbly Slim."[44] One reporter estimated that Frank now carried only 135 pounds on his five-foot, eleven-inch frame.[45] Despite Frank's handicapping condition, the IWW had picked up disgruntled IUMMSW workers, almost 50 percent.[46] Meanwhile, United Verde management successfully painted all union members broadly with anarchist and pro-German tints to justify denying union demands. As a result, the IUMMSW announced it had no intention of striking in cooperation with the IWW and disagreed on abolishing contract and check-off systems.[47] The IUMMSW leadership also said it had proof that mine operators were working *with* the IWW.[48]

At a mass meeting in Jerome's Opera House at four in the afternoon on Sunday, May 26, Frank and Grover Perry spoke to the rank and file, other sympathetic onlookers, interested mining company representatives, and local businessmen opposed to the IUMMSW's demands of union recognition. Frank and Perry counseled miners to accept the Miami wage scale (a sliding wage scale negotiated earlier in the Miami-Globe mining district, based on the market price of copper) and to return to work without union recognition, providing the companies did not retaliate. If not, they should accept the IWW's initial rallying call of $6 a day underground and $5.50

a day above ground, and two men on every drill. If this point also failed, the IWW would approach the mine operators alone with IWW demands. The IWW clearly would not participate in a strike for IUMMSW recognition.[49]

Under AFL leader Henry S. McCluskey's direction, the IUMMSW flatly rejected all IWW demands, stating, "The IWW organization was imported into the State and is being used as an auxiliary of the MOA . . . to break the back of the miners' union in Arizona."[50] McCluskey charged that the mine owners helped arrange the Opera House meeting, even asking men to join the IWW. McCluskey railed at the IWW, "There is no room for two unions of miners. Your place is in the union recognized by the American Labor Movement."[51] The IUMMSW declared the strike was won already, and anyone attempting to interview the managers on behalf of the strikers would be placed before the Labor Movement of the United States as scabs and traitors.[52] IWW members, on the other hand, charged that IUMMSW leaders double-crossed them, promising that if they joined in the strike, the only demands would be for the Miami scale.[53] That did not deter Frank and Perry from petitioning for a meeting with higher authorities.

By summer 1917, copper companies owned the Arizona government, including de facto governor Campbell and his legislature.[54] While many Arizonans had loved once-popular Governor Hunt, wartime now changed middle and working-class views. Jerome was Campbell's home. He had married a hometown girl, had been a popular postmaster and tax assessor, and a United Verde foreman. The town knew him intimately. Wearing a large sombrero, Campbell arrived in Jerome at six o'clock in the evening on May 28, along with Colonel James C. "Sunny Jim" Hornbrook, a cavalry officer known throughout the army for his affable disposition, at the request of the War Department.[55] Special conciliator John McBride had already begun to interview strike leaders.[56] The town was on the verge of chaos with crowds gathered in the streets, waiting for the mediation committee's decisions.

Frank and his grievance committee were the last to meet with the governor and colonel late that evening. Included in the small committee was Perry, whom Campbell later described as a Jew and

Karl Marx disciple.[57] Campbell's take on Frank, written in Campbell's memoirs, was far more favorable. By his own words, Campbell said he expected a "big, rough, tough, low-browed looking criminal" as publicized, a "Red and saboteur, a killer if need be." Instead he said he met "a well-dressed, well-groomed" man, "average in stature" with "clear unwavering eyes, well-shaped forehead, short straight nose and a strong chin. All in all a good looking man of about 40 years of age."[58] He further noted that Frank "had superb composure" and spoke with "a soft well-modulated voice."[59] Evidently, Frank hid his pain well.

Frank understood the politics of Campbell's election, and after thanking the governor for meeting with the committee, added that "when you [Campbell] were mining here I never expected to see you Governor of Arizona as I did not think any Republican could ever lick my good friend Governor Hunt. You know better than I do that Arizona is a very strong Democratic State and organized labor, including the Railroad Boys, are always strong for Governor Hunt."[60] Campbell was impressed that "Little was well informed on the political and labor situation in Arizona and could have conversed all night on these interesting but inappropriate and inopportune subjects."[61]

After the small talk, Frank politely presented the IWW's demands, but Governor Campbell retorted that he would not submit the demands or request the mine operators to receive Frank's committee. He considered the IWW "an Outlaw Organization, intent on destroying the old established A. F. of L. organization and the stoppage of copper production so necessary for war purposes."[62] Although clearly shocked at Campbell's blunt statement, Frank calmly replied as he prepared to leave, "I am not surprised at your attitude and action Mr. Governor but when the Supreme Court decides the election contest, now on appeal before them and Governor Hunt is again sitting on the throne, we will have a friend at Court."[63] Frank's words later proved true. With a "hearty hand-shake and a smile on his face," Frank departed, saying, "We'll be seeing you again in the near future when we are dealing the hands."[64]

By June 1, 1917, the strike was over. The IWW had won the Miami wage scale, and the IUMMSW had lost the check-off system or union recognition with a closed shop.[65] Aside from the Great War, a second war now gyrated between the IWW's MMWIU and the old WFM's IUMMSW in other Arizona camps, tilting a final win to a third party, the copper mining industry.

Three days later in Jerome, no doubt at Governor Campbell's or Colonel Hornbrook's suggestion, agents concerned about the IWW's protest plans for the next day, Registration Day, detained Frank. Following Haywood's directive, Frank told one of the agents that he had no official statement and "could not do so as the organization had taken no action."[66] Frank made no qualms about giving his personal opinion, however, repeating his statement about being opposed to all wars.

On June 9, 1917, Almira Hays Little Cox died. The family immediately wired Frank concerning their mother's death. When the telegram reached Frank is unknown, but he added the wire to other family correspondence in his valise.[67] All attention was now on Butte, Montana, where, one day earlier, the Speculator Mine fire had killed or would eventually kill 168 miners—the worst underground hard rock mining disaster ever recorded in the United States.

Frank arrived in Bisbee, probably Thursday evening, June 14, to attend the first MMWIU No. 800 Convention meeting on the following morning at Miners' Union Hall. Grover Perry joined him, bringing along his wife, Lena, and toddler son, Grover Perry Jr. The men checked into the lavish Copper Queen Hotel, reportedly under assumed names. Frank still had not found time for medical treatment.

Early in the convention's proceedings, Ben Webb, a spy for a mining company, was selected to be chairman of the Miners' Union executive committee.[68] During the next three days, Webb passed along information from "the inside" about the MMWIU's organization, demands, and strike plans.[69] At the Copper Queen Hotel, after Webb's wife had telephone conversations with a "stranger in a certain room at the hotel" concerning a proposed meeting in her home, a Bisbee city official suggested the guest was Frank Little.[70] The informants' reports reached Phelps Dodge's Walter Douglas, John C. Greenway of the Calumet and Arizona Mining Company, and M. W. Merrill, president of Bisbee's Loyalty League. While

miners elected officers, outlined demands, and endorsed supporting their brother miners in Butte where a strike had just begun,
local enforcers strategized a method to mold Bisbee into a "community of American citizens."[71] Management and city officials must
have known that Frank and Perry narrowly averted an immediate
strike by speaking adamantly for over an hour each, warning Bisbee
miners to wait for a statewide strike based on uniform demands
passed by the convention on hand.[72] On June 17, 1917, the convention concluded with a robust singing of "Hold the Fort."[73]

The same day as this first convention meeting, mining companies received the welcome news that Congress had passed the
Espionage Act. If any person or organization interfered with military operations, supported America's enemies, promoted insubor-
dination in the military, or interfered with military recruitment,
they would be arrested. Now mine operators could justify circum-
venting legalities when engaging military assistance to prevent
interruption of their copper output—it was wartime. For Bisbee leaders, it was time to finalize a clandestine plan for ridding
themselves of the IWW. For Frank, it was time to settle the issue
of conscription with Haywood and the GEB.

Before the MMWIU convention closed, both Frank and Perry
asked Bisbee miner Joe Oates to allow his name to go before the
convention for election as secretary-treasurer of the Miami-Globe
mining district.[74] Oates understood that Frank would have surgery in the near future and that neither Perry nor Frank would be
available to organize the district.[75] In fact, Perry had folded his
Arizona operation abruptly, with a final vote of approval at the
MMWIU convention. He was moving his family and office six hundred miles north to Salt Lake City to be centrally located among
all IWW western mining entities.

Could Perry have known vigilante justice was afoot? Historian
Philip Mellinger believes so because Perry had no other advantageous reason for the move. Besides, planning for a massive roundup
in a small city could not have been kept secret.[76] If Perry knew,
so did Frank.

On Monday, June 18, Frank and the Perry family surreptitiously
loaded into an auto stage heading for Globe, a distance of about 205
miles, hoping to avoid law enforcement.[77] They traveled the old

wagon road, not much improved since 1905 when Frank first traveled to Globe. As the day bled out, the small group ventured an evening journey, winding around mesas, through dark canyons and sandy washes. Well into the night, their vehicle finally crawled into Bowie, about halfway to their destination. Leaving Bowie in the early hours of June 19, the car's occupants were probably asleep, the three-year-old lying between his parents. Under a clear, starry night, the chauffeur also drifted off.[78] Suddenly, the car left the road, somersaulted into the air, and landed on a steep incline. Perry later described the accident as going off a cliff. Both Frank and Lena Perry broke their left ankles; Grover Perry, his left arm; the driver, a rib. The child was bruised.[79] For Frank, the accident must have been agonizing.

Frank remained in the Gila county hospital until June 20, when he hobbled out on crutches, his leg swathed in a cumbersome plaster cast.[80] Some historical accounts, based on local newspaper reporting, note that Frank then "holed up in a miner's cabin," where he called strikes, and as a result, narrowly missed deportation.[81] This was not true. The newly formed Loyalty League in Globe and law enforcement officers had no idea that Frank was in Miami for only one night, and not organizing a strike in Bisbee.[82]

22

THE VIGILANTES

In the middle of Miami's Sand Wash, silhouetted against the set-ting sun, Grover Perry stood in a wagon surrounded by two hundred men. Within earshot was Miners' Union Hall, close to Sullivan and Keystone Streets, and from its upstairs windows, boisterous IUMMSW men craned for a glimpse of the meeting.[1] Perry's audience was primarily "diggers"-clad Inspiration Mine and Miami Copper Mine workers, the latter known to fortify them-selves with a half-pint of ale before hiking up three hundred wooden steps at the north end of Keystone Street to work.[2] A lesser group included miners from smaller mines scattered nearby, and a few Scandinavians who trekked twenty-five miles from Supe-rior Mine to attend.[3] Noticeably absent was Frank Little, who had been hospitalized in Miami-Inspiration Hospital after the wreck the night before.

Perry began with the usual IWW talking points, urging men to organize for a statewide strike. He reminded them that with the war machine needing copper, the government would have to inter-vene in labor demands. Even if the government did not confiscate all copper mines, it should at least ensure that workers had living wages and improved working conditions. If the government did not assist the miners, the IWW would strike against Uncle Sam.[4]

Witnesses reported that Perry avowed the IWW could shut down American industry, logging, mining, and wheat production now supporting a capitalist war. Yet Joe Oates, who finally had arrived in Miami to take charge, later testified that no remarks were made about holding up wartime supplies.[5] Still, miners in the hall up the street catcalled Perry's rhetoric while law officers on horseback, armed with Winchesters, silently watched the proceedings.

When Perry retorted that the IUMMSW were no more than "traitors to other working men," Joseph Shannon, a national WFM organizer sitting in an upstairs window of Miners' Hall, began to argue loudly with Perry.[6] Oates had just asked Perry to step down in order to curb the shouting match when Frank made a dramatic appearance. When the surprised miners quieted down, Oates asked Frank to address them.[7] Bruised and on crutches, Frank was lifted into the wagon. He began to speak on the solidarity of labor, the workers forming into "one good, big organization of all of the workers, as the only way to combat conditions existing throughout Miami, Globe districts, and other places in the country."[8] Although Gila County sheriff Hi Elam later reported that Frank's speech was "rabid," Joe Oates testified that Frank never discussed war or soldiers in his speech.[9]

After the speech, Perry and Frank left Oates in charge of the roused crowd. The two joined the rest of the Perry family for a hasty retreat to Phoenix via another nighttime auto stage.[10] This time the vehicle safely reconnoitered the western route, descending through hazardous foothills and the rugged gorge at the west end of the Pinal Mountains. Travel could not have been comfortable for Frank. The road cleaved the canyon's walls, snaking below rough, puzzle-pieced outcroppings before flattening out along a string of smaller, dusty mining camps tied to Phoenix.[11]

Less than a week later, on June 28, 1917, Frank appeared at IWW headquarters on Chicago's "skid row," 1001 West Madison Street, after leaving Grover Perry in Phoenix with moving preparations. IWW headquarters was not difficult to locate—one could track lamp posts covered with IWW stickerettes, such as Jack London's "Why Be A Soldier?," or migrants stopping in to check AWO's most recent list of harvest jobs. The front windows of the former

hotel-turned-IWW headquarters were "ablaze with red IWW letter-
ing and the big IWW emblem" when Frank hobbled through the
front double doors over an inlaid-tile greeting, "Salve," welcome.[12]

Before assisting with a final audit of IWW books, Frank climbed
three flights of well-worn, wooden stairs to meet with a trusted
friend, *Solidarity* editor Ralph Chaplin.[13] When Frank arrived with
"his Stetson worn at the same jaunty angle and his twisted grin,
as aggressive as ever," Chaplin likely knew that Frank was prepared for a fight.[14] The next morning Frank planned to attend a
GEB special session to determine an official stand on conscription.[15] The last time Frank and Chaplin had met, they discussed
IWW propaganda for May Day 1917. Frank assured Chaplin that
with a production of three million stickerettes, there would be
"a 'silent agitator' on every 'son-of-a-bitch' boxcar, water tank,
pick handle, and pitchfork in the land." Bill Haywood had cautioned Frank and others on their overuse of the epithet, asking,
"What words will you use to define a real son of a bitch when you
meet one?"[16]

They had also discussed cartoons. Chaplin was a professional
artist as well as an experienced journalist. Frank had a tremendous
admiration for his drawings. He especially liked Chaplin's sketch
of a blindfolded, robotlike creature staggering out into a field of
bayonets, carrying on his back a stupid-looking jackass labeled
"The Cost of War." Chaplin later wrote that this was Frank's notion
of what IWW antiwar propaganda should be like.[17]

Frank had asked Chaplin to create a new cartoon for the MMWIU
publicity drive. He wanted it to include a flag with a coiled rattlesnake ready to strike. Above the snake Frank wanted the inscription "Don't Tread on Me," the motto first used on an American
Revolution flag. Chaplin agreed, on the condition that Frank "rustle
up" a good picture of a rattlesnake.[18] Later, when Frank was in
Bisbee, he filled out a postcard "in his small painstaking scrawl,"
spelling out the inscription above a coiled rattler's image, reminding Chaplin of his promise. Chaplin later made the drawing but it
was lost with the events that followed.[19]

The men likely discussed an official statement that they hoped
the GEB would accept. Haywood testified later that Frank had

arrived with such a statement, submitting it to the GEB for discussion and approval.[20]

A synopsis of the GEB meeting, which took place June 29 through July 6, omits the contentious discussion lasting over three days on this topic as well as the commencement of a statewide Arizona strike. The minutes record more mundane issues, certainly not worthy of an emergency session. However, three additional days of meetings, July 7 through July 9, were unrecorded. Their purpose was to draft a statement defining the organization's position on war. Omissions in the minutes pertaining to the follow-up meetings are not surprising when contrasted with Bill Haywood's testimony during the 1918 Chicago IWW trials. Haywood's vague answers nimbly detour self-incrimination when the prosecutor pinpointed his participation in the official statement. However, Ralph Chaplin's recounting confirms Haywood's uncompromising role at the meetings.

In the group were William Wiertola, a miner from Virginia, Minnesota; Richard (Dick) Brazier, a British-Canadian miner and songwriter; Charles L. Lambert, a Scottish immigrant, and jack-of-all-trades from California; Francis D. Miller, a weaver from Providence, Rhode Island; and Bill Haywood. Aside from Haywood, each represented a different section of the United States as well as a key industry.[21] Chaplin described them as "rough-and-tumble fellows, remarkable for their toughness, intelligence, and revolutionary idealism."[22] Yet this powerful group could not be compelled to consensus. By the third day, likely July 9, the committee was in a deadlock over the statement Frank had brought, and Chaplin was called in for his opinion. Chaplin explained that with a *Solidarity* deadline fast approaching, some decision had to be made to assuage readers' demands for an official position. With the committee still indecisive, Frank broke the tension by saying, "Some of these two-eyed bastards on the board want to run the show." Frank, Haywood, Lambert, and Brazier were each blind in one eye. Everyone laughed, but they knew that "the one-eyed were not unanimous" either.[23]

According to Chaplin, Dick Brazier worried, "If we oppose the draft, they'll run us out of business." Frank immediately responded,

"They'll run us out of business anyhow. Better to go out in a blaze of glory than to give in. Either we're for this capitalistic slaughterfest, or we're against it. I'm ready to face a firing squad rather than compromise."[24] When Haywood became angry, crushing the document in his hands, Chaplin quickly scribbled a compromise statement and asked permission to publish it in the next issue of *Solidarity*. This statement advised Wobblies to register for the draft but to sign as "IWW opposed to war."[25] Not one GEB member agreed to endorse Chaplin's idea but told him to "go ahead and print the damn thing" over his own signature.[26] In effect, then, they would provide a declaration without taking ownership. The statement attributed to Ralph Chaplin ultimately appeared in *Solidarity* on July 28, 1917.

Under cross-examination in the 1918 Chicago IWW trial, Haywood attributed war statements first to Frank and then to Chaplin.[27] Haywood also told federal prosecutors that he had only attended a "few, a very few, and only a part of the few" of the special-session GEB meetings, when in fact, he had only missed the June 29 meeting.[28] He dissembled further, distancing himself from the early motion to draw up the resolution, although the minutes clearly record his presence on the morning of July 5 when the motion was made.[29]

Ralph Chaplin hedged the truth as well. His memoirs state that he immediately went to his local draft board the next day to practice what he preached. In actuality, he had already registered on June 5, withholding this information from the GEB. Under exemptions, he had written, "Yes, conscientiously opposed" to the war that was enveloping the nation.[30]

Discontent continued to roil as Arizona workers expanded agitation among competing unions. Bisbee's mine workers had attacked first, ignoring instructions to wait for a "universal" strike. Grover Perry later testified that just after he and Frank left Bisbee on June 20, "the pot boiled over."[31] He firmly believed that if Frank had remained, the strike would have been delayed. On June 25, Grover

Perry had wired Haywood, warning that Arizona was on the verge of strike, asking him to come, but the GEB and Haywood were about to hold their contentious meeting.[32]

Bisbee sheriff Harry Wheeler wired Governor Campbell on June 30, requesting federal troops to take charge and prevent bloodshed. Wheeler lamented that he expected great property loss and that the majority of the strikers "seem" foreign—pro-German and anti-American.[33] Ten days later, Phelps Dodge president Walter Douglas joined him by railing that one "cannot compromise with a rattlesnake," adding his belief that "there is German influence behind this movement."[34] Wheeler pledged to perform his duties in preserving the peace, calling for every able-bodied American to assist him.[35] In response, Bisbee's Citizens' Protective League supported the "patriotic" Wheeler, publicly calling miners' demands for higher wages and better working conditions "treason."[36] Afterward, not one overt act of violence could be attributed to IWW influence, but threats such as Wheeler's increased public alarm.[37]

Just hours before the Globe IUMMSW called their strike on July 2, the IWW presented petitions simultaneously in Globe and Miami. A mass meeting the previous night of almost three thousand miners in Miami's Sand Wash had determined their demands, ultimately leading to the second strike.[38] The IWW struck at 3:00 P.M. on Sunday, July 1, shortly before the IUMMSW walked out. By the next day, with the IWW and IUMMSW picketing among law enforcement and star-wearing Loyalty Leaguers, seven thousand men were out on strike.[39] Globe's Citizens' Home Guard leader Reverend Johnson stated that the members of IWW, a "public enemy of the United States," should all be stood up against a wall and shot.[40] Thus, with explosive tensions mounting, Governor Campbell, John McBride, Henry S. McCluskey, and former governor Hunt traveled to Globe at Labor Secretary Wilson's request to mediate. The shutdown at Old Dominion had been blamed almost entirely on the IWW even though the IUMMSW dominated labor there and had been negotiating for almost a month.[41] Three hundred soldiers of the Seventeenth Cavalry stationed themselves in Globe.[42]

In Miami, where a complete shutdown was in progress, speakers openly addressed several thousand men, many wearing red badges, at the Sand Wash and at the ball field under law enforcement's eyes.[43] Sheriff Elam was concerned with speakers who spoke for supporting the strikes and not the war. He protested to a Bureau of Investigation agent that certain speakers should be shut down because their sentiments could spread. Concerned Miami citizens were also threatening to take matters into their own hands.[44]

The IUMMSW successfully shut out the IWW in Clifton-Morenci district when miners, mostly Hispanic, also struck on July 1.[45] Northwest of Clifton, on July 4, about thirty Jerome miners met on a desert hogback, listening to speeches about how profiteering copper companies could afford to pay higher wages but chose not to raise workers' standard of living.[46] Attending law enforcement officials later claimed the speakers spoke against the government, though IWW officials claimed to want government involvement against Clark mines.[47] Jerome's strike, the fourth walkout, was called for at 3:00 P.M. on July 6.[48] Ninety percent of 2,500 employees began picketing peaceably with some IUMMSW joining them, completely tying up the great United Verde mine.[49] For an Arizona industry that produced 28 percent of the nation's total supply, the decline of copper production in the ensuing days was disastrous.[50]

Frank joined Bill Haywood in sending identical telegrams to A. D. Kimball in Bisbee and Joe Oates in Miami on July 7. Besides wishing both men luck with the strikes, both telegrams stated, "I will drop all plans, and be with you. keep us posted. send all news to the papers."[51] But Haywood had no intention of traveling to Arizona, and Frank was about to head to Salt Lake City where Grover Perry had finally moved the MMWIU No. 800 office. In the meantime, Frank worked on a *Solidarity* article expounding miners' demands and asking for financial help to support their families.[52]

The night before Frank made arrangements to leave Chicago, on July 10, several hundred men, many wearing WFM buttons, registered as "emergency volunteers" at a secret meeting in Jerome High School.[53] Joining the "citizens' affair" were teachers, businessmen, company executives, and merchants. Wearing white handkerchiefs tied around their arms for identification, they were issued pick axes, pick handles, rifles, and billy clubs.[54] The vigilantes were going to clean up the town. Beginning at four in the morning, Loyalty Leaguers "swarmed over and into every rooming house, den, flop joint," or other place where Wobblies might be sleeping to seize the undesirables. The captured were taken to jail, their baggage piled up just outside the door.[55]

When the IUMMSW claimed that some of their own men had been arrested, an emergency trial was held on the steps of United Verde headquarters. A three-man review board headed by an IUMMSW leader-interrogator called "Judge" pardoned 37 men, instructing them to "keep their mouths shut" regarding the events.[56] The remaining men were loaded like cattle into two open cars on a Clark-owned short train heading for Jerome Junction, twenty-seven miles away.[57] At the junction waited about 50 members of the Prescott Home Guard, ready to intercept the Wobblies and send them on to Needles, California, with no food.[58] No policeman took part in rounding up the 112 men—it was strictly a vigilante effort.[59] Afterward Jerome's Mayor Cain remarked, "Jerome citizens have demonstrated that they know how to deal effectively with an undesirable element."[60]

Another clandestine meeting took place in Bisbee on July 11, the same day that Frank planned to leave Chicago for Salt Lake City. Among those at the meeting were Walter Douglas; Colonel John C. Greenway, who allegedly devised this secret operation; and Sheriff Harry Wheeler, who was to implement the sinister plan.[61] Rifles, machine guns, and ammunition had been stockpiled for weeks in Bisbee's YWCA.[62] More than two thousand Bisbee men would participate, at least one thousand from Douglas, and more gunmen came from as far away as England to work as scabs. Many already were secretly billeted at the Grand View Hotel on School Hill.[63] They would receive their assignments from squad leaders early the next morning.[64] Meanwhile, Citizens' Protective Leaguers prepared to block Bisbee's entrances and exits; telegraph and telephone offices were captured; court sessions adjourned; and bank withdrawals put on hold.[65] The "Great Wobbly Drive" was about to commence, and everyone would be surprised.[66]

At precisely 6:30 A.M. on July 12, newsboys circulated an early edition of the *Bisbee Daily Review*, its banner screaming, "Women and Children Keep Off Streets Today."[67] A siren at the Douglas smelter blared, not for warning of a Mexican invasion or Pancho Villa attack, but to engage more gunmen.[68] Simultaneously, vigilantes with white armbands ambushed men arriving for morning picket duty outside Bisbee mines and businesses.[69] Other men, armed with machine guns, rifles, and clubs, went door to door without warrants, waking up sleeping families. Husbands, fathers, and sons, prodded with gun butts, were ordered into the streets amid wails of protesting wives and mothers. While remembering their hats, many men dressed sockless.

A procession of over one thousand men, many of whom were not strikers or even miners, began a three-mile march to the Warren baseball park that morning at nine o'clock. Their women followed, climbing into the bleachers to observe what was happening. On the Calumet and Arizona Mining Company office roof, a machine gun was pointed downward toward the captives.

At 11:00 A.M., a train with nineteen El Paso and Southwestern Railroad cattle cars and boxcars arrived from tracks at the rear of the ball field on orders of Walter Douglas.[70] Crammed into the cars, some deep with manure, were 1,186 men, while armed guards stood on top. A few lucky husbands received hastily wrapped bundles of food from wives who fully understood the gravity of the situation.[71] As the temperature climbed above 110 degrees, the train departed. Deportees in smothering boxcars watched their women stumble alongside, slowly fading into the haze of Warren. Without food and little water, the deportees journeyed past gunmen lined on both sides of the track and machine guns on knolls leveled at them.[72] After 52 hours of travel with few stops, the train finally drew into a siding in Hermanas, New Mexico. There the undesirables were abandoned in the hot desert sun. For Bisbee residents, July 12, 1917, would be the day when "patriotism was pitted" against principles.[73]

1917 Bisbee Deportation

Frank Little's message changed after the July 12, 1917, Bisbee Deportation
when almost 1,200 men were deported. *Courtesy of Arizona Historical Society,
Photo Postcard Collection.*

Before he left for Salt Lake City, Frank hobbled up to Ralph Chaplin's office to say goodbye. Chaplin recalled that Frank was still
disturbed about the GEB's lack of action. Frank commented, "You're
wrong about registering for the draft. It would be better to go down
slugging."[74] After Utah, Frank intended to travel to Butte, Montana, to direct strike organization. Chaplin "marveled at Frank's
courage in taking on a difficult and dangerous assignment like
this in his present condition."[75] He joked to Frank, "It's a fine
specimen the IWW is sending into that tough town, one leg, one
eye, two crutches—and no brains!"[76] But Frank only laughed and
pretended to hit Chaplin with his crutch. "Don't worry, fellow-
worker, all we're going to need from now on is guts."[77]

23

BUTTE, 1917

Over the past hundred years, historians, authors, and working-men have added various sobriquets to the once bawdy city of Butte, names generally depicting the town as civilized and capti-vating, criminal and dangerous, or toxic and dead. Today the city is rejuvenated, with restored elegant mansions, humble cottages, and verdigris-encrusted buildings framed by grassy slopes and imported trees. Attractive slanted streets, newly painted gallows (gallus) head frames, and prominent historical museums and libraries add to its charm. It has outgrown the six or seven blocks that were the primary building district in 1917, an area once thronged day and night with men looking for end-of-shift drinks or female companion-ship. The old city shrugs off decline and welcomes the rebirth that proudly claims all Butte's characterizations. Butte is at peace with its history.

Traveling north on Main Street, toward what locals call "Up-town" or "up the Hill," visual reminders of Butte's connection with mining come to life. Cross streets named for the area's minerals—Copper, Quartz, Granite, Mercury, Silver, Gold, Porphyry, and Galena—intersect prominent business avenues. Victorian-frontier, red-and-mauve brick buildings, some more than six stories tall, await restoration with their toes dug solidly into the flanks of the streets. To the east are a few faded cottages and traces of barren mine dumps, some green with vegetation, surrounding the site of an infamous kidnapping in 1917.

Frank Little traveled to his death on Wyoming Street, one block east of Main Street, adjacent to the mostly barren gray slopes of old Finntown. To the north of Finntown lay Dublin Gulch, where bored Irish lads would get into rock fights with Finnish boys. Traveling south, Wyoming Street enters a former notorious red-light district that was not officially closed until 1982.[1] Nothing remains of the Steele Block at 316 Wyoming, the boarding house from which Frank was abducted. A hotel and parking lot have replaced both it and neighboring Finlandia (Finn) Hall. The Anaconda Road, where thousands of miners walked to and from work in 1917, runs north of the lot and branches eastward toward nothingness.

At the base of the East Ridge Mountains, just northeast of these neighborhood remnants, sits a 1,700-foot-deep hole filled with toxic water: the Berkeley Pit. The former open-mining pit consumed miles of copper-rich tunnels and the poor neighborhoods atop them when Anaconda Copper Mining Company determined a more efficient way to mine copper ore. Overlooking the deep yellow abyss, a monument dedicated to the Granite Mountain–Speculator Fire mining catastrophe whispers the story of a more sinister time in Butte while paying homage to those who died so tragically on June 8, 1917. Frank's death is also recorded there, as a casualty of the suppression of labor.

No union workers labor at the edge of the Butte pit today. High above sparse trees and low yellow hills, atop the pine-fringed Continental Divide, stands a ninety-foot-tall white statue. Our Lady of the Rockies spreads her arms over a city that was ripped apart by both unions and copper mining corporations.

To the Copper Kings—Marcus Daly, William A. Clark, and later, Augustus Heinze—Butte's worth was incalculable. The source of its wealth, originally silver, transformed overnight to the flame-orange metal sought by global markets. The three men battled over ownership of mineral deposits and political positioning, impacting local and Montana state policymaking and economy for over

WYOMING STREET VIEW, BUTTE, MONTANA

Frank Little traveled to his death on Wyoming Street, running northwest and southeast in the photo. Finn Hall (with Gothic windows) and the Steele Block Boarding House (below arrow) are the third and fourth buildings from the north corner of Wyoming Street. *Courtesy of the World Museum of Mining, Butte, Montana.*

twenty-five years. Butte became known as the "World's Greatest Copper Camp" because of their presence.

The Irish Diaspora heavily influenced Butte, and no other American city at the turn of the twentieth century was so overwhelmingly Hibernian.[2] When Irish immigrants landed on American shores, they regularly asked for directions to Butte, America, largest city between Pittsburgh and Spokane.[3] Even non-Irish immigrants felt their influence. Butte rug peddler Mohammed Akara purportedly had his name changed legally to Mohammed Murphy for business reasons.[4] The Irish were communal in all facets of life, which impacted labor convictions. Since underground mining had been part of their recent shared past, Butte Hill became their shared future, both good and bad. Disasters were generally accepted with collective mourning, acceptance, and fortitude. As long as Daly was alive, there never was a strike in Butte.[5] But Daly died in 1900 just after consolidating his mining interests, including the Anaconda Mine, under Amalgamated Copper Mining Corporation. By 1915, after more corporate consolidation, Anaconda Copper Mining Company emerged, known to locals simply as "the Company."[6]

Butte Miners' Union Local No. 1 had been strongest of all WFM locals, and Butte quickly earned the title "Gibraltar of Unionism" because of its success. The union remained a branch of the WFM from 1905 until 1911 when it rejoined the AFL. Generally, Butte mine workers moved in the same direction as mine operators, accepting their politics and maintaining a closed shop until 1914.[7] A challenge to Butte's relationship between labor and politics began in 1911 when citizens elected a full SPA ticket to city offices, including a new mayor. When Unitarian minister Lewis J. Duncan and his city council wanted to tax mining tonnage for the city's coffers, the Company sought political change.[8] One way to implement change was to control who would be permitted to work in Butte and, consequently, who voted.[9]

The next shift in employee-employer relationships began in 1912 when the Company reintroduced the infamous rustling card system to employ men who fit into the Company's desired social and political profile.[10] The white rustling card was actually a leave-to-look-for-work permit. Any man who came into Butte could not "rustle" a job in a mine, no matter how much demand there was for work, unless he first went to the "rustling card office" and gave his personal history, political affiliations, and past labor history.[11] If approved, he could come back and collect his card. It might take two weeks to collect the card, if he received it at all. With this system, miners were blacklisted if their political bents diverged from the Company's views.

Local Company-sponsored newspapers often neglected reporting labor abuses even as workers became increasingly outspoken

within Miners' Union Hall.[12] The Company's hiring practices, coupled with safety concerns and continuous labor contracts, increased
Local No. 1's dysfunction as men began quarreling concerning the
union's ineffectiveness in labor affairs. When Duncan was reelected
mayor in 1913, the Company redoubled its efforts to destroy Butte's
SPA politics. Local No. 1 gave the mining company an opportunity
to remove the Socialists, especially Mayor Duncan and a local
sheriff, when miners' riots broke out in June 1914.[13] The union split
into two factions: a conservative group that wanted to maintain
status quo with the Company, continuing to collect dues and special assessments through card inspections, and a progressive group,
mainly Socialists, that wanted to effect change immediately in
companies' management and labor policies, including abolishing
contractual agreements. After a series of contentious events and
possible provocation by Company-planted detectives, radical miners
blew up Miners' Union Hall on Main Street.[14] IWW agitators became
the scapegoat.

From fall 1914 until June 1917, there was no miners' organization in the Butte district, and so, the Company increased its labor
abuse. Conditions in certain mines had become so dangerous that
companies had a difficult time getting men to work. To prevent
men from taking jobs elsewhere, miners were restricted to two
rustling cards a month. This meant that when a man wanted to
work within a different mine, he had to wait two weeks before
applying for a rustling card, which might take another two weeks
to become approved.[15]

Butte was becoming a town of diverse cultures, its neighborhoods defined by ethnicity and by the mines in which men worked.
Not surprisingly, ancestral emotions tied to the European War made
for rancorous divisions, affecting the Company's labor force. The
Pearse-Connelly Club was an active presence in Butte, having sprung
from Ireland's Easter Uprising. Named after two Irish leaders—
Patrick Pearse and James Connelly—its members sympathized with
the Sinn-Féiners in Ireland who detested British rule. The Finnish,
most of whom were socialists, and their cousins, the Swedes, also
brought ethnic biases with them, condemning Russia for its attempted
"Russification" of Finland and other Baltic countries. Some of these

European cultures had an "us versus them" historic past, working class against ruling class, so fighting the mining corporations was perhaps instinctive. The United States' decision to ally with Russia and Great Britain in the Great War awakened vociferous objections, creating still more social schisms in Butte. While their fathers argued the merits of war, the rustling card system, and mine safety, children played on toxic grounds among their homes near mines and tailing piles. Air quality was so bad that virtually no trees grew within the town or on Butte Hill, and a metallic-mineral taste often disturbed the palates of anyone who ventured outside.[16]

The Justice Department had begun placing agents in locations where unions agitated and where enemy agents might be infiltrating American organizations or interfering with the war effort. Twenty-seven-year-old Bureau of Investigation agent Edward W. Byrn had just arrived in spring 1917 from Washington, D.C., to monitor Butte's union agitation among sixteen thousand mostly immigrant miners who now worked twelve-hour days to support the war machine.[17] In a report to the Bureau of Investigation headquarters on August 5, Byrn wrote that Butte's large low-grade foreign population, the "scum of the various nations of Europe," was centered largely in the mines. His word choice illustrates how even the Justice Department viewed the struggling immigrant population, let alone the Company's views.[18] Much like Arizona's copper camps, mining industries, and their agents, many of Butte's mining managers viewed unskilled immigrants with little empathy and sometimes outright disdain, even as they depended on the fruits of their labor.

A walk through the paupers' section of Butte's Mountain View Cemetery shows grave after grave of young men who died in their prime, supporting a common belief that more miners were buried in Butte's cemeteries than once living in the city itself.[19] It is no surprise that, despite a deep pride in their craftsmanship, miners constantly feared for their safety. Below their neighborhoods, a reported ten thousand miles of dangerous tunnels ran under Butte, with shafts up to one mile deep.[20] One could walk from one mine to another mine under the city. However, many considered it a victory just to be able to walk *out* of the mine each day. Children looked for fathers trudging through mine gates after work while wives and mothers constantly listened for wailing whistles heralding mining calamities. Doctors responding to companies' whitewashed health and accident reports countered that the "slaughter of miners in Butte was appalling."[21] Common fatal ailments included pneumonia, caused by sandpapered lungs from an accumulation of rock dust; silicosis; lead poisoning; and tuberculosis.[22] Accidents among recent immigrants, with and without the use of unfamiliar, modern technology, also took their toll.[23]

Instead of telling a man to "Go to hell!" he was advised to "Go to Butte!" as Butte was about as near hell as a man could go where normal underground temperatures ranged between 110 and 120 degrees.[24] Working in old timber, miners had to watch for fires that ignited easily in the oily works. To stop fires from spreading underground, mining companies installed bulkheads between tunnels to other mines. Sealed bulkheads, in which North Butte Mining Company was supposed to have installed manhole doors, contributed enormously to loss of life on June 8, 1917, when the Granite Shaft ignited in Speculator Mine after a worker accidentally touched his carbide lantern to a frayed, oily electrical cable.[25] The resulting inferno was instantaneous as oil-covered insulation burst into flames. Of the 900 men at work in tunnels, scattered on different levels with no exits below a spreading fire that discharged deadly gases and smoke downward, 168 died.[26] Ironically, miners had been installing a sprinkler system to improve safety.

When the Granite Shaft blew, a series of short bursts erupted from the mine whistle, alerting ambulances, hearses, and "dead" wagons to hasten up Broadway. Crying wives, mothers, and children waited nearby for their husbands, sons, and fathers to be discovered, peering through holes in a fence erected around the shaft.[27] Confusion abounded for days as authorities gave no official account of the death trap below. Electrician William F. Dunn, during his 1918 testimony in the Chicago IWW trial, stated that he saw the condition of charred bodies in Duggan's Morgue, their torn, bloody fingernails attesting to the men's efforts to scratch their way out.[28] The bodies had been discovered piled on top of one another next to a sealed bulkhead. Papers had only reported the results of a company-controlled inquest, ignoring accusations that the bulk-heads had been sealed.[29] Dunn also stated that he never saw a mining inspector underground in the two and a half months he worked for the Company.[30] And so, Butte was a city of widows and cemeteries in 1917. When Frank Little arrived in town, bodies were still being pulled out of the mine.

A rebellion of Irish miners acted as a preamble to the 1917 Butte strike. On Registration Day, June 5, while Frank was still in Jerome, Arizona, Butte miners launched an organizing drive to restart Butte Miners' Union. At about six in the evening, they involved themselves in antiwar agitation, holding a meeting and a parade.[31] The parade began at Finn Hall, with about one thousand Irishmen, Finns, and Swedes carrying banners with antiwar messages. Many of the Irishmen belonged to the Pearse-Connelly Club. When a disturbance broke out in front of the federal building on the corner of Main and Copper Streets, policemen and protesters began fighting. Afterward the Second Montana, which was headquartered in Butte, cleared streets and put the city under martial law for about six hours.[32]

Peter Rickman of the revitalized Butte Local No. 1 sent a letter requesting IWW help at once. He wrote, "Several of our members and sympathizers were imprisoned by authorities and consequently they have decided to declare Butte miners under strike conditions. So send us pamphlets and speakers if possible for it is the time to act. The sooner, the better."[33] Next the Electrical Workers' Union struck against Montana Power Company, and other electricians who worked for mining companies went out in sympathy. William Dunn, leader of the International Brotherhood of Electrical Workers Local No. 65, and an officer of the Montana State Metal Trades Council, led the charge. Then the Speculator Mine incinerated on June 8. Coupled with objections to mine companies' wage and hiring practices, the accident prompted a volatile reaction from most miners. The resulting strike had nothing to do with the war as far as miners were concerned.[34]

The Butte Metal Mine Workers' Union (BMMWU) officially formed on June 11, led by Tom Campbell, Joe Shannon, and Dan Shovlin, the latter two men present at the contentious 1907 WFM Convention. They decided against affiliation with the AFL and the IWW.[35] The Butte press immediately began calling the BMMWU an "outlaw" union or "Campbell's Union," while the IUMMSW formed in 1916 from the old WFM remained the "regular" union.[36] However, under Dunn's leadership, the Electricians' Union recognized the BMMWU, and others began endorsing the new union as well. Together they struck for improved safety regulations and righting of long-standing grievances.[37]

On the day before the Bisbee deportation, Frank purchased an expensive seat with a Pullman berth to Salt Lake City on the Chicago and North Western Railroad.[38] He was no longer traveling by the "side-door Pullman" as in his early days. He was in terrible physical shape and still needed the hernia surgery. With the broken ankle, some even called him a cripple. Almost a month after Almira Little's death, Frank also had no time to mourn. He now planned to spend several quiet days with Grover Perry in Salt Lake City's new home office of MMWIU No. 800, likely to discuss an IWW response to threats in Arizona and Montana mining camps.

On Monday, July 16, the day he left for the continuation of his journey to Butte, Frank wired Arizona's Governor Campbell to protest Bisbee's deportation. The exile of workers, leaving their women and children without support, had affected Frank profoundly. He wrote, "Understand that the mine owners' mob will take same action at Globe and Miami as was taken at Bisbee. The membership of the IWW is getting tired of the lawlessness of the capitalistic class and will no longer stand for such action. If you, as governor, cannot uphold the law, we will take same into our own hands. Will you act or must we?"[39] Governor Campbell bit back, claiming that with federal troops presently in the Miami-Globe district no deportations would occur. Campbell added, "I resent your untimely threats in view of my earnest efforts to bring law and order and such forces as well maintain same, and further like behavior on your part will be punished to the full extent of my authority."[40]

But Frank certainly had no trust for any governmental body, especially federal or state troops. Again purchasing an upper berth for a final overnight journey from Salt Lake City to Butte, Frank's bitterness grew.[41] The president, who had run a campaign of "He Kept Us Out of War," had broken his promise to America, and now the Great War was generating enormous profits on backs of workingmen overwhelmed by military-occupied camps and fear of deportation. As he approached Butte, Frank Little's message changed.

24

THIRTEEN DAYS

Bureau of Investigation agents were not informed that Frank Little was aboard a train rumbling into the red-brick Front Street Depot in Butte, Montana, on Wednesday, July 18, 1917. They were spying on a mustached doppelgänger in Chicago. A Thiel detective, employed by J. L. Bruce of the Butte and Superior Mining Company to infiltrate IWW headquarters in Chicago, thought he was monitoring Frank's activities. The detective's reports, copied to the Bureau of Investigation, stated that Frank was in Chicago from July 17 through July 22, in company with an IWW organizer named Miller. The detective noted that Frank and Miller had dinner in Miller's home on July 22, a testament to his close study of his target.[1] As a result of this error, the real Frank Little caught mining officials and the Bureau of Investigation unawares.

Upon his arrival, Frank proceeded to the Steele Block boarding house next door to the loftier Finn Hall, where the BMMWU was awaiting his arrival. Frank had selected his accommodations carefully. Walking south down North Wyoming Street after leaving Anaconda Road, miners regularly stopped at a saloon on the southeast corner of Copper and North Wyoming Streets just before passing Finn Hall and the Steele Block. To the west, streets were lined

with more businesses, boarding houses, and eateries that workingmen frequented. To the east and southeast sprawled Finntown,
centered on East Broadway and Granite Streets.[2]

But the Steele Block's landlady Nora Byrne was Irish. Honora
Lynch Byrne, widowed in 1910 when her young husband joined
other miners in Saint Patrick's Cemetery, had recently found work
managing the Steele Block. She and her sons had moved away
from death's dark business south of town where she had worked at
City Crematorium as a custodian.[3] Nora Byrne presented a friendly
face to her new tenant, making small talk, upon his arrival on
July 18. When Frank signed the register, Nora asked him if he was
related to Joe Little, an organizer for the new BMMWU. Distracted
by Byrne's question, and especially the name "Joe," he began to
write a capital "J" in the residence column. Quickly he scratched
out the letter and recorded Chicago, Illinois, and then paid rent up
to August 1, 1917.[4] Nora thoughtfully assigned Frank a room close
to the entrance so that he would not be encumbered with many
steps. Frank moved into room 32, next to Nora Byrne's living quarters, with his single suitcase.

By the time Frank arrived, Butte was simmering just below the
summit of the Hennessey Building's sixth-floor Company dominion
on Granite Street, derisively called the "floor next to heaven." A
molten stew of press reports, recalcitrant unions, scabbing, union
rivalries, and Company gunmen had created the tense environment,
ready to erupt if the right torch ignited the mix. Local unions' asym-
metrical organization had created obstacles for general strike organization, and the Company did not have to work hard to chip away
at craft unions and isolate the BMMWU. During the next week,
Frank would kindle great animosity among Company management
and disdain among AFL craft unions, many of whom feared and
resented his presence and interference.

Frank began igniting the flame at Columbia Gardens Baseball
Park the next day, July 19. The stadium, a magnificent structure
capable of seating thousands in grand style, was perfect for holding
a public meeting. A noisy grandstand behind home plate was filled
to capacity while the east and west side bleachers were half-full of
rank-and-file miners, union members, and union sympathizers.

Others stood shoulder to shoulder directly in front of the grandstand, interspersed with curiosity seekers, company spies, and
reporters. Labor leaders sat on a platform in the baseball diamond.[5]
The summer sky threatened rain.

By prearrangement, Tom Campbell, leader of the BMMWU,
chaired the meeting. Just after 3:00 P.M., he began his opening
address, stating the meeting's purpose to recognize Butte miners
and show them who their friends and enemies truly were.[6] Campbell emphasized that the miners' strike was yet in progress and read
a list of organizations supporting the BMWWU in order to validate
the new union's official recognition.[7] The audience fidgeted while
listening to the long list of contributors. Many knew by now that
Frank Little had arrived in Butte to address the miners, and the
audience could plainly see him waiting on the platform. Campbell next introduced Irishman Frank Mabie of the Workingmen's
Union. Mabie attacked the local press and its lies about the mines
operating at full capacity. He asserted that the reporters knew what
they were writing were lies, the editor who published the paper
knew they were lies, the newsboys who sold the papers knew they
were lies, and the men who read the paper knew they were lies.[8]
Mabie's accusations awakened the crowd, burning the ears of newspaperman A. W. Walliser of the *Butte Evening Post*, standing near
the speakers' platform; *Anaconda Standard*'s Charles S. Stevens,
standing between the platform and the grandstand; and Harold W.
Crary, sitting in the front row on the grandstand. These reporters'
selective coverage during the next two weeks would help inflame
the city, and their testimonies at the 1918 Chicago IWW trial helped
condemn Frank's speech as sedition. Next Patrick Gildea, another
Irishman of the Workingmen's Union, rose to congratulate the
miners on their conduct. The strike had been orderly and peaceful,
and he urged them to keep out of trouble and not take part in any
riots. If they stood together, they would surely win. If they lost the
strike, they could blame no one but themselves.[9] Gildea took his
seat, and Frank was next.

In his introduction, Campbell vouched for Frank as a man who
had a great deal of experience in labor movements.[10] The audience,
composed of chiefly conservative miners, peered at the slight man

on the platform, sitting with his crutches at his side and a white plaster cast showing below his right pant leg.[11] Frank hobbled to a speaking position, his face contorted with pain. Earlier he had received a letter from an IWW anxious about his weakened appearance instructing him to "throw away these crutches, F . . . they are no good to you."[12]

Frank's first words described recent events outside of Butte, setting the stage for the enormity of miners' solidarity in fighting the "Capitalist class and its warmongers." He recounted his recent trip, explaining his broken ankle. He told of his repeated abduction by thugs, and how he was "ruptured" from being thrown down and jumped on by gunmen in El Paso.[13] Frank had clearly risen from adversity—and so could the families of Butte.

He then reminded the audience of Ludlow's massacre of women and children, Cripple Creek's miner deportation, and the murder of a sleepy West Virginia tent village when machine guns brutally opened fire.[14] He told how in Butte itself, American soldiers with machine guns had been stationed on the great hill.[15] He called Bisbee's soldiers "Uncle Sam's Scabs."[16] It was natural for miners to dislike soldiers; hadn't the military interfered with the worker's right to strike? As his anger rose, Frank punctuated his statements by pounding his crutch on the wooden platform.[17]

Still rankled by Arizona governor Campbell's recent rebuff, Frank's voice rose as he recounted a story of how Campbell sent for him in late May to discuss what would happen if the companies refused to grant strikers' demands. Frank claimed that he told the governor that he would call every man out of the mines.[18] In response Campbell had said, "If you do that, I will put the mines under Federal control."[19] Frank then told the audience how he had chuckled, telling Campbell, "If you put the mines under federal control, I will call out all the workers, including the agricultural workers, lumber workers, munitions workers, miners, and all other classes of workers."[20] What Frank told the crowd next was repeated in newspapers all across the United States on August 1 and 2. He said Campbell exclaimed, "Why, Little you can't do that, this country is at war!" Frank had replied, "I don't give a damn what your country is fighting. I am fighting for the solidarity of labor."[21] He reiterated that if the demands of the striking miners were not met, all classes of labor would be called to strike, and "if the mines are taken under federal control, we will make it so damned hot for the government that it will not be able to send any troops to France."[22] But some of the men in the audience were men who had enlisted on June 5, including reporter Harold W. Crary. He looked forward to getting into military service, and Frank's description of "Pershing's yellow-legs" insulted him.[23] No matter that the term, devised by regulars, originated in identifying militia men within their ranks. That Frank called attention to the Bisbee wives and children who were starving without their deported husbands and fathers was also irrelevant. Crary afterward testified in the 1918 Chicago IWW trial that he was not impressed by what had happened in Bisbee. It was war time.[24]

The skies finally broke into a light rain, dampening the speakers, as well as those sitting in the bleachers and standing directly in front of the platform. But Frank turned his face toward the sky, raised his hands, and said, "Oh man, if this rain could only descend upon that bull pen in the hot, sun-parched desert of New Mexico, and bring some relief to the two thousand noble men held there by the uniformed federal thugs, it would be appreciated."[25] James P. Cannon later wrote that "with a wisdom never learned in books, he [Frank] seemed to sense the great historical significance of the stand he was taking," Frank's philosophy resting entirely on the solidarity of labor.[26] Thus, at the conclusion of this speech, Frank called for unity to gain liberty from oppression. He emphasized that every trade, every branch, and every walk of life must rise together and throw off the yoke of the capitalist.[27]

While not everyone in the audience was an IWW sympathizer, the *Anaconda Standard* reported that a majority radical crowd "wildly applauded" Frank's speech.[28] The paper also reported that Frank was "very adroit" and, while he made no direct statement concerning the IWW, every person knew what he meant by "the one big union."[29] Still, his inflammatory words were totally different from the other speakers on the platform, and likely defied audience expectations.

After about three hours the public meeting concluded, and everyone went to their corners to prepare for an imminent fight. In his report to Chicago headquarters, Agent Byrn stated that from the tenor of Frank's remarks, it was evident that his purpose was to bring the newly formed Miners' Union into the IWW. Company spy Warren D. Bennett confirmed Byrn's assessment.[30] That evening Agent Barry, also of the bureau, mailed a letter to the chief of police in Peoria, Illinois, requesting any records on members of the IWW's GEB and specifically on F. H. Little.[31] The bureau wanted to know Frank's past activities and if they had any reason to arrest him. Realization that Frank Little was actually in Butte, Montana, slowly filtered through telegrams and mail to federal agents. Agent Byrn stood ready to investigate.

As before, the press had its own tactics to combat the threat of organized labor. Reporter A. W. Walliser emphasized Frank's use of the terms "uniformed scabs" and "scabs in uniform" in his reporting that evening, although he later admitted that he had heard the terms thousands of times before as miners commonly used them during strikes to describe troops employed for strikebreaking.[32] Walliser had reported on the Cripple Creek strike but in Butte his disregard for the IWW colored his objectivity. He selectively reported what was best for the mining companies, omitting the failure to install bulkhead doors in the Speculator Mine in his account of the June 8 tragedy.[33] Instead of headlining the speeches at the baseball park, the July 20 edition of the *Butte Daily Post* bannered an agreement that would modify the rustling card and increase wages based on a sliding scale. C. F. Kelley, the Company's vice president, published his front page editorial explaining the agreement, which the Company had reached with the Montana State Metal Trades Council.[34] However, not all craft unions were on board with the council's decision, including Butte's Electrical Workers' Union, despite its national headquarters' mandate to fall into rank and file. *Anaconda Standard*'s Charles S. Stevens did describe the mass meeting, characterizing Frank's words as inflammatory and radical. Stevens also claimed that Frank had been driven out of Bisbee, a notion that the other papers soon replicated.[35]

Finn Hall was home to several different unions. The BMMWU met on its ground floor, near a meeting room where about four hundred people could be seated. Down a hallway, which went to the back of the building, were more meeting rooms, as well as the

Electricians' Union headquarters. The IWW, having just come to Butte to organize on June 11, was relegated to a small office on the second floor in the far back.[36] With so many different groups using this building and other union halls, informants and reporters could blend into union audiences—or "accidentally" enter the wrong meeting room or hall—with ease.

On Friday, July 20, the BMMWU held a business meeting in Finn Hall. Frank was in attendance. Along with business relating to their organization and the strike, they discussed two telegrams from Bill Haywood inviting them to affiliate with the IWW. After some discussion, they passed a motion to stay out on strike until the Arizona miners were granted their demands too, a point Frank had made in his speech the evening before.[37] Acting chairman Dan Shovlin then announced that one of their boys was currently sitting in the Butte jail and wanted to get out. Tom Hanrahan, a member of the BMMWU defense council, left quickly to see about the man's release. He swiftly returned, claiming that he had discovered a meeting being held in the elegant Finlen Hotel on Broadway Street. Hanrahan told the group that a mass of gunmen, including government officials and Police Chief Jere Murphy, were sitting at a large table "doing a lot of writing."[38]

Known as "Jere the Wise" for his gut intuition and ability to remember names and faces, Murphy ruled the city with an iron fist. At odds with Butte socialists, and especially those who met at Finn Hall, Murphy made arrests whenever the occasion arose, creating a reputation of harshness among some immigrant workers. Once when a Finn bit Murphy's hand to the bone, the 6-foot, 230-pound Murphy subdued the man with a club, a disciplinary practice commonly used by Butte police.[39] English and Finnish socialists reportedly considered efforts to remove Murphy as chief of police in 1913.[40] Perhaps wisely, they reconsidered. Besides being employed as police chief, Murphy moonlighted for Roy Alley, lawyer and private secretary of the Company's president, John D. Ryan, who controlled the Company's private army of guards or gunmen.[41] A meeting that involved any of these men meant trouble for the BMMWU.

Ragnar Johanson, a Missoula Lumber Workers' Union delegate with whom Frank had worked in the past, had arrived in Butte to speak to this same group at 2:35 P.M.[42] He and his fellow loggers were currently striking for an eight-hour day. Before Johnson was called to the podium, Shovlin cautioned everyone to stay away from the hall after the meeting, exit in an orderly fashion, and to use extreme prudence in their words with others. Frank, who had been quietly observing up to this point, reminded the men that there would soon be a move to run the new union members out of town. Everyone agreed that no matter who was left, they would try to hold a daily executive meeting.[43] What the miners did not know was that in this closed meeting, where reporters were not invited, Warren D. Bennett was taking copious notes for the Company and the bureau. In his speech, Johanson asked for solidarity between the two unions since 80 percent of the mills' output was mine lumber.[44] After his request, everyone left Finn Hall in an orderly manner.

That evening at 9:00, another group met in Finn Hall. This time Frank spoke to three hundred to four hundred workers, mostly Finns and Swedes, in an open IWW meeting.[45] A translator was provided. William Bennett also attended, still spying for his employers. Frank told the audience that this was going to be a "straight IWW" meeting.[46] Noting that he expected "prostitutes of the press" to report every word he uttered that evening, just as they had in the morning papers, Frank went on to criticize capitalists. He declared that a person could make a living three ways: by working, begging, or stealing. The only conclusion he had was that the capitalist class were thieves since they did not work or beg for a living.[47] Reiterating the phrase "uniformed thugs" for the press's benefit as he described the soldiers' massacre of women and children at Ludlow, Frank hammered the aristocratic labor union, the AFL, whose train engineers and brakemen had carried the soldiers and their guns to Ludlow. No true union man would have done that, he declared.[48] Frank also addressed the selective draft, saying, "We (the IWW) don't want to fight. If the Capitalists want to fight, we will go into the mining and munitions factories and furnish them the bullets to kill themselves off with. We don't want them here anyhow."[49] He added that any man could join the army, but if he did, then that man would not be able to carry an IWW card. Insulting the former

WFM, Frank declared that five hundred of the IUMMSW's six hundred members were probably gunmen and scabs.[50] IUMMSW members had made their own deals with Company officials and were no friends of the IWW, which had openly invited all to participate in the strikes. Finally, Frank pointed out that if miners organized properly, they could get six dollars for an eight-hour day. Eventually they could put "the officials on the 6th floor below on the end of a muck-stick!"[51]

As they returned to their rooms in the Steele Block, Frank showed Ragnar Johanson a threatening message he had received earlier that day.[52] The mysterious envelope had been placed among mail scattered on a table just inside the boarding house's front door. Inside the envelope was a single sentence: "This is the first warning, beware, 3-7-77." There was no return address. The two briefly discussed the note, and then Frank shrugged and tore up the paper.[53] However, he did not dismiss the warning entirely. Frank wired Bill Haywood the day before his death, saying he expected to pay with his life for his stand against the war but that he considered it worth the sacrifice.[54] This martyr complex, which had percolated within his heart since Spokane's free speech fight, had melded with his sense of historical position. Frank deeply understood the impact his death could have on labor, and seemed to welcome becoming a purposeful casualty of war.

IWW organization proceeded apace, as did Frank's own efforts. Agent Byrn reported on July 20 that with the large increase in the cost of living, which was higher in this part of the country than elsewhere, the average worker found it difficult to feed his family. Byrn admitted that the only apparent relief from these conditions was that offered by the IWW, and therefore, many good workingmen, while not in sympathy with IWW principles, lent their support to the organization in the hope that they might derive material benefits from it.[55] Butte miner George R. Tompkins, in writing what he called "the truth about Butte" in September 1917, differed in his assessment. Tompkins wrote that once the "bigger fish" (Anaconda Copper Mining Company) ate "the smaller" mining companies, the industrial area was swept of all competitors, with a free field to bring "under complete domination and into absolute, abject slavery and peonage the whole people of an entire state."[56] Tompkins pointed out that the working class had finally revolted after the Speculator fire and the AFL's nonresponse to their interests.[57]

The day after its closed-door business meeting, the BMMWU held a public meeting to try and gain more supporters for the strike. Reporter A. W. Walliser was in attendance, as he was at every Saturday general meeting. He reported that there were ten thousand IWW members in Butte who were "against everything and everybody," including the federal government and the state of Montana.[58] He wrote that up to three hundred IWW miners, primarily imported, were the real disturbers who terrorized everyone else. When later called to testify to circumstances during the 1917 summer in Butte, though, Walliser admitted that actually there were no more than twenty to thirty IWW organizers. [59] His colorful reporting had accentuated the heightened fear that the IWW was in control of the new strike, when in reality the strike had thus far been a product of the new BMWWU.

On Sunday morning, July 22, Ragnar Johanson finished with his charge to bring the Butte miners in line with the lumber workers and packed to leave the Steele Block. Like Frank, Johnson found an envelope addressed to him on the hall table. Late for his train, Johanson grabbed the mail without opening it until he was safely on board. Inside was a piece of paper with an identical warning to Frank's.[60] Apparently the same spies were at the IWW general meeting and the BMMWU closed meeting, and it seems more than likely that Warren Bennett was not alone in his spy efforts. Later that afternoon, miners again took a ten-minute streetcar ride over to Columbia Gardens to attend another mass meeting at the baseball park. Again Frank sat on the platform with other labor leaders in front of an audience of about two thousand people.[61] This time he did not speak, observing the audience's reaction to the speakers. The press covered the event in their usual manner, claiming IWW terrorism.

The next day, the BMMWU held a regular open meeting that was subsequently reported in the *Anaconda Standard*. When miners questioned Frank's participation in the labor conflict, Ed Bassett defended him and declared that Frank had come from "the best kind of Americans," having Cherokee blood. Bassett added that Frank's friend and fellow Wobbly Grover Perry, "descended from men who landed at Plymouth."[62] Rumors that Frank was a half-breed Indian had become more amplified, likely because strike leaders desperately wanted miners to believe that the IWW was an organic American movement. After the meeting, Frank handed out old copies of *Solidarity* with both his and Perry's articles for the miners to read. The *Standard* highlighted the publication's excerpts regarding the "Outlaw Union" in order to further antagonize miners against the IWW. But Frank had already won over the BMMWU.

On Wednesday, a week after his arrival in Butte, Frank wrote a news story for *Solidarity* that would be published on August 4, 1917, three days after his death. He reported that, despite craft unions' scabbing, the metal miners' strike was "progressing in good shape and the output of copper output . . . practically nil."[63] He told of how newspapers were unsuccessfully reporting "scare line" stories in order to coerce miners back to work and that the miners were "sticking together solidly for victory."[64] Frank ended his story by recounting an "amusing incident" whereby a BMMWU committee mistakenly entered an IUMMSW hall to present a formal resolution branding the WFM as "scabs and gunmen," the same audience in attendance. Frank humorously added that after realizing their error, the committee "decided to go through with the program," and "You can imagine the reception it got!"[65] The article's tone suggests that Frank did not consider himself in imminent danger. He was certain that the new BMWWU would become IWW affiliated.

However, between Wednesday and Thursday, craft unions broke away from the strike, threatening the BMMWU's recognition as a legitimate union and its success in the strike. On Thursday, Frank stood in the BMMWU executive meeting and, according to an *Anaconda Standard* informant, declared, "I am an IWW and as an IWW I am responsible for what I say."[66] Frank attacked the trade unions for not standing in solidarity with striking miners, calling them "scabs." He reportedly said that the BMWWU needed to use direct action against men who were going back to work, instead of sending petitions to legislators.

Being called a scab was fighting words for any worker. As an example, Waldemar Kaiyala, born in 1907 to a Butte Finnish mining family, wrote that his father was extremely proud that he never scabbed even though he had ten children to feed.[67] Kaiyala's father's stance was not exceptional. Yet, some miners crossed picket lines because of economic conditions in Butte, disgracing themselves among their peers unless they could blame their parent union for their positions. The AFL provided such an umbrella for craft unions to give in to the Company's demands, irrespective of local conditions, in order to openly oppose IWW tactics. The BMMWU then made a statement with Frank's help, demanding craft unions throw off the AFL yoke. The paper prefaced Frank's remarks with "Little, who was driven out of Bisbee, and who advocated the workers letting the crops rot on the ground."[68]

Frank received a disappointing answer from Bill Haywood, dated July 27, in response to his wire of the previous Tuesday. Frank finally had reported success with the new BMMWU, soon to be Local No. 800, but had not yet received an organizational charter. He wanted to report to the BMMWU that they could participate officially in Denver's fall IWW conference, a promise Haywood made if they affiliated. But once again Haywood had hedged. The IWW had no money to send any delegates from the new Butte local to the Denver convention. Haywood, knowing the impossibility of such a change, even suggested to Frank that the convention be moved to Butte, a more central location.[69] This was more than likely Haywood's way of placating Frank and the new local with empty promises. Butte was too political and tied to the Company.

Even more dismaying was Haywood's response to Frank's most recent request to announce the formal GEB statement on the war. Haywood continued to avoid making an overt stand, writing, "In regard to the Statement of the Board on War, will say, after the statement in this week's *Solidarity* by the Editor [Ralph Chaplin] it would be superfluous to publish the statement of the Board, as it is practically the same and covers the same essential points as *Solidarity*'s statement."[70] After promoting the IWW to the BMMWU— its organization, the Denver convention, and its stand on war—

Frank must have felt deflated. Haywood did advise Frank that he had sent IWW attorney Fred H. Moore to Arizona to secure the release of the arrested miners in Prescott, Bisbee, and Globe. This information was but a mild salve to the rest of the disheartening telegram. Frank clearly wanted union members to take a stand against the war in solidarity, and Haywood's waffling irritated him immensely.[71]

The wound that had opened between Bill Haywood and Frank at their last GEB meeting bled openly. The two men could not have been more dissimilar in their approaches. Some suggested that Haywood was a coward; while others argued that Frank was too rash. Frank's peers disagreed with the latter assessment. Contemporary James P. Cannon attributed Frank's decision-making process to his "first virtue" of "physical courage" which Frank "possessed to a superlative degree." Cannon stated that, unlike Bill Haywood, Frank "was not a 'swivel chair' leader, but a man of the field and the firing line," who did not understand the meaning of the word "fear."[72] Ralph Chaplin recalled Frank's resolve. Frank had warned him that war would "mean the end of free speech, free press, free assembly—everything we ever fought for. I'll take the firing squad first!"[73] True to character, Frank passionately made his own antiwar statement on July 28 when he wrote an editorial in *Industrial Worker*. James Cannon stated that Frank's "I stand for solidarity of labor" was transmitted all over the country's telegraph wires.[74] While Frank was bold, the GEB likely cringed.

That same night, the BMMWU held its regular meeting with reporters present, including A. W. Walliser. Frank's words at this meeting, as reported in the next day's newspapers, added an exclamation point to his overall view of Butte politics, the Company, and how the miners were handling their strike. Frank contrasted capitalist mining organizations' and workers' interests. He also clearly put the IWW on the side of neutrality regarding the Great War. He said the IWW was not interested in the country's war but should "use the war just like the business men do, to make a profit for our class. Let the capitalists fight the battle and we will go into the munitions plants and see that they get plenty of bullets."[75]

In case people still believed that Wobblies were German sympathizers, Frank added, "The IWW do not object to war, but the way
they want to fight is to put the capitalists in the front trenches and
if the Germans do not get them, the IWW will. Then the IWW will
clean [out] the Germans."[76]

Frank knew he was rousing the Company's wrath. He encouraged the miners to start picketing and packing the jails, just as
Wobblies had done in their free speech fights. Reminiscent of his
Fresno soapboxing days, Frank also told miners to challenge acting
mayor Hanratty and the corrupt Butte Police Department:

> Look the city daddies in the face and tell them to go to hell
> and their city ordinances and laws. The ordinance is only
> a piece of paper which can be torn up and the same can
> be said about the Constitution of the United States. The
> country's laws are made by congressman, not by workers.
> Two years ago, every house in the country had Wilson's pic-
> ture in it and the words "He kept us out of war." But when
> we got into the war, he told us to shut our mouths.[77]

Frank's words were explosive and vitriolic. He cast the Great War
as a war among other nations and their show of brawn, not a just
conflict spawned from an attack on American soil. *Now*, Frank
affirmed, *was the time to strike.*

The next day was Sunday, and the regular mass meeting at the
baseball park served as a pep talk to miners who might consider
going back into the mines. Strike leaders asked the miners to "stand
pat" although the strike was currently in its seventh week.[78] After
the meeting, the various unions retreated to their meeting halls
and discussed their continuance in the strike. At Finn Hall, a purported one hundred men arrived at the BMMWU evening meeting.[79]
Frank spoke to the group and advised direct action, including the
use of using women and children on picket lines. It was the last
time Frank would address the BMMWU. The day after the meeting,
newspapers reported that police had responded to calls of men
attacking scab miners directly after the past night's meeting, suggesting that these attacks were part of IWW direct action.[80] Miners
claimed that their women were being assaulted by Company

gunmen.[81] Tensions continued to build as Butte prepared for the next incident of violence.

On Tuesday, July 31, thirteen days had passed since Frank's arrival. The front page of the *Butte Daily Post* shouted Bill Haywood's threat for a general sympathy strike unless the Bisbee deported miners were brought back. Haywood had wired President Wilson personally that a nationwide walkout of 250,000 men would occur unless some action was taken. His emissary, Fred H. Moore, had been illegally removed from Bisbee where he was representing deported miners.[82] Disappointed in Moore's lack of success, Frank sent a telegram to Miami, Arizona, encouraging the IWW local to "use any tactics necessary to defend yourselves and win the strike any way."[83] To Haywood, Frank wired that miners were solid for the IWW and were determined to win at all costs. Frank wrote "We've got what it takes," concluding his last letter, dated July 31.[84] In Butte, a general walkout would stop copper production completely.

At the Company's request, Montana governor Sam Ford implored District Attorney Burton K. Wheeler to arrest Frank. Wheeler investigated and found that Frank had perpetuated no crimes but had only exercised his right to free speech.[85] With the IWW's presence threatening the national and local war effort, and with no help from the county and state attorneys general, the Company determined to use its muscle to mold Butte into submission. Rumors of some ill will planned against Frank began lingering like ghost whispers in Butte streets. On North Wyoming Street the same day, some strange men pulled in front of the Steele Block. They wanted to ask Nora Byrne questions about her tenant from Chicago. Satisfied, they left.[86]

Frank was walking back to the boarding house when, as local legend has it, a barber named Cornelius Lowney stopped him to report that a lynching party was being formed, if the scuttlebutt in town was true. He warned Frank to get out of town. Vigilantes—whether hired guns of the Company, disgruntled union men who were not receptive to his message, or insulted soldiers—were planning Frank's murder.[87] Having heard these warnings before, Frank supposedly shrugged off Lowney's words.

That evening Frank stripped to his underwear, placed his pocket watch nearby, and crawled into bed. His crutches rested underneath.

In a dozen days, he had attended a myriad of union meetings and given at least five speeches. Frank was anxious to get back to Arizona.[88] He was undoubtedly exhausted and fell asleep. Just hours afterward, at about three o'clock on the morning of August 1, 1917, a black Cadillac quietly stopped at 316 Wyoming Street.

25

3-7-77

Nora Byrne, wrapped in her robe, waited at least forty-five minutes after Frank Little's abduction before calling police. She was badly frightened by the gun that one "officer" had pointed at her.[1] The masked gunmen had left her frozen with indecisiveness. She was not certain if they were law officers from the Butte Police Department or soldiers in uniform. They seemed young and spoke English well without an Irish brogue.[2] What if she contacted the same organization that had contracted the kidnappers? She discussed the possibilities with several of the roomers, including one of her sons, before she made the call to thirty-three-year-old officer James Casey of the Butte Police Department.[3] Later Nora's recollection of the men would become suspiciously vague.

Casey rushed to the Steele Block to secure the crime scene. The room was in minor disarray. Frank had not been able to gather any clothes, his Stetson, which he never went without, or his crutches. His pocket watch lay on the floor. Casey guarded the crime scene for Coroner Lane's investigation, including the contents of Frank's suitcase: IWW documents, letters, receipts, and telegrams, many of which had recently come from Bisbee.

Federal agent Edward W. Byrn was called to the Steele Block to do his own investigation, not certain that the missing man was

IWW GEB member Frank H. Little. Frank's arrival in Butte had placed Byrn on high alert while the "other" Frank Little in Chicago still was being shadowed. Agent Byrn subsequently sent the valise's contents, with a copy of Casey's report, to the Bureau of Investigation's Chicago office. Byrn's own report stated that in Frank's belongings was correspondence from various IWW organizers, including Bill Haywood. Frank had been carrying his sister Bessie Courtright's letter informing him of his mother's illness, and the subsequent telegram, sent from Lon Little, notifying Frank of their mother's death on June 9. Byrn determined that none of the items was important but sent them to bureau headquarters anyway.[4] The Little family was never offered these personal effects.

Butte police leaked information to Company-owned newspapers regarding the crime scene. The *Anaconda Standard* and *Butte Daily Post* erroneously reported that the telegram notifying Frank of his mother's death was sent by his brother *William* Little, and that another letter from a brother named *Henry* Little who was in jail in Seattle was found.[5] The story was instantly repeated in other papers across the nation. In fact, no brother named William existed, and Henry or Hank Little was no relation to Frank. Henry was a Canadian IWW who had been arrested on July 19 for inciting a riot during a logger strike.[6] Nevertheless, with Frank's murder and collection of his personal belongings, there was no doubt that Frank Little was not the man in Chicago that the Thiel detective so vigorously reported.[7] But where was Frank? Nora Byrne, the *Butte Daily Post* reported, suspected that he had been taken from his room in the Steele Block for deportation.

The sun was just hinting silvery light behind the East Ridge at about six o'clock on the morning of Wednesday, August 1. Gray wisps of clouds above the mountains, outlined in whites and gold, promised a bright blue sky on a day forecast to be warm. Robert W. Brown, a teamster whose current job was hauling tombstones, was on his way to work when the sunlight illuminated a white-clad body swinging from the north side of the Milwaukee Railroad trestle near Centennial Avenue. Dressed only in lightweight summer underwear abbreviated at thighs and arms, it dangled just a few feet from the trestle, which was fourteen feet above the ground. Attached to one thigh was a pasteboard placard six by ten inches, reading "Others take notice! First and last warning! 3-7-77, L-D-C-S-S-W-T."[8] A shattered white plaster cast barely encased the right leg below an obscenely bloody knee.[9] Brown immediately notified desk sergeant William Taylor who in turn called Police Chief Jere Murphy at home.

Chief Murphy had surely listened to Frank's speeches with disdain. Patriotic to the core, Murphy required all his police officers to purchase Liberty Bonds with a month's salary, or he would not consider them "red-blooded American enough" to work for him. He told his men that it was their duty to aid the government in every possible way, even if they had to borrow the money to do so.[10] When Murphy called Coroner Aeneas Lane to meet him at the crime scene, he appeared to be in no hurry, arriving after the other investigators. Most likely he had heard rumors of the murder plot and suspected or even knew the participants.[11] Murphy would lead the local investigation.

Frank's body was still warm when Detective Frank White and patrol driver Ralph Wynne first arrived amid a few interested bystanders.[12] After Coroner Lane arrived about seven o'clock, they studied the position of Frank's body hanging just feet above the ground. It had the appearance of having been placed there after Frank was either unconscious or dead, as there was no evidence of a struggle. Only small trickles of blood streamed from the back of his head to his shoulder and from his nose, evidently from a bullet or blows, demanding immediate postmortem examination. After more law officers and mortician James Cassidy arrived, the men continued to study the crime scene. Cassidy was certain that Frank was indeed unconscious at the time of his death.[13]

The setting beneath the Milwaukee Railroad trestle revealed other clues. Smooth cord-tire tracks with two grooves running through the center around the outer circumference left their imprint in the sandy soils. Footprints under the trestle were smudged since shifting sand obliterated any definitive patterns.[14] Evidence indicated that with a twenty-five-foot rope looped over the trestle timber, Frank had been lynched much like Wild West outlaws. The end result was the same. Instead of astride a horse, Frank had been

placed atop the dark Cadillac. After tying off the rope to the bottom
of the trestle, the car was driven away, leaving his slight body hanging five feet above the ground.[15]

It was a well-organized plan. Frank Little, hero to the working
class, had been ignominiously hanged by a bunch of thugs, the same
type of men he often described in his speeches. The railroad trestle
was near the entrance to Williamsburg, a small German American
neighborhood outside Butte, in a clear warning to German sympathizers. Murphy and Police Lieutenant Dwyer officially identified Frank before cutting him down at 8:00 A.M. Coroner Lane, after
removing the body for autopsy, drove to room 32 in the Steele Block
to further his investigation.

As Butte rumbled awake, the news rapidly spread to every home
and hall. The morning paper, the *Butte Daily Post*, provided graphic
details of the crime, adding to the horror of the news. As if to exon-
erate the murderers and justify the homicide, the paper provided
a list of Frank's alleged treasonable statements.[16] Such reporting
only increased rancor between metal miners and the Company.
Strangely, many Montana newspapers were purported to have
printed editorials lauding Frank's death before he even arrived at
the undertaker's.[17] Will Campbell, the superpatriot editor of the
Helena Independent who warned of German airplanes flying over
Montana, wrote, "Good work, let them continue to hang every IWW
in the state."[18]

Angry men congregated around Finn Hall, many packing guns
and muttering threats of retaliation against Company gunmen.[19]
Next door, various law enforcement teams entered and exited the
Steele Block under baleful eyes of union members standing in the
street. Someone hoisted an American flag half-mast over the Gothic-
styled windows of the hall and placed a notice on matching Gothic
doors: "Frank Little was taken from his bed early this morning and
murdered by gunmen. He was not given chance to put on his clothes
or get his crutches."[20] To many, Frank's murder was an open salvo
against labor.

It did not help that soldiers had been called in, despite press
reports to the contrary. Company B, Second Montana Infantry Regiment had been camped just outside Butte at the request of U.S.

District Attorney Burton K. Wheeler since before Registration Day. Patrols stood on street corners with bayonets and machine guns fixed at principal street intersections, threatening military intrusion in civil matters, similar to what Frank had described one week earlier.[21] The Company did not intend to be shut down because a bunch of miners were upset, and definitely not because of one Wobbly's death.

Wheeler telegraphed U.S. Attorney General Thomas W. Gregory in Washington, D.C., by early afternoon, advising that he had received a report that the masked killers had worn uniforms.[22] If the military or police were involved, Butte could be a powder keg igniting the city and IWW wrath nationwide. The Bureau of Investigation swiftly ordered an investigation that Agent Byrn would head.

A fog of apprehension settled on the hillside city while everyone waited and hypothesized about the crime. A far-fetched rumor began circulating immediately, possibly at the initiation of the Company itself, that Frank Little was a spy for the Company, and when the BMMWU found out, they killed him.[23] Butte's newspapers quickly picked up the story, which continued to grow, as others claimed that Company gunmen killed him, not knowing his informant status. With so many agents provocateurs embedded within unions, the rumor was tantalizing. Adding to the allegation, a former Butte detective and sometimes-barber George Ambrose claimed that he had been present when Frank's body was cut down and that papers found in a pocket of his underwear indicated Frank was connected with a detective agency.[24] Whose underwear had pockets? Was Ambrose even there, or was this another barbershop yarn? Conn Lowney, also a barber, disagreed with Ambrose, afterward describing Frank as "a clean man and no double-crosser."[25] In subsequent testimony, William F. Dunn stated that fully half of the IWW were undercover detectives or informants. He held out the possibility that Frank was brought into Butte because an undercover Company detective enticed him to come. However, he declared that Frank was not a Company detective himself.[26] It is important to note that Dunn did not approve of the IWW although he was much involved in the new strike and antagonized the Company through his outspokenness in his prolabor publication, *Butte Daily Bulletin*.

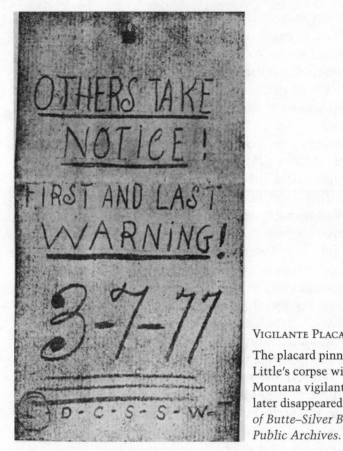

Vigilante Placard

The placard pinned to Frank Little's corpse with the old Montana vigilante code later disappeared. *Courtesy of Butte–Silver Bow Public Archives.*

    With the exception of Frank, who received his first warning on July 20, the infamous placard roused yet more speculation. Who was next? The custom of the Montana vigilantes was to send two warnings to a marked man. The warnings were usually numbered as "first warning" and "second warning." The "last warning," which often was written in red, was a final penalty, as indicated by the circled red "L" on Frank's placard.[27] Bureau of Investigation's special-agent-in-charge F. W. Kelly, along with many others, believed the figures on the placard to be dimensions of a grave (3 feet wide by 7 feet long and 77 inches deep), dire consequences for those who ignored the first two warnings.[28] Had Frank received a second warning?

Strike leaders whose initials were listed on Frank's placard spoke candidly about receiving similar warnings themselves. Everyone was certain that the "C" was for Tom Campbell. The two "S's" must have stood for two of three people—BMMWU organizers Joe Shannon and Dan Shovlin, or their attorney William Sullivan. The "T" was for BMMWU organizer L. Tomich; "W" for John Williams, an IWW organizer; and the "D" for *Butte Daily Bulletin* editor William Dunn.[29] In fact, both Campbell and Dunn received duplicates of the vigilante card through the mail on the same day Frank was hanged. The addresses on their envelopes were made of clipped numbers and letters pasted on the envelopes.[30]

Although Bill Haywood promised that "resources of the organization [IWW] would be employed to bring lynchers of Little to justice," various unions were not so sure of justice in Butte.[31] So frightened were they that their representatives went to the sheriff's department asking permission to carry arms.[32] By afternoon on August 1, the BMMWU warned their members to keep their mouths shut and tread carefully in the tense city.

Window boxes of bright flowers softened the shadow-lettered sign presenting "Duggan the Undertaker" on glass-front windows at 322 North Main Street. Along with the town's other undertakers, Larry Duggan had just finished preparing the Speculator dead during the last month, probably using all the hearses in his multicar heated garage, when Frank's body was delivered the afternoon of his death. It had first been driven uptown to Sherman and Reed's Undertaking Rooms where it was autopsied per Coroner Lane's instructions, but the union demanded that Duggan, not James Cassidy, handle the body.[33]

A trained embalmer, Duggan was quite active in Irish fraternal organizations such as the Pearse-Connelly Club and the Workingmen's Union. As such, he supported both the BMMWU and Frank. Duggan laid out Frank for public view and photographic documentation. Hundreds of morbidly curious people, many weeping Finnish women, streamed into Duggan's morgue to view the partially naked corpse.[34] Many had to see the body just to believe the murder had taken place.

At Bill Haywood's order, a death mask and two postcard photos were taken of Frank. The first showed Frank's black-and-blue body stretched out with his bruised hands clasped in repose in front of a foot bridge and floral backdrop, his mutilated kneecaps incongruous with the pastoral setting. The other unadorned photo similarly posed Frank, with his midsection modestly covered with a white sheet, his plaster cast removed, and both kneecap flaps of skin pulled back into place. The brutal injuries to his neck, arms, legs, and hands are still quite visible in both photos. The body's condition spawned macabre discussions in saloons, meat markets, barbershops, cafés, Finn Hall, and even the sixth floor of the copper-gilded Hennessey Building. Post-mortem photos were nailed on boards and poles in public places, emblazoning one more victim of the class struggle to enrage public opinion. As quickly as gunmen tore them down, more grisly photos appeared by next morning.[35] The death photos would later be sold to raise money for a General Defense Fund of the IWW.

With the body in public view and local newspapers printing lurid descriptions, various rumors of Frank's last minutes were woven into Frank Little's growing legend in Butte. One account states that Frank had been "drugged by a traitor" and had lain in a dead sleep when murderers broke in the door to his room.[36] Some said he was dead before he hanged.[37] Others reported that Frank was dragged by his neck behind the car, which could certainly have killed him before the car even arrived at the railroad trestle.[38] Henry E. McGuckin, an IWW GEB member, wrote that Frank, whose body was not only bloody and battered, was "desexed."[39] A rumor circulated among the Finns that Frank had been stabbed twenty-seven or twenty-nine times, probably a result of viewing the bruised half-naked corpse.[40] The most common rumor, still in circulation today, is that Frank Little left his kneecaps in the streets of Butte. The autopsy, performed by Dr. P. H. McCarthy early on the afternoon of August 1, did reveal gruesome details—Frank's

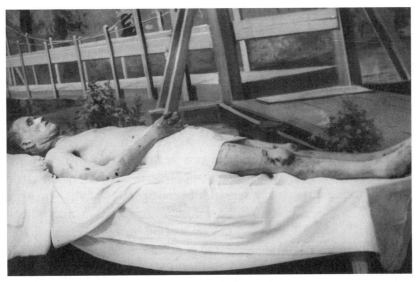

FRANK LITTLE'S CORPSE

Bill Haywood ordered photos of Frank Little's corpse in Duggan's Funeral Parlor. The IWW circulated the photo postcards immediately after Frank's murder. *Courtesy of Butte–Silver Bow Public Archives.*

shoulders and left shin were scratched, his head bloodied and both kneecaps mutilated.[41]

A coroner's jury, encompassing seven miners and ex-miners, met three times in order to make an investigation into Frank's death. At the outset of investigation, Coroner Lane voiced his opinion that the inquest would "develop nothing" beyond what was known already about the case, adding to a general assumption of futility regarding the investigation.[42] Two witnesses, who saw the big black sedan drive away from the Steele Block with Frank as they left a nearby saloon, disappeared before testifying.[43] With statements from other Steele Block witnesses, police, bystanders, and a physician, the jury swiftly finished their charge. Their final verdict read that the cause of death was strangulation by hanging at 3:15 A.M. on August 1, 1917. Frank's neck had not been broken, nor had he been

shot. After receiving blunt blows to the back of his head and muti-
lation from dragging, Frank had died of asphyxiation after being
drawn toward the trestle. He was already unconscious when he
died.[44] Yet, what should have become a file for further scrutiny
soon became a mysterious notation to the Frank Little legend. The
final coroner's report, including testimony from eleven people,
swiftly disappeared in an apparent cover-up of information that
might have revealed telltale evidence in future inspections.

In Chicago, throngs of reporters waited for words from Bill
Haywood. When Haywood finally appeared, he stated, "Frank Little
was an earnest, active advocate of the interests of the working
classes. I cannot begin to say how deeply I regret his death."[45] Haywood went on to tell reporters that he had notified Frank's sister
in Oklahoma City and sent word to Hank and Ed [Fred] Little, brothers of Frank Little.[46] Bessie Little Courtright actually received the
telegram in Perkins, Oklahoma, announcing Frank's death.[47] Haywood either did not actually know Frank's background, relying on
what the press had reported much earlier, or an informant present
at the meeting misquoted him. Nevertheless, his machinations to
use Frank's murder for the advancement of the IWW were hastily
placed in motion. Haywood wasted no time in writing an editorial
for *Solidarity* on the same day as Frank's murder, stating that it "was
not because of anything he [Frank] had said about the soldiers that
he was killed. He was murdered because of the part he was taking
in the strike at Butte, Montana." Haywood closed with, "The tragic,
brutal death of Frank Little will unite the working forces of this
country against the masters of bread. He has not died in vain, and
with his blood will be written the abolition of the wage system."[48]
The words "We never forget!" became a rallying cry for IWWs planning to march in a silent protest behind his body as it was shipped
to either Fresno, California, or Yale, Oklahoma.

The description of Frank as an unarmed cripple played well to
progressive circles, including union members, as news was wired
swiftly to newspapers across the country. One editorial stated, "In
the lurid history of Butte, no event ever occurred so startling, so
savage, of such sinister, evil portent as the inconceivably vicious
murder of Frank Little, a cripple, last Wednesday morning."[49] But

other newspapers voiced praise and even support for the gunmen, helping paint Frank's criminal portrait to justify extreme actions against other Wobblies. The Oklahoma press was particularly venomous regarding any IWW-related news, creating a frightening atmosphere for the Little family. *Tulsa World's* editor penned, "Frank Little, IWW organizer, lynched at Butte, Montana, left his will in the form of a poem. The poem could be described as beautiful had it been composed by or for a man that amounted for anything."[50]

By Thursday, August 2, Bessie Courtright and Lon Little were desperately trying to make funeral decisions in Yale. Frank's sudden death and the charged Oklahoma atmosphere made the situation delicate, and Lon was unsure as to what steps to take. From Fresno, Emma Little informed IWW headquarters that she and Fred favored Frank's burial in Chicago or Butte with an IWW demonstration. However, they ultimately deferred to Lon, the family patriarch, to make the unhappy arrangements.[51] Breaking his family's silence, Lon asked to have Chicago IWW headquarters ship Frank's body home on Sunday, August 5, 1917, where he and Bessie would bury Frank next to their mother Almira in the family plot in Ingalls.[52]

But Bill Haywood knew a good propaganda opportunity when he saw it and directly contacted Lon Little. With Frank's murder saluted across the nation by a rancorous press, a mob could destroy the family's funeral, or worse, harass the rest of the Little family if the body were returned to Oklahoma. Five neighboring Oklahoma counties had erupted into violence after Frank's murder when armed bands of tenant farmers decided to protest the draft under the light of a new Green Corn moon. A vigilante posse led by sheriffs was attempting to identify and capture the "slackers" using violence. Haywood urged Lon and Bessie to reconsider bringing Frank home to the unsettled state.[53] On August 4, Lon and Bessie came to a sound decision. Bessie wired IWW headquarters in Chicago, "Bury Frank Little where the Organization thinks best."[54] Frank Little now belonged to Butte.

Joe Shannon, William Sullivan, and Tom Campbell began making final arrangements for Frank's funeral to be held the next day, August 5, on "fighting ground," as IWW headquarters immediately directed.[55] The parade route would begin near the Federal Building on Main Street and end at Mountain View Cemetery. Larry Duggan placed the funeral announcement in the *Anaconda Standard,* where it was buried in the sports page between baseball scores and "want ads."[56] Despite the Company's efforts to play down the funeral, no advertising was necessary. Emma Little, who according to one paper had been supported in Fresno by her brother-in-law, sent the following message to Chicago: "Telegram Frank's funeral arrangements. Save a few of Joe Hill's ashes for me."[57] Her telegram indicated that she intended to be present for the funeral. It is doubtful Emma or Fred made the trip as the funeral location was suddenly changed to Butte, although Emma fervently would have desired to attend. Other IWWs arrived by the train load and were met by BMMWU pickets, who directed them to lodging. Over two hundred telegrams had been delivered in condemnation of Frank's murder, and IWW locals planned demonstrations across the nation.[58] The Second Montana Infantry stood prepared for chaos.

The largest funeral procession in Butte's history commenced at 1:30 P.M. on Sunday, August 5.[59] Over 3,500 men and women marched in the funeral parade, led by a color bearer from the Electrical Workers' Union. At his right was Tom Campbell, president of the BMMWU, and to his left walked R. L. Dunn of the electrical workers.[60] Behind the American flag came a volunteer band, consisting of members of the musicians' union from various bands, playing Beethoven's *Eroica* Symphony no. 3.[61] Next marched the Pearse-Connelly Club, with 120 members in large emerald sashes adorned with yellow and green rosettes. After the Irish organization, about 200 Finnish women and children marched.[62] Many carried babies or pulled their children in go-carts. Union members followed in solemn procession walking four abreast. Committee members of the BMMWU marched in front of the Electrical Workers' Union banner, the sole banner in the entire parade. Behind them marched the Street Railway Union, Hod Carriers' Union, Workingmen's Union, and other sundry craft unions finally brought together through a death. Lastly members of the BMMWU appeared during the parade, with almost 2,500 men, walking in a tight formation.[63] And then came the hearse.

FRANK LITTLE'S FUNERAL PROCESSION ON ARIZONA STREET

A portion of Frank Little's funeral procession on Arizona Street in Butte, Montana, said to be the largest funeral the city has ever witnessed. *Author's photo.*

Larry Duggan in a black top hat sat ramrod straight as he solemnly drove the empty hearse in front of three honorary pallbearers wearing scarlet sashes. Behind them six-foot-tall men, also in red sashes, carried Frank's pale-gray casket on their shoulders for their sections of the parade route. Twenty BMMWU members would take turns carrying it on their shoulders to the cemetery.[64] The ornately carved coffin was decorated with lacy-green ferns and blood-red carnations, wrapped with bright red ribbons proclaiming "Martyr for Solidarity" draped over the sides. After the pall-bearers, more bare-headed men marched in double file in silent lockstep, also wearing scarlet sashes.[65] Many were immigrants who had arrived in Butte to attend the funeral. After the guard of mourners, about a dozen automobiles carried friends and a delegation of miners.[66]

Ten thousand people stood on the streets or quietly hung out of windows, some waiting as long as two hours for the procession to appear along the four-mile route to the cemetery.[67] The parade took thirty minutes to pass each group of silent spectators along the route to the cemetery south of the city.[68] In death Frank Little was too large for the Company and Police Chief Jere Murphy to control. Amid the crowds, Murphy's entire police force, scores of deputy sheriffs, and four hundred members of the National Guard were on hand in case the funeral was used for labor agitation or demonstration.[69] But instead of rousting demonstrators, the detectives, police, and Company gunmen could only observe union men and women in their disciplined procession. A moving camera filmed the orderly event for the IWW.

When the procession reached the city limits close to Mountain View Cemetery, the American flag was replaced with a red banner bearing the word "Solidarity."[70] With the American flag removed, Frank's body was placed in the hearse and driven the remaining distance to the cemetery where a brief graveside ceremony was held. No minister or family member was present to give spiritual solace or attest to Frank's personal information. Instead, a eulogy delivered by Tom Rimmer expressed outrage at the murder. A few short speeches underlined that Frank had died for the solidarity of the working class. As Frank's casket was about to be lowered into the grave, the camera was directed to capture the message Bill Haywood wanted the world to see. A red silk banner reading "The One Big Union, Universal, the IWW" was turned so the camera could record its image along with other red banners reading "A Martyr for Solidarity." Red carnations, red roses, and red silk handkerchiefs were tossed onto the casket as a last tribute to a man who was devoted to liberty and the class struggle. After the eulogy, mourners sang "The Marseillaise," the revolutionary song of the Industrialists.[71] The moving camera captured it all for the OBU—but the film, like the autopsy report, would mysteriously disappear.[72]

Frank's general strike took effect through his death. The great Anaconda, the largest copper mine in the world, was shut down as a citywide strike ensued. A member of the IWW wrote on August 18 that no smoke was coming out of the big stack at Anaconda, and that "just so surely as they dragged Little to his death, just so surely will retribution be meted out to them [Anaconda Copper Mining Company], and when law exacts from them the full penalty, not one of them will die as gamely as did Frank Little."[73] William Dunn proudly added that "we stopped completely the production of that primary war necessity—copper—when it was selling for 26 1/2¢ per pound."[74] The strike would last almost six months. Federal troops under future five-star general Omar Bradley later appeared in Butte, relieving many citizens since Company gunmen continued to patrol streets.

Unsurprisingly, no murderers were ever convicted of the crime despite early warnings, tire tracks, footprints, and reluctant witnesses. A patsy, transient miner Charles McCarty (alias Charles Albright), was hastily identified as a suspect so that the government could move on to more serious matters. A prominent BMMWU member, McCarty was held for vagrancy despite his claim that the arrest was a frame-up as on the night in question, he had visited about town with several friends until eleven at night and then had gone to his room to sleep.[75] Just one day after investigating the murder, Montana attorney general Sam Ford threw up his hands and stated, "It is very improbable that the men will ever be brought to justice. There is not a single piece of tangible evidence."[76] Less than a week afterward, he went fishing.[77] Only Congresswoman Jeannette Rankin pushed for a federal investigation of the Company's practices leading to the violence, although her male peers derisively referred to her actions as "hoopskirt hysteria."[78]

Attorney William Sullivan said he could name five of the men on the spot, all Company guards and gunmen, but he would not testify at the coroner's hearing.[79] After the *Butte Strike Bulletin* named Billy Oates, Herman Gillis, Peter Beaudin, H. B. Middleton, and Jack Ryan—all Company gunmen—the alleged murderers took offense at their names being bandied around and demanded Sullivan produce evidence in court.[80] No one presented proof after the union received death threats.[81] Despite authorities' dismissiveness of Sullivan's claim, he subsequently testified that he had hired a detective to find out who had mailed a vigilante card to him. The detective concluded that the card was mailed out of a James F. Taylor's office in Butte's Silver Bow Block.[82] Known as a "stool pigeon" and "gunman," Taylor at one time ran a mercantile collection agency in Butte and had been employed by various mining companies in the capacity of deputy sheriff, gunman, and detective.[83] Besides Taylor, Company lawyer and head of the Company "guard," Roy Alley; Colonel D'Gay Stivers; L. O. Evans; John Berkin, a sometimes-deputy; Oscar Rohn; and James Rowe, a prominent Butte businessman, were named as having knowledge of or participating in Frank's murder.[84]

The BMMWU did issue a provocative bulletin stating that two murderers were gunmen, two were businessmen, and one was connected with law enforcement in the city.[85] Chief of Detectives Ed Morrissey, generally assumed by many to be the law-enforcement murderer, met a fate similar to that which he imposed on others during his long ruthless career: he was severely beaten and died alone in his boarding house room from a brain hemorrhage on February 3, 1922.[86] Other possible murderers who met untimely deaths in an automobile accident, included Howard Pierce, owner of a car dealership that sold Cadillacs, and his chauffeur Alex Loiselle.[87] Years later, former Pinkerton spy-turned-detective-novelist Dashiell Hammett stated he had been offered $5,000 to murder Frank. Originally hired as a Butte strikebreaker by the Pinkerton Detective Agency, he made the admission to his girlfriend, playwright Lillian Hellman. Hammett contended that an officer of the Company approached him with the offer, upsetting him so much that he left the Agency.[88] Afterward he wrote *Red Harvest* based on 1917 events in Butte, renaming the city to Poisonville.

The *Tulsa World's* editor perceptively stated on August 13, "The men who lynched Frank Little have not been found. . . . So far we have heard nobody ever expected them to be found."[89] Even today no assassins' names have emerged, despite whispers within families of both the victim and murderers.[90] At the time, many people in Butte could have revealed them—but only if motivated to do so without fear of retaliation. U.S. District Attorney Burton K. Wheeler, who had upheld Frank's constitutional right to free speech despite his inflammatory rhetoric, was blamed for the vigilante violence in Butte. Had he arrested Frank for his alleged seditious comments immediately after Frank first spoke at the ball field, the murder could have been prevented. According to the Montana State Legislature, Wheeler and Frank himself were both guilty of causing general unrest and ultimately, Frank's death.[91] Perhaps William Dunn stated it best when he wrote years afterward that the only entity responsible for the murder was the Company, which had squeezed the life out of Frank Little.[92]

With the murder in mind, zealot William C. Campbell, editor of the *Helena Independent*, pushed Montana governor Sam Stewart to encourage legislation that persecuted anyone who spoke out against the war effort in January 1918. The resulting Montana Sedition Act became a cookie-cutter pattern for other states, causing a multitude of unconstitutional arrests across the nation.[93] Within a few short months, the federal government would pass similar legislation that flat out contradicted the First Amendment of the U.S. Constitution, allowing for arrests of those who disparaged the military in times of war.

Complicity among the press, corporations, and federal agencies, before and after the passing of the Sedition Act, ensured that Frank Little—who had been described as selfless, honest, and courageous by those who knew the man, and whose actions illustrate his empathy for the working class—became dishonestly chronicled as a villain and traitor. With Frank's death, capitalist corporations could blame radicals and inspire American patriotic vigilantism through their press, the federal government could put a face on an enemy within the homeland and motivate support for the Great War, and the IWW gained a new martyr to rejuvenate the organization toward economic revolution. But Bill Haywood's vision of IWW victory would be stymied. Frank's death would become the spark that changed America.[94]

26

✦ ✦ ✦ ✦

THE BIG PINCH

Fred and Emma Little viewed the destruction of Fresno's IWW Hall, home to Local 66 at 816 I Street, from afar. Inside, the building was a shell of its previous organization, with all office furniture, equipment, books, posters, documents, publications, recruiting forms, and even the trash can with its contents removed. Fortunately, their jobs prevented them from being present when federal agents raided the building at noon on Wednesday, September 5, 1917.

Since Frank's funeral, Fred and Emma had resumed their daily routines in Fresno. Fred remained a carpet cleaner, and Emma worked at Griffin and Shelley Canning Company.[1] Instead, twenty-five other men, some of whom happened to be at the wrong place at the wrong time, men looking for work or who had slept in the hall the night before, were arrested and hauled off to the red-brick Fresno County Jail, where both Fred and Frank had been incarcerated some seven years earlier.[2] Just a little more than a month after Frank's death, the "Big Pinch" was on.

The IWW finally had voted for a national strike, but as Bill Haywood adamantly testified later, their intention was not to interfere with conscription but to fight for the solidarity of the worker. Using Frank's martyrdom as a catalyst, Haywood emphasized to workers that the real enemies were lumber barons, copper barons, and railroad magnates. The murder inspired thousands of bindle stiffs to participate in the IWW's call to grow membership to about 105,000 members by September 1917.[3] Fearing their general strike, the U.S. government had spurred into action.

The Fresno IWW had no reason to believe they would be invaded by federal agents and local law enforcement. Instead of focusing on street meetings, Local 66 had been organizing membership on the job during the summer of 1917. The IWW hall was full of migrants coming into Fresno seeking work. If a man had no money, he could sleep in the hall. If he needed a job, Local 66 would help him find one, operating as an employment office as well as a membership recruitment headquarters.[4] But Local 66 was guilty of joining in solidarity with the Butte miners' strike, and so it became a target.

In cities across the nation, federal agents prepared for simultaneous raids on IWW local halls and Chicago IWW headquarters on September 5. The greatest secrecy had been ordered.[5] In Fresno, Deputy U.S. Marshal Albert Sidney Shannon and federal agent George H. Hudson had made plans to invade IWW headquarters on I Street. Fifty-year-old Shannon was a hard-drinking, college-educated Fresno law officer who worked because he enjoyed the power of his position, not because he had to earn a livelihood. What he lacked in personal integrity, he offset with quid pro quo among forgiving county residents who had appointed him to the authoritative title.[6] The younger Hudson had been a Fresno area farmer just a few years before becoming a special agent of the U.S. Justice Department. He looked to Shannon for his orders. Both men were intent on making arrests at 816 I Street. After planting a Dictaphone in Fresno IWW headquarters, Shannon and Hudson had eavesdropped from an adjoining office in the same building for some time.[7] Now they were ready to act. Their warrant, just received from the bureau's Los Angeles district office, was issued to search the premises for evidence of treason as defined by the new Espionage Act.[8]

The morning of September 5 began normally at local headquarters. Oak tables were strewn with newspapers in different languages, applications for union credentials, stickerettes, various handbills, and *Joe Hill's Memorial Songbook*, all laid out for Wobblies to read while they sat in folding chairs awaiting their turns. A Remington typewriter and Edison mimeograph machine stood ready to produce correspondence, membership lists, and bulletins. A large back room, serving as a hall for union activities, held enough chairs to seat an audience of about twenty-five people.[9] Tacked onto walls were posters, postcards, sketches, and circulars promoting IWW membership. One drawing of a bindle stiff walking down a railroad track with his bundle over his arm read: "He built the road with others of his class, he built the road and now for many a mile he packs his load and wonders why the hell he built the road. The Bindle Stiff."[10] On another wall was a postcard illustrating a member of the Colorado National Guard standing over dead bodies of women and children, including one small child frozen with stiff arms upward and blood on its breast. The soldier's bayoneted gun was pointed upward with an impaled baby. The caption read "Ludlow, Colorado, USA, in the year of our Lord 1914," and below that "My conscience acquits me, John Rockefeller, Jr."[11] In adjacent rooms were two rolltop oak desks belonging to district AWO secretary James Elliott and new local secretary Glen A. Roberts, covered with dues books, stamps, constitutions, receipts, ledgers and files of correspondence, indicating that the men had no clue as to the impending storm.[12] All of this was incriminating and seditious, according to the Espionage Act.

Four cars pulled up to 816 I Street just as whistles signaled the noon hour. When Shannon and his agents entered the building, James Elliott claimed they had no warrant.[13] However, a newspaper account stated that Shannon sought out Secretary Roberts to read him the presidential search warrant as agents began to load IWW men into a patrol wagon.[14] The officer and agents seized about $1,200 in cash from Elliott and Roberts, along with about five thousand assorted issues of *Solidarity* and *Industrial Worker*, the official publications and recruiting materials of the IWW.[15] Papers and postcards with Frank's photo were in abundance.[16] Equally dangerous were subscription and membership lists that named a great number of individuals along with their addresses.[17] A pistol, found in a desk drawer, was the lone weapon on the premises.[18]

Leaving IWW headquarters, agents proceeded to the California Labor Bureau on Kern Street to make more arrests, primarily targeting "chief agitators" who were, according to the local newspaper, attempting to keep men from going to work on the farms and vineyards.[19] In all, about one hundred IWWs were herded back to the hall where they were searched, questioned by officers, and in many cases released.[20] By 4:00 P.M. the last man had been booked in jail, and by 7:00 P.M. the last load of papers and books had been bundled and delivered to Shannon's office in the Federal Building. The documents would be separated and examined for seditious content. Guards remained stationed at Local 66's headquarters for the remainder of the evening.

For the past four years, Fred Little had not been an active IWW member, since he was running a business.[21] Although they were steadfastly engaged with the union, Emma was the one who had grown with the organization. After his resignation as secretary of Local 66 in 1910, Fred had lost status. Now he had an opportunity to take a lead again. Fred helped compose a temporary defense committee, called the Fresno Liberation Workers Committee.[22] The problem was that the committee had no place to establish an office, since anyone approaching the IWW hall on I Street shortly after the raid could be questioned or worse, arrested.[23] They needed their office furniture, typewriter and mimeograph machine, and cash returned to get out a defense bulletin. The new committee sought the help of Fresno attorney Harry M. McKee, the same Socialist who had spoken in Bisbee in 1903, just after Frank's arrival there. McKee and the firm of Fred H. Moore and C. Schapiro of Los Angeles demanded to hear the charges against the jailed men since no justification for their arrests were given. Twenty-five men had been held incommunicado for at least eight days before their lawyers finally could interview them.[24] The lawyers' demand for return of all IWW property was denied after a federal agent, possibly Agent Hudson, determined that the supplies, office furniture, and cash were intended to be used in committing a felony.[25] Eventually ten men were released.[26]

With their attorneys' help, the Fresno Liberation Workers Committee published Defense Bulletin No. 1, which proclaimed: "At the present time, no meeting of the IWW can be held in a hall or advertised. In this land of democracy and freedom an organization without a blemish upon its character is denied the use of the mail, the use of halls or of public meeting."[27] Operative No. 7 promptly collected the document, turning it over to the Bureau of Investigation's Agent Hudson. This volunteer informant, who was a member of Local 66 and close to the inner circle, would become an effective tool for the bureau. On September 8, Operative No. 7 reported to Agent Freeman that between fifteen and twenty female IWW members lived in Fresno, out of about 2,300 female members nationwide. They had two leaders: Marie Williams and Emma Little.[28] Marie Williams seems to have faded out of history, but Emma left her mark by both her activities and her words. Emma had continued writing, even taking a typewriting and shorthand course to improve her skills the past January.[29] Agent Freeman reported to the Los Angeles field office that Emma had written some satirical verse recently in regard to the raid, investigation, and prosecution of the Fresno IWWs.[30]

Emma also was not afraid to address authority, often questioning motives of government officials to their faces with courtesy but bold audaciousness. Three days later, Fred and Emma called the Bureau of Investigation office, which had been organized in the Federal Building in Fresno, regarding a one-dollar money order confiscated during the September 5 raid. Emma wanted it back, stating that she had given the dollar, in the form of a postal money order, to secretary James Elliott to be forwarded to Joe Kennedy, secretary of the Butte IWW local. Emma claimed that the money was in return for Kennedy's mailed photos of her deceased brother-in-law.[31] She also spoke harshly to the federal agent about President Wilson, whom she claimed to have once admired and supported, for not sending federal troops to prevent deportations in Arizona.

She admitted that deported IWWs had written to her that they had been well fed and well treated by authorities in Columbus, New Mexico, and that was why she was sorry the president had not dealt the same way with all IWWs.[32] Her plucky phone call only aroused the curiosity of federal agents.

While the bureau sorted out names on the lists they had seized from I Street, Agent Freeman contacted Wells Fargo, the post office, and telegraph office regarding materials en route to the IWW office. Individuals found on the IWW delegate list from Fresno IWW headquarters were to have their packages and mail confiscated and sent to the bureau for review. Emma B. Little was on the list.[33] Immediately everything she wrote and received would be scrutinized. Yet Emma would never be arrested. Instead she would be used as a golden conduit for information regarding IWW members, activities, and California's IWW state of mind.

As the nation was whipped into hysteria by yet more accounts of German influence within the IWW, the bureau's chief of investigation A. Bruce Bielaski investigated rumors of California enemy involvement. He wrote a letter to the State Department after his investigation, claiming that no evidence had been secured to indicate that there was any German financial influence in IWW disturbances in California.[34] Still, Shannon and agents Freeman and Hudson, with help from the Los Angeles and Washington, D.C. bureau offices, worked aggressively to put together lists and addresses of disloyal Americans living in Fresno, including those raising funds for defense committees. Across the United States other law enforcement did the same, so that no alleged traitor could escape the wrath of the federal government.

By September 26, the Bureau of Investigation had nearly finished its hard lists based on information they seized in the earlier raids. Which members of the IWW might turn evidence or testify to IWW activities from various localities? Which union members, newspapers and magazines, and professors and other professionals were in sympathy of the IWW? Who did field agents determine were radicals? Who had donated money at any time to the IWW? Who subscribed to *Solidarity* and *Industrial Worker*, or *El Rebelde* and other foreign radical publications? What other organizations, such as the Civil Liberties Union, supported the IWW? Who were the radical writers of the period? Who corresponded with IWW officials? When the Bureau of Investigation finished compiling, at least one thousand individuals were named. More arrests were inevitable. Furthermore, the National Civil Liberties Bureau reported that membership in local Loyalty Leagues had increased. A number of towns and cities were rife with incidents of horse whipping, tarring and feathering, deportations, and mock trials with mock hangings of Non-Partisan League members and IWWs for refusal to support the YMCA and Red Cross.[35]

Oklahoma communities were particularly rabid, alarming Little family members. In September 1917, four wealthy Bartlesville oil men put a price on German sympathizers, offering ten dollars for every pro-German brought in, with an extra five dollars for men from Washington County.[36] On November 9 in Tulsa, as the nationwide search for radicals widened, eleven Wobblies who had been convicted for not owning war bonds and five others who testified in the accused's defenses were arrested and jailed. Several hours later, policemen escorted the prisoners out of the city jail into waiting cars and the muscled grip of the Knights of Liberty. Some of the heavily armed, black-robed Knights were the same police who originally made the arrests, while others were Chamber of Commerce members, well-respected businessmen, and a preacher. At midnight, the shirtless prisoners were driven three miles out of town on a country road where a mob of Tulsa citizens was waiting, roused by *Tulsa World*'s editor. Illuminated by police car headlights, the prisoners were tied to trees and whipped "in the name of the women and children of Belgium," and their bloody wounds were tarred and feathered. The incident nationally became known as the Tulsa Outrage.[37]

New reports within the *Yale Record* of arrested slackers and Drumright Oilfield Workers' Union members, who were claimed to have IWW sympathies or membership, increased the Little families' anxieties. Shortly afterward, Lon Little's worst fears were realized as he was arrested and his home searched in Drumright. About two months earlier on Sunday, September 9, the Drumright IWW hall had been raided and its furniture and windows demolished. Federal agents removed letters, correspondence, supplies, and a daybook while the locals ran union members out of town.[38] Whether Lon was arrested because his name was found on a list or because he was Frank Little's brother is unknown. Lon had no IWW materials in his possession, not even a photo of Frank, and had never been an IWW member.[39] After he was released back to his terrified family, they hastily made plans to move back to Yale. The family alerted Emma and Fred, who immediately immersed themselves with their defense committee.

The IWW worked diligently for the newly arrested Wobblies. No German gold would be used to pay for defending imprisoned IWWs, as the press had railed, but other unions and radical presses were called to help solicit funds. Since the mail was disturbed at its point of destination, collecting donations was practically impossible. Instead, defense committees were established in almost every town or city where there was a recruiting union or industrial union. Sympathizers could purchase Freedom or Liberty Certificates to help defray defense expenses. Memorial postcards of Frank were sold for seventy-five cents each as well as Frank Little buttons— all to raise money for the IWW.[40] Unfortunately, those arrested with buttons or photos of Frank in their possession were usually judged pro-German, while those who purchased Liberty Certificates left their names in a paper trail of lists.

On Monday, November 12, Agent Hudson accompanied Shannon and two other deputies to 742 California Street, home of Fred and Emma Little. They were armed with a presidential search warrant to comb for IWW literature and supplies based on reports from operatives in Shannon's office.[41] Upon entering the home, the agents ordered Emma to open a trunk containing her intimate clothing and to remove everything for their scrutiny. They then searched the rooms, finally finding what they sought. Included in items removed from the house were IWW Constitutions and preambles, red membership books, copies of *Industrial Worker*, stickerettes, IWW stationary, strike bulletins, and various report forms.[42] As agents collected the IWW materials, Emma overheard Shannon giving Fred a veiled threat, "something about Tulsa."[43] Although an agent would write later that Fred had "no papers of much importance," Fresno U.S. Attorney Lawson instructed Hudson and Shannon to arrest Fred and lock him into Fresno County Jail.[44]

Emma fumed over the raid on her house. She abhorred Shannon and his methods, but she was quite relieved that he had not found her personal papers and the manuscript of short stories, essays, and other articles she had written over the years. They had been hidden in a kitchen table drawer. Nor did Shannon and his men find the big rolls of newspaper clippings she had painstakingly saved from the Fresno and San Diego Free Speech Fights and from Frank's death and burial. She still had Minderman's diary, as well as personal letters and photos from "some of the boys" who were involved in the free speech fight and who were now dead. They also did not find her book that the U.S. Industrial Relations Commission had returned to her after its report in 1915. She commented to her children that at least the officers "didn't get everything."[45] But Emma was certain they would come back, and so the next day she bundled all these pieces of memorabilia into a gunny sack and hid it as securely as possible, expecting to remove the bag to a safer place as soon as it was dark. What Emma did not know was that Shannon had stationed an agent below her window to observe her.

After lunch Emma went to the Fresno County Jail to visit Fred. To her dismay, Emma was informed that she would have to get permission from Shannon in room 8 in the Federal Building, on the corner of K and Tulare, a brisk walk from the jailhouse. At his office, Shannon informed her that he would have Fred brought over in about two hours, at 4:00 P.M. When Emma retraced her steps to Shannon's office just before four, Fred was not there. Instead, Shannon told her that they would need to go to the jail, and together they walked back to Fresno County Courthouse Square.

During the conversation between Emma and Fred at the jail under Shannon's watchful eyes, Fred worried about the Defense Liberation Committee. He asked what Shannon was going to do with the furniture impounded from the September 5 raid. Shannon replied, "I think I will just burn it!" Then, turning to Emma, he asked, "Where is the money?"[46] As Shannon and Emma left the jail together after the visit, Shannon let Emma know that while she was at the jail, his agents had just raided her house again. In fact,

Emma had been under the Secret Service's surveillance and just as soon as she got busy again, there would be another raid. Uncharacteristically intimidated, Emma defended herself and Fred, stating that they had always been anti-German, even before the country entered the war.[47] She was worried. Not only had the gunny sack not been secured, but the boys and Victoria were alone at home.

When Emma reached her house she found the gunny sack gone, just as she feared. The agents left the scrapbook and roll of clippings but seized everything else, including family photos of Frank. Her neighbors, curious about the raid, told Emma they had watched the agents as they methodically searched around the house, even inside an outhouse slop hole and under a washtub.[48] Walter and Lawrence told her that officers had asked them where the "stuff" was and, when they faltered, reminded them of what had happened to Uncle Frank and threatened to send them to reform school. The men continued intimidating the boys by making slighting remarks in regard to the U.S. Constitution and reminding them of Tulsa.[49] Agent Hudson never reported the removal of Emma's personal papers, book, and memorabilia to Washington, D.C. headquarters. Indeed, he reported that the only thing discovered in Fred and Emma's house on Tuesday, November 13, was one tin box containing seven blasting caps used for dynamiting. Hudson also claimed that Shannon was with him in the raid, hiding the strategy in which Shannon had removed Emma from her home while Hudson and other agents gained access without a warrant.[50]

The agents soon came back with a search warrant, this time for Emma's neighbors at 738 California Street. Since operatives reported that Emma had been seen making trips back and forth from their house, Hudson and Shannon determined that she was hiding more materials, if not cash. The Taylor family, which had resided at the address for the past month, claimed to not know the Littles. Although they were probably the same neighbors who let Emma know where agents had searched on November 13, Mr. Taylor indignantly stated, "I am an American and don't even allow my family to mix with the Littles."[51] He claimed the previous occupants had been friends of the Littles, not his family. Nothing was discovered. Federal agents raided Fred and Emma's home on Saturday,

November 17. Again nothing else was discovered.[52] The agents had already succeeded in taking almost anything of value from Fred and Emma.

Local newspapers went wild with stories of IWW arrests, and not surprisingly, Fred's arrest made national news. The *Morning Republican* reported on November 17 that "a quantity of literature of a seditious nature" was seized from his home, intended for distribution among IWWs in central California. The paper furthermore reported that Fred was considered one of Fresno's IWW leaders since it was learned he had been a delegate to a recent conference of IWWs in San Francisco and secretary of the Fresno local. However, the only conference Fred would have attended was a meeting regarding the new defense committee. The article ended by stating that Fred had been booked as a federal prisoner who would receive an early hearing on charge of violating the espionage law.[53] Next to headlines about Pancho Villa's move on Juárez, national papers called attention to Fred's relationship with lynched IWW leader Frank Little and repeated that Fred had taken charge of the Fresno IWW local.[54]

Just as the *Morning Republican* predicted, Fred was brought before a federal grand jury in the second floor courtroom in the Federal Building for an early hearing on Friday, November 16. Fred now increased the number of jailed IWWs in Fresno as he joined the fifteen men whom he was working to defend. He was arraigned before U.S. Commissioner R. G. Retallick and held to the grand jury in a $2,500 bond.[55] The U.S. authorities had succeeded in dismantling the Fresno Liberation Workers Committee. Fred now joined other IWW prisoners in thirty federal court districts awaiting a test trial's outcome in a Chicago federal court that would use the new Espionage Law against IWW leaders. On the evening of November 20, Walter Frederick Little was indicted for sedition and conspiracy to defeat the war measure of the United States.[56] He finally had achieved national notoriety as an IWW leader.

It was Thursday, February 7, 1918, and Emma sat at her typewriter composing a letter to a recipient she hoped would take her seriously.

She had written many letters to this point, often regarding defense funds or morale-lifting news, since she was now the acting secretary of Local 66. Everyone else was in jail.

Five days earlier, the United States had formally charged fifty-five IWW members in Sacramento, California, after combining Fresno and Sacramento indictments. Fred was charged with the same indictments as the 166 men in Chicago, but his trial would occur in Sacramento.[57] He had been in the Fresno County Jail for two and a half months with a hefty bond. Because of all the press in Fresno, Fred and Emma's daughter, Victoria, who had walked frequently with her father to the IWW Hall, was being tormented at school. A teacher put a stop to the harassment, but Victoria would carry the hurt all the way through her adult life.[58] However, Emma was not writing a letter to complain about Fred's incarceration or her daughter's bullying. She began the letter to the president of the United States to ask for his intercession in the return of her personal belongings. She wanted her manuscript back. Emma decided to begin her letter by appealing to President Woodrow Wilson as one writer to another: "I do not believe that you would be willing to allow an injustice to be done to the humblest citizen—to the most insignificant writer, if it were possible for you to correct it. Much less, would you allow such an injustice not only to be committed but to be continued in your name."[59]

Surely he would understand how her heart was ripped at the loss of her manuscript. In fact, the IWW used to be "all fours with President Wilson" and his campaign to keep America out of the European War, although he had moved the country into the conflict.[60] The Wobblies had Wilson's book *New Freedom* in their office, and many were reading it. Emma also reminded Wilson that the IWWs were "getting a new light on the invincible government as a result."[61] She had waited two and a half months for return of her belongings and now asked him to intervene.

Emma gave President Wilson a detailed account of government raids on November 12 and 13, calling the second raid "a dirty sneaking trick."[62] She stated that Shannon knew that her husband had not been a member of the IWW between the dates described in the indictment, nor had he handled any of the literature of the organization between those dates. She accused Shannon of arresting

Fred only because he did his best to provide legal defense for other IWWs who had been arrested. In fact, Emma wrote, Shannon had systemically arrested everyone who had done any work on the defense in Fresno except herself, and he told her he had Secret Service men watching her constantly.[63] Since her husband's arrest, neither Shannon nor any other federal agent had bothered to ask if she had any means of providing for herself and her children.

Still enraged about the duplicity that Deputy U.S. Marshal Shannon had used to get into her home the second time, Emma declared Shannon "an Irish incompetent who is a disgrace to any employer and who should never have had office at all," adding, "One look at his face would convince you of this."[64] How could Shannon, "who by his looks is a drunken Irishman," take "my writings, the work of my hand and brain, and keep them from me?" she asked Wilson.[65]

People on Fresno streets were saying that the sole reason for Fred's arrest was because he was Frank Little's brother, Emma wrote. Even her brother-in-law Lon was arrested and investigated by the authorities, and he was just a farmer. The Littles had not a drop of German blood in their veins, she explained. They were of Scottish heritage. Finally, Emma explained that Lon was "one of those people who might call themselves real Americans, having a small quantity of Cherokee blood."[66] Emma boldly asked the president of the United States, "Do you think this is right, President Wilson? I do not believe that you do."[67]

Emma concluded her letter by offering her services to the president of the United States as a card-carrying IWW member, adding that there were lots of "our boys" in the army, more than there were of any other organization. The IWWs were just "young lads" whose "feelings have been hurt by the treatment meted out to their Fellow Workers."[68] Then gutsy as ever, Emma B. Little signed her name with a flourish to the five-page typed letter under the closing— *Yours for the OBU.*

Fred, perhaps coincidentally, was released about one week later.

27

SLEUTHS AND
STOOL PIGEONS

Jack Dymond appreciated a good audience. A cellmate of Fred
Little's for two and a half months, he just happened to be in Fresno
after a brief absence before the September 5 raids.[1] He, too, had
been lassoed by the Bureau of Investigation's noose at the IWW hall
on I street, incriminated by at least one letter he wrote to IWW
secretary James Elliott.[2] Fred easily made friends with forty-five-
year-old Dymond while the two sat in jail with nothing else to do
but get to know each other better. In his jailhouse interview with
Agent Freeman on the day of his arrest, Dymond was extraordinarily talkative. His interview, full of volunteered information
regarding the IWW, filled four typewritten pages. During the interrogation, the Bureau of Investigation detected a curious crack in
his character.

Singling out and approaching a man with the purpose of asking
him to spy or report on his associates and even friends or family
was a delicate operation. Spies may well have been down-and-out
Wobblies, who needed either protection or money, or had nothing
to lose. Some just hated the IWW. At what point Jack Dymond
made his deal with the Bureau of Investigation is unknown, but
likely he turned informant while in jail between November 1917
and February 1918. Fred, who was released on a $1,500 bond at the

same time, surely did not know that Dymond had turned informant.[3] Informants usually did not know who other snitches were,
a safety mechanism for protecting the bureau's continual stream
of information.

Fred and Dymond established a new defense hall at 1430 Kern
Street in Fresno in a red-brick building next door to a tall wooden
Buddhist temple.[4] The hall would serve as a collection center
and clearing house for defense funds and a communications center
operating among other defense committees, including the General Defense Committee in Chicago and the California District
Defense Committee. Emma worked feverishly as the Hall's secretary, greeting Wobblies while answering all incoming correspondence, managing defense funds, and fundraising. It also would serve
as a snare of unfortunate IWWs who corresponded with Fred and
Emma, or Dymond.

Even Emma's letter to President Wilson had been stopped by the
post office and routed to A. Bruce Bielaski, chief of the Bureau of
Investigation in Washington, D.C. Seemingly the only thing in
Emma's letter that concerned Bielaski was her assessment of Deputy
U.S. Marshal Shannon. After a four month investigation, Shannon
was affirmed to be a man of substantial property and higher education—and therefore, a true patriot—and the matter forgotten.
The investigator did agree to Emma's charge that one look at Shannon's ruddy face would convince anyone of his incompetency,
admitting "that his [Shannon's] face was not a work of art."[5] Instead
of Shannon's bullying behavior, the bureau was more interested
in the wealth of information being mailed or telegrammed to and
from Fresno.

Arousing some suspicion about six weeks after Emma wrote
her letter to President Wilson, Bill Haywood met privately with
other IWW leaders at Chicago headquarters to discuss defense strategies and funding. The leaders had just been released on bond from
Cook County Jail after a three-month incarceration. A spy from
the Office of Naval Intelligence described the meeting as incendiary and subsequently reported to Washington, D.C. that Haywood
had urged his fellow Wobblies to send messages to the West and

Northeast to prepare for a bloody "Class War" and to get arms and ammunition ready. One of the people to be notified was Fred Little.[6] On March 25, the same informant reported that IWW leaders Vincent St. John and Ralph Chaplin had proposed and carried a motion for a forthcoming plan of sabotage involving various IWW local leaders, including Fred Little in Fresno.[7] No action was taken on the government's part, indicating lack of trust in the spy's report. The notion that IWW leaders, who hoped for permanent freedom from their federal indictments, would immediately attack United States' industry was ludicrous. Fred was not thrown back in jail as a conspiring saboteur, nor were St. John and Chaplin, though all three men were indicted and awaiting trial. Still, the operator's singling out of Fred as a potential conspirator, even if untrue, invites closer inspection. Fred's reputation as an enemy of the government had been echoed, yet he was never rearrested.

The IWW continued to raise money to cover its mounting legal expenses. In May 1918, Fred corresponded with the new Butte IWW local about selling the newest photo of Frank for defense funds. Five days later Agent Hudson confiscated a sample photo mailed to Fred, now considered seditious material. He described it as a picture of Frank Little in the upper center of picture and with the following words inscribed underneath: "IN MEMORY OF THE DEAD FELLOW WORKER F. H. LITTLE MURDERED BY THE COPPER TRUST BUTTE, MONT. AUG. I, 1917. WE NEVER FORGET."[8] Photos of Frank's corpse framed the pledge.

Carrying or owning Frank's photo had become an indicator of extreme radicalism in the federal purview since early August 1917. An elderly Oklahoma farmer named Wallace Cargill lost his life in Oklahoma on his ranch when he was shot after refusing to surrender during the Green Corn Rebellion. Joining Cargill were mostly young radical tenant farmers, many of them American Indians and members of the Working Class Union, as well as men who had resisted the draft or had met Frank previously to discuss joining the IWW.[9] After the mob was broken, a posse was rumored to have found a fifteen-cent photo of Frank stuffed in a pocket on Cargill's bleeding body. Not surprisingly, the Justice Department generated a future count for federal indictment: conspiring with Frank H. Little, now deceased, and with other persons to prevent by force the execution of federal laws pertaining to the prosecution of war.

Fred never received the "seditious" photo, but he did receive his brother's battered valise. The suitcase, removed from the boarding house room in Butte, had been shipped from the public administration in Seattle via Wells Fargo after a warranted search of its contents. Hidden in Frank's old underwear were fifty-four IWW membership cards that someone was able to conceal en route.[10] Just like other parcels of IWW materials, which were confiscated on their way to Fred, the valise had been emptied. When it arrived, it contained nothing but the underwear.

While the Fresno Defense Hall ensnared visiting Wobblies, the Post Office Department accessed IWW mail to catch those who defied entrapment. Emma wrote to one Wobbly "that any old thing is good enough an excuse" for an arrest, and evidence suggests that federal agents detained people identified through her letters, which had been read and copied from the post office.[11] Defense committee members mentioned in the Fresno Defense Hall's letters, documents, and defense funds, unwittingly stood ready to be snatched by federal agents. Until May 1918, arrests were made precariously as no special law was applicable for the IWW apprehensions. Bielaski admitted as much to a Canadian police chief, who questioned how to arrest IWWs in his locale.[12] However, the United States had just made it much easier for federal agents to justify arrests of dissenters. Following Montana's model, the federal government extended the Espionage Act of 1917 with a national Sedition Act, overreaching its powers beyond the limits of the First Amendment. Speech and expression of opinion that cast the government or the war effort in a negative light, or interfered with sale of government bonds, would be a felony. Specifically, the act forbade the use of disloyal, profane, scurrilous, or abusive language about the United States, its flag, or its armed forces. It also allowed the U.S. postmaster general to refuse delivery of mail that met those same standards for punishable speech or opinion.

On the same day the federal act was passed, one Wobbly from Oregon wrote Emma, "The Sleuths and Stool Pigeons are very

numerous around here."[13] It did not take long for the General
Defense Hall to discern that someone was opening their mail, and
that anticipated materials were being confiscated en route. Emma
derisively called the sleuths "Paul Pry Sneaks," yet she continued
to write.[14] The confiscated materials subsequently would be used
as evidence—and any IWW speech and opinions used as a condemnation. Federal authorities were also invading defense attorneys'
mail and scouring offices for documents and money that could be
used to damage IWW defenses, while lawyers voiced strong objections to trampling their client-attorney relationships and stealing
their correspondence. George Vandeveer, a Seattle attorney, was
targeted as he prepared his defense for the Chicago Wobblies. He
had trouble even getting his list of defendants.[15] The federal government had placed its mighty thumb on the scale of justice.

Emma was concerned about the prisoners' welfare, and now
saw her principal business as the defense of Class War prisoners.
Reports that Fresno and Sacramento prisoners' clothes were wearing out and that any available prison clothing was of exceedingly
poor quality led Emma to solicit help in her correspondence. Various IWW bulletins now asked for contributions of food and clothing.[16] Emma was particularly sensitive to "the boys," trying to
meet their simple needs such as tobacco and socks. Additionally,
Fresno and Sacramento men who were not out on bond had been
consolidated into the old Sacramento County Jail, not the new
modern jail. Sanitary conditions were absolutely filthy in their
21-by-21-foot cell. Forty-three men were packed so densely that
half of them had to stand or sit so that others could lie down to
sleep on a cold concrete floor with thin cotton blankets.[17] Some
contracted tuberculosis, and others' health began to degenerate,
making them susceptible to Spanish flu. Prison food was deficient:
coffee, two ounces of mush, and less than two ounces of bread at
breakfast, and three small smelts and less than two ounces of pota-
toes for supper.[18] When prisoners protested that their food was
inadequate, defense committees sent wholesome food to them
that a jailer placed outside their cages in full view, allowing it to
rot.[19] A planted Dictaphone secretly recorded all their complaints
and conversations.[20]

As IWWs faced mounting challenges, Fresno's former AWO secretary James Elliott sat in Chicago's Cook County Jail. However, he exchanged many letters with Emma, who was hungry for information regarding the impending trial in Judge Landis's court. The jury's decision in this test case would determine the fate of Fred, other IWWs out on bail, and the Fresno Wobblies jailed in Sacramento. Lean and slightly built, Elliott's long pale face exuded kindness and honesty—an expression that expected fair play in return. Elliott wanted to share his daily activities, his certainties that he would be found innocent, and his perceptions of the prosecution's farcical actions. He was certain that the right to strike and organize was on trial—not sedition.[21]

Elliott was not far off base. The original indictment against Fred Little and other indicted Wobblies read:

> The defendants are charged with having conspired to injure, intimidate and oppress certain citizens of the United States ... by demanding stated wages and certain terms from the employers throughout the United States and unless the employers of labor will agree to pay the stated wages and agree to the certain terms demanded, the said defendants and the said persons, with whom said defendants conspired, would refuse to work for or give "their services to said employers, and would engage in what is known in every day parlance as a strike."[22]

In the Chicago IWW trial, the prosecution expounded the belief that any man who struck in wartime was not loyal to his country.[23] Later the antistrike clause would be removed from the formal indictment against the Sacramento defendants.

Meanwhile, Herbert Stredwick and R. V. Lewis, who served on the California District Defense Committee in San Francisco, were working hard to get Sacramento prisoners out on bond. Both wrote Emma to reiterate their need for accurate recording of defense stamp sales and subscriptions. The next day, Lewis and Stredwick sent a curious notice to Emma and others. No more information regarding what was taking place with the Sacramento trial would be included in letters. If anyone wanted to get information, they had to come to their office in San Francisco.[24] Clearly, Lewis and Stredwick had begun to suspect that something or someone was interfering in their organization.

On Saturday, August 17, 1918, all one hundred defendants in the Chicago IWW trial stood before white-haired Judge Landis, dwarfed behind his enormous mahogany bench. In the huge white marble room, decorated with gilt and murals, each man was found guilty on all four counts in the indictment and charged with sedition and conspiracy.[25] The jury was out merely one hour. The first count read: "That the defendants conspired with Frank H. Little, now deceased, and with other persons to prevent by force the execution of federal laws pertaining to the prosecution of war."[26] Frank had been indicted and tried posthumously. The press and big business had done their jobs. Immediately California defense committees focused all their attention on the Sacramento IWWs, despite realizing the end game. Their nucleus fractured instantly as agents swooped in and arrested most California Defense Committee members. By the time of the Sacramento trial, the entire IWW District Defense Committee of California had been arrested and indicted. As each defense secretary was arrested, another took his place, and was arrested in turn. In the Fresno Defense Hall, the arrests left Fred and Emma as sole committee members, and Jack Dymond was often absent.

Perhaps receiving Frank's empty valise, haunted with its emptiness and defeat, sparked the split. Or perhaps it was a matrimonial infidelity, or new whispers about something amiss, that were to blame. Whatever the cause, Emma was not happy with her husband, and soon Emma and Victoria were living in their home alone.[27] Fred, one of the indicted out on bond, moved to 2010 Harvey Avenue in Fresno by September 1918.[28] Even so, they continued to share communications regarding the Fresno Local.

At 1:30 P.M. on October 1, after living in jail for more than a year, forty-three prisoners were divided into groups of about twenty in the basement of the old Sacramento County Prison and marched

in chains to the federal courthouse for a preliminary hearing. They
filed down a brick street with detectives guarding them on each
side and on street corners. Many wore prison-blue woolen shirts,
a sharp contrast to their pale faces. Federal agents blocked subway
entrances in case of some foolhardy escape attempt.[29] Tall window-
bespectacled buildings, in the heart of Sacramento's local, state,
and federal judicial systems, loomed over the ragged bunch of men.
As the groups entered into the federal courtroom, Judge Frank H.
Rudkin opened court proceedings by asking for their lawyer. In a
surprise appearance, Jack Dymond, along with a shady ex-convict
named Elbert Coutts, stood and declared themselves to be IWW
legal representatives. A loud uproar broke out among the prisoners.
How could Dymond represent the Wobblies? The men bellowed
their objections, some jumping to their feet. The defendants did not
want Dymond to represent them, stating that he had really never
served in their interests anyway. Rather than use any lawyer, the
Wobblies, with the exception of three prisoners who were out on
bond, declared they would use no legal representation, as "in our
experience in Capitalist Courts there does not exist what we call
Justice."[30] When Judge Rudkin responded with a lecture about justice and democracy, the prisoners broke out in laughter. The courtroom's federal agents and detectives were in shock.

In a packed courtroom of reporters, detectives, and lawyers, the
prisoners were granted a public IWW business meeting to discuss
their nondefense. After prisoners elected a chairman to represent
them, they collectively pled not guilty. Each prisoner's name was
called, including Fred Little's. However, Fred was not present to
make a plea.[31] He had not been rearrested but was home in Fresno,
the only indicted Wobbly not to appear. Three weeks later, U.S. Attorney Robert Duncan stood before Judge Rudkin, representing Fred
Little and two others for pretrial motions. Duncan formally asked
that charges against the three be dropped. Judge Rudkin agreed.[32]

At last the Sacramento trial commenced at 11:00 A.M. on
December 18, 1918. The Fresno IWWs' indictments had changed
four times to suit inclusion of other members. The final indictment
covered sixty-nine typewritten pages and grouped everyone together,
even if an individual was obviously not present where an alleged

"crime" occurred.[33] Harry Gray (Hime Grau), a Russian immigrant who moved with his parents to the United States when he was two years old and who had been arrested in Fresno, wrote, "perhaps it will be that they will charge us with going down into the bowels of the earth and removing the ball bearings upon which the earth revolves, then again some gumshoe artist may discover us in trying to put a blanket over the sun, in so doing shut out the light."[34] Many of the individuals did not know one another until they met in jail. Yet they were charged with conspiring together. Others were defense secretaries who recently had been indicted for committing overt acts of sedition by receiving letters from men in Chicago's Cook County Jail and sending telegrams protesting against jail conditions, the same activities in which Fred and Emma had engaged.[35]

Besides law enforcement, the prosecution relied on testimony from their three star witnesses, two of them originally defendants: Wilford Dennis, Elbert Coutts, and, of course, Jack Dymond. Dennis sat just a few days in Sacramento County Jail before his name was stricken from the indictment, at the same time as Fred's, on condition that he would testify against other IWWs.[36] Coutts was not indicted with Fresno and Sacramento Wobblies but was an admitted arsonist and former San Quentin convict who had served time for grand larceny.[37] He admitted on the witness stand that his testimony was a product of making a deal with the prosecution for release from his most recent incarceration. Jack Dymond evidently began his betrayal upon his release the past February when he and Fred opened the Fresno Defense Hall. His treachery over the months and his courtroom perjury were disastrous for the Wobblies.

The trial opened with one hundred pictures of Frank, Joe Hill posters, pamphlets with captions exclaiming "War—what for?" and many other documents that the prosecution alleged violated the Sedition Act, in an attempt to lay a foundation for the prosecution's case.[38] Compensated informants, law enforcement, and sundry witnesses testified in front of a jury that were all subscribers to the *Sacramento Bee*, which regularly agitated against the IWW.[39] Testimonies typically included assertions from witnesses that defendants said something against the war or, in one specific case, a witness overheard a Wobbly speak a foreign language to some of his former countrymen on the same day as the draft. No matter that the immigrant defendant had registered previously for the draft or that the witness had no idea what the immigrant was telling his peers.[40] Others were guilty of having simply stood in picket lines protesting low wages.

With Dymond's help, prosecutors presented various, far-fetched conspiracy theories such as German gold switching hands with IWW agents. Some of the men were accused of setting fires while they were sitting in jail cells. Some, for mailing letters to prisoners already serving time in Leavenworth. Wobblies supposedly caused sheep poisoning, sugar shortages, all fires in the state, and even an attempted assassination of the California governor. The paper published letters from Oklahoma Chamber of Commerce members who urged that Sacramento apply the same justice as that which had prevailed in Tulsa.[41] Most IWW prisoners sat silently, some reading and some taking notes. Others wore humorous expressions while a few simply slept, all believing a prejudiced jury guaranteed the trial's outcome.[42]

The year 1919 opened with continued fears of the Spanish flu killing still more Americans, the very old and very young. The flu finally found its way into Sacramento County Jail, where its weakened victims waited. In court everyone was provided a mask, except for the prisoners.[43] At exactly 4:35 P.M. on Thursday, January 16, the Sacramento jury received final instructions from Judge Rudkin: "The mere fact that these defendants are Industrial Workers of the World should not justify a verdict of guilty. The fact that they may be found to be conscientious objectors to war should not be held against them in the consideration of this case."[44] Yet just one hour and twenty-five minutes later, the jury returned its unanimous verdict. Guilty. An eyewitness remarked that all prisoners marched out of the courtroom singing "Solidarity Forever!" in "splendid spirit."[45]

The next day, the day of sentencing, most men at last spoke, claiming that government witnesses were compensated perjurers and denouncing the prosecution's methods. When IWW Mortimer Downing's turn came to speak, he cried out, "Dymond said I was pro-Ally and against the war. And he charges me with being against the war in 1916, when President Wilson was 'too proud to fight!' I *am* against war. There never was a good war or a bad peace. Now sentence me!"[46] The government agents appeared to be embarrassed. Perjury, it would seem, was patriotic.

California Wobblies would serve time in Leavenworth Prison, known as "Hell's Forty Acres," and a few would be deported to their home countries. Most of the prisoners were "straight American" sons and daughters with "names of the old type."[47] Of those who were tried, the three who engaged legal representation received light sentences. Others of the silent defense received varying prison terms, with half the men sentenced to twenty years and no one eligible for appeal since there was not a record of a defense on hand.[48]

Wobblies were furious with Elbert Coutts and especially Jack Dymond. The bureau planned to use their testimonies in a Kansas IWW trial in December 1919, so the IWW determined to discredit Dymond. They knew Fred had been in jail with Dymond and could provide what the "army men who came to see him [Dymond] in jail said."[49] When a Wobbly named Stumpy Garrigan wrote to Fred regarding Dymond's whereabouts, Fred ignored the letter. He apparently wanted to distance himself from Dymond as quickly as possible.

A Wobbly-turned–stool pigeon aroused great bitterness and anger among IWW prisoners. The Bureau of Investigation reported that revelation of an informant could mean assassination, and that greatest secrecy should be maintained in protecting names. Believing that California Wobblies would not pursue Jack Dymond, prisoners in "Uncle Sam's Hotel at Leavenworth" organized from within to retaliate against him. One group apparently met to discuss defense matters outside of prison and specifically how to get Dymond. They decided to send "out an underground to give him [Dymond] a good dose of direct action."[50]

Fred may have begun experiencing a tightening in his gut as nameless ghost whisperers in numbered, gray garb pointed their bony fingers in his direction. Like many Wobblies who felt betrayed and found themselves in Leavenworth Prison, Herbert Stredwick, just beginning his ten-year sentence, had been doing some serious contemplating. On April 20, 1919, Stredwick wrote to IWW Charles

Hutchinson, who was working with the defense committee in Fresno. The prisoner said, "I wish you would make it your business to know Fred Little. Study him well. Fresno has more than one Dymond, so beware! This does not say Little is one. You will please destroy this letter to save misunderstanding."[51] Both Fred and Dymond had worked closely with the California Defense Committee the past year, and one of the two was a proven informant. Now Stredwick and others suspected Fred's motives and activities.

Ironically, just two months later in June 1919, a letter, which may have been composed by federal authorities to agitate IWWs, claimed that both Fred Little and Charles Hutchinson were informants working for the Thiel Detective Agency in San Francisco. The writer, William Dyer, claimed to have followed Hutchinson and a known "Thiel man" as they visited Fred and Emma for about an hour at Fred's work place. The author stated that Hutchinson had broken up the local at Fresno so that he could be elected as the new secretary and find out "everything that was going on." The author warned, "Take a tip and don't get to [sic] confidential with Hutchinson till you investigate his record."[52]

With both real and phony allegations of duplicity woven together, Emma must have had questions about her husband. Why had Fred's indictment been dropped at the urging of a U.S. Attorney, along with Wilford Dennis, who was a public informant? Why had she never been arrested, despite taking leadership on the Fresno Defense Committee, as well as receiving and sending alleged seditious materials? Hadn't Fred been important enough to be tried as a conspirator with the rest of the boys? Had Fred known about Jack Dymond? But Jack Dymond never went to jail either. Instead, he joined Coutts in a string of paid testimonies thanks to the recent passing of the California Syndicalism Bill on April 19, 1919.[53] They made perfect witnesses for the Justice Department's new Quaker attorney general, Alexander Mitchell Palmer, when he was just beginning his career of notorious police raids. At his side was his eager young recruit, J. Edgar Hoover, at the helm of the new General Intelligence Unit.

Minor players remained free but not for long. The Bureau of Investigation continued to use Fred's and Emma's communications outside of Fresno as a source of information for constricting IWW activities. Now Emma worked from home, using her address as a point of distribution for IWW mail. She had moved with the children to a different residence, perhaps because of financial worries or because her former address had been compromised by the Bureau of Investigation. However, the bureau continued to seize letters to and from her new address at 2160 Fairview in Fresno just as quickly as they had at her previous address.[54] More IWW leaders were arrested and indicted, including those who had continued to maintain a relationship with Fred and Emma through the California General Defense Committee. In one confiscated letter, Emma confessed to C. F. Bentley from Stockton, California, that she was in a "broke condition most of the time."[55] She asked for any piece of news and for Bentley to remember her to the boys in Stockton who knew her.

Emma arrived at attorney Harry McKee's office on January 24, 1920, to officially sever her marriage to Fred. Their intimacy had dissolved years ago, and perhaps with suspicions of his betrayal, Emma wanted Fred out of her life completely. She had once written to Vincent St. John that "As for me and the majority of the Fellow Workers I have met, we are Wobblies regardless, and if we are dead we are dead Wobblies and if we are alive we are alive Wobblies," indicating her willingness to sacrifice herself for the OBU.[56] Had Fred, through his actions, made a deal for an umbrella of protection for himself *and* Emma? If true, no doubt Emma would never have agreed to such an arrangement. Neglecting to say that Fred had been in and out of the Little home during the past year, Emma claimed to McKee that Fred had deserted her mid-December 1918, without any cause or reason and against her will. She wanted custody of Victoria and ten dollars a month support. They had no other property to share.[57] McKee subpoenaed Fred to appear in court to answer a complaint for divorce two days later.[58]

By all appearances, Fred lost no time grieving the situation. He was not considering his marital situation but planning involvement with a rebuilt California Defense Committee. Fred had just received new delegate credentials and a duplicate of his 1909 IWW membership card.[59] In a letter to Emma shortly before February 14, 1920, Fred discussed his new role in a Hod Carriers' Union.[60] Walter Frederick Little, once an Oklahoma college student aspiring to strike it rich, had settled for pushing a wheel barrow carrying muck. Agent George Hudson, who read and copied the letter, dismissed Fred as an old-time IWW delegate and brother of Frank Little, but took note of Emma, a radical writer in constant contact with IWW prisoners in Leavenworth.[61] Still, Emma's "overt acts" of sedition would never place her under arrest.

Emma continued to write James Elliott, who was counting off his days in Leavenworth. She had thoughtfully mailed him a 1920 calendar that he hung on a wall in his jail cell.[62] In a letter two weeks later, Elliott wrote "this is the 2nd day of our 18th month in here, 4th day of my 30th month in jail, for being born in the United States of America and believing in the constitutional right of FREE SPEECH—committed for the joining of the Industrial Workers of the World."[63] He had nothing to do but mark time.

Emma was also counting the days. On March 4, 1920, she legally ended her marriage to Walter Frederick Little.[64] Almost twenty-two years of marriage were dissolved with no contest. Unknown to her, their life decisions had already begun leaching downward, staining the Little family for future generations.

BRING OUT THE WHITEWASH

Don't read the Declaration, boys, it's un-American,
That's what the cops will tell you in little old Spokane,
Instead of the Constitution, Post Mortems now you'll get,
The capitalists are killing off the working men, you bet.
Bring out the whitewash,
Bring out the whitewash,
Spread it on as thick as you can;
Bring out the whitewash,
Bring out the whitewash,

We've murdered another working man.
Down in Bisbee you ought to see the fun,
When we rounded up the working men and made the
	Bisbee run.
And while we were about it, we took in all their cash,
We knew they wouldn't need it, in the desert there's no hash.
Bring out the whitewash,
Bring out the whitewash,
Spread it on as thick as you can;
Bring out the whitewash,
Bring out the whitewash,
We've murdered another working man.
Frank Little was an agitator, he made people think,
We thought we'd better get him or else he'd raise a stink,
And so we planned the murder well, the cops were nowhere
	near,
Everyone had gone to get another glass of beer.
Bring out the whitewash,
Bring out the whitewash,
Spread it on as thick as you can;
Bring out the whitewash,
Bring out the whitewash,
We've murdered another working man.
We've got another bunch picked out and we'll get them too,
We've planned the murders carefully and just know how
	we will do,
There'll be no interference, for the cops will all be wise.
We're killing off the working men because they organize.
Bring out the whitewash,
Bring out the whitewash,
Spread it on as thick as you can;
Bring out the whitewash,
Bring out the whitewash,
We've murdered another working man.[65]

Emma B. Little

EPILOGUE

Frank H. Little's story reveals unpleasant truths about American history that are often glossed over in history survey courses and political discourse, even as our history tends to repeat itself, for better or worse. Often obscured is the harsh treatment of Americans who spoke or wrote against socioeconomic injustices prior to and during World War I, creating suspicious relationships among citizens, politicians, and governments, and even neighbors, friends, and families. Americans' collective common sense wavered while propaganda-fueled zealots destroyed constitutional rights and muddied patriotism's character in the name of national loyalty. Abetting the country's xenophobic fervor, political repression profoundly strangled the voices of the men and women who possessed the civic courage to dissent within this fearful national climate. The resulting arrests, searches, seizures, and trials destroyed many individuals and families, resulting in a generation of children, including the Little family members, who could not trust the American justice system and hesitated to express themselves out of shame or fear.[1]

With the 1918 Sedition Act, government agents legally made hundreds of arrests across the country while spying on the American population. Lumped along with true traitors, saboteurs, and draft evaders were those who had German surnames, had not purchased Liberty Bonds, had criticized the government, had possessed radical literature, were associates of radicals, and were members of or had consorted with the IWW. Burton K. Wheeler later wrote that the "most bizarre element of the war hysteria was the spy fever, which made many people completely lose their sense of justice."[2]

The Sedition Act was repealed on December 13, 1920, but by then innocent families and their loved ones had incurred much hardship. Even A. Bruce Bielaski, chief of the Bureau of Investigation during the first Red Scare, admitted that widespread prosecution of IWWs would cure nothing. He had learned in the course of his investigation that most of the labor troubles in big cities were caused by miserable working conditions maintained by large corporations.[3] Had these conditions been fairly addressed, the IWW would have not required such a threatening presence. Instead, the organization gained an undeserved reputation for violence and political upheaval.

One hundred and fifty men and women were tried and convicted in IWW cases brought at Chicago, Wichita, and Sacramento. Of these, the Chicago and Wichita cases were brought to the court of appeals, where the charges of sabotage were thrown out but not the charge of speaking and writing against the war and the draft. The Sacramento prisoners had no trial record to appeal due to their silent defense. No one was imprisoned for an act of violence. For expressing their beliefs, prisoners received fines as well as five-to-twenty-year sentences.[4] Of the 1,186 Bisbee deportees, only 50 were German, with Mexicans and Americans the majority of other ethnicities. Almost a third had registered for the draft, over half owned property, 312 had taken out citizenship papers, 281 men had bank accounts, 230 had families, and 169 men owned Liberty Bonds.[5] In 1920 only one Citizens' Protective League member stood trial for the Bisbee kidnappings but was acquitted after a sixteen-minute jury deliberation.[6]

On April 13, 2006, Montana righted some of its wartime atrocities. Seventy-nine people who were convicted of sedition by the Montana Council for Defense, led by *Helena Independent* editor

William Campbell, were pardoned posthumously by Governor Brian Schweitzer. "[The sedition law's] victims were not traitors," said Professor Clemons P. Work, whose own research inspired the project to pardon the individuals. "They were ordinary people with ordinary sentiments, who spoke their minds or voiced their conscience, who said critical or derogatory things about the government, but no more. They went to prison . . . for their words and passed into history, all but forgotten, their convictions a black mark that most sought to hide—a black mark that rippled through families for generations."[7]

No pardons or apologies were planned for the Little family. The family bore its scars until forgetfulness and ignorance finally fragmented its history into piecemeal puzzle pieces, much like the federal government's redacted documents describing unlawful actions taken against family members. A generation of photographs, letters, and memories are gone, taken away, or destroyed, as are the primary players who lived and breathed these times.

Almira Hays Little died on June 9, 1917, just weeks before her youngest son was murdered. Her obituary states, "She leaves two sons, A. C. Little, who now lives at Yale, and Frank, who travels most of the time, and one daughter, Mrs. Charley Courtright, of Perkins."[8] Fred, perhaps disgraced because of his life decisions, was omitted. Demonstrating the continued enmity between Almira and Ella Little, Ella objected to Almira being buried next to Walter. She was overruled, but no tombstone was placed on her mother-in-law's grave.[9] Almira rests on the left of Walter's marked grave in Ingalls Cemetery in the old ghost town.

Frank's antiwar agitation caused other divisions in the extended family. Oscar Newland, who had moved in with the Little family as early as 1880 and married Almira's niece Minnie Boyle, once had a portrait of Lon hanging in the Newland family's parlor, illustrating a close bond between the two men. However, the Newland family distanced itself from the Littles after Lon paid a visit to Oscar, who was grieving over the death of his son Frank Newland, a casualty during the Great War in the spring of 1918. The Newlands simply could not understand Frank Little's beliefs. In future conversations, Oscar told his family members that Frank had been

ALONZO LITTLE FAMILY, 1918

1918 Alonzo Little family reunion about eight months after the "Big Pinch."
Little Family Papers.

hanged for horse-thievery.[10] A horse thief was better than having
a traitor for a cousin. The Littles and Newlands grew apart until
contact between the families ceased.[11]

In late 1917, Lon and Ella Evans Little moved back to Yale,
ostensibly so that their youngest daughter Thaylia could attend
school.[12] In reality, living there was safer than weathering Drumright's vigilante justice. Despite Lon's arrest and the search of his
home for radical connections in the fall of 1917, a family photo
taken about June 1918 shows the family gathered together for
an important occasion: the send-off of a family member to war.
Among Lon and Ella's children, their spouses, and grandchildren
is a World War I uniform worn proudly by Tommie Little Warfield's
husband, Bill.

Lon managed to hold on to the Oklahoma farm. He and Ella
would move back and forth between the farm and town until

April 22, 1931, when he died in Yale of stomach cancer. Lon was sixty-nine years old.[13] Always his best helpmate, Ella slept on the floor where she could be close to her husband while he lay dying. Seventy years after the Oklahoma Land Run, the governor of Oklahoma honored Ella Evans Little as a heroic pioneer woman, a surviving eighty-niner who helped shape Oklahoma Territory into a great state. On June 15, 1960, Ella died at her Yale home after a long illness.[14] She was nearly ninety-one years old. She and Lon are both buried in Lawson Cemetery, originally called Quay, near Yale.

After his divorce from Emma in March 1920, Walter Frederick Little left Fresno for good. Not only had the local IWW chapter been crushed, but whisperings of his being a stool pigeon finished Fred's affiliation with the organization. The last written record of his connection to the IWW occurred in 1920. Fred's daughter later commented, "It seems my father was gold mining," referencing the more innocuous reason for Fred's betrayal and desertion of his family that Emma gave the family.[15] After working as a lather in 1921, Fred found work as a hod carrier in Sacramento, California, joining Hod Carriers' Union Local 294. His Fresno carpet-cleaning business was taken over by his son Walter. Walter R. Little II later helped build the Golden Gate Bridge, working as a structural steelworker. Lawrence continued to live with Emma and Victoria.[16]

On May 10, 1922, Fred was found sleeping on a park bench in front of the courthouse in downtown Stockton, California. He appeared homeless and disoriented and had been known to wander aimlessly in the area for some time. Customary of the era, transients suspected of being alcoholics were often arrested and sent to state hospitals for evaluation. Fred was taken for examination to Stockton State Hospital, today home to a portion of California State University, Stanislaus. During Fred's interview with doctors, he denied ever drinking and stated that his physician father Walter also had been temperate. Fred claimed to have a job, earning eight dollars a day.[17] But when he claimed to have a brother who was hit on the head with a revolver and hanged from a bridge in Butte, Montana, the evaluating doctors regarded this information as "incoherent and irrelevant . . . and not reliable."[18] Fred was admitted into Stockton State Hospital where he began treatment not for alcoholism but for neurosyphilis, an aspect of late stage syphilis that takes between ten and twenty years to manifest itself after first infection. On March 19, 1924, Fred died at Stockton State hospital of general paralysis of the insane.[19] Victoria was told that her father had died of pneumonia while he panned for gold in the Sierra Madre.[20] Obviously his alcohol use had not been the sole reason for past erratic behaviors. His unmarked grave is located in Stockton Rural Cemetery, paid for and arranged by the Hod Carriers' Union of Sacramento.[21] Under manicured green grass and layers of soil, a small disc-shaped plate marks grave 313 as his final resting place.

Despite Fred's exclusion from the Oklahoma Little family, Bessie Little Courtright continued a relationship with Emma Harper Little, her children becoming friends with their cousins. Bessie passed away on August 4, 1967, at the age of eighty-three in Moore, Oklahoma. She is buried next to Charles Courtright, her husband of almost fifty-seven years, in Fairlawn Cemetery in Stillwater, Oklahoma. A true and loving sister, Bessie protected the sole family photo of Frank.

Emma continued to live in Fresno. After Frank's death and Fred's desertion, Emma worked tirelessly to answer Leavenworth-incarcerated Wobblies' letters with optimism. If she worried about being arrested, she never wrote of her fears, despite federal arrests of Wobblies continuing for the next three years. Unemployed during the months that the U.S. government tried IWW members for conspiracy and sedition, Emma later launched her own small business, a lunch stand where she worked until late in her life.[22] She continued to voice her opinions via letters to area newspapers. On March 13, 1977, Emma died from complications from a stroke in Twin Harte, Tuolumne County, California. She was ninety-seven years old.[23] Emma lies next to her son Lawrence in the IOOF Cemetery (today part of Mountain View Cemetery) in Fresno, California.[24] A simple, flat steel-gray marker speaks the dates of her birth and death but no details of her extraordinary life. Still, Emma's involvement within the industrial labor movement has not gone unnoticed. In one publication, which was translated into a 2008 French edition, Emma's story is included with those of other notable female labor organizers, including Emma Goldman, Elizabeth Gurley Flynn, Lucy Parsons, and Mother Jones.[25]

And Franklin Henry Little? All details relating to his death, coroner's inquest, and murder investigation are buried with the men who made the decision to cover up the vicious crime. Witnesses suddenly became vague. Statements, reports, and minutes from meetings disappeared. The infamous placard pinned to Frank's underwear and photographed at the crime scene vanished. Other items disappeared as well; Frank's death mask, formed out of clay by Henry Myers, a Wobbly known for his creation of martyred IWW leaders' death masks, vanished after hanging on a Chicago IWW office wall.[26] It is certain that President Woodrow Wilson never replied to Emma's bold letter requesting the return of personal belongings. Frank's valise—which held his clothing, letters, telegrams, and photos—was returned to the family with only the dingy underwear inside. The final cover-up of Frank's murder ensured that the investigation would conclude without identifying a single individual responsible for the heinous crime. On January 13, 1921, the Bureau of Investigation officially closed its investigation of Frank H. Little.[27] The day after the investigation closed, Bureau of Investigation director W. J. Flynn added photos of the missing placard, along with other Little personal effects, to his personal Frank Little collection in Washington, D.C.[28]

In March 1918, Helen Keller pointed out that a "society that permits the conditions out of which the IWWs have sprung, stands self-condemned."[29] She further stated that IWWs who had been arrested without warrants, thrown into bull pens without access to attorneys, denied bail and trial by jury, and even shot, illustrated cruel and undemocratic actions praised by newspapers and patriots alike. "A cripple, Frank Little, who was forced out of bed at 3:00 in the morning by masked citizens, dragged behind an automobile and hanged on a railroad trestle" reminded American individualists that "it takes courage to steer one's course through a storm of abuse and ignominy."[30] Frank's ultimate sacrifice was best depicted in a caption under his portrait found in a run-down Seattle IWW office in the 1950s: "Tell the boys I died for my class."[31]

"Oh Bury Me Not on the Lone Prairie" was Frank's favorite song.[32] And on the lonesome prairie, far from his loved ones, he lies buried in Mountain View Cemetery in Butte, Montana. The tombstone simply reads, "Frank Little: 1879–1917, Slain by Capitalist Interests for Organizing and Inspiring His Fellow Man."[33] He is surrounded by the hundreds of unnamed souls to whom he gave voice.

Lee, Zora, Tommie, Hazel, Glen, and Thaylia Little continued their silence concerning Frank and his prewar and wartime activities, just as their father Lon had instructed them. Their children and grandchildren were simply told that Lon had a brother, a socialist, who was hanged in Butte, Montana. Butte was a long way from Oklahoma, and the murder was decades in the past. Frank became the ghost in the family closet, easily put away with old scrapbooks, family Bibles, photos, and the truth.

NOTES

CHAPTER ONE

1. *History of Cass and Bates Counties, Missouri* (St. Joseph, MO: National Historical Company, 1883), 1217.

2. Mary Ann Riley was born in 1819 in Lewis, Mason County, Kentucky, to William Riley and Mary McIlvain. Her father, William Riley, was born in Somerset County, Pennsylvania, in 1778, and her mother, Mary McIlvain, in Cabin Creek, Mason County, Kentucky, in 1779. Mary McIlvain Riley's parents were both McIlvains, the two branches having emigrated from Antrim, Ireland, in 1740, eventually settling in Chester County, Pennsylvania. Mary Ann Riley Little's great-grandfather John McIlvain married his second wife, Laura Barnard, a Quaker. Patrick Sullivan Little was born in 1811 in Perryopolis, Fayette County, Pennsylvania.

3. Victoria Little Burris to Carolyn Leverich Atkinson, October 4, 1995, Victoria Little Burris Letters. Victoria is the only daughter of Walter Frederick Little and Emma Barbara Harper Little. Victoria was born on February 28, 1911, in Fresno, California. She passed away on July 23, 2003, in Elk Grove, California. Carolyn L. Atkinson is the great-granddaughter of Bessie Little Courtright. In all branches of the Little family, the family story that the Littles were related to notable Scots was passed down.

4. Barbara Clapper Lewis, e-mail to Carolyn Leverich Atkinson, July 29, 2010. Barbara Lewis is the great-granddaughter of Emaline Hays Boyle, Almira Hays Little's sister.

5. Wanda Clancy Kinsey, e-mail to Carolyn Leverich Atkinson and author, July 1, 2010. Wanda C. Kinsey is the granddaughter of Bessie Little,

and Carolyn L. Atkinson's mother. See also Delce Courtright Copeland Notes, undated, Courtright Family Papers. Delce C. Copeland is the daughter of Bessie Little Courtright. Delce was born August 27, 1915, in Clayton, Payne County, Oklahoma, and passed away on March 17, 1995, in Oklahoma City, Oklahoma.

6. James L. Little is buried in Vermont Cemetery in Vermont, Fulton County, Illinois. He was born in 1863 and died in 1866.

7. Delce Courtright Copeland to Carolyn Leverich Atkinson, undated, Courtright Family Papers.

8. 1880 U.S. Federal Census, Grant, Cass County, MO, Roll 680, Family History Film 1254680, p. 199C, Enumeration District 91, Image 0059.

9. Barbara Clapper Lewis to Dolores Little Adams, November 16, 1992, Little Family Papers. This letter resulted from Dolores Little Adams's visit to Butte, Montana, to view Frank Little memorabilia. Dolores Little Adams is the granddaughter of Alonzo Little. Dolores was born on July 13, 1919, in Kay County, Oklahoma. She passed away November 8, 2001, in Albuquerque, New Mexico.

10. Earl Carson, "Early History of Bird Creek, District and Construction of the Mission Related by Pioneer," Hillside Quaker Mission Collection, Archives, Bartlesville Area History Museum (BAHM). See "History of Skiatook, Oklahoma," abstracted from *Tulsa County Historic Sites* (July 1982), prepared by the Community Planning Division Indian Nations Council of Governments for the Tulsa County Historical Society, http://www.tulsaokhistory.com/cities/skiatook.html (accessed June 15, 2010).

11. "The Skiatook Mission Story," Hillside Quaker Mission Collection, BAHM. Missionary John Murdock is considered to be the actual founder of Hillside Mission. "Hillside Town, School, and Church History," Hillside Quaker Mission Collection, BAHM; "Hillside Mission," Hillside Quaker Mission Collection, BAHM; Floyd Miller, "Hillside Mission," *Chronicles of Oklahoma* 4, no. 3 (September 1926): 225, http://digital.library.okstate.edu/chronicles/v004/v004p223.html (accessed May 10, 2010); "Hillside Mission Alumni Set Meeting Sunday," September 3, 1974, Hillside Quaker Mission Collection, BAHM.

12. "The Skiatook Mission Story."

13. Ibid.

14. "Friends School," *Bartlesville Magnet*, December 17, 1897, p. 1.

15. W. C. Jacobs, interview by Leone Bryan, March 31, 1937, Indian-Pioneer Papers 47: 245, Western History Collection, University of Oklahoma Libraries, http://digital.libraries.ou.edu/whc/pioneer/paper.asp?pID=3097&vID=47 (accessed May 10, 2010).

16. Victoria Little Burris to Carolyn Leverich Atkinson, October 4, 1995. Victoria states she was told that she was one-sixty-fourth Cherokee, which would make Almira Hays Little one-sixteenth Cherokee. See Thaylia

Little Farris to author, January 23, 1985, Little Family Papers. Thaylia states that Almira was one-half Cherokee, and that Almira was ashamed of her heritage. Thaylia L. Farris is the youngest child of Alonzo and Ella Evans Little. She was born August 3, 1910, in Payne County, Oklahoma. She passed away on December 5, 2005, in Yale, Payne County, Oklahoma. First cousins Victoria and Thaylia were handed down the same general information as were Almira's great-grandchildren.

17. 1850 U.S. Federal Census, Vermont, Fulton County, Illinois, Roll M432_107, p. 94A, Image 55.

18. *The History of Fulton County, Illinois* (Peoria: Charles C. Chapman, 1879), 902. The 1850 Federal Census cites Julia Williams's birthplace as Indiana, but her children reported both Ohio and Kentucky at various times in later census records.

19. Jack Allen Little, interview by the author, August 25, 2010, Little Family Papers. Jack A. Little is the grandson of Alonzo and Ella Little. He was born on the Alonzo Little homestead near Yale, Payne County, Oklahoma. Jane L. Botkin is the great-granddaughter of Lon and Ella Little.

20. Tommie Little Warfield, interview by the author, August 1981, Little Family Papers. Esther "Tommie" Little Warfield is the daughter of Alonzo and Ella Evans Little. Tommie L. Warfield was born on March 25, 1901, in Payne County, Oklahoma, and passed away on May 20, 1998, in Turney, Missouri. Tommie, her sister Thaylia Little Farris, and their first cousin Jewel Sykes visited the author during the 1981 summer to do a series of interviews. These interviews were followed by letters with pertinent family information.

21. Cherokee Nation Intruders' Report No. 316, U.S. Board of Appraisers of the Improvements of Intruders in the Cherokee Nation, NARG 75, BIA-E411-Intruders 33008-1895, Cherokee Census of Intruders 1893, Roll 2601; *Annual Report of the Commissioner of Indian Affairs 1895* (Washington, D.C.: Government Printing Office, 1896), 84–85.

22. Jewel Evans Sykes, interview by the author, August 1981, Little Family Papers. Jewel Sykes is the niece of Alonzo and Ella Evans Little. Jewel was born in 1908 in northeastern Oklahoma to Ella Evans Little's sister, Susan Alice Evans.

23. Thaylia Little Farris to author, January 23, 1985.

24. Victoria Little Burris to Carolyn Leverich Atkinson, October 21, 1996.

25. Thaylia Little Farris to author, January 23, 1985.

26. Jack Allen Little, e-mail to author, July 2, 2010.

27. "Land of Oklahoma Where the Milk and Honey Flows," *Kansas City Star*, July 30, 1885, p. 4.

28. "Settlers Stop!" *Kansas City Times*, March 13, 1885, p. 1.

29. "For Settlers," *Kansas City Times*, October 31, 1887, p. 4.

30. Carl Rister, *Land Hunger* (Norman: University of Oklahoma Press, 1942), 207.

31. Homestead Certificate No. 7335, Patent Record, July 6, 1898, General Land Records, Oklahoma, vol. 11, p. 216, U.S. Bureau of Land Management, U.S. Department of the Interior. The claim was located on lots 3, 6, 7, and 8 in the northeast quarter of the southwest quarter of section 19 in township 18, north of range 4, east of the Indian Meridian, containing 159 and 84/100 acres.

32. Earl D. Newsom, *The Story of Exciting Payne County* (Stillwater: New Forums Press, 1997), 181. The first wagon bridge built across the Cimarron crossing was completed July 31, 1900.

33. Thaylia Little Farris to author, January 23, 1985.

34. Homestead Certificate No. 1599, Patent Record, April 3, 1896, General Land Records, Oklahoma, vol. 4, p. 14. U.S. Bureau of Land Management, U.S. Department of the Interior. The legal description is the northeast quarter of section 13, township 19, north of range 4, and east of the Indian Meridian.

35. J. J. Fleming, interview by James H. Fleming, June 15, 1937, Indian-Pioneer Papers 30: 237, Western History Collection, University of Oklahoma Libraries, http://digital.libraries.ou.edu/whc/pioneer/paper.asp?pID=1924&vID=30 (accessed May 10, 2010).

36. Thaylia Little Farris to author, January 23, 1985.

CHAPTER TWO

1. "Early Memories of the Berry Sisters," in *Cimarron Valley Family Legends*, vol. 1 (Perkins, OK: Evans Publishing, 1978), 16.

2. Tommie Little Warfield, interview. See "Early Memories of the Berry Sisters," 17. Ruby Berry, whose parents purchased the Walter R. Little homestead from Almira Little in 1899, recalls that a bridge was built across Stillwater Creek going south from the cabin and that the road traveled around the bluff of the Little's homestead. The road was a section-line road that carried people to where the first Cimarron River bridge crossing was built. The half-section road cut directly across the homestead west to Clayton, about one-half mile south and one-half mile west of the cabin.

3. Anna B. Little, interview by Goldie Turner, September 2, 1937, Indian-Pioneer Papers 54, Western History Collection, University of Oklahoma Libraries, http://digital.libraries.ou.edu/whc/pioneer/paper.asp?pID=3397&vID=54 (accessed May 10, 2010). Anna B. Little is the wife of Porter Little, Walter R. Little's brother. She was born June 9, 1849, in Ripley, Illinois, and died in Shidler, Osage County, Oklahoma, in 1947.

4. Mary Ann Anders, ed., "Resource Protection Planning: Project Settlement Patterns in the Unassigned Lands, Region Six," Oklahoma Historic Preservation Survey (Stillwater: History Department, Oklahoma State University, 1984), 19–20.

5. George Milburn, "Oklahoma," first appeared in *Yale Review* (March 1946), 515–26, in *"An Oklahoma I Had Never Seen Before": Alternative Views of Oklahoma History*, ed. Davis D. Joyce (Norman: University of Oklahoma Press, 1994), 9–10.

6. *History of Cass and Bates Counties*, 1217.

7. Ibid.; 1870 U.S. Federal Census, Littleton, Schuyler County, IL, Roll M593_276, Family History Library Film 545775, p. 153A, Image 310. Walter R. Little is listed as a physician after receiving his college degree from Abingdon College in Illinois. After Patrick S. Little's death, James Little bought out his siblings' interests in the family farm and continued to own the family homestead until his death in 1925. See Alexander McLean, ed., *History of McDonough County*, vol. 2 (Chicago: Munsell Publishing, 1907), 940–41.

8. Frank's birthdate has been reported erroneously in histories written about him, and his tombstone, which states 1879, is also inaccurate. While Hancock County, Illinois, began recording births in 1877, no state requirement to file birth certificates existed until 1916. For determining the year of his birth, see the 1880 U.S. Federal Census, Grant, Cass County, MO, Roll 680, Family History Film 1254680, p. 199C, Enumeration District 91, Image 0059. On June 5, Frank was cited as being 2 years old. The Oklahoma Territorial Census Index, page 1173, states that Frank H. Little, born in Illinois, was 12 years old in June 1890. The census may be accessed from the Oklahoma Historical Society, http://www.okhistory.org/research /terr. Walter R. Little's probate dated January 21, 1899, Little Family Papers, states that Frank was 20 years old. He would turn 21 before mid-June 1899. Frank was 39 at the time of his death, not 38.

9. "Drove of Doctors," *Keokuk Constitution*, June 18, 1878. See Delce Courtright Copeland Notes; Victoria Little Burris to Carolyn Leverich Atkinson, October 21, 1996.

10. Anna B. Little, interview.

11. Tommie Little Warfield, interview. Walter doctored in Pawnee County at times. Don Riley Courtright, interview by the author, October 9, 2013. Delce Courtright Copeland wrote that Dr. Walter R. Little practiced medicine in Ripley and possibly Chandler, Oklahoma. See Delce Courtright Copeland Notes; Leola Courtright Kelley, interview by the author, October 14, 2013, Little Family Papers. Leola is the granddaughter of Bessie Little Courtright. "Gunfight at Ingalls—1893," Little Family Papers. Ingalls had four other doctors who had offices—Dr. D. H. Selph, Dr. W. R. Call, Dr. J. H. Pickering, and Dr. McCurdy (a pharmacist).

12. Homestead Certificate No. 2335, Patent Record, July 6, 1898, General Land Records, Oklahoma, vol. 5, p. 216, U.S. Bureau of Land Management, U.S. Department of the Interior.

13. Tommie Little Warfield, interview.

14. Ibid. Summer complaint presented symptoms of diarrhea and vomiting. Babies typically died of dehydration.

15. Ibid.

16. Homestead Certificate No. 1599, Patent Record, April 3, 1896, General Land Records, Oklahoma, vol. 4, p. 14, U.S. Bureau of Land Management, U.S. Department of the Interior.

17. Anna B. Little, interview. Porter Sullivan Little's claim sat upon a great lake of oil that extended from Pawnee County to Osage County, Oklahoma. Any time a member of the extended Little family needed financial assistance, Port provided funds, especially for Lon Little's family.

18. Thaylia Little Farris to author, January 23, 1985.

19. Victoria Little Burris to Carolyn Leverich Atkinson, March 11, 1995.

20. Newsom, *Exciting Payne County*, 183.

21. Michael Punke, *Fire and Brimstone: The North Butte Mining Disaster of 1917* (New York: Hyperion Books, 2006), 202. Despite Dunn's condemnation of Frank Little during Dunn's sedition trial, perhaps in an attempt to separate himself, William Dunn (Dunne) memorialized Frank ten years after his death. See William F. Dunne, "August 1917, in Butte: The Murder of Frank Little," *Labor Defender* 1, no. 8 (August 1928): 123–24, 142.

22. *History of Cass and Bates Counties*, 1217.

23. A typical statement repeated in various scholarly works reads that Frank Little was born of a Quaker doctor and an Indian mother. Philip S. Foner claimed that Frank was son of a Cherokee Indian mother and a Quaker father. See Philip S. Foner, ed., *Fellow Workers and Friends: I.W.W. Free-Speech Fights as Told by Participants* (Westport, CT: Greenwood Press, 1981), 217. Nigel Sellars provides a more detailed description of "a Quaker physician father of English extraction and a southern mother who was one-eighth Cherokee." See Nigel Anthony Sellars, *Oil, Wheat, and Wobblies* (Norman: University of Oklahoma Press, 1998), 30. How and where the misinformation regarding Frank Little's ancestry originated is unknown, but even a recent author asserts that "W. H. Little" (actually W. R. Little) was "unanimously identified" as Quaker in scholarly accounts, and the myth continues. Arnold Stead, *Always on Strike* (Chicago: Haymarket Books, 2014), 8.

24. William Ordway, *House of Grimmet, a Family Genealogy* (1993), 360; John Smith Futhey and Gilbert Cope, *The History of Chester County* (Philadelphia: L. J. Everts, 1881), 473, 643.

25. On April 8, 1859, Frank's mother, fifteen-year-old Almira Hays, was one of sixteen founding members of New Salem Christian Church

in New Salem Township in McDonough County, Illinois, under Reverend Joseph B. Royal, father of Almira's sister-in-law Eleanor Royal (married to James M. Little, Walter's brother). Reverend Royal also baptized Walter Little, her husband-to-be, and married the couple on September 11, 1859, in the same Christian church. From inscription on back of photo of Reverend J. B. Royal, Courtright Papers. *Illinois Marriages, 1851–1900*, online database (Provo, UT: Ancestry.com, 2005); County Court Records located at Macomb. Mary Ann Riley Little transferred her membership to Reverend Royal's New Salem Christian Church when it was organized, joining her children and becoming a prominent member. "Death Record—Mary Ann Little," *Vermont Union*, May 5, 1910.

26. Victoria Little Burris to Carolyn Leverich Atkinson, October 21, 1995.

27. Thaylia Little Farris to author, January 23, 1985; Barbara Clapper Lewis, e-mails to author, January 10, 2011, and June 5, 2013. Almira Little's niece Minnie Boyle Newland also made the decision to avoid registration, purportedly because the family was afraid they could be moved forcibly if registered as Indians. Other family members reported shame for having American Indian blood, which may have influenced avoiding the Dawes Roll.

Chapter Three

1. Modicus, "Personal Recollections," *Cincinnati Daily Gazette*, May 5, 1869, p. 1. This editorial presents a passionate response to Quantrill's raid on Lawrence, Kansas, August 21, 1863.

2. "Scientist Finds Buried History of Border War," originally from *Kansas City Star*, May 12, 2010, republished in *Columbia Daily Tribune* May 12, 2010, p. A7. For a thorough examination of factors that led to General Order No. 11 and its aftermath, see Ann Davis Niepman, "General Orders No. 11 and Border Warfare During the Civil War," in *Kansas City, America's Crossroads: Essays from the Missouri Historical Review, 1906–2006*, Diane Mutti Burke and John Herron, eds. (Columbia, MO: State Historical Society of Missouri, 2007), 96–121.

3. Niepman, "General Orders," 96–121. Historian Albert Castel is quoted, "With the exception of the hysteria-motivated herding of Japanese-Americans into concentration camps during World War II, it stands as the harshest treatment ever imposed on U.S. citizens under the plea of military necessity in our nation's history." See "Scientist Finds Buried History of Border War."

4. Richard Slotkin, *Gunfighter Nation: The Myth of the Frontier in Twentieth-Century America* (Norman: University of Oklahoma Press, 1998), 133.

5. Jennie Edwards, *John N. Edwards, Biography, Memoirs, Reminiscences and Recollections* (Kansas City, MO: Jennie Edwards, 1889), 163.

6. Slotkin, *Gunfighter Nation*, 125–26.

7. Michael Denning, *Mechanic Accents: Dime Novels and Working Class Culture in America*, 1987, quoted in Slotkin, *Gunfighter Nation*, 128.

8. Slotkin, *Gunfighter Nation*, 128.

9. 1880 U.S. Federal Census, Grant, Cass County, MO, Roll 680, Family History Film 1254680, p. 199C, Enumeration District 91, Image 0059.

10. *History of Cass and Bates Counties*, 1217.

11. "Scientist Finds Buried History of Border War."

12. Charles H. Rogers, interview by W. T. Holland, Indian-Pioneer Papers 77, Western History Collection, University of Oklahoma Libraries, August 17, 1937, http://digital.libraries.ou.edu/whc/pioneer/paper.asp?pID=5106&vID=77 (accessed May 10, 2010).

13. Milburn in Joyce, *"An Oklahoma I Had Never Seen Before,"* 12.

14. Sue Buzzard, "Lawmen and Outlaws," *The History of Craig County*, vol. 1, available at http://www.okgenweb.org/~okcraig/history/people/lawmen.htm (accessed December 1, 2010); Emmett Dalton, *When the Daltons Rode* (Gretna, LA: Pelican Publishing, 2012), 42.

15. Included in their gang at one time or another were Grat, Bob, and Emmett Dalton; Charley Pierce; George "Bitter Creek" Newcomb; Dick Broadwell; Bill Powers; William McElhanie; Charley Bryant; and Bill Doolin. While "Arkansas" Tom Jones, a.k.a. Roy Daugherty; "Dynamite" Dick (Dan) Clifton; George "Red Buck" Weightman; and Bill "Tulsa Jack" Blake are mentioned as riding with the Dalton gang at times, Emmett Dalton claims they were never connected with his lawless enterprises. Dalton, *When the Daltons Rode*, 103.

16. W. F. Little, Case #27402, California State Hospital. When interviewed by admitting doctors, Fred stated that he had spent five months in jail in Tulare. The date is uncertain, and he could have confused Tulare for Fresno due to his psychological condition at the time.

17. Jack Allen Little, interview.

18. Tommie Little Warfield, interview.

19. William Elliott, interview by Grace Kelley, August 15, 1937, Indian-Pioneer History 27: 418, Western History Collection, University of Oklahoma Libraries, http://digital.libraries.ou.edu/whc/pioneer/paper.asp?pID=1414&vID=27 (accessed May 10, 2010).

20. Ibid.

21. Ward Hays, *Drifting Down Memory Lane* (Perkins, OK: Evans Publications, 1985), 33. Hays's parents and grandparents participated in the Land Run of April 22, 1889. His parents claimed land in Payne County near present-day Stillwater.

22. Newsom, *Exciting Payne County*, 181–82.

23. Jack Allen Little, interview.

24. Newsom, *Exciting Payne County*, 188. The William T. Dunn Ranch was located in Pawnee Township, Payne County, southeast of Ingalls.

The legal description is the southeast quarter of section 26, township 19, north of range 4, east of the Indian Meridian. Council Creek runs through the 160 acres. Homestead Certificate No. 1877, Patent Record, June 19, 1896, General Land Records, Oklahoma, vol. 10, p. 284, U.S. Bureau of Land Management, U.S. Department of the Interior. The Doolin-Dalton gang was known to camp on the Dunn ranch, the Creek Nation Cave located in Payne County, Oklahoma southeast of Ingalls, and the Doolin-Dalton Cave to the east of Ingalls in Creek County, Oklahoma, near the Cimarron River northeast of today's Oilton community.

   25. Newsom, *Exciting Payne County*, 186.

   26. "Cal Owens Recalls Ingalls' Past," *Cimarron Valley Legends*, vol. 1 (Perkins: Evans Publications, 1978), 79.

   27. Tommie Little Warfield, interview.

   28. Jack Allen Little, interview.

   29. Tommie Little Warfield, interview. Dr. Walter R. Little had a medical accounts journal where he recorded all patient charges. This charge is included in the journal, today in the possession of Little descendants.

   30. "Gunfight at Ingalls—1893," Little Family Papers. For a thorough firsthand account, see William Ray Kerr, "In Defense of Ingalls, Oklahoma," *Cimarron Family Legends*, vol. 2 (Perkins, OK: Evans Press, 1980), 362–66. Kerr claims that Ingalls was not an outlaw town as the press advertised and that the outlaws came often to do business and visit family and friends. He blames the press for exaggerating events in Ingalls, causing the railroad to bypass the town. See Elsie Shoemaker, "Oldtimers Recall Ingalls, September 1st, 1893," *Stillwater New-Press*, September 6, 1964, p. 4–5. The majority of accounts name Murray's Saloon and the Pierce Hotel.

   31. Tommie Little Warfield, interview.

   32. Jack Allen Little, interview. Bill Doolin's son, Bill Doolin Jr., owned a bar known for its backroom gambling and bootleg whiskey in Oilton, Oklahoma. Jack recalls going to Doolin's Bar with his father, Glen Little, to play pool during the late 1930s and early 1940s. Doolin carried sidearms to keep the peace in his establishment since the law typically avoided Oilton's main street where at least five bars had established themselves in one block.

   33. *The Fourth Annual Catalogue of the Oklahoma Agricultural and Mechanical College*, Office of the Registrar, Oklahoma State University, Stillwater, Oklahoma.

CHAPTER FOUR

   1. Victoria Little Burris to Carolyn Leverich Atkinson, March 11, 1995.

   2. Frank C. Young, "Yellow Metal in Colorado," reprinted from the *Boston Daily Advertiser, Guthrie Daily Leader*, March 9, 1894, p. 2.

   3. Ibid.

4. Dr. Jim Foster, "Ten Day Tramps," *Labor History* 23, no. 4 (1982), Arizona Pioneer and Cemetery Research Project, http://www.apcrp.org /TRAMPS,%20The%20Ten%20Day/THE_TEN_DAY_TRAMPS.htm (accessed August 15, 2011).

5. Ibid.

6. Ibid.

7. Susie Harper, e-mail to author, August 2, 2010. See also "Whatever Happened to Alice?" Rand-McNally Advertisement, 1972, Harper Family Papers. Susie Harper is the grandniece of Emma Harper Little.

8. Susie Harper, e-mail to author, May 24, 2010.

9. Helen Freudengerger Holmes, ed., *Logan County History*, vol. 1 (1978), 248; Victoria Little Burris to Carolyn Leverich Atkinson, March 11, 1995.

10. "Mrs. Emma Harper Taken by Death," Emmarilla J. Harper Obituary, Los Angeles, CA, August 1946, Harper Family Papers; Victoria Little Burris to Carolyn Leverich Atkinson, March 11, 1995; Susie Harper, e-mail to author, August 5, 2010.

11. Emma J. Frisbie and William H. Harper, November 21, 1877, Gilpin County Bride's and Groom's Marriage Index, 1864–1944, Colorado State Archives (CSA): vol. 1, 280; Susie Harper, e-mail to author, August 2, 2010.

12. 1850 U.S. Federal Census, Magnolia, Rock County, WI, Roll M 432_1005, p. 289A, Image 157.

13. Historical Data Systems, comp., *American Civil War Soldiers*, online database (Provo, UT: Ancestry.com, 1999), Source 97; Report of Wm. L. Utley, Col., Cmdg. Twenty-second Regt. Wisconsin Volunteers, 1863, Engagement at Thompson's Station, TN," in *The War of the Rebellion: A Compilation of the Official Records of the Union and Confederate Armies* (Official Records), Robert N. Scott, ed., series I, vol. 23, ch. 35, serial no. 34, Part I—Reports (1889): 106–34. See also *The Union Army*, vol. 4, 58.

14. Emma B. Little to President Woodrow Wilson, February 7, 1918, p. 5, Case #8000-144363, Investigative Reports of the Bureau of Investigation 1908–1922, Old German Files (OGF), 1909–1921, FBI Case Files, National Archives Microfilm Publication M1085, Roll 536, NARA, Washington, D.C. The Bureau of Investigation (BOI), formed on March 16, 1909, investigated espionage, sabotage, and threats to a nation in wartime. The OGF, from which this particular case is found, contains investigative records relating to German aliens who were politically suspect before and during World War I. Since at the time the IWW was considered an organization of spies and anarchists supporting Kaiser Wilhelm, members of the IWW were investigated as traitors to the United States in a time of war. This particular case involves a February 1918 letter that Emma

sent to President Woodrow Wilson complaining about Fred Little's and Lon Little's arrests in the fall of 1917. The letter is rich with details relating to search and seizure methods, intimidation, and details of Emma's life.

15. 1880 U.S. Federal Census, La Fayette, Clinton County, MO, Roll 682, Family History Film 1254682, p. 451A, Enumeration District 100, Image 0084.

16. 1880 U.S. Federal Census, Black Hawk, Gilpin County, CO, Roll 90, Family History Film 1254090, p. 32A, Enumeration District 50, Image 0448.

17. "Mrs. Emma Harper Taken by Death."

18. Susie Harper, e-mail to author, July 7, 2010. The Alice-Yankee Placer district was also known as the Lincoln Placer district.

19. Victoria Little Burris to Carolyn Leverich Atkinson, March 11, 1995. See also Sandra L. Palcic-Erman, ed., *The Alice School 1906, Commemorative Booklet Marking the 75th Anniversary of the Alice School*, Alice Historical Society (July 4, 1982). Emma was the second teacher hired for the Alice School.

20. Palcic-Erman, *The Alice School*.

21. "The State Normal Institute, a Splendid Attendance—Interesting Introductory Proceedings," *Colorado Transcript*, August 11, 1897, p. 4.

22. Ibid.

23. Holmes, *Logan County History*, 248.

24. Palcic-Erman, *The Alice School*.

25. Ibid.

26. "State Normal Institute," 4. The Scripture is from Luke 6:31.

27. Victoria Little Burris to Carolyn Leverich Atkinson, March 11, 1995.

28. Walter F. Little and Emma B. Harper Marriage License No. 27852, Arapahoe County, Denver, CO, October 6, 1898, CSA.

CHAPTER FIVE

1. George Fetherling, *The Gold Crusades: A Social History of Gold Rushes, 1849–1929* (University of Toronto Press, 1997), 92. The popular song "There'll Be a Hot Time in Town Tonight" originated in Cripple Creek during the gold rush era.

2. Robert Guilford Taylor, *Cripple Creek Mining District* (Palm Lake, CO: Filter Press, 1973), 203–205.

3. Digital Gallery, Cripple Creek District Museum, http://cripple creek museum.com/PhotoCollection.htm (accessed August 15, 2011). Photographs from the Denver Public Library Western History/Genealogy Digital Collection, http://digital.denverlibrary.org/cdm (accessed August 15, 2011), also provided clues as to daily street scenes in Cripple Creek, Colorado, during 1898–99.

4. "Mines Go on as Usual," *Denver Rocky Mountain News*, May 3, 1896, p. 4.

5. "National Register of Historical Places Inventory Form," Historical National Parks Service, U.S. Department of the Interior, 1975, Item 7, 2.

6. Elizabeth Jameson, "History, Memory, and Commemoration: The Cripple Creek Strike Remembered," in *The Colorado Labor Wars, Cripple Creek District 1903–1904*, eds. Tim Blevins, Chris Nichol, and Calvin P. Otto (Colorado Springs: Pikes Peak Library District, 2006), 4; Mine Owners' Association, *Criminal Record of the Western Federation of Miners, Coeur d'Alene to Cripple Creek, 1894–1904* (Colorado Springs: Colorado Mine Operators' Association, 1904).

7. Elizabeth Jameson, *All That Glitters: Class, Conflict, and Community in Cripple Creek* (Chicago: University of Illinois Press, 1998), 59. Perhaps the most thorough, analytical assessment of class studies within the western labor movement, Jameson magnifies the Cripple Creek mining district using the 1900 Federal Census, local newspapers, interviews, and other sources to depict life within the mining town.

8. Clara Stiverson, interview by Elizabeth Jameson, July 29, 1975, as quoted in Elizabeth Jameson, "Imperfect Unions, Class, and Gender," *Frontiers: A Journal of Women Studies* 1, no. 2 (Spring 1976), 91.

9. Ibid.

10. Jameson, *All That Glitters*, 118.

11. George G. Suggs, *Colorado's War on Militant Unionism: James H. Peabody and the Western Federation of Miners* (Norman: University of Oklahoma Press, 1991), 20.

12. Ibid., 25.

13. Ibid., 40.

14. Ibid., 152.

15. Ibid., 33.

16. Victoria Little Burris to Carolyn Leverich Atkinson, March 11, 1995.

17. Dr. W. R. Little Obituary, *Stillwater Gazette*, January 19, 1899.

18. Almira Little Petition of Probate, Walter R. Little Estate, January 21, 1899, in Walter R. Little Probate Papers, January 13–July 28, 1899, p. 1. Originals filed in Probate Records, Payne County Courthouse, Stillwater, OK.

CHAPTER SIX

1. Sellars, *Oil, Wheat, and Wobblies*, 6.

2. See Nigel A. Sellars, "Treasonous Tenant Farmers and Seditious Sharecroppers: The 1917 Green Corn Rebellion Trials," *Oklahoma City University Law Review* 27 (2002): 1110–11, available at http://www.

NationalAgLawCenter.org, for statistics relating to tenancy in Oklahoma counties.

3. F. H. Little, "Conditions in Oklahoma," *Solidarity*, December 2, 1911, p. 4. This letter to the editor of *Solidarity* was dated November 23, 1911, written from Guthrie, Oklahoma, where Frank was convalescing at his mother's home. *Solidarity*, an IWW newspaper, was first published in late 1909.

4. 1900 U.S. Federal Census, Pawnee, Payne County, OK, Roll 1341, FHL microfilm 1241341, p. 2B, Enumeration District 0189.

5. Walter R. Little Probate Papers. Included in the probate is a Creditor's Claim for $15.90 from W. E. Berry and the original promissory note. Walter was to have begun payments November 1, 1889, concluding his financial obligation by March 1, 1890.

6. William E. Berry participated in the Land Run of 1889 and the Cherokee Strip Land Run of 1893. In both instances his land claims were disqualified for having resided and run a stock operation in Indian Territory prior to the land openings. See "Thomas Nelson Berry," originally published in "History of Oklahoma," in *Cimarron Valley Family Legends*, vol. 1 (Perkins, OK: Evans Publishing, 1978), 15. He and his brother-partner owned about two thousand cattle and three hundred horses and mules that they sold to eighty-niners after the run. William, in an effort to gain the original lease land back, purchased relinquishments and other land amounting to about one thousand acres in the southern part of Payne County. By 1907 his son Thomas N. Berry became owner of at least 880 acres purchased by either his father or other Berry family members. See both 1907 Clayton Township and Cimarron Township maps. Thomas originally farmed, later becoming a successful businessman and founder of several oil companies. His son (William E. Berry's grandson) Thomas E. Berry recalled that the mouth of Stillwater Creek at the Cimarron River was part of a relinquishment claim purchased from a man who had only held on to his land for two years. Actually, Walter R. Little owned lot 6 where Stillwater Creek poured into the Cimarron. See Homestead Certificate No. 7335, Patent Record, July 6, 1898, General Land Records, Oklahoma, vol. 11, p. 216, U.S. Bureau of Land Management, U.S. Department of the Interior. See also La Veta M. Randall, "Thomas E. Berry," in *Cimarron Valley Family Legends*, vol. 1 (Perkins, OK: Evans Publishing, 1978), 20.

7. Randall, "Thomas E. Berry," 20. Berry claimed that some men who made the 1889 Land Run sold their claims for a fine team of horses. Many relinquishments could be purchased at practically nothing. See William W. Howard, "The Rush to Oklahoma, *Harper's Weekly* 33 (May 18, 1889): 394. Howard participated in the 1889 Land Run.

8. Almira Little Petition of Probate, Layton and Sain General Store Creditor's Claim to Walter R. Little Estate, July 28, 1899, in Walter R. Little Probate Papers.

9. Tommie Little Warfield to Barbara Clapper Lewis, July 11, 1983, Little Family Papers.

10. "A. C. Little and Bessie to Almira Little," Warranty Records 5, p. 497, May 29, 1899, County Clerk, Payne County, Stillwater, OK. See "Almira Little to Harriet Berry," Warranty Records 5, p. 498. In order to acquire Walter R. Little's property, William E. Berry's daughter-in-law Harriet completed the transaction. Thomas N. and Harriet Berry's children recall the old cabin in "Early Memories of the Berry Sisters," 16–19. The Little family homestead cabin on Doc Little Hill burned down before 1925.

11. Charles Courtright and Bessie Little Marriage Record No. 324, June 11, 1899 (Payne County), Oklahoma State Archives (OSA). See 1900 U.S. Federal Census, Mound, Payne County, OK, Roll 1341, FHL microfilm 1241341, p. 17A, Enumeration District 0187.

12. Both Fred and Frank Little were not included in the Warranty Records as receiving one dollar each for relinquishing property claims to the Walter and Almira Little homestead. Their exclusion indicates that they had left Oklahoma by May 1899.

13. 1900 U.S. Federal Census, Guthrie, Logan County, OK, Roll T623_1339, p. 7B, Enumeration District 138. On June 15, 1900, Emma is listed as living with her Frisbie grandparents on the family dairy in Guthrie, Logan County, Oklahoma. Instead of her maiden name, she was listed as Emma Little, married in 1898, with a one-year-old baby, Walter R. Little. Her little brother Guy was also with her grandparents, having attended school in Guthrie that year. Nora G. Frisbie, ed., *Bulletin of the Frisbie-Frisbee Family Association of America* 21, no. 4 (October 1971): 73.

14. Elihu Cox and Mrs. Almira Little Marriage Record, June 20, 1899, Logan County Marriage Records, 339, County Clerk, Logan County, Guthrie, OK. William Judd officiated. Cox lost his first wife Rhoda Clark Cox in January 1898.

15. James P. Cannon, *Notebook of an Agitator*, 3rd ed. (New York: Pathfinder Press, 1993), 59.

16. 1900 U.S. Federal Census, San Jose, San Luis Obispo County, CA, Roll 109, FHL microfilm 1240109, p. 4A, Enumeration District 0030. Frank is not living with Fred in 1900. Researchers may confuse another Frank Hamilton Little of Indian Territory. This Little is the son of William Little, a rancher from Georgia, who married an American Indian woman. In 1900 this Frank H. Little of Vinita, Indian Territory, is living with his widower father. Still another Frank Little is recorded in 1900 in the Chickasaw Nation, building railroad ties and living in a boarding house. His birthplace, as well as his parents', is cited as Kansas with his birthday November 1875. This livelihood certainly fits a future IWW's résumé despite other mismatching information. Yet it is inconceivable

that Almira would not have included Frank, along with Bessie and Alonzo, in the sale transactions of the family farm if Frank were still living in Oklahoma. It is this author's opinion that Frank left the territory before the farm sale with his brother Fred as neither of them was involved in the customary one-dollar heir transaction.

Chapter Seven

1. "Copper Queen Arrivals," *Bisbee Daily Review*, October 10, 1903, p. 5. The Copper Queen Hotel published its daily ledger of new occupants in the order they registered. The hotel also recorded the home residence of each guest. George Delaporte and Frank Little signed the register, one after another. Phelps, Dodge & Co. changed its name in 1916 to Phelps Dodge Corporation in order to include its various business acquisitions.

2. "Impressions of Bisbee the Big Mining Camp Does Not Boast of Beauty but Claims to be Money Producer," *Tucson Daily Citizen*, August 30, 1905, p. 8. The newspaper story fully compares the positives and negatives of living and working in Bisbee, Arizona, with the "nauseating odor" a definite negative.

3. "Woman Clerk Left Major Part of Estate," *Oakland Tribune*, March 4, 1910, p. 3. Delaporte, reported to have been a dissenter against the French Commune, escaped to America where he financed his success as a chemist who was talented with concocting whiskey. "Aged Woman Tells of Privation," *Oakland Tribune*, September 6, 1918, p. 3; "That's All," *Daily Nevada State Journal*, May 9, 1903, p. 1.

4. R. W. Graeme, "Bisbee, Arizona's Dowager Queen of Mining Camps, A Look at Her First Fifty Years," in *History of Mining in Arizona*, vol. 1, J. M. Canty and M. N. Greeley, eds. (Tucson: Mining Club of the Southwest Foundation, 1987): 52.

5. Ibid.

6. Ibid.

7. Ibid.

8. Dan Finck, interview by the author, August 20, 2012. Finck and his wife Connie are the current owners (2012) of the Copper Queen Hotel in Bisbee, Arizona.

9. "Impressions of Bisbee," 8.

10. Ibid.

11. Interview and tour of Copper Queen Mine, August 19, 2012. A former Phelps Dodge miner provided a complete description of a miner's daily activities specific to the geological attributes of the Copper Queen Mine.

12. James Douglas to Phelps Dodge, June 11, 1903, Lewis W. Douglas Collection, Folder 5, Box 42, Special Collections, University of Arizona (UA), as quoted in James McBride, "Gaining a Foothold in the Paradise of Capitalism, *Journal of Arizona History* 23 (Autumn 1982): 304.

13. Interview and tour of Copper Queen Mine.

14. Vernon Perry, interview by the author, August 23, 2012. Perry is the president of the Gila Historical Museum in Globe, Arizona.

15. Interview and tour of Copper Queen Mine.

16. Ibid.

17. Vernon H. Jensen, *Heritage of Conflict* (Ithaca, New York: Cornell University Press, 1950), 357.

18. John Michal Benson, interview by the author, August 23, 2012. Benson is the son of a mine manager who worked for the Inspiration Mine and grandson of immigrants who moved to Arizona Territory to work. Born in Cananea, Mexico, where his father was employed, Benson has a deep knowledge and understanding of ethnic division and labor practices within the Miami mining culture. Benson worked various jobs for the mining company as his father rose within the company.

19. Ibid.

20. "Impressions of Bisbee," 8.

21. Graeme, "Bisbee," 57.

22. McBride, "Gaining a Foothold," 305.

23. Jim Bissett, *Agrarian Socialism in America* (Norman, Oklahoma: University of Oklahoma Press, 1999), 63. The Socialist Party of America (SPA) and the Socialist Labor Party (SLP) are two distinctly different organizations. The SLP, the original socialist party in America, supported an alliance of trade unions but battled direct action. The SLP was led by Marxist Daniel De Leon, a founding IWW member, who split from the IWW in favor of political action using the ballot. He formed a short-lived variant IWW in Detroit called Workers' International Industrial Union. The SPA, formed in 1901 by disgruntled former SLP members, and primarily led by Eugene Debs, identified with social democrats wherein workers share and control production. It too was an economic and political party, but supported capitalist reforms. Harry A. McKee and Joseph D. Cannon were early members of the SPA. Frank Little later became apolitical, believing only in workplace or economic democracy.

24. McBride, "Gaining a Foothold," 305.

25. Almira L. Cox, Petition for Temporary Alimony, no. 4748, October 29, 1904, Logan County, Oklahoma.

26. Ibid.

27. *R. L. Polk & Co.'s Guthrie City Directory*, 1907–1908.

28. Cox, Petition for Temporary Alimony.

29. "Wants Alimony, Crescent City Woman Will Be Satisfied Without Divorce," *Oklahoman*, Oklahoma City, Oklahoma, May 10, 1905; *Logan County News*, May 12, 1905, p. 5.

30. Cox, Petition for Temporary Alimony. Almira claimed that she had been owner of a claim of 80 acres of land in Payne County, OK, which

Elihu forced her to sell for $750, probably the Mound Farm. She invested $500 for a house and lot in Stillwater, which she was renting for $4 a month and which Elihu took.

CHAPTER EIGHT

1. "Labor Day in Globe," *Solidarity,* September 24, 1910, p. 2; "May Day Demonstration," *Arizona Silver Belt,* April 26, 1906, p. 1. The latter article presented the official program to be held on May 1, 1906, in Globe, Arizona.

2. "May Day Demonstration," May 3, 1906, p. 1.

3. "Labor Day in Globe," 2.

4. "May Day Demonstration," May 3, 1906, p. 1; "Labor Day in Globe," 2. The two periodicals give vastly different accounts of the Globe May Day parade. The *Solidarity* article recalls May 1, 1906, with great victory compared to the 1910 May Day parade when gunmen rode in the parade, controlling the holiday's program.

5. "May Day Demonstration," April 26, 1906, p. 1; "May Day Demonstration," May 3, 1906, p. 1. Joseph D. Cannon was also an executive board member of the Western Federation of Miners and the Arizona Socialist party's nominee for Congress in 1906 and 1908. David R. Berman, *Radicalism in the Mountain West, 1890–1920* (Boulder: University of Colorado, 2007), 196.

6. Berman, *Radicalism,* 196.

7. *Official Proceedings of the Fifteenth Annual Convention of the Western Federation of Miners,* Stenographic Report, June 10–July 3, 1907, Denver, Colorado, 194.

8. "Labor Day in Globe," 2.

9. William D. Haywood, *Bill Haywood's Book: Autobiography of Big Bill Haywood* (New York: International Publishers, 1929), 171.

10. "May Day Demonstration," April 26, 1906, p. 1.

11. Ralph Chaplin, *Wobbly: The Rough-and-Tumble Story of an American Radical* (Chicago: University of Chicago Press, 1948), 196.

12. Elizabeth Gurley Flynn, *Rebel Girl, An Autobiography,* rev. ed. (New York: International Publishers, 1994), 232.

13. Ibid.; Chaplin, *Wobbly,* 195–96. Frank Little began wearing a glass eye by 1909.

14. Tom C. Stewart to Aaron C. Marsh, August 22, 1906, File AZ 549, Special Collections, University of Arizona (UA). The letter provides a colorful description of life in Globe.

15. Stewart to Aaron C. Marsh.

16. Lester Ward Ruffner, "Arizona's First Governor, George W. P. Hunt, Was the Consummate Politician" in "Days Past," *Prescott Daily Courier,*

June 26, 2005, http://www.sharlot.org/library-archives/arizonas-first-governor-george-w-p-hunt-was-the-consummate-politician/ (accessed January 31, 2016). The original quote from the *Daily Arizona Silver Belt,* 1911, attributed the comment to Prescott banker and political opponent Edmund W. Wells during the 1911 fall gubernatorial campaign.

17. Stewart to Aaron C. Marsh.

18. Ibid.

19. Alexander Ziede, "The Territorial History of Globe Mining District" (thesis manuscript, University of Southern California, 1939), 16.

20. Clyde Elrod, "The Old Dominion Mine" (unpublished manuscript, 1965), Vertical Files, Gila County Historical Society (GCHS); Wilbur A. Haak, "The Old Dominion Copper Mine," in *History of Mining in Arizona,* vol. 3, eds. J. M. Canty and M. N. Greeley (Tucson, Arizona: Mining Club of the Southwest Foundation, 1999), 83–102.

21. George W. P. Hunt, personal journal entry dated March 27, 1915, George W. P. Hunt Papers, Box 26, Folder 5 (MSS48), Haydon Library, Arizona Collection, Arizona State University (ASU).

22. Philip Mellinger, "'The Men Have Become Organizers': Labor Conflict and Unionization in the Mexican Mines of Arizona, 1900–1915," *Western Historical Quarterly* 23, no. 3 (1992), 326; Michael Casillas, "The PLM in Territorial Arizona: A Survey for, and Results of Mexican Unionizational Attempts" (unpublished manuscript, Arizona State University, 1975), Chicano Collection, Box 6, Folder 2 (CHSM), Haydon Library, ASU.

23. Berman, *Radicalism,* 152. See T. H. Watkins, "Requiem for the Federation," *American West* 3, no. 1 (Winter 1966): 10. By July 26, 1904, 238 Cripple Creek miners had been deported beyond the Colorado state border and dumped on the open prairie.

24. James McClintock, *Arizona: The Youngest State,* vol. 2: 387.

25. Ibid.; John Michal Benson, interview.

26. James B. Tenney, *History of Mining in Arizona,* 1 (1929): 76, AZ 198, Special Collections, UA. Tenney was an assistant geologist for the Arizona Bureau of Mines.

27. Daphne Overstreet, "On Strike! The 1917 Walkout at Globe, Arizona," *Journal of Arizona History* (1977): 198; Phylis Cancilla Martinelli, *Undermining Race* (Tucson: University of Arizona Press, 2009), 83. See Casillas, "PLM in Territorial Arizona," for a thorough job exploring relationships among Anglo and Mexican labor in Arizona.

28. *Scabs* were men who broke strike lines to work, usually non-union workers.

29. James D. McBride, "The Development of Labor Unions in Arizona Mining, 1884–1919" (thesis manuscript, Arizona State University, 1975), Arizona Collection, Haydon Library, ASU, 60.

30. The Citizens Alliance of Denver is credited with the new acronym. See Watkins, "Requiem for the Federation," 10.

31. Theodore Roosevelt to Edward H. Harriman, April 2, 1907, in Henry F. Pringle, *Theodore Roosevelt* (New York: Konecky & Konecky, 1931), 316–20. This biography has been criticized for its "muckraking" style. Roosevelt tried to qualify his predetermination of William Haywood's, George Pettibone's, and Charles Moyer's guilt after a storm of criticism in a letter dated April 23, 1907, to Chairman Jaxon of the Cook County Moyer-Haywood Conference. See "Roosevelt Replies to Labor Attacks," *New York Times*, April 24, 1907. See also *Miner's Magazine*, May 5, 1907, p. 4.

32. *Official Proceedings of the Fifteenth Annual Convention*, 107–109.

33. Harry Orchard died in Idaho State Prison on April 13, 1954, where he spent forty-nine of his eighty-one years.

34. The Immigration Act of 1907 was signed into law by President Theodore Roosevelt to help regulate and restrict certain classes and ethnicities from immigrating. Within Section Two of the law, "undesirable" immigrants included those who were considered political threats or anarchists. Roosevelt's description of certain groups of immigrants as "undesirable citizens" prompted hundreds of thousands of the American Left to proudly wear "I am an Undesirable Citizen" lapel buttons. See the Immigration Act of 1907 (34 Stat. 898).

35. F. H. Little, "Correspondence," *Miner's Magazine*, February 8, 1906, pp. 11–12.

Chapter Nine

1. Linda Gordon, *The Great Arizona Orphan Abduction* (Cambridge: Harvard University Press, 1999).

2. *Arizona Bulletin*, as quoted by Margaret Regan, "The Orphan Abduction," *Tucson Weekly*, March 15, 2007.

3. "Joyous Home Coming of Clifton Orphans," *Arizona Silver Belt*, February 2, 1905, p. 5.

4. Originally called Copper Street, the street acquired its second name when a Captain Chase led a troop of cavalrymen in pursuit of horse-stealing Apaches. "Charles A. Spezia's Walking Tour of Historic Chase Creek, Clifton, AZ, 1900–29," Greenlee County Historical Society, Clifton, AZ, 1990, p. 2.

5. H. W. (F.) Kane, "Arizona Labor Conditions," *Miner's Magazine*, February 2, 1907, p. 8; Jane Eppinga, "Ethnic Diversity in Mining Camps," in *History of Mining in Arizona*, vol. 2, eds. J. Michael Canty and Michael N. Greeley (Tucson: Mining Club of the Southwest Foundation, 1991), 53.

6. Rodolfo F. Acuña, *Corridors of Migration* (Tucson: University of Arizona Press, 2007), 58.

7. Allen H. Rogers, "Characters and Habits of the Mexican Miner," *Engineering and Mining Journal* 85 (1908): 702.

8. See James Colquhoun, *The History of Clifton-Morenci Mining District* (London: John Murray, 1924), for his description of early mining communities.

9. "History," *Morenci*, available at http://www.morencitown.com/2143/History. Freeport-McMoRan published that the Morenci mine, which continues to hold most of North America's copper reserves, is one of the highest copper-producing mines in the world. See Freeport-McMoRan Annual Report, *Value at Our Core*, 2014, pp. 8–9.

10. President's Mediation Commission, 1917, Reel 11, pp. 37–40, as quoted in Andrea Yvette Huginnie, "'Strikitos': Race, Class, and Work in the Arizona Copper Industry, 1870–1920" (thesis manuscript, Arizona State University, 1971), Chicano Research Collection (HD 939.C7), Haydon Library, Arizona State University (ASU), 210.

11. Huginnie, "'Strikitos,'" 211.

12. Jennie Parks Ringgold, *Frontier Days in the Southwest* (San Antonio: Naylor, 1952), 165–66. Ringgold is the sister of James V. Parks, leading sheriff during the 1903 miners' strike.

13. Eppinga, "Ethnic Diversity," 53; Acuña, *Corridors of Migration*, 113.

14. Acuña, *Corridors of Migration*, 113.

15. Ibid., 113; Michael Casillas, "Ethnic Factors Leading to the Clifton-Morenci Strike of 1915–1916" (manuscript, Arizona State University, 1973), Chicano Research Collection, Small Manuscripts (MM CHSM-20), Haydon Library, ASU. See Philip Mellinger for a thorough discussion of the 1903 Clifton-Morenci strike in "The Men Have Become Organizers," 323–47.

16. "Wages at Clifton-Morenci," *Bisbee Daily Review*, June 2, 1903, p. 1.

17. "3,500 Men Are Now Idle," *Bisbee Daily Review*, June 3, 1903, p. 1. The number of strikers on June 3, 1903, differs, anywhere between 1,500 and 3,000, mostly Mexicans. Acuña, *Corridors of Migration*, 113.

18. "Morenci Men Have Support," *Bisbee Daily Review*, June 12, 1903, p. 1; Acuña, *Corridors of Migration*, 140. Moyer, who sometimes called Mexicans "greasers," blamed Mexicans for organizational failures. The WFM's general antipathy and prejudice toward Hispanics isolated them and contributed to their solidarity. One WFM organizer was sent to Clifton-Morenci, arriving too late to assist the strike. *Official Proceedings of the Eleventh Annual Convention of the Western Federation of Miners*, Stenographic Report, May 25–June 10, 1903, Denver, Colorado, 224.

19. "3,500 Men Are Now Idle," 1; Evan Fraser-Campbell, "The Management of Mexican Labor," *Engineering and Mining Journal* 91 (1911):

1140; *Los Mineros,* documentary, directed by Hector Galen (Scottsdale: Espinosa Productions, 1992), DVD.

20. "Mining in Clifton and Morenci," *Arizona Silver Belt,* June 18, 1903, p. 2.

21. Arizona-acting Governor Isaac Stoddard's telegram to President Theodore Roosevelt, June 9, 1903, Clifton-Morenci Ephemeral Files (MS 1101), Arizona Historical Society (AHS). Roosevelt authorized troops for which he subsequently received criticism.

22. Acuña, *Corridors of Migration,* 114. For a detailed account of the 1903 Morenci strike, see Ringgold, "Frontier Days," 164–76. Sheriff James V. Parks was credited with helping prevent bloodshed.

23. Roy Talbert Jr., *Negative Intelligence, The Army and the American Left, 1917–1941* (Jackson, MS: University Press of Mississippi, 1991), 38–39. Talbert states that the Pinkerton National Detective Agency, most famous of detective agencies, became tainted by its violent antilabor record. The Burns Detective Agency became their main rival. The Thiel Detective Service Company was also active in labor disputes and conducted successful operations in Oklahoma, with agents infiltrating senior positions in the IWW.

24. "The Rangers at Morenci," *Bisbee Daily Review,* June 3, 1903, p. 1.

25. Acuña, *Corridors of Migration,* 115. Arizona territorial legislation in 1901 passed a bill enabling the governor to create a special body called the Arizona Rangers. Their personnel, whose identification was to be kept as secret as possible "for strategic purposes," were authorized to command the services of cattlemen and law officers when necessary. Joseph E. Park, "The 1903 'Mexican Affair' at Clifton," *Journal of Arizona History* 18 (1977): 119–48; McClintock, *Arizona,* 584–85. In June 1906 Captain Rynning led an Arizona Rangers contingent into Cananea, Mexico, to put down a Mexican strike, upon orders of Colonel William Greene, owner of Cananea Mining Company. In order to legalize what should have been an illegal international operation into a neighboring country, Socorro Governor Izábal deputized each ranger individually. Author Colonel James McClintock commanded the First Arizona Infantry and its involvement in the 1903 Morenci Miners' strike.

26. Eppinga, "Ethnic Diversity," 53. Phylis Cancilla Martinelli states in *Undermining Race* that local papers also exaggerated the labor situation, putting fear into the public regarding unruly Italians and Mexicans. Italians participated in *mutualistas* and were heavily involved in the strike. Italians brought a sense of radicalism to the workplace including familiarity with European socialistic tendencies.

27. Jennie Parks Ringgold describes Charles Mills as a coward, an obstinate man who was much disliked by his employees, and partly responsible for the 1903 Morenci strike. See Ringgold, *Frontier Days,* 165; Stoddard, telegram, June 9, 1903.

28. See "Morenci Now Surrounded by Soldiers," *Bisbee Daily Review,* June 12, 1903, p. 1, for a full description of the flood and its aftermath.

29. Acuña, *Corridors of Migration,* 116.

30. *Official Proceedings of the Fifteenth Annual Convention,* 148.

31. Ibid.

32. "The Hanging at Butte," *Daily Missoulian,* August 2, 1917, p. 2. Vernon Jensen describes the evolution of the Goldfield conflict, making no mention of Frank Little, in *Heritage of Conflict,* 219–35. For a complete chronology and description of the Goldfield labor conflict, see Russell R. Elliott, "Labor Troubles in the Mining Camp at Goldfield, Nevada, 1906–1908, *Pacific Historical Review,* 19, no. 4 (Nov. 1950): 369–84. Elliott states that there were basically four different labor conflicts in Goldfield, Nevada, between 1906 and 1908. The first began in December 1906, a second in March 1907, a third in August 1907, and the final strike in November 1907. No Nevada newspapers report Frank Little's presence although he would have been a relatively unknown agitator at the time. In addition, MaryJoy Martin, biographer of Vincent St. John who led IWW organization in Goldfield, has found no corroborating evidence to support Frank Little's participation in the Goldfield conflict. Finally, Frank's labor organization is clearly documented, principally in Arizona, during the four periods of Goldfield labor conflict. In November 1906, he organized the Clifton WFM local; in March 1907, he organized the Metcalf WFM local; in June 1907, he attended the WFM convention; and he was back in Morenci by late July 1907, where he was trying to organize a local. While the final Goldfield strike was occurring in November 1907, Frank, by his own narrative, was about to leave Prescott, Arizona, where he had been working. After a series of stops in Arizona and California, he arrived in Nevada in mid-to-late 1908 where he unsuccessfully tried to organize a Reno IWW local. See F. H. Little, "Experiences of a Hobo Miner," *Industrial Union Bulletin,* December 12, 1908, p. 4.

33. D. Habersoll, "Conditions in Clifton, Metcalf, and Morenci, Arizona," *Miner's Magazine,* September 23, 1907, pp. 14–15.

34. Article IV, Sections 7–9, "Duties of the Executive Board," *Constitution of the Western Federation of Miners, Affiliated with the AFL,* Butte City, Montana, May 19, 1893, p. 13. WFM executive board members were required to organize in the field and provide monthly reports for four dollars per diem and other "legitimate" expenses, such as transportation.

35. *Official Proceedings of the Fifteenth Annual Convention,* 295, 893–95. Frank was paid $46.80 for his mileage to Denver. *Official Proceedings of the Sixteenth Annual Convention Western Federation of Miners,* July 13–July 29, 1908, Denver, Colorado. Officers were paid $150 a month in 1907, the executive board members and organizers were paid per diem

($5) plus transportation. See also *Constitution and by-Laws of the Western Federation of Miners* (Butte, MT: 1883), 21.

36. While the IWW supported industrial unionism, the American Federation of Labor (AFL) excluded different ethnicities and unskilled workers, supported collective bargaining, and tended to support traditional political parties, such as the Democratic Party. The IWW considered the AFL to have much more in common with the employing class than the working class.

37. Kane, "Arizona Labor Conditions," 8.

38. "Purely Personal," *Copper Era*, November 29, 1906, p. 3.

39. Kane, "Arizona Labor Conditions," 8.

40. "Dissolution Notice," *Copper Era*, August 30, 1906, p. 2; "A Three-Man Strike," *Copper Era*, December 1907, p. 3. H. F. Kane broke his partnership with Major Lattin, a Republican.

41. Philip J. Mellinger, *Race and Labor in Western Copper* (Tucson: University of Arizona Press, 1995), 70.

42. Kane, "Arizona Labor Conditions," 8.

43. Ibid.

44. Ibid.

45. Ibid.

46. Mellinger, *Race and Labor*, 70–72.

47. "Notice," *Miner's Magazine*, March 21, 1907, p. 1; *Official Proceedings of the Fifteenth Annual Convention*, 147.

48. Mellinger, *Race and Labor*, 70.

49. "Clifton Miners Want Increase in Wages," *Bisbee Daily Review*, April 6, 1907, p. 5.

50. Kane, "Arizona Labor Conditions," 8.

51. *Los Mineros*, documentary.

52. "Moyer-Haywood Demonstration," *Copper Era*, May 16, 1907, p. 2.

53. "Roosevelt Replies to Labor Attacks," *New York Times*, April 24, 1907; *Miner's Magazine*, May 5, 1907, p. 4.

54. "Moyer-Haywood Demonstration," 2; *Official Proceedings of the Fifteenth Annual Convention*, 36.

55. "Moyer-Haywood Demonstration," 2.

56. See *Proceedings of the Second Annual Convention of the Industrial Workers of the World*, Sept. 17 to Oct. 3, 1906 (Chicago: International Workers of the World, 1906) for a stenographic report.

57. Ibid. For excellent analysis, see Eric L. Clements, "Pragmatic Revolutionaries?: Tactics, Ideologies, and the Western Federation of Miners in the Progressive Era," *Western Historical Quarterly* 40, no. 4 (2009): 445–67.

58. Ibid. Vernon Jensen states that those supporting the minority or Trautmann position in Arizona met informally before going to Denver.

These delegates included Frank Little, Albert Ryan, Joe Cannon, John Riordan, P. W. Galentine, and Percy Rawlings. They did not all stand together, however, when they reached the convention in Denver. *Heritage of Conflict*, 360–61. Jensen interviewed Joseph Cannon in 1945.

59. *Official Proceedings of the Fifteenth Annual Convention*, 13.

60. Ibid., 331.

61. Ibid., 579, 611, 742.

62. Ibid., 744.

63. Ibid., 680.

64. *Morenci Leader*, July 27, 1907, p. 1

65. Ibid.

66. Ibid.

67. Ibid.

68. Ibid.

69. Joseph D. Cannon, "The Report of the President of the Arizona State Union WFM," 8.

70. "Convention of Arizona Miners," *Arizona Silver Belt*, August 13, 1907, p. 1.

CHAPTER TEN

1. "Conversation Anent the Bridge," *Daily Missoulian*, October 16, 1909, p. 3.

2. "IWW Occupies 'Prominent Positions,'" *Butte Miner*, September 30, 1909; "County Jail Offers Better Care," *Butte Miner*, September 30, 1909.

3. Flynn, *Rebel Girl*, 102. Her autobiography includes firsthand accounts of free speech fights, which she originally furnished to the U.S. Industrial Relations Commission in Washington, D.C., in 1914. Philip S. Foner included Flynn's and other Wobblies' free speech accounts for his book *Fellow Workers and Friends*.

4. "Democratic Institutions Are Assailed," *Montana News*, October 14, 1909, p. 1.

5. See Foner, *Fellow Workers and Friends*, 12–22, for a closer look at the evolution of the IWW free speech technique. Foner suggests that some of the most competent organizers who participated in the free speech fights limited their efficacy instead of using their talents elsewhere.

6. Flynn, *Rebel Girl*, 104; "Street Orators Get Into Trouble," *Daily Missoulian*, October 1, 1909, p. 10; "Gurley Flynn Sends Horrible Story," *Daily Missoulian*, October 6, 1909, p. 2.

7. F. H. Little, "The Beating of Jones by the Missoula Sheriff," *Industrial Worker*, October 29, 1910, p. 1.

8. Ibid. "Street Orators Get Into Trouble," 10.

9. Flynn, *Rebel Girl*, 104. Flynn's plea for rebels to join the Missoula Free Speech Fight was published in the September 30, 1909, issue of *Industrial Worker*. The *Industrial Worker* was the official newspaper of the IWW organization.

10. The first free speech fight was actually held in San Francisco in April 1906, according to Paul Brissenden. Elizabeth Gurley Flynn and others perfected the strategy. Paul Frederick Brissenden, *An IWW Study of American Syndicalism* (New York: 1919), 365. Brissenden lists twenty-six free speech fights in total. Missoula was the second protest.

11. Paul Houlb, testimony before U.S. District Court of Illinois, July 13, 1918, transcript available from U.S. vs. Haywood et al., 1917–1918, Legal Problems, Trials, and Defense, File 2: 7207, Box 104, Subseries B, Walter P. Reuther Library, Wayne State University (WSU). Houlb was typical of young loggers who had worked in so many logging camps that they had lost count. Testimony from the trial on July 13, 1918, revealed numerous accounts of unsanitary conditions, inadequate housing, work hazards, and general disregard for workers in logging camps.

12. Ibid., 7182; Hulbert Engebritson, testimony before U.S. District Court of Illinois, July 13, 1918, transcript available from U.S. vs. Haywood et al., 1917–1918, Legal Problems, Trials, and Defense, File 2: 7166, Box 104, Subseries B, Walter P. Reuther Library, WSU. Engebritson, a Norwegian immigrant, claimed to have worked in thirty camps overall, and he was thirty-three years old at the time.

13. Ibid., 7165, 7182–83.

14. Ibid., 7184, 7189.

15. Flynn, *Rebel Girl*, 102.

16. Ibid., 103.

17. "Democratic Institutions Are Assailed," 1.

18. Flynn, *Rebel Girl*, 103–104.

19. Ibid., 103.

20. "The Report of the Secretary-Treasurer of the Arizona State Union WFM," *Miner's Magazine*, August 27, 1908, p. 9. Frank received $240 for his final year of service.

21. Thomas E. Campbell, "True Copy of the Notes of Honorable Thomas E. Campbell," written between 1934 and 1939, Arizona Historical Society Library (AHS), Campbell Family Papers (MS 132), Folder 6, p. 20, http://www.library.arizona.edu/exhibits/bisbee/docs/rec_camp.html (accessed August 12, 2013).

22. In the 1916 Arizona gubernatorial election, Thomas E. Campbell beat incumbent George W. P. Hunt by thirty votes. Hunt claimed fraud, and after a lengthy court battle, Hunt was reinstated as Arizona governor at the end of 1917. From January 1917 until December 1917, Campbell

was considered the "de facto" governor. "Hunt Wins Governorship," *Tucson Daily Citizen*," December 22, 1917, pp. 1–2.

23. Campbell, "True Copy of the Notes," 20.

24. E. M. J. Alenius, "A Brief History of the United Verde Open Pit, Jerome, Arizona," *Arizona Bureau of Mines Bulletin*, 178 (Tucson: University of Arizona, 1968): iii. The mine was opened for open-pit excavation in 1922.

25. Campbell, "True Copy of the Notes," 20.

26. *Official Proceedings of the Fifteenth Annual Convention*, 148.

27. "Organizer Frank Little," *Prescott Evening Courier*, November 30, 1907, p. 4.

28. "Two Industrial Unionists," *Industrial Union Bulletin*, January 11, 1908, p. 2.

29. F. H. Little, "Experiences of a Hobo Miner," p. 4. This article provides Frank Little's personal narrative of his activities between December 1907 and December 1908.

30. Ibid.

31. Foner, *Fellow Workers and Friends*, 7.

32. Fred W. Thompson to Joel W. Watne, June 12, 1967, Fred Thompson Collection, Subseries A, Box 9, File 18, Walter P. Reuther Library, WSU.

33. Chaplin, *Wobbly*, 89.

34. See Ed Nolan, "From Frisco to Denver," in Foner, *Fellow Workers and Friends*, 146–52, for a complete account of the journey to Denver.

35. F. H. Little, "Experiences of a Hobo Miner," 4.

36. Ibid.

37. Ibid.

38. Ibid.

39. Joyce L. Kornbluh, ed., *Rebel Voices, An IWW Anthology* (Chicago: Charles H. Kerr, 1988), 405–408. See Kornbluh for other words attributed to the IWW worker. Some believe that *Los Angeles Times* owner/editor Harrison Gray Otis is credited with first publishing the word *Wobbly* while others, such as IWW Mortimer Downing, reported that Chinese speakers said "I Wobbly Wobbly" instead of "IWW."

40. Ibid.

41. F. H. Little, "Experiences of a Hobo Miner," 4.

42. F. H. Little, "Life and Prospects of the Blanket Stiff," *Solidarity*, February 12, 1916, p. 5.

43. Ibid.

44. Victoria Little Burris to Carolyn Atkinson, January 5, 1995.

45. 1900 U.S. Federal Census, Tulare, Tulare County, CA, Roll 115, FHL microfilm 1240115, p. 1B, Enumeration District 0065. Alvin Church is also listed as living in Liberty Township, Tulare County, in the *1898 Tulare County Great Register*, 16.

46. *1904–05 Tulare County Business & Resident Directory*, 125.

47. "Big Republican Majority in the Next Legislature," *San Francisco Call*, October 25, 1906, p. 10; "Partial Returns Tulare Co. Vote," *Daily Tulare Advance Register*, November 7, 1906, p. 1. The Republican and Democrat candidates each tied with seventy-one votes, while Fred Little had sixteen.

48. Eugene L. Menefee and Fred A. Dodge eds., *History of Tulare and King Counties, CA* (Los Angeles: Historic Record, 1913), 595.

49. *1907 Fresno City Directory*, 232. Emma is not listed, but the city directory is clear to mention that female spouses and unmarried children are excluded. "Jeff D. Statham, City Trustee, Is Dead," *Fresno Morning Republican*, May 29, 1914, p. 8.

50. J. M. Guinn, ed., *History of the State of California and Biographical Record of the San Joaquin Valley, California* (Chicago: Chapman Publishing, 1905), 1338–39. The Fresno Police Department Headquarters building stands on the site of the hotel, which burned down in 1913. See "Jeff D. Statham, City Trustee, Is Dead," 8; "Police Building Is Set For Civic Center," *Fresno Bee*, July 23, 1958, p. 1A; "Police Complete Move into New Headquarters," *Fresno Bee*, December 12, 1960, p. 1C.

51. 1910 U.S. Federal Census, Fresno Ward 4, Fresno County, CA, Roll T624_76, FHL microfilm 1374089, p. 7A, Enumeration District 004.

52. "Various," Case #8000-78852: 44, Investigative Reports of the Bureau of Investigation 1908–1922, Old German Files (OGF), 1909–1921, FBI Case Files, National Archives Microfilm Publication M1085, NARA, Washington, D.C.; "Notice," *Industrial Worker*, December 25, 1909, p. 3; "New Unions," *Industrial Worker*, December 25, 1909, p. 4.

53. F. H. Little, "Experiences of a Hobo Miner," 4.

54. Ibid.

55. Flynn, *Rebel Girl*, 105.

56. F. H. Little, "The Beating of Jones," 1.

57. Ibid.

58. "Democratic Institutions Are Assailed," 1.

59. F. H. Little, "The Beating of Jones," 1.

60. "Street Orators Get Into Trouble," 10.

61. "Garden City Mayor Says Laborites Are Trying to Embarrass Officials," *Butte Miner*, October 2, 1909; Foner, *Fellow Workers and Friends*, 5. The author has chosen to use the term "Wobbly" to label IWWs at times from this point on within this manuscript. However, the term "Wobbly" was not first used until about 1911.

62. "Street Speakers Go to Jail Again," *Daily Missoulian*, October 2, 1909, p. 12.

63. Elizabeth Gurley Flynn, "Free-Speech Fight Diary, Missoula, Montana," in Foner, *Fellow Workers and Friends*, 27, originally published in *International Socialist Review*, November 1909.

64. "Socialists Continue Their Former Tactics," *Daily Missoulian*, October 4, 1909, p. 4.

65. "Police Arrest Nine More," *Daily Missoulian*, October 4, 1909, p. 2. Flynn was charged with inciting a riot.

66. Flynn, *Rebel Girl*, 104. "IWW Defies Law; Busy Bulls in Missoula," *Industrial Worker*, October 7, 1909, p. 1.

67. "IWW Defies Law," 1.

68. "Union Miners Take Decided Stand," *Daily Missoulian*, October 7, 1909, p. 5.

69. Foner, *Fellow Workers and Friends*, 28; "Crowd Is Unruly Missile Is Thrown," *Anaconda Standard*, October 6, 1909, p. 1.

70. Flynn, *Rebel Girl*, 104. Wisconsin Senator Robert La Follette Sr., a progressive Republican, delivered his address in the Harnois Opera House above IWW headquarters.

71. "This Day in Court," *Daily Missoulian*, October 8, 1909, p. 10.

CHAPTER ELEVEN

1. "Little Becomes Real Martyr to His Cause," *Fresno Morning Republican*, September 3, 1910, p. 10.

2. "Industrial Worker is Defiant and Insults Officers," *Fresno Herald*, August 25, 1910, p. 8; "Jury in Police Court Renders Four Verdicts in Afternoon," *Fresno Morning Republican*, September 1, 1910, p. 8. The other arrested men were W. C. Flannigan and Victor Vagol [Vogel].

3. "Industrial Worker is Defiant," 8.

4. "I.W.W. Plans to Wage War on Police," *Fresno Morning Republican*, August 27, 1910, p. 5.

5. Ibid.

6. "Industrial Worker is Defiant," 8; "Jury in Police Court Renders Four," 8. See W. F. Little, "Fresno Free Speech Fight On to Finish," *New York Evening Call*, March 1, 1911, p. 2. At the conclusion of the Fresno Free Speech Fight, Fred Little submitted a summary of the events to the paper. The *New York Call* was a socialist daily newspaper published in 1908. The *Call's* opposition to U.S. involvement in the First World War resulted in its prosecution under the Espionage Act.

7. "Police Witness is Accused of Perjury," *Fresno Morning Republican*, September 3, 1910, p. 16. Hapgood was arrested on the perjury charges but released on bond until a preliminary hearing. See "Hapgood Released on Bond of $500," *Fresno Morning Republican*, September 4, 1910, p. 10. At the preliminary hearing, Hapgood was again released on a one-hundred-dollar bond, but evidently never tried for false testimony. See Mrs. W. F. Little, "Court Crookedness in Fresno," *The Class War*, n.d., 117, first printed in *Appeal*, February 11, 1911, Frank Little Bio,

Vertical File VF0528, Silver Bow Archives (SBA). Emma B. Little writes a detailed account of arrests during the Fresno Free Speech Fight when a large group of men were still in jail. She details the corruption within the courts and police department. She claims that Hapgood was found guilty and bound over to the superior court where he was released on bond, never to be arrested again.

8. "Free Speech Must Be Won in Fresno," *Industrial Worker,* September 10, 1910, p. 1; W. F. Little, "Fresno Free Speech Fight," 2.

9. "IWW Worker Will Get Taste of Jail," *Fresno Morning Republican,* September 2, 1910, p. 6.

10. Ibid.; "H. F. Little (sic) Sent to Jail to Work Out Sentence," *Fresno Herald,* September 1, 1910, p. 8.

11. "Little Says He Preferred Dark Cell," *Industrial Worker,* October 8, 1910, p. 1.

12. "Little Would Not Work and Was Put in Dungeon," *Fresno Herald,* September 2, 1910; "Little Becomes Real Martyr," 10.

13. John Pancner, "The Free-Speech Fight," in Foner, *Fellow Workers and Friends,* 72; "The Spokane Fight," *Solidarity,* January 29, 1910, p. 3.

14. Fred W. Heslewood, "Barbarous Spokane," *International Socialist Review* 5, no. 8 (February 1910): 711. Heslewood was a general organizer for the IWW.

15. "Ask Council to Make New Ordinance," *Spokane Press,* November 10, 1909, p. 2.

16. Victoria Little Burris to Carolyn Leverich Atkinson, January 5, 1995.

17. Carl Sandburg, "Billy Sunday," *International Socialist Review* 16, no. 4 (September 1915): 152–53. William Ashley Sunday, a Christian evangelist who lived from 1862 until 1935, was noted for his colloquial sermons and frenetic delivery. He also became wealthy and was welcomed into the homes of the affluent and influential, an example of hypocrisy to the IWW.

18. Frank Little and IWW I. G. Nobles arrived in Kalispell mid-October 1910 to agitate workers in lumber camps. Nobles later joined the Wobblies in the Fresno Free Speech Fight. "Union News Items," *Industrial Worker,* October 27, 1909, p. 1; "Fight On; Send Men," *Spokane Press,* November 19, 1909, p. 1. C. L. Filigno's telegram to Frank Little was used against Filigno as evidence of conspiracy in the Spokane Free Speech Fight trials. Haywood, *Bill Haywood's Book,* 186. Haywood gives David C. Coates credit for the IWW slogan that had been amended for the IWW preamble during the founding convention of the IWW. The Knights of Labor used the old slogan, "An injury to one is the concern of all."

19. "Buy Scrubbing Brushes for Use on the Street Speakers," *Spokane Daily Chronicle,* November 5, 1909, p. 1; "IWW Men Plan to Block Police

Court; Will Demand Separate Jury Trials," *Spokane Daily Chronicle,* November 3, 1909, pp. 1–2.

20. Elizabeth Gurley Flynn, "The Free-Speech Fight at Spokane," in Foner, *Fellow Workers and Friends,* 52.

21. "Sullivan Dies from Assassin's Bullet—State Reward Asked," *Olympia Daily Recorder,* January 7, 1911, p. 1; H. Minderman, "The Fresno Free-Speech Fight," in Foner, *Fellow Workers and Friends,* 115. Wobblies were sitting in the Fresno County Jail when they received a telegram that Sullivan had been killed.

22. "Men Begin 'Starvation Strike'; Refuse to Eat Nice Hot Breakfast," *Spokane Daily Chronicle,* November 6, 1909, p. 1; "Will Police Use Stomach Pump Now?" *Spokane Press,* November 6, 1909, p. 1; "Buy Scrubbing Brushes for Use on the Street Speakers," 1; "The Press Believes in Fair Play and Free Speech," *Spokane Press,* November 6, 1909, p. 1.

23. City of Spokane vs. F. J. [*sic*] Little, Case No. 42563, Complaint for Violation of Ordinance No. A1324, "Disorderly Conduct," Police Justice Court, November 5, 1909. Police Chief J. T. Sullivan was the arresting officer. The charge from the original ordinance "prohibiting street speaking" was changed to "disorderly conduct" for all IWW arrests just before Frank Little was arrested. Flynn, "Free-Speech Fight," 37. The majority of the rank-and-file IWWs, such as Frank Little, were given a $200 bond and $30 or thirty days.

24. Heslewood, "Barbarous Spokane," 706.

25. Robert Ross to the Industrial Relations Commission, September 19, 1914, in "The Spokane Free-Speech Fight," in Foner, *Fellow Workers and Friends,* 69–70; Flynn, *Rebel Girl,* 107.

26. "Allege Gag on Free Press," *Spokane Press,* November 6, 1909, p. 2.

27. "Men in Jail Refuse to Work on Rock Pile," *Spokane Daily Chronicle,* November 4, 1909, p. 2.

28. Ibid.; "Plan Red and Black Uniform for IWW," *Spokane Press,* November 29, 1909, p. 1.

29. Foner, *Fellow Workers and Friends,* 65.

30. Ibid., 63.

31. "Tells of Spokane Industrial Fight," *Fresno Morning Republican,* November 16, 1909, p. 6; Chaplin, *Wobbly,* 150; "Contributions to Defense Fund," *Industrial Worker,* November 24, 1909, p. 3. Fred Little collected twelve dollars to send to the Spokane Defense Fund upon receiving information that Frank Little had been arrested.

32. Foner, *Fellow Workers and Friends,* 63; James Stark, "Diary of a Released Free Speech Fighter, *Industrial Worker,* January 8, 1909, pp. 1, 4; Chaplin, *Wobbly,* 150.

33. Ross in Foner, *Fellow Workers and Friends,* 32, 70. Foner reports that the men were given one-fifth of a five-cent loaf twice daily.

34. "Take IWW Prisoners to Fort; Seventeen Eat," *Spokane Daily Chronicle*, November 10, 1909, pp. 1–2.

35. "'Wash Day' for the IWWs," *Spokane Daily Chronicle*, November 13, 1909, p. 1.

36. City of Spokane vs. F. H. Little, Case No. 3943, Note of Issue and Notice of Trial for Trial Docket, Superior Court of the State of Washington and County of Spokane, November 17, 1909. Fred H. Moore was a Socialist lawyer whose most famous defense was in the Ettor-Giovannitti trial, which arose from the Lawrence, Massachusetts, textile strike in 1912.

37. "Speech Fight Appeals Grow," *Spokane Press*, November 17, 1909, p. 1; "Synopsis of Free Speech Fight," *Industrial Worker*, March 19, 1910, p. 3.

38. Ross in Foner, *Fellow Workers and Friends*, 71.

39. "Offers $1 for Half a Loaf," *Spokane Press*, November 22, 1909, p. 2.

40. "Bread and Water Tastes Good to Franklin School Prisoners," *Spokane Daily Chronicle*, November 11, 1909, pp. 1–2; "Starvation Strike is Over; Beg for Food and Eat Like Wild Creatures," *Spokane Daily Chronicle*, November 12, 1909, pp. 1–2.

41. "Synopsis of Free Speech Fight," 3.

42. "No Turkeys for the IWW. They Still Feed on Bread and Water Rather Than Work," *Portland Oregonian*, November 26, 1909, p. 6; "Bread and Water Is Thanksgiving Feast In and Out of Jail," *Spokane Press*, November 25, 1909, p. 1.

43. "Events of the Week," *Industrial Worker*, December 1, 1909, p. 1; Foner, *Fellow Workers and Friends*, 41.

44. "Proclamation by the IWW," *Spokane Press*, November 25, 1909, p. 1; "Synopsis of Free Speech Fight," 3.

45. "Officials Try to Force Confession," *Spokane Press*, December 2, 1909, pp. 1–2. The boys were between 11 and 16 years old.

46. Foner, *Fellow Workers and Friends*, 33.

47. Chaplin, *Wobbly*, 150; "Officials Emulate Díaz of Mexico," *Industrial Worker*, February 5, 1910, 1; Ross in Foner, *Fellow Workers and Friends*, 70. A report in the *Spokesman-Review* on January 3, 1910, states that emergency physician Dr. O'Shea treated 334 men in the hospital and 1,600 treatments overall for a period of 60 days. These cases excluded a regular run of accidents and jail cases. See Heslewood, "Barbarous Spokane," 708–709. Men from railroad and logging camps who were used to eating the poorest food succumbed to the ills that the Spokane jail produced. Heslewood writes that robust men, many of whom never knew a day's sickness in their lives, called O'Shea the "horse doctor" who dispensed green pills for everything from a broken jaw to a starving stomach.

48. "On to Spokane March First," *Industrial Worker*, February 19, 1910, p. 1. Following Fred Heslewood's appeal, the IWW adopted "The

Marseillaise" as their official song for the first time during the Spokane Free Speech Fight.

49. "IWW Chiefs Make Peace, Spokane Street Speakers to be Released, Pending Settlement," *Portland Oregonian*, March 4, 1910, p. 4. See details of the agreement between the City of Spokane and the IWW in William Z. Foster, "Spokane Fight for Free Speech Settled," *Industrial Worker*, March 12, 1910, p. 1. The city agreed to the release of IWW prisoners on a sliding scale, noninterference with landlords who could rent halls to IWW locals, free press on street corners, and free speech. The IWW agreed to drop all lawsuits.

Chapter Twelve

1. W. F. Little, "Fresno Free Speech Fight," 2; "Fresno Fight Won," *Solidarity*, March 11, 1911, p. 1.

2. "Fresno Extends Welcome to President Taft Today," *Fresno Morning Republican*, October 10, 1909, p. 1; William Howard Taft, "'He Who Conquers Himself Is Greater Than He Who Takes a City,' Address at City Hall Park, Fresno, California, at a Union Religious Service, October 10, 1909," *Presidential Addresses and State Papers of William Howard Taft, March 4, 1909, to March 4, 1910* (New York: Doubleday, Page, 1910), 1: 338.

3. "Notice," *Industrial Worker*, December 25, 1909, p. 3; "New Unions," *Industrial Worker*, December 25, 1909, p. 4.

4. "Various," Case #8000-78852: 44.

5. E. B. Harper, "Says Slavery Here; Remedy, Socialism," *Fresno Morning Republican*, November 23, 1909, p. 8.

6. E. B. Harper, "Says Working Man Is Without Rights," *Fresno Morning Republican*, December 12, 1909, p. 23.

7. W. F. Little, "One Union, One Card, One Common Enemy," *Fresno Morning Republican*, December 17, 1909, p. 11; E. B. Harper, "Every Man Must Join Labor Trust to Live," *Fresno Morning Republican*, December 17, 1909, p. 11.

8. F. H. Little, "Free Speech in Spokane," *Industrial Worker*, January 8, 1910, p. 3.

9. J. S. B., "On the Road from Sunny California," *Industrial Worker*, March 5, 1910, p. 3.

10. "Correspondence," *Industrialist Worker*, January 29, 1910, p. 4.

11. "Correspondence," *Miner's Magazine*, April 14, 1910, p. 9. *Miner's Magazine* reported that on April 4, 1910, Fred sent four dollars from the Fresno SPA to the Black Hills Lockout in care of Mr. Ernest Mills, Denver, Colorado.

12. A simplified explanation follows: poverty + immigrant = socialism; "revolutionary socialism" = yellow socialism; and "revolutionary

industrial unionism" = red socialism, as explained in *The Hobo Agitator*, documentary, KUSM (Missoula: Montana PBS, 1995), Television.

13. Fred Little uses this address for receiving correspondence on all his notices in *Industrial Worker* during 1909–10.

14. W. F. Little, "Fresno Free Speech Fight," 2.

15. Mrs. W. F. Little, "Court Crookedness." 117.

16. W. F. Little, "From Fresno California," *Industrial Worker*, May 21, 1910, p. 4; "Industrial Workers Here to Aid Fellow Workers in Fresno, California," *Industrial Worker*, December 29, 1910, p. 3; Martin Dodd, "The IWW, Fresno, and the Free Speech Fight of 1910–11: A Case Study in Hobo Activism" (thesis manuscript, 1974), Fred Thompson Collection, Subseries A, Box 14, Folder 10, Walter P. Reuther Library, WSU. Dodd writes that Wobbly agitation on the Santa Fe Railroad included work slowdowns, appropriation of provisions from the company store, and minor sabotage, such as tool breakage. Fred Thompson joined the IWW in 1922, later serving as editor of *Industrial Worker*, general secretary-treasurer, and historian.

17. F. H. Little, "Struggle for Free Speech in North and West," *Industrial Worker*, June 4, 1910, p. 1; Fred Thompson to Stephen J. Schwoegler, dated February 13, 1982, Fred Thompson Collection, Box 14, Folder 9, Walter P. Reuther Library, WSU.

18. "Mexican Speaker is Stopped by Police: Socialist Agitator Has No Permit; Is to Enter Protest," *Fresno Morning Republican*, April 17, 1910, p. 12. Fred Thompson incorrectly identifies Frank Little as the speaker. Fred Thompson to Stephen J. Schwoegler, dated November 11, 1982, Fred Thompson Collection, Box 14, Folder 10, Walter P. Reuther Library, WSU.

19. F. H. Little, "Struggle for Free Speech," 1; "Mexican Speaker is Stopped," 1. See Dodd, "The IWW." Dodd writes that Police Chief Shaw responded, "Take the name of every man who refuses a job and I will put him in jail."

20. W. F. Little, "Fresno Free Speech Fight," 2; Mrs. W. F. Little, "Court Crookedness," 117.

21. "Industrial Workers' Meeting Was a Fizzle," *Fresno Morning Republican*, May 30, 1910, p. 10.

22. Ibid.; W. F. Little, "Fresno Free Speech Fight," 2.

23. W. F. Little, "Fresno Free Speech Fight," 2; Mrs. W. F. Little, "Court Crookedness," 117.

24. *Fresno Morning Republican*, May 26, 1910, p. 4. The *Fresno Morning Republican* was managed and edited by Chester Harvey Rowell, nephew of the mayor of Fresno from 1909–12 by the same name and who also owned the paper. Often the two Rowells are confused, but both worked to rid Fresno of the IWW.

25. "I.W.W. Activity," *Solidarity*, August 20, 1910, p. 1; Mrs. W. F. Little, "Court Crookedness," 117.

26. F. H. Little, "Struggle for Free Speech," 1.

27. W. F. Little, "From Fresno, California," *Industrial Worker*, May 21, 1910, p. 4.

28. *Industrial Worker*, May 14, 1910, p. 4.

29. "Chartered Since Last Convention," *Industrial Worker*, April 29, 1910, p. 3.

30. Unnamed male, born July 19, 1909, *Index to Fresno Births*, California Birth Records, recorded in Book B: 359. The child died July 19, 1909, *Index to Deaths, Fresno County*, as recorded in Book C: 164. Fred Thompson notes in his letter to Ellen Herman, dated December 11, 1978, that radical families somehow had few children and few abortions. See Fred Thompson Collection, Box 15, Folder 2, Walter P. Reuther Library, WSU.

31. *Solidarity*, August 27, 1910, p. 1; F. H. Little, "The California Fruit Belt," *Solidarity*, August 27, 1910, p. 4.

32. "Labor and Its Day," *Fresno Herald*, September 3, 1910, illegible page.

33. F. H. Little, "The California Fruit Belt," 4.

34. "Crowds See Labor Day Parade," *Fresno Herald*, September 5, 1910, pp. 1, 8; "Industrial Worker is Still Confined in Dungeon," *Fresno Herald*, September 5, 1910, p. 8.

35. "Looking for Man Who Disowned Flag," *Fresno Morning Republican*, September 7, 1910, p. 12. Tom Seaward, secretary of the Federated Trades, suggested that an IWW tore down the American flag on Union Hall. Seaward had a close relationship with Police Chief Shaw and Chester H. Rowell, editor of the *Fresno Morning Republican*.

36. W. F. Little, "Little Declares Flag Story Untrue," *Fresno Morning Republican*, September 8, 1910, p. 3.

37. "Industrial Worker Declines to Do Any Work," *Fresno Herald*, September 7, 1910, p. 1.

38. W. F. Little, "Fresno Free Speech Fight," 2; "IWW Orders Little to Work in the Park," *Fresno Morning Republican*, September 9, 1910, p. 3.

CHAPTER THIRTEEN

1. "Determine to Harrass [sic] the Police," *Fresno Herald*, September 28, 1910, p. 1; "Industrial Workers to Invade This City—Free Speech to Be Tried," *Industrial Worker*, October 8, 1910, p. 4.

2. "Determine to Harrass [sic]," 1, 3.

3. Paul E. Vandor, *History of Fresno County* (Los Angeles: Historic Recording Company, 1919), 833–34; "Robert Dean Chittenden," Fresno County Sheriff's Office, Former Sheriffs of Fresno County, online database, http://www.fresnosheriff.org/admin/history/former-sheriffs.html (accessed July 13, 2014).

4. "Robert Dean Chittenden."

5. "Woman Is Insulted on Street by a Member of the IWW," *Fresno Morning Republican*, October 22, 1910, p. 12.

6. Ibid.

7. "Spokane Journalist Speaks About the Industrial Worker," *Fresno Herald*, October 10, 1910.

8. "Thirty IWWs Now in Custody; 23 Enter Pleas in Court," *Fresno Morning Republican*, December 2, 1910.

9. "IWW Agitator in Wrong at Coalinga," *Fresno Morning Republican*, October 4, 1910, p. 7.

10. "IWW Man Suspected in Dynamiting Case," *Fresno Morning Republican*, October 25, 1910, p. 16.

11. "Vicious Capitalist Tool," *Solidarity*, October 22, 1910, p. 4.

12. "Determine to Harrass [sic]," 3.

13. Ibid.

14. "Thirteen IWW Men Are Thrown into Jail by the Police," *Fresno Morning Republican*, October 17, 1910, p. 2.

15. "Fight on in Fresno," *Solidarity*, October 29, 1910, p. 2.

16. "7 More IWW Men Are Thrown in Jail by Officers," *Fresno Morning Republican*, October 18, 1910, p. 12; "Thirteen IWW Men Are Thrown into Jail," 2.

17. "Fight on in Fresno," 2.

18. "7 More IWW Men Are Thrown in Jail," 12. *Solidarity* reported only men taken to jail with one underage youth released when his father retrieved him. See "Fight on in Fresno," 2.

19. "3 of IWW Members Join Fellow Workers in Jail," *Fresno Morning Republican*, October 19, 1910, p. 12.

20. "7 More IWW Men Are Thrown in Jail," 12.

21. "Thirty-Three Members of IWW Now in County Jail," *Fresno Morning Republican*, October 21, 1910, p. 9. E. F. (Red) Doree made his appearance in court on October 20, 1910, pleading not guilty.

22. William M. Adler, *The Man Who Never Died* (New York: Bloomsbury, 2012), 147. Adler states that many of the Wobblies who were arrested used aliases. He suggests that "Joe Dock" was Joe Hill, a former dockworker. IWW historian Fred Thompson doubted Hill's presence in the Fresno Free Speech Fight. See Fred Thompson to F. W. Sheetz dated February 14, 1975, Fred Thompson Collection, Subseries A, Box 9, File 18, Walter P. Reuther Library, WSU.

23. "Thirty-three Members of IWW Now in County Jail," 9.

24. Ibid.

25. H. Minderman was originally arrested with Frank Little on October 16, 1910. His diary was reprinted as "The Fresno Free-Speech Fight," in Foner, *Fellow Workers and Friends*, 105–22; "5 Industrial Workers

Arrested Last Night," *Fresno Morning Republican*, October 25, 1910, p. 16;
"Fresno County Jail Is Unsanitary Report Health Officers," *Fresno Morning Republican*, January 11, 1911. Emma Little reported the Fresno bull
pen to be 28 by 47 feet. Mrs. W. F. Little, "Court Crookedness." 118. In
January 1912, the state health department pronounced the bull pen to be
40 by 50 feet, inadequate for the numbers incarcerated within.

26. "Armed Guards on Duty to Prevent Escape," *Fresno Morning Republican*, October 28, 1910, p. 12.

27. Minderman in Foner, *Fellow Workers and Friends*, 107.

28. "Industrial Workers on Verge of Abandoning Battlefield," *Fresno Morning Republican*, October 29, 1910, p. 16; "Industrial' Speakers Allude
to Possible Dynamiting," *Fresno Morning Republican*, October 30, 1910,
p. 7. Fred Little's first appearance in court was on Monday, October 24,
1910. He pled not guilty and posted bail. See "5 Industrial Workers Arrested
Last Night," 16.

29. "Large Crowd Gathers; IWW Members Do Not Show Up," *Fresno Morning Republican*, October 23, 1910, p. 15; "5 Industrial Workers
Arrested Last Night," 16.

30. Bylaws, Article VI, Section 1, *Preamble and Constitution of the
Industrial Workers of the World* (Chicago: Industrial Workers of the
World, 1908).

31. "Woman Is Insulted on Street," 12.

32. "Industrial Workers on Verge," 16.

33. Ibid. Fresno County Sheriff Chittenden confiscated the diary of a
prisoner, using selected passages to discourage Wobblies who remained
eager to get into jail. "Industrial Speakers Allude to Possible Dynamiting," *Fresno Morning Republican*, October 30, 1910, p. 7.

34. "Industrial Workers on Verge," 16; Minderman in Foner, *Fellow
Workers and Friends*, 105.

35. "3 of IWW Members Join Fellow Workers," 12.

36. Minderman in Foner, *Fellow Workers and Friends*, 107. Twenty
of thirty men voted against the hunger strike.

37. W. [U.] L. Leister, "Free Speech News from the Front," *Industrial
Worker*, November 2, 1910, p. 1.

38. "Two Industrial Workers Left in the County Jail," *Fresno Herald*,
November 3, 1910. William Storey posted bail for Frank Little. Minderman in Foner, *Fellow Workers and Friends*, 107–108. Minderman states
that on October 27, 1910, the men sent Frank Little out on bond to "communicate with the outside." The rank and file may have viewed Frank's
release as a defeat.

39. "Industrial Workers Are Beaten in Fight for Speech on Streets,"
Fresno Morning Republican, November 3, 1910, p. 6.

40. "Free Speech Fight Is Now All History," *Fresno Morning Republican*, November 5, 1910.

41. "Fresno Fight Postponed," *Industrial Worker*, November 9, 1910, p. 3.

42. Ibid.

43. Ibid.

44. Ibid.

45. W. F. Little, "Fresno Free Speech Fight," 2; "Fresno Fight Won," *Solidarity*, March 11, 1911, p. 12.

46. E. Flawith, "Barbarous Fresno," *Solidarity*, December 31, 1910, p. 3.

47. *1911 Fresno City Directory*, 232.

48. "Riots Put End to IWW Troubles," *Los Angeles Herald*, December 11, 1910, p. 6.

49. "Two Industrial Workers Left in the County Jail."

50. "Thirty-three Members of IWW," 9; "Woman Is Insulted on Street," 12.

51. "Fresno Fight Continues," *Solidarity*, November 12, 1910, p. 4.

52. Leister, "Everybody Get Busy," *Industrial Worker*, November 17, 1910, p. 1.

53. "California Free Speech Fight," *Solidarity*, December 17, 1910, p. 2.

54. "Industrial Workers Will Break Loose Tonight," *Fresno Morning Republican*, November 28, 1910; "F. H. Little Acquitted; IWWs Speak on Streets Again," *Fresno Morning Republican*, December 9, 1910, p. 2. Shaw stated that he had issued permits to Little, Merrill, Murdock, and Filigno, the "big four" of the local organization.

55. "Industrial Workers Are Marching on This City," *Fresno Herald*, November 26, 1910, p. 2.

56. The *Boy with the Leaky Boot* drinking fountain was a gift from the Salvation Army in 1895. The fountain, located at the intersection of Mariposa and K [Van Ness] Streets, had six tin cups and several faucets available for the public to use for drinking water.

57. Minderman in Foner, *Fellow Workers and Friends*, 108.

58. See Fred Little's account of the second round of the Fresno Free Speech Fight in "Fresno Free Speech Fight," 2.

59. Minderman in Foner, *Fellow Workers and Friends*, 109.

60. "2 Industrial Workers Join 'Comrades' at Local Jail," *Fresno Morning Republican*, December 1, 1910; "Fresno Fighters Encouraged," *Solidarity*, February 8, 1911, p. 2. The late posting of this news indicates that the Wobblies were having difficulty getting out news from Fresno.

61. "2 Industrial Workers Join 'Comrades'"; "Industrial Workers at Their Same Old Game," *Fresno Herald*, November 30, 1910, p. 1.

62. "F. H. Little Acquitted," 2.

63. Ibid.

64. "Fifty-Five IWWs Confined in Jail," *Fresno Morning Republican*, December 5, 1910. See Minderman in Foner, *Fellow Workers and Friends*, 109.

65. "F. H. Little Acquitted," 2; "7 More IWW Men Are Thrown in Jail," 12. Police knew as early as mid-October that local merchants were discussing methods to rid the city of undesirables. They announced a mass meeting to organize a force to drive the Wobblies from Fresno.

66. Minderman in Foner, *Fellow Workers and Friends*, 110; "IWW Leader Found Guilty of Vagrancy," *Fresno Morning Republican*, December 10, 1910, p. 1.

67. "IWW Appeals to State for Protection from Fresno Mob," *Fresno Morning Republican*, December 11, 1910, p. 1.

68. Ted Lehman, "The Constitution Guarantees Freedom of Speech—Rats!: The Fresno Free Speech Fight" (unpublished manuscript, 1971), Fred Thompson Collection, Box 14, Folder 9, Walter P. Reuther Library, WSU. Ted Lehman interviewed Billy Mahoney, a contemporary and friend of Nig Normart's, and Nig Normart's son, William Normart. Normart stated that his father was "probably just drunk."

69. "Lower Court Daily Grind," *Fresno Morning Republican*, September 6, 1906, p. 4; "Firemen Doubt Smith Will Give Fair Trial," *Fresno Morning Republican*, October 6, 1906, p. 2. Normart later became assistant chief of the Fresno Fire Department.

70. "Mob Attacks IWW Speakers, Surrounds Jail," *Fresno Morning Republican*, December 10, 1910, p. 1.

71. Ibid.

72. "Mob Attacks IWW Speakers," 1.

73. Ibid.

74. Ibid.; "The Disgrace of Sunny Fresno," *Industrial Worker*, December 22, 1910, p. 1.

75. "IWW Appeals to State for Protection," 4; "Will Make No More Camps Here," *Fresno Herald*, December 10, 1910, p. 1. Frank Shuck admitted in his public statement that he went to the scene of the IWW camp but never left his car. Quinn and Normart claimed that they stood on the outer edge of the crowd, witnessing the rioting from a distance. "Capitalist Sluggers in Fresno," *Industrial Worker*, December 15, 1910, p. 1.

76. W. F. Little, "Fresno Free Speech Fight," 2.

77. "IWW Appeals to State for Protection," 1.

78. Ibid.; "Report That IWW Will File Suit in Court," *Fresno Herald*, December 10, 1910, p. 1.

79. "IWW Appeals to State for Protection," 1.

80. "Riots Put End to IWW Troubles," *Los Angeles Herald*, December 11, 1910, p. 6.

81. "IWW Appeals to State for Protection," 1.

82. "Riots Put End to IWW Troubles," 6.

CHAPTER FOURTEEN

1. Melvyn Dubofsky, *We Shall Be All: A History of the Industrial Workers of the World*, abridged edition, ed. Joseph A. McCartin (Chicago: University of Illinois Press, 2000), 98.

2. "Industrial Workers Will Break Loose Tonight," *Fresno Morning Republican*, November 28, 1910; "Industrial Workers Charged with Vagrancy," *Fresno Herald*, November 29, 1910, p. 8.

3. "IWW Appeals to State for Protection from Fresno Mob," *Fresno Morning Republican*, December 11, 1910, p. 4.

4. Ibid.

5. "Another IWW Found Guilty in Police Court," *Fresno Morning Republican*, December 14, 1910.

6. "Another IWW Gets 180 Days Behind Bars," *Fresno Morning Republican*, December 15, 1910.

7. Patrick Renshaw, *The Wobblies, The Story of Syndicalism in the United States* (Garden City, New York: Double Day, 1967), 160–61.

8. Chaplin, *Wobbly*, 196.

9. "Industrial Workers Appear on Streets under the Red Flag," *Fresno Morning Republican*, December 12, 1910, p. 12.

10. "Industrialists Refuse to Abide by Terms of Agreement," *Fresno Morning Republican*, December 20, 1910.

11. Minderman in Foner, *Fellow Workers and Friends*, 111; "IWWs Agree to Quit City If Let Out of Jail," *Fresno Morning Republican*, December 19, 1910, p. 1; "Industrials to Renew Fight," *Fresno Herald*, December 1910, p. 1.

12. "Ordinance Is Passed to Forbid Speeches in Streets," *Fresno Morning Republican*, December 20, 1910.

13. W. F. Little, "Fresno Free Speech Fight," 2; "Fresno Fight Won," *Solidarity*, March 11, 1911, p. 12.

14. See William M. Adler for analysis in *Man Who Never Died*, 148.

15. "Soap Box Orators Fail to Materialize at Street Corners," *Fresno Morning Republican*, December 21, 1910.

16. "Police Secure a Third Conviction against Industrialists," *Fresno Morning Republican*, December 21, 1910.

17. "IWWs Start Riot in Jail," *Fresno Morning Republican*, December 23, 1910, p. 1.

18. W. F. Little, "Fresno Free Speech Fight," 2; "IWWs Start Riot in Jail," 1.

19. "Hurled Back Bread at Jailers, *Fresno Herald*, December 23, 1910, pp. 1–2.

20. "Quell IWWs with Stream from Fire Engine," *Fresno Morning Republican*, December 24, 1910, p. 1; Minderman in Foner, *Fellow Workers and Friends*, 112.

21. O. N., "The 'Law' in Fresno," *Solidarity*, January 21, 1911, p. 4; W. F. Little, "Fresno Free Speech Fight," 2.

22. W. F. Little, "Fresno Free Speech Fight," 2; "Quell IWWs with Stream," 1.

23. W. F. Little, "Fresno on Trial," *Solidarity*, January 21, 1911, p. 1. The *Fresno Morning Republican* reported that the fire hose exerted fifty pounds of pressure, a figure contradicted by most accounts. "Quell IWWs with Stream," 1. Melvin Dubofsky confirms 150 pounds of pressure washed men, who were lying prone on the floor, upward into the air. Dubofsky, *We Shall Be All*, 107 and Minderman in Foner, *Fellow Workers and Friends*, 113. "Kind Treatment by the Master," *Industrial Worker*, December 29, 1910, p. 1.

24. W. F. Little, "Fresno Free Speech Fight," 2.

25. Jack Whyte, "Fresno Police Show Brutality," *Industrial Worker*, January 5, 1911, p. 1, and "Help the Fresno Fighters," *Solidarity*, January 13, 1911, p. 2. Paul Vandor claims that Mayor Rowell, Sheriff Chittenden, and Fire Chief Ward did not know who had given the orders for the employment of the fire engine hose and engine crews to flood the jail. IWW prisoners heard Chittenden make the order. Vandor, *History of Fresno County*, 504–505.

26. Minderman in Foner, *Fellow Workers and Friends*, 114.

27. "Raise Funds for Fresno Fighters," *Solidarity*, December 24, 1910, p. 1; "Help the Fresno Fight," *Solidarity*, December 31, 1910, p. 3.

28. O. N., "The 'Law' in Fresno," 4.

29. W. F. Little, "Fresno on Trial," 1.

30. "Walter S. McSwain," Fresno County Sheriff's Office, Former Sheriffs of Fresno County, online database, http://www.fresnosheriff.org/admin/history/former-sheriffs.html (accessed July 13, 2014).

31. Minderman in Foner, *Fellow Workers and Friends*, 116.

32. "Fresno County Jail Is Unsanitary Report Health Officers," *Fresno Morning Republican*, January 11, 1911.

33. Minderman in Foner, *Fellow Workers and Friends*, 117. See "Fresno County Jail Is Unsanitary."

34. W. F. Little, "Fresno Free Speech Fight," 2; "Fresno Fighters Encouraged," *Solidarity*, February 8, 1911, p. 2. The article, most likely written by Fred Little, reports that thirty Wobblies had been released on January 18, 2014. See Minderman in Foner, *Fellow Workers and Friends*, 115.

35. Mrs. W. F. Little, "Court Crookedness," 116–18. H. Minderman states the prisoners received two hours of free air on January 14, 1912. Minderman in Foner, *Fellow Workers and Friends*, 116.

NOTES TO PAGES 163–66

36. "Pastor Favors A Chain Gang for Industrial Workers Here," *Fresno Morning Republican*, December 12, 1910.

37. Minderman in Foner, *Fellow Workers and Friends*, 118.

38. "'The Rock Pile' Is Located as an Extension of County Jail," *Fresno Morning Republican*, January 14, 1911.

39. "Industrials Reported Coming to Fresno from North," *Fresno Morning Republican*, February 15, 1911, p. 12.

40. "Fresno Authorities Flim Flammed by IWW," *Solidarity*, February 25, 1911, p. 3.

41. Minderman in Foner, *Fellow Workers and Friends*, 118; "Exodus of IWWs from Fresno Due to Jealousy," *Fresno Morning Republican*, February 3, 1911; "Fresno Authorities Flim Flammed," 3. *Solidarity* also printed a disclaimer from the Fresno Committee that "no participant of this fight receives compensation for his work whether in or out of jail." IWW organizers were receiving three dollars a day. "From the Fresno Committee," *Solidarity*, February 25, 1911, p. 1.

42. "Sheriff Makes Claim for Board of IWWs," *Fresno Morning Republican*, February 4, 1911; "They Were Anxious to Return to Jail," *Fresno Morning Republican*, February 6, 1911; "An Even 100 Is in County Jail," *Fresno Morning Republican*, February 13, 1911.

43. "Lone IWW Tried to Interest a Crowd," *Fresno Morning Republican*, February 12, 1911.

44. "Convict Three IWWs on First Ballot," *Fresno Morning Republican*, February 15, 1911, p. 12.

45. Ibid.

46. "Police Break Up Street Meeting of IWWs, Eleven Arrested," *Fresno Morning Republican*, February 7, 1911.

47. "Arrest Six IWWs; Now Record Number in Jail Here," *Fresno Morning Republican*, February 8, 1911.

48. "The IWW Problem," *Fresno Morning Republican*, February 15, 1911; "Ministers Protest Against IWW Policy," *Fresno Morning Republican*, February 14, 1911, p. 15.

49. "Frank H. Little Is Arrested by Police," *Fresno Morning Republican*, February 16, 1911, p. 6.

50. "Convict Three IWWs on First Ballot," 12.

51. "Dr. Burks Reports on Jail Conditions," *Fresno Morning Republican*, February 18, 1911.

52. "IWW Bound for Mexico; Talk of Fresno a Blind," *Fresno Morning Republican*, February 18, 1911.

53. "Industrial Workers on California Soil," *Fresno Morning Republican*, February 19, 1911; "Invasion of California," *Solidarity*, March 4, 1911, p. 1. On February 16, 1911, 112 members of the IWW left Portland on freight trains bound for Fresno, California. Nearly a hundred Wobblies made the

hazardous trek south by foot through the snow-covered Siskiyou Mountains after being kicked out of the boxcars in Ashland. Except for a dozen miles from Mount Shasta to Dunsmuir when the group rode on a private train car, they walked roughly 150 miles south from Ashland.

54. "IWW 'Army' Now Much Reduced; Agitators in East Active," *Fresno Morning Republican*, February 21, 1911.

55. Ibid. See "To Join a Free Speech Army," *Kansas City Star*, February 26, 1911, p. 1.

56. "Supervisors Set Aside Place for Public Speaking," *Fresno Morning Republican*, February 19, 1911; "Citizens Vote to Sustain City Government in Dealing with IWW," *Fresno Morning Republican*, February 22, 1911.

57. "Citizens Vote to Sustain."

58. "IWW Straggle in Snow 3 Feet Deep," *Fresno Morning Republican*, February 23, 1911.

59. "IWW Frame Demands to be Presented to Committee, *Fresno Morning Republican*, February 23, 1911.

60. "Sustain Authorities," *Fresno Morning Republican*, February 23, 1911.

61. "Call Citizens Together to Hear Report on IWW Situation," *Fresno Morning Republican*, March 1, 1911.

62. "IWW Trouble Ends; Invasion of City to Stop," *Fresno Morning Republican*, March 2, 1911; Minderman in Foner, *Fellow Workers and Friends*, 121.

63. "Victoria Little," *Index to Births, H–Z (1882–1950)*, GSU Film Number: 1548579, California State Archives, Sacramento, California.

64. Minderman in Foner, *Fellow Workers and Friends*, 121.

65. "IWW Trouble Ends; Invasion of City to Stop." See "Industrialists Speak to Large Crowd in Oriental Quarter," *Fresno Morning Republican*, March 5, 1911. A total of 37 men were released on March 2, 28 men on March 3, 46 men on March 4, and 5 on March 5. Free speech was established one year to the month from the Spokane Free Speech Fight. For a summary of the free speech fight, see Press Committee, "Solidarity Wins in Fresno," *International Socialist Review* 11, no. 10 (April 1911): 634–36; "A Skirmish in a Great War," *Solidarity*, March 18, 1911, p. 3; "Fresno Fight Won," *Solidarity*, March 11, 1911, pp. 1, 4; "The Closing Sounds of the Fresno Fight," *Industrial Worker*, March 16, 1911, p. 1. The *San Francisco Call* reported that Frank threatened to renew the fight if he was not released. This is doubtful since an orderly release was in place and McSwain had announced that Frank would be the last to see freedom. See "IWW Men Are Allowed to Speak," *San Francisco Call*, March 6, 1911, p. 1. Frank spoke to a crowd, unmolested, the evening he was freed.

66. "On the Road to Fresno," *Industrial Worker*, April 6, 1911, p. 4.

67. "Interior of Jail Is Cleaned by Trusties [sic]," *Fresno Morning Republican*, March 7, 1911.

68. "Pastor Says Mob Worse Than the Industrial Workers Here," *Fresno Morning Republican*, December 12, 1910, p. 12. Reverend Thomas Boyd, pastor of the First Presbyterian Church, gave the sermon.

CHAPTER FIFTEEN

1. "Convention Report," *Solidarity*, October 7, 1911, p. 1. No songwriter has been attributed to the song "Hallelujah! I'm A Bum." Richard Brazier, Spokane local secretary 1911–12, reported that Captain Richard Speed first heard the song in Coxey's army when it marched to Washington, D.C., in 1894. Richard Brazier to Fred W. Thompson, December 21, 1966, Fred Thompson Collection, Subseries VI, Box 12, Folder 25, Walter P. Reuther Library, WSU. A genuine folk song, "Hallelujah! I'm A Bum!" has many versions although the original verses have never been supplanted. The song was first recorded by Harry "Mac" McClintock in 1928. Archie Green et al., eds., *The Big Red Songbook* (Chicago: Charles H. Kerr, 1907), 52–54. *Industrial Worker*, October 19, 1911, p. 3.

2. *Industrial Worker*, October 19, 1911, p. 3. Today the Reid-Murdock Center sits on the site of Schweizer-Turner Hall in Chicago.

3. Carl Sandburg, "Clark Street Bridge," *Chicago Poems* (New York: Henry Holt, 1916), 183. Carl Sandburg, son of Swedish immigrants, hoboed when he was nineteen years old, jumping westward-traveling trains, before volunteering for the military. Sandburg was a member of the Socialist Democratic Party (Socialist Party of America).

4. "Convention in Action," *Industrial Worker*, September 28, 1911, p. 4.

5. "Convention Report," 1. Dedicated on June 25, 1893, the Haymarket Martyrs' Monument by sculptor Albert Weinert consists of a monumental figure of a woman standing over the body of a fallen worker, both in bronze. The inscription reads "1887," the year of the executions, and August Spies's words, recorded just before his execution. On the back of the monument are listed the names of the men. On the top of the monument, a bronze plaque contains text of a pardon later issued by Illinois governor John Peter Altgeld, who criticized the trial. The Haymarket Affair, which occurred on May 4, 1886, is generally considered the origin of international May Day observances for workers. In 1997 the monument was designated a National Historic Landmark.

6. *Industrial Worker*, October 19, 1911, p. 3.

7. "Convention Report," 1.

8. Owners of the Triangle Shirtwaist Factory were found innocent in their negligence almost a year later.

9. Jack Whyte, "Activity in Fresno," *Solidarity,* April 29, 1911, p. 3.

10. Ibid.; Grace V. Silver, "Refused to Help IWW," reprinted from the *New York Call, Solidarity,* March 25, 1911, p. 4.

11. Whyte, "Activity in Fresno," 3.

12. Ibid.; "Local Union Directory," *Industrial Worker,* October 19, 1911, p. 3.

13. William Haywood was rejected by the Socialist Party of America in 1913 for his preference of direct action over the ballot box.

14. "The Crime of the Century," *Los Angeles Times,* October 16, 1910, p. 1.

15. James B. McNamara was illegally detained by Detective William J. Burns in Chicago until Burns could coerce another witness into testifying against McNamara. After Burns received extradition papers from California, he traveled to Indiana and arrested John J. McNamara. McNamara was denied a lawyer. On September 19, 1911, the convention approved sending telegrams to the McNamaras, expressing assurances of IWW moral, financial, and physical support. "Convention Report," 1. A motion carried that the IWW would go on record as inviting all members and supporters to go on a general strike on the day the McNamara trial was scheduled to begin. "Strike When McNamara Goes on Trial," *Industrial Worker,* October 5, 1911, p. 1.

16. "McNamara Makes Startling Confession," *Industrial Worker,* December 7, 1911, pp. 1, 4; "Death, Labor Says," *Kansas City Star,* December 3, 1911, p. 1. Amid much criticism, Clarence Darrow wrote a letter to newspapers explaining why he took the McNamara case and what led to the men's declaration of guilt. See Darrow, "Statement Given to Newspapers the Day of Plea of Guilty by McNamara Brothers in Los Angeles," Clarence Darrow Digital Collection, Law School, University of Minnesota, http://darrow.law.umn.edu/documents/Darrow_statement_to_newspaper _guilty_plea_OCR_cropped.pdf (accessed August 30, 2014).

17. *Industrial Relations: Final Report and Testimony Submitted to Congress by the Commission on Industrial Relations,* Document No. 415, vol. 1 (Washington, D.C.: Washington Government Printing Office, 1916). For Paterson silk worker accounts, see Jane Wallerstein, *Voices from the Paterson Silk Mills* (Charleston, SC: Arcadia Publishing, 2000). For an account of all events relating to the Illinois Central and Harriman Lines labor conflict, see Carl E. Person, *The Lizard's Tail* (Chicago: Lake Publishing, 1918). Person was editor of the *Illinois Strike Bulletin* at the time of the conflict. He was indicted and acquitted of murdering a chief strikebreaker in 1914.

18. Ethel Duffy Turner, *Revolution in Baja California: Ricardo Flores Magon's High Noon,* ed. Rey Davis (Detroit: Blaine Ethridge Books, 1981),

39. Ethel Turner was former editor for the English version of the Magonista periodical *El Regeneración*. Otis's son-in-law Harry Chandler was in constant contact with President Taft's administration and Francisco Madero. In a telegram dated May 29, 1911, Chandler asked Madero to wire Taft regarding moving U.S. troops to Lower California. Two days later the U.S. Senate authorized federal troops to occupy Lower California. F. I. de La Barra [Provisional President], Telegram to F. I. Madero, June 1, 1911, p. 40. In addition, the Mexican army was allowed to travel through the United States in order to arrive quickly in Baja. E. Rascon, Telegram to Francisco I. Madero, June 2, 1911, p. 41. Turner wrote and edited the last page of *Regeneración* in English for six months during the Mexican Revolution. In the first issue, Flores Magón's lead editorial asserted that he would foment armed revolution against Porfirio Díaz. See Chaz Bufe and Mitchell Cowen Verter, eds., *Dreams of Freedom* (AK Press: Oakland, CA, 2005), 73. See Turner's interview in *"Writers and Revolutionists: Oral History Transcript and Related material, 1966–1967"* (Berkeley, CA: University of California, 1967), 23.

19. "More Industrial Workers to Go Free," *San Francisco Chronicle*, March 4, 1911, p. 3. The *San Francisco Call* reported that half of the twenty-eight Wobblies released on March 4 had left for Los Angeles and Mexico where the abortive attempt at liberating Baja California was in progress. "To Arms, Ye Braves," *Industrial Worker*, June 8, 1911, p. 1. The letter was dated May 24, 1911. The article reports about half of the 250 *insurrectos* in Tijuana were Wobblies.

20. Adolfo Gilly, *The Mexican Revolution*, English translation (New York: The New Press, 2005), 87.

21. "37 Industrial Workers Freed," *San Francisco Call*, March 3, 1911, p. 3. Magón warned Mexicans that Francisco Madero did not represent the proletariat. When Magón split from Madero and called for direct action, the Socialist Party of America and American Federation of Labor withdrew their support. The IWW supplied most of the support to the Magonistas.

22. Thomas C. Langham, *Border Trials: Ricardo Flores Magón and the Mexican Liberals* (El Paso: Texas Western Press, 1981), 33. Langham states that disorganization, shortage of supplies, inadequate leadership, and uncertainty of purpose prevented the PLM from winning.

23. Hyman Weintraub, "The I.W.W. in California, 1905–1931" (unpublished M.A. thesis, University of California, Los Angeles, 1947), 32. Weintraub may have been the source of Frank Little's alleged participation in the Tijuana battle. Both Joe Hill and Fred Little were reported to have organized at other unusual locations. Harry "Mac" McClintock placed both Joe Hill and Fred Little in Hawaii during 1910. IWW historian Fred Thompson could make no definite conclusion and strongly denied McClintock's credibility. See Fred Thompson to F. W. Sheetz, February 14, 1975,

Fred Thompson Collection, Subseries A, Box 9, File 18, Walter P. Reuther Library, WSU. A call for Wobblies to come to Honolulu went out in the 1910 fall. "Rebels Wanted in Honolulu," *Solidarity*, October 8, 1910, p. 2.

24. After the first Battle of Tijuana on May 11, 1911, San Diegans, who had been watching the battle from the border, entered Mexico where a red flag flew above the customs house. Amid the celebration in days following, the Magonistas taxed proceeds from gambling houses and saloons as well as sold battle artifacts to raise money for the Liberales. Photographers seized the opportunity to create penny postcards for mementos of the battle.

25. Turner, *Revolution in Baja California*, 63. Joe Hill arrived in Tijuana on June 1, 1911, and Sam Murray, on June 8, 1911, both men participating in the second Tijuana battle on June 22, 1911. It would seem that had Frank Little been to the Mexican Baja during the Mexican Revolution in the summer of 1911, Sam Murray would have included this observation in his eyewitness testimony since Frank Little was equally famous to IWW martyr Joe Hill by 1955. In the interview, Murray recalled that at night Joe Hill would play his violin and sing his workers' songs, mocking the situation at hand, adding greatly to camp morale. Among the other rebels, Murray noted that Hill spoke little but drew amusing cartoons. Langham, *Border Trials*, 33. Langham writes that 106 Liberales retreated across the border where U.S. soldiers placed them under arrest.

26. "To Arms, Ye Brave," 1. The 1911 IWW Convention gave full endorsement to the rebels in Mexico. "Endorses the Rebels," *Industrial Worker*, October 5, 1911, p. 1.

27. "Kansas City Historical Timeline," Kansas City Police Department Historical Section, http://www.kcpolicememorial.com/history (accessed September 7, 2014).

28. Local No. 61, a mixed local, organized in March 1911, meeting at 211 East Missouri Avenue. A. B. Carson was its local leader with Don Hugh Scott taking the helm of the local by fall 1911.

29. T. Doyle, "Telegram," *Industrial Worker*, October 19, 1911, p. 1; "Free Speech Fight Is On," *Industrial Worker*, October 26, 1911, p. 4; G. H. Perry, "Free Speech Fight Is On in Kansas City," *Industrial Worker*, October 26, 1911, p. 1. A parking lot occupies the site of the beginning of the Kansas City Free Speech Fight, the corner of 6th Street and Main in Kansas City, Missouri.

30. "Saturday Night in Kansas City," *Industrial Worker*, November 2, 1911, p. 3.

31. On October 23, 1911, the *Kansas City Star* published a statement from current Spokane police chief W. J. Doust who detailed the city's experiences with the Spokane Free Speech Fight. Doust stated that if they had arrested the IWW leaders first, the city could have ended the conflict

sooner and cheaply. "Chief Griffin Gets the Details of the Washington City's Fight Against the Organization Now in Trouble Here," *Kansas City Star*, October 23, 1911, p. 2; "Kansas City Is After News," *Industrial Worker*, November 2, 1911, p. 4.

32. G. H. Perry, "Quit Bothering Us," *Solidarity*, October 28, 1911, p. 1.

33. Perry, "Free Speech Fight Is On," 1; "Saturday Night in Kansas City," 3.

34. "Saturday Night in Kansas City," 3. The six men, who originally had been arrested with Frank Little and then released, were all arrested again on Wednesday, October 18, 1911. One account states that Frank was fined twenty-five dollars or a fifty-day sentence. G. H. Perry, "Kansas City Tamed," *Solidarity*, November 11, 1911, p. 1.

35. *Kansas City Journal*, October 19, 1911, p. 1. Wentworth E. Griffin served as Kansas City police chief from July 9, 1910, to June 23, 1913. "Wentworth E. Griffin," in Carrie Westlake Whitney, *Kansas City, Missouri: Its History and Its People 1800–1908*, vol. 2 (Chicago: S. J. Clarke, 1908), 483–84.

36. Vincent St. John notified all locals to enlist volunteers for the free speech fight in Kansas City. "Telegram," *Solidarity*, October 28, 1911, p. 1; "Up to IWW Locals!" *Solidarity*, October 21, 1911, p. 1.

37. Kristina Stilwell, "After the Stench Cleared: Prison Life and Labor at Leeds Farm" (paper presented to the Missouri Conference on History, Columbia, Missouri, 1998), 10. Stilwell relies heavily on the papers of Robert S. Saunders. "The Road," Robert S. Saunders Collection, Western Historical Manuscripts Collection, University of Missouri–St. Louis, 108. Saunders, an IWW, was arrested in 1915 for direct action during a waiter-waitress strike. He was assigned one hundred days in Leeds Farm to work off his sentence.

38. Perry, "Free Speech Fight Is On," 1.

39. "Want No Walls at Leeds," *Kansas City Star*, November 1, 1911, p. 5. Leeds Municipal Farm compound was located on Ozark Road near Interstate 435 and Raytown Road in Jackson County, Missouri. In July 1910, a Kansas City bond issue was held for approval of $50,000 in order to construct a building for the House of Corrections at the Leeds Farm. On approval, construction began with the labor being supplied by the male prisoners. "Ready to Build Workhouse," *Kansas City Star*, June 3, 1911, p. 3.

40. "Plan Potter's Field at Leeds," *Kansas City Star*, May 13, 1911, p. 1.

41. "K.C. Afraid of Agitation," *Industrial Worker*, November 9, 1911, p. 4; "A Special Jail for IWW," *Kansas City Star*, October 25, 1911, p. 12.

42. Stilwell, "After the Stench Cleared," 11; "A Special Jail for IWW," 12.

43. Perry, "Kansas City Tamed," 1; Perry, "Quit Bothering Us," 1.

44. "A Special Jail for IWW," 12; Perry, "Quit Bothering Us," 1. Perry claimed that 250 men were housed at Leeds Municipal Farm.

45. "Want No Walls at Leeds," 5; "Fewer Escape From Leeds Now," *Kansas City Star*, November 3, 1911, p. 2.

46. *Industrial Worker*, November 2, 1911, p. 1.

47. "K.C. Fight in Closing Round," *Industrial Worker*, November 9, 1911, p. 4; "Kansas City Has Been Placed on the Map," *Industrial Worker*, November 9, 1911, p. 1.

48. "Not Jails Enough for Them," *Kansas City Star*, October 24, 1911, p. 4.

49. "IWW Still Court Jails," *Kansas City Star*, October 27, 1911, p. 1.

50. "Won't Arrest IWW Men," *Kansas City Star*, October 29, 1911, p. 1.

51. Ibid. IWWs Thomas Halcro, William Volker, and Walter C. Smith negotiated the deal with Police Chief Griffin and C. D. Mill, president of the Board of Public Welfare. Walker C. Smith, "City Ready to Quit," *Solidarity*, November 4, 1911, p. 1.

52. Ibid.

53. "Kansas City Has Been Placed on the Map," 1, 4.

54. "Paroles Today for IWW," *Kansas City Star*, November 1, 1911, p. 11.

55. Perry, "Kansas City Tamed," 1.

56. "Industrial Workers Are Free," *Kansas City Star*, November 2, 1911, p. 1; "Paroles Today for IWW," 1.

CHAPTER SIXTEEN

1. "Elihu H. Cox," *Logan County News*," October 9, 1914, p. 6. See Almira L. Cox, Petition for Temporary Alimony.

Elihu H. Cox claimed to have become disabled by a heat stroke during the Battle of Peach Tree Creek in Georgia, July 1864, while enlisted in Company C, Indiana Twelfth Infantry Regiment. Historical Data Systems, comp., *U.S. Civil War Soldier Records and Profiles, 1861–1865*, online database (Provo, UT: Ancestry.com, 2009). Elihu H. Cox, Application File #1073678, *U.S. Civil War Pension Index: General Index to Pension Files, 1861–1934*, online database (Provo, UT: Ancestry.com, 2000), original data: *General Index to Pension Files, 1861–1934*, Washington, D.C.: NARA, T288, 546 rolls.

2. "Out at Bethany," *Oklahoma Christian*, May 23, 1901, p. 1; "Who Is She?" *Oklahoma State Register*, May 18, 1905, p. 1; "Indiana Association," *Oklahoma State Register*, May 21, 1908, p. 4; "Elihu H. Cox," 1.

3. Cox, Petition for Temporary Alimony.

4. Warranty Deeds 277 and 307 for lots 15 and 16 respectively in St. Andrews Bay Development Company, Lynn Haven, Washington County,

Florida, March 15, 1911, Little Family Papers. Lynn Haven was established in January 1911 as a Union Veteran Colony in Florida.

5. "Plaintiff Union Central Life Insurance Company vs. Elihu H. Cox and Almira Cox, Defendants," *Oklahoma State Register*, May 8, 1913, p. 4. In November 1912, the court decided in favor of the plaintiff.

6. The Cox home was located at 1119 West Logan Street, Guthrie, Oklahoma. Frank Little asked that mail be sent in care of his mother, Allie L. Cox, Rural Route 3, Guthrie, Oklahoma. F. H. Little, "Conditions in Oklahoma," 2.

7. Ibid.

8. Ibid. During his recuperation in the Cox home, Frank initiated organizational meetings among farmers.

9. Nigel Sellars, "Wobblies in the Oilfields: The Suppression of the Industrial Workers of the World in Oklahoma," in Joyce, *"An Oklahoma I Had Never Seen Before,"* 132.

10. F. H. Little, "Conditions in Oklahoma," 2.

11. Covington Hall, *Labor Struggles in the Deep South* (unpublished manuscript), 218–19, Walter P. Reuther Library, WSU. Covington Hall was a labor journalist and organizer for the IWW. He organized dock workers and timber workers in Texas and Louisiana, and edited the Lumber Workers' Industrial Union's newspaper, *Voice of the People.*

12. Sellars, "Treasonous Tenant Farmers," 1110. Sellars's statistics come from William Spillman and E. A. Goldenweiser, "Farm Tenantry in the United States," in *Yearbook of the United States Department of Agriculture* (1917).

13. Sellars, *Oil, Wheat, and Wobblies*, 79–80; 1910 U.S. Federal; Census, Elm Grove, Payne County, OK, Roll T624_1269, p. 2A, Enumeration District 0190; Delce Courtland Copeland, *The Past to Remember*, undated, 58.

14. L. D. Gillespie, "Hunger in the Midst of Plenty," *International Socialist Review*, vol. 17, no. 5 (November 1916): 283; 1910 U.S. Federal Census, Pawnee, Payne County, OK, Roll T624_1269, p. 12B, Enumeration District 0196.

15. Sellars, *Oil, Wheat, and Wobblies*, 80; W. E. Reynolds, "Capturing Political Power in Oklahoma," *International Socialist Review* 17, no. 7 (January 1917): 416.

16. Sellars, *Oil, Wheat, and Wobblies*, 80; Reynolds, "Capturing Political Power in Oklahoma," 416.

17. Hall, *Labor Struggles*, 218–19.

18. F. H. Little, "Conditions in Oklahoma," 2.

19. "Murdering Free Speech Fighters in San Diego," *Solidarity*, March 30, 1912, p. 1. John Spreckels owned both the *San Diego Union* and *San Diego Evening Tribune*. San Diego's Ordinance 4623 was passed

on December 8, 1911. For a chronological listing of all events relating to the San Diego Free Speech Fight, see "Six Workers Found Guilty," *Industrial Worker*, August 8, 1912, pp. 1, 3.

20. San Francisco won the federally backed Panama-Pacific International Exhibition in 1915. San Diego continued to hold a smaller, successful exhibition but had to leave "International" out of the event's name, calling it the Panama-California Exhibition. Rosalie Shanks, "The IWW Free Speech Movement: San Diego, 1912," *San Diego Historical Society Quarterly* 19, no. 1 (Winter 1973).

21. "Councils Grants Permit for Protest Parade," *San Diego Union*, February 22, 1912, p. 3; "Claim 2000 Men Will Parade Tonight," *San Diego Evening Tribune*, February 26, 1912, p. 5; Kevin Starr, *Endangered Dreams: The Great Depression in California* (New York: Oxford Press, 1996), 34; "The Shame of San Diego," *Industrial Worker*, February 29, 1912, p. 4.

22. "Jail Life to Attract 'Martyrs,'" *San Diego Evening Tribune*, February 27, 1912, p. 1. *Industrial Worker* reported 2,500 participants. "Six Workers Found Guilty," 1.

23. Ernest J. Hopkins, "Meaning of San Diego Fight," *Solidarity*, April 12, 1912, p. 4, originally published in the *San Francisco Bulletin*, March 30, 1912; "Police Commit Murder in San Diego," *Industrial Worker*, April 4, 1912, p. 1; "Police Murder in San Diego," *Industrial Worker*, April 11, 1912, p. 1. San Diego authorities claimed that Michael Hoey died from advanced age and tuberculosis while the IWW claimed he was kicked in the stomach. "Autopsy Performed on Remains of Hoy [sic]," *San Diego Union*, April 4, 1912, p. 5.

24. "Raising Vagrants to the Great Dignity of Great Criminals," *San Diego Evening Tribune*, March 4, 1912, p. 4.

25. "Under Which Flag, San Diegan?" *San Diego Union*, May 24, 1912, p. 4.

26. Alfred R. Tucker, "San Diego Free-Speech Fight," in Foner, *Fellow Workers and Friends*, 138–41. Alfred R. Tucker and Charles Hanson submitted similar accounts of the infamous gauntlet to IWW secretary-treasurer Vincent St. John for the Commission on Industrial Relations' investigation, which Foner includes in his book. Charles Hanson and Chris Hansen, who traveled with Frank Little from Arizona to California in 1907, are reported to have been the same individual. Hanson (or Hansen) nearly died from his injuries, spending over eight months in a hospital. Charles Hanson, "My Experience during the San Diego Free-Speech Fight," in Foner, *Fellow Workers and Friends*, 135–38. Two other IWWs were reported to have been separated from the group and clubbed to death. Stumpy (Garrigan), "Two More Men Murdered in San Diego!" *Industrial Worker*, April 18, 1912, p. 4.

27. Jack Whyte, "Call from San Diego," *Solidarity*, February 24, 1912, p. 1. Whyte wrote the appeal on February 12, 1912, where he reported eighty-four men and women being held in jail.

28. "Murdering Free Speech Fighters in San Diego," *Solidarity*, March 30, 1912, p. 1.

29. *1912 Fresno City Directory*, 22. The directory lists Walter F. Little as a laborer working for J. T. (Traynham) Anderson, a plumber, whose workplace was situated at 1254 K Street. Fred's residence on Fairview Avenue no longer exists. The vicinity would be just east of what is today Edison High School.

30. "San Diego Vigilantes," *Solidarity*, May 18, 1912, p. 4.

31. Emma Goldman, *Living My Life* (New York: Alfred A. Knopf, 1931), http://theanarchistlibrary.org/library/emma-goldman-living-my-life#toc42 (accessed January 9, 2015). A detailed account of the San Diego vigilante attack on Ben Reitman may be found in Part One, Chapter 38. Caroline Nelson, "Emma Goldman and Ben Reitman Tell of San Diego Experience," *Industrial Worker*, June 6, 1912, p. 4; Citizens of San Diego the Night of May 14th, 1912, from a Sworn Statement, "What Was Done to Ben Reitman," *Industrial Worker*, June 6, 1912, p. 4.

32. "Why This Encouragement of San Diego's Peace Disturbers?" *San Diego Evening Tribune*, April 22, 1912, p. 4. Weinstock was a San Franciscan clothier, sociologist, and economist who, the editor of the *Tribune* claimed, was a crony of the governor's.

33. Stumpy (Garrigan), "San Diego Situation," *Solidarity*, April 13, 1912, p. 4. "Stumpy" authored the most thorough IWW accounts of the San Diego Free Speech Fight in *Industrial Worker*.

34. Jacob Fuchsenberger, "Status of the Fight," *Solidarity*, May 11, 1912, pp. 1, 4. Fuchsenberger became acting secretary of San Diego Local 13.

35. Ibid.

36. "Kidnappers in Auto Seize Editor on Street," *San Diego Union*, April 6, 1912, p. 1; "IWWs Purchase Tents; New Move Is Mystery to Officers," *San Diego Union*, April 11, 1912, p. 6; "Kidnappers to Not Be Prosecuted," *San Diego Evening Tribune*, April 11, 1912, p. 10. See Saur's testimony in "Twenty Testify Hearing Held by Weinstock," *San Diego Union*, April 19, 1912, p. 12. Stanley M. Gue, "Loyalty League Makes Appeal," *Industrial Worker*, April 25, 1912, p. 3.

37. Hopkins, 4. "Vigilante Murderers," *Solidarity*, April 20, 1912, p. 1; "San Diego on Trial," *Solidarity*, June 1, 1912, p. 1.

38. "Vigilante Murderers," 1.

39. "San Diego on Trial," pp. 1, 4.

40. Ibid., 4.

41. Ibid.

42. Ibid.

43. "Why This Encouragement of San Diego's Peace Disturbers?" 4.

44. "Colonel Weinstock's Accusation," *San Diego Union*, May 20, 1912, p. 4.

45. F. H. Little, "The Rank and File," *Solidarity*, August 10, 1912, p. 2.
46. "IWW Chiefs Fined and Sentenced to Jail," *San Diego Union*, August 6, 1912, p. 9. McKee, a member of the SPA, was at odds with IWW attorney Fred Moore throughout the trial. Coincidentally McKee had run against Judge Sloan for the San Diego judgeship just six months earlier.
47. F. H. Little, "The Rank and File," 2.
48. Ibid.; "The Shame of San Diego," *Solidarity*, May 25, 1912, p. 1. Joseph Mikolasek was shot several times by San Diego police after defending himself with an axe in a police raid. The IWW considered his killing an assassination. "Court Victory in San Diego," *Solidarity*, August 17, 1912, p. 4; "Eye Witness Tells of Police Murder," *Industrial Worker*, May 23, 1912, p. 3.
49. "Jack Whyte's Defiance," *Solidarity*, August 17, 1912, p. 4.
50. See Judge Sloane's opinion in "IWW Chiefs Fined and Sentenced to Jail," *San Diego Union*, 12.
51. Charles Grant, "Held 97 Days—No Evidence," *Industrial Worker*, August 29, 1912, pp. 1, 3.
52. Goldman, *Living My Life*.

CHAPTER SEVENTEEN

1. The Great Northern Railway built the Great Northern Allouez Ore Dock Facility in Superior, Wisconsin, the first dock completed in 1892. John Hill controlled the Great Northern Railway but leased his Great Northern Iron Ore Properties to U.S. Steel. Ralph W. Hidy et al., *The Great Northern Railway: A History* (Minneapolis: University of Minnesota Press, 2004). In 1893 the Duluth ore docks were constructed by the Merritt family's Duluth, Missabe & Northern Railway Company, adding to the family's Mesabi Range mining interests. In 1893 the Merritt family syndicate formed a partnership with John D. Rockefeller which lasted one year. After that, Rockefeller purchased their interests through U.S. Steel for $81 million. "Huett Clinton Merritt," *The Successful American* 5, no. 5 (May 1902): 276.
2. James P. Cannon, "On the Anniversary of His Death," *Labor Defender* (August 1926): 133. The event, as described by Cannon, most likely occurred on the morning of Tuesday, August 12, 1913. Born in Kansas, Cannon first joined the Socialist Party of America, then the IWW, and finally the Communist Party of the United States, an organization that few IWWs would join later. He supported Trotskyism and the Socialist Party, became a founding member of the Communist Labor Party, and later worked for the Socialist Workers' Party. Cannon, who never believed in ignoring political action, describes the IWW's general anti-Communism views in "The I.W.W.: On the Fiftieth Anniversary of the

Founding Convention," *Fourth International* (New York: Pioneer Publishers, 1955). He claims that the ultimate failure of the IWW can be linked to their exclusion of political party interests.

3. Dubofsky, *We Shall Be All*, 186.

4. Douglas Ollila Jr., "Ethnic Radicalism and the 1916 Mesabi Strike," *Range History*, Iron Range Research Center, Chisholm, MN 3, no. 4 (December 1978): 2, 4. Finns, derisively called "Mongolians" or "jackpine savages," became considered too radical to employ, socialists who held no allegiance to their employers. The newly imported immigrant labor force took their jobs instead.

5. Richard Hudelson and Carl Ross, *By the Ore Docks* (Minneapolis: University of Minnesota Press, 2006), 52. Hudelson and Ross provide a detailed description of Finnish communities and a review of how ethnicities impacted labor in the Upper Midwest. See also "Millions Made on the Mesaba," *International Socialist Review* 17, no. 4 (October 1916): 231. In 1892 Pittsburgh Irishman Henry W. Oliver, a close friend of Andrew Carnegie's, formed a company to operate the Mesabi Mountain Mine on the Mesabi Range in order to secure a supply of high-grade iron ore for his Pittsburgh mills. Andrew Carnegie, in exchange for half the stock in the Oliver Iron Mining Company, loaned Oliver money to be spent specifically in development work, ensuring future rewards for his investment. In 1896 the Oliver Iron Mining Company leased other mines on the Mesabi Range from John D. Rockefeller on a royalty basis. In exchange, Rockefeller received a guarantee that the ore be shipped over Rockefeller railroads, specifically the Duluth, Missabe & Northern Railroad, and steamships on the Great Lakes. The United States Steel Trust was born. American Barge Company eventually became the Bessemer Steamship Company. A Chippewa word for "giant," *Mesabi* has various spellings, including *Mesaba* and *Missabe*. Harrison George, "The Mesaba Iron Range," *International Socialist Review* 17, no. 6 (December 1916): 329–32.

6. George P. West, "The Mesaba Strike," *International Socialist Review* 17, no. 3 (September 1916): 158.

7. "Possible Dock Strike 'Cock and Bull' Story," *Duluth News-Tribune*, May 11, 1913, p. 7.

8. Chaplin, *Wobbly*, 195.

9. *Solidarity* entitled James P. Cannon's report from his jail cell regarding matters in Peoria as "folly" in May 1913. "Peoria's Folly," *Solidarity*, June 7, 1913, p. 1. Following recommendations from Frederick W. Taylor's 1911 book, *Principles of Scientific Management*, many factories implemented sped-up assembly-line operations that required less skill from easily replaceable labor. Factories could maximize production and profits using systems that required workers whose simple, repetitive actions in specially designed workstations collectively increased factory

output. In this case, Peoria's Avery Farm Implement Company was the target of an IWW strike.

10. "Various," Case #26759: 294. See *Industrial Worker,* July 17, 1913, for notes from the GEB meeting.

11. "Why the IWW Left Town," *Peoria Herald-Transcript,* June 17, 1913, as quoted in "Catching 'Em Going and Coming," *Solidarity,* June 28, 1913, p. 2.

12. "Free Speech in Duluth," *Solidarity,* July 15, 1911, p. 1. Frank Little participated in the special session getting organizers their credentials. "IWW Organizers," *Solidarity,* July 26, 1913, p. 3.

13. Hudelson and Ross, *By the Ore Docks,* 65. Leo Laukki was an instructor and director of the Finnish Work People's College in Smithville, a suburb of Duluth. The college became connected to the IWW because of Laukki.

14. "Minneapolis Police Assist Bosses," *Solidarity,* July 26, 1913, p. 1.

15. Ibid.

16. "Possible Dock Strike 'Cock and Bull' Story," 7.

17. "Demands to be Made Monday. If Great Northern Fails to Agree to Wage Raise the Ore Dock Employees Will Strike," *Duluth News-Tribune,* May 11, 1913, p. 13.

18. F. H. Little, "Rebels Wanted in Duluth," *Solidarity,* August 9, 1913, p. 1.

19. "No Fight in Duluth," *Solidarity,* July 22, 1911, p. 1. The SPA promoted AFL's craft unionism while aspiring toward a neutral stance regarding economic organization of the working class and at times standing directly against immigration of "backward races." Hudelson and Ross, *By the Ore Docks,* 63; Fred W. Thompson and Patrick Murfin, *The I.W.W.: Its First Seventy Years 1905–1975* (Chicago: Industrial Workers of the World, 1976), 77.

20. "2 Dead, 4 Are Fatally Hurt in Train Crash," *Duluth News-Tribune,* August 1, 1913, p. 1.

21. "Three Accidents at Two Harbors," *Duluth News-Tribune,* July 1, 1913, p. 3.

22. Hudelson and Ross, *By the Ore Docks,* 61; "Allouez Ore Workers Out on Strike as Result of Accident Thursday Night 500 Men," *Duluth News-Tribune,* August 2, 1913, p. 1.

23. "Dock Strike to Be Settled," *Duluth News-Tribune,* August 5, 1913, p. 4.

24. Ibid.; "600 Men at Missabe Dock Quit Work," *Duluth News-Tribune,* August 7, 1913, p. 1; "Supt. C. O. Jenks Issues Ultimatum," *Duluth News-Tribune,* August 6, 1913, p. 4.

25. "News and Views," *International Socialist Review* 14, no. 3 (September 1913): 184; *Duluth News-Tribune,* August 8, 1913.

26. "Ore Dock Strike Was Short Lived," *Duluth Labor World*, August 16, 1913, p. 3; James P. Cannon, "Special to *Solidarity*" August 9, 1913, in *Solidarity*, August 16, 1913, p. 1. In 1908 Oliver Mining Company controlled more than 75 percent of the ore resources on the Mesabi Range. This mining company would target Frank Little in 1916. Robert M. Eleff, "The 1916 Minnesota Miners' Strike against U.S. Steel," *Minnesota History* 51, no. 2 (Summer 1988): 63.

27. "News and Views," 184.

28. "Supt. C. O. Jenks Issues Ultimatum," 4. A cartoon on the front of the *Duluth News-Tribune*, August 8, 1913, shows a boot labeled "Public Opinion" stomping a bearded and mustached snake labeled "IWW Agitator."

29. "Majority of Ore Handlers Will Resume Work Today; Little Arrives in Duluth," *Duluth News-Tribune* August 11, 1913, p. 1; "The Steel Trust Thugs Kidnapped Little," *Industrial Worker*, August 21, 1913, p. 1.

30. "Majority of Ore Handlers," 1; "The Steel Trust Thugs Kidnapped Little," 1.

31. "Majority of Ore Handlers," 4. Railroad detectives were stated to be Frank Little's captors in most reports. "Released by His Friends," *New Ulm Review*, August 20, 1913, p. 2; 1910 U.S. Federal Census, Duluth Ward 2, St. Louis County, MN, Roll T624_725, Family History Film 1374738, p. 1B, Enumeration District 0160. Matt Ronald Mannheim's physical description is detailed in World War I Selective Service System Draft Registration Cards, 1917–18, Wayne County, Michigan, June 5, 1917, National Archives Microfilm Publication, Roll #2023692, NARA, Washington, D.C. The *Duluth-News Tribune* recounts several society events involving Getty and Mannheim (Manheim) families during 1912–13.

32. Cannon, "On the Anniversary of His Death," 133.

33. Ibid.

34. "The Steel Trust Thugs Kidnapped Little," 1.

35. Cannon, "Special to *Solidarity*," 1.

36. Ibid., 1; "Ore Dock Strike Was Short Lived, 1; "Superior Mayor May Call Out Troops," *Duluth News-Tribune*, August 8, 1913, p. 4.

37. "Work at Ore Docks Fast Assuming Normal Phase; IWW Men Go to Find Little," *Duluth News-Tribune*, August 10, 1913, pp. 1–2.

38. Toby [No last name] to Fred W. Thompson, July 16, 1982, Fred Thompson Collection, Series VI, Box 14, Folder 9, Walter P. Reuther Library, WSU. The author recalled meeting Mr. Sihto in Cleveland years ago when this story was recounted. Originally the author used the word "Buddy" instead of "Mister" but corrected the quote later for Fred Thompson.

39. "Majority of Ore Handlers," 1.

40. Document No. 21162, BLM Serial No. MN NO S/N, "Joseph Getty," State Volume Patent MN, vol. 321: 148, General Land Office Records,

U.S. Bureau of Land Management, U.S. Department of the Interior. Eighty acres were purchased in May 1905.

41. "Majority of Ore Handlers," 4.

42. "Work at Ore Docks Fast Assuming Normal Phase," 1.

43. "Majority of Ore Handlers," 4; "News and Views," 184.

44. "Majority of Ore Handlers," 4.

45. "The Steel Trust Thugs Kidnapped Little," 1.

46. "Majority of Ore Handlers," 4.

47. Ibid.

48. Ibid.; "News and Views," 184; "The Steel Trust Thugs Kidnapped Little, 1. One account states Frank walked out of the shack toward the rescuers.

49. W. I. Fisher, "On 'Worker' and GEB," *Voice of the People* 2, no. 33 (August 21, 1913): 4.

50. James P. Cannon, "Strike of Seamen & Dockmen in Fine Shape," *Solidarity*, August 16, 1913, p. 1.

51. "Majority of Ore Handlers," 4.

52. "The Steel Trust Thugs Kidnapped Little," 1.

53. "Released by His Friends," 2; "'Strike A Thing of the Past,' Says Pres. M'Gonagle," *Duluth News-Tribune*, August 12, 1913, p. 1. McGonagle withdrew the offer a day later.

54. "Strike A Thing of the Past," 2. C. O. Jenks announced that the Great Northern Railway would rehire strikers with the exception of the Finnish.

55. Ibid., 1.

56. "Ore Dock Strike Was Short Lived, 1.

57. F. H. Little, "Duluth Strike Still On," *Solidarity*, August 30, 1913, p. 4.

58. "Ore Dock Strike Was Short Lived," 3.

59. Ibid., 1.

60. *Miner's Magazine*, August 28, 1913, p. 3.

61. Thompson and Murfin, *I.W.W.: Its First Seventy Years*, 78.

62. "IWW Convention," *Solidarity*, September 27, 1913, p. 1. See *Industrial Worker*, August 14, 1913, for various articles relating to the controversy. Cannon, "On the Anniversary of His Death," 133; "A Critical Period," *Solidarity*, September 27, 1913, p. 2. For complete minutes of the IWW convention, see *Stenographic Report of the Eighth Annual Convention of the Industrial Workers of the World*, September 14–29, 1913 (Chicago: Industrial Workers of the World, 1913).

63. Cited from a letter dated September 7, 1913, to the Eighth Convention of the IWW from Industrial Union No. 66, Fresno, California. *Stenographic Report of the Eighth Annual Convention.*

64. "Convention Deals with Press," *Solidarity*, September 27, 1913, p. 2.

65. Cannon, *Notebook of an Agitator*, 61.

66. *Stenographic Report of the Eighth Annual Convention*. No delegate from Fresno attended nor is Emma Little's name included anywhere in the report. She was merely an observer.

67. Frank Little never married. His relationship with sister-in-law Emma Little was evidently close. Pursuits to assert that Frank was homosexual are illogical, as the evidence of Frank's life points only to a passionate relationship with the IWW, which took up most of his time. In addition, Frank's enemies, including the spies and informants who easily interspersed within the IWW, would have seized any opportunity to declare his sexual orientation as aberrant or unacceptable in the context of the time period. In investigating many of the Wobbly organizers and migratory workers during this time period, many men simply never married.

CHAPTER EIGHTEEN

1. Jack Allen Little, e-mail to author, August 7, 2011; Jack Allen Little, interview. Glen Porter Little, youngest son of Alonzo C. Little, was born April 8, 1907, in Payne County, Oklahoma, and died on December 28, 1975, in Yale, Payne County, Oklahoma. Lee Melvin Little, eldest son of Alonzo C. Little, was born February 12, 1893, on the Alonzo Little homestead in Payne County, Oklahoma, and died on January 10, 1976, in Roswell, Chaves County, New Mexico. Author Jane Little Botkin is the granddaughter of Lee and Louise Little.

2. Steven B. Oates, "Boom Oil! Oklahoma Strikes it Rich!" *The American West* 5, no. 1 (January 1968): 12.

3. Ibid.

4. D. Karl Newsom, *Drumright! The Glory Days of a Boom Town* (Perkins, OK: Evans Publications, 1985), 24.

5. 1910 U.S. Federal Census, Pawnee, Payne County, OK, Roll T624_1269, p. 12B, Enumeration District 0196.

6. Jack Allen Little, e-mail to author, August 7, 2011.

7. Jack Allen Little, interview.

8. "Drumright, Oklahoma," *Voice of the People*, June 30, 1914, p. 4.

9. Zora Mae Little met Harry H. Harper at her parents' boarding house, where she worked. She married Harper in Drumright on July 3, 1914, in Drumright. Frank likely attended this wedding. Harry founded Harper Drilling Company and Harper Oil Company. He is not related to Emma B. Harper. All marriages are recorded in the Alonzo Little Family Bible in the possession of Jack A. Little.

10. Eileen Huff, *Drumright's Unique History* (Stillwater, OK: New Forums Press, 1995), 14.

11. D. Karl Newsom, *Drumright II: A Thousand Memories* (Perkins, OK: Evans Publications, 1987), 113.

12. Jack Allen Little, interview.

13. "Drumright is Substantial City: Growth Outrivals Any in State," *Drumright Daily Derrick*, 1914, from *Items and Articles Taken from Newspapers and Clippings Found in a Scrap Book Kept by Mayor W. E. Nicodemus During the Years 1916–1922 and From Items and Pictures Saved for Many Years by Mrs. Lille Reynolds and Harold O. Ford*," W. E. Nicodemus Scrapbook, Archives, Drumright Historical Society Museum (DHS).

14. Ibid.

15. Oates, "Boom Oil," 11.

16. "Drumright, Oklahoma," 4.

17. Oates, "Boom Oil," 12.

18. "Drumright Not Wild and Wooley," *Drumright Derrick*, November 27, 1914, p. 1.

19. Newsom, *Drumright! The Glory Days of a Boom Town*, 47.

20. Jack Allen Little, interview.

21. "Oilfield Workers, If You Are Satisfied, Don't Read This," *Voice of the People*, July 7, 1914, p. 2.

22. Ibid.

23. Newsom, *Drumright! The Glory Days of a Boom Town*, 45.

24. "Oklahoma Field News," *Voice of the People*, June 4, 1914, p. 4.

25. Foner, *Fellow Workers and Friends*, 178.

26. F. Little et al., "Free Speech and Police Brutality in Kansas City," *Voice of the People*, January 8, 1914, p. 3. Frank Little led a contingent of men to Kansas City in early January 1914, and the number in Leeds soon grew to eighty-five. For detailed accounts of the second Leeds Farm incarcerations, see F. W. C. Deal to Vincent St. John, September 26, 1914, in "Kansas City Free-Speech Fight," in Foner, *Fellow Workers and Friends*, 180–81. See also William Ford, "Free-Speech Fight in Kansas City," in Foner, *Fellow Workers and Friends*, 181–82.

27. Sellars, *Oil, Wheat, and Wobblies*, 67.

28. Ibid.; "To the Oil Workers of Louisiana, Texas, Oklahoma," *Voice of the People*, February 26, 1914, p. 1.

29. Erica S. Maniez, e-mails to author, August 29 and September 3, 2012. Maniez, director of the Issaquah History Museum in Issaquah, Washington (2012), reports an example of an IWW who possibly tried to emulate Frank's reputation. IWW Benjamin Legg was arrested after the 1919 Everett Massacre in Washington State. Legg was described as being part American Indian although both his parents were born in England. Other examples of Frank's impact on younger men, especially, may be found in poetry, songs, and personal stories.

30. Flynn, *Rebel Girl*, 188–89.

31. Sellars, *Oil, Wheat, and Wobblies*, 68.

32. "Oklahoma Field News," *Voice of the People*, June 4, 1914, p. 4.

33. "Oil Workers, Attention," *Voice of the People*, July 21, 1914, p. 3.
34. Sellars, *Oil, Wheat, and Wobblies*, 69.
35. Ibid.
36. "Rockefellers' Thugs Busy in Dixie," *Voice of the People*, September 3, 1914, p. 4.
37. Newsom, *Drumright II: A Thousand Memories*, 211, 222.
38. Ibid., 210–11, 222.
39. Ibid.
40. "Rockefellers' Thugs Busy in Dixie," *Voice of the People*, September 3, 1914, p. 4.
41. Ibid., 211.
42. Oates, "Boom Oil," 12.
43. Sellars, "Wobblies in the Oilfields," in Joyce, *"An Oklahoma I Had Never Seen Before,"* 130.
44. Newsom, *Drumright II: A Thousand Memories*, 219.
45. "Tremendous Gas Well Burning at Cushing Well Making 25,000,000 Ft. of Gas is Burning Fiercely Other Storm Damages," *Tulsa Star*, 6.
46. Blay, Sheila, "The Early Boom Days of Drumright," *News Journal*, October 7, 1987.
47. Newsom, *Drumright! The Glory Days of a Boom Town*, 47–48.
48. Jack Allen Little, e-mails to author, May 21, 2010 and May 24, 2010. The family story about how Frank killed a man with a knife was told to Jack A. Little (and Frank Little's other nieces and nephews) by his father Glen with little variation. Lon was so frightened for his family and Frank that he ordered everyone to never discuss Frank with others. He feared that federal or local authorities would retaliate against the family for their relationship with Frank and the IWW, and justifiably so. While no arrest warrant was issued for Frank, Lon was arrested and his house searched after Frank's death in the fall of 1917. Not until the early 1990s, when a union member came to interview Thaylia Little Farris in Yale, Oklahoma, about Frank, did the family as a whole begin discussing Frank again.
49. Oates, "Boom Oil," 12.
50. Newsom, *Drumright II: A Thousand Memories*, 213.
51. Ibid., 214.

CHAPTER NINETEEN

1. Otto Christensen, "Invading Miners' Homes," *International Socialist Review* 17, no. 3 (September 1916): 160. Christensen, a Chicago defense attorney, later assisted in the 1918 IWW trial of William D. Haywood and others. "Labor Troubles," *The Public* 19, no. 963 (September 15, 1916): 878; "Inquiry Begins Before Smallwood," *Duluth News Tribune*, July 22,

1916, p. 6. The deputy sheriffs changed their account of why they were delivering arrest warrants to the Masonovich house. According to trial testimony, the deputies were serving a warrant for stopping a bus and restraining miners from working. West, "Mesaba Strike," 158. West reported to the Commission on Industrial Relations that a warrant had been issued for the illegal sale of liquor with the intent of arresting strike leaders and removing them to jail. Various sources spell Malitza Masonovich's name differently: Malitza, Makitza, Malika, Malica, etc. In census and draft registration records, recorders used Melissa.

2. West, "Mesaba Strike," 159.

3. Eleff, "1916 Minnesota Miners' Strike," 70. See West, "Mesaba Strike," 158. West's investigation revealed that Sheriff John R. Meining admitted deputizing those who "might possibly" be thugs. West also reported that the governor expected the sheriff "to approach a group of men anywhere and proceed to go through their pockets without formality-simply strong-arm them; . . . to enter without warrant the homes of the miners and search for firearms, and if there was resistance to arrest the miners and slap them into jail, or beat them into insensibility with a bill."

4. Christensen, "Invading Miners' Homes," 162; Hudelson and Ross, *By the Ore Docks*, 70.

5. Christensen, "Invading Miners' Homes," 162.

6. "Minnesota Like Colorado, Says Industrial Investigator," *Solidarity*, August 12, 1916, 1; "Steel Trust Gun Law Only Strengthens Strikers' Determination," *Solidarity*, July 22, 1916, p. 1. The *Duluth Labor World* states that officials knew that the Biwabik shootings occurred because of Nick Dillon's aggressiveness.

7. Christensen, "Invading Miners' Homes," 162.

8. Ibid.; "Suppression Order of Day in Iron Range Strike," *Solidarity*, July 15, 1916, p. 4.

9. John A. Keyes, "Facts in Range Case," *Solidarity*, September 23, 1916, p. 4. Keyes, a Duluth attorney, helped defend the IWWs and Montenegrins in the preliminary hearing.

10. "Suppression in Miners' Strike," *Solidarity*, July 15, 1916, p. 4; Flynn, *Rebel Girl*, 207. Flynn states that Ladvalla was sitting on his "pop" wagon when shot with direct fire from Nick Dillon's gun. Other sources report that Ladvalla was at the Masonovich door. "Death Claims Two in Biwabik Riot," *Duluth News Tribune*, July 4, 1916, p. 1 and 6. The paper states that the "pop man" Ladvalla was one hundred feet from the house and shot by a stray bullet, instead of near the Masonovich door and Nick Dillon.

11. Christensen, "Invading Miners' Homes," 162; "Death Claims Two in Biwabik Riot," 1; "Deputy Sheriff J. C. Myron of Duluth and T. Ladvalla Hit by Strikers' Bullets," *Duluth News Tribune*, July 4, 1916, p. 1.

The paper reported that Deputy Schubisky dropped to the ground and pretended to be dead, later remarking, "I could not attack a woman." He changed his story at the preliminary investigation. "Tresca and Others Held after Infamous Hearing," *Solidarity*, August 5, 1916, p. 1.

12. Christensen, "Invading Miners' Homes," 162; "Inquiry Begins before Smallwood," 6. The story presents a different account in which Deputy Sheriff Schubisky claimed to have become overpowered by the boarders who appeared from the rear of the house, instead of knocked to the ground by Militza Masonovich.

13. "Deputy Sheriff J. C. Myron of Duluth and T. Ladvalla Hit," 1. Other news reports across Minnesota inaccurately stated that IWW agitators were on the scene and caused a riot. "Strikers Accused of Murder in Jail under Heavy Guard," *Bemidji Daily Pioneer*, July 5, 1916, p. 1.

14. "Tresca and Others Held after Infamous Hearing," *Solidarity*, August 5, 1916, p. 1. Frank Little began organizing almost 200 miles away according to various reports. Historian Melvin Dubofsky excludes Frank Little as having been arrested with other organizers on July 4, 1916, or as one of the men whose cases were dismissed on August 5, 1916. See Dubofsky, *We Shall Be All*, 189. However, Frank wired both his arrest and release to *Solidarity*. "Letter from Little," *Solidarity*, July 22, 1916, p. 1; "Tresca and Others Held," 1.

15. Nunzio Pemicone, *Carlo Tresca: Portrait of a Rebel* (Oakland: AK Press, 2010), 179. Carlo Tresca, an Italian American, vociferously opposed fascism and communism but his own anarchist activities caused bitterness. Working as an IWW agitator, he helped mobilize Italian workers. He primarily helped organize on the East Coast where he maintained a close relationship with Elizabeth Gurley Flynn. In 1943 the mafia purportedly assassinated Tresca in New York City, supposedly because of Tresca's antifascism statements.

16. Leslie H. Marcy, "The Iron Heel on the Mesaba Range," *International Socialist Review* 17, no. 2 (August 1916): 76.

17. "Letter from Little," 1; "Police Surround Jail to Keep Out IWWs," *Duluth News Tribune*, July 5, 1916, p. 1. While Frank Little slept unconcerned in jail, a police cordon dramatically surrounded the facility until dawn on July 5, 1916, to prevent a daring rescue. Arthur Lesueur, "Legal Side Lights on Murder," *International Socialist Review* 17, no. 5 (November 1916): 299. Non-Partisan League attorney Lesueur helped defend IWW organizers Carlo Tresca, Sam Scarlett, and Joseph Schmidt in the Mesabi Range trial.

18. West, "Mesaba Strike," 160. The Commission of Industrial Relations met in Washington, D.C., in November 1916, to discuss findings. The report was released in print April 1916.

19. "Situation Reviewed," *Solidarity*, July 29, 1916, p. 1. See Eleff, "1916 Minnesota Miners' Strike," 65, for extensive discussion on bribery.

20. Michael G. Karni, "Elizabeth Gurley Flynn and the Mesabi Strike of 1916," *Range History*, Iron Range Research Center, Chisholm, MN, 5, no. 4 (Winter 1981): 3.

21. Ollila, "Ethnic Radicalism," 3.

22. Karni, "Elizabeth Gurley Flynn," 1.

23. Eleff, "1916 Minnesota Miners' Strike," 67.

24. William D. Haywood, "Declaration of War," *International Socialist Review* 17, no. 2 (August 1916): 132. The Biwabik Branch of Metal Mine Workers' Industrial Union (MMWIU) No. 490 and Virginia Branch of the MMWIU No. 490 chartered on June 12, 1916. The following branches of the MMWIU No. 490 chartered on June 19, 1916: Eveleth, Gilbert, Chisholm, Kinney, Hibbing, Crosby, Aurora, and Buhl. See *Proceedings of the Tenth Convention of the Industrial Workers of the World, Held at Chicago, Illinois, November 20 to December 1, 1916* (Chicago: Industrial Workers of the World, 1917), 36.

25. "Suppression Order of Day," 1.

26. Eleff, "1916 Minnesota Miners' Strike," 69.

27. "Suppression Order of Day," 1; West, "Mesaba Strike," 160.

28. "Letter from Little," 1.

29. "Stark Tells of Mesaba Strike," *Solidarity*, August 26, 1916, p. 1. The author may mean "shakes" or tremors associated with extreme alcoholism.

30. See "The Ninth IWW Convention, *Solidarity*, September 21, 1914, p. 4, for discussion.

31. "Various," Case #26759: 295.

32. "Various," Case #8000-17030: 35. Volunteer Operative Maurice Curran reported that Frank Little had lived with Vincent and Clara St. John in 1915. Vincent St. John biographer MaryJoy Martin suggests that the St. Johns offered their home to various IWW organizers who had brief business in Chicago, including Frank Little. Frank Little never actually resided with Vincent St. John as Operative Curran insinuates.

33. *Proceedings of the Tenth Convention*, 154. The Tenth Convention also included minutes from GEB meetings back to 1914. "Various," Case #26759: 295. Frank Little was Chairman of the IWW General Executive Board from 1914–17.

34. Chaplin, *Wobbly*, 195.

35. "The Ninth I.W.W. Convention," *Solidarity*, September 26, 1914, p. 4.

36. Flynn, *Rebel Girl*, 199–200; William D. Haywood, Testimony before U.S. District Court of Illinois, August 12, 1918, transcript available from U.S. vs. Haywood et al., 1917–18, Legal Problems, Trials, and Defense, File 3: 11359–11376, Box 117, Subseries B, Walter P. Reuther Library, WSU. In his testimony, Bill Haywood never took responsibility for an IWW statement against World War I.

37. "The Ninth I.W.W. Convention," September 26, 1914, p. 1.

38. Ibid.

39. Fred and Emma Little were now living at 1809 California Street in Fresno, California.

40. "To Investigate Municipal Work," *Fresno Morning Republican*, October 6, 1914, p. 16.

41. "Ask Raisin Company to Patronize Unions," *Fresno Morning Republican*, October 24, 1914, p. 10; "Union Label League to Go After Members," *Fresno Morning Republican*, October 20, 1914, p. 8; "Mother Jones of West Coast to Hold Meetings Here," *Fresno Morning Republican*, October 26, 1914, p. 12. Sarah Crossfield first established the Women's Union Label League in 1899. The Fresno WULL was formed in early 1912 by the Fresno Labor Council.

42. "Union Label League to Go After Members," 8.

43. "Information on Free Speech Fights Wanted," *Solidarity*, September 19, 1914, p. 3. Paul U. Kellogg, "The Field before the Committee on Industrial Relations," *Political Science Quarterly* 28 (1913): 593–609. The detailed article describes reasons for addressing the relationship between labor and employers since the Civil War. The emergence of the IWW profoundly raised awareness of conditions specifically pertaining to unskilled workers.

44. Emma B. Little to President Woodrow Wilson, February 7, 1918, p. 3.

45. *Industrial Relations: Final Report and Testimony Submitted to Congress by the Commission on Industrial Relations*, Document No. 415, vol. 1 (Washington D.C.: Washington Government Printing Office, 1916), 144. Frank P. Walsh chaired the U.S. Committee on Industrial Relations.

46. Ibid.

47. Ibid.

48. Theodore Roosevelt, "Hyphenated American Speech," Address to the Knights of Columbus, New York City, New York, October 12, 1915. The Knights of Columbus is a Catholic organization.

49. Woodrow Wilson, *Final Address in Support of the League of Nations*, Pueblo, Colorado, September 24, 1919. Instead of speaking directly to Congress, Wilson conducted a series of public "barnstorming" speeches across the West. Exactly one week after the Pueblo speech, Wilson suffered a stroke that incapacitated him.

50. As quoted in Eleff, "1916 Minnesota Miners' Strike," 72.

51. *Solidarity*, July 24, 1915, p. 4.

52. Copeland, *Past to Remember*, 58. In January 1919, Charles H. Courtright purchased an eighty-acre farm in Payne County, Oklahoma. "James B. and Emma Basar to Charles H. Courtright," Warranty Deed, 46: 610, January 30, 1919, County Clerk, Payne County, Stillwater, Oklahoma.

53. Nils H. Hanson, "Among the Harvesters," *International Socialist Review* 16, no. 2 (August 1915): 76.

54. Ibid.

55. See "Oklahoma Field News," *Voice of the People*, June 4, 1914, p. 4, for earlier tactics of flooding labor into locales in order to drive down wages. The press assisted in calling men to come to areas where fewer jobs would be available. See "Prosperity in Kansas," *Voice of the People*, June 30, 1914, p. 3, for another example of flooding workers in Wichita, Kansas.

56. Fred Thompson to Joel W. Watne, June 12, 1967, Fred Thompson Collection, File 18, Box 9, Subseries A, Walter P. Reuther Library, WSU. *Proceedings of the Tenth Convention*, 36. Elizabeth Gurley Flynn cites the 1915 membership figure in her autobiography in *Rebel Girl*, 201.

57. Ed Rowan, "Dock Wages Go Up," *Solidarity*, July 29, 1916, p. 1; "Rally Against the Monster Steel Trust," *Solidarity*, July 8, 1916, p. 1; "Rally to the Strikers!" *Solidarity*, July 1, 1916, p. 1. See Eleff, "1916 Minnesota Miners' Strike," 64. Eleff cites the Minnesota Department of Labor and Industries' estimated contract rates during 1915–16 averaged between $2.80 and $3.25 a day.

58. "Trouble is on at Webb City, MO," *International Socialist Review* 17, no. 1 (July 1916): 57. See "Golden West a Myth," *Solidarity*, June 3, 1916, p. 1, for Elizabeth Gurley Flynn's description of living conditions in Webb City and Carterville, Missouri. Metal, Mine, and Smelter Workers' Industrial Union No. 603 was chartered February 15, 1916.

59. "Deputy Sheriff J. C. Myron of Duluth and T. Ladvalla Hit," 1; Fred Thompson to Joel W. Watne.

60. "Ashurst Denounces IWW: Says Initials Really Mean Imperial Wilhelm's Warriors," *Evening Star*, August 17, 1917, p. 2.

Chapter Twenty

1. "Hillstrom Guilty Murder in the First Degree, No Recommendation for Mercy Contained in the Verdict, *Salt Lake Telegram*, June 7, 1914, p. 1. The crime occurred January 10, 1914.

2. "Officers Winding Evidence about Hillstrom, Wounded Suspect in Murder Case," *Salt Lake Telegram*, January 14, 1914, p. 1; Adler, *Man Who Never Died*, 216–17.

3. Adler, *Man Who Never Died*, 57. Adler examines why Magnus Olson was never arrested for Morrison's murder despite evidence. See pp. 56–69.

4. Woody Guthrie, *American Folksong* (New York: Oak Publications, 1961), 22–23 (reprint of 1947 edition by Disc Company of America). Guthrie was a native Oklahoman.

5. Adler, *Man Who Never Died*, 285.

6. Hilda Erickson letters to Aubrey Haan, June 22, 1949, and June 30, 1949, personal papers of William M. Adler, in Adler, *Man Who Never Died*, 73.

7. "Joe Hill Convicted," *Solidarity*, July 11, 1914, p. 1; Richard Brazier to Fred W. Thompson, December 21, 1966, and H. M. E. to Fred W. Thompson, December 26, 1966, Fred Thompson Collection, Subseries VI, Box 12, Folder 25, Walter P. Reuther Library, WSU. This file contains correspondence between Fred Thompson and old-time IWW contemporaries of Joe Hill. They dispel insinuations that Hill could have committed murder.

8. "Hillstrom Will be Shot, 'I Am Used to That,' He Said when Asked to Express Choice," *Evening Telegram* (Salt Lake City), July 8, 1914, p. 1.

9. *Solidarity*, September 25, 1915, p. 2; "Threatening Letters Demand New Trial for Hillstrom Governor Spry is Threatened by 500 Working Men," *Evening Telegram* (Salt Lake City), August 1, 1914, p. 18.

10. E. B. Little, "Editorial," *Solidarity*, September 25, 1915, p. 2.

11. The state of Utah later disbarred Judge Hilton after Hilton gave a eulogy at Joe Hill's funeral on Thanksgiving Day, 1915. Ralph Chaplin, "Joe Hill's Funeral," *International Socialist Review* 16, no. 7 (January 1915): 401.

12. Chaplin, *Wobbly*, 189.

13. "Hillstrom Battles with Executors," *Salt Lake Telegram*, November 19, 1915, p. 11. This local editorial does not paint a heroic picture of Joe Hill. Other sources state that Joe Hill declined a blindfold, facing his execution with bravery. Ralph Chaplin claimed that a red cardboard heart was pinned to Hill's chest instead of a bullseye. Chaplin, *Wobbly*, 189; Adler, *Man Who Never Died*, 332.

14. "Hillstrom Battles with Executors," 11; "In Memoriam of Joe Hill," *International Socialist Review* 17, no. 6 (December 1916): 326.

15. An envelope of Joe Hill's ashes was seized by the Department of Justice and placed into evidence in the 1918 IWW trial in Chicago. It is not known if this is the same envelope that was seized in Frank H. Little's Steele Block boarding house room after his death.

16. *Proceedings of the Tenth Convention of the Industrial Workers of the World, November 20 to December 1, 1916* (Chicago: Industrial Workers of the World, 1917), 142. Because of Frank's decision to go to Roseville, he was overdrawn on his expenses by one day.

17. F. H. Little, "Life and Prospects of the Blanket Stiff," *Solidarity*, February 12, 1916, p. 5.

18. "California Miners Strike," *Solidarity*, May 13, 1916, p. 4. A strike was called May 1, 1916, in the Porterville and Lindsay districts. The strikers called for $3.50 a day, an eight-hour day, good wholesome food and sleeping accommodations to be provided by the employer, at a per

diem rate not to exceed seventy-five cents. Ironically the lowest paid workers, the Mexicans, "came out to a man" while others refused to participate in the strike.

19. "House Maids Form Union in Denver," *Solidarity*, April 1, 1916, pp. 1, 4; "Denver House Maids Join IWW," *Solidarity*, April 22, 1916, p. 1; Sellars, *Oil, Wheat, and Wobblies*, 20. Domestic Workers' Industrial Union No. 113, was chartered March 27, 1916, under Frank Little's direction.

20. *Proceedings of the Tenth Convention*, 134.

21. "Labor Defense League Holds Protest Meet Tomorrow," *Day Book* (Chicago), April 1, 1916, p. 31.

22. "Various," Case #26759: 295; *Proceedings of the Tenth Convention*, 143.

23. F. H. Little, "Calif. Miners Take Note," *Solidarity*, March 4, 1916, p. 3. Metal, Mine, and Smelter Workers' Industrial Union No. 313, Branch 1, was chartered on March 14, 1916, under Frank Little's direction. *Proceedings of the Tenth Convention* 143, 146. At the April 1916 GEB meeting, the committee responded to a letter from some of the "Western Locals" complaining about Frank Little's activities. The letter was not recorded in the minutes to reveal the source of their protests. Subsequent letters from Porterville refuted the previous insinuations and apparent declarations of Frank's incompetence.

24. "Defends Seven Steel Strike Leaders," *Evening News* (Sault Ste. Marie, MI), August 11, 1916, p. 5.

25. "IWW Inquiry Begins," *Duluth News Tribune*, July 22, 1916, p. 6; Christensen, "Invading Miners' Homes," 162.

26. "Tresca and Others Held After Infamous Hearing," *Solidarity*, August 5, 1916, p. 1; West, "Mesaba Strike," 160.

27. "IWW Inquiry Begins," 1; "Suppression Order of Day," 1.

28. "IWW Inquiry Begins," 6.

29. Ibid.; Louis Freeland Post, Alice Thatcher Post, and Stoughton Cooley, "Labor Troubles," *The Public* 19, no. 963 (September 15, 1916): 878; "Tresca and Others Held," 1.

30. "Tresca and Others Held," 1.

31. "Smallwood Holds Ten IWW for Grand Jury Charge of Murder," *Duluth News Tribune*, July 28, 1916, p. 1.

32. "IWW Inquiry Begins," 6; Post, "Labor Troubles," 878; "Tresca and Others Held," 1. See Bill Haywood's letter to Tresca. "Haywood is Directing IWW Leaders; Notorious Agitator Sends Tresca," *Duluth News Tribune*, July 3, 1916, p. 1.

33. "Iron Ore Strikers in Deadly Grapple with Steel Trust," *Solidarity*, July 1, 1916, p. 1. See Marcy, "Iron Heel," 74–78, for an account of the murder. Eleff, "1916 Minnesota Miners' Strike," 68. The name "Aller" may have originally been *Alar* although censuses record "Aller."

34. Marcy, "Iron Heel," 74, 76.

35. Ibid., 76.

36. Ollila, "Ethnic Radicalism," 3; "Says IWW Urged Killing of Brother," *Duluth News Tribune,* July 27, 1916, p. 1.

37. "Says IWW Urged Killing of Brother," 1, 5.

38. West, "Mesaba Strike," 160.

39. F. H. Little, "Special Telegram," *Solidarity,* August 5, 1916, p. 4.

40. "Various," Case #26759: 298.

41. Flynn, *Rebel Girl,* 152. Elizabeth Gurley Flynn and Carlo Tresca had a thirteen-year-long relationship although they were married to others.

42. "Demeanor of IWW Viewed Seriously," *Duluth News Tribune,* July 30, 1916, p. 12a. The *News Tribune* reported that Frank was nowhere to be found after the trial; however, he remained in Duluth near the jail calling for the other agitators' release.

43. "Winter Not to Halt Range Strike, Says Elizabeth G. Flynn," *Duluth News Tribune,* August 28, 1916, p. 10; Karni, "Elizabeth Gurley Flynn," 3.

44. "Doesn't Wish to be Called 'Fat,'" *Duluth News Tribune,* July 26, 1916, p. 5.

45. "Penury May Put End to Strike of IWW," *Duluth News Tribune,* August 2, 1916, p. 5.

46. "Calls Force to Open Jail," *Duluth New Tribune,* July 31, 1916, p. 1.

47. Ibid.

48. Joseph Ettor telegram to *Solidarity,* August 1, 1916; "Strike Grows More Tense," *Solidarity,* August 5, 1916, p. 1.

49. "Strikers' Firm despite Violence, *Solidarity,* August 5, 1916, p. 4.

50. "Like Real War at Mines," *Kansas City Star,* July 31, 1916, p. 9.

51. Ibid.

52. "IWW to Meet," *Duluth News Tribune,* August 2, 1916, p. 5.

53. "Frank Little Tells Chisholm Strikers How to Win Strike," *Duluth News Tribune,* August 4, 1916, p. 5.

54. Ibid.

55. "Buhl Sends Call for More Deputies," *Duluth News Tribune,* August 4, 1916, p. 5.

56. "Socialists in Line with Haywoodmen," *Duluth News Tribune,* August 5, 1916, pp. 1–2.

57. Ibid., 1.

58. "Little Hits at Authorities," *Duluth News Tribune,* August 5, 1916, p. 2; "Savage Criticism of Gov. Burnquist by Little," *Duluth News Tribune,* August 5, 1916, p. 1.

59. "Little Hits at Authorities," 11.

60. "Leader Insinuates Action Yet to Come," *Duluth News Tribune,* August 4, 1916, p. 5.

61. "IWW Claims Big Membership," *Duluth News Tribune,* August 5, 1916, p. 11.

62. "Organizers Mysteriously Disappear," *Solidarity*, August 12, 1916, p. 1. Joe Greeni, the miner who walked off his job after receiving a heavily deducted paycheck thus beginning the strike, was one of the deported strikers.

63. Ibid.

64. Flynn, *Rebel Girl*, 211; "Various," Case #26759: 298. Bill Haywood wrote Pancner on August 8, 1916, that organizing iron-ore miners was urgent in Michigan. Pancner was to discuss this with Frank Little, Elizabeth Gurley Flynn, and Joseph Ettor. Frank took the assignment.

65. Kornbluh, *Rebel Voices*, 295.

66. "Attempts Settlement at Chisholm," *Solidarity*, August 26, 1916, p. 1. *Solidarity* reported that Frank was deported to Wisconsin from Michigan. He was escorted out of state after he was found near Watersmeet. Thompson and Murfin, *I.W.W.: Its First Seventy Years*, 104.

67. Thompson and Murfin, *I.W.W.: Its First Seventy Years*, 103. Fred W. Thompson asserts that Elizabeth Gurley Flynn was behind the proposal to get Carlo Tresca and others freed at the expense of the Montenegrin miners. No trial was ever held for Tresca. Elizabeth Gurley Flynn and Joseph Ettor were heavily criticized for putting the IWW organizers' needs above the rights of the miners they were organizing. 1920 U.S. Federal Census, Stillwater, Washington County, MN, Roll T625_866, p. 3B, Enumeration District 182, Image 909. Ironically by 1920, Philip Masonovich's son, Nick, became a laborer for Oliver Mining Company.

CHAPTER TWENTY-ONE

1. After being discovered near Watersmeet, Michigan, Frank Little was taken to an undisclosed location in Wisconsin. "Attempts Settlement at Chisholm," *Solidarity*, August 26, 1916, p. 1. An affidavit of his extensive injuries was entered into evidence during the Chicago IWW trial of 1918. "IWW Activities" in "Various," Case #36190: 189-90.

2. "Frank Little Lynched in Butte," *Solidarity*, August 4, 1917, p. 1.

3. Robert Barclay Riell, "Copper Mine Strikes of 1917, Globe, Arizona," Gila County Historical Society (GCHS), undated, 2. Riell's memoirs detail oppositional views to the IWW.

4. Phil Mellinger, "How the IWW Lost Its Heartland," *Western Labor Historical Quarterly* 27, no. 3 (1996): 319. By February's end, 1917, Frank had organized Chandler and was well into organizing the Miami-Globe district. Grover H. Perry, "IWW Spreading Rapidly in Arizona," *Solidarity*, March 3, 1917, p. 1; Grover H. Perry, "Good News from Arizona," *Solidarity*, March 10, 1917, p. 1.

5. Riell, "Copper Mine Strikes," 1.

6. Riell paid the spy the difference between his mining wages and Thiel's salary every payday. Riell, "Copper Mine Strikes," 2; Elrod, "Old Dominion Mine."

7. James W. Byrkit, *Forging the Copper Collar: Arizona's Labor Management War of 1901–1921* (Tucson: University of Arizona Press, 1982), 120–21; Campbell, "True Copy of the Notes," 7.

8. Byrkit, *Forging the Copper Collar*, 120; John Joseph Oates, Testimony before U.S. District Court of Illinois, August 3, 1918, transcript available from U.S. vs. Haywood et al., 1917–1918, Legal Problems, Trials, and Defense, File 4: 10060, Box 115, Subseries B, Walter P. Reuther Library, WSU.

9. Byrkit, *Forging the Copper Collar*, 141, 158, 299.

10. Ibid., 120. Byrkit cites John McBride, a federal mediator sent to Arizona in 1917, whose report describes mine operators employing Pinkertons as miners to create trouble and terrorize both miners and the public.

11. F. H. Little, "IWW Wins Strike in Prescott, Arizona," *Solidarity*, May 19, 1917, p. 1.

12. The Russian Revolution began in February 1917 when Czar Nicholas II abdicated and the government was replaced with a Communist or Bolshevik government. Since the IWW was believed, erroneously but widely, to be Communist, its members were labeled "Reds" or Bolsheviks, enhancing America's first Red Scare.

13. Jerome Miners' Union No. 79 of IUMMSW to the Committee of the IWW, May 27, 1917, MSS54, Box 2, Folder 2, Henry S. McCluskey Papers 1911–1956, Haydon Library, Arizona State University (ASU).

14. "A Critical Period," *Solidarity*, September 27, 1913, p. 2. Grover H. Perry, Testimony before U.S. District Court of Illinois, August 8, 1918, transcript available from U.S. vs. Haywood et al., 1917–1918, Legal Problems, Trials, and Defense, File 3: 10917, Box 116, Subseries B, Walter P. Reuther Library, WSU; George Powell to H. S. McCluskey, February 8, 1917, MSS54, Box 2, Folder 8, Henry S. McCluskey Papers 1911–1956, Haydon Library, ASU. Powell claims that Grover Perry had only thirty-five dollars to organize Arizona.

15. "Free Speech Fight Is On," *Industrial Worker*, October 26, 1911, p. 4.

16. Chaplin, *Wobbly*, 201.

17. E. J. MacCasham to Grover Perry, June 9, 1917, File AZ 114, Box 1, Folder 2, Special Collections, University of Arizona (UA); Perry, Testimony, August 8, 1918, 10946–10947.

18. U.S. v. Haywood et al., 10970, as quoted in Mellinger, "How the IWW Lost Its Heartland," 321; James W. Byrkit, "The IWW in Wartime Arizona," *Journal of Arizona History* 19 (Summer 1977): 43; Paul Frederick Brissenden, *The IWW, A Study of American Syndicalism* (New York: 1919), 264.

19. Chaplin, *Wobbly*, 206. Frank used the expression when arguing to the GEB that they needed to continue circulating *The Deadly Parallel,* an official bulletin that contrasted the IWW's militant antiwar position with the AFL's pro-war position.

20. Grover H. Perry to William D. Haywood, April 20, 1917, AZ 114, Box 1, Folder 1, Special Collections, UA; "Display Old Glory Over Globe Union Houses," *Tombstone Weekly Epitaph,* June 5, 1917, p. 5.

21. "Citizens of Globe Brand IWW Enemy to Nation," *Bisbee Daily Review,* July 7, 1917, p. 1; "Globe IWW Fear Citizens Planning Raid," *Bisbee Daily Review,* July 13, 1917, p. 1. Loyalty League merchants posted their loyalty cards in their storefronts. Overstreet, "On Strike!," 211.

22. Sellars, "Treasonous Tenant Farmers," 1123; Grover Perry, "Does Arizona Need Cheap Labor?" *Solidarity,* May 19, 1917, p. 1. Perry believed that Mexicans would continue to flood Arizona for cheap wages.

23. Perry, Testimony, August 8, 1918, 10962. "Registration Day" for the National Draft required all males between 21 and 30 years of age to register. Failure to register resulted in arrest. A lottery later determined who would be inducted.

24. Chaplin, *Wobbly*, 208. See Butte miner Albert Jahn's letter to Grover H. Perry, May 31, 1917, asking for an official IWW statement regarding registration. Perry answered Jahn by informing him about what other locals had chosen to do, explaining the issue as "an individual matter." Grover H. Perry to Albert Jahn, May 31, 1917, AZ 114, Box 1, Folder 3, Special Collections, UA.

25. F. H. Little, Telegram to William D. Haywood, April 10, 1917, Bisbee Deportation Legal Papers and Exhibits, Special Collections, AZ 114, Box 1, Folder 1, UA.

26. F. H. Little to Grover H. Perry, April 11, 1917, and Grover H. Perry to William D. Haywood, May 9, 1917, as quoted in Eric Thomas Chester, *The Wobblies in Their Heyday: The Rise and Fall of the Industrial Workers of the World during the World War I Era* (Santa Barbara, CA: Praeger, 2014), 34.

27. Grover H. Perry to F. H. Little, April 11, 1917, AZ 114, Box 1, Folder 2, Special Collections, UA. Perry planned to avoid registration and expressed concern that he would be arrested. He needed Frank to take charge if necessary. Yet Perry did register for the draft, citing need for an exemption due to a bad heart and crippled right arm. World War I *Selective Service System Draft Registration Cards, 1917–1918,* Maricopa County, Arizona, June 5, 1917, National Archives Microfilm Publication, Roll #1522456, NARA, Washington, D.C.

28. Grover H. Perry to F. H. Little, April 11, 1917, p. 3; Chaplin, *Wobbly*, 196.

29. F. H. Little, "Statement of Work for the Week Ending April 14, 1917," submitted to Grover Perry, AZ 114, Box 1, Folder 2, Special Collections, UA.

30. F. H. Little to William D. Haywood, April 16, 1917, Bisbee Deportation Legal Papers and Exhibits, Special Collections, AZ 114, Box 1, Folder 1, UA; William D. Haywood, Testimony before U.S. District Court of Illinois, August 12, 1918, transcript available from U.S. vs. Haywood et al., 1917–1918, Legal Problems, Trials, and Defense, File 3: 11510–11511, Box 117, Subseries B, Walter P. Reuther Library, WSU.

31. F. H. Little, "Miners in Arizona Lining Up," *Solidarity*, April 21, 1917, p. 4. Frank expected this article to be published a week earlier.

32. Haywood, Testimony, August 12, 1918, 11511.

33. F. H. Little to Grover H. Perry, May 9, 1917, as quoted in Chester, *Wobblies in Their Heyday*, 34.

34. F. H. Little, "IWW Wins Strike in Prescott, Arizona," 1. Frank spoke to about one hundred men in Humboldt, near Prescott, Arizona. Pedro Coria helped Frank coordinate the Humboldt smelter strike. John R. Baskett, Testimony before U.S. District Court of Illinois, August 8, 1918, transcript available from U.S. vs. Haywood et al., 1917–1918, Legal Problems, Trials, and Defense, File 3: 10865, Box 116, Subseries B, Walter P. Reuther Library, WSU. Baskett, an electrician, was a Jerome camp delegate on salary from the IWW.

35. A. D. Kimball, "Arizona on the Job," *Solidarity*, May 26, 1917, p. 4; *Solidarity*, March 10, 1917, p. 4. Frank spoke at the first open air meeting in 1917 at the Warren baseball field in Bisbee, March 1917. Later speeches occurred at Bisbee's City Park, up the hill in Brewery Gulch.

36. Grover H. Perry to William D. Haywood, May 16, 1917, as quoted in Chester, *Wobblies in Their Heyday*, 33.

37. F. H. Little to Grover H. Perry, May 17, 1917, as quoted in Chester, *Wobblies in Their Heyday*, 34.

38. Almira Little Cox filed for her husband's pension on September 18, 1916. Elihu H. Cox, Application File #1073678, *U.S. Civil War Pension Index: General Index to Pension Files, 1861–1934*, online database (Provo, UT: Ancestry.com, 2000). Original data: *General Index to Pension Files, 1861–1934*. Washington, D.C.: NARA, T288, 546 rolls. Elihu H. Cox died in Guthrie, Oklahoma, on September 30, 1914.

39. "I.W.W. Activities," Case #8000-15817: 21, Investigative Reports of the Bureau of Investigation 1908–1922, OGF, 1909–1921, FBI Case Files, National Archives Microfilm Publication M1085, NARA, Washington, D.C. The letter was postmarked from Perkins, Oklahoma.

40. "Various," Case #8000-197638: 68, Roll 603; "Butte Hangs an IWW Agitator," *El Paso Herald*, August 1, 1917, p. 5.

41. Grover H. Perry to William D. Haywood, May 9, 1917, as quoted in Chester, *Wobblies in Their Heyday*, 34.

42. F. H. Little to Grover H. Perry, May 17, 1917, as quoted in Chester, *Wobblies in Their Heyday*, 34.

43. "Jerome District Is Paralyzed by Strikes," *Prescott Journal Miner*, May 26, 1917, p. 1. See Mellinger, *Race and Labor*, 182–84, for further information regarding the first Jerome strike.

44. "'Wobbly Slim' Known Here, Hanged at Butte for Insult to Troops," *Jerome News*, August 3, 1917, p. 1.

45. Ibid.; "Frank Little Is Lynched," *Jerome Sun*, August 1, 1917, p. 1.

46. F. H. Little, "Strike in Jerome, Ariz.," *Solidarity*, May 26, 1917, p. 3; Grover H. Perry, "The IWW in Arizona," *Solidarity*, June 23, 1917, p. 4.

47. The check-off system is where companies deduct union dues for union management, and no worker can work without union membership. A comparison of IWW to IUMMSW benefits is listed in an IWW bulletin "Do You Want a Contract," Bisbee Deportation Legal Papers and Exhibits, Special Collections, AZ 114, Box 1, Folder 2, UA; "Various," Case #8000-197638: 68.

48. Robert W. Bruere, "Following the Trail of the IWW," *New York Evening Post*, 1918, Box 2, Folder 3, Henry S. McCluskey Papers, Haydon Library, ASU.

49. "IWW Members Claim They Were Misled by False Promises of the Union Strike Leaders" *Prescott Journal Miner* May 27, 1917, p. 1; "Sympathy Strike Now in Jerome," *Tombstone Weekly Epitaph*, June 3, 1917, p. 5.

50. "IWW Members Claim They Were Misled," 1. See resolution attached to Thomas J. Crooff to Henry S. McCluskey, March 20, 1918, p. 2, MSS 54, Box 2, Folder 8, Henry S. McCluskey Papers, Haydon Library, ASU; Jerome Miners' Union No. 79 of IUMMSW to the Committee of the IWW, May 26, 1917, p. 1, MS54 Box 2, Folder 2, Henry S. McCluskey Papers 1911–1956, Haydon Library, ASU. Attorney Henry S. McCluskey, an organizer for the AFL, was called to Arizona in January 1917 due to mounting IWW interruption within the IUMMSW. For a thorough account of McCluskey's work, see James David McBride, "Henry S. McCluskey: Workingman's Advocate" (dissertation, Arizona State University, May 1982), LD179.15, Special Collections, Haydon Library, ASU.

51. H. S. McCluskey to the "Committee Purporting to Represent the IWW," May 26, 1917, MS54 Box 2, Folder 2, Henry S. McCluskey Papers 1911–1956, Haydon Library, ASU.

52. Jerome Miners' Union No. 79 of IUMMSW to the Committee of the IWW, May 27, 1917, p. 2.

53. "IWW Members Claim They Were Misled," 1.

54. In the 1916 Arizona gubernatorial election, Thomas E. Campbell beat incumbent George W. P. Hunt by thirty votes. Hunt claimed fraud, and after a lengthy court battle, was reinstated as Arizona governor at

the end of 1917. From January 1917 until December 1917, Campbell was considered the de facto governor.

55. Thomas E. Campbell described Colonel James Hornbrook as an "easy mixer" with all types of people and who possessed much common sense and good judgment. Campbell, "True Copy of the Notes," 19.

56. "Governor Campbell Declares He Will Stay in Jerome until Strike Is Settled without Danger of Repetition," *Prescott Journal Miner,* May 29, 1917, p. 1. John McBride, a former judge and WFM president, was sent to Jerome at Labor Secretary W. B. Wilson's behest.

57. Campbell, "True Copy of the Notes," 20.

58. Ibid.

59. Ibid.

60. Ibid.

61. Ibid.

62. Ibid., 21.

63. Ibid. According to historian James W. Byrkit, Campbell's failure to censure mine operators' illegal activities, for which he later was embarrassed, may have contributed to Arizona's extensive labor problems. Whether he knew in advance about deportations is unknown, but he joined mine operators by repeatedly calling for federal troops into several mining camps. Ultimately he condemned both the deportation and IWWs. Byrkit, *Forging the Copper Collar: Arizona's Labor Management War of 1901–1921* (Tucson: University of Arizona Press, 1982.)

64. Campbell, "True Copy of the Notes," 22.

65. See "IWW Wins in Jerome Arizona," *Solidarity,* June 9, 1917, for an overview of the first Jerome strike. For an opposing viewpoint, see Campbell, "True Copy of the Notes." Grover H. Perry to Charles H. MacKinnon, June 5, 1917, Bisbee Deportation Legal Papers and Exhibits, Special Collections, AZ 114, Box 1, Folder 2, UA; Thomas J. Dorich, "This is a Tough Place to Work," *Journal of Arizona History* 38 (Autumn 1997) 233–56.

66. F. H. Little to William D. Haywood, June 5, 1917, as quoted in Bill Haywood, George F. Vanderveer, and Frank Knowlton, *Evidence and Cross Examination of William D. Haywood in the Case of the USA versus Wm. D. Haywood, et al.* (Chicago: General Defense Committee, 1918), 97.

67. "Butte's Name Tarnished by the Stain of Lynch Law, Frank Little Hanged at Trestle by Unknown Mob," *Anaconda Standard,* August 2, 1917, p. 1.

68. "Various," Case #8000-36190: 486–87. Ben Webb was considered to be a most valuable Bisbee witness since he was believed to be working for a mining company while serving on Bisbee's IWW executive, organization, and audit committees. Other valuable Bisbee informants included Bisbee Postmaster L. R. Bailey, Western Union Telegraph operator R. M.

Henderson, H. B. Scott, Thomas Mooney, W. H. Minshull, Dave Foster, E. A. Tovres, John Caretto, and H. Howe. The Bureau of Investigation report stated that these people would be "annihilated" if their names were revealed.

69. Ibid. For a complete record of the convention's minutes, see "Minutes of First Convention Metal Mine Workers Industrial Union 800, Bisbee, Arizona June 15–June 17 1917," AZ 114, Box 1, Folder 2, Special Collections, UA. The Loyalty League of America organized in Phoenix as a statewide organization. Its avowed purpose was "to exterminate the IWW."

70. "Bisbee Thinks Little Was Secret Visitor," El Paso Herald, August 1, 1917, p. 5. The city official stated that Frank registered under a different name.

71. "IWW Wins in Jerome," Solidarity, June 9, 1917, p. 4; "Mining Conditions in Bisbee, Arizona," August 29, 1917, L9791, B62, Pamphlet 15, Special Collections, UA.

72. A. S. Embree to Grover H. Perry, June 26, 1917, AZ 114, Box 1, Folder 2, Special Collections, UA; Grover H. Perry to the Executive Committee, Bisbee, AZ, July 10, 1917, AZ 114, Box 2, Folder 3, Special Collections, UA; Perry, Testimony, August 8, 1918, 10928.

73. "Minutes of First Convention Metal Mine Workers Industrial Union 800, Bisbee, Arizona June 15–June 17 1917."

74. Oates, Testimony, August 3, 1918, 10036; "Various," Case #8000-36190: 471.

75. "Various," Case #8000-36190: 471. Frank sent Joe Oates to organize Jerome in March 1917 until the strike was over about six weeks later.

76. Mellinger, Race and Labor, 183.

77. "Butte Vigilantes Hang Little, I.W.W. Agitator, at Bridge as a Warning," El Paso Herald, August 1, 1917, p. 5.

78. Perry, Testimony, August 8, 1918, 10930.

79. Ibid.; "Recovering from the Auto Accident," Daily Arizona Silver Belt, June 20, 1917, p. 1. Joe Oates claimed he would have been with the group but had remained in Bisbee to get his final pay. Oates, Testimony, August 3, 1918, 10036.

80. "Recovering from the Auto Accident," 1; Perry, Testimony, August 8, 1918, 10930. The county hospital was Inspiration Hospital in Miami.

81. "Little's Lameness Due to Injury in Miami," El Paso Herald, August 1, 1917, p. 5. Both Grover H. Perry and John Joseph Oates confirmed Frank Little spent only one night in Miami. Perry, Testimony, August 8, 1918, 10930; Oates, Testimony, August 3, 1918, 10074–10075.

82. "Butte Vigilantes Hang Little," 5.

CHAPTER TWENTY-TWO

1. "Various," Case #8000-36190: 477, Roll 603. Perry first spoke in Globe at the Bankers' Gardens on June 19, 1917, the same day as the auto accident. Perry, Testimony, August 8, 1918, 10931; Oates, Testimony, August 3, 1918, 10056–10057. Fred Barcón, grandson of a Miami Copper Company miner, reported that the Sand Wash was part of Bloody Tanks Wash, running between Sullivan and Live Oak Streets, about a mile west of the stairs on Keystone Street. Fred Barcón, interview by the author, March 29, 2013. A 1917 Sanborn map places the Sand Wash two blocks east at the entrance of Adonis Avenue. Delvan Hayward recalled that Miners' Union Hall was on the corner of Sullivan and Cordova Streets where a basketball court presently occupies. Delvan Burch Hayward, interview by the author, August 23, 2012. While the Miners' Union Hall was located on this location in 1922, it had not yet been built there in 1917. Hayward's grandfather and father were miners in the Miami mining district. She is currently (2012) library manager of Miami Memorial Library in Miami, Arizona

2. John Michal Benson, interview. "Miami Arizona Historic Tour," Globe/Miami Chamber of Commerce and City of Miami, AZ, n.d., 14.

3. Delvan Burch Hayward, interview. Hayward stated that it was not uncommon for miners to walk great distances between the mines in which they worked and Miami.

4. For statements as to the content of Grover Perry's speech, see "Various," Case #8000-36190: 450, 476–78.

5. Oates, Testimony, August 3, 1918, 10056.

6. "Various," Case #8000-36190: 477–78.

7. Perry, Testimony, August 8, 1918, 10931; Oates, Testimony, August 3, 1918, 10056–10057.

8. Perry, Testimony, August 8, 1918, 10931; Oates, Testimony, August 3, 1918, 10057, 10075.

9. Hiram "Hi" Elam, a former Texas Ranger, was deputy sheriff of Miami. Elam is also the grandfather of famous actor Jack Elam. "Various," Case #8000-36190: 474; Oates, Testimony, August 3, 1918, 10057, 10075.

10. Oates, Testimony, August 3, 1918, 10055; Perry, Testimony, August 8, 1918, 10931.

11. When Frank Little was called from Miami-Globe to WFM headquarters, Arizona State Union No. 3, or MMWIU No. 800 headquarters in Phoenix, he had to follow the Bellamy Trail (or Swift Trail, as it was sometimes known) west to Superior, which served travel needs until 1922 when U.S. Highway 60 was completed between Superior and Globe.

12. Chaplin, Wobbly, 199–200. Chaplin was elected Solidarity's new editor during the Tenth Annual IWW Convention. Leslie Marcy, "The

Tenth Annual IWW Convention," *International Socialist Review*, 17, no. 3 (January 1917): 407.

13. "Synopsis of Minutes of Meeting of General Executive Board, Held June 29th–July 6th, 1917," Bisbee Deportation Legal Papers and Exhibits, Special Collections, AZ 114, Box 1, Folder 2, University of Arizona (UA).

14. Chaplin, *Wobbly*, 200.

15. Ibid., 208.

16. Ibid., 200.

17. Ibid., 206. The cartoon was published in *Solidarity*.

18. Ibid., 196.

19. Ibid.

20. William Haywood, Testimony before U.S. District Court of Illinois, August 12, 1918, transcript available from U.S. vs. Haywood et al., 1917–1918, Legal Problems, Trials, and Defense, File 3: 11368, Box 117, Subseries B, Walter P. Reuther Library, WSU. For the war statement that Haywood attributes to Frank Little, see "Statement of the General Executive Board of the IWW on War," Bisbee Deportation Legal Papers and Exhibits, Special Collections, AZ 114, Box 1, Folder 2, UA.

21. "Synopsis of Minutes."

22. Chaplin, *Wobbly*, 200.

23. Ibid., 209.

24. Ibid.

25. Ibid.; "Various," Case #8000-36190: 366.

26. Chaplin, *Wobbly*, 209.

27. William Haywood to F. H. Little, July 27, 1917, Bisbee Deportation Legal Papers and Exhibits, Special Collections, AZ 114, Box 1, Folder 1, UA. Haywood, Testimony, August 12, 1918, 11368.

28. Bill Haywood, George F. Vanderveer, and Frank Knowlton, *Evidence and Cross Examination of William D. Haywood in the Case of the USA versus Wm. D. Haywood, et al.* (Chicago: General Defense Committee, 1918), 195.

29. Haywood, Testimony, August 12, 1918, 11368; "Synopsis of Minutes."

30. World War I Selective Service System Draft Registration Cards, 1917–1918, Cook County, Illinois, June 5, 1917, National Archives Microfilm Publication M1509, Roll #1503877, NARA, Washington, D.C.

31. Perry, Testimony, August 8, 1918, 10928.

32. Grover H. Perry, Telegram to William D. Haywood, June 25, 1917, Bisbee Deportation Legal Papers and Exhibits, Special Collections, AZ 114, Box 1, Folder 1, UA. No mention was made in the GEB minutes of the Bisbee strike. See "Bisbee Branch IWW Makes Demand on Local Mines; Walkout Called," *Bisbee Daily Review*, June 27, 1917, p. 1, for a list of demands.

33. Sheriff Wheeler, Telegram to Governor Thomas Campbell, June 30, 1917, Bisbee Deportation Legal Papers and Exhibits, Special Collections, AZ 114, Box 2, Folder 5, UA; Campbell, "True Copy of the Notes," 58. Col. James J. Hornbrook was assigned to investigate Wheeler's claim. He reported on June 30 and July 2 that the solution did not warrant troops, and if it did, that a squadron of cavalry was stationed a few miles away and was ready for service at a moment's notice.

34. "Compromise with 'Rattlesnakes' Impossible, Declares Douglas," *Bisbee Daily Review,* July 11, 1917, p. 1.

35. "Sheriff Announces He Will Use Force to Prevent Any Disorders During Trouble," *Bisbee Daily Review,* June 27, 1917, p. 1.

36. "Citizens and Business Men Condemn Action of IWW in Calling Strike as Treason," *Bisbee Daily Review,* June 28, 1917, p. 1.

37. For a closer look at Sheriff Wheeler's mischaracterizations of the IWW, see Byrkit, "IWW in Wartime Arizona," 149–70.

38. Oates, Testimony, August 3, 1918, 10072; "State-wide Strike in Copper Industry," 4. *Solidarity* reported that all mines, mills, and smelters in the Miami-Globe district were closed by June 20, 1917.

39. "Shut-Down in Arizona Complete," *Solidarity,* July 7, 1917, p. 1.

40. Stanley J. Clark, Testimony before U.S. District Court of Illinois, August 8, 1918, transcript available from U.S. vs. Haywood et al., 1917–1918, Legal Problems, Trials, and Defense, File 3: 10878, Box 116, Subseries B, Walter P. Reuther Library, WSU; "Citizens of Globe Brand IWW Enemy to Nation," *Bisbee Daily Review,* July 7, 1917, p. 1. Governor Campbell had been in close communication with Mayor Keegan of Globe and Episcopal Minister Johnson, who had been elected major of the Citizens' Home Guard. Johnson had experience as a noncommissioned officer in the army before entering the episcopate. Johnson followed the communication from Sheriff Armer that the situation was so tense that he had to mobilize the Home Guard and prepare to protect Globe against mob violence. Johnson also urged Campbell for immediate action. Campbell, "True Copy of the Notes," 27.

41. Oates, Testimony, August 3, 1918, 10039, 10041–10043. Oates testified that craft unions came out in solidarity for the IWW. In comparison, Oates stated that the WFM specifically struck for union recognition and a grievance committee. Perry, Testimony, August 12, 1918, 10936. Perry states that the IMMSU had given the company ten days to meet demands, which had been discussed as much as two weeks beforehand. "Miami Union Defers Action; Situation in Globe is Improving," *Bisbee Daily Review,* June 27, 1917, p. 3.

42. "State-wide Strike in Copper Industry," *Solidarity,* July 7, 1917, p. 4.

43. Joseph Oates to Grover H. Perry, July 6, 1917, Bisbee Deportation Legal Papers and Exhibits, Special Collections, AZ 114, Box 2, Folder 3,

UA. Oates also mentions needing cash for helping poor Mexican families from going hungry. "Various," Case #8000-36190: 432.

44. "Various," Case #8000-36190: 439.

45. IWW Agitators Coria and Costillo were jailed in Clifton and registered with the WFM against their will. "'Union' Conscription in Arizona," *Solidarity*, June 2, 1917, p. 4. See Clifton-Morenci mining district's demands in "Refuse to Work until Demand Is Won," *Copper Era*, July 6, 1917, p. 1. See Mellinger, *Race and Labor*, 189–90, for discussion of the 1917 Clifton-Morenci strike.

46. John Robert Baskett, Testimony before U.S. District Court of Illinois, August 8, 1918, transcript available from U.S. vs. Haywood et al., 1917–1918, Legal Problems, Trials, and Defense, File 3: 10824–10025, 10833, 10859–10860, Box 116, Subseries B, Walter P. Reuther Library, WSU. No business would rent a proper hall for their meetings.

47. Ibid., 10829–10830, 10859.

48. Ibid., 10825–10826. Underground miners struck for six dollars for six hours, later amending their demands to six dollars for eight hours at a strike meeting the next day, July 7, 1917. See Mellinger, *Race and Labor*, 182–84, for discussion of union politics in the Jerome strike.

49. J. MacDonald and Bisbee Press Committee to Grover H. Perry, July 6, 1917, AZ 114, Bisbee Deportation Legal Papers and Exhibits, Special Collections, AZ 114, Box 2, Folder 3, UA. Dr. Thomas J. Dorich suggests no WFM member assisted the IWW with the strike. Dorich, "Tough Place to Work," 243; "State-wide Strike in Copper Industry," 4; "Metal Miners Organize for Victory," *Solidarity*, July 14, 1917, p. 7.

50. Dubofsky, *We Shall Be All*, 210–11; "Shut-Down in Arizona Complete," 1.

51. Frank Little and William D. Haywood, Telegrams to A. D. Kimball and Joseph Oates, July 6, 1917, Bisbee Deportation Legal Papers and Exhibits, Special Collections, AZ 114, Box 1, Folder 1, UA.

52. Frank Little, "What the Metal Miners Are Striking For and Why They Need Your Support," *Solidarity*, July 21, 1917, p. 4.

53. "Strike! The IWW and the Jerome Deportation," *Jerome Chronicle* (Spring 1997): 5; Baskett, Testimony, August 8, 1918, 10842. John R. Baskett, a Spanish-American War veteran, was arrested but released after interrogation in the United Verde Mine office.

54. "Strike! The IWW and the Jerome Deportation," 5.

55. Baskett, Testimony, August 8, 1918, 10829.

56. "Strike! The IWW and the Jerome Deportation," 6; "67 'Wobblies' Are Shipped from Jerome in Cattle Cars," *Bisbee Daily Review*, July 11, 1917, p. 1.

57. Baskett, Testimony, August 8, 1918, 10861.

58. California law enforcement officials met the train at Needles and ordered the posse to return to Arizona. The local sheriff held the detainees

in the Kingman, Arizona, courthouse until Governor Campbell ordered them released if no charges were pending. *Jerome News*, July 13, 1917; "Jerome Agitators Are Chased from Needles, Dispersed at Kingman," *Prescott Journal Miner*, July 11, 1917, p. 1; Dorich, "Tough Place to Work," 233–56.

59. "Strike! The IWW and the Jerome Deportation," 5. Governor Thomas E. Campbell writes that mine operators also took part in the deportation. Campbell, "True Copy of the Notes," 23.

60. "67 'Wobblies' are Shipped," 1. For an analysis of the Jerome deportation, see John H. Lindquist, "The Jerome Deportation of 1917," *Arizona and the West* 11, no. 3 (Autumn 1969): 233–46.

61. Gilbert Mere to Fred Thompson, June 9, 1976, Fred Thompson Collection, Subseries A, Box 8, File 23, Walter P. Reuther Library, WSU. A. S. [Sam] Embree reported that Wheeler was just a puppet, controlled by Walter Douglas, who followed plans drawn by a former captain in the German army working in the Copper Queen office. Gilbert Mere to Fred Thompson, October 8, 1976, Fred Thompson Collection, Subseries A, Box 8, File 23, Walter P. Reuther Library, WSU. The rumor of a German officer who assisted Douglas in devising the deportation plan is highly doubtful, perhaps a red herring to protect John C. Greenway, the real architect.

62. Gilbert Mere to Fred Thompson, June 9, 1976; Frederick Watson, "A Deportee Deposition," August 30, 1970, in Robert E. Hanson, *The Great Bisbee IWW Deportation of July 12, 1917*, Montana: Signature Press, 1987.

63. "The Great Wobbly Drive," *Bisbee Daily Review*, July 13, 1917, p. 1. See discussion of Sam Embree's recollections in Gilbert Mere to Fred Thompson, June 9, 1976. Ray Ewing, "The Big Drive," originally published in *Souvenir of Bisbee*, by a Recycled Miner, 1979, in Hanson. Ewing reports that many of these Englishmen were deported erroneously on July 12, 1917, when they reported that they were unemployed in the mines.

64. "Deportation Records Reveal Original List of Deputies," in Hanson. A black box discovered in the Cochise County recorder's office in 1987 revealed that Sheriff Wheeler originally deputized 572 men, some registrations predated as early as June 1917. Byrkit suggests that the group of vigilantes grew immediately after the arrests.

65. Gilbert Mere to Robert W. Houston, January 17, 1977, Fred Thompson Collection, Subseries A, Box 8, File 24, Walter P. Reuther Library, WSU.

66. Gilbert Mere to Fred Thompson, May 25, 1976, Fred Thompson Collection, Subseries A, Box 8 File 23, Walter P. Reuther Library, WSU. On the evening of July 11, 1917, the Local 800 strike committee received a "vague" warning. Gilbert Mere to Fred Thompson, June 9, 1976. Some of the imported English scabs had talked at a Brewery Gulch brothel run by "Oklahoma Joe," before July 12, 1917. Ewing, "The Big Drive."

67. "Notes on the Big Drive,' *Bisbee Daily Review*, July 13, 1917, p. 4.

68. See Fred Watson's memoirs of the Bisbee deportation in "Still on Strike! Recollections of a Bisbee Deportee," *Journal of Arizona History* 18 (Summer 1977): 171–84.

69. Gilbert Mere to Fred Thompson, June 9, 1976.

70. Ewing, "The Big Drive." Gilbert Mere to Fred Thompson, May 25, 1976; Watson, "Still on Strike!"

71. For historical accounting of the Bisbee Deportation, see Hanson. See also James Byrkit, *Forging the Copper Collar* (Tucson: University of Arizona, 1982), 187–15. For contemporary local views, see "The Great Wobbly Drive," 4.

72. Watson, "A Deportee Deposition"; Ewing, "The Big Drive." Ray Ewing reported one barrel of water per boxcar, which emptied quickly. See Byrkit, *Forging the Copper Collar*, 210–15, for descriptions of the train ride.

73. Richard Byrd, "Bisbee's Darkest Day Recalled 69 Years Later," *Bisbee Observer*, June 16, 1986, p. 6.

74. Chaplin, *Wobbly*, 209.

75. Ibid.

76. Ibid.

77. Ibid.

CHAPTER TWENTY-THREE

1. Richard I. Gibson, *Lost Butte, Montana* (Charleston: The History Press, 2012), 65.

2. David M. Emmons, *The Butte Irish: Class and Ethnicity in an American Mining Town 1875–1925* (Chicago: University of Illinois, 1989), 13. Emmons cites statistics from 1900 when approximately 25 percent or 12,000 of Silver Bow County's population of 47,635 were Irish. In Butte proper, 26 percent of the population was Irish, a higher percentage of Irish than in any other American city at the time according to Emmons. (The Irish include immigrants and second-generation residents.)

3. Richard I. Gibson, interview by the author, June 24, 2013.

4. Gibson, *Lost Butte*, 11; Emmons, *Butte Irish*, 116.

5. George D. Marsh, ed., *Copper Camp*, Workers of the Writers' Program (WPA), Montana State Department of Agriculture (New York: Hastings House, 1943), 39.

6. *Hobo Agitator*, documentary; Jerry Calvert, "The Destruction of the Butte Miners' Union: A Study of Labor, Socialism, a Company, and the State" (unpublished manuscript), 3, Fred Thompson Collection, Subseries A, Box 8, Folder 26–27, Walter P. Reuther Library, WSU. Amalgamated Mining Corporation acquired Heinze's United Copper Company by 1907.

7. See Paul F. Brissenden, "The Butte Miners and the Rustling Card," *American Economic Review* 10, no. 4 (Dec. 1920): 755–75, for a concise history of Butte mining. Brissenden was an investigator for the U.S. Department of Labor in western mining districts. Jerry W. Calvert, *The Gibraltar: Socialism and Labor in Butte, Montana, 1895–1920* (Helena: Montana Historical Society Press, 1988). The Writers' Program (WPA), Montana State Department of Agriculture (New York: Hastings House, 1943) has a timeline of Butte events from 1856–1941.

8. Kornbluh, *Rebel Voices*, 291.

9. Calvert, "Destruction of the Butte Miners' Union," 14–16.

10. "The Infamous Rustling Card System in Butte, Montana," *Industrial Worker*, January 2, 1913, p. 1. The *Worker* reports that the card had been known by old-time miners for years, first appearing in Cripple Creek and Coeur d'Alene. The miners called the card the "Employment Office Plan." A. W. Walliser, Testimony before U.S. District Court of Illinois, May 23, 1918, transcript available from U.S. vs. Haywood et al., 1917–1918, Legal Problems, Trials, and Defense, File 12: 1370, Box 104, Subseries B, Walter P. Reuther Library, WSU. For an extensive examination of Butte politics in relation to labor, see Calvert, *The Gibraltar*.

11. Brissenden, "The Butte Miners and the Rustling Card," 755. Fred Thompson cites Brissenden's work as an accurate assessment of miners' reception to the rustling card while disagreeing with historian Arnon Gutfeld's generalization of the rustling card as "particularly obnoxious to labor." Fred Thompson states that the Silver Bow trades and labor leaders generally welcomed use of the rustling card since it minimized Finnish job opportunities and punished them for voting Socialist. Fred Thompson, "Distortions re Frank Little," Fred Thompson Collection, Subseries VI, Box 14, Folder 9, Walter P. Reuther Library, WSU. See Arnon Gutfeld, "The Murder of Frank Little: Radical Labor Agitation in Butte, Montana," *Labor History* 10, no. 2 (Spring 1969): 178. Historian Jerry Calvert clarifies progressive and conservative views and their participation regarding the card's reinstatement. Calvert, "Destruction of the Butte Miners' Union," 14–16. See correspondence between Fred Thompson and Jerry Calvert, dated April 1979 and June 1981, Fred Thompson Collection, Subseries A, Box 8, Folder 25, Walter P. Reuther Library, WSU. See also George R. Tompkins, *The Truth about Butte: A Little History for Thoughtful People* (Butte: October 20, 1917), Folder 1985455, File AWT011, SBA, 8. This small publication, a product of the IWW Butte Local, presents a personal response to the actions leading to the labor finale during the summer of 1917.

12. Charles L. Stevens, Testimony before U.S. District Court of Illinois, May 23, 1918, transcript available from U.S. vs. Haywood et al., 1917–1918, Legal Problems, Trials, and Defense, File 12: 1397, Box 104,

Subseries B, Walter P. Reuther Library, WSU. Stevens testified that the *Anaconda Standard* had called attention to the fact that the questionnaire used in the rustling card system was not nearly as drastic as those asked by a man applying for a job with the U.S. government.

13. Marsh, *Copper Camp*, 53. See also William F. Dunn, Testimony before U.S. District Court of Illinois, July 13, 1918, transcript available from U.S. vs. Haywood et al., 1917–1918, Legal Problems, Trials, and Defense, File 2: 7233–7235, Box 104, Subseries B, Walter P. Reuther Library, WSU.

14. Marsh, *Copper Camp*, 65; Jerry W. Calvert to Fred Thompson, April 26, 1979, Fred Thompson Collection, Subseries A, Box 8, Folder 25, Walter P. Reuther Library, WSU; Calvert, "Destruction of the Butte Miners' Union," 19–23, 36–37. Politicians blamed the IWW for the bombing of Miners' Union Hall with tacit agreement of WFM partisans. Anaconda Copper Mining Company operatives, portraying themselves as progressive, radical miners, helped create the false narrative. Vernon H. Jensen also points out the use of company detectives, acting as miner provocateurs, to destroy union organization from within—the same practice used in Arizona mining camps. He cites contradictory reports where many insist the dynamiters were not Butte miners since they freely accessed the dynamite. Jensen, *Heritage of Conflict*, 326, 335; Reid Robinson, "Town without History," 1936, File AWR014, SBA. Robinson also asserts that only Anaconda Copper Mining Company operatives would have had access to the dynamite used to blow up Miners' Union Hall. See Tompkins, *Truth about Butte*, 13–16, for an IWW perspective regarding the riots.

15. Dunn, Testimony, 7226; Tompkins, *Truth about Butte*, 33.

16. Richard I. Gibson, interview. Gibson stated that at turn of the century the Butte hill was barren with some reports of just four trees standing. Once all mining operations shut down and the air was cleaner, the city began to green.

17. "Edward W. Byrn, Jr.," World War I Selective Service System Draft Registration Cards, 1917–1918, Silver Bow County, Montana, June 5, 1917, National Archives Microfilm Publication M1509, Roll 1684100, NARA, Washington, D.C.; 1920 U.S. Federal Census, Butte Ward 2B, Silver Bow County, Montana, Roll T625_976, p. 7A, Enumeration District 206, Image 165; *Butte, America*, documentary, directed by Pamela Roberts (2008, Independent Lens PBS Television, 2009), DVD.

18. "Frank H. Little," Case #8000-15817: 18, Investigative Reports of the Bureau of Investigation 1908–1922, Old German Files (OGF), 1909–1921, FBI Case Files, National Archives Microfilm Publication M1085, NARA, Washington, D.C.

19. Henry E. McGuckin, *Memoirs of a Wobbly* (Chicago: Charles H. Kerr, 1987), 211. This statement has been repeated variously over different decades.

20. *Butte, America*, documentary.

21. *Hobo Agitator*, documentary.

22. David M. Emmons, "Immigrant Workers and Industrial Hazards: The Irish Miners of Butte, 1880–1919," *Journal of American Ethnic History* 5, no. 1 (Fall 1985), University of Illinois Press, 45, 47. The U.S. Census Bureau compiled mortality statistics from 1905 to 1917. In 1916 Butte was one of the bureau's registration cities, and the figures for that year showed it to have one of the highest rates of respiratory disease in the nation. Butte's average death rate per 100,000 for all forms of tuberculosis between 1911 and 1916 was 237.45, more than twice the national average. Butte's mortality rate for all respiratory disease was 513.8 per 100,000. The Irish seemed to have more susceptibility to TB than others with Corktown and Dublin's Gulch most vulnerable.

23. Brian Shovers, "On the Perils of Working in Butte Underground: Underground Fatalities in the Copper Mines," *Montana: The Magazine of Western History* 37, no. 2 (Spring 1987), 26–39. Shovers states that safer, ancestral hard rock practices gave way to immediate frenzied technological development engineered by corporations intent on satisfying an insatiable work demand for nonferrous metals. This required a highly trained workforce. The Butte underground was peopled by many untrained, rural southern European immigrants completely unfamiliar with and ignorant of the industrial workplace.

24. McGuckin, *Memoirs of a Wobbly*, 84.

25. A month later Frank Little called for the use of wax candles instead of the cheaper carbide lamps since hundreds of lives had been lost to their use. Frank Little, "What the Metal Miners Are Striking For and Why They Need Your Support," *Solidarity*, July 21, 1917, p. 4. North Butte Mining Company, incorporated in 1905, was not affiliated with Anaconda Copper Mining Company.

26. See Marsh, *Copper Camp*, 166–72, for a description of the immediate aftermath of the Speculator fire. For an examination of the Speculator tragedy, see Punke, *Fire and Brimstone*.

27. Waldemar Kaiyala, "My Memories in Butte, Montana," Date Unknown, File 11, Box 1 (LH021), SBA; "Death Exacts Enormous Toll from Miners, Butte Stands Appalled at Great Sacrifice," *Anaconda Standard*, June 10, 1917, p. 1.

28. Dunn, Testimony, 7223–7224; Chaplin, *Wobbly*, 210. William F. Dunn, a twenty-nine-year-old electrician living in Butte in 1917, began spelling his name *Dunne* sometime after 1919, which may cause some confusion to researchers. His actual surname was *Dunn* as evidenced in his parents' marriage application and his World War I registration where he clearly signed his name *William F. Dunn*. He also identified himself as Dunn during his time as editor of the *Butte Daily Bulletin* and while

he campaigned for political office and served in the 1919 Montana State Legislature. Other governmental documents recorded during the Montana sedition trials and 1918 Chicago IWW trial record his Dunn surname. Later Dunn as Dunne became a founding member of the American Communist Party. See World War I Selective Service System Draft Registration Cards, 1917–1918, Silver Bow County, Montana, June 5, 1917, National Archives Microfilm Publication M1509, Roll #1684100, NARA, Washington, D.C. See also the marriage application and marriage of William Dunn and Della Raymond on October 27, 1886, in Kansas City, Missouri. *Missouri Marriage Records*, Jefferson City, MO: Missouri State Archives, Microfilm, 459; "Close Contest for Many Offices Silver Bow County," *Anaconda Standard*, November 6, 1918, p. 1.

29. Walliser, Testimony, 1365.

30. Dunn, Testimony, 7226.

31. Harold W. Crary, Testimony before U.S. District Court of Illinois, May 23, 1918, transcript available from U.S. vs. Haywood et al., 1917–1918, Legal Problems, Trials, and Defense, File12: 1423, Box 104, Subseries B, Walter P. Reuther Library, WSU. The *Anaconda Standard*, owned by the Anaconda Copper Mining Company, had a Butte office where it reported news compatible with its shareholders' views. Crary stated that he received a circular enclosed in an envelope under his door on June 3, 1917, opposing the draft.

32. Ibid., 1416.

33. Peter Rickman, Butte [Local No. 1] to Harry Lloyd, June 5, 1917, Bisbee Deportation Legal Papers and Exhibits, AZ 114, Box 1, Folder 1, Special Collections, University of Arizona (UA).

34. Dunn, Testimony, 7228–7229, 7233.

35. "Butte Miners Turn Down A. F. of L.," *Solidarity*, July 21, 1917, p. 3.

36. "Butte Miners Take Up Fight to Oust IWW," *Anaconda Standard*, July 20, 1917, p. 7.

37. See "The Labor Troubles in Butte," *Mining and Scientific Press* 115, September 1, 1917, p. 305, for a detailed list of demands.

38. "Frank H. Little," Case #8000-15817: 21. Agent Byrn reported receipts, including one for $4.75 for a Pullman berth, in Frank's belongings in his room in Butte.

39. "Little's Tart Telegram to Governor of Arizona," *Anaconda Standard*, August 2, 1917, p. 2. It should be noted that Agent Byrn reported a receipt from Western Union Telegraph Company, Salt Lake City, dated July 16, 1917, in Frank's belongings in his room at the Steele Block in Butte, Montana. Frank may have sent the telegram to Governor Campbell on July 16, and not July 17, 1917, as reported in the *Standard*. "Frank H. Little," Case #8000-15817: 21.

40. "Little's Tart Telegram," 2.

41. "Frank H. Little," Case #8000-15817: 21.

CHAPTER TWENTY-FOUR

1. "Frank H. Little," [IWW Activities], Case #8000-15817: 20–21, Investigative Reports of the Bureau of Investigation 1908–1922, Old German Files (OGF), 1909–1921, FBI Case Files, National Archives Microfilm Publication M1085, NARA, Washington, D.C. It is unknown if the mistaken identity of Frank Little was the result of a deliberate subterfuge.

2. Richard I. Gibson, interview. Dick Gibson researched architectural remains of Butte, Montana, and their inhabitants. See Richard I. Gibson, ed., "Butte Day: Field Guide for the 30th Annual Meeting, Butte, Montana, June 10–13, 2009," *Vernacular Architecture Forum*, 2009, pp. 98–154, and a living catalog of buildings in the Butte-Anaconda National Historic Landmark District at http://butte-anacondanhld.blogspot.com, which includes more of Gibson's work.

3. Butte City Directories, 1911 and 1913. *Anaconda Standard*, November 16, 1910, p. 8. Nora Byrne took her deceased husband's City Crematorium custodian job upon his death.

4. "Frank H. Little," Case #8000-15817: 25–26, 30. The Bureau of Investigation was charged with getting a verified copy of Frank Little's signature. The guest ledger page was torn out of the Steele Block ledger, so that Ms. Byrne could testify to Frank's arrival at the boarding house and his signature in the Chicago IWW trial. A search of Frank's signature in Butte financial institutions was not successful when agents searched for a connection to German financing.

5. A. W. Walliser, Testimony before U.S. District Court of Illinois, May 23, 1918, transcript available from U.S. vs. Haywood et al., 1917–1918, Legal Problems, Trials, and Defense, File12: 1380, Box 104, Subseries B, Walter P. Reuther Library, WSU. Walliser wrote a story for the next day's paper describing the speech in front of 4,000 to 5,000 spectators. Charles S. Stevens stated more like 3,000 to 4,000 people were at the ball park, mainly miners. Stevens's story appeared the morning of July 20, 1917. Charles L. Stevens, Testimony before U.S. District Court of Illinois, May 23, 1918, transcript available from U.S. vs. Haywood et al., 1917–1918, Legal Problems, Trials, and Defense, File12: 1386, Box 104, Subseries B, Walter P. Reuther Library, WSU. Anaconda Company spies also infiltrated the meeting. Informant Warren D. Bennett, a mining company employee and spy, prepared a statement for the Bureau of Investigation describing the speeches in detail, corroborating reporters' accounts. "Frank H. Little," Case #8000-15817: 5; *Hobo Agitator*, documentary.

6. "Frank H. Little," Case #8000-15817: 2.

7. Ibid., 2–3; Walliser, Testimony, 1380. There were fifty to sixty unions in Butte.

8. "Frank H. Little," Case #8000-15817: 3.

9. Ibid.

10. Ibid.

11. Walliser, Testimony, 1380–81. Walliser testified that the audience was made up of curiosity seekers and rank-and-file miners who were law-abiding citizens. Stevens, 1397–99. Stevens testified that the audience was made up of miners who were "low" citizens. He stated that Frank was not supposed to be on the meeting agenda but was a last minute entry.

12. "Butte Vigilantes Hang Little," p. 5.

13. Walliser, Testimony, 1374.

14. Frank Little made reference to the Paint Creek–Cabin Creek strike of 1912–13, in which coal operators attempted to break a miners' strike by hiring Baldwin-Felts detective agents as professional strikebreakers. In February 1913, the gunmen drove a heavily armored train through a tent colony at night, opening fire on families with machine guns.

15. Harold W. Crary, Testimony before U.S. District Court of Illinois, May 23, 1918, transcript available from U.S. vs. Haywood et al., 1917–1918, Legal Problems, Trials, and Defense, File12: 1437, Box 104, Subseries B, Walter P. Reuther Library, WSU.

16. Ibid.

17. Ibid.

18. "Frank H. Little," Case #8000-15817: 3.

19. Ibid.

20. Ibid.

21. Ibid.

22. Ibid., 4.; "Butte Vigilantes Hang Little," 5.

23. Crary, Testimony, 1435

24. Ibid.

25. "Frank H. Little," Case #8000-15817: 4. Walliser, Testimony, 1345–46.

26. Cannon, "On the Anniversary of His Death," 133.

27. Ibid.

28. "To Keep Army From France," *Anaconda Standard,* July 20, 1917, p. 7. Charles L. Stevens wrote the story per his testimony in the 1918 Chicago IWW trial.

29. Ibid.

30. "Frank H. Little," Case #8000-15817: 3. See the entire file, Investigative Reports of the Bureau of Investigation 1908–1922, OGF, 1909–1921, "Frank H. Little," Case #8000-15817, for Warren D. Bennett's reports.

31. Ibid., 31.

32. Walliser, Testimony, 1374.

33. Ibid., 1348.

34. "Substantial Wage Increase Provided by Agreement Modified Rustling Card System and Weekly Payroll," *Butte Daily Post,* July 20, 1917, p. 1.

35. "To Keep Army from France," 7.

36. Crary, Testimony, 1444; Walliser, Testimony, 1367.

37. "Frank H. Little," Case #8000-15817: 6; "IWW Soon to Claim Butte Miners' Union," *Butte Miner*, July 21, 1917, p. 1.

38. "Frank H. Little," Case #8000-15817: 7; "IWW Soon to Claim Butte," 1.

39. "Frank H. Little," Case #8000-15817: 26–29. The Bureau of Investigation could not rely on testimony produced by witnesses who were subjected to physical intimidation. Detective Morrissey beat one victim into signing his name for Company and Bureau of Investigation operatives. Calvert, "Destruction of the Butte Miners' Union," 12. Calvert states that due to Finlanders' radical political beliefs, ethnic prejudice was "whipped up in which the terms 'damn Finlander' and 'those damned dirty anarchists and socialists' were frequently used." Jere Murphy's view of those who met at Finlander Hall would be influenced also by local prejudices. "Two Finlanders in Fight with Police," *Anaconda Standard*, August 29, 1910, p. 5.

40. "Socialist Committee Decides to Take Away Maury's Job," *Anaconda Standard*, April 17, 1913, p. 1. In 1917 political appointments ceased after a new city police system was adopted.

41. "Frank H. Little," Case #8000-15817: 29.

42. Ibid., 6. Johanson was a young Swedish millworker and IWW.

43. "IWW Soon to Claim Butte," 1.

44. Ragnar Johanson, Testimony before U.S. District Court of Illinois, August 3, 1918, transcript available from U.S. vs. Haywood et al., 1917–1918, Legal Problems, Trials, and Defense, File 4: 10093, Box 115, Subseries B, Walter P. Reuther Library, WSU.

45. "Frank H. Little," Case #8000-15817: 8.

46. Ibid.

47. Ibid., 8–9; "Not to Accept Agreement, Vote of Electricians," *Anaconda Standard*, July 21, 1917, p. 7.

48. "Frank H. Little," Case #8000-15817: 9; "Not to Accept Agreement," 7.

49. Ibid. "Treasonable Talk of Little in Butte May be Cause of Hanging," *Butte Daily Post*, August 1, 1917, p. 14.

50. "Frank H. Little," Case #8000-15817: 9; "Not to Accept Agreement," 7.

51. Ibid.

52. Johanson, Testimony, 100102.

53. Ibid., 10098.

54. Cannon, "On the Anniversary of His Death," 133. Ralph Chaplin states the letter was dated July 31, 1917. Chaplin, *Wobbly*, 210.

55. "Frank H. Little," Case #8000-15817: 10.

56. Tompkins, *Truth about Butte*, 6.

57. Ibid., 36.

58. Walliser, Testimony, 1369.

59. Ibid.

60. Johanson, Testimony, 10096–10097.

61. "Agitators Against Everything," *Anaconda Standard*, July 23, 1917, p. 8.

62. "Picketing Discussed by Campbell Union," *Anaconda Standard*, July 24, 1917, p. 7.

63. F. H. Little, "Butte Miners Still Firm," *Solidarity*, August 4, 1917, p. 1.

64. Ibid.

65. Ibid.

66. "Engineers to Decide Today," *Anaconda Standard*, July 27, 1917, p. 7.

67. Waldemar Kaiyala, "My Memories in Butte, Montana," Date Unknown, File 11, Box 1 (LH021), Silver Bow Archives (SBA).

68. "Engineers to Decide Today," 7.

69. William Haywood to F. H. Little, July 27, 1917, Bisbee Deportation Legal Papers and Exhibits, Special Collections, AZ 114, Box 1, Folder 1, Exhibit 50, UA.

70. Ibid.

71. Chaplin, *Wobbly*, 206, 209. Besides being disturbed at the General Executive Board's action regarding an IWW antiwar statement, Frank Little "dissented violently" when Haywood changed his mind about publishing the *Deadly Parallel*, which also took an antiwar position. The *Deadly Parallel* had initially been Haywood's idea in contrasting the militant antiwar position of the IWW with the pro-war position of the AFL.

72. Cannon, "On the Anniversary of His Death," 132.

73. Chaplin, *Wobbly*, 196.

74. Cannon, *Notebook of an Agitator*, 61.

75. "Lynching of Little Denounced in Butte," *Anaconda Standard*, August 2, 1917, p. 2.

76. Ibid.

77. Ibid.

78. "Electricians in New Move," *Anaconda Standard*, July 30, 1917, p. 7.

79. Ibid.

80. Ibid.

81. Reid Robinson, "Town without History," 1936, File AWR014, SBA.

82. "Haywood Directs Threat to President, Declaring He May Call on IWWs," *Butte Daily Post*, July 31, 1917, p. 1.

83. "Evidence Seized by Government to Indict IWW Leaders," *Tucson Daily Citizen*, September 6, 1917, p. 1.

84. Chaplin, *Wobbly*, 210.

85. "Burton K. Wheeler," Case #15029: 1–2. Investigative Reports of the Bureau of Investigation 1908–1922, Miscellaneous Files, 1909–1921, FBI Case Files, National Archives Microfilm Publication M1085, NARA, Washington, D.C. See also *Hobo Agitator*, documentary.

86. "Little Inquest Is Begun Before Coroner Lane and a Jury of Seven Miners," *Butte Daily Post*, August 3, 1917, p. 12.

87. *Hobo Agitator*, documentary; Will Roscoe, "Unsolved Murder," *Montana Standard*, October 7, 2006, p. 1. Roscoe heard the story as a youngster in Helena, Montana. While many authors have repeated the notion that Conn Lowney was the barber who warned Frank Little of a murder plot, other barbers have been named. Nelson Algren, "Come In If You Love Money," *The Last Carousel* (New York: Seven Stories Press), 1997, p. 88. Algren states in his essay that he met an old miner who had turned barber in 1964 named Cornelius (Conn) Lowney. Lowney was ninety-one years old but had a clear but bitter memory of the 1917 summer events in Butte, Montana. He claimed to have warned Frank Little of a murder plot after a public meeting at the ballpark on July 31, 1917. Lowney stated that Frank surely had other warnings. After the meeting, Frank had gone back to his room.

88. C. L. Lambert, "Frank Little—Rebel," *Solidarity*, August 11, 1917, p. 3. Lambert, an IWW GEB member, wrote that Frank wanted to get back to Arizona where the miners were striking in sympathy with the Butte miners after their meeting in Chicago.

CHAPTER TWENTY-FIVE

1. "Butte's Name Tarnished by the Stain of Lynch Law, Frank Little Hanged from Trestle by Unknown Mob," *Anaconda Standard*, August 2, 1917, p. 1; "Not One Clew as to Lynchers," *Anaconda Standard*, August 4, 1917, p. 2.

2. "Little Inquest Is Begun Before Coroner Lane and a Jury of Seven Miners," *Butte Daily Post*, August 3, 1917, p. 12.

3. Ibid.; "Butte's Name Tarnished," 1; "Frank H. Little," Case #8000-15817: 24, Investigative Reports of the Bureau of Investigation 1908–1922, Old German Files (OGF), 1909–1921, FBI Case Files, National Archives Microfilm Publication M1085, NARA, Washington, D.C.

4. "Frank H. Little," Case #8000-15817: 24.

5. "Butte's Name Tarnished," 1; "Victim of Vigilantes Made Seditious Speeches Openly since His Arrival in Butte," *Butte Daily Post*, August 1, 1917, p. 1.

6. "Henry Little," Case #8000-391088: 1, Investigative Reports of the Bureau of Investigation 1908–1922, OGF, 1909–1921, FBI Case Files,

National Archives Microfilm Publication M1085, Roll 849, NARA, Washington, D.C.; *Seattle Times*, August 1, 1917, p. 3. The paper reported Henry Little, who had been arrested on July 19, 1917, as a ringleader of the lumber strike.

7. "Frank H. Little," Case #8000-15817: 21.

8. "Butte's Name Tarnished," 1.

9. Chaplin, *Wobbly*, 210.

10. "Police Subscribe to Liberty Bonds," *Anaconda Standard*, October 17, 1917, p. 3.

11. Richard I. Gibson, interview. Gibson stated that it is conceivable that Jere Murphy had at least prior knowledge of the murder plot although he may not have been directly involved. Butte police generally did what the Anaconda Copper Mining Company wanted.

12. "Little Executed by Masked Men," *Butte Daily Post*, August 1, 1917, p. 3; "Not One Clew as to Lynchers," 2.

13. "Little Inquest Is Begun," 12; "Not One Clew as to Lynchers," 2.

14. Ibid.; Patrolman W. H. Ingraham testified to the physical details of the crime scene at the coroner's inquest on August 2, 1917.

15. "Butte's Name Tarnished," 1. Some sources contend that the rope was tied to the back of the car used to hoist the body. *Hobo Agitator*, documentary.

16. "Treasonable Talk of Little in Butte May be Cause of Hanging," *Butte Daily Post*, August 1, 1917, p. 14.

17. Dunne, "August 1917," 142. This author is the same William Francis Dunn, editor of the *Butte Strike Bulletin*. Dunne asserts that Anaconda Copper Mining Company alerted various news organizations of the murder plot before it happened.

18. Michael Punke, "Extraordinary Session of 1918," L1985.369, AWP021, Silver Bow Archives (SBA).

19. "Little Executed by Masked Men," 3.

20. "Lynching of Little Denounced by Butte," *Anaconda Standard*, August 2, 1917, p. 2.

21. Dunne, "August 1917," 123.

22. Burton K. Wheeler [Montana district attorney], telegram to Thomas W. Gregory [U.S. attorney general], August 1, 1917, Case #186701-54, Investigative Reports of the Bureau of Investigation 1908–1922, Bureau Section Files (BSF), 1909–1921, FBI Case Files, National Archives Microfilm Publication M1085, Roll 917, NARA, Washington, D.C. Immediately, the Justice Department sent back a telegram ordering officials in Butte to ascertain whether persons in the U.S. military took part in hanging Little. See Thomas W. Gregory [U.S. attorney general], Telegram to Burton K. Wheeler [Montana district attorney], August 1, 1917, Case #186701-54, Investigative Reports of the Bureau of Investigation 1908–1922, BSF,

1909–1921, FBI Case Files, National Archives Microfilm Publication M1085, Roll 917, NARA, Washington, D.C.

23. "Butte Vigilantes Hang Little," p. 1.

24. *Butte Daily Post*, August 1, 1917, p. 3.

25. Algren, "Come In," 88.

26. William F. Dunn, Testimony before Montana Council of Defense at Montana State Capitol, June 5–6, 1918, transcript available from Files 2 and 3, Box 6, Montana Council of Defense Records, Montana Historical Society Library, Helena, MT.

27. "Butte Vigilantes Hang Little," 1.

28. Roy Talbert Jr., *Negative Intelligence, the Army and the American Left, 1917–1941* (Jackson: University Press of Mississippi, 1991), 99. Talbert writes that several of William Dunn's colleagues at the *Butte Daily Bulletin* received similar warnings. F. W. Kelly to W. J. Flynn, Director of Bureau of Investigation, January 14, 1921; Case #186701-54-11: 1, Investigative Reports of the Bureau of Investigation 1908–1922, OGF, 1909–1921, FBI Case Files, National Archives Microfilm Publication M1085, Roll 536, NARA, Washington, D.C. Kelly states in his letter to Bureau of Investigation Director W. J. Flynn that the warning was taken from the Montana Vigilantes of the early sixties, 3-7-77 being the dimensions of a grave. For a study of various interpretations of the Montana Vigilante Code and its origin, see Frederick Allen, *A Decent Orderly Lynching: The Montana Vigilantes*, 2nd ed. (Norman: University of Oklahoma Press, 2009), 356–60. Allen states that the code's origin was to warn vagrants to purchase a three-dollar train ticket on a 7 A.M. stagecoach, as ordered by a secret committee of seventy-seven men in Helena, Montana.

29. "Little Executed by Masked Men," 3. There is some confusion as to which Dunn the "D" represented. R. L. Dunn was the business agent for the Butte Electrical Workers' Union. He had been chairman of the recent strike committee of the electrical workers. William F. Dunn, also an electrician, put out the *Butte Daily Bulletin*, a thorn in the ACM's side.

30. Dunne, "August 1917," 124.

31. "IWW Strike Chief Lynched at Butte," *New York Times*, August 2, 1917, p. 1; "Victim of Vigilantes Made Seditious Speeches Openly," 1.

32. "Lynching of Little Denounced by Butte," 2.

33. "Butte's Name Tarnished," 1.

34. Ibid.; "Lynching Mob Still at Large," *Anaconda Standard*, August 3, 1917, p. 1.

35. Dunne, "August 1917," 124.

36. George Wesley Davis, *Sketches of Butte* (Boston: Cornhill, 1921), 136, Folder L1985.551, File AW D003.001, SBA.

37. Jensen, *Heritage of Conflict*, 437.

38. William D. Haywood, *Bill Haywood's Book: Autobiography of Big Bill Haywood* (New York: International Publishers, 1929), 301. The

newspaper reported that Coroner Lane's investigation determined that Frank Little was not dragged by a rope behind a car although his kneecaps indicated otherwise. "Lynching Mob Still at Large," 1.

39. McGuckin, *Memoirs of a Wobbly*, 85.

40. Waldemar Kaiyala, "My Memories in Butte, Montana," date unknown, File 11, Box 1 (LH021), SBA.

41. "Various," Case #36190: 190, Roll 383; "Not One Clew as to Lynchers," 2, 4; Tompkins, *Truth about Butte*, 42. Tompkins, an IWW in Butte in 1917, writes that Frank's skull had been cracked and that bits of flesh were found under his fingernails, indicative of a great struggle for life.

42. "Little Inquest Is Begun," 1.

43. "Sullivan Refuses to Give Evidence," *Anaconda Standard*, August 7, 1917, p. 12.

44. "Little Inquest Is Begun," 12. Testimony concluded that Frank Little had not been dragged down Butte streets, as if to lessen the horrific actions. In addition, testimony claimed that sand embedded in his bloody knees was evident of a struggle at the site of the hanging. More likely the sand was from his unconscious body being dropped to the ground at some point. Frank Little Death Certificate, August 1, 1917. Frank Little Coroner's Verdict, August 7, 1917, Butte, Silver Bow County, Montana. All documents relating to the coroner's inquest and its three-day investigation mysteriously disappeared. "Little Executed by Masked Men," 3.

45. "Butte Vigilantes Hang Little," 5.

46. "Frank H. Little," Case #8000-15817: 16. A Thiel detective, reporting this information, possibly erred in naming Frank's siblings, and not Haywood.

47. Carolyn Leverich Atkinson, e-mail to author, May 15, 2010. Carolyn is Bessie Little Courtright's great-granddaughter.

48. "Frank Little Has Not Died in Vain," *Solidarity*, August 11, 1917, p. 2.

49. "Frank Little's Funeral," *Solidarity*, August 18, 1917, p. 1.

50. "Editorials," *Tulsa World*, August 13, 1917, p. 4. No poetic will has surfaced for Frank H. Little as far as this author has found.

51. Ibid.; "Funeral Details Left to Brother in South," *Butte Daily Post*, August 3, 1917, p. 12.

52. "Will Bury Little in Butte Cemetery," *Anaconda Standard*, August 4, 1917, p. 7; "Little Inquest Is Begun before Coroner Lane," 1.

53. "Little's Body Will Be Sent to Yale, Oklahoma," *Tulsa World*, August 4, 1917, p. 1; "Little May Be Buried at Yale," *Drumright Derrick*, August 4, 1917, p. 4.

54. "What They Think of It," *Solidarity*, August 11, 1917, p. 1.

55. "Frank H. Little," Case #8000-15817: p. 12.

56. "Undertakers," *Anaconda Standard*, August 5, 1917, p. 14.

57. "What They Think of It," 1; "Little Kept Some Ashes of Late Frank Hillstrom," *Anaconda Standard*, August 2, 1917, p. 7. Purportedly while examining Frank's personal effects, Public Administrator Harrington found an envelope containing ashes from the body of Joe Hill. Agent E. W. Byrn does not make mention of these ashes in his report to Chicago Bureau of Investigation offices although Emma Little later refers to the ashes. "Organizer for IWW Hung from a Trestle by Masked Murderers," *New York Call*, August 2, 1917, p. 1.

58. "Silent Protest to IWW Slaying to Be Made," *Salt Lake Telegram*, August 3, 1917, p. 6.

59. In comparison, approximately 3,500 people attended legendary daredevil Evel Knievel's funeral on December 10, 2007, in Butte.

60. "Large Funeral No Disorder," *Anaconda Standard*, August 6, 1917, p. 5.

61. "Editorial Correspondence, Butte—Aug. 9," *Engineering and Mining Journal* 104, no. 7, August 18, 1917, p. 321; "Large Funeral No Disorder," 5; *The Hobo Agitator*, documentary; Kornbluh, *Rebel Voices*, 296.

62. "Editorial Correspondence, Butte—Aug. 9," 321; "Large Funeral No Disorder," 5.

63. "Large Funeral No Disorder," 5.

64. "Little's Body Buried and Butte is Quiet," *El Paso Herald*, August 6, 1917, p. 2.

65. Ibid.

66. "Large Funeral No Disorder," 5.

67. *The Hobo Agitator*, documentary; "Large Funeral No Disorder," 5.

68. "Large Funeral No Disorder," 5.

69. "Heavy Guard on Duty of Funeral of Frank Little," *Lexington Herald*, August 6, 1917, p. 2.

70. Harold W. Crary, Testimony before U.S. District Court of Illinois, May 23, 1918, transcript available from U.S. vs. Haywood et al., 1917–1918, Legal Problems, Trials, and Defense, File 12: 1419, 1421, Box 104, Subseries B, Walter P. Reuther Library, WSU. Butte Mayor Malone ordered that the American flag be displayed at all public meetings held in Butte. Malone declared that the ruling applied to Frank Little's funeral procession as well.

71. "Large Funeral No Disorder," 5.

72. Haywood, *Bill Haywood's Book*, 302. Haywood claims that a photographer named George Dawson took the motion picture from IWW headquarters. Haywood further claimed that Dawson was subsequently found to be a federal agent.

73. "Butte Situation Unchanged," *Solidarity*, August 18, 1917, p. 3.

74. Dunne, "August 1917," 124.

75. "I.W.W. Official Denies Part in Lynching Little," *El Paso Herald*, August 27, 1917, p. 1.

76. "Butte Police Lack Clews to Lynchers," *Idaho Statesman*, August 3, 1917, p. 1. See Governor Sam Stewart, Telegrams and Telephone Calls Record, "Frank Little," VF0528, SBA, regarding Frank's murder.

77. Clemens P. Work, *Darkest Before Dawn* (Albuquerque, NM: University of New Mexico Press, 2005), 96.

78. "Editorial Correspondence—Butte, Aug. 7," *Engineering and Mining Journal* 104, no. 6 (August 11, 1917), 277.

79. Crary, Testimony, 1444; "IWW Strike Chief Lynched at Butte," *New York Times*, August 1, 1917; "No Evidence Put before Authorities Today as to Men Who Lynched Little," *Butte Daily Post*, August 2, 1917, p. 1.

80. "No Evidence Put before Authorities," 1.

81. "Butte on Hunt for Lynchers," *Morning Olympian*, August 3, 1917, p. 3.

82. Dunn, Testimony, 7246; *Butte City Directory*, 1917.

83. Dunn, Testimony, 7243; Calvert, *The Gibraltar*, 110.

84. Calvert, *The Gibraltar*, 109–10; Burton K. Wheeler, *Yankee from the West* (New York: Octagon Books, 1977), 183–84; Algren, "Come In," 88.

85. "Butte Offers Big Reward," *New York Times*, August 3, 1917.

86. Morrissey, a well-known Anaconda Operations detective and a watchman on the Company's payroll at the same time as his city employment, has a historic-newspaper-rap-sheet record filled with years of brutality accusations and dropped charges. Gibson stated that the general belief in Butte was that Detective Ed Morrissey was involved in Frank's murder. Gibson, interview by the author. Butte police finally fired Morrissey in an attempt to clean up its image three years after Frank Little's death and his wife's uncertain death. "Brain Injury is Cause of Death Autopsy Shows That Ed Morrissey Probably had Sustained Blow on Head," *Anaconda Standard*, February 5, 1922, p. 2.

87. Will Roscoe, "Unsolved Mystery, Writer Delves into Controversial 1917 Death of Union Leader," *Montana Standard*, October 8, 2006, C1; "Frank Little," VF0528, SBA.

88. Lillian Hellman, *Scoundrel Time* (New York: Little, Brown, 1976), 47. Some doubt Hammett's claim to have been offered money to kill Frank Little. He worked for the Pinkerton Detective Agency from 1915 to 1922, and using his knowledge of the inner workings of the agency and Butte labor troubles, he created plots and characters for his detective novels. See *Shadow Man, The Life of Dashiell Hammett* by Richard Layman for a thorough biography of Hammett.

89. "Editorials," *Tulsa World*, August 13, 1917, p. 4.

90. In a deathbed confession, a person close to the Little family revealed that his/her relative, who had lived in Anaconda, Montana, had participated in the murder. The individual has never been discussed publicly.

91. "Burton K. Wheeler," Case #15029: 1, Investigative Reports of the Bureau of Investigation 1908–1922, Miscellaneous Files, 1909–1921, FBI Case Files, National Archives Microfilm Publication M1085 NARA, Washington, D.C. Agent E. W. Byrn reported on March 3, 1918, that the Montana State Legislature in special session narrowly missed passing a resolution to remove Wheeler from office (29 in favor to 30 against), stating that Wheeler had been importuned time and again to take action against Frank Little, but that Mr. Wheeler refused to do so with the threat of mob action. Montana newspapers also condemned Wheeler, aiding in the firestorm after Frank's death. See Agent E. W. Byrn's report on August 6, 1917, "Frank H. Little," Case #15817: 17. See also Wheeler's autobiography *Yankee from the West*, 1977, for his version of the event.

92. Dunne, "August 1917," 141.

93. Punke, "Extraordinary Session of 1918."

94. "Various," Case #67: 77, Roll 916. Bill Haywood is credited for this statement about Frank's death.

Chapter Twenty-Six

1. "Various." Case #8000-78852: 2. Emma told Agent Hudson that she worked under the direction of Mr. Drew, "one employer at least who treated her well."

2. Ibid.; "IWW Matter," Case #363668: 170, Investigative Reports of the Bureau of Investigation 1908–1922, OGF, 1909–1921, FBI Case Files, National Archives Microfilm Publication M1085, Roll 799, NARA, Washington, D.C.

3. William D. Haywood, Testimony before U.S. District Court of Illinois, August 12, 1918, transcript available from U.S. vs. Haywood et al., 1917–1918, Legal Problems, Trials, and Defense, File 3: 11291, 11286–87, 11385, Box 117, Subseries B, Walter P. Reuther Library, WSU.

4. James Elliott, Testimony before U.S. District Court of Illinois, August 3, 1918, transcript available from U.S. vs. Haywood et al., 1917–1918, Legal Problems, Trials, and Defense, File 4: 9981, Box 115, Subseries B, Walter P. Reuther Library, WSU.

5. "Various," Case #67: 273, Roll 916.

6. "Various," Case #8000-144363: 7–8, Roll 536.

7. "Sabotage Plan is Related at Trial," *San Diego Evening Tribune*, November 21, 1919, p. 5.

8. "Nineteen IWWs Taken in Raid of Fresno Local," *Fresno Morning Republican*, September 6, 1917, p. 2.

9. "Various," Case #67: 46, 96–97.

10. Ibid., 45.

11. Ibid., 40.

12. See "Various," Case #67: 1–100, for a complete inventory of items seized in the Fresno raid of September 5, 1917.

13. James Elliott, Testimony, 9977.

14. "Nineteen IWWs Taken in Raid," 1.

15. James Elliott, Testimony, 9986. "News from Agricultural Workers Industrial Union No. 400," *Solidarity,* September 29, 1917, p. 3.

16. "Nineteen IWWs Taken in Raid," 1.

17. "IWW Matter," Case #363668: 169.

18. "Nineteen IWWs Taken in Raid," 1.

19. Ibid.

20. Ibid.

21. Emma B. Little to President Woodrow Wilson, February 7, 1918, p. 6.

22. "IWW Matter," Case #363668: 169. Mortimer Downing, "Story of Fresno Arrests," *Solidarity,* October 13, 1917, p. 1.

23. "News from Agricultural Workers," 3.

24. "IWW Matter," Case #363668: 170; James Elliott, Testimony, 9978.

25. "IWW Matter," Case #363668, 170; James Elliott, Testimony, 9978.

26. James Elliott, Testimony, 9978.

27. "IWW Matter," Case #363668: 169.

28. "Various," Case #8000-78852: 2.

29. Emma B. Little to President Woodrow Wilson, 2.

30. "Various," Case #8000-78852: 1. Agent William Freeman also reported that Emma wrote an article against the use of lye when canning peaches since she said the lye was injurious to the peelers, fruit, and consumer. This had been called to the attention of the health department, but nothing had been done.

31. Ibid.

32. Ibid., 2.

33. "IWW Activities," Case #8000-71322: 33, Investigative Reports of the Bureau of Investigation 1908–1922, OGF, 1909–1921, FBI Case Files, National Archives Microfilm Publication M1085, Roll 536, NARA, Washington, D.C.

34. "Various," Case #67: 247. A. Bruce Bielaski joined the Justice Department in 1904, and worked his way through the department to become the second chief of the Bureau of Investigation in 1912. Under his direction, the department grew, and in 1919, just before the department was transformed into the Federal Bureau of Investigation under J. Edgar Hoover, Bielaski left to enter private law practice.

35. National Civil Liberties Bureau, *War-Time Prosecutions and Mob Violence, Involving the Rights of Free Speech, Free Press, and Peaceful*

Assemblage, 1919, reprint, Amsterdam: Fredonia Books, 2004. The book includes an annotated list of prosecutions under war statutes and cases of mob violence due to World War I.

36. "Reward for Pro-Germans," *Yale Record,* September 27, 1917, p. 5.

37. "IWW Members Flogged, Tarred, and Feathered," *Tulsa World,* November 10, 1917, p. 1.

38. "Various," Case #67: 288; *The Truth about the IWW Prisoners* (New York: American Civil Liberties Bureau, 1922), 22.

39. Emma B. Little to President Woodrow Wilson, 6.

40. "Anarchist Activities," Case #8000-357986: 25, Investigative Reports of the Bureau of Investigation 1908–1922, OGF, 1909–1921, FBI Case Files, National Archives Microfilm Publication M1085, Roll 791, NARA, Washington, D.C. See "Various," Case #36190: 227–30, for a September 1917 receipt list as example.

41. "Various," Case #67: 100. Emma is listed as *boarding* at 742 California Street where Fred lives, the only time where she is listed along with her husband at the same residence. The entry seems to indicate that their marriage had dissolved by this time. *Polk-Husted Directory Co.'s Fresno City and Fresno County Directory,* 1917.

42. "Various," Case #67: 100.

43. Emma B. Little to President Woodrow Wilson, 2. Emma's letter details events regarding two of the raids at her home. It is rich with the details of Fred's arrest, what items she had in the house, her neighbors' involvement, and particularly Deputy U.S. Marshal Sidney Shannon's demeanor.

44. "Various," Case #8000-78852: 3.

45. Emma B. Little to President Woodrow Wilson, 3–4.

46. Ibid.

47. Ibid.

48. Ibid.

49. Ibid.

50. "Various," Case #67: 101.

51. "Various," Case #8000-78852: 4.

52. "E. L. Laroche," Case #8000-275528: 35, Investigative Reports of the Bureau of Investigation 1908–1922, OGF, 1909–1921, FBI Case Files, National Archives Microfilm Publication M1085, Roll 690, NARA, Washington, D.C.

53. "I.W.W. Leaders Arrested in Several Cities," *Fresno Morning Republican,* November 17, 1917, p. 1.

54. "Fred Little Arrested," *Colorado Gazette Telegraph,* November 14, 1917, p. 4. The story was repeated throughout national newspapers.

55. "Fred Little and Mortimer Downing Held to Grand Jury. Now 17 Held," *Fresno Morning Republican,* November 16, 1917, p. 18.

56. "Charge Sedition!" *Pueblo Chieftain*, November 21, 1917, p. 3.

57. *The Truth about the IWW Prisoners*, 19, 25.

58. Victoria Little Burris to Carolyn Leverich Atkinson, undated.

59. Emma B. Little to President Woodrow Wilson, 2.

60. Haywood, Testimony, 11384.

61. Emma B. Little to President Woodrow Wilson, 5.

62. Ibid., 4.

63. Ibid., 6.

64. Ibid., 5.

65. Ibid.

66. Ibid.

67. Ibid., 6.

68. Ibid.

Chapter Twenty-Seven

1. "IWW Matter," Case #73294: 36–38. John Dymond went by Jack.

2. "Various," Case #67: 93, Roll 916.

3. "Various," Case #67: 210.

4. Ibid.; "IWW Activities," Case #67-7: 614, Investigative Reports of the Bureau of Investigation 1908–1922, OGF, 1909–1921, FBI Case Files, National Archives Microfilm Publication M1085, NARA, Washington, D.C. The red brick building holding Local 66's IWW office is today a bank parking lot (2013).

5. "Various," Case #8000-144363: 8, Roll 536.

6. "IWW Meeting," Case #171646: 2, Investigative Reports of the Bureau of Investigation, 1908–1922, BSF, 1909–1921, FBI Case Files, National Archives Microfilm Publication M1085, Roll 922, NARA, Washington, D.C.

7. Ibid.

8. "Various," Case #8000-78852: 14–15. The suitcase was shipped to W. F. Little from T. J. Harrington, Public Administration in Seattle, Washington, via Wells Fargo.

9. "Backbone of Draft Rebellion Believed Broken," *Tulsa World*, August 5, 1917, p. 1; *The Truth about the IWW Prisoners* (New York: American Civil Liberties Bureau, 1922), 21; Sellars, "Treasonous Tenant Farmers," 1118–19. The Working Class Union was formed to embrace mostly tenant farmers who did not qualify for membership in the IWW. Founded in Louisiana, the organization determined to support all working men and women in their struggle against capitalism, using violence when necessary. The secret organization publicly was called "the Jones Family." "Death for Agitators." *Mangum Mirror*, August 10, 1917, p. 2; "Resister

Shot Down When He Refuses to Surrender to Konawa and Shawnee Possee," *Shawnee Daily News-Herald*, August 5, 1917, p. 1.

10. "Various," Case #8000-78852: 8, 29.

11. Ibid., 7.

12. "Various Files," Case #67: 143.

13. "Various," Case #8000-78852: 17.

14. Ibid., 11–12.

15. "Nation-wide IWW Arrests Continuing," *Tucson Daily Citizen*, September 29, 1917, p. 7.

16. "IWW Activities," Case #67-7: 614.

17. *The Truth about the IWW Prisoners*, 26.

18. "The Silent Defense" (Chicago: Industrial Workers of the World, n.d.), 5.

19. Harvey Duff, *The Silent Defenders, Courts and Capitalism in California* (Chicago: Industrial Workers of the World, 1920), 26.

20. "Sabotage Plan is Related at Trial," *San Diego Evening Tribune*, November 21, 1919, p. 5.

21. "Various," Case #8000-78852: 21–22.

22. Duff, *Silent Defenders*, 22.

23. Ibid.

24. "Various," Case #8000-78852, 18.

25. See Chaplin, *Wobbly*, for memoirs of the 1918 IWW trial in Chicago.

26. "IWW Found Guilty on First Ballot," *Rockford Daily Register Gazette*, August 19, 1918, p. 2. For Bill Haywood's account of the 1918 IWW trial, see *Bill Haywood's Book: Autobiography of Big Bill Haywood* (New York: International Publishers, 1929), 313–24.

27. Victoria Little Burris to Carolyn Leverich Atkinson, undated. Victoria recalled being in first or second grade when they left her father. See also Emma B. Little vs. W. F. Little, Petition for Divorce, No. 24697, January 24, 1920, Superior Court, Fresno, California, 1.

28. Walter Raleigh Little (II), World War I Draft Registration Card, September 12, 1918, California, Fresno, Roll 1530714, Draft Board 1. Fred and Emma's son Walter Raleigh Little (II) was working as an ironworker when he registered for the draft. For some reason, Walter R. Little cites Fred as the next living relative living at 209 Harvey Avenue in Fresno. Perhaps Emma would not have endorsed his registration.

29. "Various," Case #224877: 294, Roll 636.

30. Ibid.

31. Ibid., 295; "Who Is Who in California," *Defense Bulletin of the Seattle District*, no. 32 (Seattle: Industrial Workers of the World, October 14, 1918): 4.

32. "Various," Case #224877: 298. The charges were also dropped against Wilford Dennis and W. C. Kelly.

33. Zechariah Chafee Jr., "California Justice," *New Republic* 36 (September 19, 1923): 99. Grand Jury, Indictment of IWW Members, April 8, 1918, U.S. District of California, Northern Division of California, Northern District, First Division, Series 5, Legal Problems, Trials, and Defense Cases, File 7, Box 125 Subseries B, Walter P. Reuther Library, WSU; "Application for Passport," Case #8000-355539: 4, Investigative Reports of the Bureau of Investigation 1908–1922, OGF, 1909–1921, FBI Case Files, National Archives Microfilm Publication M1085, NARA, Washington, D.C.

34. "IWW Activities," Case #8000-71322: 18, Investigative Reports of the Bureau of Investigation 1908–1922, OGF, 1909–1921, FBI Case Files, National Archives Microfilm Publication M1085, NARA, Washington, D.C.

35. Chafee, "California Justice," 99; "Application for Passport," Case #8000-355539: 4.

36. Duff, *Silent Defenders*, 35; "Various," Case #224877: 298.

37. *The Truth about the IWW Prisoners*, 27.

38. "Marshal Shows Relics Taken in Raid of IWW," *Tucson Daily Citizen*, December 13, 1918, p. 1.

39. Duff, *Silent Defenders*, 33.

40. Ibid., 47.

41. Ibid., 29.

42. Theodora Pollok, A. L. Fox, and Basil Saffores, who were out on bail, dissented and employed attorneys.

43. William D. Haywood, *Bill Haywood's Book: Autobiography of Big Bill Haywood* (New York: International Publishers, 1929), 311.

44. "Find 46 IWWs Guilty of Plot," *New York Times*, January 19, 1919, p. 1.

45. See "Final Scene in the Courtroom" in "Application for Passport," Case #8000-355539: 1.

46. Ibid.; Duff, *Silent Defenders*, 38.

47. Chafee, "California Justice," 99. See "Application for Passport," Case #8000-355539: 4.

48. Ibid. See Duff for a complete description of the prisoners and their punishments.

49. "IWW Matter," Case #334127: 44, Roll 757.

50. "Various," Case #311343: 460, Roll 731. See Chaplin for his memoirs of incarceration in Cook County Jail and Leavenworth Prison.

51. H. Stredwick to Charles Hutchinson, April 20, 1919, in "Various," Case #345429: 78, Roll 774.

52. "Various," Case #311343: 471. Federal agent F. W. Kelly was of the opinion that the letter was faked by the federal authorities interested in new IWW investigations in Fresno.

53. "IWW Activities," Case #73294: 1–40. By January 5, 1920, the IWW strategy to discredit John Dymond obviously worked, although too late

for the Kansas indictments. When interviewed, Deputy Marshal Sid Shannon of Fresno and Agent F. W. Kelley of the Bureau's San Francisco office seemed to think that Mr. Dymond had been of considerable use to the government in former IWW investigations. They said that Dymond would probably say the first thing that came into his head in answer to any interrogation, but on the stand would tell the truth.

54. Emma B. Little to C. F. Bentley, in "IWW Matter," Case #334127: 45.

55. Ibid.

56. Emma B. Little to Vincent St. John, May 15, 1918, in "Various," Case #8000-78852: 11–12.

57. Emma B. Little vs. W. F. Little Petition for Divorce.

58. Superior Court Summons, January 26, 1920, No. 24197, Fresno, CA. Fred was renting a room in a two-story red brick building at 749 Van Ness Avenue.

59. "Various," Case #8000-78852: 43–44.

60. Ibid., 47.

61. Ibid.

62. "IWW Activities," Case #8000-71322: 2.

63. Ibid., 4.

64. Emma B. Little vs. W. F. Little Petition for Divorce.

65. Emma B. Little, "Bring Out the Whitewash," *Solidarity*, August 11, 1917. Agent William Freeman reported this satirical verse to authorities in September 1917. See "Various," Case #8000-78852: 1.

EPILOGUE

1. The author is not referring to the demographic group born between 1925 and 1945 called the Silent Generation, but to the children whose family members were persecuted as traitors before and during World War I. The author encountered descendants of several participants in Arizona's 1917 labor unrest who were willing to provide information, but only "off the record."

2. Wheeler, *Yankee from the West*, 142.

3. Ibid., 153.

4. *The Truth about the IWW Prisoners*, American Civil Liberties Bureau (New York, 1922), 1.

5. Data provided by the Bisbee Mining and Historical Museum.

6. Harry E. Wootton took the place of Sheriff Harry Wheeler as an indicted representative for an en masse trial. See James Byrkit, *Forging the Copper Collar* (Tucson: University of Arizona, 1982), 287–94.

7. "The Pardons," *The Montana Sedition Project*, Professor Clemens P. Work, Project Director, University of Montana School of Journalism, http://www.seditionproject.net/pardons.html (accessed March 20,

2012). Dr. Clemons authored a study of the early free speech restrictions and consequent arrests, inspiring the project. See *Darkest Before Dawn, Sedition and Free Speech in the American West* (Albuquerque: University of New Mexico Press, 2005).

8. Almira Little Obituary, *Stillwater Gazette,* June 15, 1917, p. 4.

9. Jack Allen Little, e-mail to author, July 2, 2010.

10. Barbara Clapper Lewis to Dolores Little Adams, November 16, 1992.

11. Barbara Clapper Lewis to Carolyn Leverich Atkinson, 1995, Courtright Family Papers.

12. Jack Allen Little, interview; Thaylia Little Farris to author, January 23, 1985.

13. Alonzo C. Little, Death Certificate Register No 1132, State Department of Health, State of Oklahoma.

14. "Pritchett Rites Are Held Saturday," Obituary, June 1960, Little Family Papers.

15. Victoria Little Burris to Carolyn Leverich Atkinson, undated.

16. Ibid.

17. W. F. Little, Case #27402, California State Hospital.

18. Ibid.

19. W. F. Little, California Death Index, State File #24-15665: 6376. The onset of psychiatric symptoms of general paresis can be insidious, first noticed by family and friends rather than the patient. These include loss of ambition at work, memory lapses, irritability, unusual giddiness, apathy, withdrawal, and a decline in attention to personal affairs. Fred may have begun showing these symptoms as early as five years before his death. To most, he appeared to have a drinking problem.

20. Victoria Little Burris to Carolyn Leverich Atkinson, May 5, 1995. Victoria Little Burris Letters.

21. W. F. Little Death Certificate, Stockton, California, County of San Joaquin. Facts on the death certificate, based on Fred's vague and confusing interview with the hospital staff, are erroneous. Fred is buried in Stockton Rural Cemetery, block 7A, grave 313, Stockton, California. John Surby to Stockton State Hospital, dated May 10, 1923, Little Family papers. John Surby was the secretary of the International Hod Carriers, Building, and Common Laborers Union of America, Local 294. In the letter, he requests that the union be informed as to Fred Little's condition, and states that Fred has a death benefit from the union. Apparently no family member claimed Fred's body or provided accurate information. The Hod Carriers' Union took care of final arrangements. Ultimately, the union paid for burial expenses but not a tombstone.

22. 1930 U.S. Federal Census, Fresno, Fresno County, CA, Roll 116, FHL microfilm 2339851, p. 3A, Enumeration District 0014, Image 6. The earliest census record to show Emma working at her lunch stand is 1930.

"Organizer for IWW Hung from a Trestle by Masked Murderers," *New York Call*, August 2, 1917. The article, published the day after Frank's murder, states, "Frank was the support of his mother and his sister-in-law."

23. Emma B. Little Death Certificate #5550-46, State of California, 1965. Victoria Little Burris wrote that Emma died in Sonora, California, not Tuolumne, California. Victoria Little Burris to Carolyn L. Atkinson, May 5, 1995.

24. Emma's grave lies in the International Organization of Odd Fellows Cemetery (IOOF), today part of Mountain View Cemetery, at 1411 Belmont Avenue, Fresno, California. The grave is located in block 2, lot 62 B, grave 2.

25. Franklin Rosemont, *Joe Hill, les IWW et la création d'une contreculture ouvrière révolutionnaire* (Paris: CNT-RP, 2008), translated from *Joe Hill, the IWW and Making of the Revolutionary Working-Class Counterculture* (Chicago: Charles H. Kerr, 2002).

26. William Haywood, "On the Inside," in *Rebel Voices: An IWW Anthology*, ed. Joyce Kornbluh (Chicago: Charles H. Kerr, 1988), 337.

27. "Frank H. Little," Case #186701-54-10: 1, Investigative Reports of the Bureau of Investigation 1908–1922, Bureau Section Files (BSF), 1909–1921, FBI Case Files, National Archives Microfilm Publication M1085, Roll 917, NARA, Washington, D.C.

28. Ibid. The case file includes Special Agent F. W. Kelly's letter to Bureau of Investigation Director W. J. Flynn, dated January 14, 1921. The letter, labeled *"Personal,"* states, "I am enclosing herewith for your personal collection three photographs of a placard pinned on the body of Frank Little by his executioners, and ante and postmortem photographs of the same person." William J. Flynn spent twenty-five years in federal government work. He was head of the Secret Service in New York, and when World War I began, he had a large part in crippling the German espionage system. At President Woodrow Wilson's request, he took the helm of the Bureau of Intelligence. His work resulted in the deportation of radical Emma Goldman, among others. After his retirement, he opened his own private detective business, stating that he would never furnish strikebreakers or enter the labor field again. "W. J. Flynn Opens Agency," *New York Times*, October 3, 1921.

29. Helen Keller, "In Behalf of the IWW," *The Liberator* (March 1918): 13.

30. Ibid.

31. Kornbluh, *Rebel Voices*, 357. The quote was attributed originally to Wesley Everest, who was murdered in 1919 in Centralia, Washington.

32. Victoria Little Burris to Carolyn Leverich Atkinson, October 21, 1996.

33. Frank's birthdate as recorded on the tombstone is incorrect. He was born in 1878.

BIBLIOGRAPHY

PRIMARY SOURCES

Archives and Other Collections

Arizona Collection. Haydon Library, Arizona State University, Tempe (ASU).
Arizona and Southwest Collection. Special Collections, University of Arizona, Tucson (UA).
Bisbee Deportation Legal Papers and Exhibits. Special Collections, UA.
California State Archives, Sacramento.
Campbell Family Papers. Arizona Historical Society, Tucson.
Chicano Research Collection. ASU.
Clarence Darrow Digital Collection. Law Library, University of Minnesota, St. Paul.
Clifton-Morenci Ephemeral Files. Arizona Historical Society, Tucson (AHS).
Colorado State Archives, Denver.
Digital Gallery. Cripple Creek District Museum, Cripple Creek, Colorado.
Fred Thompson Collection. Walter P. Reuther Library, Wayne State University, Detroit, Michigan (WSU).
Genealogy Digital Collection. Western History Collection, Denver Public Library.
Greenlee County Historical Society, Clifton, Arizona.
Henry S. McCluskey Papers. Haydon Library, ASU.
Hillside Quaker Mission Collection. Archives, Bartlesville Area History Museum, Bartlesville, Oklahoma (BAHM).

Indian-Pioneer Papers. Western History Collection, University of Oklahoma, Norman.
Industrial Workers of the World Collection, WSU.
Joseph A. Labadie Collection. Special Collections Library, University of Michigan, Ann Arbor.
Kaiyala Collection. Silver Bow Public Archives, Butte, Montana (SBA).
Lewis W. Douglas Collection. Special Collections, UA.
Montana Historical Society Library, Helena.
Oklahoma State Archives, Oklahoma City.
Photo Postcard Collection. Arizona Historical Society, Tucson.
Robert S. Saunders Collection. Western Historical Manuscripts Collection, University of Missouri–St. Louis.
Vernon Jensen Collection. Kheel Center, Cornell University, Ithaca, New York.
Vertical Files. Gila County Historical Society, Globe, Arizona.
Vertical Files. SBA.
W. E. Nicodemus Scrapbook. Archives, Drumright Historical Society Museum, Drumright, Oklahoma.

Directories

1904–05 Tulare County Business & Resident Directory
1907 Fresno City Directory
1911 Butte City Directory
1911 Fresno City Directory
1912 Fresno City Directory
1913 Butte City Directory
1917 Butte City Directory
1917 Fresno City Directory
Polk-Husted Directory Co.'s Fresno City and Fresno County Directory, 1917
Polk-Husted Directory Co.'s Fresno City and Fresno County Directory, 1919
R. L. Polk & Co.'s Guthrie City Directory 1907–1908.

Newspapers

IWW Publications

Industrial Union Bulletin (Chicago)
Industrial Worker (Spokane and Seattle, WA, 1909–17)
The Lumberjack (New Orleans)
Solidarity (Chicago, Cleveland)

Labor and Radical Publications

Miner's Magazine (Western Federation of Miners, Denver, CO)
Montana News (Helena, MT)
The New York Evening Call (New York, NY)
The Voice of the People (New Orleans, LA)

Other Newspapers and Magazines

Anaconda Standard (Anaconda, MT)
Arizona Bulletin (Solomonville, AZ)
Arizona Silver Belt (Globe, AZ)
Bartlesville Magnet (Bartlesville, OK)
Bemidji Daily Pioneer (Bemidji, MN)
Bisbee Daily Review (Bisbee, AZ)
Bisbee Observer (Bisbee, AZ)
Butte Daily Post (Butte, MT)
Butte Miner (Butte, MT)
Cincinnati Daily Gazette (Cincinnati, OH)
Colorado Gazette Telegraph (Colorado Springs, CO)
Colorado Transcript (Golden, CO)
Columbia Daily Tribune (Columbia, MO)
Copper Era (Clifton, AZ)
Cripple Creek Evening Star (Cripple Creek, CO)
Daily Missoulian (Missoula, MT)
Daily Nevada State Journal (Reno, NV)
Daily Tulare Advance Register (Tulare, CA)
Day Book (Chicago, IL)
Denver Rocky Mountain News (Denver, CO)
Drumright Derrick (Drumright, OK)
Duluth Labor World (Duluth, MN)
Duluth News-Tribune (Duluth, MN)
El Paso Herald (El Paso, TX)
Evening News (Sault St. Marie, MI)
Evening Telegram (Salt Lake City, UT)
Fresno Bee (Fresno, CA)
Fresno Herald (Fresno, CA)
Fresno Morning Republican (Fresno, CA)
Guthrie Daily Leader (Guthrie, OK)
Idaho Statesman (Boise, ID)
Jerome News (Jerome, AZ)
Jerome Sun (Jerome, AZ)

Kansas City Journal (Kansas City, MO)
Kansas City Star (Kansas City, MO)
Kansas City Times (Kansas City, MO)
Keokuk Constitution (Keokuk, IA)
Lexington Herald (Lexington, KY)
Logan County News (Guthrie, OK)
Los Angeles Herald (Los Angeles, CA)
Magnum Mirror (Magnum, OK)
Montana Standard (Butte, MT)
Morenci Leader (Morenci, AZ)
Morning Olympian (Olympia, WA)
New Ulm Review (New Ulm, MN)
New York Times (New York, NY)
News Journal (Mannford, OK)
Oakland Tribune (Oakland, CA)
Oklahoman (Oklahoma City, OK)
Oklahoma State Register (Guthrie, OK)
Olympia Daily Recorder (Olympia, WA)
Peoria Herald-Transcript (Peoria, IL)
Portland Oregonian (Portland, OR)
Prescott Evening Courier (Prescott, AZ)
Prescott Journal Miner (Prescott, AZ)
Pueblo Chieftain (Pueblo, CO)
Rockford Daily Register Gazette (Rockford, IL)
Sacramento Bee (Sacramento, CA)
Salt Lake Telegram (Salt Lake City, UT)
San Diego Evening Tribune (San Diego, CA)
San Diego Union (San Diego, CA)
San Francisco Call (San Francisco, CA)
San Francisco Chronicle (San Francisco, CA)
Shawnee Daily News-Herald (Shawnee, OK)
Spokane Daily Chronicle (Spokane, WA)
Spokane Press (Spokane, WA)
Spokesman-Review (Spokane, WA)
Stillwater Gazette (Stillwater, OK)
Stillwater New-Press (Stillwater, OK)
Tombstone Weekly Epitaph (Tombstone, AZ)
Tucson Daily Citizen (Tucson, AZ)
Tulsa Star (Tulsa, OK)
Tulsa World (Tulsa, OK)
Vermont Union (Vermont, IL)
Yale Record (Yale, OK)

Family Documents, Personal Letters, and Other Papers

Basar, James B. and Emma to Charles H. Courtright. Warranty Records 46, 610. January 30, 1919. County Clerk, Payne County, Stillwater, OK.

Burris, Victoria Little. Letters.

Copeland, Delce Courtland. *The Past to Remember*, n.d.

Courtright Family Papers. Includes family interviews.

Cox, Almira L., Petition for Temporary Alimony, no. 4748. October 29, 1904. Logan County, OK.

Cox, Elihu and Almira. Warranty Deeds, nos. 277 and 307. March 15, 1911. St. Andrews Bay Development Company, Lynn Haven, FL.

Cox, Elihu and Mrs. Almira Little. Marriage Record. June 20, 1899. Logan County Marriage Records, 339. County Clerk, Logan County, Guthrie, OK.

Frisbie, Nora, ed. *Bulletins of the Frisbie-Frisbee Family Association of America*. 1971.

Harper Family Papers.

Little, A. C. and Bessie (no last name) to Almira Little. Warranty Records 5, 497. May 29, 1899. County Clerk, Payne County, Stillwater, OK.

Little, Almira to Henrietta Berry. Warranty Records 5, 498. May 29, 1899. County Clerk, Payne County, Stillwater, OK.

Little, Alonzo. *Alonzo Little Family Bible*.

Little, Alonzo C., Death Certificate Register, no. 1132. State Department of Health, State of Oklahoma.

Little, Emma B., Death Certificate, no. 5550-46. State of California.

Little, Emma B., Emma B. Little vs. W. F. Little. Petition for Divorce, no. 24697. January 24, 1920. Superior Court, Fresno, CA.

Little Family Papers. Includes family interviews.

Little, Frank. Coroner's Verdict. August 7, 1917. Butte, Silver Bow County, MT.

Little, Frank. Death Certificate. August 1, 1917. Butte, Silver Bow County, MT.

Little, Unnamed Male. July 19, 1909. *Index to Deaths, Fresno County*, C: 164.

Little, Unnamed Male. July 19, 1909. *Index to Fresno Births*, B: 359. California Birth Records.

Little, W. F., California Death Index, State File 24-15665. W. F. Little Death Certificate. San Joaquin County, Stockton, CA.

Little, W. F., Case no. 27402. California State Hospital.

Little, Walter F. and Emma B. Harper. Marriage License, no. 27852. October 6, 1898. Arapahoe County, Denver, CO.

Little, Walter R., Probate Papers. January 13, 1899 to July 28, 1899. Originals filed in Probate Records, Payne County Courthouse, Stillwater, OK.

County, State, and Federal Government Documents and Collections

Annual Report of the Commissioner of Indian Affairs 1895. Washington, D.C.: U.S. Government Printing Office, 1896.

Cherokee Nation Intruders' Report No. 316. U.S. Board of Appraisers of the Improvements of Intruders in the Cherokee Nation. NARG 75, BIA-E411-Intruders 33008-1895. Cherokee Census of Intruders, 1893, Roll no. 2601.

General Land Office Records. U.S. Bureau of Land Management. U.S. Department of the Interior.

Industrial Relations: Final Report and Testimony Submitted to Congress by the Commission on Industrial Relations. Document no. 415, vol. 1. Washington, D.C.: U.S. Government Printing Office, 1916.

Investigative Reports of the Bureau of Investigation 1908–22. FBI Case Files. National Archives and Records Administration, Washington, D.C.

    Bureau Section Files, 1909–21.
    Miscellaneous Files, 1909–21.
    Old German Files (OGF), 1909–21.

Marriage Records. Microfilm, 459. Missouri State Archives, Jefferson City, MO.

National Register of Historical Places Inventory Form. Item 7, 2. Historical National Parks Service, U.S. Department of the Interior, 1975.

Oklahoma Territorial Census Index, 1890. Oklahoma Historical Society, available at http://www.okhistory.org/research/terr.

"Report of Wm. L. Utley, Col., Cmdg. Twenty-second Regt. Wisconsin Volunteers, 1863, Engagement at Thompson's Station, TN." *The War of the Rebellion: A Compilation of the Official Records of the Union and Confederate Armies* (Official Records). Edited by Robert N. Scott. Series I, vol. 23, ch. 35, serial no. 34. Part I—Reports (1889): 106–34.

Tulare County Great Register, 1898, California.

U.S. Federal Census Records, 1850–1940.

Weinstock, Harris. *Report on Recent Disturbances in the City of San Diego and the County of San Diego, California.* Sacramento: State Printing Office, 1912.

World War I Selective Service System Draft Registration Cards, 1917–18. NARA, Washington, D.C.

Memoirs and Oral Histories

"Cal Owens Recalls Ingalls' Past." In vol. 1 of *Cimarron Valley Legends*. Perkins: Evans Publications, 1978.

Campbell, Thomas E. "True Copy of the Notes of Honorable Thomas E. Campbell." Written between 1934 and 1939. Campbell Family Papers. MS 132, Folder 6. Arizona Historical Society, Tucson. Available at http://www.library.arizona.edu/exhibits/bisbee/docs/rec_camp.html.

Cannon, James P. *Notebook of an Agitator*. 3rd ed. New York: Pathfinder, 2009.

Chaplin, Ralph. *Wobbly: The Rough-and-Tumble Story of an American Radical*. Chicago: University of Chicago Press, 1948.

Colquhoun, James. *The History of Clifton-Morenci Mining District*. London: John Murray, 1924.

Dalton, Emmett. *When the Daltons Rode*. Gretna, LA: Pelican Publishing, 2012.

Darrow, Clarence. "Statement Given to Newspapers the Day of Plea of Guilty by McNamara Brothers in Los Angeles." Clarence Darrow Digital Collection, Law School, University of Minnesota. Accessed August 30, 2014, http://darrow.law.umn.edu/documents/Darrow_statement_to_newspaper_guilty_plea_OCR_cropped.pdf.

Davis, George Wesley. *Sketches of Butte*. Boston: The Cornhill Company, 1921. Folder L1985.551, File AW D003.001, SBA.

"Early Memories of the Berry Sisters." In vol. 1 of *Cimarron Valley Family Legends*, 16–19. Perkins, OK: Evans Publishing, 1978.

Edwards, Jennie. *John N. Edwards, Biography, Memoirs, Reminiscences and Recollections*. Kansas City, MO: Jennie Edwards, 1889.

Elliott, William. Interview by Grace Kelley. August 15, 1937. Indian-Pioneer Papers 27. Western History Collection, University of Oklahoma Libraries.

Fleming, Mrs. J. J. Interview by James H. Fleming. June 15, 1937. Indian-Pioneer Papers 30. Western History Collection, University of Oklahoma Libraries.

Flynn, Elizabeth Gurley. *The Rebel Girl: An Autobiography*. Revised ed. 1973. New York: International Publishers, 1994.

Goldman, Emma. *Living My Life*. New York: Alfred A. Knopf, 1931. Accessed January 9, 2015, http://theanarchistlibrary.org/library/emma-goldman-living-my-life#toc42.

Green, Archie, David Roediger, Franklin Rosemont, and Salvatore Salerno, eds. *The Big Red Songbook*. Chicago: Charles H. Kerr, 1907.

Hays, Ward. *Drifting Down Memory Lane*. Perkins, OK: Evans Publications, 1985.

Haywood, William D. *Bill Haywood's Book: Autobiography of Big Bill Haywood*. New York: International Publishers, 1929.

———. "On the Inside." In *Rebel Voices: An IWW Anthology*, 2nd ed., edited by Joyce L. Kornbluh, 334–37. Chicago: Charles H. Kerr, 1988.

Hellman, Lillian. *Scoundrel Time*. New York: Little, Brown, 1976.

Jacobs, W. C. Interview by Leone Bryan. March 31, 1937. Indian-Pioneer Papers 47. Western History Collection, University of Oklahoma Libraries.

Kaiyala, Waldemar. "My Memories in Butte, Montana." Date unknown. File 11, Box 1, LH021, SBA.

Kerr, William Ray. "In Defense of Ingalls, Oklahoma." In vol. 2 of *Cimarron Family Legends*, 362–66. Perkins, OK: Evans Press, 1980.

Langdon, Emma Florence. *The Cripple Creek Strike 1903–1904*. Victor, Colorado: 1904.

Little, Anna B. Interview by Goldie Turner. September 2, 1937. Indian-Pioneer Papers 54, Western History Collection, University of Oklahoma Libraries.

McGuckin, Henry E. *Memoirs of a Wobbly*. Chicago: Charles H. Kerr, 1987.

Miller, Floyd E. "Hillside Mission." *Chronicles of Oklahoma* 4, no. 3 (1926): 223–38.

Person, Carl E. *The Lizard's Tail*. Chicago: Lake Publishing, 1918.

Randall, La Veta M. "Thomas E. Berry." In vol. 1 of *Cimarron Valley Family Legends*, 20–21. Perkins, OK: Evans Publishing, 1978.

Riell, Robert Barclay. "Copper Mine Strikes of 1917, Globe, Arizona." Vertical Files. Gila County Historical Society, undated.

Ringgold, Jeanne Parks. *Frontier Days in the Southwest*. San Antonio: Naylor Company, 1952.

Rogers, Charles H. Interview by W. T. Holland. August 17, 1937. Indian-Pioneer Papers 77, Western History Collection, University of Oklahoma Libraries.

Rosen, Ellen Doree. *A Wobbly Life, IWW Organizer E. F. Doree*. Detroit: Wayne State University Press, 2004.

Spell, Leslie Doye and Hazel M. *Forgotten Men of Cripple Creek*. United States: Kessinger Publishing, 1959.

Stiverson, Clara. Interview by Elizabeth Jameson. July 29, 1975. As quoted in Elizabeth Jameson, "Imperfect Unions, Class, and Gender," *Frontiers: A Journal of Women Studies* 1, no. 2 (Spring 1976): 91.

Tompkins, George R. *The Truth about Butte: A Little History for Thoughtful People*. Butte: October 20, 1917. Butte File, Folder 1985455, File AWT011, SBA.

Turner, Ethel Duffy. Interview. In *Writers and Revolutionists: Oral History Transcript and Related Material, 1966–1967*. Oral History Manuscript. Berkeley, CA: University of California, 1967.

———. *Revolution in Baja California: Ricardo Flores Magon's High Noon*. Edited by Rey Davis. Detroit: Blaine Ethridge Books, 1981.

Watson, Fred. "Still on Strike! Recollections of a Bisbee Deportee." *Journal of Arizona History* 18 (Summer 1977): 171–84.

Wheeler, Burton K. with Paul F. Healy. *Yankee from the West.* New York: Farrar, Straus, and Giroux, 1977.

Books, Documents, and Pamphlets

Industrial Workers of the World and Western Federation of Miners

Constitution and By-Laws of the Western Federation of Miners. Butte, Montana: 1883.

Constitution of the Western Federation of Miners, Affiliated with the AFL. Butte City, Montana, May 19, 1893.

Duff, Harvey. *The Silent Defenders, Courts and Capitalism in California.* Chicago: Industrial Workers of the World, 1920.

Hall, Covington. "Labor Struggles in the Deep South." Unpublished manuscript. Walter P. Reuther Library, WSU.

Haywood, Bill, George F. Vanderveer, and Frank Knowlton. *Evidence and Cross Examination of William D. Haywood in the Case of the USA versus Wm. D. Haywood, et al.* Chicago: General Defense Committee, 1918.

Official Proceedings of the Eleventh Annual Convention of the Western Federation of Miners, Stenographic Report. May 25–June 10, 1903. Denver, Colorado.

Official Proceedings of the Fifteenth Annual Convention of the Western Federation of Miners, Stenographic Report. June 10–July 12, 1907. Denver, Colorado.

Official Proceedings of the Sixteenth Annual Convention Western Federation of Miners. July 13–July 29, 1908. Denver, Colorado.

Preamble and Constitution of the Industrial Workers of the World. Chicago: Industrial Workers of the World, 1908.

Proceedings of the First Convention of the Industrial Workers of the World, Founded at Chicago. June 27–July 2, 1905. New York: New York Labor News, 1905.

Proceedings of the Second Annual Convention of the Industrial Workers of the World. Sept. 17 to Oct. 3, 1906. Chicago: International Workers of the World, 1906.

Proceedings of the Tenth Convention of the Industrial Workers of the World, Held at Chicago, Illinois, November 20 to December 1, 1916. Chicago: Industrial Workers of the World, 1917.

The Silent Defense. Chicago: Industrial Workers of the World, n.d.

Stenographic Report of the Eighth Annual Convention of the Industrial Workers of the World. September 14–29, 1913. Chicago: Industrial Workers of the World, 1913.

St. John, Vincent. *The I.W.W.: Its History, Structure, and Methods.* Revised ed. Chicago: Industrial Workers of the World, 1919.

Thompson, Fred W. and Patrick Murfin. *The I. W. W.: Its First Seventy Years 1905-1975.* Chicago: Industrial Workers of the World, 1976.

"Who Is Who in California." *Defense Bulletin of the Seattle District,* no. 32. Seattle: Industrial Workers of the World, October 14, 1918.

Articles and Chapters

Brissenden, Paul F. "The Butte Miners and the Rustling Card." *The American Economic Review* 10, no. 4 (December 1920): 755-75.

Cannon, James P. "On the Anniversary of His Death." *Labor Defender* 1, no. 8 (August 1926): 132-33.

———. "The I. W. W.: On the Fiftieth Anniversary of the Founding Convention." In *Fourth International.* New York: Pioneer Publishers, 1955.

Chafee, Zechariah, Jr. "California Justice." *New Republic* 36 (September 19, 1923): 97-99.

Chaplin, Ralph. "Joe Hill's Funeral." *International Socialist Review* 16, no. 7 (January 1915): 400-405.

Christensen, Otto. "Invading Miners' Homes." *International Socialist Review* 17, no. 3 (September 1916): 160-62.

"Drumright is Substantial City: Growth Outrivals Any in State." *Drumright Daily Derrick,* 1914. *Items and Articles Taken from Newspapers and Clippings Found in a Scrap Book Kept by Mayor W. E. Nicodemus During the Years 1916-1922 and From Items and Pictures Saved for Many Years by Mrs. Lille Reynolds and Harold O. Ford.* W. E. Nicodemus Scrapbook, Archives, Drumright Historical Society Museum.

Dunne, William F. "August, 1917, in Butte, the Murder of Frank Little." *Labor Defender* 1, no. 8 (August 1928): 123-14, 142-43.

"Editorial Correspondence, Butte—Aug. 7." *Engineering and Mining Journal* 104, no. 6 (August 11, 1917): 277.

"Editorial Correspondence, Butte—Aug. 9." *Engineering and Mining Journal* 104, no. 7 (August 18, 1917): 321.

Fraser-Campbell, Evan. "The Management of Mexican Labor." *Engineering and Mining Journal* 91 (1911): 1104-1105.

George, Harrison. "The Mesaba Iron Range." *International Socialist Review* 17, no. 6 (December 1916): 329-32.

Gillespie, L. D. "Hunger in the Midst of Plenty," *International Socialist Review* 17, no. 5 (November 1916): 283-85.

Hall, Sharlot M. "The Making of a Great Mine." *Out West* 25, no. 1 (July 1906): 3-26.

Hanson, Nils H. "Among the Harvesters." *International Socialist Review* 16, no. 2 (August 1915): 76-87.

Haywood, William D. "Declaration of War." *International Socialist Review* 17, no. 2 (August 1916): 132.

Heslewood, Fred W. "Barbarous Spokane." *International Socialist Review* 5, no. 8 (February 1910): 705–13.

Hill, Joe. "In Memoriam of Joe Hill." *The International Socialist Review* 17, no. 6 (December 1916): 326.

Howard, William W. "The Rush to Oklahoma." *Harper's Weekly* 33 (May 18, 1889): 394.

"Huett Clinton Merritt." *The Successful American* 5, no. 5 (May 1902): 276.

Keller, Helen. "In Behalf of the IWW." *The Liberator*, March 1918, 13.

Kellogg, Paul U. "The Field before the Committee on Industrial Relations." *Political Science Quarterly* 28 (1913): 593–609.

"Labor Troubles." *The Public 19*, no. 963 (September 15, 1916): 878–79.

"The Labor Troubles in Butte." *Mining and Scientific Press* 115 (September 1, 1917): 305.

Lesueur, Arthur. "Legal Side Lights on Murder." *International Socialist Review* 17, no. 5 (November 1916): 298–300.

Little, Mrs. W. F. "Court Crookedness in Fresno." *The Class War*, n.d., 117, first printed in *Appeal*, February 11, 1911, Frank Little Bio, Vertical File VF0528, SBA.

Marcy, Leslie H. "The Iron Heel on the Mesaba Range." *International Socialist Review* 17, no. 2 (August 1916): 74–80.

Marcy, Leslie H. "The Tenth Annual IWW Convention." *International Socialist Review* 17, no. 3 (January 1917): 406–409.

"Millions Made on the Mesaba." *International Socialist Review* 17, no. 4 (October 1916): 231.

Press Committee. "Solidarity Wins in Fresno." *International Socialist Review* 11, no. 10 (April 1911): 634–36.

Reynolds, W. E. "Capturing Political Power in Oklahoma." *International Socialist Review* 17, no. 7 (January 1917): 416–17.

Robinson, Reid. "Town without History," 1936. File AWR014, SBA.

Rogers, Allen H. "Characters and Habits of the Mexican Miner." *Engineering and Mining Journal* 85 (1908): 700–702.

Sandburg, Carl. "Billy Sunday." *International Socialist Review* 16, no. 4 (September 1915): 152–53.

———. "Clark Street Bridge." *Chicago Poems.* New York: Henry Holt, 1916.

Shoemaker, Elsie. "Oldtimers Recall Ingalls, September 1st, 1893." *Stillwater New-Press*, September 6, 1964, pp. 4–5.

"Trouble is on at Webb City, MO." *International Socialist Review* 17, no. 1 (July 1916): 57.

West, George P. "The Mesaba Strike." *International Socialist Review* 17, no. 3 (September 1916): 158–61.

Court Cases

Baskett, John R. Testimony before U.S. District Court of Illinois, August 8, 1918. Transcript available from U.S. vs. Haywood et al., 1917–1918.

Series 5: Legal Problems, Trials, and Defense, File 3, pages 10818–10868, Box 116, Subseries B. Walter P. Reuther Library, WSU.

City of Spokane vs. F. H. Little. Case No. 3943, Note of Issue and Notice of Trial for Trial Docket, Superior Court of the State of Washington and County of Spokane. November 17, 1909.

City of Spokane vs. F. J. [sic] Little. Case No. 42563, Complaint for Violation of Ordinance No. A1324, "Disorderly Conduct." Police Justice Court, November 5, 1909.

Clark, Stanley J. Testimony before U.S. District Court of Illinois, August 8, 1918. Transcript available from U.S. vs. Haywood et al., 1917–1918. Series 5: Legal Problems, Trials, and Defense, File 3, pages 10872–10913, Box 116, Subseries B. Walter P. Reuther Library, WSU.

Crary, Harold W. Testimony before U.S. District Court of Illinois, May 23, 1918. Transcript available from U.S. vs. Haywood et al., 1917–1918. Series 5: Legal Problems, Trials, and Defense, File 12, pages 1423–1452, Box 104, Subseries B. Walter P. Reuther Library, WSU.

Dunn, William F. Testimony before Montana Council of Defense at Montana State Capitol, June 5–6, 1918. Transcript available from Box 6, Files 2 and 3, Montana Council of Defense Records. Montana Historical Society Library, Helena, MT.

———. Testimony before U.S. District Court of Illinois, July 13, 1918. Transcript available from U.S. vs. Haywood et al., 1917–1918. Series 5: Legal Problems, Trials, and Defense, File 2, pages 7220–7260, Box 104, Subseries B. Walter P. Reuther Library, WSU.

Elliott, James. Testimony before U.S. District Court of Illinois, August 3, 1918. Transcript available from U.S. vs. Haywood et al., 1917–1918. Series 5: Legal Problems, Trials, and Defense, File 4, pages 9977–9995, Box 115, Subseries B. Walter P. Reuther Library, WSU.

Engebritson, Hulbert. Testimony before U.S. District Court of Illinois, July 13, 1918. Transcript available from U.S. vs. Haywood et al., 1917–1918. Series 5: Legal Problems, Trials, and Defense, File 2, pages 7162–7177, Box 104, Subseries B. Walter P. Reuther Library, WSU.

Grand Jury, Indictment of IWW Members, April 8, 1918. U.S. District of California, Northern Division of California, Northern District, First Division. Series 5. Legal Problems, Trials, and Defense Cases, File 7, Box 125 Subseries B. Walter P. Reuther Library, WSU.

Haywood, William D. Testimony before U.S. District Court of Illinois, August 12, 1918. Transcript available from U.S. vs. Haywood et al., 1917–1918. Series 5: Legal Problems, Trials, and Defense, File 3, pages 11359–11376, Box 117, Subseries B. Walter P. Reuther Library, WSU.

Houlb, Paul. Testimony before U.S. District Court of Illinois, July 13, 1918. Transcript available from U.S. vs. Haywood et al., 1917–1918. Series 5: Legal Problems, Trials, and Defense, File 2, pages 7180–7208, Box 104, Subseries B. Walter P. Reuther Library, WSU.

Johanson, Ragnar. Testimony before U.S. District Court of Illinois, August 3, 1918. Transcript available from U.S. vs. Haywood et al., 1917–1918. Series 5: Legal Problems, Trials, and Defense, File 4, pages 10087–10112, Box 115, Subseries B. Walter P. Reuther Library, WSU.

Oates, John Joseph. Testimony before U.S. District Court of Illinois, August 3, 1918. Transcript available from U.S. vs. Haywood et al., 1917–1918. Series 5: Legal Problems, Trials, and Defense, File 4, pages 10034–10086, Box 115, Subseries B. Walter P. Reuther Library, WSU.

Perry, Grover H. Testimony before U.S. District Court of Illinois, August 8, 1918. Transcript available from U.S. vs. Haywood et al., 1917–1918. Series 5: Legal Problems, Trials, and Defense, File 3, pages 10914–10963, Box 116, Subseries B. Walter P. Reuther Library, WSU.

Stevens, Charles L. Testimony before U.S. District Court of Illinois, May 23, 1918. Transcript available from U.S. vs. Haywood et al., 1917–1918. Series 5: Legal Problems, Trials, and Defense, File 12, pages 1384–1411, Box 104, Subseries B. Walter P. Reuther Library, WSU.

Walliser, A. W. Testimony before U.S. District Court of Illinois, May 23, 1918. Transcript available from U.S. vs. Haywood et al., 1917–1918. Series 5: Legal Problems, Trials, and Defense, File 12, pages 1341–1383, Box 104, Subseries B. Walter P. Reuther Library, WSU.

Other Histories and Pamphlets

The Fourth Annual Catalogue of the Oklahoma Agricultural and Mechanical College. Office of the Registrar, Oklahoma State University, Stillwater, Oklahoma.

Futhey, John Smith and Gilbert Cope. *The History of Chester County.* N.p.: L. J. Everts, 1881.

Guinn, J. M., ed. *History of the State of California and Biographical Record of the San Joaquin Valley, California.* Chicago: Chapman Publishing, 1905.

History of Cass and Bates Counties, Missouri. St. Joseph, MO: National Historical Company, 1883.

The History of Fulton County, Illinois. Peoria: Charles C. Chapman, 1879.

Holmes, Helen Freudengerger, ed. Vol. 1 of *Logan County History.* 1978.

"Kansas City Historical Timeline." Kansas City Police Department Historical Section. Accessed September 7, 2014, http://www.kcpolice memorial.com/history.

Kansas City, Missouri: Its History and Its People 1808–1908, vol. 2. Chicago: S. J. Clarke Publishing, 1908, 483–84.

Ordway, William. *House of Grimmet, a Family Genealogy.* 1993.

McClintock, James H. Vol. 2 of *Arizona, the Youngest State.* Chicago: S. J. Clarke, 1916.

McLean, Alexander, ed. Vol. 2 of *History of McDonough County.* Chicago: Munsell Publishing, 1907.

Marsh, George D., ed. *Copper Camp*. Workers of the Writers' Program (WPA), Montana State Department of Agriculture. New York: Hastings House, 1943.

Menefee, Eugene L. and Fred A. Dodge, eds. *History of Tulare and King Counties, CA*. Los Angeles: Historic Record, 1913.

Mine Owners' Association. *Criminal Record of the Western Federation of Miners, Coeur d'Alene to Cripple Creek, 1894–1904*. Colorado Springs: Colorado Mine Operators' Association, 1904.

National Civil Liberties Bureau. *War-Time Prosecutions and Mob Violence, Involving the Rights of Free Speech, Free Press, and Peaceful Assemblage*. 1919. Reprint, Amsterdam: Fredonia Books, 2004.

Stevens, Horace J., ed. *The Mines Handbook*. Houghton, MI: H. J. Stevens, 1909.

Tenney, James B. Vol. 1 of *History of Mining in Arizona*. 1929. Special Collections (AZ198), UA.

Thomas, Agnes Boss. "Columbia Gardens." *Overland Monthly* 60, no. 5 (1912): 494–500.

"Thomas Nelson Berry." Originally published in *History of Oklahoma*. Vol. 1 of *Cimarron Valley Family Legends*. (Perkins, OK: Evans Publishing, 1978), 15–16.

The Truth about the IWW Prisoners. New York: American Civil Liberties Bureau, 1922.

Vandor, Paul E. *History of Fresno County*. Los Angeles: Historic Recording Company, 1919.

The Writers' Program (WPA). Montana State Department of Agriculture. New York: Hastings House, 1943.

Speeches

Roosevelt, Theodore. "Hyphenated American Speech." Address to the Knights of Columbus, New York City, October 12, 1915.

Taft, William Howard. "'He Who Conquers Himself Is Greater Than He Who Takes a City,' Address at City Hall Park, Fresno, California, at a Union Religious Service, October 10, 1909." In *Presidential Addresses and State Papers of William Howard Taft, March 4, 1909, to March 4, 1910*. New York: Doubleday, Page, 1910.

Wilson, Woodrow. "Final Address in Support of the League of Nations." Pueblo, Colorado, September 24, 1919.

Databases

American Civil War Soldiers. Historical Data Systems. Source 97. Online database. Provo, UT: Ancestry.com, 1999.

Cox, Elihu H. Application File, no. 1073678. *U.S. Civil War Pension Index: General Index to Pension Files, 1861–1934*. Online database. Provo, UT: Ancestry.com, 2000. Original data: *General Index to Pension Files, 1861–1934*. T288, 546 rolls. Washington, D.C.: NARA.

Fresno County Sheriff's Office. Former Sheriffs of Fresno County. Online database. Accessed July 13, 2014, http://www.fresnosheriff.org/admin/history/former-sheriffs.html.

Illinois Marriages, 1851–1900. Online database. Provo, UT: Ancestry.com, 2005.

U.S. Civil War Soldier Records and Profiles, 1861–1865. Historical Data Systems. Online database. Provo, UT: Ancestry.com, 2009.

SECONDARY SOURCES

Dissertations, Theses, and Unpublished Material

Calvert, Jerry. "The Destruction of the Butte Miners' Union: A Study of Labor, Socialism, a Company, and the State." Unpublished manuscript. Fred Thompson Collection, Subseries A, Box 8, Folder 26–27. Walter P. Reuther Library, WSU.

Casillas, Michael. "Ethnic Factors Leading to the Clifton-Morenci Strike of 1915–1916." Unpublished manuscript, Arizona State University, 1973. Chicano Research Collection, Small Manuscripts (MM CHSM-20). Haydon Library, ASU.

———. "Mexicans, Labor, & Strife in Arizona." Unpublished manuscript, Chicano Research Collection, Small Manuscripts (MM CHSM-20). Haydon Library, ASU.

———. "The PLM in Territorial Arizona: A Survey of Reasons for, and Results of, Mexican Unionizational Attempts." Unpublished manuscript, Arizona State University, 1976. Chicano Collection, Box 6, Folder 2 (CHSM). Haydon Library, ASU.

Dodd, Martin. "The I.W.W., Fresno, and the Free Speech Fight of 1910–1911: A Case Study in Hobo Activism." Thesis manuscript, Wayne State University, 1974. Fred Thompson Collection, Subseries A, Box 14, Folder 10. Walter P. Reuther Library, WSU.

Elrod, Clyde. "The Old Dominion Mine," Unpublished Manuscript, 1965. Vertical Files. Gila County Historical Society.

Huginnie, Andrea Yvette. "'Strikitos': Race, Class, and Work in the Arizona Copper Industry, 1870–1920." Thesis manuscript, Arizona State University, 1991. Chicano Research Collection (HD 939.C7). Haydon Library, ASU.

Lehman, Ted. "The Constitution Guarantees Freedom of Speech—Rats!: The Fresno Free Speech Fight." Unpublished manuscript, 1971. Fred Thompson Collection, Box 14, Folder 9. Walter P. Reuther Library, WSU.

McBride, James D. "The Development of Labor Unions in Arizona Mining, 1884–1919." Thesis manuscript, Arizona State University, 1975. Arizona Collection, Haydon Library, ASU.

————. "Henry S. McCluskey: Workingman's Advocate." Thesis manu-
script, Arizona State University, 1982. Special Collections (LD179.15).
Haydon Library, ASU.
"Resource Protection Planning: Project Settlement Patterns in the Unas-
signed Lands, Region Six." Edited by Mary Ann Anders. Oklahoma
Historic Preservation Survey. Stillwater: History Department, Okla-
homa State University, 1984.
Walker, William R. "Only the Heretics Are Burning: Democracy and
Repression in World War I America." Thesis dissertation, Univer-
sity of Wisconsin-Madison, 2008.
Weintraub, Hyman. "The I.W.W. in California, 1905–1931." Unpublished
manuscript, University of California, 1947.
Ziede, Alexander. "The Territorial History of Globe Mining District."
Thesis manuscript, University of Southern California, 1939.

Books

Acuña, Rodolfo. *Corridors of Migration.* Tucson: University of Arizona
Press, 2007.
Adler, William M. *The Man Who Never Died.* New York: Bloomsbury, 2012.
Allen, Frederick. *A Decent Orderly Lunching: The Montana Vigilantes.*
Norman: University of Oklahoma Press, 2009.
Bancroft, Carolyn. *Gulch of Gold: A History of Central City, Colorado.*
Denver: Sage Books, 1958.
Benton-Cohen, Katherine. *Borderline Americans, Racial Division and
Labor War in the Arizona Borderlands.* Cambridge, MA: Harvard
University Press, 2009.
Berman, David R. *Radicalism in the Mountain West, 1890–1920.* Boulder:
University Press of Colorado, 2007.
Bissett, Jim. *Agrarian Socialism in America: Marx, Jefferson, and Jesus in
the Oklahoma Countryside, 1904–1920.* Norman: University of
Oklahoma Press, 2002.
Blevins, Tim, Chris Nicholl, and Calvin P. Otto, eds. *The Colorado Labor
Wars, 1903–1904.* Colorado Springs: Pikes Peak Library District, 2006.
Brissenden, Paul Frederick. *The IWW: A Study of American Syndicalism.*
New York, 1919.
Bufe, Chaz, and Mitchell Cowen Verter, eds. *Dreams of Freedom.* Oak-
land, CA: AK Press, 2005.
Byrkit, James W. *Forging the Copper Collar.* Tucson: University of Ari-
zona Press, 1982.
Calvert, Jerry W. *The Gibraltar: Socialism and Labor in Butte, Montana,
1895–1920.* Helena: Montana Historical Society Press, 1988.
Chester, Eric Thomas. *The Wobblies in Their Heyday: The Rise and
Fall of the Industrial Workers of the World during the World War
I Era.* Santa Barbara, CA: Praeger, 2014.

Dubofsky, Melvyn, ed. *The Industrial Workers of the World: A Guide to Department of Justice Investigative Files, Part I.* Bethesda, MD: University Publications of America, 1989.

———. *We Shall Be All: A History of the Industrial Workers of the World.* Abridged ed. Edited by Joseph A. McCartin. Urbana: University of Illinois Press, 2000.

Emmons, David M. *The Butte Irish: Class and Ethnicity in an American Mining Town, 1875–1925.* Urbana: University of Illinois Press, 1989.

Fethering, George. *The Gold Crusades: A Social History of Gold Rushes, 1849–1929.* Toronto: University of Toronto Press, 1997.

Foner, Philip S., ed. *Fellow Workers and Friends, IWW Free-Speech Fights as Told by Participants.* Westport, CT: Greenwood Press, 1981.

Gibson, Richard I. *Lost Butte, Montana.* Charleston, SC: History Press, 2012.

Gilly, Adolfo. *The Mexican Revolution.* English Translation. New York: New Press, 2005.

Glasscock, C. B. *The War of the Copper Kings.* 1935. Reprint, Helena: Riverbend Publishing, 2002.

Gordon, Linda. *The Great Arizona Orphan Abduction.* Cambridge: Harvard University Press, 1999.

Guthrie, Woody. *American Folksong.* Reprint 1947. New York: Oak Publications, 1961.

Hanson, Robert E. *The Great Bisbee IWW Deportation of July 12, 1917.* Montana: Signature Press, 1987.

Hidy, Ralph W., Muriel E. Hidy, Roy V. Scott, and Don L. Hofsommer. *The Great Northern Railway: A History.* Minneapolis: University of Minnesota Press, 2004.

Hudelson, Richard and Carl Ross. *By the Ore Docks: A Working People's History of Duluth.* Minneapolis: University of Minnesota Press, 2006.

Huff, Eileen. *Drumright's Unique History.* Stillwater, OK: New Forums Press, 1995.

Jameson, Elizabeth. *All That Glitters: Class, Conflict, and Community in Cripple Creek.* Chicago: University of Illinois Press, 1998.

Jantzen, Steven. *Hooray for Peace, Hurrah for War.* New York: Alfred A. Knopf, 1971.

Jensen, Vernon H. *Heritage of Conflict.* Ithaca, NY: Cornell University Press, 1950.

Kemp, Donald C. *Colorado's Little Kingdom.* Denver: Sage Books, 1949.

Kornbluh, Joyce L. *Rebel Voices, An IWW Anthology.* 2nd ed. Chicago: Charles H. Kerr, 1988.

Knowles, Ruth Sheldon. *The Greatest Gambler: The Epic of American Oil Exploration.* Norman: University of Oklahoma Press, 1978.

Langham, Thomas C. *Border Trials, Ricardo Flores Magón and the Mexican Liberals.* El Paso: Texas Western Press, 1981.

Layman, Richard. *Shadow Man: The Life of Dashiell Hammett.* San Diego: Harcourt Brace, 1981.

MacLachlan, Colin M. *Anarchism and the Mexican Revolution.* Los Angeles: University of California Press, 1991.

Martinelli, Phylis Cancilla. *Undermining Race, Ethnic Identities in Arizona Copper Camps, 1880–1920.* Tucson: University of Arizona Press, 2009.

Mellinger, Philip J. *Race and Labor in Western Copper.* Tucson: University of Arizona Press, 1995.

Newsom, D. Earl. *Drumright! The Glory Days of a Boom Town.* Perkins, OK: Evans Publications, 1985.

———. *Drumright II: A Thousand Memories.* Perkins, OK: Evans Publications, 1987.

———. *The Story of Exciting Payne County.* Stillwater, OK: New Forums Press, 1997.

Pemicone, Nunzio. *Carlo Tresca: Portrait of a Rebel.* Oakland, CA: AK Press, 2010.

Preston, William, Jr. *Aliens & Dissenters, Federal Suppression of Radicals, 1903–1933.* 2nd ed. Chicago: University of Illinois Press, 1994.

Pringle, Henry F. *Theodore Roosevelt.* New York: Konecky & Konecky, 1931.

Punke, Michael. *Fire and Brimstone, the North Butte Mining Disaster of 1917.* New York: Hyperion Books, 2006.

Renshaw, Patrick. *The Wobblies: The Story of the IWW and Syndicalism in the United States.* Updated edition. Chicago: Ivan R. Dee, 1999.

Rister, Carl. *Land Hunger.* Norman: University of Oklahoma Press, 1942.

Rosemont, Franklin. *Joe Hill, les IWW et la création d'une contre-culture ouvrière révolutionnaire (Paris: CNT-RP, 2008),* translated from *Joe Hill, the IWW and Making of the Revolutionary Working-class Counterculture.* Chicago: Charles H. Kerr, 2002.

Rouse, A. L. *The Cousin Jacks: The Cornish in America.* New York: Charles Scribner's Sons, 1969.

Sellars, Nigel A. *Oil, Wheat, and Wobblies.* Norman: University of Oklahoma Press, 1998.

Slotkin, Richard. *Gunfighter Nation: The Myth of the Frontier in Twentieth-Century America.* Norman: University of Oklahoma Press, 1998.

Starr, Kevin. *Endangered Dreams: The Great Depression in California.* New York: Oxford University Press, 1996.

Stevens, Horace J., ed. *The Mines Handbook.* Houghton, MI: H. J. Stevens, 1909.

Suggs, George. *Colorado's War on Militant Unionism: James H. Peabody and the Western Federation of Miners.* Norman: University of Oklahoma Press, 1991.

Talbert, Roy, Jr. *Negative Intelligence, The Army and the American Left, 1917–1941.* Jackson: University Press of Mississippi, 1991.

Taylor, Robert Guilford. *Cripple Creek Mining District.* Palmer Lake, CO: Filter Press, 1973.

Wallerstein, Jane. *Voices from the Paterson Silk Mills.* Charleston, SC: Arcadia Publishing, 2000.

Winters, Donald E. *The Soul of the Wobblies: The I.W.W., Religion, and American Culture in the Progressive Era, 1905–1917.* Westport, CT: Greenwood Press, 1985.

Work, Clemens P. *Darkest Before Dawn: Sedition and Free Speech in the American West.* Albuquerque: University of New Mexico Press, 2005.

World Museum of Mining. *Mining in Butte.* Charleston, SC: Arcadia Publishing, 2011.

Articles, Chapters, and Pamphlets

Alenius, E. M. J. "A Brief History of the United Verde Open Pit, Jerome, Arizona." *Arizona Bureau of Mines Bulletin* 178. Tucson: University of Arizona, 1968.

Algren, Nelson. "Come in If You Love Money." *The Last Carousel.* New York: Seven Stories Press, 1997, 83–96.

Buzzard, Sue. "Lawmen and Outlaws." Vol. 1 of *The History of Craig County.* Accessed December 1, 2010, http://www.okgenweb.org/~okcraig/history/people/lawmen.htm.

Byrkit, James W. "The IWW in Wartime Arizona." *Journal of Arizona History* 19 (Summer 1977): 149–70.

"A Changing Society, Life and Culture, 1907–1945." In *Not in Precious Metals Alone: A Manuscript History of Montana,* 190–203. Helena: Montana Historical Society, 1976.

Clements, Eric L. "Pragmatic Revolutionaries?: Tactics, Ideologies, and the Western Federation of Miners in the Progressive Era." *Western Historical Quarterly* 40, no. 4 (2009): 445–67.

Conger, W. C. "History of Clifton-Morenci District." In vol. 1 of The History of Mining in Arizona, edited by J. M. Canty and M. N. Greeley. Tucson: Mining Club of the Southwest Foundation, 1987, 99–128.

Del Castillo, Richard Griswold. "The Discredited Revolution: The Magonista Capture of Tijuana in 1911." *San Diego Historical Society Quarterly* 26, no. 4 (1980). Accessed August 5, 2014, http://www.sandiegohistory.org/journal/80fall/revolution.htm.

Denning, Michael. *Mechanic Accents: Dime Novels and Working Class Culture in America.* London: Verso, 1987.

Dorich, Thomas J. "This Is a Tough Place to Work." *Journal of Arizona History* 38 (Autumn 1997): 233–56.

Eleff, Robert M. "The 1916 Minnesota Miners' Strike against U.S. Steel." *Minnesota History* 51, no. 2 (Summer 1988): 63–74.

Elliott, Russell R. "Labor Troubles in the Mining Camp at Goldfield, Nevada, 1906–1908." *Pacific Historical Review*, 19, no. 4 (1950): 369–84.

Emmons, David. M. "Immigrant Workers and Industrial Hazards: The Irish of Butte 1880–1919." *Journal of American Ethnic History* 5, no. 1 (1985): 41–64.

Eppinga, Jane. "Ethnic Diversity in Mining Camps." In vol. 2 of *The History of Mining in Arizona*, edited by J. M. Canty and M. N. Greeley. Tucson: Mining Club of the Southwest Foundation, 1991, 49–72.

Foster, Jim. "The Ten Day Tramps." *Labor History* 23, no. 4 (1982): 606–23.

Graeme, R. W. "Bisbee, Arizona's Dowager Queen of Mining Camps: A Look at Her First Fifty Years." In vol. 1 of *The History of Mining in Arizona*, edited by J. M. Canty and M. N. Greeley. Tucson: Mining Club of the Southwest Foundation, 1987, 51–57.

Gutfield, Arnon. "The Speculator Disaster in 1917: Labor Resurgence at Butte, Montana." *Arizona and the West* 2, no. 1 (1969): 27–38.

———. "The Murder of Frank Little: Radical Labor Agitation in Butte, Montana, 1917." *Labor History* 10, no. 2 (1969): 177–92.

Haak, Wilbur A. "The Old Dominion Mine." In vol. 3 of *The History of Mining in Arizona*, edited by J. M. Canty, H. Mason Coggins, and M. N. Greeley. Tucson: Mining Club of the Southwest Foundation, 1999, 88–102.

Harrington, James D. "A Re-examination of the Granite Mountain Speculator Fire." Special Butte Issue, *Montana The Magazine of Western History* 48, no. 3 (1998): 62–69.

"Hillside Mission Alumni Set Meeting Sunday." September 3, 1974. Archives, BAHM.

"History Skiatook, Oklahoma." Abstracted from *Tulsa County Historic Sites* (1982), Tulsa County Historical Society. www.tulsaokhistory.com/cities/skiatook.html.

Hobsbawm, E. J. "Tramping Artisan." *Economic History Review*, New Series 3, no. 3 (1951).

Jameson, Elizabeth. "History, Memory, and Commemoration: The Cripple Creek Strike Remembered." Edited by Tim Blevins, Chris Nichol, and Calvin P. Otto. *The Colorado Labor Wars, Cripple Creek District 1903–1904*. Colorado Springs: Pikes Peak Library District, 2006.

———. "Imperfect Unions Class and Gender in Cripple Creek, 1894–1904." *Frontiers: A Journal of Women Studies* 1, no. 2 (1976): 88–117.

Karni, Michael G. "Elizabeth Gurley Flynn and the Mesabi Strike of 1916." *Range History* (Iron Range Research Center, Chisholm, MN) 5, no. 4 (Winter 1981): 1–6.

Lake, Ted. "Old Dominion Property . . . A Lot of Owners." "Classic Times," *Copper Country News*, December 13, 2006. Vertical Files, Gila County Historical Society, Globe, Arizona.

Lindquist, John H. "The Jerome Deportation of 1917." *Arizona and the West* 11, no. 3 (Autumn 1969): 233–46.

McBride, James D. "Gaining a Foothold in the Paradise of Capitalism." *Journal of Arizona History* 23 (1982): 299–316.

"Miami Arizona Historic Tour." Globe/Miami Chamber of Commerce and City of Miami, AZ, n.d.

Mellinger, Phil. "How the IWW Lost its Heartland." *Western Labor Historical Quarterly* 27, no. 3 (1996): 303–24.

———. "The Men Have Become Organizers: Labor Conflict and Unionization in the Mexican Mining Communities of Arizona, 1900–1915." *Western Historical Quarterly* 23, no. 3 (1992): 323–47.

Milburn, George. "Oklahoma." Originally published in *Yale Review* (March 1946): 515–26. Reprinted in *"An Oklahoma I Had Never Seen Before": Alternative Views of Oklahoma History*, edited by Davis D. Joyce. Norman: University of Oklahoma Press, 1994.

Nelson, Mark and Maurice Isserman, eds. "A Guide to the Microfilm Edition of Part I. The Industrial Workers of the World." *Department of Justice Investigative Files*. Bethesda, MA: University Publications of America, 1989.

Niepman, Ann Davis. "General Orders No. 11 and Border Warfare During the Civil War." In *Kansas City, America's Crossroads: Essays from the Missouri Historical Review, 1906–2006*, edited by Diane Mutti Burke and John Herron, 96–121. Columbia, MO: State Historical Society of Missouri, 2007.

Oates, Steven B. "Boom Oil! Oklahoma Strikes it Rich!" *The American West* 5, no. 1 (1968): 11–15, 64–66.

Ollila, Douglas, Jr. "Ethnic Radicalism and the 1916 Mesabi Strike." *Range History*, Iron Range Research Center, Chisholm, MN 3, no. 4 (December 1978): 3.

Overstreet, Daphne. "On Strike! The 1917 Walkout at Globe, Arizona." *Journal of Arizona History* 18 (1977): 197–218.

Palcic-Erman, Sandra L., ed. *The Alice School 1906, Commemorative Booklet Marking the 75th Anniversary of the Alice School*. Alice Historical Society, Alice (St. Mary's), CO, July 4, 1982.

Park, Joseph E. "The 1903 'Mexican Affair' at Clifton." *Journal of Arizona History* 18 (1977): 119–48.

Punke, Michael. "Extraordinary Session of 1918." L1985.369, AWP021, SBA.

Roscoe, Will. "Unsolved Mystery, Writer Delves into Controversial 1917 Death of Union Leader." *Montana Standard*, October 8, 2006, C1, "Frank Little," VF0528, SBA.

Sellars, Nigel A. "Treasonous Tenant Farmers and Seditious Sharecroppers: The 1917 Green Corn Rebellion Trials." *Oklahoma City University Law Review* 27 (2002): 1097–1141.

————. "Wobblies in the Oil Fields: The Suppression of the Industrial Workers of the World in Oklahoma." In *"An Oklahoma I Had Never Seen Before": Alternative Views of Oklahoma History*, edited by Davis D. Joyce. Norman: University of Oklahoma Press, 1994.

Shanks, Rosalie. "The IWW Free Speech Movement: San Diego, 1912." *San Diego Historical Society Quarterly* 19, no. 1 (Winter 1973). Accessed February 3, 2015, http://www.sandiegohistory.org/journal /73winter/speech.htm

Shovers, Brian. "On the Perils of Working in Butte Underground: Underground Fatalities in the Copper Mines." *Montana: The Magazine of Western History* 37, no. 2 (1987): 26–39.

Stilwell, Kristina. "After the Stench Cleared: Prison Life and Labor at Leeds Farm." Paper presented to the Missouri Conference on History, Columbia, Missouri, 1998.

"Strike! The IWW and the Jerome Deportation." *Jerome Chronicle*, Spring 1997, 5.

Taylor, Lawrence D. "The Magonista Revolt in Baja California." *San Diego Historical Society Quarterly* 45, no. 1 (1999). Accessed August 5, 2014, http://www.sandiegohistory.org/journal/99winter/magonista .htm.

Watkins, T. H. "Requiem for the Federation." *The American West* 3, no. 1 (1966): 4–12, 91–95.

"Whatever Happened to Alice?" Rand-McNally Advertisement, 1972.

Documentaries

Butte, America. Documentary. Directed by Pamela Roberts. 2008. Independent Lens PBS, 2009. DVD.

The Hobo Agitator. Documentary. KUSM. 1995. Missoula: Montana PBS, 1995. Television.

Los Mineros. Documentary. Directed by Hector Galen. 1992. Scottsdale: Espinosa Productions, 1992. DVD.

INDEX